RICHARD
MORRIS
HUNT

RICHARD MORRIS HUNT

PAUL R. BAKER

The MIT Press
Cambridge,
Massachusetts,
and London,
England

Publication of this volume has been aided by a grant from the National Endowment for the Humanities.

First paperback edition, 1986
© 1980 by The Massachusetts Institute of Technology

This book was set in VIP Palatino by Grafacon, Inc. and printed and bound by Halliday Lithograph Corporation in the United States of America.

Library of Congress Cataloging in Publication Data

Baker, Paul R
  Richard Morris Hunt.

  Bibliography: p.
  Includes index.
  1. Hunt, Richard Morris, 1827–
1895. 2. Architects—United States—
Biography.
  NA737.H86B34   720′.92′4[B]   79-25008
  ISBN 0-262-52109-1

For
Elizabeth Kemp Baker

CONTENTS

Several years ago, in my studies of American culture in the latter half of the nineteenth century, I became interested in Richard Morris Hunt, whose name frequently appears in accounts of the artistic life of the Gilded Age. I quickly discovered, however, that little detailed information could easily be found on his life and his architectural works and that what was available often was manifestly biased and inaccurate. As I began to study Hunt, I became aware of the great diversity of his activities and the immense variety of his creative work. The trail of research I followed involved many paths into libraries, archives, and manuscript collections and brought several unexpected discoveries as I became intimately acquainted with the architect, his family, and his friends. My investigations, moreover, led to new friendships for me and numerous debts to those who helped me. The Acknowledgments at the end of this volume include the names of many people to whom I am grateful for assistance.

This study is based on both a large body of unpublished manuscript materials and a large number of contemporary published sources, as well as on-site visits to many Hunt buildings. Especially useful for this book have been the available resources of the Hunt Collection (denoted as "HC" in the endnotes), at the American Institute of Architects Foundation, The Octagon, Washington, D.C., and the Hunt Papers (denoted in the endnotes as "HP"), relating to the Hunt family and privately held by descendants of Richard Morris Hunt. Both collections are rich in journals, letters, and financial accounts, while the Hunt Collection contains as well a wealth of drawings and photographs of Hunt's buildings. A description of the materials used from these two collections, as well as from other archival and manuscript sources, is to be found in the note on Selected Sources.

Of particular importance for this study has been the manuscript biography of Richard Morris Hunt, written by his widow, Catharine Clinton Howland Hunt, and completed about 1907. In 1940, Mr. Alan Burnham transcribed and edited this biography from the original manuscript, and his typed and edited version is included in the Richard Morris Hunt Papers in the American Architectural Archive. Mr. Burnham was most generous in giving me access to this transcription early in my researches. A second copy of the typed transcript of the Catharine Hunt biography, located in the Hunt (family) Papers, with some annotations by family members, has been used for this present study; it is denoted in the endnotes as "CCHH, HP." The original manuscript is now in the Hunt Collection. The Catharine Hunt work, chatty and adulatory, is a valuable source of information about Hunt's activities and his architectural work, but it must be used with caution, for it is sometimes inaccurate. Specific corrections are indicated in some endnotes.

INTRODUCTION On a rainy day in October 1966, a handful of people gathered at the eastern edge of New York's Central Park on Fifth Avenue between Seventieth and Seventy-First streets. They had come to join in the rededication of the Richard Morris Hunt Memorial, originally erected in 1898, the only piece of civic art in New York honoring an architect and one of the very few public monuments to an American artist. Four years earlier, two large bronze allegorical figures had been stolen from the memorial, the thieves apparently intending to dispose of them as scrap metal. Fortunately, the statues were recovered, and the memorial was restored. Within a short time after the rededication, however, like so much else in New York City, the stone had been defaced by graffiti, and the monument looked sadly uncared for and decayed.[1]

In spite of its present condition, the Hunt Memorial (figure 1) is an elegant construction, graceful in its proportions. Some thirty feet in length, it includes a semielliptical seat raised three steps above the sidewalk; behind the low curving seat rises an Ionic colonnade of polished detached columns, surmounted by a finely worked and ornamented entablature. A central pedestal holds a larger-than-life-size bronze bust of the architect. At each end, pedestals attached in front of the terminal piers support bronze allegorical figures: the one on the left represents "Painting and Sculpture" and holds a painter's palette, a sculptor's mallet, and a small figure copied from the pediment of the Parthenon, while that on the right personifies "Architecture" and holds a model of Hunt's Administration Building from the World's Columbian Exposition of 1893. On panels at the base of the columns are listed the names of the art societies that contributed to the memorial.[2]

Few people today passing by the Hunt Memorial give it a glance or linger to rest on the elevated seat, perhaps apprehensive that they themselves might thus be considered a part of the public sculpture of the city and a target for graffiti-makers. The inscription on the central pedestal goes largely unnoticed:

To
RICHARD MORRIS HUNT
October 31, 1828*
July 31, 1895
In Recognition
Of his Services to
The Cause of Art
In America,
This Memorial
Was Erected in 1898 by
The Art Societies
Of New York

* The birth date is incorrect; see chapter 1, note 1.

Figure 1
Richard Morris Hunt
Memorial, Fifth Avenue
between Seventieth and
Seventy-First streets,
New York (1898).

And to those who do read the inscription it probably means little, for the man who was known as the dean of American architects in the latter part of the nineteenth century has largely been forgotten. Most of the buildings he erected in New York City have been destroyed. The great Fifth Avenue mansions he designed are now all gone. Only the large central section of the principal front of the Metropolitan Museum of Art remains of the many works that Hunt built along Fifth Avenue. When the memorial was erected, it was placed so as to face the imposing Lenox Library—"the finest design Richard M. Hunt ever composed," according to one late-nineteenth-century art critic. But within a few years the Lenox Library was torn down to make way for Henry Clay Frick's mansion, which now houses the Frick Collection.[3]

The fate of these buildings and the neglect of the memorial only duplicate the course of Hunt's reputation, his name now largely unknown to the public at large and his lifetime work—at least until recently—remembered negatively by many twentieth-century writers on American architecture and historians of the Gilded Age. The twentieth-century characterizations come easily: Hunt was "the Vanderbilt architect," "château builder to Fifth Avenue," "a Beaux-Arts copyist," always looking to the past and designing buildings that were alien to the American experience.[4]

That he stood outside the early developments of architectural modernism has placed him beyond the pale for many architectural historians. Some writers have concluded that Hunt was capable of little more than cribbing historical styles and copying details from work he already knew, with none of the creative originality of a Henry Hobson Richardson or a Louis Sullivan. His Beaux-Arts training—considered during his lifetime one of his greatest assets—later represented for some critics an indoctrination into styles that were irrelevant to American life. In his most conspicuous buildings, Hunt was decidedly not the architect of democracy whom Sullivan called for in his Whitmanesque prose. The great mansions he designed for the very rich of his day probably as much as anything else helped identify the new American plutocracy in the public eye by providing striking symbols of its wealth and power. Russell Lynes put the matter of Hunt's reputation bluntly in 1955: "To most critics of architecture today Hunt is anathema. . . . His influence on American building is looked upon darkly. . . . The style that he played so large a part in setting has, in many expert opinions, been a disastrous backwater in the progress of our architecture." One should note here the use of the word "progress," implying movement from a lower to a higher state.[5]

Figure 2
Richard Morris Hunt.
Courtesy The American
Institute of Architects
Foundation/Prints and
Drawings Collection,
Washington, D.C. Re-
production by James
Garrison.

Recently there has been a critical reassessment of the American cultural achievement, including the artistic accomplishments of the once-disparaged Gilded Age. In part this serious and often scholarly reconsideration of past endeavors has come as a reaction to earlier negative assessments and neglect. The sons reject their fathers, while the grandchildren, in their turn, react against *their* fathers and find that their grandfathers were not so bad after all. Obviously, too, America's bicentennial celebration awakened interest not only in the achievements of the Revolutionary period but also in the total body of American creative accomplishment, and especially the years around the centennial of the nation. Moreover, after years of destruction of the architectural remnants of the past through city expansion, private construction, and urban renewal, a vast public beyond professional preservationists has come to accept the urgency of keeping and maintaining what is left. Then, too, a reaction against modernism in architecture has developed. Modern design has not brought the social betterment in the form of new ways of living appropriate to urban-industrial life that some advocates assumed would naturally follow stylistic changes. In addition, the austerities of modern design seem to many to have led to aesthetic malnutrition. Decoration beyond functional needs, once so scorned, is being sought again. And the elements of conspicuous display which so delighted people in the past have taken on new importance. Critics and historians have begun to look with sympathetic understanding on neo-classicism and the eclecticism of the Beaux-Arts tradition. The 1975 exhibition at the Museum of Modern Art in New York City of student work at the Ecole des Beaux-Arts and of Beaux-Arts-inspired buildings signaled both scholarly and general interest in an output until recently widely scorned.[6]

Within this context of reassessment, this study aims to show the many dimensions of Richard Morris Hunt. To his contemporaries in the second half of the nineteenth century, Hunt was more than a prominent architect—the first American trained at the Ecole des Beaux-Arts—who had designed some very striking buildings. By his early forties he was becoming known as the dean of American architects; during his latter years he was generally acknowledged as the leading figure of his profession. Richardson's buildings were more admired than those of Hunt by their peers, but Hunt, who had a much longer career, was accorded greater honors. During his lifetime, he was one of the most widely honored of nineteenth-century Americans, both at home and abroad. In the decades since his death, however, this major American figure has been very much neglected.[7]

One problem in dealing with Hunt, then, is this question of his reputation: How did it arise, and how was it supported? What went into its making? Was it the man himself as much as, or more than, his buildings that impressed his contemporaries? Why did his professional colleagues by and large afford him such unreserved praise?

The problem of the man shades into the development of the profession of architecture in the United States. One of the more intriguing aspects of social history is the crystallization and growth of specialization and of professionalism in emergent modern industrial nations. In the second half of the nineteenth century, architecture became a respected profession in the United States, and Hunt more than anyone else was instrumental in shaping its dimensions and standards. Moreover, he did significant work in establishing professional education in architecture in this country. For many years, he was the best-known spokesman of his profession in the United States.

Throughout his career, Hunt served the diverse needs of a rapidly expanding nation. In his commissions for clients of great wealth, he was able to shape and to fulfill dreams and ideals in a way that few other Americans ever have. And yet his output was immensely varied, and he designed buildings for many private, commercial, and public purposes. His designs for several monuments and memorials helped forward the renewed unifying nationalism which followed the Civil War and Reconstruction.

Paradoxes envelop Hunt. He was a man of refined aesthetic perceptions, who throughout his lifetime felt the need to work to elevate public taste in the arts; yet he was proud of his ability to adapt his ideas to his clients' wishes and emphasized that he would do the work they wanted him to do. He looked to the past for artistic inspiration; yet he was very much involved with the needs of his time and the most advanced technology of his day. He was concerned in his work with order and discipline; yet he always sought a free and individual expression in his designs. One finds in his work a fabric of balanced tensions between the past and the present, tradition and uniqueness, order and freedom. An elitist in his education, travel experience, and tastes, and a member of the upper class, he was nonetheless very much the democrat in his manner and in many of his attitudes and opinions. He prided himself on his Americanness, and his emphasis on hard work, reliability, and seriousness of endeavor showed his Puritan-Yankee heritage; nevertheless, he had an affinity for Europe, to which he returned again and again for extended periods of time, and there was always in him something of the European aesthete.

Hunt's many designs, his public and private activities, and his meaning for his own time provide us with important documentation of the attitudes, values, and ideals of his age. He was a key figure of America's Gilded Age, and his buildings are an important part of our national cultural heritage.

RICHARD
MORRIS
HUNT

I

NEW ENGLAND ROOTS

Richard Morris Hunt always took pride in his American birth and in the knowledge that his ancestral roots were deeply planted in American soil. Since the early seventeenth century, Hunts had been leaders in politics, community service, and business in New England, and his childhood as a member of an old family of prominence and wealth undoubtedly provided him with a firm sense of place and of belonging and a solid cultural foundation for his later years of travel, schooling, and professional training in Europe. Although he became one of the most cosmopolitan of nineteenth-century Americans, living abroad for extended periods, traveling widely throughout Europe, Egypt and the Near East, and Russia, and associating himself closely with leading European artists, he was constantly drawn back to the United States, where he could find his opportunities and his challenges, where he could achieve a sense of artistic and civic fulfillment, and where he knew that he belonged.

The fourth of five children of Jonathan and Jane Maria Hunt, Richard was born in Brattleboro, Vermont, on October 31, 1827.[1] He was named after Lieutenant Richard Hunt Morris (1803–1837), an officer in the United States Navy, who was Richard's much older cousin, the son of his father's sister.[2] The other children already in the family when Richard arrived were his sister Jane, five years older; his brother William Morris, some three and a half years older; and his brother Jonathan, known in the family as John or Jack, about sixteen months his senior. Another brother, Leavitt, was born more than two years later.[3]

Jonathan Hunt, Richard's father, was a leading citizen of Brattleboro. A Dartmouth graduate, he was a prominent lawyer, banker, landowner, and politician. On Main Street at the corner of High Street, he constructed in 1822 "the first house built entirely of brick in Brattleboro and Windham County," and it was said that "people came from miles distant to see the wonderful sight." The large, two-and-one-half-story structure, painted white, was surrounded by tall trees, a sweep of lawn, and shrubbery plantings (figure 3). It had, as one commentator put it, "an air of superior elegance." Behind the house stood a large barn, and close to the street was Jonathan's one-story law office, where he worked when he was in Brattleboro. In 1830, Hunt had a staff of two men and two women to maintain the property and help his wife care for the five small children. At the church on the common, the Hunt family occupied a second-row pew. They lived very comfortably, even luxuriously.[4]

At the time of Richard's birth, Brattleboro was already more than one hundred years old. It had been the first permanent white settlement in the area that later became Vermont. Brattleborough (as it was first

Figure 3
Jonathan Hunt house,
Brattleboro, Vermont.
From an old photograph,
Hunt Papers.

spelled) was located a few miles north of the Massachusetts border on the west bank of the upper Connecticut River, near Fort Dummer, built by the Massachusetts colonial government in 1724 for protection against the Indians. Fort Dummer had been erected in the southeastern corner of the large area of land between Lake Champlain and the Connecticut River known as the New Hampshire Grants, which was at various times claimed by New Hampshire, Massachusetts, and New York. In 1777, after the outbreak of the Revolutionary War, the inhabitants of the New Hampshire Grants rejected all outside claims and established the independent state of Vermont, which was admitted to the Union as the fourteenth state in 1791.[5]

Brattleboro soon became the principal town of Windham County in the southeastern corner of the state. Here, Royall Tyler, the early American dramatist, novelist, and jurist lived from 1801 to his death in 1826. Tyler held various state offices, including that of chief justice of the Vermont Supreme Court. His widow kept a nursery school in Brattleboro, which Jane, William, and John Hunt all attended. Here also in Brattleboro, John Humphrey Noyes, the famous Oneida utopianist, was born sixteen years before Richard Hunt in 1811. His father, John Noyes, like Richard's father, was a Dartmouth graduate, a state representative, and a national Congressman, and the two families must have been well acquainted. John Humphrey Noyes's mother was an aunt of Rutherford B. Hayes, and his sister Mary became the mother of William Rutherford Mead, born in Brattleboro in 1846, who later achieved fame in the architectural firm of McKim, Mead & White and collaborated with Hunt on designs for the World's Columbian Exposition. "Jubilee Jim" Fisk, who attained notoriety in Gilded Age railroad speculations, spent his youthful years in Brattleboro in the 1830s and 1840s. For a town with a population of only 2,141 in 1830 and 2,624 in 1840, Brattleboro produced a surprising number of notable offspring.[6]

The Hunt family had been prominent in New England for several generations. The American founder of the family was Jonathan Hunt (ca. 1610–1661), who came from England to the Massachusetts Bay Colony in about 1630 and moved to the Connecticut River Valley in 1636. Richard's great-grandfather, Samuel Hunt (1703–1770), was the source of much of the family's fortune. Samuel Hunt, who lived in Northfield, Massachusetts, reputedly amassed the largest land holdings in the New Hampshire Grants and owned other large tracts as well in New Hampshire proper and in Canada. In his will, Samuel divided his property among his four sons and three daughters. His youngest son, Arad Hunt (1743–1825), who was Richard's great-uncle, served as representative of Vernon, just south of Brattleboro, in the Vermont Assembly and as a general in the state militia. General Arad Hunt was involved in many land transactions and in 1813 contributed 5,000 acres of land to help support Middlebury College.[7]

The second son of the land magnate Samuel was another Jonathan Hunt, Richard's grandfather, who was born on September 12, 1738, and who also lived in Vernon. He married Levinah Swan (1749–1834) in 1779. He became a major in the militia during the Revolution, and in 1780 he was sent to the Continental Congress to inform that body that the independent state of Vermont proposed to enforce its authority over the inhabitants in the New Hampshire Grants. He represented Vernon in the Vermont Assembly in 1783 and was elected a councilor of the state from 1786 to 1794. In 1787, he was named an agent to appear before Congress to present the case for Vermont's entering the Union, but he was excused from the mission at the last moment. When a convention was called in Bennington in January 1791 to ratify the Constitution, he served as a delegate from Vernon. In 1794, the Vermont legislature chose Jonathan Hunt lieutenant governor, and he was re-elected by the voters of the state in 1795. He also served as a trustee of the University of Vermont. He died on June 1, 1823, at the age of nearly eighty-five. His will, drawn up in July 1813, left most of his very extensive real estate holdings in Massachusetts and in several towns in Windham County, along with shares in the Windham Turnpike Company, to his eldest son, Jonathan.[8]

Lieutenant-Governor Jonathan Hunt was much revered by his associates. An obituary written at Vernon on June 1, 1823, commented: "The principles and practice of industry, virtue, and religion he greatly respected and encouraged, and the ministry of the gospel he liberally supported; and, while his hospitality and kindness to the deserving were extensively exercised, indolence and vice found in him an open and uniform reprover. He preserved through his long life, and amidst his temporal prosperity the most unassuming and unaffected deportment, and, what is always highly honourable in the rich as well as the poor, the reputation of an honest man." Except for the support of religion, to which he was indifferent, Richard Morris Hunt would have much the same reputation as did his grandfather.[9]

Richard's father, Jonathan Hunt, was born to Jonathan and Levinah Hunt on May 12, 1787, in Vernon. He attended secondary school at Chesterfield, and in 1807 graduated from Dartmouth College, where he was elected to Phi Beta Kappa. Subsequently, he studied law at the school conducted by Tapping Reeve in Litchfield, Connecticut, entering the regular course in 1808. He later settled in Brattleboro to practice law, gained admission to the Vermont bar in 1812, and soon became active in Vermont affairs. He was named a captain in the Vermont artillery in 1811 and was known to have provided support for the state militia from his own funds. He represented Brattleboro in the Vermont legislature in 1816, 1817, and 1824. From 1822 until his death he was president of the Bank of Brattleboro. His political career culminated with his election in February 1827 as a candidate of the National Republican Party to the Twentieth Congress. He was re-elected to the Twenty-First and the Twenty-Second congresses. In the House of Representatives, Jonathan Hunt was member of the Committee for Revolutionary Claims in 1827 and the Committee on Public Lands in 1829.[10]

Less is known of Richard's maternal line, though this family was also distinguished. Richard's mother was Jane Maria Leavitt, the eldest of four children of Judge Thaddeus and Jemima Loomis Leavitt of Suffield, Connecticut. Thaddeus Leavitt, one of thirteen children of Thaddeus Leavitt (1750–1813) and Elizabeth King Leavitt (1751–1826), was born on February 16, 1778; he was educated at Yale College and became, like his father, a merchant at Suffield and was also a colonel in the state militia and a judge. On January 1, 1800, Thaddeus was married to Jemima Loomis, who had been born on September 24, 1779, the daughter of Colonel Luther Loomis (1754–1812) and Jemima Bronson Loomis (1762–1834). Judge Leavitt, Richard's grandfather, died on October 12, 1828; his wife lived until April 10, 1846. Within the family, Judge Leavitt was remembered for heavy drinking and a bad temper.[11]

Jane Maria Leavitt was born on October 16, 1801. She was educated at Miss Clarke's Boarding School in Northampton, Massachusetts, and later at Colonel Dunham's School in Windsor, Vermont. It was at the inn at Windsor that she first encountered Jonathan Hunt, who was fourteen years her senior and at the time already well established in Brattleboro. Judge Leavitt was then taking Jane Maria back to school, and he and his daughter had stopped for dinner at the Windsor inn. The landlord asked them if they would share their table with a gentleman and lady who had just driven up. They did so, and the gentleman, Jonathan Hunt, was apparently immediately attracted to the schoolgirl. A short while later he was reintroduced to Judge Leavitt by Colonel Dunham, the schoolmaster, who characterized Jonathan as "the finest fellow in the state of Vermont." After Jane left the school in 1819, Jonathan went to the Leavitt home in Suffield to court her, and soon they were engaged. They were married on May 15, 1820.[12]

Jane Maria Hunt was a woman of great spirit and forceful character, noted for her beauty, and, in later life, her artistic talent. If Richard inherited his energy and his sharp intelligence from his father, surely his love of art and his artistic ability came largely from his mother. Mrs. Hunt had a very strong impact on the lives of her children, making, it was said, "her own ambitious ideals the standards for them."[13]

As a child, Jane Maria had felt an urge to draw and paint, but Judge Leavitt was outspoken in opposing such activities as a waste of time. While at boarding school, she was fascinated by the class in painting, which she wanted to join but felt she could not because of her father's attitude. Finally, after the painting teacher had repeatedly encouraged her, she did attend the class and commenced to paint. But when she returned home and showed her work to her parents, her father brusquely ordered her to stop. Only many years later as a mature woman did she again take up drawing and painting, this time determined that she would satisfy her artistic yearnings and that her children would have the opportunities that had been forbidden to her.[14]

Of the children, Jane and William, the two eldest, exhibited their creative talents at a very early age. At Mrs. Amelia S. Tyler's nursery school in Brattleboro, the effervescent William, then four or five years old, and his sister, then six or seven, learned to sew. The two children made a patchwork calico quilt of scarlet and yellow with a gray and violet border, which their mother carefully preserved. In later years she would occasionally bring it out to show the children, promising them that it would be given to the first of them to marry. The quilt was therefore eventually handed on to William, and at the exhibition of his paintings and sketches held shortly after his death in 1879 at the Museum of Fine Arts in Boston, it was displayed along with a few other personal articles. William's first preserved drawing was done when he was seven years old. Jane, who never married and spent her later years in Newport, Rhode Island, and in California, was subsequently recognized as a talented watercolorist.[15]

According to Hunt family tradition, Richard's earliest years were "remarkably happy." His mother and sister later recalled "that he cooed for hours over his toys, crying so little that his mother was almost anxious. His distinguishing quality, from a very early age, was his persistent industry." That characteristic of industry was also noted by a neighbor who remembered Richard as a three-year-old in Washington, D.C., "struggling with a spade nearly twice as large as himself, cleaning away the snow, and shoveling in the coal . . . returning to the charge again and again." One summer a few years later he spent most of his days busily collecting the silken seeds of milkweed in hopes of selling them to an upholsterer.[16]

After Jonathan Hunt was first elected to Congress in 1827, much of his time was spent in Washington, D.C., away from his family. Jonathan left Brattleboro on November 25, 1827, only three weeks after Richard was born, to begin his service in the first session of the Twentieth Congress. The absence of her husband and the burden of four small children made life very difficult for Jane Maria Hunt. From the capital, scarcely three weeks after he had left home, Congressman Hunt tried to console his young wife:

From certain expressions in your letter, it seems that you feel unhappy, as if you were in some measure deserted. Do not, I beseech you, think so—your friends around you I am sure will be kind to you, & altho I cannot at present be with you to afford you assistance, yet believe that my thoughts do hourly attend you, & my heart is irretrievably attached to you, that no inducement in the world can seduce my faith. Make yourself happy; the time I hope will shortly come when I shall meet you again, & rejoice in the frolicks & prattling innocence of our children & with you be happy.[17]

A few days after this letter was written, Jonathan attempted to cheer his wife with an account of a "levée" he had just attended at the White House, although his letter indicates something of his own loneliness:

About 8 o'clock in the evening, I took a hack with one of our boarders for the Royal Mansion. We entered without any ceremony. Three rooms are devoted to the Company; the centre one is circular, or rather a circle, and is, I conclude, the drawing room for Mrs. President. In this, the crowd was so dense, that one could hardly pass thru it. The ladies were principally upon one side of it and dressed with much splendour, *I mean in comparison with our ladies*. Their heads, I thought, monopolised the most brilliant ornaments. Mrs. [John Quincy] Adams was dressed in light blue, with a cap or turban of similar colour, surmounted with a broad rich feather, forming an undulating circle. Her countenance indicates ill health; she has not much beauty at present, but her chaste & courtly manners inspire the purest sentiments of respect. I moved around in this mass about one hour—when I felt willing to retire. Many members of Congress were present—all the heads of departments—foreigners, officers of the Army & Navy—and of all these I scarcely knew by sight over ten or twelve.[18]

In January 1828, a few months after Richard's birth, Mrs. Hunt left her sons William and John in Mrs. Tyler's nursery school in Brattleboro and took Jane and the baby with her to join her husband in Washington for a short time. He was at that time living in B. O. Tyler's boarding house close to the Capitol. Senator Daniel Webster from Massachusetts, a friend of Congressman Hunt, was then in Washington. Years afterward, Jane remembered seeing Webster, after his wife had died, hand over to her mother the keys to his wife's trunks, so that she might repack them to be sent back to Massachusetts.[19]

Daniel Webster and Jonathan Hunt had a close and continuing personal and working relationship, and Webster often visited the Hunts in Brattleboro. In September 1828, Webster wrote Jonathan Hunt informing him that he and his daughter would soon be coming to Brattleboro and suggesting that he and Hunt might share lodgings in Washington at the next session of Congress. According to Hunt family tradition, Webster lived with the Hunt household in Washington for some months, but there is no evidence to support this. Nonetheless, the two families remained intimate. In early August 1829, the Hunt family visited Webster and his daughter in Boston. Mrs. Hunt was very fond of Webster's daughter Julia, and after Webster remarried in December 1829, Mrs. Hunt became close to his second wife. During one visit to Brattleboro, Webster worked with Hunt on strategy for a land distribution bill at Hunt's office next to the residence on Main Street.[20]

When Jonathan Hunt returned to Washington for the first session of the Twenty-First Congress, beginning on December 7, 1829, he left his wife at home in Brattleboro in an advanced state of pregnancy. He was absent at the capital when their last child, Leavitt, was born in February 1830. His letters from Washington just before the baby's birth attempted from a distance to give what support he could to Jane Maria and buoy up her spirits. At her request, Jonathan described as best he could the belles of the national capital, but he had to admit that she had applied to "a bad source for information. I don't know who they are." After attending a reception given by President Andrew Jackson in the East Room of the White House, Jonathan reported that "there was a prodigious crowd, most of them entirely new faces." The notorious Peggy Eaton, a tavern keeper recently married to the Secretary of War and one whom the president had befriended, was not present for this gathering, Jonathan reported. Her absence, he concluded, meant that "she thinks herself entirely down, & that it is best to give up for the present." For the Vermont Congressman, the Jackson reception obviously lacked the restrained elegance that had characterized the Adams presidency.[21]

When Hunt returned to Washington in November 1830 for the second session of his second term, Jane Maria and the five children accompanied him. They took nearly two weeks to make the journey from

Brattleboro to Washington, driving much of the way in their own carriage. Probably they stopped for a day or two with Mrs. Hunt's widowed mother in Suffield, Connecticut, before going on to New Haven. There they took a steamer to New York and thence traveled south by way of Philadelphia and Baltimore. The trip was rigorous, and it must have been especially hard with the infant Leavitt and the four other youngsters to be cared for.[22]

In Washington, the Hunts took rooms in Denny's boarding house on Four and One-Half Street near City Hall during the second session of the Twenty-First Congress; and during the first session of the Twenty-Second Congress, they were at Richard Ballard's boarding house on Pennsylvania Avenue. Besides the Websters, Jonathan and Jane Maria Hunt had a few other close friends whom they saw frequently: Representative and Mrs. Edward Everett from Massachusetts, Representative Horace Everett from Vermont, and Senator and Mrs. Peleg Sprague from Maine, among them. They also came to know well the Comte de Menou, French chargé d'affaires, whom Mrs. Hunt and her children in later years often visited in France. The family's residence in the national capital undoubtedly opened up a fuller and more interesting social life for Mrs. Hunt than she had previously experienced in the small towns of New England, and probably helped shape the course that she subsequently chose for herself and her children.[23]

While living in the capital, Mrs. Hunt was also able to gratify her desire to draw. During the summer of 1831 she regularly visited the Congressional Library, where she copied from illustrations in one of the recently published volumes by John James Audubon. Proud of what she had accomplished, she presented some of her drawings to friends, including Edward Everett.[24]

In the spring of 1831, Jonathan Hunt left his wife and children in Washington while he traveled through western Virginia and Kentucky to Ohio to look over land he held near Cincinnati. His trip was difficult, since the roads were often blocked by rising waters from heavy spring rains. By this time, he was anticipating retiring from Congress at the end of his third term to devote himself to land sales and speculation. He was considering settling in Cincinnati.[25]

At the end of 1831, Hunt was back in the House of Representatives, when the first session of the Twenty-Second Congress convened. Suddenly, in April of 1832, the vigorous, active congressman was taken very ill. The doctor who was summoned diagnosed his illness as cholera. His condition worsened, and on May 15, 1832, he died, only forty-five years of age. In the House of Representatives, Horace Everett, the Vermont congressman, announced Hunt's death and offered a resolution that House members wear crepe bands on their arms for the remainder of the session. This resolution was unanimously agreed to, and the House adjourned through the following day, when funeral ceremonies were held. The Senate, too, resolved unanimously to go into mourning and wear crepe armbands for thirty days; the Senate also adjourned "as a testimony of respect for the memory of the deceased" so that members might attend the funeral. Jane Hunt remembered watching the funeral procession for her father from an upstairs window with her four younger brothers.[26]

After the funeral in Washington, Mrs. Hunt's brother, John G. Leavitt, escorted the widow and her five children and a servant back to Brattleboro, and on June 8, 1832, the body of Jonathan Hunt was interred at the Brattleboro Prospect Hill Cemetery. One "C. W." composed some lines read at the graveside; behind the sentimentality of the verse is a very apparent sense of loss:

The statesman, husband, father, friend, is dead;
    Hence all who know him feel an awful gloom!
O'er many miles his sable hearse was led;—
    His much lov'd native valley is his tomb.

Senseless his frame, his head, his heart, all cold,
    Where usefulness and science used to dwell;
Speechless his lips and tongue, which never told
    A word, that Truth and Virtue would not tell.

His face, which almost ev'ry heart could please,
    His limbs, his form, in symmetry so just,
Where late, true dignity combin'd with ease,
    Are gone, all gone to moulder in the dust.

Rever'd departed Friend, long to thy grave
    Shall SCIENCE, LOVE, and FRIENDSHIP oft' repair,
And Sympathy, in mourning join to lave
    With tears the turf or stone which holds Thee there.

May the sweet hope of joining Thee be ours,
    When we in faith and hope shall end our days,
To tune our tongues and hearts and noblest powers,
    To sing, enraptur'd, our CREATOR'S Praise.

Surviving Friends, accept these humble lays,
    From one, to whom the DEAD was very dear;
Who knew his many virtues;—and whose praise
    Cannot be more imperfect—than sincere.[27]

One can only speculate as to the impact of his father's early death on Richard, who was four and one-half years old, for the surviving documents give no indication as to his feelings about this event or the effect it may have had on his behavior. Probably, since Jonathan Hunt's death occurred when Richard was so very young and since the congressman had been apart from the family for so much of the time since Richard's birth, his death had relatively little direct impact on the boy. As Richard grew older, moreover, his two elder brothers could provide him with some of the masculine companionship he needed. But Jonathan's death did most certainly influence Richard's life in an indirect way. It brought an immediate cutting of old ties in Washington and, soon, in Brattleboro. It led to new homes and new friends and, eventually, the biggest break with the past of all—the family's move to Europe.

On her return to Brattleboro, Mrs. Hunt faced many new responsibilities as the head of a household. She was by no means alone in the world, however, for her own family and Jonathan's stood ready to help her, and many other persons who had been associated with her husband were willing to advise her. Nor had she been left in straitened financial circumstances. Jonathan Hunt's estate, mostly in real property and personal loans and in canal and turnpike bonds, was valued in excess of $150,000. The estate was apportioned directly to the five children as well as to the widow. Nonetheless, the following months were very difficult for Jane Maria Hunt.[1]

In his will, Jonathan had named one Epaphroditus Seymour, cashier of the Bank of Brattleboro, as an executor of his estate, along with Jane Maria Hunt and his brother-in-law Gardiner C. Hall. Seymour succeeded Hunt as president of the bank and for a time largely managed his former associate's estate. Seymour persuaded Mrs. Hunt to relinquish the guardianship of her children for legal reasons. She followed his advice but soon regretted this course and was later involved in extended litigation to regain her rights. Subsequently, when she took her children to Europe, she employed a Boston lawyer named Pelham Hayward to manage the family estate, most of which was then invested in railroad and municipal bonds and in mortgages. Over the years, however, Hayward, either through dishonesty or inefficiency, misappropriated funds and got Mrs. Hunt involved in further litigation.[2]

For some months after her return to Brattleboro, Jane Maria Hunt lived in the large house on Main Street and put her older children in the Brattleboro school. But by autumn she decided, at the suggestion of Daniel Webster, to move to Boston, where the children could get a better education. She left them in Brattleboro with their nursemaid and went to Boston to arrange for a house. When her mother, Mrs. Thaddeus Leavitt, in Suffield, heard about this projected move, she argued that it would be unwise to bring up the children in the city, and she soon persuaded her daughter to abandon her plans and move to New Haven instead.[3]

In October 1832, Mrs. Hunt moved with her children to New Haven. For a while they lived in the Tontine Hotel, but when the young widow found that she was losing control over the youngsters in the hotel, she purchased a house on Chapel Street. Although the house was small, it had a playroom for the children, who often performed theatricals there, a favorite amusement of Richard even as an adult. A close playmate of the Hunt children was Theodore Winthrop, who in later years as a writer would sketch a figure based on Richard in one of his novels. Mrs. Hunt regularly took the family to the Unitarian Church, and the children were enrolled in schools. Richard first attended Mrs. Smith's boys' school and then Mr. French's school. But the small boy intensely disliked going to classes, and at one point he would agree to attend school only when his mother in effect bribed him with "a mulberry colored coat with gilt buttons which he had long desired." The family spent summers at Suffield near the Leavitt family.[4]

Jane Maria Hunt apparently found New Haven rather quiet for her taste, however, and she spent the winter of 1835–1836 in New York City. Leaving William and John in New Haven as boarders in Mr. Skinner's school, she took Jane, Richard, and Leavitt with her to New York, where they took rooms on Fourth Street near Washington Square. Jane was enrolled in a school for young ladies on Fifth Avenue; Richard and Leavitt probably did not attend classes. At the age of eight years, then, Richard first came to know something of the city and even the very neighborhood which would be his future home and would bear the impress of his artistic personality. Mrs. Hunt returned to New York for a shorter period in the winter of 1836–1837.[5]

In the summer of 1837, Mrs. Hunt became acquainted with three Italian political refugees. Gaetano de Castillia, who came to New Haven with letters of introduction to Mrs. Hunt from the writer Catherine Maria Sedgwick of Stockbridge, Massachusetts, introduced in turn Eleuthere Felix Foresti, from whom Mrs. Hunt for a time took Italian lessons. Foresti, who was subsequently a language teacher at Columbia College, in his turn introduced a painter friend named Spiridione Gambardella.[6]

Gambardella had fled to the United States for political reasons and was trying to make a living teaching painting. Mrs. Hunt was so impressed with his artistic ability that she tried to organize a painting class for him, but she found no one else in the neighborhood who was interested. She therefore provided the painter with a studio in her own home, preparing the room herself, and she, Jane, and William became Gambardella's pupils. The Italian artist worked hard that summer; he not only instructed his students and painted a portrait of the two youngest boys, but he also regularly played with and entertained the youngsters. Under his supervision, Jane Maria Hunt herself did a portrait of William. When some of the neighbors saw the work going on in the studio, they asked to enroll, but Mrs. Hunt then declared that they were too late. Gambardella left New Haven after a few months, and Mrs. Hunt proudly showed off the work done during the summer.[7]

Although Richard did not join in the painting class, he had already begun to show artistic and architectural inclinations. At the age of about eight, he built a small brick and wood house in the yard. "In spite of constant punishment for getting himself dirty," he dug a cellar and very carefully laid bricks for the foundation, "determined to have it right from the very beginning." The finished cottage even had decorated cross beams, which William carved with his penknife. Sometime in 1836, Richard became acquainted with the architect Richard Upjohn, who though a generation older would be a friend for many years.[8]

In the spring of 1838, when William expressed interest in attending Harvard College, Mrs. Hunt decided to leave New Haven and move the entire family to Boston in order to be near her eldest son. In Boston she took a house on Mt. Vernon Street and later at 54 Chestnut Street, and the fourteen-year-old William was soon entered in a preparatory school in Cambridge. Already well acquainted with Edward Everett, now governor of Massachusetts, and Senator Daniel Webster, Mrs. Hunt was soon caught up in the social life of the Boston elite. She developed lasting friendships with such prominent families as those of C. P. Brooks, Abbott Lawrence, Josiah Quincy, George Ticknor (a classmate of her husband at Dartmouth College), and Rufus Choate. Moreover, the Chestnut Street house became a gathering place for neighborhood children, and here Richard and the other Hunt children also made many lifelong friends, including Martin Brimmer and Joseph Choate. In the summers there were games in the yard south of the house, and in the winter sledding on the steep streets of Beacon Hill.[9]

Richard was enrolled in the Boston Latin School. Although he was interested in his schoolwork, the boy was not particularly studious, and he often did the minimal work necessary for his lessons while walking to school. But apparently his recitations and behavior satisfied his teachers, and at least once, on February 22, 1840, he received "a public expression of approbation for industry and good conduct during the past week." During the summer vacation of 1842, Richard was enrolled in a Quaker school in Sandwich, Massachusetts, but because of the death of the schoolmaster, he stayed only a short time. He also attended the Boston English High School. As a fourteen-year-old, he was described by one acquaintance as "a rather slight boy, of active build, with a very full head of brown hair, with bright, eager looking eyes."[10]

Even though he was not always attentive to his studies in these years, Richard's Puritan heritage asserted itself in the Franklin-like New Year's resolutions he wrote out for himself for the year 1843:

My Resolutions—1843
I hereby certify that I, Richard M. Hunt, will hereafter abide by the resolutions, which are written as follows;

Firstly;   I will rise at 6 o'clock in summer and at 6½ o'clock in winter.

Secondly;   I will never cheat any one.

Thirdly;   I will strive to merit the approbation of every person with whom I associate.

Fourthly;   I will keep good hours.

Fifthly;   I will not spend my money foolishly.

Sixthly;   I will attend divine service regularly.

Seventhly;   I will be moderate in all things.

Eighthly;   I will keep the commandments strictly.

Ninthly;   [blank]

Amendments to these resolutions may be made if I can with justice do the same, never however *abolishing* any of the resolutions: This set of resolutions shall take place after the first day of January in the year of our Lord one thousand eight hundred and forty three.

Je suis   R. M. Hunt[11]

At this time William, whose interest in art had been greatly stimulated by the painting lessons in New Haven, wanted to continue his artistic studies. Already it was evident that he possessed considerable talent. With either John C. King or Peter Stephenson, in Boston, he took up the art of cutting cameos, and he executed several miniature cameo portraits of members of the family. The Museum of Fine Arts in Boston later acquired a shell bracelet with cameo portraits of the four Hunt brothers, which William had carved.[12]

William was admitted to Harvard College in the fall of 1840 as a member of the class of 1844, which also included Francis Parkman, the future historian. John, who had graduated from the Boston Latin School, entered Harvard in the fall of 1841. It must have been planned that Richard would enroll in Harvard College in the fall of 1843, for an extant note of May 29, 1843, from President Josiah Quincy to Mrs. Hunt, apparently responding to an inquiry she had made, indicated that her son was "at liberty to offer himself for admission in August next."[13]

William Morris Hunt was obviously a young man who made considerable impact on those about him. A cheerful, witty person and something of a raconteur, he was elected to the most exclusive college clubs—Hasty Pudding, Porcellian, and Pierian Sodality—and for the funeral ceremonies for President William Henry Harrison, conducted in Boston on April 20, 1841, he was named chief marshal of his class. "Ever ready to amuse and delight those about him with his quick and life-like sketches," he was always "bubbling over with fun and innocent mirth." He loved music as well as art and sang with a rich bass voice, accompanying himself on the guitar. But he was decidedly "not in his element in the recitation room. Latin and Greek and mathematics were foreign to his nature." During his sophomore year, because he was "too fond of amusement," he was temporarily suspended from college, rusticated to the Reverend Samuel Parker's school in Stockbridge, on the recommendation of the Harvard faculty. As William later said about his formal academic experience: "I was not interested."[14]

William was readmitted to college in the fall of 1842. One evening in the following summer he caught a cold while serenading and had such a bad and persistent cough that he was sent home to his mother in Boston. When the cough continued, his physician advised Mrs. Hunt that William should spend the following winter away from the damp and biting New England winter, preferably in the South or in Italy.[15]

With the counsel of Reverend Frothingham, Mrs. Hunt decided that not only would William leave New England for the winter but also that the whole family would accompany him. At first she intended to pass the winter in southern France but later she changed her goal to Italy. She planned to be away for no more than one year, and when they returned William would complete his Harvard education and go on to study surgery. John arranged to leave the college in good standing and planned to take along books to help prepare him for his advanced work on his return. Richard, whose mother wanted him to enter Harvard, was seriously considering going to the United States Military Academy to prepare for a military career on their return.[16]

Mrs. Hunt's decision to take the entire family to Europe was in fact sudden and not really thought through. Her friends were astonished at what she intended to do. Reverend Samuel Parker and his wife in Stockbridge, with whom William had stayed and with whom John and Leavitt had studied, urged Jane Maria Hunt to send William to the West rather than to Italy since there would be less excitement and less exposure to damp churches and ruins there. The climate of Missouri, Parker suggested, was far better for "pectoral complaints" than that of Italy. But she had made up her mind and was determined to go. She enlisted the aid of Daniel Webster, who had recently resigned as secretary of state, to get letters of introduction to the United States ministers in Paris and Naples and the consuls in Le Havre, Marseilles, and Rome. Webster wrote her that he regretted the necessity that took his "dear friend" and her entire family abroad, but that he hoped that William's health might be restored by this "arduous undertaking." After putting the furniture from the Chestnut Street house in storage, Mrs. Hunt went on with her five children to New York City, where they remained for a short time in a boarding house on Bowling Green, while she made final arrangements for their transatlantic passage. On October 9, 1843, they sailed for France on the *Duchesse d'Orléans*.[17]

Some years later Mrs. Hunt reminisced about their hurried departure for Europe:

People did not then go abroad to study; and I was regarded as venturesome in the extreme. In truth, I did not realize what I was doing until we were half way across the ocean. My friends had done their best to discourage me, and the greatness of the undertaking was indeed oppressive; yet there was no way but to go on.[18]

She obviously had many misgivings about what she was doing by the time the trip was well under way. But since she planned a stay of no more than a year, she could not envision this experience as such a major break with the past and so crucial a determinant of their future as it was to be. For better or worse, the departure from America would have a profound influence on all their lives and, more important, on the history of American architecture and painting. In breaking away from the American homeland, the Hunts to a decided degree were released from American standards and values. The pressures to pursue a conventional "American" career would be greatly lessened for the Hunt sons in these years of absence from the United States. Here indeed were fortunate pilgrims journeying from the New World to the Old, ready to absorb new sensations and become involved in new experiences, and, in so doing, add new dimensions to their lives.[19]

The eastward voyage of the *Duchesse d'Orléans* was a good one. Although on the first six days out of New York, the ship encountered high winds and heavy seas and Richard's sister Jane became violently seasick, they eventually came upon calmer waters, and the quiet relaxed hours in the open air on the upper deck seemed to improve William's health. The Hunt family found several congenial companions among the other twenty-six cabin passengers. Mrs. Hunt became particularly friendly with Mr. and Mrs. Elisha Dyer of Providence, Rhode Island, whom they later saw in Paris and in Rome. The crossing to Le Havre took eighteen days. At the French port, debarkation and customs inspection delayed them some time, but all the procedures and activities were new to them and very interesting, for this was their very first taste of a foreign land. From Le Havre they traveled by diligence coach to Rouen, where they spent the night and the next morning climbed to the top of one of the cathedral towers. From there they went to Paris, where they took rooms in a small hotel on the rue du Helder. The Dyers, who had many friends in Paris, helped ease the way for the widow and her children, even sending a servant to assist them in getting settled in their quarters.[20]

Almost immediately the Hunts embarked on a strenuous program of sightseeing and shopping, opera-going and balls. Within the first few days the entire family visited the art gallery at the Ecole des Beaux-Arts, Richard's first introduction to the school that would shortly have so much importance for him. The Gobelins tapestry factory was another high point of their early days in Paris. At the Palais-Royal, when Richard tried to step up on the platform holding the throne he was summarily pulled away by one of the guards. Before long, Mrs. Hunt and Jane were presented at court to King Louis Philippe, who briefly stopped to chat with the widow and recounted his own visit to Boston. By November 21, Richard and Leavitt were enrolled in a boys' boarding school. Four days after entering, however, Richard had to leave because of a severe boil on his neck, a condition that plagued him for some years. After he recovered and returned to the school, he often spent weekends with a Mrs. Moulton, an acquaintance of Mrs. Hunt, whose town house and country place attracted many artists, writers, and musicians. Here and in school Richard rapidly acquired facility in the French language.[21]

When Mrs. Hunt consulted Parisian doctors about William's condition and they too advised that he go to Italy for the winter, she was ready to carry out her plan, even though she was apparently reluctant to leave Paris, which she was enjoying greatly. On February 22, 1844, after nearly four months in Paris, the family started out for Italy. They journeyed by diligence to Lyons, by river steamer down the Rhône to Marseilles, and by coastal steamer to Genoa. A journal that Richard kept intermittently from February 1844 to April 1848 opened with his first impressions of Italy at Genoa. He explored the fortifications of the port city with Leavitt and saw "for the first time a church full of Catholics!" The Hunts took a coastal steamer from Genoa to Leghorn, with a side trip to the Campo Santo at Pisa, where in the bapistery Richard was captivated by the "most beautiful echo." The voyage along the coast to Civitavecchia, the entry port for Rome, was very rough, and "at dinner most of the passengers got sick, and crept silently into their berths one after the other, like so many mud turtles." The delay at customs was tiresome, and when they arrived in Rome at three o'clock in the morning on March 3, after a long moonlight drive, they had great difficulty in finding a place to stay.[22]

Like most other nineteenth-century American visitors to Rome, the Hunts took an apartment near the Piazza di Spagna. Here they were close to most of the studios of the foreign painters and sculptors who made Rome their home, and nearby was the famous Caffè Greco, long a gathering place of foreign visitors. It was easy to become widely acquainted in Rome, with so many Americans there, and always there was much to see and do. Together, the Hunts visited many of the artists' studios, took drives to Frascati and Lake Albano as well as to Tivoli, and went to the circus and the opera. The Dyers had also come south to Rome, adding to Mrs. Hunt's enjoyment. Moreover, William's health was obviously much better.[23]

Above all, the remnants of the ancient past attracted them. Richard, who was now sixteen years old, was an avid sightseer, and the Eternal City took a strong hold on him. He filled the pages of his journal with descriptions of the many monuments and ruins he visited. Like many other American visitors in the nineteenth century, he began to sketch some of the more picturesque scenes of the city. He also commenced taking Italian lessons from "a pretty good teacher," who "gives lessons on very moderate terms." Frequently, Richard and Leavitt slipped away from the others to explore the city by themselves, and they found relief from the serious labors of sightseeing in an occasional horse race or game of billiards. Rome provided him with a sense of a vast extension of time and of the rich texture of the past that he had never known before. But he was concerned that the precious monuments were deteriorating daily. "'T is a shame, but modern Rome has robbed ancient Rome of all its moveables," he wrote in his journal. And he felt that the atmosphere of the city had an ominous quality as well: "It is a bad place, Rome, dark streets; two men have been guilotined [sic] very lately for stabbing in the street."[24]

Richard's attitude toward the Roman Catholic observances was typical of nineteenth-century Protestant Americans, who were fascinated by the colorful ceremonies while condemning them as superstitious and idolatrous. "It is sport," he wrote, "to see the persons confess. My stars!" And he returned to St. Peter's again and again, delighted especially by the singing of vespers, which "surpasses everything of this kind in the world," and by the baldachin over the altar "as high as the Astor House." During Holy Week, Richard and the others in his family rushed about from one church to another and one ceremony to another, so that by the day before Easter he was "about sick of ceremonies." On Easter Sunday morning, nevertheless, he joined the crowd at St. Peter's for the papal blessing and in the evening returned for the illumination of the dome.[25]

William, who was now turning twenty, was fully caught up in the artistic atmosphere of Rome, and he began to sketch regularly in the galleries as well as to study in the studio of the American sculptor Henry Kirke Brown, one of several American sculptors established in Roman workshops. Here, directed, encouraged, and criticized by a recognized artist, William again carved cameos and modeled a copy of the Naples *Psyche*, which his mother arranged to have cut in marble.[26]

Very shortly after their arrival in Rome, William joined his Harvard classmate Francis Parkman for a tour of the Apennines. When Parkman came to Rome, he was delighted to find that "the whole family of the Hunts are here." He and William hired a guide and donkeys and followed the road up the course of the Aniene River to the Convent of San Cosimato, stopping at a nearby inn, where the dirt and filth were compensated for by the very good wine at three cents a liter. At Subiaco they found the narrow streets crowded and dirty, but intensely picturesque; village women gathered with their water jars at the fountains, while the men wearing their red breeches sat and smoked and stared at them. Proceeding on to Rocca di San Stephano, they stopped at a good inn at the village of Civitella, with a magnificent view, where "Hunt betook himself to sketching at once." At Palestrina they found an inn kept by two young sisters, "both handsome as the sun," with whom they spent the evening talking before the fire, "though Hunt, who does not speak a word of Italian, kept up his share of the conversation by sign. . . . The girls were as intelligent as they were handsome, and . . . as virtuous." At Cana, in a dirty little inn filled with silent peasants, Parkman and William told each other college stories. Then on to Velletri and back to Rome. In this sketching tour, William was establishing a practice that all the Hunts would follow for some years.[27]

Later that spring, the entire family visited Naples, taking excursions to Mt. Vesuvius, Pompeii, and Baia, and then in late April they traveled by steamer north to Leghorn and thence by coach to Pisa and Florence. After weeks of travel, Richard was still an insatiable sightseer. He found Florence filled with fine streets and he was "immediately reminded of home, everything was quiet, yet the streets were filled, every one looked neat and happy." The bapistery gates beside the cathedral he praised as "of magnificent workmanship." Years later, he would recall these gates when he made his own designs for entrance doors to Trinity Church in New York City. Mrs. Hunt had engaged a courier, Giovanni, to help them with their travel arrangements, and the young Italian became almost a member of the family, so delighted with him were all of them.[28]

Since William had by this time decided not to return to Harvard but rather to pursue an artistic career, he wanted to become acquainted with art other than that of antiquity and the Italian Renaissance and therefore to travel in northern Europe. Moreover, the two youngest boys needed further schooling. So it was determined to go on to Switzerland to find a school and to establish a centrally located family headquarters. Journeying northward from Florence, the Hunts first visited Bologna, where Richard got involved in a card game and lost fifteen dollars. After Ferrara and Padua, they stopped briefly at Venice, and then by way of Vicenza, Verona, and Brescia, they went on to Milan. In the last city, Richard was tremendously impressed by the Grand Hospital, a vast establishment housing two thousand patients and employing four hundred doctors. A quarter of a century later, he would design a hospital in New York which, though smaller, would impress New Yorkers with its admirable medical facilities. The cathedral in Milan was a high point of the entire Italian visit: it was simply, Richard concluded, "the handsomest church I ever saw." As they left Italy, the Hunts also took leave of Giovanni, from whom they all parted with considerable regret. Geneva was their destination.[29]

By the end of May 1844, Richard and Leavitt were enrolled in a boys' academy in Geneva, which was directed by a schoolmaster named Alphonse Briquet. The two hundred and fifty or so students in Briquet's school were a highly cosmopolitan group, including some twenty other Americans as well as English and French youngsters among the foreign contingent. Richard, who was known to his classmates as Dick, and Leavitt called themselves "the Green Mountain boys," proudly proclaiming their New England origins. Richard took up playing the cornet, and he was chosen to command one of the school companies for military exercises. Moreover, the brothers acquired a horse, which they named Jacob, but they soon grew tired of caring for the animal and sold him in exchange for three watches and twenty Swiss francs. Richard had already built up a good foundation in French, and soon after entering Briquet's school he began to write his journal entries in French. Increasingly, during the following months, the names of young ladies, often characterized as *"très amusantes,"* appeared in his journal. He was a popular young man and attended many parties and balls. "I am," he wrote his mother in January 1845, "acquainted with about a dozen young ladies, *rather handsome,* as you might suppose."[30]

In August of 1844, Briquet gave permission for Richard and Leavitt to join their mother and sister for a holiday trip. After visiting Lausanne and Fribourg, they traveled to Bern, where they saw the fountains with bear figures, a motif that Hunt used many years later in his fountain design for Geneseo, New York. Going on to Basel, Strasbourg, Baden-Baden, and Wiesbaden, they lingered briefly at the watering place of Schwalbach, to which Richard would return more than once in later years. After visits to Mainz and a return to Wiesbaden, they went on to Frankfurt and Heidelberg, where Leavitt would soon go to study. On their return to Switzerland, near Zurich they unexpectedly encountered William and John exploring the countryside on horseback. Needless to say, the members of this closely knit family delighted in this unlooked-for reunion. The two youngest boys, their sister, and their mother then spent some days in the Swiss mountains, but they were back in Geneva by September 3. Briquet's classes commenced on September 4, and ten days later Richard was writing in his journal: "Same old routine in school!"[31]

In the spring of 1845, while the two youngest boys remained in school in Geneva, Mrs. Hunt with Jane, William, and John took an extensive trip to the eastern Mediterranean in the company of Thomas Gold Appleton, the son and heir of a highly successful Boston merchant and a later client of Richard Morris Hunt. They sailed early in April from Ancona, Italy, on an Austrian steamer, and spent a few hours on the island of Corfu and a day at Corinth before reaching Athens. For several days they remained in Athens, "visiting all there was to be seen of interest, going to the Piraeus and to Marathon," and carefully filling the pages of their sketchbooks with watercolors. An excursion to Eleusis was the culmination of their Greek visit. As Appleton exclaimed in a letter to his sister, Fanny Appleton Longfellow, "When we drove beside the sparkling sea, blue as the eyes of Minerva, we were wild with delight." In the small church at Daphne, the mosaic of Christ Pantocrator was "so quaint and fierce as to seem almost a robber." And at Eleusis they came upon "a party of English officers pottering over an incomprehensible monument, once a sort of huge medallion, with a head in *alto-rilievo*, but now destroyed."[32]

The Hunts decided to continue on with Appleton to Constantinople, for the group was "delightfully congenial." After a stop at Smyrna and a few hours at Gallipoli, their French steamer captain halted his vessel so that they "might have a sunrise impression for the first" view of the great city, coming so slowly that they might drink in "every slight change of this unrivaled panorama." As they rounded Seraglio Point, with its gardens and latticed kiosks, "the Golden Horn, then, like a cornucopia, poured its treasures at our feet, and, amid ships and steamers, and thousands of caïques, we dropped our anchor." Having settled in a lodging house overlooking a burial ground, "with tombstones like petrified Turks," they rushed out to catch a glimpse of the Sultan going to a mosque: He "stumbled along, almost supported by two officers, to his phaeton, rather gay with gold, and, after taking one long, sleepy look at us, he drove off with a grand chatter of attendants." The Hunts stayed in Istanbul for nearly a fortnight, remaining for the Orthodox Easter celebrations and joining the American consul for a festive picnic on the shores of the Black Sea. They returned westward by ship to Trieste.[33]

Meanwhile, at Briquet's school in Geneva, Richard was anxious to settle on a vocation. Early in January 1845, in a long letter to his mother, who was then in Paris, Richard reassured her about his health and his work at school and stated that he still remained committed to a military career:

It seems that you have spoken to Mr. Kimberly concerning the profession that I should lead in after life. My opinion is as it always has been, that I am destined to lead a military career, and for this reason, should enter West Point. I was well prepared for admission when I left America, the only thing that might be an obstacle is my age, but this be as it may, I was 17 yrs. old October/44. I will enumerate my several *accomplishments:* I have a schoolboy's knowledge of history. Quite a decent knowledge of Geography. Nearly ignorant of Greek and Latin. Know something about German, can translate easy Italian, and understand perfectly the French. My strongest point is Mathematiques. . . . This with a schoolboy's knowledge of Mechanics, Hydrostatics, Pneumatics, Astronomy, & Bookkeeping, is the sum total of all my *Gumption.*

Thus, being sufficiently prepared, I think, at least, that a West Point education should not be passed, if one is able to partake of its benefits.[34]

Four months later, in another letter to his mother, who had returned to Paris from her travels in the East, Richard came back once more to his plans for the future: He emphasized that the Hunt family had "always distinguished itself" and the idea that he and his three brothers, "who have had all the advantages in the world," would be "only 'small potatoes'" was *"outrageous."* He wrote that he was determined if not admitted to West Point or the navy to study architecture, and after "getting a good ground work" in Geneva would "endeavor to take a degree at the 'Ecole Centrale' at Paris, or some other *first rate* academy in Europe." Then he would "return to America where an architect of the *first* quality would be much sought for." Monsieur Briquet had said that he thought "I would make a first rate one."[35]

Apparently, his interest in architecture had been stimulated during his stay in Geneva. In 1844, he had commenced the study of architectural drawing and design outside Briquet's school with Samuel Darier, a Geneva architect who had attended the Ecole des Beaux-Arts in Paris in the 1830s. At this time he had also begun his collection of architectural books. Then, early in the summer of 1845, Richard went to Paris to visit his mother, who was staying there with his brother John, and he undoubtedly discussed his future plans with them. Most likely at this time he made the decision to begin preparations for the entrance examinations for the Ecole des Beaux-Arts. Upon returning to Switzerland, however, he evidently felt reluctant to cut his ties there yet. Obviously, he enjoyed his way of life in Geneva immensely. Leavitt, with whom among his brothers he was closest, was with him in Briquet's school, and his sister Jane was also then staying in Geneva, studying piano and drawing, and living not far from her two youngest brothers. Late in July, Richard wrote his mother that he was getting along very well in his studies, and "really, I don't think that I could do better at Paris." On August 1st, the day after his examinations were completed, however, he and his sister left for Paris.[36]

During the following months, Richard attempted to gain admission to the Ecole des Beaux-Arts. On September 4, he obtained a formal introduction to the school from the chargé d'affaires of the United States legation in Paris certifying that he was an American citizen. Then, on September 12, he obtained a second obligatory introduction to the school establishing himself as an *aspirant* (applicant). This came from Hector Martin Lefuel, a noted French architect, who had agreed to take Hunt into his atelier and thus serve as his *patron* at the Ecole.[37]

Within a few months most of the other members of the Hunt family were also settled in Paris. Mrs. Hunt and Jane shared an apartment there. John entered the Ecole de Médecine. Although William had been persuaded by the painter Emanuel Leutze to go to Düsseldorf to study, he remained in Germany only nine months and then came on to Paris first to study sculpture and then painting. Leavitt decided to prepare himself for a career in the law and went to Heidelberg for his advanced studies. Richard thus had most of his family close by during the years he was at the Ecole des Beaux-Arts. Paris would be his home for the next decade.[38]

The year 1845 had been a very important one for him, since his vocational direction had now been set. But Richard was not looking behind but to what lay before him. On December 31, 1845, he wrote in his journal just at midnight: "I watch the old year out and the new one in writing my journal exact 12. . . . Janvier 1er commençant à la minute. May my deeds this year keep pace with my good intentions. . . . Eighteen hundred and forty six, this date in your memory fix." Late in 1846 he would begin his formal studies at the Ecole des Beaux-Arts.[39]

3

A PARIS
EDUCATION

Paris was still largely a medieval city in the 1840s. Most of the streets were narrow and twisting, usually strewn with garbage. Facilities for the supply of fresh water and for the removal of sewage were highly inadequate, and only a few acres of land were available as public parks. Since many streets were badly lighted, it was unsafe for a well-dressed person to venture forth after dark in most quarters. During the decade that Richard Morris Hunt spent in Paris, however, the face of the city would be markedly changed.[1]

American visitors, used to a general physical uniformity in their own towns and cities and a sameness in appearance of the inhabitants, found Paris a highly colorful place. Guidebooks, travelers' accounts, and paintings and sketches had led them to expect a picturesque quality in European cities, and Americans coming to Paris in the first half of the nineteenth century were seldom disappointed with what they found. "I am very much amused in the streets with everything, soldiers, peasants, *bonnes,* hand-bills and signs," Richard's friend Theodore Winthrop wrote home to his mother in 1849. Winthrop was particularly struck by "the contrast between the fashion and splendor of the Boulevards, and the narrow and ancient streets, where you find a life so different that you might think yourself in another world—lofty old houses, crammed with people from cellar to skylight, but in all their darkness preserving something of the attempt at elegance that makes *any* house in Paris prettier than *any* house elsewhere. The women, in nice caps, go about as if life were pleasant, and the muddy street a ball-room." For many American visitors, the poor of the cities and the peasants of the countryside were pleasantly picturesque characters playing their roles as if on a stage; seldom did the New World visitors get to know such people as individuals. Moreover, the quaint houses, the stately churches, and the grand palaces were like stage backdrops to the human actors. Because the architecture of Paris and other European cities was decidedly different from what the Americans had known at home, many visitors from across the sea who had formerly had little interest in building styles and the details of architectural design found themselves avidly studying the structures they encountered.[2]

As a student of architecture, Richard would surely have been very interested in the principal new buildings recently completed or then under construction in Paris. Since his accession in 1830, Louis Philippe had undertaken several major building projects in the city. To strengthen his regime, the king wanted to identify the July monarchy with the glories of the Napoleonic empire. He had directed completion of Napoleon's Arc de Triomphe de l'Etoile and his Church of the

Madeleine, finished in 1837 and 1845 respectively. He planned to have Napoleon's remains brought to Paris and placed in the elaborate crypt at Les Invalides designed by Louis Visconti in 1842 and constructed 1843–1853. An obelisk, given by the Khedive of Egypt to Louis Philippe, was placed in the Place de la Concorde in 1833, where it might remind Parisians of Napoleon's Egyptian campaign. Subsequently, from 1836 to 1840, the Place de la Concorde, the Champs Elysées, and the Place de l'Etoile were decorated in imperial style, with grand fountains and ornate lamp standards.[3]

The 1840s brought a surge of architectural activity, though nothing like the efflorescence of the 1850s. Planning for the enlargement and redesign of the Palais de Justice was begun by Eugène-Emanuel Viollet-le-Duc in 1840, although the most important parts of the structure were built later on in the Second Empire. The foreign ministry headquarters on the Quai d'Orsay, designed by Jacques Lacornée in a Venetian adaptation of Renaissance forms, was begun in 1846. The great church of Sainte-Clotilde, built by Franz-Christian Gau in a fourteenth-century Rayonnant (radiating tracery) style, was started in 1846 and completed in 1857, while the chapter house at the Cathedral of Notre-Dame was begun by Viollet-le-Duc in 1847. The restoration of the old Palais du Louvre was begun in 1848, under the direction of Jacques-Félix Duban. Several Parisian hospitals and prisons also date from these years. New railway stations were built in iron and glass, including the Gare Montparnasse, 1848–1852, designed by V.-B. Lenoir and Eugène Flachat, and the Gare de Strasbourg (Gare de l'Est), 1847–1852, by F.-A. Duquesnay.[4]

The most notable and historically significant structure built in Paris during the 1840s was the Bibliothèque Sainte-Geneviève, designed by Henri P.-F. Labrouste in 1839 and constructed from 1843 to 1850. Effectively utilizing new cast-iron construction techniques, the library is notable for the refinement and originality of its masonry and ironwork. "Almost universally admired ever since its completion," the building, as Henry-Russell Hitchcock notes, is "the finest structure of the forties in France."[5]

Also on the left bank of the Seine, not far from the Bibliothèque Sainte-Geneviève though somewhat nearer to the river, stood the Ecole des Beaux-Arts, an impressive array of buildings, gateways, courtyards, and architectural fragments, with the principal entrance on the Rue Bonaparte. The Ecole was located on the tract once occupied by the church, cloisters, and other buildings of the convent of the Petits Augustins, an order which had been suppressed in 1789, at the outbreak of the

Revolution; the confiscated property had subsequently been made into a museum of French monuments. In 1816, the buildings of the museum were established as quarters for the Ecole des Beaux-Arts; later on, new structures for the school were erected in the former convent gardens.[6]

In the 1840s, a visitor entering the main gate of the Ecole would come into the outer forecourt, which centered on a red marble Corinthian column whose high base formed a seat. To the right stood a portal brought from the Château d'Anet, built by Philibert Delorme between 1548 and 1554 for Diane de Poitiers, a mistress of Henri II. Behind it was the Musée du Moyen-Age, containing sculpture casts from the Middle Ages and the Renaissance, and the small, gemlike Chapelle Michel-Ange. The main courtyard was separated from the forecourt by fragments of a chateau from Gaillon, beyond which rose the main building, the Palais des Etudes, begun by François Debret and completed by Jacques-Félix Duban in 1839–1840; it contained large galleries, filled with sculptural and architectural fragments, statuary, vases, and basins, surrounding a central, glass-covered courtyard, which served as a museum of plaster casts from antiquity. To the rear of the enclosed courtyard was a hemicycle auditorium used for ceremonial occasions. A library was located on the second floor.[7]

Although the Ecole Nationale et Spéciale des Beaux-Arts de Paris had been installed in the Rue Bonaparte location for only a few decades when Richard arrived, it was an established institution which had long played an important role in French life. The Ecole had its origins in the seventeenth century, when the French government had organized schools for the education of artists, modeled on the Accademia di San Luca in Rome and the Accademia delle arti del disegno in Florence. In earlier times architects and other artists had been trained as apprentices under guild supervision. The Académie Royale de Peinture et de Sculpture was established in 1648 as both an honorary society and a teaching body. The Académie Royale d'Architecture, founded in 1671, was originally composed of a small group of the most prominent architects, who regularly met to discuss the problems of their craft and to act as advisers to the government. This academy organized classes of instruction in architectural design, which looked back to Vitruvius for inspiration and promulgated the architectural ideals of Roman antiquity. Lectures were given as well in mathematics, perspective, mechanics, construction, and the principles of fortification. Architectural competitions had been set up in the academy by the early eighteenth century, the premier award being the Grand Prix, which allowed the winner to complete his architectural studies at the French Academy in Rome.[8]

In August 1793, during the Revolution, the two academies were suppressed. Thereafter some architectural instruction continued under private teachers; however, it was quickly recognized that the needs for trained architects were not being met, and the disbanded academy classes were soon revived and in 1795 renamed the Ecole Spéciale de l'Architecture, under the new Institut National des Sciences et des Arts. Napoleon reorganized the school, providing instruction in architecture, painting, sculpture, and engraving, and in 1816, Louis XVIII placed it under the supervision of the Académie des Beaux-Arts of the Institut de France. The Ecole was rechartered in 1819, and in 1863, Napoleon III put it directly under the control of the Ministre des Beaux-Arts of the central government.[9]

Competition for entry into the architectural section of the prestigious Ecole des Beaux-Arts was always intense. The school was open free to any young man, from age fifteen to thirty, French or foreign, who could pass the entrance examinations. These examinations, which were given annually, were difficult, and usually only a small proportion of those applying were successful. Many who failed to gain entry returned to try again and again. Applicants for admission had to belong to one of the recognized architectural ateliers (or private studios) or, in any case, to be presented for the entrance examinations as an applicant, or *aspirant,* by one of the atelier directors, or *patrons.* Students could choose their own ateliers.[10]

As an *aspirant,* Hunt began in September 1845 to prepare for the entrance examinations under the general supervision of Hector Martin Lefuel, who had agreed to be his *patron.* Like other *aspirants* he was permitted to attend lectures, use the library, and sketch casts at the Ecole even before being formally admitted. On October 1, he began going to the Ecole, and he soon was also working regularly in the Lefuel atelier. According to his journal, Richard took the entrance examinations at this time. Early in October, he took the examination in mathematics and was notified at the end of the month that he had been "received in mathematics." The graphic examination in descriptive geometry came in the first week in November, and around the 15th of November he had an oral examination in descriptive geometry; on the 17th of December he learned that he had been "received in descriptive geometry." That same day he presented himself for the *concours en architecture,* the all-important entrance test in architectural design. Hunt and the other *as-*

pirants were let into a large room with stalls around the sides and, after they were given instructions for a plan, an elevation, and a section of a specified building, with the dimensions and other particulars set forth, they had to complete their drawings, working in one of the stalls, in a straight twelve-hour stretch. The following day an exhibition of the work of the *aspirants* was held at the Ecole, and a jury decided which designs were acceptable. On December 19, 1845, Hunt wrote a terse entry in his journal: *"Décision pas reçu"* ("Decision not received"). He had failed the most crucial entrance test and was therefore denied admission. He would have to wait a full year before trying once again. Seriously resolving to make the effort to gain admission, he wrote in his journal the next day: *"Aujourd'hui nous commençons bien étudier l'architecture"* ("Today we really begin to study architecture").[11]

That is just what he did. The young American, who as a small child had astonished others by his industry, worked hard during the following months to carry out his resolution. He became familiar with the practices of the school and established a place for himself in Lefuel's atelier, going there regularly. He also studied the specifications of past architectural *concours*. Late in 1846, Hunt took the entrance examinations once again, this time successfully. He was admitted to the second, or lower, class of the Ecole on December 11, 1846.[12]

Once students were admitted to the second class, they advanced through the required work at their own pace. The best ones usually completed the work in two to four years, passing from the second class to the first or upper class when they had received the requisite numerical points (or *valeurs*) from their competitions (*concours*) both in architectural projects and in certain academic subjects. Promotion to the first class came only through competitive honors and prizes, which brought *valeurs*. Rivalry among the students was therefore intense but was mitigated by the aid that students gave one another in completing their projects. The students had a good deal of freedom in the school; they were not compelled to attend any classes and could remain enrolled even though they did very little serious work. In order to maintain good standing, however, students were obliged to enter at least one competition a year. Before 1869, they were allowed to stay in the school until they reached the age of thirty. A great many who were admitted to the second class never succeeded in getting into the first class.[13]

Architectural education at the Ecole was divided between the academic lectures, which few students attended, and the more practical design work in the private ateliers, located in the neighborhood of the Ecole. In the classroom, lectures were regularly offered on architectural subjects. Professors lectured to the lower class on architectural history, the theory of architecture, perspective, the elements of building construction, and mathematics. Students in the upper class might attend courses on building construction and professional practice. The architectural faculty of the Ecole consisted of distinguished men who had done exceptional professional work. Ordinarily the professors taught only a course or two while devoting themselves mainly to their own private practices. The students' most important instruction, that in architectural design, was, however, chiefly carried on in the informal atmosphere of the ateliers.[14]

The atelier system, the second foundational element of architectural education in France, was no doubt more influential in training architects than the systematic instruction given at the Ecole. Although the many design projects assigned to the students were formulated at the Ecole, the preliminary sketches were made there, and the final results were brought there to be judged and later exhibited, the actual work of preparing the designs for the competitions was mainly done in the ateliers. Here twenty or more students worked on their individual projects, helping one another and criticizing each other's work under the guidance and direction of the *patron*. The *patrons* were experienced and successful architects, who had their own professional practices and came perhaps two or three times a week to their ateliers to look over the work of the students. Lefuel, whose atelier Hunt joined, had studied at the Ecole and had won the Grand Prix in 1839; he was elected a member of the Académie des Beaux-Arts in 1855. Instruction in the atelier was usually casual, and the work done there was not always well integrated with the course instruction offered in the lecture rooms at the Ecole. There was great rivalry among the ateliers: the students in each generally were intensely loyal to their own group and to their *patron*.[15]

The student members themselves administered the ateliers, paying a fee to the *patrons* and contributing to a common fund for fuel and supplies. The *anciens,* or senior student members, of the ateliers were by custom severe taskmasters of the *nouveaux,* the junior members, who were under the general supervision of the *caporal des nouveaux.* The *nouveaux* were supposed to be at the beck and call of the *anciens* at all times, running errands, going out for food and drink, and cleaning up the workshop rooms. The meanest tasks of all were assigned to the most recent newcomer, *le dernier nouveau,* who was made to pull the cart, or *charrette,* on the day that drawings were taken to the Ecole for judging. The *anciens* selected one of their number as the administrator of the atelier; he served as treasurer and also acted as master of ceremonies on special occasions. Usually the ateliers had an assistant treasurer, as well as a librarian and an assistant librarian.[16]

Student life in the ateliers was filled with periods of intense work, relieved by a great deal of fun and pranks. Initiation dinners for the *nouveaux* were usually rowdy affairs, with the wine flowly freely and lots of singing, the initiates providing the entertainment for the evening. Newcomers were always expected to treat all the others in the atelier to drink. For Charles F. McKim, who came to study architecture in Paris in 1867, the most memorable characteristic of the atelier was the incessant noise: the shouting, howling, singing, and arguing made for an unending uproar. And in the evenings, the students customarily went to cafés to drink, sing, play cards, or talk politics until the early hours of the morning.[17]

The most important work of the students in their professional education, as Hunt discovered, came in their competitions, or *concours*, in architectural design. These *concours* were of two types, *projets rendus*, or finished drawings, completed in two months, and *esquisse* competitions (sometimes called *esquisse-esquisse*), done in a single twelve-hour period. For the first type of *concours*, six times a year, each class was assigned specified programs, issued in alternative months to the second class and to the first, which were to be developed into fully rendered projects with carefully executed drawings. On a selected day, the students came to the Ecole, where during a twelve-hour period in the stalls (*en loge*) of the competition room, they were each required, without the assistance of any reference materials, to make a preliminary sketch (*esquisse*) in accord with specifications handed out to them. The need to solve given architectural problems in a limited period of time forced the students to concentrate on the essential aspects and subordinate the less important elements of the program provided them. *Nouveaux* coming for the first time were initiated here once more before the serious work was begun; they were expected to provide drink for the others in the competition room. Sometimes the horseplay or the heated political discussions got out of hand, and guards had to be sent in to restore order. Experienced students made the preliminary *esquisse* as vague and noncommital as they could get by with to allow as much scope as possible for later changes in the proportions and the details. At the end of the day the students left their original signed sketches at the school, taking a tracing to show their *patrons* at the ateliers. If the *patron* approved the *esquisse*, the student might then proceed to "render" it, studying the problems presented and making the detailed, finished drawings. If the *patron* rejected the sketch, however, the student had to wait for two months before trying once more. After the preliminary sketch was made, students would often devote themselves to their other subjects or take a holiday excursion away from Paris before beginning the serious work of preparing the final drawings for the project. The final drawings were made under the guidance of the *patron*, and they clearly had to conform to the main ideas of the preliminary sketches; otherwise, they would not be considered by the jury, and the student would be disqualified. On the appointed day, the *projets rendus*, or finished drawings, including a plan, a section, and an elevation, were taken by cart (*en charrette*) to the Ecole, where a jury evaluated them, awarding honorable mentions and medals or cash prizes, all bringing numerical points, to those they judged best. The drawings were then placed on exhibit for all to see.[18]

Besides the *projets rendus*, students also came to the stalls six times a year, in alternate months, for a sketching competition that had to be composed, developed in detail, and completed in one twelve-hour period. As with the preliminary *projet* sketches, no reference materials or advice were allowed. An honorable mention for this difficult one-day effort would count for as many points toward advancement in the Ecole as a mention awarded for the *projet rendu*. In addition, the students in the second class had to participate in and receive a mention in four construction competitions, one each for wood, iron, stone, and general construction, lasting about four months each, and in competitions in mathematics and perspective before being admitted to the first class. For the students in the first class, the programs for the *projets rendus* and the one-day *esquisses* were considerably more complicated than those handed out to the lower class.[19]

Richard was committed to his architectural studies and, like most of the other students, worked day and night when the deadlines approached for completing the *projets*. He worked, however, not from a sense of duty but because he really enjoyed what he was doing and found, as he would later on, that the greatest satisfactions and gratifications of his life came from his occupation. Years later his wife recorded that Richard had begun his lifelong habit of drinking pots of tea during all-night sessions to complete his drawings.[20]

In the design competitions, the students of the Ecole des Beaux-Arts were exposed to a variety of architectural problems. Through the competitions as well as in the course of study, central architectural ideas or principles were to be mastered. The emphasis of the instruction was in solving problems rather than in developing competence in using particular styles, for the school aimed to teach the fundamentals of architecture, and, more important, a well thought-out system of planning, design, and construction.[21]

At the Ecole, the principles of composition taught were those of unity, proportion, scale, and balance of architectural forms, but, above all, the working out of a logical solution to the particular problems encountered in a structure. The term *parti* was used to refer to this concept of the most reasonable or logically right solution, from both an artistic and a practical point of view. Indeed, as the American architect Ernest Flagg put it toward the end of the century, "success or failure at the school so far as the architect is concerned depends chiefly upon his ability to seize the *parti*." Flagg saw the ability to find the best *parti* as a natural gift which could only be acquired in a limited way. Only the most talented could hope to use the *parti* in an original manner; however, others might learn traditional solutions and do work creditable enough to gain the necessary mentions. Originality in developing the *parti* was encouraged by the judges in their awards. The *parti* was supposed to take into account such things as the uses and needs of the building being designed, lighting and air circulation in the rooms, convenience of movement through the structure, appropriateness of the forms and decorative elements, fitness of scale and proportions, economy of means, and, though often ignored, relationships of buildings to one another in large-scale planning. Each design, then, should be based on the functions of particular structures.[22]

Since the *parti* was most clearly set forth in the plan, the plan itself was of primary importance for the Beaux-Arts students in their compositions. In Flagg's view, it was "scarcely an exaggeration to say that in making awards the plan counts for nine parts out of ten." Purely artistic considerations, imposed decorative elements, and stylistic consistency were always to remain secondary to the plan. Those Beaux-Arts plans judged best were usually symmetrical and often axial and usually involved an openness and a sense of flow of spaces from one room to another.[23]

Much of the Beaux-Arts training was in the design of public buildings, formal in composition and frequently monumental in scale. The enframement of the mass of the building was stressed, so that each structure had a well-defined base, middle, and terminating roofline. Exteriors were closed compositions, solidly placed and usually static in appearance. Considerable emphasis was placed on the relationship of interior spaces; and the way a viewer moving into and through the building might experience the different areas in a logical and orderly progression of architectural elements to climaxes of form and space (*la marche*) was considered of primary importance. The Beaux-Arts tradition was derived, of course, from Renaissance classicism. Picturesque elements and individual fantasies and eccentricities were to be eschewed. Only within the guidelines of the tradition was there scope for individual creativity.[24]

The students at the Ecole des Beaux-Arts were expected, as a matter of course, to learn to draw well. Drawings had to be rendered precisely, so that the *parti* was clearly evident, but also imaginatively, especially in elevations, where immediate settings were often delineated. The drawings for student *projets* could frequently stand on their own as fascinating compositions of line and form and light and shade, highly decorative, stimulating the viewer's imagination.[25]

While Hunt was studying in Paris, a great ferment of ideas and agitation for reform was building at the Ecole. The demands for teaching reform were led by Eugène-Emanuel Viollet-le-Duc, who had not himself studied at the Ecole. For some years, Viollet-le-Duc had been working on the restoration of medieval structures in France, and in analyzing medieval modes of building he had found a rational structural system that he believed should be followed in principle, in contemporary work. Just as in Romanesque and Gothic building the methods of construction, the plans, and the materials used all logically determined the design, so, he urged, the design of buildings in the nineteenth century should freely express the plans, the materials, and the character and purpose of those structures rather than being concealed by traditional applied decoration. By contrast, the members of the Académie des Beaux-Arts, who controlled the Ecole, clung to an idealized Roman-French classical tradition and strongly opposed the rationalism and the picturesque character of the Gothic and the Gothic Revival. The reformers wished to have less of a conservative, classical, fine-arts emphasis in the curriculum at the Ecole and more work on practical architectural problems relevant to the nineteenth century, utilizing rationalist principles. Eventually, in 1863, after Hunt had left, the Ecole was reorganized, new professors were brought in, three new official ateliers were set up, and some curricular changes were made. A new council to oversee the Ecole was established, including Lefuel, who was sympathetic to the rationalist ideas and yet was still very much a traditionalist. Viollet-le-Duc was named a professor, but students were so hostile to him that he quickly resigned his post. The "progressive" reforms ultimately had little impact, as traditionalists continued to dominate the school. Hunt later became well acquainted with Viollet-le-Duc, and the new ideas had considerable impact on Hunt's own architectural thinking.[26]

As a student in the lower class, Hunt was first successful in winning honorable mentions in his four construction competitions in 1847 and 1848, followed by one in mathematics in 1848 and in the *concours* in perspective in 1849. He received mentions in architectural composition only in 1849, 1850, and 1851. On June 6, 1851, he received two mentions in architectural composition, the project for one of which is pictured in figure 4, and with these finally gained the points he needed for admission to the first class, four and a half years after he had entered the school. Like other students there, Hunt failed in numerous competitions both in his subjects and in his *projets rendus* and his one-day *esquisse* sessions. After he was admitted to the first class, Hunt continued to enter competitions, although during much of 1852 and 1853 he was away from Paris on travels. He did enroll in competitions in August, September, and October 1853, and again as late as April 4, 1854. But while a student in the first class, he was completely unsuccessful in the competitions and received no further mentions. By and large, the official record suggests that Hunt's work at the Ecole des Beaux-Arts was rather undistinguished.[27]

In a few years other Americans followed Hunt to study architecture at the Ecole. In 1852, after he had been promoted to the first class, Arthur Dexter and Francis Peabody enrolled and joined Lefuel's atelier, but both men remained only a short time. Henry Hobson Richardson, who came to France in 1859, gained entry in 1860, after having failed the entrance examinations on his first try. In the 1860s nine other Americans besides Richardson studied there, and in the 1870s thirty-three Americans were enrolled; in the 1880s there were twenty-nine Americans and one hundred and fifty-two in the 1890s.[28]

Hunt's years in Paris were very happy ones. His days were filled with study and work at Lefuel's atelier and at the Ecole, and he had ample means to explore the city and to enjoy the amusements of Paris, especially the theater, and to go off for extended sightseeing and sketching excursions, another important aspect of his architectural education. His social contacts gave him admission to circles at the upper reaches of Parisian society, and he numbered both French and American students among his closest friends. Soon after arriving in the capital he was presented to King Louis Philippe and invited to balls at the Tuileries Palace. His mother, sister, and brothers (figure 5) were often in the city

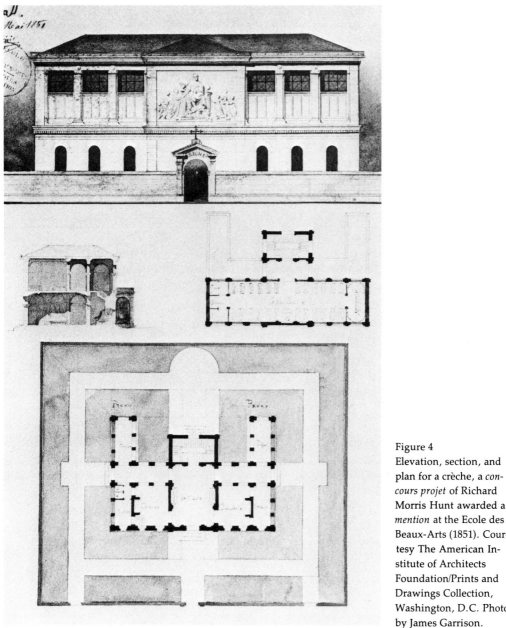

Figure 4
Elevation, section, and
plan for a crèche, a *concours projet* of Richard
Morris Hunt awarded a
mention at the Ecole des
Beaux-Arts (1851). Cour-
tesy The American In-
stitute of Architects
Foundation/Prints and
Drawings Collection,
Washington, D.C. Photo
by James Garrison.

Figure 5
Jane Maria Hunt and her
children, Paris, about
1848 (l. to r.): Richard
Morris, Jane, Leavitt,
Mrs. Jane Maria Hunt,
William Morris, and
John. From an old
photograph, Hunt
Papers.

and undoubtedly gave him the special sympathy and family companionship that he sometimes needed.[29]

The pattern of his life in Paris involved not only long periods of sustained work at the atelier and the Ecole but also many journeys away from the city. On August 4, 1846, while he was still preparing for the entrance examinations, Richard, along with his brothers John and Leavitt and his mother and sister, crossed the English Channel from Dieppe to Brighton to spend a month traveling in England, Scotland, and Ireland. This was Richard's first trip to Britain; subsequently, he often returned to spend satisfying days in London and the English countryside. On this first trip the family were thorough sightseers and avid opera- and ballet-goers. Near London, Greenwich Hospital and the Observatory impressed Richard as much as anything else. They stopped briefly at Oxford, Stratford-on-Avon, Kenilworth Castle, Matlock, Sheffield, York, and Manchester, and then went on to Preston, Carlisle, Melrose Abbey, Abbotsford, Edinburgh, and Glasgow. For a few days they saw something of Ireland, then in the midst of the Great Famine, but they were interested in places and not people, in architecture and not social conditions, and as well-to-do travelers were largely insulated from the terrible suffering around them. Richard and John left the others in Ireland to hurry back to Paris by September 5.[30]

That same month, September 1846, Richard's brother William came to Paris after a brief trip back to the United States following a period of study in Düsseldorf. In Paris, he had hoped to become a pupil of the sculptor James Pradier, but the French artist was traveling in Italy when William arrived. Sometime later, while trying to decide just what he might do, William chanced to see in an art supply store window a painting by Thomas Couture, which so delighted him that he at once applied to join Couture's class in painting. He was accepted into Couture's atelier, opened in 1847, and continued to study with this artist for over five years. Couture had become highly successful in utilizing a freer and more open technique than that of most of the academic painters, and his studio became one of the most popular in Paris. In the Couture atelier, William, always attracting others by his charm and wit, was given the name of "Maurice," adapted from his middle name, Morris; he quickly became a favorite pupil of the artist and was invited to paint in Couture's private studio. It was said that he so mastered Couture's style that his paintings were sometimes mistaken for the Frenchman's own works. William also studied sculpture with Antoine Louis Barye, the noted animal sculptor. In 1847 he modeled a large plaque in high relief of galloping horses, based on a Persian poem about Anahita, the goddess of night, sent him by his brother Leavitt; this composition formed a major element of many studies he continued to work and rework for the rest of his life, and it was central to one of the ceiling frescoes he prepared for the New York State Capitol in Albany in 1878.[31]

Richard Hunt was always interested in arts other than the one he had chosen for his profession, and he enrolled in Couture's atelier, while William was working there, for periods of study in painting and drawing in 1849 and 1851. On a subsequent visit to Paris, Richard also studied sculpture with Barye. In later years, he would work closely with decorators, sculptors, and woodcarvers on many of his buildings, making good use of the training he had received in Paris.[32]

For some years Richard and William shared an apartment at 1 Rue Jacob, while Mrs. Hunt and Jane, who often copied at the Louvre galleries, lived nearby at 22 Rue Jacob. John lived on the Rue des Beaux-Arts and later just opposite his brothers on the Rue Jacob. Leavitt frequently came to Paris for short visits. The Hunt brothers collected old paintings, antique furniture, and a variety of *objets d'art*, many of which they later took back to the United States. Richard's treasures would adorn his New York studios and his homes, and many of his pieces became family heirlooms. One especially cherished possession was an old carved bookcase, which was filled with costumes for amateur theatricals. On one occasion Richard and some friends donned costumes to go on stage as extras, posing as court dignitaries in a public performance. Richard also enlarged his book collection, the nucleus of what came to be probably the best library of architectural books in the United States. The brothers hired a cook, and the meals they served made a visit to their apartment a special occasion for their many French and American friends.[33]

But Richard and William frequently overspent and then had to scrimp while waiting for remittances from the United States. For a time they met regularly with a group of Americans living in Paris who called themselves the "O.M.C.'s," or the "Out of Money Club." Benjamin Champney, an American who was studying painting in Paris, later reminisced that William "was the soul of the club, full of fun, having the wittiest jokes and stories at his command. He could sing the jolliest songs, give the drollest imitations, and do queer things with a most nonchalant air. He was pervaded with good nature, and we all voted him the Prince of Good Fellows." The meetings of the club always closed with a spirited rendition of "The Star Spangled Banner."[34]

The year 1847, as the events and activities Richard noted in his journal indicate, was filled with a pleasant combination of hard work at the

atelier, with occasional *concours* and *charrettes,* and considerable play.
The pages of the journal include accounts of his visits to the theater, his attendance at balls, and his evenings on the town, as well as the comings and goings of members of the family, mention of American friends he saw, and descriptions of excursions in and around Paris. The masked ball of January 9, 1847, was especially noteworthy for him, since all the young men from Lefuel's atelier went in costume, but so boisterous were they when they got to the hall that most of them were not allowed inside. The morning after, "Frank [Francis Peabody] and I accompanied Clarisse and Francine to their place at 10 o'clock." In August, Mrs. Hunt with Jane and Leavitt toured Germany once again, and in October they left for Liverpool to take a steamer to Boston.[35]

Richard was in Paris during the coup d'état of February 1848, which brought down the July monarchy. Although he was caught up in the excitement of the political upheaval, Richard was always the observer rather than the participant in the political violence. On February 22, with a fellow student from the Ecole, he went to look at the barricades on the Boulevard de la Madeleine and view the damage on the Champs Elysées, where sidewalks had been upturned, benches broken, and trees torn down. When a rioting mob came too close they took refuge for a time in a billiard saloon. In his journal he recorded his experiences on the next day:

On the 23rd. everything was upset, processions of workingmen in the streets crying: 'A bas Guizot, vive la réforme.' The day before they attacked the Chambre des Députés. The Tirailleurs de Vincennes fired on the people in the Rue St. Martin and in that quarter. During the day the King changed his ministers. In the evening Paris was illuminated. It would be impossible to imagine a more beautiful spectacle than the imense city, everyone given over to gayety, without restrictions from the police, and the illuminated streets, through which they raced, singing in the light of their torches. There is only one place, in this great and beautiful city, where one cannot pass; this is before Guizot's hotel. People press from all sides on the cuirassiers-de-ligne, who are planted at this point, to defend the deposed minister from attack. But now an accident happens! A shot wounds the horse of a lieutenant of a company. Where did it come from? Nobody knows. We were too near to be pleasant, we saw the flash and we heard the noise of the guns; for a moment we thought it was fireworks. We were pushed on by the crowd who all rushed to the opposite side, on and on, stopped from time to time by the soldiers who will not let us advance. We cannot believe that they have drawn on the people. A man says to us 'If you do not believe it, go into the first tobacco shop and look about you.' Jack wanted to stay with them, then I realized that we had had no dinner and we went quickly home so that Jack might prepare himself to return and be of use. . . .

Soon we heard cries of 'Aux armes, on assassine nos frères.' Then the Tocsin rings and the Revolution is declared. . . .[36]

Henry Chauncey, who later became Richard's brother-in-law, arrived in Paris during the days of turmoil and long remembered the vivid accounts the Hunt brothers gave of the demonstrations and the fighting they had witnessed. William, as usual, dominated the discussions, with his brilliant and picturesque descriptions. Yet Chauncey recalled that Richard was "a keen observer and an acute judge of men and things," and that many of his observations were more vivid and shrewder than those of his elder brother. "Richard had been everywhere, taking no account of the danger, and he seemed to have seen everything."[37]

Even at the height of the revolutionary upheavals, Paris could still provide good drama in the theater as well as in the streets. Richard continued to go to the theater and found the famous actress Rachel supporting the revolutionary cause: in later years he "never ceased to speak of the wonderful way in which Rachel chanted the 'Marseillaise' during the Revolution of 1848, between the acts of her plays, enveloping herself with a swift movement in the folds of the French flag."[38]

Late in the spring of 1848, while John and William remained in Paris, Richard returned for a visit to the United States. He sailed on the *Bavaria* from Le Havre and joined his mother and Jane and Leavitt in Brattleboro. With them he took a four months' tour of the upper South and the trans-Appalachian West. This was the first time he had been in the United States for almost five years, and the newness and the rawness of much of the country he visited must have struck him by contrast with the antiquity and the sophistication of the Europe he had come to know. Unfortunately, Richard ended his own journal just as he started out for America, and we must rely on his sister Jane's diary for details of the 1848 visit.

The Hunts left Brattleboro on June 13 for Albany, going from there by steamboat to New York City and by train to Philadelphia. There they went to see the Girard College buildings, Thomas U. Walter's remarkable Greek Revival undertaking, which had just been opened, but they were not admitted to the school since they had no written permit. They visited Benjamin Latrobe's waterworks, and Mrs. Hunt and Jane also paid their respects to Hiram Powers's *Greek Slave,* the most famous statue sculpted by an American in the mid-nineteenth century, then on exhibit in Philadelphia. The family shortly went on by steamer to Baltimore, where they attended Sunday services at the Roman Catholic Cathedral, designed by Benjamin Latrobe, and were surprised to find themselves locked into a pew. Point Comfort, Virginia, at Hampton Roads, was their primary goal, however, and here they spent a fortnight, strolling on the beach and bathing and fishing in the waters nearby. They made excursions to Fort Monroe and to Hampton. Several years later Richard would contribute his architectural services to the Hampton Institute. After a steamer trip to Richmond, the Hunts traveled westward to Charlottesville and to Staunton, stopping to sketch at the Natural Bridge, and then on to the hot springs area of western Virginia, lingering there for six weeks more. By early September, they were on their way down the Ohio River by riverboat to Maysville, Kentucky, where they detoured to the south to pay a visit to Henry Clay at his home, Ashland, near Lexington. Clay received Mrs. Hunt, whom he had known nearly two decades earlier in Washington, and her three children "very cordially," showed them presents he had been given, including a wine glass used by General Washington during the Revolutionary War, and delighted them with gifts of delicious grapes, apples, and pears. In Cincinnati, they took care of some legal matters connected with their real estate holdings. Later they traveled overland to Nashville, Tennessee, admiring there William Strickland's magnificently situated capitol, and then went on by riverboat to St. Louis. Their eastward return took them to Chicago, across Lake Michigan and Michigan to Detroit, and by steamer across Lake Erie to Buffalo and Niagara Falls. It was mid-October before they got back to Vermont. Toward the end of the year, Richard returned to France, arriving in Paris in mid-December, after a placid transatlantic voyage lasting twenty-one days. Lefuel and others in the atelier were very happy to see him back, he wrote to his mother, and in the annual rating of the scholars at the Ecole, after his second year there, he was pleased to note that he had been ranked as number seven.[39]

Soon Richard was once more immersed in his studies and his work at the atelier, already thinking about making a career in the United States when he was fully prepared. Probably the short visit to his homeland had stimulated his plans for what he might be able to do there as an architect, and like other young Americans studying in Europe he patriotically envisioned his life work as an endeavor to help improve the national condition. Theodore Winthrop, Richard's boyhood friend, wrote to his own mother from Paris in 1849 about Richard as follows:

I see my old schoolmate, Dick Hunt, all the time; he is working hard at architecture, with a manly and patriotic feeling, to make himself of use at home. He has passed rapidly and successfully through all the examinations. The French system is calculated to bring out any original powers a man has. I am in the Louvre all the time, admiring, and full of plans for improving the condition of the fine arts in my own country. I am inclined to think that few men place their hopes higher than their powers, and therefore expect my friend Dick Hunt will do good work at home.

In his journal young Winthrop confided that he had "talked with Dick Hunt about changing our seat of government, and laying out a grand new city as a national monument." With irrepressible optimism, Winthrop concluded: "Hurrah! We'll do it."[40]

Although Hunt expressed enthusiasm about working to improve the state of the arts in his own country, several years were to pass before he could begin to act on his hopes. In the early 1850s his education continued both in his work at the Ecole des Beaux-Arts and in extensive travel throughout western and southern Europe and Egypt and the Near East. In his journeys he attempted to broaden his knowledge of the history of architecture by becoming personally acquainted with as many of the great buildings of the past as he could visit. In 1854 he was invited to participate in one of the most important French public projects of the time. The first half of the 1850s, then, was for Hunt a period of learning and expanding horizons and at mid-decade an initiation into valuable practical experience.

Increasingly while at the Ecole, Richard was taking time from his studies and projects to become better acquainted with Europe. He traveled regularly each summer. He again journeyed to England in the summer of 1850, this time by way of Normandy and the Isle of Jersey, accompanied by his brothers William and John for a good part of the excursion. After visiting Rouen they went on to Le Havre, where the port area especially fascinated them. A coastal steamer then took them across the Bay of the Seine. They were enchanted by Caen, with its clean, broad streets, its quiet, and its comforts, and particularly by the architecture of St. Etienne and the Hôtel Dieu. "During our promenade we seemed to agree very well that Caen was the grandest ville that we had ever seen of its size," Richard commented in his sketchbook. The following day they went on to Cherbourg by way of St. Lô, catching a glimpse of the cathedral at Bayeux. At Cherbourg they requested and received permission to visit the forts in the harbor. Their tour of Normandy then took them south by way of Coutances, Granville, Avranches, and Pontorson to Mont-St.-Michel, which they thoroughly inspected: "We . . . were somewhat disappointed as regards architectural details, but were much astonished at its imposing and grand appearance *comme ensemble*. On returning we made the acquaintance of two charming young ladies from Jersey in company with whom we visited the hospital here, a well-directed establishment where we were much amused by some of its *cracked* inmates." At St. Malo, on July 29, they strolled on the rocky beach, visited Chateaubriand's tomb, attended the theater, and went to a *fête*, where they "had a fine chance of studying the Bretagne profile."[1]

Another steamer ferried them across the rough waters of the Gulf of St. Malo to the Isle of Jersey, "a deservedly termed paradise." John became seasick on the way, but he recovered quickly enough, and on

4

TRAVEL AND
APPRENTICESHIP

the ramparts they "accosted two pretty girls who had quite an interesting conversation. John was more especially interested than I, what with her speaking English and his Sp.-French they got along pretty well." Jersey was decidedly a most agreeable place, and since they paid no duties the inhabitants seemed to enjoy every luxury, "but as regards art they dream not what it is."[2]

Their boat from Jersey touched at Guernsey and Aldernay on the way to Southampton, where they encountered the royal yacht in the harbor and saluted the royal family. On landing, the brothers went to a recommended hotel, but quickly changed to another when they discovered that it was a temperance establishment. Southampton proved to be unbearably dull, lacking in art and in any decent public entertainment. But, short of money, they were stuck there for a few days until their banker in London forwarded funds to them. When their purses were once more stocked, the brothers went by train to Salisbury, recording along the way their astonishment at how intensively cultivated the English fields were. Salisbury Cathedral was "remarkably impressive," but all in all the churches and cathedrals of England, Richard felt, just did not compare with those in France. The final entry in the 1850 sketchbook was made at Portsmouth, and most likely they returned to France after only a few more days in England.[3]

Again in each of the two following years, Richard visited England, recording the journeys with notes and drawings in his small sketchbooks. With Leavitt, he went to London to see the Great Exhibition in June 1851. His first visit to the Crystal Palace on June 9 elicited: "Not much for a traveller"; and returning three days later he decided that "the oriental countries [were] the only [ones] interesting to *me*." He made no comments about the remarkable glass and iron structure itself. But London still had much to offer the young Americans—book buying, a night on the town ending in a 4:00 A. M. supper in the Haymarket, visits to the Houses of Parliament, and, of course, the theater. Crossing back to the Continent, Richard and Leavitt visited Lille and Ghent, enjoying lively balls in both cities. Traveling eastward to Liège and Aix-la-Chapelle (Aachen), Richard noted that they "were bored as is usual with Germans in our carriage." At Düsseldorf, where William had studied five years before, they called on Emanuel Leutze, who "was very polite indeed," played tenpins at an artists' club, and went hunting with pistols. If they saw Leutze's most famous painting, *Washington Crossing the Delaware*, completed that year, they made no mention of it. On the boat trip up the Rhine River from Cologne it rained hard, but the day was saved by a pretty young lady they met, one of many whom Richard noted on this

trip. By June 22 they were in Heidelberg, where Leavitt had been studying law for some years. Within the week, Leavitt, who scarcely had time
to unpack from his journey, took his law examinations and was notified
on June 30 that he had passed. Richard was bored in Heidelberg, though
he encountered several American friends there and was happy to arrange a walking excursion through the Tyrol with a friend before returning to Paris. The notes for this 1851 tour conclude with the July 3rd
entry: "Had a fine time in the diligence with a young girl from Mann-
heim."[4]

The next year, 1852, Richard's English visit focused on London and
its environs, including Hampton Court and Windsor Castle. Hunt always found England far less picturesque and architecturally less interesting than France, and on this visit he wrote down his impressions
of the contrasts between London and Paris:

What a hub bub, bustling, murky town is London, in itself, on arriving
from Paris. Not a church, house, shop, fountain, or monument of any
kind that displays the slightest knowledge or even desire of such a thing
in the way of fine arts; every detail from the mouldings in their architectural details down to the balustrades and lamp posts shows the greatest
ignorance and the most profound bad taste conceivable. Luckily, however, Nature has done her best toward embellishing the city. She has
endowed it with a foggy climate which obstructs the view and thereby
making it more interesting. This however would not suffice altogether;
the Londoners have therefore set up their infernal smoke jacks in all
quarters so that the houses have all a peculiar tint resembling much a
badly blacked boot. Add to this the advantage of having the streets
badly lighted, shops shut,—And one may be able to drive quickly
through the town in a Hansome cab without feeling ill.[5]

Meanwhile, public events in France were to intrude on the Hunt
family once more, though only briefly and with only a slight jar to their
lives. The downfall of the Second Republic came with the coup d'état of
December 1851, bringing Louis Napoleon to a position of great power
leading the following year to the establishment of the Second Empire. At
the beginning of the turmoil the entire family except Leavitt was in
Paris, and Mrs. Hunt drew out all her available funds from her bankers
and insisted that they all leave immediately for England. But the three
brothers refused to go, whereupon Mrs. Hunt and her daughter moved
in with the sons for safety. John and a friend, who marched on the
boulevards shouting, "Vive la République," got caught in a clash with
soldiers and were arrested. John was slightly wounded in the encounter
and was released at the police station.[6]

By this time William's artistic talent was beginning to be widely recognized. Richard felt that his eldest brother had made great progress, both in painting and in modeling. Many Americans coming to Paris sought William out for advice on the purchase of works of art, and at the same time his own paintings were becoming known. In 1850 he did a sober, realistic portrait of his mother, and in 1852 he painted *The Girl at the Fountain*, for which his sister Jane posed. His *La Marguerite*, a three-quarter-length portrait of a young woman, her head bent forward as she pulls petals from a daisy, was greatly admired when it was shown in the Paris Salon of 1852, along with his *La Bonne Aventure*; they were the only paintings exhibited in the Salon that year by an American. *La Marguerite* was one of ten paintings that Louis Napoleon chose to purchase from this Salon for his own collection, but when the imperial messenger came to William's studio to get the painting, Richard, who was there in William's absence, knowing that this work had been promised to an American buyer, refused to release it. Nor would Richard let it go when a second messenger came from the emperor demanding the painting. The American for whom it was intended turned out to be uninterested in the work, however, and it was sent to Boston for exhibit. Hunt's boyhood friend Martin Brimmer later purchased another version of the painting. When Thomas G. Appleton, William's former traveling companion in Greece and Constantinople, came to Paris in the autumn of 1852, he saw the Hunt brothers often and wrote home that William was indeed "doing uncommonly well."[7]

Sometime late in 1852, or early in 1853, William left the Paris apartment to move to the hamlet of Barbizon, about thirty-five miles southeast of Paris, close to the Forest of Fontainebleau. He wanted to be near Jean-François Millet, whose work he had first come to know some two or three years before. After seeing Millet's somberly realistic *Sower* in the Salon of 1850, William obtained an introduction to the painter, probably through William Perkins Babcock of Boston, who had studied with Millet since 1849. Soon William was going frequently to Barbizon to talk with the French artist, coming more and more under his influence. William bought a version of *The Sower* for three hundred francs (about sixty dollars) as well as other paintings and drawings Millet had done, and he arranged for friends to acquire Millet's work as well. He eventually rented a house in Barbizon, kept a team of two horses there, and lived very comfortably, often affecting the blouse and sabots of French peasants. Millet's canvases were far more direct and personal than those of Couture, and William had come to feel that Couture had little more to teach him, while from the peasant artist he could learn a great deal. "[Millet] taught me," Hunt said, "to see nature, to appreciate the Bible, and he gave me broad ideas of humanity. I felt with him the infinitude of art. With Couture, there was a limit." For nearly two years William remained with Millet, painting alongside him, joining him for long walks, and occasionally visiting painting exhibitions with him in Paris. With his artistic change, Hunt moved into the forefront of the innovative and vital forces in mid-nineteenth-century French art, characterized by the work of such figures as Millet, Narcisse Diaz, Gustave Courbet, Jean-Baptiste Camille Corot, and Théodore Rousseau; and he himself became a link introducing these new ideas of direct, expressive realism to the United States.[8]

During the spring of 1852, Richard largely concluded his work at the Ecole des Beaux-Arts. In the course of the past seven years his association with Lefuel had become increasingly close, and the French architect had obviously become very fond of his American protégé and respected his abilities. Probably Richard found in the older man something of the father he had lost when so young, and he sought out his advice as to how he might best continue his preparations for his career. Lefuel had encouraged him to travel extensively but urged him to learn from what he saw: "If other countries teach you as France has taught you," Lefuel prophesied, "you will do great things." With his formal education mostly completed, Richard decided to undertake a much longer trip than his several earlier excursions. For more than a year he was engaged in almost continuous travel as he became acquainted with much more of the Continent and the Mediterranean world.[9]

His travels began in July 1852 with a short excursion with his mother and sister to the Loire Valley châteaux, whose forms would have such a strong influence on several of his own designs in later years. Richard made many sketches and noted some of the discomforts they encountered. At Chambord, Mrs. Hunt and Jane had to spend the night in a convent, there being no hotel rooms available, while at Blois they all found lodgings together at the Hôtel Lion d'Or, which, though "quite bad," was convenient to the château. At Blois, Richard sketched the façade and noted that the château, which was being temporarily used as a prison for a group of Arabs, was terribly dirty. He found the Château of Amboise immensely impressive, but the high point of the Loire Valley excursion was a July 14 visit to Chenonceaux, which was "beautifully kept up; everything exists as formerly; the most interesting and comfortable chateau I ever saw." He also recorded that he was doing considerable photography, perhaps having learned this skill from his brother Leavitt, who, after completing his work at Heidelberg, had already traveled to Egypt and the Near East, taking many photographs there.[10]

On August 1, 1852, Richard left Paris with William for his most extensive journey of all. He went, he said, drawn by "the sense of obligation to my profession, and to get by travel a larger and more extended experience." Taking along photographic equipment as well as their sketchbooks and watercolors, the two brothers first traveled northward to Brussels and Rotterdam. At the Dutch border, Richard told the customs agent that he was a professional photographer in order to get his equipment into the country without paying a duty. William, whose musical talents were noteworthy, was "enchanted with the music" they heard at The Hague. Throughout Holland they searched for and purchased antiques, which they had sent for them back to Paris. At Edam, the town crier even announced to the residents that foreign visitors were in town who would buy any and all antiques they would bring to the café, "and they came with antiquities of all sorts. Quite amusing." The brothers stopped at Düsseldorf and dined with Leutze on August 20. The next day they got to Berlin, where they took many photographs, but they were becoming increasingly irritated by the cumbersome apparatus they were carting around. Richard also noted here that "on returning to [the] hotel I caught a very pretty bird," and when they got to Prague on September 1, he and his brother amused themselves by "catching swallows all the morning from our windows, and tying strings to their legs before letting them fly again." In Vienna on September 4, Richard recorded that the picture gallery was "quite fine but tedious," while a performance of *The Magic Flute* was only "pretty good." They then went on to Trieste and Venice, where William painted at the Academy, while Richard savored the architectural delights with his comrade Paul Baudry from Paris and some young architectural students from the French Academy in Rome.[11]

Apparently parting from William in Venice, Richard then traveled about Italy for almost three months, often joining friends for a time. He was an unhurried tourist who let impressions sink in, took pains to make many careful sketches, and obviously had a good time. A journey of three weeks through Lombardy and Piedmont brought him to Florence, where he stayed for a month. Architectural sketching, visits to the galleries, lessons in Italian, and excursions to nearby towns kept him occupied, and several American friends were with him to provide companionship. When he and one friend visited the Church of San Miniato in Florence, dragging along Richard's heavy and awkward photographic equipment, his friend took such good pictures that he had no difficulty selling them almost right away. Subsequently, Richard spent twelve days in Spoleto and about ten days in Rome, which, of course, he already knew well. From Rome, he and a friend named Daniel Stuart Elliott took a *vettura* coach to Civitàvecchia and sailed from there to Naples, Messina, Sicily, past Etna, and on to the Island of Malta. At Valletta on Malta, on December 15, Richard recorded that the streets had "somewhat an Oriental look," though all in all the island had a "most forlorn" appearance, like "one immense rock, dark gray on the surface, covered with little stone walls, with here and there small stone square houses, terraced, with one or two grated windows or port holes, or a door." At the end of December he and Elliott sailed for Egypt.[12]

At the time Richard arrived in Egypt, in January 1853, a visit there for an American was still something of a novelty. The Napoleonic expedition of 1798 had led to the collecting of considerable scholarly information, which was reflected in articles in popular journals, and in the early years of the nineteenth century interest in Egypt grew immensely in both Europe and America. An Egyptian collection at the Peabody Museum in Salem, Massachusetts, Egyptian stylistic elements in American architecture, and a mummy presented to "the good people of Boston" by a Smyrna merchant and placed in the operating room of the Massachusetts General Hospital all stimulated American interest in the country. John Lowell, Jr., of Boston, visited Luxor in 1835 and sent back to Boston a large granite block from Karnak. George Gliddon, who had served as American consul in Cairo, began in 1842 to give illustrated lectures in the United States on ancient Egypt, while a book derived from his lectures, *Ancient Egypt*, sold thousands of copies. Most important of all for Richard, of course, was the trip his younger brother Leavitt had made the year before, when he took some of the first photographs of the area. Later on, toward the close of the century, an Egyptian tour became for many Americans less an adventuresome excursion and more a fashionable necessity.[13]

Richard's introduction to Egypt and the Muslim world came at the port of Alexandria, where he and his companion landed on January 3, 1853. The dress of the people in the streets appeared very curious to him, and the camels, he thought "the ugliest, slowest and most uncouth looking animals you could imagine." The antique ruins there were of little interest. All in all, Alexandria was "the nastiest hole I ever saw."[14]

The trip by dahabeah up the Nile to Cairo took six days. During the leisurely days on the houseboat Richard and his traveling companions amused themselves with reading, smoking, and sometimes shooting with their pistols at the wild birds and game along the shore of the river. If there were no breeze at nightfall, the craft would anchor for the night, and the passengers would go ashore to some village, where the "houses

cafés, etc." struck Richard as "very funny and very nasty." The structures were made of camel's dung and mud and were always filled with
smoke. In the cafés, "the fire smokes, and so does everybody in the
room. A few glasses of liquor, distributed promiscuously amongst males
and females renders the community quite jolly, and then the fun begins;
such banging away at tambourines, cracking of castanets, piping, yel-
ling, howling and dancing soon creates a disgust only to be conceived
by one who knows how disgustingly nasty and filthy these people
are."[15]

"Nasty" though he may have found them, the people he encountered
nonetheless fascinated Richard. He filled his notebooks with sketches of
the colorful types (figure 6)—water carriers, vendors, veiled women,
belly dancers, pipe smokers, boatmen, dervishes, and tourists with their
noses buried in John Murray's guidebooks—as well as with architectural
details of ancient temples and with views of the Nile and feluccas and
dahabeahs. Getting in the spirit of the place, Richard shaved his head
and donned a turban: "But it don't make me look like a Turk they say."[16]

The two American travelers met others of their countrymen in Cairo,
and after several days in and around the city, they went further upriver
by dahabeah, a slow trip with many delays on account of headwinds
and shallow waters. At Philae, on March 1, they had an excellent view of
the island ruins. The well-preserved wall paintings detailing customs in
the daily lives of ancient Egyptians made the bat-filled tomb of Eilethyia
at El-Kab highly interesting. At Thebes, Richard commented on the
details of construction of the Pasha's palace, part of it apparently composed of pottery shards. At Karnak, the obelisks, the Avenue of the
Sphinxes, and the Temple of Lupar, then being excavated, were memorable, but at a small granite temple, Richard found "some of the finest
scenes" he had yet come upon. They took photographs, haggled with
donkey boys over mummy fragments, lunched in the great hall, and shot
a fox at Karnak. By April 2, they were back in Cairo, remaining there a
few days and making an excursion into the desert.[17]

On the next segment of this long journey, Richard and his companions sailed eastward from Alexandria to Gaza in Palestine; they had to
remain in quarantine at Gaza for several days. Traveling on to
Jerusalem, a long and arduous horseback trip, over rocky and desolate
terrain, Richard was badly shaken up and bruised when the horse he
was riding got into a fight with another animal and threw him. At
Jerusalem on April 29, he visited the Church of the Holy Sepulchre but
was disgusted by the riotous behavior of the noisy, confused, trampling
crowd. From Jerusalem, he and his traveling companions went on to

Figure 6
Egyptian sketches by
Richard Morris Hunt
(1853). Courtesy The
American Institute of
Architects Foundation/
Prints and Drawings
Collection, Washington,
D.C. Photo by James
Garrison.

Jericho, swam in and inadvertently swallowed some of the waters of the Dead Sea, and stopped briefly at Bethlehem, a place of "filthy streets." Back in Jerusalem, Richard was exhausted; he was still badly bruised from his fall, his leg and feet pained him, and he had broken out in boils; but he still had a long way to go. "I hope to get through with this fatiguing journey safe," he confided to his journal, apprehensive about what he still had to face. The Armenian Convent in Jerusalem, however, revived his spirits, with its "blue and white porcelain pictures, doors of mother of pearl, tortoise shell and ebony, fine grills, ostrich egg lights in abundance, rich embroidered carpets and rich altars."[18]

The worst of the trip was indeed to come. Riding northward into Syria by horseback, the travelers were stopped by suspicious Bedouins, one tribe warring against another. Richard kept his pistols handy and confided that they all now feared for their lives. Not only was there the danger of being stabbed or shot, but also the possibility of being eaten alive by the fleas and vermin which infested their clothing. May 14: "We were all scratching all night." Fortunately, no harm came to the travelers. They passed Mt. Tabor and lingered briefly at Tiberias on the Sea of Galilee, before finally reaching Beirut toward the end of May. Here they embarked by ship, stopping overnight at Tripoli, going on to Iskenderun, and landing at the island of Rhodes. From Rhodes they sailed along the coast of Asia Minor to Smyrna, where they remained for five days, before continuing by ship through the Dardanelles to Constantinople, which they reached on June 10. Richard still was unwell, afflicted with more boils and blisters, but he nevertheless immersed himself in the delicious atmosphere of Constantinople and made many sketches. For years he had longed to see this city, which other members of his family had visited in the spring of 1845.[19]

The final part of the long trip brought the Americans by ship to Piraeus, Greece, where they arrived on June 22. Richard exulted in the magnificent temples of antiquity. While sketching on the Acropolis, his eye was caught by sunlight reflecting from a small object, which he later picked up. It was a little piece of gold repoussé, considered by archaeologists, whom Hunt afterward consulted, to have been one of the ornaments with which the Statue of Athena had been inlaid. Embarking again on July 2, they sailed around the Peloponnesos and northward through the Adriatic Sea to Trieste, arriving on July 6. There Richard, who was "delighted to get back to a civilized world," indulged in the luxury of a good bath, the best cleansing he had apparently had for a long, long time. Venice, a few days later, was even more relaxing, for he was now back in familiar territory; the young men's spirits rose with the "usual ices at Florians" on the Piazza San Marco, a gondola ride, and strolling, singing, and smoking through the Venetian alleyways. Returning to Trieste, they arranged to send to New York some of the things they had collected on their trip, and then headed north to Graz, Vienna, Salzburg, and Munich.[20]

Richard arrived back in Paris on July 29, 1853. For some weeks he was obviously at odds with himself and found it difficult to settle down. "It is funny," he wrote in his journal, "how I bore myself given a year travelling; I wanted to be still, *no go*. I wished to be in Paris; poste haste I came to P.; in a week I was heartily sick of P. Now I am trying Fontaine-bleau. . . . I think I will plunge to the bottom (go to Barbizon) and come up the surface at Paris." And, indeed, shortly, he had resurfaced. By September 9, he was at work once more, he reported in a letter, "and a happier man you do not see often. The spirit moved me and I moved with it."[21]

But Richard's intense happiness was rather short-lived, for his resumption of serious architectural work in Paris was brief. Sometime late in 1853, he joined his mother and his sister, who had returned to Europe, for a trip to the south of France, with visits at Nîmes and Avignon, before going on to Italy for the winter. Their sojourn in Rome was a homecoming, a return to the city that they had all enjoyed so much when they had first arrived in Europe ten years earlier and that Richard had come to know once again on his trip the previous year. In Rome they could once more indulge themselves in the well-known ruins of the ancient city, the evocative remnants of the Middle Ages, and the living presence of the Renaissance. In Rome they found many American friends—William Page, the painter, and his wife; Thomas Crawford, the sculptor, who was working on his sketches for the pediment figures for the United States Capitol extensions, and Mrs. Crawford; and Martin Van Buren, the former president. On February 4, Van Buren gave Richard a letter of introduction to Richard Upjohn, then perhaps the most prominent architect in the United States, asking the experienced older man to give the novice advice. Upjohn had known Richard as a boy in New Haven, and in a few years the two would become friends and professional associates in New York. According to Van Buren, Hunt at this time had already decided to return to the United States to practice his profession. In Naples a short time later, with another letter of introduction, the Hunts were fortunate to gain the privilege of being allowed to sketch in the museum from early morning until sunset. At Pompeii they stopped in a little hotel just outside the gate. One wonders just how the sophisticated Richard in the company of his mother and sister responded to the more salacious aspects of Pompeian decorations which even then male visitors were encouraged, for a special fee, to view. Were they seen as nasty and the work of a degraded people? We have no evidence.[22]

Back in Paris in the spring of 1854, Richard finally began serious architectural work. For almost three years, he had been on the move much of the time and obviously had been unable to devote himself to sustained architectural endeavors. Early in 1854, his *patron,* Lefuel, was made architect to the emperor Napoleon III, and director of works of the new structures being built to connect the Tuileries and the Louvre, succeeding Louis Visconti, who had died the year before. In April 1854, Lefuel invited Richard to join his staff as Inspecteur des Travaux at an annual salary of two thousand francs. The invitation to participate in this work was a great honor and a splendid opportunity to gain excellent experience, and Richard was proud to accept the position. Lefuel had long appreciated his American pupil's talents and apparently was delighted to be able to offer him this governmental post. In later years Richard and his wife regularly visited Lefuel on their trips to Paris, and the two men maintained an "intimate and affectionate" relationship for the rest of Lefuel's life.[23]

In his work on the Louvre extensions, Richard joined a massive endeavor, one of the great building projects of the nineteenth century—the remaking of the city of Paris, instituted by Napoleon III. Even before Louis Napoleon had returned from exile to become president of the Second Republic, he had envisioned a rebuilding of the French capital to make it a great modern city suitable to the needs and the activities of mid-nineteenth-century French society. He wished not only to improve the health and the well-being of the inhabitants of the city but also to provide public works that would stimulate economic prosperity and establish a great and elegant setting for his regime. As president he initiated many projects, advising even on the details of the plans and taking a close interest in the progress of the works. Then, after the establishment of the Second Empire, when he became the emperor Napoleon III, the pace of his rebuilding of Paris was stepped up. On June 29, 1853, Baron Georges-Eugène von Haussmann was placed in charge of the program and, as prefect of the Department of the Seine, he directed the transformation of the city.[24]

The scale of the changes was truly impressive. The old city walls were torn down and replaced by broad new tree-lined boulevards giving an openness to formerly congested neighborhoods. Many of the boulevards were arranged so as to provide vistas of monuments and monumental buildings, as well as to assist transportation from one part of the city to another. New bridges were constructed over the Seine. By 1870, about five thousand acres of public parks had been laid out in the city, including the great Bois de Boulogne, established on governmental property. New aqueducts and an elaborate sewer system extending hundreds of miles underground provided for the city's needs. New schools, hospitals, military barracks, and railroad stations also helped transform the face of Paris. By the end of the Second Empire, Napoleon III's vision of a great imperial city had to a large extent been realized; and with the physical changes throughout the city, the living conditions of the Parisian people had been considerably improved.[25]

Magnificent buildings began to take shape. Les Halles Centrales, the main food market of the city, was, as suggested by the emperor himself, a series of glass and iron pavilions, modeled on the train shed of the Gare de l'Est. The Hôtel Dieu was renovated and the reading room of the Bibliothèque Nationale completed. Viollet-le-Duc rebuilt the Sainte-Chapelle and parts of Notre Dame, as well as the Château of Pierrefonds, the walled city of Carcassonne, and the papal palace at Avignon elsewhere in France. Charles Garnier's Théâtre de l'Opéra, in the Place de l'Opéra, begun in 1860 and completed after the fall of Napoleon III, has perhaps to later times most fully epitomized the splendors of the prosperous, materialistic Second Empire.[26]

The lush neobaroque of the Opéra or the technically advanced glass and iron construction of Les Halles, however, were not typical of French Second Empire architecture. Building commissions largely went to those providing designs which expressed continuity with the past and thus by association connected the new imperial regime with the glories of France under the monarchy before the Revolution. Many older architects favored by the government clung rather rigidly to academic classical modes, utilizing masonry construction with hard and dry "Néo-Grec" details. Much of the Second Empire work, though, was an architecture of elegance, with a plasticity that lent itself to a richness of ornamentation and display. For example, the additions to the Louvre were conceived in a richly opulent style.[27]

The completion of the Louvre and its connection with the Tuileries Palace was a major undertaking in the Second Empire reconstruction of Paris. For several hundred years the original fortress of the Louvre and the adjacent Tuileries Palace, where the imperial family resided, had been reconstructed and enlarged again and again. The first Napoleon had begun building a wing along the Rue de Rivoli to join the two palaces, but the connection remained unfinished at the end of his regime. The government of the Second Republic in October 1849 ordered the clearing away of the jumble of old buildings standing between the two palaces, and in March 1852 the connecting wings were authorized under the direction of the architect Louis Visconti. The foundations were laid in July 1852. By the following year some three thousand workers were employed on the project. The emperor himself was very much involved, and he often stopped by to watch the construction and sometimes suggested changes or additions, occasionally to the dismay of those responsible for the work. In the design of the new Louvre, Visconti utilized a High Renaissance style; his use of the mansard roof and tower was one of the few instances in Paris of those elements which became so characteristic of American adaptations of the French Empire style. When Visconti died in 1853, the project was, however, little more than begun. Lefuel, who was shortly appointed director of the Louvre works, modified Visconti's plans and put his own stamp on the extensions, including far more elaborate sculptured ornamentation of the façades, inspired by the earlier Louvre designs of Pierre Lescot in the sixteenth century and Jacques Lemercier in the seventeenth century. Lefuel completed the connections of the Louvre and the Tuileries in 1857.[28]

Hunt later expressed the view that it was a "godsend" that Visconti had been replaced by Lefuel. Visconti, Hunt believed, had not really been representative of the traditions of French architecture, and Lefuel had been hampered when he took over by what Visconti had already planned to do. Lefuel, for example, had been unable to reproduce as he wished in the new Louvre the precise character of some of the work of the sixteenth-century French architect Philibert Delorme because of Visconti's blunders.[29]

Richard's own work on the Louvre extensions under Lefuel obviously gave him excellent practical experience. As one notice after his death half a century later described this apprenticeship: "It was a practical training in exactly the school which pleased him most—the French school of academic architecture, the school of a style which takes splendor, dignity and a certain monumental feeling as the most necessary merits of its construction." Hunt reputedly drew the working plans and designed many of the details for the Pavillon de la Bibliothèque (figure 7), opposite the Palais Royal, including the façades and the archway leading from the Rue de Rivoli to the inner courtyard. Three full stories in height, with an uppermost mansard story, and with an elaboration of balconies, columns, caryatids, antifixae, pedimental sculpture, and acroteria, the Pavillon presents a surfeit of decoration to the modern eye

Figure 7
Pavillon de la Bib-
liothèque, Palais du
Louvre, Paris (Hunt's
work: 1854–1855). From
L'Architecture et la Déco-
ration aux Palais du
Louvre et des Tuileries
(1905–1907) I, Pl. XXIII.

but was welcomed as most suitable to the new Paris of the Second Empire. Lefuel was highly satisfied with his protégé's work on the project. Thirteen years later, Lefuel wrote to Catharine Hunt, Richard's wife, that his own "greatest work was done while dear Dick worked with me, and he can justly claim a great share of its success. I do not hide from you those circumstances of which his own modesty does not permit him to speak."[30]

When his work on the Louvre extension was nearing completion, Richard finally decided that if he were ever going to practice his profession in the United States, now was surely the time for him to return to his native land. At first, Lefuel vigorously opposed Richard's decision. He felt that the young man's future would be too uncertain in the United States, and he "offered him any government position within his control if he would remain in Paris." Richard did stay on in Paris until the Rue de Rivoli façade of the Pavillon was completed, and he then worked for some months in general construction.[31]

At the beginning of 1855, it was evident that he was comfortably established in Paris. William had just returned to Paris after another trip to the United States, though he intended within a short time to go back to make his permanent home in New England. Richard was continuing to purchase books on a lavish scale, and he wrote his mother, who was back in the United States, that he had run out of funds and could not get her a New Year's present since he had spent all his available money on books. "The fact is," he wrote, "we ought to have, after spending half of our lives in France, a good French library. You can count upon me for that." Although he sent no present to his mother, he did relay the good news that he had recently been promoted on his job at the Louvre from a fifth-class inspector to a fourth-class inspector, with a salary increase of five hundred francs. He was pleased, too, that his position allowed him a good amount of free time to pursue his own interests, studying music and reading, and to enjoy an extensive social life. He revealed that he had even taken up cooking—a *"nouveau genre d'amusement."* It would not be easy for him to break the ties he had in Paris.[32]

Two months later, on March 15, 1855, Richard wrote to his mother that he had been suffering from his old enemy, boils—"'t is irksome not to be able to sit down with any comfort"—but that he nonetheless intended to go to England shortly and was pleased that Lefuel had offered him some letters of introduction to acquaintances there. Lefuel had asked him to dine with him and had requested that Richard remember him to his mother. Before going to England, Richard hoped once more to

visit Paris thoroughly, for there was "an immense deal" to see "on
account of the preparations for visitors to the Exhibition," scheduled to
open shortly. "In England I shall make the most of my time, after which I
shall return to Paris for the Exhibition, attend to whatever business I
may have unfinished, & then nothing will remain for me to do but to
traverse the Great Lake." Both William and Leavitt, he suggested to his
mother, would also return permanently to the United States in the
months to come. Leavitt, he thought, would most likely come back with
him. Since Leavitt was hoping for a public career, Richard thought that
he ought to settle in Brattleboro, where family connections and the respected position held by their father would help him to advance. Not
only for Richard but also for two of his brothers, a major turning point in
their lives was once more at hand.[33]

Richard's visit to England was a short one. He traveled with Gus
Perkins, whose sister Louisa would soon become William's bride. The
two young men apparently spent most of their time in London. On his
return to Paris, Richard had much to do, getting his affairs settled and
packing up to ship home the accumulations of ten years. He sent his
furniture, books, and art objects, along with some things his mother had
left in Paris, back to Boston, in care of Pelham Hayward, the family
financial adviser, and toward the end of August he sailed for home. In
early September 1855, Richard was back in the United States, prepared
to commence professional work.[34]

The temptations for him to remain in France had been great. After a
thorough training at the Ecole des Beaux-Arts, he was recognized as a
remarkably talented person. The opportunities for an interesting and
successful career in France appeared excellent; it was evident that he
could go a long way there. Then, too, the buildings and monuments of
Europe offered him an imaginative stimulus he could never hope to find
in his own country. He had many friends in Paris and enjoyed a full and
satisfying social life there. Some of his friends thought that he had
already become more French than the French. But, on the other hand,
Richard was strongly drawn back to his native land.

Here, he recognized, there were great opportunities for an architect
with skill, sound training, and good experience. His own education and
practical training in his art had been better than that of any other American. And here, in America, was the place where he had his roots.
Richard was still the person who as a young student in Geneva had
styled himself as one of "the Green Mountain Boys," always remaining
very much the American while immersed in European culture. Indeed,

his feeling for his own country had probably been stimulated by his experiences abroad, and his interest in the artistic development of the United States was sincere.

In another letter to his mother, Richard discussed the opportunities for the arts in the United States and his own hopes for the future. He was convinced that it was an error to think that America was not yet ready for the fine arts. "There is no place in the world where they are more needed, or where they should be more encouraged." Greater numbers of luxurious houses were now being built in New York City than in Paris, and if the money were spent and good architecture not obtained, then this was the fault of the architects. Surely in architecture, as well as in painting and the other arts, the United States should rival or surpass Europe. "Merit must eventually command its position with us. . . . The only thing is that the Professional man with us has got to make his own standing." Hunt intended to do just that.[35]

And so, as Henry Van Brunt half a century later put the matter, "Hunt returned to his native land, accredited as an ambassador of art from the abounding wealth of the old world to the infinite possibilities of the new [even though]. . . . the new world was not then hospitable to such high ideals, such noble enthusiasms, as this first American thoroughbred brought with him from the schools of Paris." He came back "inspired by a patriotic ardor and hopefulness," leaving behind "the more congenial atmosphere of the old world." Despite the fact that "he found himself an exile in his own country . . . . his natural loyalty was unshaken, and he stayed because he loved his country and because he modestly believed that, sooner or later, he could do something to direct a part of its crude but tremendous energy to the service of beauty and truth in art."[36]

Hunt returned to the United States in his twenty-seventh year. Handsome, with deep-set, piercing eyes, he wore a luxuriant moustache and a tuft of hair on his chin. He was well-trained, knowledgeable, and decidedly a man of the world. Through his years of study and his extended travels, he had personal acquaintance with more Western European architecture than any other American of his time. Self-assured and confident of his own abilities, he was convinced that he could make an important contribution to the arts in the United States. The enthusiasm, drive, and energy that he displayed from the start of his career were undoubtedly fostered in large part by his great confidence in himself and his sense of a secure social position.[1]

Hunt never had to face the turmoil experienced by many young men in antebellum America who were pressured to accept business careers but felt disinclined to do so; nor was he beset by the tensions of men of leisure who feared their social positions threatened by *arrivistes*. His situation was quite different, for example, from that of his friend Thomas Gold Appleton, who had been his brother William's traveling companion a few years before. Appleton, who was the son of a highly successful self-made businessman, considered a career in commerce or industry distasteful, and, with neither the talent nor the commitment for an artistic career, chose the role of gentleman artist; however, without general social support and understanding, he found himself useless and socially alienated. Although Hunt was not rich like Appleton, he had ample means. His social position was a respected one. Above all, he had a sense of purpose for his life. He strongly believed that the arts were necessary for an advanced civilization and that he would be able to contribute a great deal as a professional architect in the United States. Perhaps the country might not be ready for him, but he felt that he was ready for it.[2]

The common idea that American artists have always been alienated from the larger society has been considerably modified in recent years. The position of artists has no doubt varied from one period of time to another in the course of American history. Probably too often critics and historians have used a few individuals to characterize the artistic life of a time, while neglecting the experience of the many. During the mid-nineteenth century the alienation of those working in the visual and plastic arts was in fact minimal. This condition came about not because the society absorbed artistic perspectives and ideals but because the artists themselves by and large accepted the perspectives and ideals of the mainstream culture.[3]

Indeed, from the establishment of the new nation, the arts were

5

A NEW YORK HOME

manifestly supportive of the new republic. John Trumbull, in his Capitol paintings, sought to show Americans that they had a worthy past filled with heroes and heroic deeds. Later on, Horatio Greenough, like many others, tried, as in his statue of George Washington as an Olympian Zeus, to associate the greatness of American heroes and their nation with the heroic aspects of antiquity. In the literary realm, too, countless poems and essays dealt with the glory of the new nation.

Throughout the first half of the nineteenth century, American artists and writers called for the development of the arts as instruments of general happiness, social advancement, and national glory. A major thrust of the pervasive cultural nationalism was the search for new forms and new modes of expression that would be appropriate to the political and social conditions of the nation. It was recognized, of course, that the arts had not yet developed to any great extent in the United States, but that very lack made the opportunities all the greater. When Richard and his companion Theodore Winthrop talked in Paris of improving the fine arts in their own country and building a great new capital city, they were expressing sentiments similar to those of many other American artists of the time. Indeed, artist-commentators frequently indicated that American artists had a responsibility to do their work in their own country and thus improve the state of the arts at home. They might study abroad and be inspired by the European achievement, but their duty lay at home. Too long a residence abroad, it was felt, could be dangerous, destroying the artist's originality. Except for a small number of permanent expatriates, American artists believed that their life work must be done in their native land. Thus American artists by and large maintained a firm identification with the national culture and patriotically associated the development of art with the progress of the nation.[4]

The larger American community responded by accepting the artists as fulfilling a necessary function. By the 1850s, an artistic career was widely recognized as useful and legitimate, providing not only for aesthetic needs but also for the teaching of moral truths and spiritual inspiration, as did the religious vocation. Moreover, an artistic career was often viewed by midcentury commentators not as an outlet for personal indulgence and a foil to materialism but rather as a job wherein industry and perseverance could make for successful achievement, just as in business. Artists were usually looked upon as somehow more sensitive and otherworldly than other people, but still as individuals who could and should share the goals and the rewards of the most respected members of the community. By the onset of the Gilded Age, the artistic ideal was well absorbed into the American ethic of success.[5]

Architecture is, of course, both an art and a business. To see his designs realized, the architect, unlike the painter, the sculptor, or the poet, must work closely with a client and provide him with just what he is willing to pay for. When the architect supervises the construction of his buildings, as was generally done in the nineteenth century, he must deal with craftsmen, suppliers, and others as a businessman. And so in a society that valued above all the shrewd and active man of affairs who got things done, the architect as one type of creative artist did not stand so far out from the mainstream of business activity as did artists working in other media. Furthermore, in an expanding, increasingly urbanized, prosperous society, the building designer manifestly played a far more necessary and central role than did those whose endeavors were aimed at pleasing a very few or perhaps not even at pleasing anyone but the creative artist himself. Hunt always considered himself above all an artist, and throughout his life he was closely associated with artists. At the same time he was a businessman and deeply involved with many of the most central concerns of the Gilded Age.

By midcentury, in some circles there was still less than full social acceptance of the artist, but for a man with good family position and social connections, and with the background of European training and experience that Hunt had, the way to success was relatively open. Obviously the best opportunities were to be found where the number of buildings to be erected was greatest and where wealth was most concentrated, and for a beginning architect in 1855 the best chances for advancement in the United States decidedly were to be found in New York City. Moreover, New York was the artistic center of the nation, and with the variety of city life it could perhaps best provide the urban stimulation that Hunt had already enjoyed for so many years in Paris. Hunt chose New York City as his primary home and the focus of his architectural activity. From this urban base he became in a few years a figure of national importance.

Returning from Europe, Hunt landed in Boston, and by mid-September 1855 he was settled in New York, although a few months passed before he was established in a permanent residence. As of February 1, 1856, he rented a studio at the University of the City of New York (New York University) on the northeast side of Washington Square, and here for a time established his office and home. His studio, in room 12, was on the northeast corner of the second floor of the University Building. Hunt kept the studio for three years, until May 1, 1859, paying $300 rent a year until May 1, 1857, when the rent was raised to $400 annually. After the Studio Building on West Tenth Street was completed in 1858, he established his office in the new structure. When his mother purchased a house at 49 West Thirty-Fifth Street in 1859, he moved there to live with her, his sister Jane, and his brother Leavitt, remaining there for almost two years.[6]

The great Gothic pile of the university was one of the showplaces of New York and had become a center of artistic and cultural life in the city. The university had been founded in 1831 as a new urban educational institution modeled on the University of London, opened in 1828. Classes commenced in temporary quarters in 1832, and the following year construction began on the University Building (figure 8). James H. Dakin of the architectural firm of Town and Davis, working with David B. Douglass, who had been named professor of engineering and architecture, was primarily responsible for the design. At first Dakin was not particularly pleased with the style decided upon and called the design "a half-barbarous thing" and "a half savage gothic," but he later judged that "on the whole it will do quite well."[7]

No doubt the final decision on the design for the University Building was made by Chancellor James M. Mathews, a clergyman of the Dutch Reformed Church, whose own church building, later constructed just across the street on the south part of the east side of Washington Square, echoed the English Perpendicular style he wanted for the New York University Building. The University of London may have been the institutional model for the new American school, but the Gothic Revival quality of the structure obviously was meant to recall the buildings of Oxford and Cambridge. Here was a New World academic building that associated itself with a long tradition and provided the accepted architectural symbol of learning. Unfortunately, however, Chancellor Mathews spent so lavishly on the building, using money that had been allocated for equipment and books, that soon after it was dedicated in 1837 a legislative investigation was instituted and Mathews was forced to resign. The fledgling university had been left deeply in debt by Mathews's extravagance.[8]

The chancellor had, nonetheless, directed the creation of a very impressive structure, which shortly became one of the chief architectural attractions of the city. With a frontage of 180 feet on the square and extending 100 feet back on the sides, the University Building dominated the east side of Washington Square in the heart of what soon was the most fashionable residential section of the city. The main building contained, besides classrooms, a library and a reading room, a small chapel, and a great hall. To bring in income, many of the nearly sixty rooms were rented out as studios to private individuals or as offices for associa-

Figure 8
The University Building,
Washington Square,
New York. Museum of
the City of New York.

tions. From the start, it had been planned that the university would bring in tenants to provide continuing financial support. Two separate residences behind the main structure provided additional rentable space.[9]

The dominant feature of the building was the great hall or chapel, its inner space indicated on the exterior by the large, traceried west window, some twenty-four feet wide and fifty-two feet high, placed between castellated central towers. The interior of the chapel was derived from the choir of Oxford Cathedral, while exterior features recalled King's College Chapel at Cambridge. Adjoining the central section on both sides were flanking wings framed by corner towers. The exterior was faced with marble, which was also used on the interior stairways and corridors. As a widely known precedent, the University Building was influential in establishing the Gothic style for American colleges. Although the Gothic Revival had already made its appearance at Kenyon College in Ohio, the Washington Square building appears to have been the first American college with specific historical Gothic elements. Gothic Revival became shortly the new collegiate fashion. Some came to know the building at second hand through the evocative romantic painting *Allegorical Landscape Showing the University*, executed in 1836 by Samuel F. B. Morse, who moved into the newly completed building in 1835.[10]

Morse was the nucleus of a group of scientists, artists, writers, and bohemians who made the new University Building their home. A faculty member of the university from 1832 until his death in 1872, he was professor of the literature of the arts of design, the first professor of fine arts in the United States. Even before the building was completed, Morse had rented the room in the northwest tower and had taken five rooms on the floor below, subletting four of these rooms to his own students, one of them the painter Daniel Huntington. Morse gave instruction in painting and also established a laboratory, probably located in the tower room, where he conducted experiments that led to the development of the telegraph. He was assisted in his early work by Professor John W. Draper, who with Morse helped develop techniques of the daguerreotype in the building, and by Alfred Vail, a recent graduate, who later helped promote the telegraph.[11]

The university boasted many other talented people among the tenants. Alexander Jackson Davis, the architect, moved into quarters there soon after the building was opened. Samuel Colt lived in the southwest tower room for a time and worked on the design of his revolver there. Henry T. Tuckerman, an early historian of American art, made the University Building his headquarters for a few years. And during the mid-nineteenth century such well-known painters as George Inness, Eastman Johnson, Eugene Benson, Edwin Austin Abbey, Winslow Homer, and J. H. Twachtman took studios there. Contact between the students in the university classes and the youngsters at a classical school on the lower floor and the artists and scientists in the studios above usually remained limited, but the famous tenants and the work they were doing engendered an atmosphere of creative activity and scholarly endeavor. The scholarly atmosphere was reinforced, too, by the presence of various associations. While Hunt had his studio at the university, the New-York Historical Society, the American Geographical Society, the New York Academy of Medicine, and the American Institute of Architects made their headquarters in the building. The Broadway Tabernacle and St. Ann's Church for Deaf Mutes also met there.[12]

In his studio, Hunt gathered his "spoils of foreign travel," bringing to New York what Henry Van Brunt, who was soon to be one of his pupils, called "the mellow atmosphere of the old world." The "carved antique cabinets, filled with bronzes, medallions, precious glass of Venice and curiosities of fine handiwork in all the arts," stood by "the walls . . . rich with hangings, old panels, sculptured or painted and modern studies from the studios of Paris." Scattered about the spacious room were "mediaeval missals and embroideries, instruments of music, masterpieces of forged and wrought metal work and of Faience, [and] strange and costly toys of every era of civilization." Best of all to Van Brunt were the many books, "by far the richest, most comprehensive, and most curious collection of books on architecture and the other fine arts which at that time had been brought together in the new world." Hunt made his books readily available to others. For Van Brunt, looking back years later, "the hours spent in the gracious seclusion of that dim chamber were the most fruitful of my life."[13]

Living in the University Building was very pleasant for Hunt. There was much coming and going and socializing with the painters, as well as friends who stopped by and pupils who lingered over the architectural books. Hunt hired a woman named Kate to keep the studio clean, but Kate gave the janitor of the building considerable trouble, since she did not keep to the standards of "cleanliness and good order" he wished to maintain. Within a short time after making New York University his home, Hunt had become a well-known figure there and he was even portrayed in a lurid Gothic novel, which was set in the building.[14]

The novel, *Cecil Dreeme*, had been written by Theodore Winthrop some years before it was published posthumously in October 1861.

Winthrop and Hunt had first become friends as schoolmates during the Hunt family's brief stay in New Haven in the early 1830s. "A grave, delicate, rather precocious child," Winthrop entered Yale College when he was sixteen, graduating in the class of 1848. In his subsequent European travels, he saw a good deal of Richard and his brother William in Paris, where, it will be recalled, they made plans to build up the arts in America on their return to the United States. In Italy, Winthrop became acquainted with William H. Aspinwall, a wealthy merchant, who hired him to become tutor to his son. Returning to New York, Winthrop entered Aspinwall's firm, Howland and Aspinwall, and traveled to Panama and to the Pacific Northwest for the company. Although he also studied law and was admitted to the bar in 1855, he did not relish either business or a law practice and turned instead to writing tales and novels, mixing with the artistic and bohemian set of New York. Winthrop apparently never lived in the University Building, but he did have a writing room in the Studio Building. When the Civil War broke out, he immediately enlisted in the artillery corps of the Seventh Regiment, and a few weeks later, on June 10, 1861, Major Winthrop was killed at the Battle of Great Bethel.[15]

The secondary characters in *Cecil Dreeme* include Henry Stillfleet, obviously modeled after Hunt. Stillfleet is a young architect who has just returned to New York from ten years of study and travel in Europe and establishes a studio filled with "a fair bag of plunder" in the north rear corner room of the second story (the room Hunt occupied) of a "big, battlemented, buttressed marble" building called "Chrysalis College." Henry, who sports a moustache and goatee (as Hunt did), is "a fellow of the practical and artistic natures well combined," very much the ironist and wit, providing "the merry element" in this "sombre story" of murder, disguises, dark, locked rooms, and nameless evils. The narrator-observer sublets Stillfleet's studio room when the architect goes off to Washington to work on the "big abortion of a new Capitol." Stillfleet thinks that the college is "without vitality . . . an ineffectual high-low school," clinging to "traditional methods of education" and so unappealing to students that the halls and lecture rooms must be rented to lodgers. The building's "interior was singularly ill-constructed," with long, dim, marble-tiled corridors, clumsy marble staircases, large Gothic doorways, and, in the lobby, a fan-tracery vaulting of plaster reminiscent of King's College Chapel but so peeling and crumbling that it seemed "deciduous." The building and college were pretentious and lent themselves to easy ridicule, but Stillfleet's studio, though known as "the Rubbish Palace," was something else. "There were models of the most mythological temples, and the most Christian spires and towers. There were prints and pictures, old and young. There were curiosities in iron and steel, in enamel and ivory, in glass and gem, in armor and weapon." Casts, busts, and elaborately carved furniture were scattered about. The collection obviously fascinated the narrator-observer, and it provided an appropriately romantic setting for the story of the strange events that took place in the building.[16]

The experience of living at the University Building was important to Hunt, for there he was in close association with other American artists and came to know many people influential in the city. In the room next door to him was Joseph Howland, the son of a wealthy merchant, who had grown up in a house on the north side of Washington Square. Howland would in a few years be Hunt's brother-in-law and patron. Nearby, on Fifth Avenue at Eighth Street, lived John Taylor Johnston, who was soon associated with Hunt in the Studio Building project and later at the Metropolitan Museum of Art. One block east, on Washington Place, Commodore Cornelius Vanderbilt had erected his Greek Revival townhouse; many years in the future Hunt would dispose of a good part of the Commodore's handed-down fortune in the great houses he designed for some of his grandsons. Hunt put down his roots in the New York community during these years in the University Building. In the early 1890s, when the old New York University Building was torn down to make way for a graceless, multipurpose building that could be used for commercial as well as academic purposes, Richard, his wife wrote, "said that he felt as if it was pulling down some of the foundation stones of his life."[17]

During the late 1850s, then, Hunt came to know well the metropolis of New York. With some 675,000 inhabitants in 1855, it was the most cosmopolitan city in the United States and in most ways the center of American culture. Residents and foreign visitors remarked upon the excitement of life in New York City. It boasted a concentration of theaters, concert halls, restaurants and hotels, art galleries, and publishing houses not found elsewhere in the country. Notable foreigners frequently came to New York to lecture, and musicians and entertainers from abroad drew large audiences. The streets were crowded, noisy, and bustling. New enterprises sprang up constantly, as fortunes were rapidly being made. Native Americans coming from farms and country towns and foreign-born immigrants, especially from Ireland and Germany, crowded into the city in ever-increasing numbers, most of them with few skills suitable for city life. With much poverty, the violence of robbery and murder was commonplace.[18]

Flux and turmoil characterized the national scene in the mid-1850s. By 1855 the tensions of American life were rapidly growing. Besides the urban strains of prejudice against the foreign newcomers and the difficulties of immigrant adjustment, large-scale unemployment, and widespread poverty and crime, a growing division over sectional differences and the question of slavery agitated the nation. *Uncle Tom's Cabin*, published three years earlier, had brought home to Northerners the tragedy of slavery as nothing else had. In the year before Hunt's return, George Fitzhugh's *Sociology for the South* had set forth a Southern viewpoint which made Northerners realize the dangers to their institutions posed by aggressive, expansionist pro-Southerners. Already the new Republican Party, to which Hunt would soon give his allegiance, had been organized to oppose the further extension of slavery to the territories. In the presidential election of 1856, the Democrat James Buchanan seemed to many Americans to be a safe candidate who might heal sectional divisions. Differences between South and North had been eased in the past by compromises, and probably most Americans believed that compromises would continue.

The sectional tensions of the nation and the social problems of the city, however, little concerned Hunt on his return to the United States. As an architect involved in his craft and his art, he was most interested in the physical aspects of the city. Grimy and dirty, noisy and congested, committed to commercialism, New York was more like London than Paris, especially the redesigned Paris of the Second Empire, with its elegant boulevards and monuments. In place of the great boulevards, New York had Broadway, its main thoroughfare and the focus of commercial life. From its lower reaches at Bowling Green nearly three miles north to Union Square, Broadway was lined with "one grand succession of commercial palaces." To one British visitor, Charles Mackay, who came to the city in 1857, there was "no street in London that can be declared superior, or even equal, all things considered, to Broadway." Lined by elms, willows, and mountain ash much of the way, Broadway was paved with granite and was, Mackay noted, the cleanest street in the city, a great contrast to the dirty and uneven side streets. Prosperous, elegantly garbed merchants and women shoppers in extravagant hoopskirts shared the crowded sidewalks with ragged porters and vendors and barefoot newsboys. Omnibuses lumbered up and down, often delayed by the delivery wagons which jammed the avenue as well as the adjacent streets. Coaches and cabs added to the congestion.[19]

From its beginning, the city had been expanding northward on Manhattan Island. In the early nineteenth century, the best private residences had been located south of Chambers and Beekman Streets, but as this area had increasingly been taken over for commercial purposes, the well-to-do had moved northward. Around midcentury, the most desirable residential area was considered to be the thirteen blocks between Houston (or First) Street and Union Square, especially the streets surrounding Washington Square and the lower part of Fifth Avenue. Union Square itself was a choice place in which to live, surrounded by some of the finest dwellings of the city. Just to the south of the square on Broadway, James Renwick's delicate Gothic Revival Grace Church, completed in 1846, was by 1855 the most fashionable church in the most fashionable part of Manhattan.[20]

Many years afterward, Edith Wharton looked back upon the New York City that she had known in her childhood, just two decades later in the 1870s. She recalled the city disparagingly as "this little low-studded rectangular New York, cursed with its universal chocolate-coloured coating of the most hideous stone ever quarried, this cramped horizontal gridiron of a town without towers, porticoes, fountains or perspectives, hide-bound in its deadly uniformity of mean ugliness." But, as John Maass has pointed out, her memory had played her false, for the New York of the 1870s, and likewise the city of two decades earlier, had a considerable architectural variety in styles and building materials, even though it was dominated by brownstone houses set in the monotonous gridiron pattern. The impress of varying architectural styles had already become characteristic in the mid-1850s as new building fashions and techniques came to the fore. Squares and small parks, tree-lined streets, and even some statuary, fountains, steeples and spires, and domes broke the uniformity of the skyline.[21]

By midcentury, the classical revival had passed out of favor in New York City. The impressive row of Greek Revival houses on the north side of Washington Square dated from the early 1830s, and, though elegant and dignified, they were by this time generally considered rather old fashioned. The outstanding Greek Revival design in New York was the Customs House (later the Subtreasury Building) on Wall Street at Broad, a Doric temple, designed by the firm of Town and Davis and completed in 1842. Nearby was the Merchants' Exchange, a three-story Ionic temple with a central trading hall, also completed in 1842. One commentator a few years later found the Exchange handsome in exterior design but very inconvenient and "the dreariest, least inviting, and most expensive place of business in the city." The same commentator was unsparing in his ridicule of the Greek Revival façades of several of the banks along Wall Street: "Granite dowagers," he called them,

which once "bloomed with grace. . . . Yet to our eyes these grim temples . . . are matter only for lamentation." They appeared "out of
place, out of proportion, like a crowd of briefly-petticoated ballet dancers, who stand shivering and unregarded after the play and its
applauses are over, [waiting] for their carriages to carry them home."
New York, he felt, had best be rid of their like.[22]

At midcentury, the Gothic Revival was dominant in ecclesiastical
and educational buildings. Richard Upjohn's Trinity Church, conse-
crated in 1845, appeared to one commentator in 1855 "a noble building,"
yet coarse and clumsy in many details. The same anonymous observer
found Grace Church "a very showy building, very florid, and of bad
white marble." The old Columbia College, on Park Place, Murray and
Church streets, with pseudo-Tudor cloisters and oriels, seemed to the
observer "worthy of no notice . . . as a work of art." By contrast, the
New York University building on the east side of Washington Square
was, he judged, "much more magnificent," although some of its details
were false and inappropriate. Leopold Eidlitz's St. Peter's Church (1853)
in the Bronx and Jacob Wrey Mould's All Souls Unitarian Church and
Parsonage (1853–1855) were notable Gothic Revival structures, the latter
showing the influence of Victorian Gothic design. Within a few years,
new decorative details, color contrasts, and additional ornamentation
would transmute the Gothic Revival into the fussier and more florid
Victorian Gothic.[23]

The 1850s brought an increasing eclecticism to American building.
As early as the 1840s, an Italianate style had come into use both in city
and country houses, and by midcentury it had become one of the most
influential modes. Italianate details characterized many of the
brownstone dwellings of New York. But clients were asking for and
architects were providing other designs, too. Egyptian forms were tried,
most notably in the Tombs (1840), the main prison of New York City. In
business buildings, new glass and iron construction began to be used,
with masonry forms imitated in cast iron. From the middle of the
nineteenth century on to World War I and after, the eclecticism of a
self-conscious choice of style came to dominate American architecture.
Elements from different historical styles were intermixed, and often
widely variant stylistic details were juxtaposed. Looking back on the
period from about 1850 to 1870 and after, historians have generally
judged the architectural work done then as the most tasteless and the
least successful aesthetically in American history.[24]

The most important new current of the 1850s was the emergence of
an American version of the French Second Empire style. Anthony Trol-

lope, visiting the United States in 1860–1861, wrote that things French had become all the fashion in America: "The taste of America is becoming French in its conversation, French in its comforts, and French in its discomforts, French in its eating and French in its dress, French in its manners, and will become French in its art." American journals gave much attention to the lives of Napoleon III and the Empress Eugénie. From the latter 1850s to the early 1870s, the French mode was dominant in both private and public architecture in the United States. The most characteristic feature of the style was the mansard roof (named after François Mansart, 1598–1666), having a double pitch, the lower slope very steep, the upper relatively flat, allowing for large dormer windows, and prominent cornices at the top and bottom of the lower slope. Brackets usually supported the lower cornice, and cast-iron cresting was often placed at the top edge. Sometimes the roof slope was made convex or concave, or a combination of both. On the first floor of Empire-style houses, floor-to-ceiling French windows with louvered shutters were also characteristic. Occasionally the mansard was added to basically Gothic Revival or Italianate houses. French Empire designs were also often used for banks and hotels. Probably the first architect to utilize the mansard roof in the United States was Detlef Lienau, a German-Dane who came to New York in 1848 after working with Henri Labrouste in Paris and brought something of the Beaux-Arts discipline he had absorbed in France. His early (1850) mansard-roofed house for the New York banker Hart M. Shiff was especially influential.[25]

When Hunt came to New York in the fall of 1855 he would have remembered from his earlier visits to the city the more important older public buildings. City Hall was surely the most attractive and the only New York structure that would have appeared completely at home in France. Probably modeled largely on the Parisian Hôtel de Monaco, the Renaissance classicism of which was infused with the elegance of the American Federal style, City Hall had been designed by Joseph F. Mangin, a French-born architect, who had won the commission for the building in 1802, together with John McComb, Jr., a New Yorker. It was first occupied in 1811 and completed in 1812. Near the Battery stood Castle Garden, designed in its original form as a fort by McComb and later used for public concerts, receptions, and other festivities. Castle Garden was roofed over in 1845 and thereafter housed operas and other musical events, including the famous New York concert of Jenny Lind in 1850. The year Hunt settled in the city, Castle Garden was turned into an immigrant reception center.[26]

Of more interest to Hunt, however, would have been some of the most recently constructed buildings in the city and some still being built. Many of the city's commercial buildings were especially impressive, and many of them embraced new styles and new construction elements. On lower Broadway, occupying the entire block between Reade and Chambers streets, was the city's largest "commercial palace," the A. T. Stewart Department Store, which had been opened a decade earlier in 1846 and was enlarged in 1850. Five stories high and divided into five sections on its long Broadway front, the store was faced with a light, cream-colored marble and had large plate-glass windows at street level. Stewart's store centered inside on a spacious, domed hall. It was the most elegant example of the Italian palazzo style in a commercial building and a structure pointed to with pride by New Yorkers. To the north on Broadway, the Brown and McNamee Silk Warehouse, designed by Joseph C. Wells and built in 1849–1850, combined Italianate Venetian elements with Tudor detail. At Grand and Chrystie streets stood the Lord and Taylor Store, finished in 1853, with large double plate-glass windows separated by cast-iron piers at the street level. One of the most ornate of the new business buildings was that designed for Harper and Brothers, the publishers, by James Bogardus and completed in 1853, at Franklin Square and Pearl Street. Bogardus, a master of iron-front design, had been working in this medium since 1848. The regular rhythm of the cast-iron columns, piers, and arches echoed Venetian Renaissance designs. The Harper Brothers Building, however, was surpassed in 1857 by the Haughwout Building on Broadway at Broome Street, designed by John P. Gaynor; this most elegant of the New York cast-iron structures was modeled after Sansovino's Library of St. Mark in Venice. These and other commercial palaces by the end of the decade of the 1850s were giving a particular architectural image to the streets of New York.[27]

Other new structures were bringing variety to the city. Uptown on Reservoir Square on the west end of what is now Bryant Park stood New York's Crystal Palace, an iron and glass pavilion, built in 1853 for the "Exhibition of the Industry of all Nations" and patterned after the Crystal Palace that Hunt had visited in London in 1851, though smaller in scale. Three years after Hunt's return, the New York Exhibition Hall caught fire and was completely destroyed in a few minutes. Soon under construction was what is now the central wing of the Astor Library Building at 425 Lafayette Street, the first great library to be made available to the public in New York and one of the institutions whose collections were later united to form the New York Public Library. Designed by Griffith Thomas in a North Italian Renaissance style, the central wing was begun in 1856 and finished in 1859 and joined to the earlier south wing, completed in 1853. Close by the Astor Library stood the Cooper Union Foundation Building, designed by Frederick A. Peterson. The five-story educational facility had been begun in 1853 and was completed in 1859.[28]

As a young and well-off bachelor, Hunt frequently dined out in New York hotels and restaurants. Delmonico's hotel-restaurant, five stories in height, had been opened on Broadway in 1846 and was the best-known of the fashionable eating establishments of the city. Isaiah Rogers's Astor House, a 340-room hotel overlooking St. Paul's Chapel, had been opened in 1836. The Metropolitan Hotel on Broadway between Prince and Houston streets, designed by John Butler Snook and Joseph Trench in brownstone with cast-iron columns and piers at the street level and large plate-glass windows, was opened in 1852. The more opulent St. Nicholas Hotel, opened in 1853 on Broadway near Prince Street, with luxurious interior decor, central heating, and hot and cold running water in every room, was faced with marble.[29]

Hunt was devoted to painting almost as much as to architecture. He was himself not only an accomplished draftsman but also a talented sketcher and watercolorist, and many of his close friends were painters. The New York City to which he came in 1855 offered the interested viewer a considerable accumulation of paintings, obviously not impressive by European standards but far greater than could be seen anywhere else in the country. American painters who came to New York found the companionship of fellow artists along with various institutions in which to exhibit their works and agencies to sell them. The National Academy of Design, organized in 1825, held the most prestigious exhibitions of contemporary art works in the country. The galleries of the American Art Union showed American paintings, as did the galleries at the International Art Union. The New York Gallery of Fine Arts was formed in 1844 from the private collection of the merchant Luman Reed, who had built an art gallery in his own home on Greenwich Street; Reed's son-in-law Jonathan Sturges organized the gallery with nearly fifty other leading merchants as a supervisory board of trustees. In 1858 the New York Gallery of Fine Arts collections were transferred to the New-York Historical Society, which subsequently acquired various other major collections as well. The Düsseldorf Gallery exhibited the works of German-trained artists; it was established in 1849 in a hall of the Church of Divine Unity on Broadway by John G. Boker, who had lived in Düsseldorf for twenty years and served as Prussian consul in New York. P. T. Barnum's American Museum on Broadway had taken over the American Museum of John Scudder and Peale's Museum and Gallery of

Fine Arts. Other galleries, temporary exhibits, and private collections were regularly open to public visitors as well. Hunt often visited the painting galleries.[30]

Finally, among the important artistic and cultural organizations of the city, there was the Century Association. Hunt's artistic promise and social position were given almost immediate recognition when, shortly after his move to New York, he was invited to become a member of this prestigious group. The Century Association had been formed in 1847 by men prominent in the arts in one way or another, including Asher B. Durand, John G. Chapman, Francis W. Edmonds, Henry T. Tuckerman, and William Cullen Bryant, who felt the need for centrally located rooms where men involved in the arts might gather socially. According to the constitution of the Century, members were to consist of "authors, artists, and amateurs of letters and the fine arts, resident of the city of New York and vicinity. Its objects shall be the cultivation of a taste for letters and the fine arts, and social enjoyment." Club rooms were set up first on Clinton Place and after 1857 on East Fifteenth Street. To promote "the advancement of art and literature," a library, a reading room, and an art gallery were organized, under the terms of the state charter granted to the association in 1857. Prominent figures in commerce, finance, law, medicine, and politics—presumably talented "amateurs" in the arts—were invited to join those working in the arts as members. Leavitt Hunt followed his brother Richard as a member in 1858, and in 1859 Hunt's later antagonist and still later collaborator, Frederick Law Olmsted, became a Centurion.[31]

Throughout the second half of the nineteenth century, the Century was a social stronghold of men of distinction and wealth in New York City, and its success signified in a way the social recognition of artists in the United States. Although first limited to one hundred, membership was expanded to four hundred in 1862, to five hundred in 1866, and by 1893 to over eight hundred. Most of the leading painters, sculptors, architects, and writers living in New York became Century members, and distinguished foreigners in the arts coming to the city were customarily entertained by the club. William Makepeace Thackeray, visiting New York in 1852–1853 and in 1855–1856, reveled in the conviviality of the Century and pronounced it "the most enjoyable club in the world." The editor Henry Holt, reminiscing years later, considered the Century "unquestionably the most active center of culture in New York," and the fun there "simply colossal." Saturday night was club night, with oyster and cheese suppers, and Hunt made it a point to attend once a month when he was in the city. In 1858, club members began a tradition of

Twelfth Night revels, with masks and toy musical instruments, and a show of lampoons, satirical sketches, and extemporaneous stunts, in which Hunt occasionally participated. Until he joined the University Club many years later, the Century Association was Hunt's favorite New York retreat.[32]

New York City thus provided a very congenial atmosphere for the newly arrived bachelor. Hunt greatly enjoyed the variety of the city and was pleased by the many congenial friends and associations it provided. Although crude and unbeautiful in comparison with the Paris he had known, New York nonetheless had a vitality and a sense of promise that the young architect found stimulating. Above all, he found in the city opportunity to do his work. Immediately on his return he was involved in an important private commission that would bring him considerable public notice.

6

**GETTING
STARTED**

For several months after coming to New York, while he was living at the University Building, Hunt devoted much of his time seeing to completion the construction of the Rossiter house at 17 West Thirty-Eighth Street, built for a dentist and his painter son-in-law. This first important American commission, however, turned out to be a baptism under fire for the young architect. Many details of the design and of the actual construction of this house were to become a source of considerable contention, which eventuated in February 1861 in a trial in the Superior Court of New York City. The trial testimony in *Hunt* v. *Parmly* revealed a slackness on Hunt's part both in the specifics of design and in the business arrangements. But from the controversy over the house and the litigation that ensued, Hunt undoubtedly learned a great deal about the need for absolute precision in design and complete clarity in contractual arrangements. The court case itself helped establish an important precedent for the architectural profession in the United States.[1]

Well before the trial, the Rossiter house (figure 9) had attracted attention in New York. A writer in *The Crayon* in May 1859, for instance, reported on his recent visit to the residence: "The columns, the panels, the cornices, the niches, the pilasters of this house, are all arranged in accordance with the principles of the Renaissance style; all are suggestive of purpose, controlled by Taste, which in that school seems to be to render a façade as attractive and joyous as possible. . . . Of the interior of this house, all we can say is that convenience for every domestic purpose is thoroughly studied and provided for. The rooms are of suitable dimensions, and are elegant without being ostentatious. . . . [The studios] are so arranged as to meet every artistic requirement." From the large, high-ceilinged upper studio on the fourth floor, the panoramic view over the city was magnificent, especially at twilight, the writer reported.[2]

The façade of the Rossiter house was, in Hunt's opinion, "different from any in the city, in its way." And "its way" was decidedly the Second Empire manner of Hector Martin Lefuel, toned down, simplified, and domesticated for a New York side street. Indeed, the formal, symmetrical façade strongly echoed the Pavillon de la Bibliothèque on which Hunt had worked the year before construction began on the New York house. The Rossiter house recalled the Louvre work in several aspects: the symmetrical, tripartite division; the pediment surmounting the central section (though a segmental-arched parapet in this case); the single-windowed lateral bays; the banded column shafts on the street level flanking the entrance; the smooth rustication of the lower-wall sandstone masonry; the balustrades forming balconies under the sec-

Figure 9
Thomas P. Rossiter
house, 17 West Thirty-
Eighth Street, New York
(1855–1857). Courtesy
The American Institute
of Architects
Foundation/Prints and
Drawings Collection,
Washington, D.C. Re-
production by James
Garrison.

ond- and third-story windows; and the blind round-arched niches (similar to the deeply recessed round-arched windows of Lefuel's structure).

The Rossiter house, nevertheless, was not merely echoes. The overall integrity of the façade elements is evident, although the abundance of projecting balconies, pediments, cornices, lintels, pilasters, columns, window jambs, and stringcourses gives the front an overly fussy and rather mottled appearance. And the breaking of the stringcourse above the third story by the window lintels is a jarring discordance. All in all, the façade is restless and awkward. Even though the lush ornamentation of the Louvre pavilion is absent here, one must assume that if there had been funds available the niches of the house would have been provided with statuary; and if more money and skilled stonecutters had been available, Hunt would have done more with the barren panels on the second and fourth stories.[3]

When construction began on the house in 1856, Hunt had already known Thomas P. Rossiter for several years. They may well have been acquainted as small boys in New Haven; later, in Paris, Hunt and Rossiter saw one another frequently. Rossiter lived for some years with his wife and three small children in Paris, where he painted. In March or April 1855, in Paris, Rossiter drew a rough sketch of his concept of a town house he planned to have built in New York. His father-in-law, Dr. Eleazer Parmly, a dentist and real estate speculator, had agreed to pay for the house. Rossiter later testified that when he showed Hunt the sketch, the architect said that "the best thing I could do, if I wanted a proper plan was to submit it to some man then in Paris who would give me a motive, or lay it down to a scale—that it would save me a good deal of trouble." Rossiter said that he had known "very little about architecture at that time," and consequently that he had asked Hunt "if he would take it and put it in shape." Hunt told Rossiter that he was very busy but that he would try to do the work when he had some leisure in the evenings. "So he took the sketch and laid it down to a scale, amplifying and adding to it, making it a very different thing ultimately from my original design, changing the whole character of it before he got through with it." Hunt's first sketch had provided for a house with a fifty-foot frontage, and it took account of Rossiter's specifications for a dwelling that incorporated space for private living facilities and for a public exhibition room, a portrait studio, and a teaching room, while keeping the two sets of rooms separate.[4]

Immediately upon his return to the United States in September 1855, Hunt called on Dr. Parmly in New York City and showed him the plan he had drawn in Paris. Apparently the dentist and the young architect did not hit it off well. Dr. Parmly at once said that the house was far more elaborate than what he had wanted and would be much too expensive for him. When Hunt estimated that the house would cost between $40,000 and $45,000, Dr. Parmly responded that Hunt did not know what he was talking about, since he had been abroad and was not acquainted with building costs in the city. Parmly therefore had a separate estimate made, but this came to about the same amount that Hunt had projected. The dentist thereupon decided that this sum was more than he wanted to spend and discussed with Hunt cutting down the size of the house to a thirty-seven-and-one-half-foot frontage.[5]

What subsequently happened became a matter of later dispute. Hunt eventually brought suit against Parmly for nonpayment of architect's fees, claiming that he had been "not only employed to prepare the plans and specifications, but that he superintended the entire conduct of the work." Hunt testified that at Parmly's direction he then made half a dozen or so sketches until finally, early in 1856, the dentist approved a plan with a thirty-seven-and-one-half-foot frontage. Hunt thereupon provided detailed plans, elevations, and sections and between two and three hundred working drawings. Hunt also said that Parmly had asked his advice about specific lots on West Thirty-Eighth Street and that he had told his client that he thought the site was a good one. Since Hunt was going to Washington, D.C., to work on the United States Capitol early in March 1856—encouraged by Dr. Parmly—he suggested that Joseph C. Wells, who had designed the austere Plymouth Church of the Pilgrims in Brooklyn for Henry Ward Beecher and the Gothic Revival First Presbyterian Church on Fifth Avenue between Eleventh and Twelfth Streets, might temporarily serve as supervising architect. Wells was provided with Hunt's plans and was paid by Hunt, who kept in touch with Dr. Parmly when he was in Washington. On his return to New York in late May, Hunt went to the construction site regularly every day and sometimes twice a day as the work progressed. Hunt employed two draftsmen to prepare the working drawings.[6]

In the meantime, however, a tragedy had occurred. While the plans for the house were moving along, the Rossiter family had remained in Paris, where Mrs. Rossiter suddenly became very ill. Her father, Dr. Parmly, hastened to Europe, but she died before he could get to her bedside. Thomas Rossiter then returned to New York with his children, about the same time that Hunt got back to New York from Washington in May, and Dr. Parmly returned to the city in mid-June, 1856. On his arrival, Dr. Parmly decided that he himself would live in the house with his son-in-law and his grandchildren; therefore, in June or July, in the midst of the construction of the foundations and the cellar walls, he directed that the house be considerably altered and enlarged from three to four stories, with modifications of the façade. Dr. Parmly asked Hunt to have only the simplest work done on the house and to carry on all negotiations concerning construction matters with Rossiter. Hunt testified that he had agreed to these terms.[7]

At the 1861 trial, Dr. Parmly's testimony directly contradicted Hunt's. Parmly said that when he found Hunt's proposal too expensive, he suggested a small house to John Thomson, a local builder, who drew up a new plan for him. This plan was sent in December 1855 to Rossiter in Paris, who elaborated the idea and sent it back to his father-in-law. The dentist liked the new plan and had Thomson take it to a certain William Thomas, who in two weeks produced working drawings. Parmly stated that at that point he got estimates from builders and gave the job to William Lambier, a mason-builder, who himself testified that his estimates had been based on the Thomas plans. Lambier said that he had worked closely under the direction of John Thomson. A stonecutter, Francis Duncan, also testified that his original estimate for stonework on the house had been based on the Thomas plans. At the trial, Parmly asserted bluntly: "I never engaged Mr. Hunt to make a line of architecture for me in my life, in any way, shape or manner, and never authorized any one else to do so." He admitted that Hunt had been asked to draw a façade for the house, but he knew of no other services that Hunt had given. Parmly disclosed that he had paid Hunt $300 for his work on the façade.[8]

The house was completed in November 1857, at which time Rossiter and his family occupied it and Rossiter began to make use of the painting studios. They remained there until May 1860, subsequently putting the house up for sale. It was empty in February 1861, at the time of the trial. Dr. Parmly revealed that the house had actually cost $46,465.45, not including the $300 payment to Hunt for the façade design and other payments for interest, taxes, and insurance, and only when the house had been completed, he asserted, did he become aware that Hunt wanted further payment. Hunt had sent his bill to Dr. Parmly on November 22, 1857.[9]

When Rossiter apprised his father-in-law that "the usual rates of architects' fees were five per cent on the cost of the building, he [Parmly] said he had never paid such a fee, and had never heard of it before; he objected to the price." He continued to refuse to pay. Hunt based his suit against Parmly on his claim of five percent of the cost of the building in return for providing preliminary drawings and working drawings with specifications and details and for supervising construction of the house. This claim amounted to $1,750, computed on five percent of a low estimate of $35,000 for the house, less the $300 he had already received, or a balance of $1,450. At the trial, Hunt brought several prominent fellow-architects, including Henry Dudley, Detlef Lienau, Jacob Wrey Mould, Frederick A. Peterson, and Richard Upjohn to testify on his behalf as to customary fees for architectural services. All these witnesses supported his claim that a five percent commission was usual for the full drawings and construction supervision.[10]

The questions of whether Hunt's plans for the house had actually been followed and whether he had in fact supervised construction were central to the trial. John Thomson, the carpenter-builder, testified that the Rossiter house was erected largely as Hunt had designed it, with only a few minor alterations, but that Dr. Parmly had so often found fault with what he himself had done that he was reluctant to go along with changes that Hunt or Rossiter wanted unless Parmly specifically agreed. William Lambier, the mason-builder, who worked closely under Thomson's direction, said that he had never heard Hunt spoken of as the architect until the work was well along, and that he too bore the brunt of the dentist's anger when he did extra work that Rossiter, Hunt, or Thomson wanted him to do. Francis Duncan, a stonecutter, testified that he drew up estimates for designs that Thomas, Wells, and Hunt had prepared, and that Hunt's designs involved work beyond what seemed to him to have originally been decided upon. Thus, even among those working directly on the house, the authorship of some of the elements was unclear, and Parmly, Hunt, Rossiter, and Thomson all at various times acted as supervisors and gave orders about construction details.[11]

Moreover, it was brought out in the trial testimony that Hunt had made some serious errors in his design and working drawings. After the house had been enlarged from three to four stories, the windows of the third floor were found to extend above the beams of the third-floor ceiling. Thomson, who did not think that Hunt's plans were an improvement on Thomas's, reported what happened: "Hunt came there one morning and said, 'Thomson, there is something wrong here; I have made a sad mistake; will you raise those beams? I am a little above the beams with the head of these windows.' Said I, 'You need not trouble yourself; I will raise these beams up so that it will be all right'; and I done so." Thomson had the ceiling beams raised between seven and eight inches after they had already been put in place and then filled in the ends. As a result, he reported, "the window trimmings cut into the cornices . . . [and I did] not consider that desirable architecture but the reverse." Thomson also revealed that a mistake had been made in the plans for some of the doorways so that he had to cut through a sixteen-inch wall in order to make door jambs: "That was the fault of Mr. Hunt's drawings: the openings were not in the right place to set the trimmings."[12]

The stonecutter Francis Duncan also had trouble with Hunt's drawings. When he went to Hunt's studio to get working drawings for the façade, he found that "there were alterations from the plan that I estimated for: but in fact it was not a plan—it was not an elevation such as stone-cutters get from architects elsewhere; it did not show the work as it is: it was a sketch of a front." Duncan was asked to make certain changes, which he found would cost $1,165 beyond the original estimate, but when he told Hunt of the extra expense, "he [Hunt] got angry at me for mentioning it." Duncan went ahead and did the extra work of fluting the columns and carving the bands, but there was more difficulty when he presented the bill for the additional amount. In Duncan's view, "Mr. Hunt's designs were not suited for moldings; the moldings were too small for Connecticut brown stone, because you could not cut a sharp edge upon it—the stone is too porous." But Hunt was very anxious to have the ornamented work on the column bands, and at one point, Duncan revealed, Hunt "said in my hearing that he wanted to show something to New York, and he would give $150 out of his own pocket on Rossiter's account to have it done."[13]

It therefore appears from the trial testimony that Hunt had been careless in some of the design details as well as lax in establishing precisely what his contractual rights and obligations actually were in this, his first American commission. There had been no written contract. It was evident that some of the witnesses in the Parmly trial were hostile to him, especially Thomson, who denigrated using a professional architect at all. Indeed, Thomson felt that an artisan could do just as good a job, and he said that he threw out many of the architect's drawings as quite useless. Thomson testified proudly that he had been the superintendent as well as the carpenter-builder, though he had received no compensation as superintendent. Hunt, of course, claimed that he rather than Thomson had been hired as superintendent.[14]

To a large degree Hunt lost his case, even though the decision was for him as plaintiff, since the trial jury verdict awarded to him only "two-and-one-half percent on $46,000 ($1,150), deducting therefrom $450, with interest from November 22, 1857." In other words, the jury, following the explicit instructions of the trial judge, decided that Hunt had provided plans and working drawings for the Rossiter house, but that he had not actually superintended construction. The Parmly case did, however, have considerable significance in helping to establish a recognized fixed set of charges for the work done by professional architects, who were clearly differentiated from carpenter-builders. For some years the members of the newly formed American Institute of Architects would concern themselves with establishing with even more precision what work merited what percentage fees. Hunt gained public attention from the case, becoming more widely known to potential clients. An editorial in the *Architects' and Mechanics' Journal* unreservedly took Hunt's part in the dispute and lauded "one so distinguished in his profession" in his defense of the architect's professionalism, citing the "talent, education, energy, character, [and] variety of accomplishments" necessary for the skilled professional.[15]

Hunt's work on the Rossiter house taught him a great deal. His only previous professional experience, on a government-funded and bureaucratically administered project, had not really prepared him for a private commission. Obviously, the architect had much to learn—and possibly to unlearn as well. Given the continuous division of authority and of design and construction responsibility that obtained, it was a wonder that the house finally had as logical and coherent appearance as it did.

Soon after work on the Rossiter house had begun, Hunt had accepted an offer from Thomas U. Walter to work on the extension of the United States Capitol in Washington. How Walter learned of Hunt is not known, but it is evident that negotiations for Hunt to go to Washington were under way early in 1856. In a letter to Walter, on March 3, 1856, Hunt reported that he had been endeavoring to find "some suitable person" to take charge of his professional affairs in New York during his projected stay with Walter and that he was now ready to come to Washington to be Walter's "assistant" if the architect still felt that this was advisable. Hunt left for Washington a few days later. For a time his mother and sister Jane joined him at Willard's Hotel. Going to the national capital was a return to one of his childhood homes, the place where his father had carried on a good part of his public career and where some people possibly still remembered him after almost a quarter of a century. The appointment was a prestigious one, for not only was Hunt joining the architectural staff of the most important public building project then going on in the United States, but he was also to work with one of the foremost architects in the nation.[16]

A native of Philadelphia and apprenticed as a youth to his father, a master bricklayer and stonemason, Walter had studied architecture with William Strickland and had started his own architectural practice by the early 1830s. Beginning in 1833 he had designed and built the impressive Greek Revival buildings for Girard College in Philadelphia. His architectural abilities were soon widely recognized: he was named professor of architecture at the Franklin Institute in Philadelphia; he built up a large private practice, including consultation work in Latin America; and in 1841 he was elected to the American Philosophical Society. Highly successful and respected, Walter was immensely qualified to take on the important work of enlarging the Capitol.[17]

The Capitol building had for some years been inadequate for the needs of the legislative branch as new states were admitted and additional senators and representatives came to Washington. The original building had been designed by Dr. William Thornton, modified by Benjamin Latrobe, and completed by Charles Bulfinch in 1828; but within a decade and a half moves were instituted to enlarge the building in order to relieve congestion, while at the same time removing evident fire hazards. In 1843, William Strickland, who had designed the United States Mint in Philadelphia (1829–1833), among other buildings, presented a plan for new wings for the central structure; and in 1850, Robert Mills, then architect of public buildings, who had designed parts of the Treasury, Patent Office, and Post Office buildings in Washington, D.C., submitted his ideas for enlarging the Capitol. Although a Senate committee recommended that Mills's plans be accepted, the full Senate decided that a competition was in order. Four designs were selected as suitable, one of them by Thomas U. Walter. Mills was then asked to draw up a new plan for the Capitol enlargement combining the best features of the four sets of drawings. But President Millard S. Fillmore, who liked Walter's plan, rejected this procedure by naming Walter on June 11, 1851, as the architect of the United States Capitol extension. On July 4, 1851, the cornerstone for the Capitol extension was laid.[18]

In his revised plans for the new Senate and House wings, Walter included some of the ideas of the other architects whose designs had originally been selected. As the work on the Capitol extension was beginning, a fire on December 24, 1851, destroyed the old Library of Congress rooms in the building. Walter resolved to reconstruct the library rooms and the new extensions in so far as possible with fireproof materials. By March of the next year, Walter's designs for new quarters for the library, largely built of cast iron, had been approved by Congress. Considerable cast-iron construction was incorporated in the new wings.[19]

In an administrative shift on March 23, 1853, control over the construction of the Capitol extension was transferred from the Secretary of the Interior to the Secretary of War, and the following month Captain Montgomery C. Meigs, a West Point graduate and an officer in the Corps of Engineers, was named superintendent of construction of the Capitol. For a time Walter and Meigs got along amiably, and it was during this period that Hunt joined the architect's office. Later on, Meigs, who took a significant role in planning the wings, became so overbearing that on November 1, 1859, he was relieved of his duties. During the Civil War, the Capitol enlargement was put back in the Interior Department. Walter remained in charge of the operation until he resigned on May 26, 1865.[20]

As the enlargement took shape, the low, flat, wooden dome over the central section of the Capitol increasingly seemed to be inadequate. Studies for a new dome proportionate to the enlarged structure were begun, and just before Congress adjourned in March 1855, the legislature authorized the replacement of the old dome by a much larger cast-iron dome. Walter modeled the outer shell of the new dome chiefly on the dome of St. Paul's Cathedral in London, but the new dome also looked back to those of St. Peter's in Rome, St. Isaac's (a cast-iron dome) in St. Petersburg, and Les Invalides and the Panthéon in Paris. It was a truly monumental design and eventually became an important symbol of the newly reunited nation after the Civil War.[21]

Although the remarkable design of the Capitol dome is customarily attributed to Walter, some of the credit for it, as well as for elements of the Capitol extension, must go to August Gottlieb Schoenborn (1827–1902), who was Walter's chief architectural draftsman during most of the time that he was architect of the Capitol extension. Schoenborn was a stonemason from Thuringia who had been given training in architectural design at the Erfurt Technical Institute and Art School. He had emigrated to Wisconsin in 1849 and came on to Washington in June 1851, seeking to work on the enlargement of the Capitol. As construction progressed, Walter increasingly depended on Schoenborn both for routine work and for some original design elements and working drawings. Walter thought very highly of Schoenborn, referring to him as "the best architectural draughtsman that has ever come under my notice," and as "my right hand."[22]

In the spring of 1856, when Hunt joined Walter's office, the work of constructing the iron ceilings and the copper and glass roofing over the new Senate and House wings was coming to completion. On the exterior of the two wings, the marble work up to the top of the architrave and much of the cornice were also nearly finished. Work was continuing on the columned basement corridors and on the several stairways, and the floor tiling was progressing. Part of the foundations for the connecting sections between the new wings and the old building had been laid, and vaults were being built below ground for heating apparatus. Much of the work on the interior marble finish and iron ceilings was in progress. The frescoes in some of the committee rooms had already been begun. The old dome was being dismantled, old supporting masonry was being tested, and the derricks and hoisting machinery were being set up. The dome itself had not yet been begun.[23]

Hunt stated a few years later, in 1861, that as an assistant to Walter he had "superintended the whole bureau," and "got a monthly salary of $200, the highest pay of any except Walter himself, and with the stipulation that I could leave [go away] whenever I chose." On one or two occasions, he said, he was absent for about three days in a week, apparently going back to New York City to inspect the work on the Rossiter house.[24]

But just what Hunt actually did in Walter's office, what his position was, and how long he remained have been obscure points. Hunt said that he "superintended" Walter's office and implied by stating that he had "a monthly salary of $200" that he had remained there for at least a few months. Moreover, it was a part of the later public information about Hunt that he had worked on the Capitol for six months. But the evidence does not fully support Hunt's contentions. At the crux of the matter is Hunt's relationship to August Schoenborn, Walter's assistant. Walter's high regard for Schoenborn appeared to have been based not only on the skilled services and the personal loyalty the young German gave, but also on the fact that Schoenborn had a prominent role in creating design elements for the Capitol extension and the new dome. In his autobiographical sketch, written in 1895–1898, Schoenborn said that he had made the "original drawings" for the new dome, "as I have always done for work furnished by this office." And for the Capitol work generally, he wrote: "I can truly say, that I made all the original drawings of this work, including all plans, sections, details, all architectural ornamentation and enrichment, Column-Capitals and even working drawings. The other draughtsmen, who were employed being mere copyists." Although Schoenborn also referred to "personell [*sic*] of the Office" before 1865, he did not include any mention of Hunt, a curious omission considering that this autobiographical sketch was written just after Hunt's death in 1895, when the latter's fame was solidly established. Did Schoenborn not mention Hunt because of jealousy? Or because he forgot that Hunt had even worked in Walter's office at all, so short a time was he there and so unimportant was the work he did? The correct answer probably relates to both of these questions.[25]

On July 28, 1856, Captain Meigs, then superintendent of the Capitol works, sent a report to his superior, the Secretary of War, detailing a breakdown of expenditures on the Capitol extension, in response to inquiries made by the House of Representatives about the work. Not only did Meigs list the cost of the materials and work on the building, reprinting the relevant work contracts and job specifications, but he also listed the various employees by name, with information as to their duties and their compensation. Richard M. Hunt was listed as a "draughtsman," working under the architect Thomas U. Walter at a rate of $4.50 per day, but he was employed for only twenty-eight days in April and May of 1856. Hunt's rate of pay at $4.50 a day was the highest of any of the twelve draftsmen employed. "August Schonborn" [sic] was paid "$4.25 per day from Jan. 1 to May 21, and thereafter $5." Both men's duties were described as "making and copying drawings." This evidence establishes that Hunt did come into Walter's office in the spring of 1856 as the chief draftsman, receiving a higher rate of pay than Schoenborn, who was almost his contemporary and who had already been working with Walter for almost five years. Surely this was not an easy situation for the German immigrant to stomach. One can only speculate as to how the less professionally trained German must have felt about the self-confident and sophisticated, French-educated American, who had already worked on the Louvre (and who once indicated that he did not like Germans). There must have been a certain amount of tension. But whatever resentment Schoenborn might have felt could have lasted just a short time, since Hunt worked in Walter's office for only twenty-eight days, leaving sometime in May. Hunt later said that he was back in New York City by May 14. Probably his departure precipitated Schoenborn's pay raise on May 21 to a rate higher than Hunt had been getting, for Schoenborn then took over the position of chief draftsman to which his experience on the Capitol works entitled him.[26]

Hunt, then, did serve as the most highly paid draftsman for a brief time and probably "superintended the whole bureau." His stay, however, was briefer than he remembered it and his pay lower. Perhaps Hunt's recollection of the Washington experience was somewhat different from the facts because he wanted to be known as one who had had substantial experience in important public works projects both in Europe and in the United States. The record of such experience would obviously have been helpful for his professional career. In fact, the work he did during his stay in Washington was of little significance, though the great dome of the national Capitol was recalled many years later in his Administration Building at the World's Columbian Exposition.

Returning from Washington to New York in May, Hunt stopped briefly in Philadelphia, where he jotted in his sketchbook-journal: "Women pretty and small—plump and pretty . . . classic architecture predominated; last generation more sensible than N. Yorkers in architecture; Furness family charming & polite." The visit to the Furness household, to whom he brought letters of introduction, made a vivid impression on Frank Furness, then sixteen years old. Frank's older brother William, a painter, who had become acquainted with Hunt in Paris, recalled that Richard "had the reputation of being by far the brightest man in the Ecole des Beaux-Arts." Young Frank found himself "fascinated by his [Hunt's] appearance. At that time he had not the thoughtful look which he bore in later years, but seemed a bunch of joyous, energetic nerves." Frank had already begun to study architectural drawing, "and the moment Mr. Hunt spoke of his profession, I became absorbed and shall never forget seeing him describe a tower, I think of one of the European cathedrals—He quickly picked up a piece of paper and, taking a pencil out of his pocket, made one of those wonderful cobweb sketches of his. . . . Every line was emphasized in the right place and thoroughly fulfilled its purpose." Hunt seemed to the admiring neophyte "an altogether wonderful fellow." Three years later Furness would go to New York to study at Hunt's new Tenth Street Studio, joining what was to be the first American architectural atelier on the French model.[27]

While he lived at the University Building, Hunt was engaged on one other major project besides the Rossiter house. The Studio Building at 15 West Tenth Street, in New York City, was commissioned by James Boorman Johnston and his brother John Taylor Johnston. The Johnstons were sons of John Johnston, a wealthy merchant who had been a founder and a member and vice-president of the Council of New York University. John Taylor Johnston, who became a railroad executive and an art collector, was a graduate of the university and also served on the University Council. The Johnstons were well acquainted with the way in which the University Building had been put to use by artists and knew how unsuitable the facilities were. They decided that a building specifically designed to provide studios and gallery exhibition space for artists was needed in New York City, and they selected Hunt as their architect, his experience in France undoubtedly counting much with them.[1]

Hunt fortunately did not encounter the problems that had bedeviled him with the Rossiter house; moreover, the Johnstons were far more gracious and understanding than the irascible dentist. Hunt's preliminary designs and plans proved acceptable to the Johnstons, and the construction was carried out with little difficulty. Less ornate and less pretentious than the Rossiter house, though much larger, the Tenth Street Studios provided the first specialized quarters for artists in New York City and on completion displaced the old University Building as a center of activity in the visual and plastic arts. The Studio Building was begun in 1857 and was ready for occupancy early in 1858. It was razed in the mid-1950s. For almost a century, it remained an important center of artistic life.[2]

The three-story building (figure 10) contained some twenty-five studios as well as various small rooms. The workrooms were substantial in size, averaging fifteen by twenty feet to twenty by thirty feet, with high ceilings and excellent lighting. Directly inside the main entrance was the janitor's office, placed like the room of a French concierge, where supervision over entry into the building could be maintained. Straight ahead at the back of the structure was the large two-story exhibition room, "fine in proportion, and beautifully lighted" from a domed skylight. On either side narrow corridors gave access to the studios, and two wide staircases rose to the upper floors. Bedrooms were attached to some of the studios, and some of the tenants made the building their home as well as their workshop. Connecting doors joined several of the studios on each floor so that during an open house guests could wander directly from one artist's quarters to another's.[3]

7

**THE TENTH
STREET STUDIOS**

Figure 10
Studio Building, 51 West
Tenth Street, New York
(1858). Ware Collection,
Avery Library, Colum-
bia University.

The exterior of the structure was dark red brick with brown sandstone trim. Somewhat more austere and more utilitarian than the front of the Rossiter house, the Studio Building street side was dominated by the dramatic fenestration, the huge recessed studio windows extending almost from floor to ceiling. The façade had a tripartite division, the central section emphasized by windows larger than those on the sides, by the entrance itself, and by the four small jutting balconies. The flat-arched segmental brick lintels, together with the two low-arched parapet sections (recalling a feature of the Rossiter house) surmounting the wall sections adjacent to the central division interjected variety and contrast into the bold horizontals of the intricate geometric brickwork cornice and the sandstone stringcourse above the second story. The four small balconies, with elaborate black iron grillwork, the first-story brickwork panels, with decorative circles set in square frames, the brick piers topped with Greek crosses, and the boldly defined entrance surmounted by a triangular pediment and the word *Studios* chiseled directly above the door all made for an interesting play of surface elements. All in all, the design was most pleasing and appropriate for a singularly important building.[4]

The Studio Building was an immediate success. The first tenants, including some of the best-known painters of the day, moved into the building early in 1858. By the spring of 1858, Hunt himself was established in one of the larger studios on the upper floor, although he also kept his room at the university for about a year. In November 1859, *The Crayon* reported that the Tenth Street Studios were "as full as a Broadway omnibus on a rainy day" and not nearly all the applicants could be accommodated. Among the early arrivals were the painters John W. Casilaer, John La Farge, Frederic Church, William M. Hart, William Beard, Sanford Gifford, Jervis McEntee, and William S. Haseltine. Launt Thompson, a sculptor, occupied a workroom cluttered with statuary, busts, and medallion portraits, all of them usually coated with marble dust. Hunt's friend Theodore Winthrop took the room where he wrote *Cecil Dreeme*. The art critic Henry T. Tuckerman and the poet-essayist Thomas Bailey Aldrich had rooms there in the 1860s. Later on, the painters Albert Bierstadt, Eastman Johnson, Emanuel Leutze, John G. Brown, William Page, Worthington Whittredge, and Winslow Homer also rented studios in the building. Francis William Edmonds, a bank cashier by day and a painter in the evening, worked there for a time. Many of the painters were members of the National Academy of Design, and for years works by tenants of the Studio Building dominated the exhibitions of the Academy.[5]

The lighting was excellent, the atmosphere was congenial, the rooms were large, and the rents were modest, averaging $200 a year. Artists considered the studios very desirable, and newcomers quickly took over any vacancies. Some of the artists stayed on for many years: John G. Brown had quarters there for fifty-three years and Seymour Guy was in the building for forty-eight years. Homer D. Martin found a "little skylighted room on the top corridor" and remained for seventeen years. John La Farge, who had studied painting with Couture in Paris, came in 1858 as one of the first tenants, but he felt that he needed more instruction, and the next spring at Hunt's suggestion he went to Newport to study with William Hunt; nonetheless, La Farge kept quarters in the building until his death in 1910. Many of the artists taught pupils in their studios, a custom which lingered for a long time; many years later, Dwight David Eisenhower, when president of Columbia University, took painting lessons in the building.[6]

Two of the most attractive aspects of the Studio Building were the gala receptions, held three or four times each winter season, and the regular Saturday afternoon open houses. For the big evening receptions most of the artists invited visitors to their studios. Punch bowls and tea tables were set up and the connecting doors were opened. Visitors were perhaps intrigued as much by the seeming bohemian atmosphere of the cluttered rooms as by the works of art on display. Bierstadt filled his studio with Indian objects, such as war clubs, peace pipes, and wampum, while Frederic Church surrounded himself with tropical plants which he had gathered in his travels. If an artist had a new work he especially wanted to show, he might organize a private reception, sending out invitations to those who might be interested. Often food and wine were brought in, and there might be musical entertainment too. For some years a housekeeper, Mrs. Winter, who supplied breakfast for those lodging in the building, on special occasions cooked and served elaborate dinners for the resident artists and their guests. It was reported that Emanuel Leutze, after using birds and fish as subjects for painted panels, called on Mrs. Winter to have the objects served up for a dinner party. The receptions and the open houses greatly stimulated interest in art and helped the artists to display and sell their works. Just as important, the social affairs encouraged feelings of fellowship and a sense of community among those working in the building. When John G. Brown died after over half a century in residence, the New York *Herald* commented that there was "a peculiarly friendly quality about the old structure."[7]

Yet life in the Studio Building was relatively constrained, certainly not wildly bohemian. By and large the tenants were well established. Young, inexperienced artists sometimes complained that they were not welcome, except as paying pupils. Most of the artists in residence wanted to maintain an atmosphere of propriety. During the 1860s, when Jervis McEntee and his wife were for a time the only married couple living in the building, Mrs. McEntee was often called upon to act as a chaperon for bachelor artists when they entertained young ladies. Possibly the superb facilities helped mold the life style of the residents. The artists were mostly hard-working; and when the building was completed, *The Crayon* commented that the new quarters were "models of neatness, order, and even elegance," which, it was felt, would encourage artists to receive visitors with a refined "style of elegance and taste that should always characterize the man who is by profession a cultivator of those excellent qualities."[8]

William Merritt Chase, a painter who moved into the Studio Building in 1878, was too flamboyant and unconventional for some of the more staid residents. Chase occupied a small upstairs room but later managed to secure the large exhibition gallery as his private studio. He sported a pointed beard and a waxed mustache, looking, in his French silk cap and soft tie, "as if he had just escaped from the Latin Quarter," and he attracted considerable attention with his wolfhound, his black servant wearing a red fez, and the exotic birds and the "colossal collection of impediments" he kept in the large room. Chase gave painting lessons there and did a great deal of serious work, including about 1879 a magnificent view of the interior of his studio. But he was noted at the time as much for his receptions, musicales, and lavish parties as for his paintings. Chase's studio was considered the best in the city, and in the 1880s it became the focal point of New York artistic life. On Saturdays he regularly opened his studio to visitors, and for years various art societies used the large gallery as a meeting place. Here, one evening in 1890, Carmencita, the renowned Spanish dancer, came to perform. John Singer Sargent, who was painting her portrait, had arranged the event, and Mrs. Jack Gardner was there. But the dancer arrived at the studio in a bad mood, lost her temper, and threw a rose in Mrs. Gardner's face. When a gentleman retrieved the flower, pretending it was for him, Carmencita was mollified by the act and then danced brilliantly. The enthusiasm of the audience was unrestrained: the women threw jewels at her feet, and Mrs. Jack even did an odd little dance.[9]

The commission for the Tenth Street Studio Building probably assisted Hunt's career as few others could have done. Not only did the building immediately become the nucleus of artistic life in New York

City, but also Hunt's establishment of his own studio there identified him with the building. The artists working there invariably were enthusiastic about the quarters he had created, and he must have been looked upon by the residents as an important person who had provided them with a congenial home. Even though he was not much older than many of them, he perhaps came to be viewed with a certain respect because of his training at the Ecole and for what he had so quickly accomplished in New York. And to the public interested in art, Hunt was soon known as a leader in local artistic circles. Moreover, what he was doing in his own studio was of considerable importance in building up his position within the architectural profession and ultimately in making a decided impact on the course of American architectural development.

Even before he moved from the University Building to his new studio, Hunt had begun to provide architectural instruction to a few pupils, modeling his teaching on the French system of instruction. The new quarters in the Tenth Street Studios became then both a studio-workshop for Hunt and an atelier for a group of students. Although this was not the first instance of systematic architectural instruction in the United States, Hunt's atelier was the first to utilize many elements of Beaux-Arts teaching. There, Hunt attempted to pass on much that he had learned in Paris.

For some time Hunt had thought of involving himself in art education in the United States, realizing the importance of professional training in elevating standards of accomplishment and of public taste. In 1855, the year he and William returned to America, the two brothers seriously considered setting up an art school in New York City in which both architecture and painting would be taught. They contemplated an academy, modeled on the Ecole des Beaux-Arts, at which leading artists would contribute a day or so of their time each week for teaching. The young students would be exposed both to systematic instruction in the elements of the arts and to the inspiration and example of leading practicing artists. Although the idea was never carried out, both brothers nevertheless devoted themselves to teaching, Richard for a few years in his atelier and William throughout his life, first in informal instruction at his Newport studio and later in formal classes in Boston. William Morris Hunt became one of the great art teachers of the nineteenth century in the United States.[10]

At this time the primary method of architectural training in the United States was office training. Those who wished to learn architecture served as apprentices to practicing architects, though, of course, without any formal guild standards or other outside supervision. This means of preparation was similar to the tradition of other fields, such as law, in which most neophytes learned by clerking with a practicing lawyer, or medicine, in which many young men were instructed by assisting a physician in his work. Academic training had already been established in these fields, however, and graduates of such programs were in fact much better prepared than those who had served as apprentices. In architecture, Benjamin Latrobe early in the century took on apprentices in his Philadelphia office; Charles Bulfinch accepted young men to work with him in his office in Boston; and Richard Upjohn and Alexander Jackson Davis in New York took in assistants for training. The apprentice-assistants, who often had already been given some systematic training in drawing, were expected not only to help in the preparation of working plans but also to make themselves generally useful, providing measurements, inspecting materials, and overseeing the work of carpenters and masons. Robert Mills, the first American trained specifically as an architect, took a classical course at Charleston College and then worked as an assistant to James Hoban, Thomas Jefferson, and Benjamin Latrobe. William Strickland also worked as a pupil-assistant to Latrobe.[11]

Attempts had already been made to provide more formal instruction. Thomas Jefferson had hoped to include a professional course in architecture at the University of Virginia. Indeed, he designed the pavilions of the university so that the buildings would show examples of a variety of architectural elements, which might be used for instructional purposes. But a professional program was not established there, since no one was found to teach the full program of necessary courses. Systematic training in engineering, including drawing, was set up at West Point, established in 1802, and at the Rensselaer Institute, founded in 1825; and at New York University Professor David Bates Douglass organized a course in engineering and architecture when the school opened in 1832. A year after the Franklin Institute was founded in Philadephia in 1824 to promote study of applied science and the mechanical arts, William Strickland, by then the leading architect of Philadelphia, gave lectures there on architecture, while his brother George Strickland taught classes in architectural drawing. Thomas U. Walter, who studied under William Strickland at the Franklin Institute, was later selected to give architectural instruction there. Another short-lived architectural school was that established by Robert Mills in Washington, D.C. in the late 1830s. Mills, who was by then architect of federal buildings, wanted both to add to his own income and to train men to meet public building needs. Although his school was accorded a good reception, it lasted only about three years.[12]

Like Hunt's quarters in the University Building, his new studio on Tenth Street (figure 11) was soon filled with a clutter of objects— paintings, prints, drawings, photographs, plaster casts, pieces of panels, moldings, and stained glass, old furniture, and relics from Egyptian, Greek, and Roman antiquity. An old carved chimneypiece dominated one wall of the workroom. Hunt also arranged in the new studio much of his by now substantial library, one of the largest collections of books in New York City. By the end of the 1850s he had acquired between three and four thousand volumes, perhaps two thousand of which were books on architecture; the others were largely books on painting, sculpture, interior decoration, and travel. Hunt also collected books dealing with the hospitalization and treatment of the insane. Most of the works were in French, but other modern languages were also represented. By 1860, Hunt also possessed a collection of some five thousand photographs of famous buildings and monuments. The architect willingly lent his books to his pupils, but he was always very careful to see that they were returned in good condition and put back in their proper places. The books and photographs, as well as the art objects, were used as aides in teaching architecture, enlarging the students' awareness of what had been done in the past and therefore of the possibilities for the future. Large drafting tables, drawing boards on trestles, and a blackboard provided working equipment for the young master and his atelier pupils.[13]

Hunt's first pupil was George Bradbury, one of the two draftsmen who worked with him on the Rossiter house. Bradbury, along with James S. Wightman, who assisted Hunt for only two or three weeks, came to work for Hunt in the spring of 1857; he continued in the architect's employ as a pupil-assistant at a salary of ten dollars a week until late August, after which he remained as a pupil until January or February 1858. In the meantime, late in the summer of 1857, two others came to Hunt for instruction at his University Building studio. Henry Van Brunt and Charles D. Gambrill, who had both graduated from Harvard College in 1854, had been attempting to obtain instruction in architecture and asked Hunt to take them on as students. The next year George B. Post, who had graduated in civil engineering from New York University, came into the atelier. Early in 1859, the three pupils were joined by William R. Ware, who had known Van Brunt and Gambrill at Harvard, and by Frank Furness of Philadelphia, whose brother had known Van Brunt, Gambrill, and Ware at Harvard and whom Hunt had

Figure 11
Hunt's studio, Studio
Building (ca. 1859).
Courtesy American Ar-
chitectural Archive.

met three years earlier. Then Edward Quincy and E. L. Hyde entered the atelier. The last two did not continue in architecture, however; Quincy turned to painting and Hyde became a clergyman. The other five—Van Brunt, Gambrill, Post, Ware, and Furness—all became prominent architects and all retained an attachment to Hunt. Through his system of instruction and these pupils, Hunt had considerable influence on American architectural education. Indeed, by 1876 he was being called "the father of high and successful architectural education in this country."[14]

In his atelier, which, unlike its French prototype, also served as his office, Hunt formulated specific problems for his students, whose work he then guided and criticized. Since he gave his students one major problem and additional minor problems each month, the projects were more limited in scope than the Beaux-Arts *projets*, on which the Parisian students spent two months. Hunt's pupils, of course, did not have the systematic and formal instruction in various subjects that the Beaux-Arts students had, but Hunt did attempt to direct their reading as well as give instruction in the principles of architectural design. Basically, he tried to provide the students with a solid foundation in historical architecture, exposing them to a wide variety of styles, elements of design, and problems. He did not attempt to make his students accept a particular style as best. But he did discourage eccentricity, teaching principles of care and attention to proportion and the logic and appropriateness of solutions. He required the young men in the atelier to learn the classical orders thoroughly, insisting that even if they were never to make use of classical styles, the orders would give them a certain idea or instinct of proportion essential to good design, which they would always retain.[15]

Fundamental to architectural design, Hunt believed, was the ability to draw well. He himself had a remarkable drawing talent, and he was resolute that his students must "draw, draw, draw, sketch, sketch, sketch!" He always insisted, "If you can't draw anything else, draw your boots, it doesn't matter, it will ultimately give you a control of your pencil so that you can the more rapidly express on paper your thoughts in designing. The greater facility you have in expressing these thoughts the freer and better your designs will be."[16]

To his pupils the teacher constantly stressed the need for hard work and thorough study. He was very demanding, often severe, in his criticism of their work and sometimes harsh with them if he encountered them in social activities when he felt that they should be working. Hunt worked hard himself and expected others to do so too. His students recalled that he constantly endeavored to convey to them his own sense of commitment to his art and the short time available to do what might be done. On the bookplates for his library volumes he had printed the two mottos: *Ars Longa, Vita Brevis Est* and *Laborare Est Orare,* and the first of these, George Post related, he frequently wrote on the blackboard in the studio. Post also recalled Hunt's exhortations: "You have not got long to live, you won't live half long enough to be a really accomplished architect. You have got to work at day, and you have got to work at night. When you wake up at night, you have got to think about it!"[17]

Despite his rough manner, Hunt inspired his students both by his teachings and by his example. To William Ware, who studied with Hunt for only a few months, the master had an "electric influence," breathing into his New York atelier "the atmosphere of the Paris school," and making his studio "a real home of art, a real fountain of inspiration." In Ware's view, Hunt's teachings opened up a whole new realm of experience to his disciples. Almost every day he set them "at some new line of work, spurring us and whipping us along paths then new to this part of the world." Sometimes in the evening the whole group would go out to dinner together, and then the young men would sit, delighted to hear Hunt talk of his Beaux-Arts days and the scheme of instruction there. Ware's estimate of the atelier was unreserved: "I think we all of us feel that it was then that we learned all we knew."[18]

Both George Post and Henry Van Brunt later asserted that Hunt's teachings had given them a firm grasp of architectural principles and a sense of direction in the midst of the confusion of mid-nineteenth-century American building practices. Post remembered "the inspiring nature of his instruction," with his "vehement and strenuous manner" and the wealth of resources placed at their disposal. Van Brunt recalled "the excitement and enthusiasm" of working under "the almost tempestuous zeal of the master," the atmosphere of the workroom "quickened by his energy and illuminated by his inexhaustible humor." Above all, "Hunt ever insisted upon the pre-eminent importance of academical discipline and order in design," inculcating "respect for authority and discipline" in contrast to the "romantic license" of the time. The experience of studying with him, Van Brunt concluded, "was a liberal education in the fullest sense" and all were "enlarged and enlightened by his influence."[19]

Frank Furness had joined the atelier after Hunt paid another visit to the Furness family in Philadelphia in 1858 and had described what he was doing in New York. Frank, who had been so dazzled by Hunt two years before, pleaded with his father, the Reverend William Henry Furness, to allow him to go to New York to study. When Reverend Furness agreed and wrote Hunt to inquire if he would take his son, Hunt was apparently very flattered by the request and welcomed the young Philadelphian to his studio. Furness remained with Hunt for two years, until the outbreak of the Civil War. During the summer of 1860, he joined his teacher in Newport, studying drawing with William, while Richard recuperated there from an illness. Late in 1864, after he had served for three years in the Sixth Pennsylvania Cavalry and received the Congressional Medal of Honor, Furness returned to New York to join Hunt's office staff and probably remained with him through 1865.[20]

The first days that young Furness spent in the atelier were rather uncomfortable at the time but in retrospect seemed "indeed delightful":

The first morning I spent at the studio, when Mr. Hunt came in he nodded to the other fellows and shaking hands with me, said he was very glad to see me among the rest of them. He then made the address which I found afterward was made to all newcomers, and which proved a great incentive to industrious work. It ran somewhat after this fashion: "Now look here, don't you see I am not going to be any kind of a bear leader, schoolmaster or taskmaster to you in any way. You pay me to get out of me everything I know about architecture, and for what you pay me I am willing to give you the benefit of what I know. If you choose to loaf and throw away the opportunity of getting all that you might out of me that is your lookout not mine; you will never by word, look or action on my part know that I do not think you are doing quite right. In short I am here to teach you if you want to be taught; I am not here to force you in any way."

The first careful drawing in Indian ink in Mr. Hunt's studio was a frightful ordeal. He had such perfect control over both his pencil and his brush that it seemed to him impossible that everybody else should not have the same facility. The consequence was that the pupil had indeed a terrible time, generally ending by Mr. Hunt's snatching the brush from his pupil's hand, and saying, "There, you clumsy idiot, don't you see it is perfectly easy to do? Why don't you do it?"

The scene over the first drawing was so well known that when my turn came, all my fellow students stopped work, and listened with evident enjoyment, well remembering that they themselves had previously gone through the same ordeal. . . .

The whip used by Mr. Hunt to keep us well up to the mark was a critical bludgeon, with now and then between the blows a very small dose of praise, of course greatly prized by all on account of its rarity; the bitter medicine was always administered first, and then came the currant jelly, in the way of praise, to palliate the sometimes fearful dose.[21]

The students worked very hard, Furness later related, but also played hard. Sometimes they would cook an oyster stew in the studio, Hunt enjoying the moments of relaxation with them. But despite his familiar manner on these special occasions, the students remained in awe of him and were always respectful. To Furness, Hunt "was indeed so far above us all in ability, capacity for work, and knowledge, that I cannot imagine any young man who could fail to be rather awe-stricken in his presence. He never did anything by halves; he was the hardest worker I have ever known, and when he played he did it just as energetically, and as earnestly as he worked."[22]

Hunt's most important direct influence on architectural education in the United States came through his pupil William R. Ware. Ware left the atelier late in 1859 to open his own architectural office in Boston, where Henry Van Brunt joined him in 1863 as a partner. Ware and Van Brunt both thought so highly of the training they had received in Hunt's office that in 1864 they established a similar atelier in their own office, lecturing and setting up problems for their students to work on, over a two-year course of study. They achieved, Ware later wrote, "a very satisfactory success." When administrators at the Massachusetts Institute of Technology in 1865 began to investigate the possibility of setting up a professional course in architecture, Ware and his atelier came to their attention, and in 1866 he was invited to organize and direct the school of architecture there, the first professional architectural school in the United States. It opened in September 1868 with four students enrolled. By 1879, the M.I.T. school had thirty students, two-thirds of them enrolled in a two-year course of study, the remainder in a four-year course. Ware's program at M.I.T., as described in his *Outline of a Course for Architectural Instruction* (1866), echoed that of the Ecole des Beaux-Arts. In 1881, Ware was brought to Columbia College to organize a new Department of Architecture, under the School of Mines. Apparently, the trustees of Columbia had first offered the position to Hunt, who turned it down because he felt that it would limit his private practice and recommended Ware for the job. Ware headed the Columbia department until his retirement in 1903. During the latter part of the nineteenth century, Ware was undoubtedly the most influential single individual in American architectural education, and he acknowledged that "everything that has been done at the institute and at the college has followed that precept . . . [of] the whole scheme of the Ecole. . . ." In 1898, Ware wrote to Furness that the Columbia department was "a direct outcome of the Tenth Street Studio of thirty-nine years ago."[23]

Ware's work in establishing the two important architectural schools at M.I.T. and Columbia was an impressive achievement: he has been called "the virtual creator of the American system of architectural education." Through Ware, the Beaux-Arts tradition, which he had encountered at second hand in Hunt's atelier, moved into formal architectural education in the United States. Up to this point what collegiate instruction in architecture there was had been closely tied to the teaching of basic engineering. At New York University, for example, the professor in charge of architectural drawing, Thomas S. Cummings, was in the School of Civil Engineering and Architecture, organized in 1854, which was an outgrowth of the engineering course of Professor Douglass. Ware's work significantly developed the distinction between architecture and engineering. The architectural student, Ware believed, must be liberally cultivated, with a grounding in history, science, and the arts. The French system and methods which he accepted, however, had to be adapted to American needs.[24]

For thirty years after the founding of the architectural course at M.I.T., Beaux-Arts influences were pronounced in the two schools that Ware had set up. By the mid-1890s, seven additional collegiate architectural courses had been established: Illinois (1870), Cornell (1871), Syracuse (1873), Pennsylvania (1874), Columbian University (George Washington; 1884), Armour (now Illinois) Institute of Technology (1889), and Harvard (1895). These seven programs focused largely on practical construction problems and specific academic technical study, rather than on broadly liberal, historically and art-oriented courses, with large, formal, competitive design projects, such as Ware favored. Organized within existing colleges, some in schools of engineering, the new architectural courses were adapted to the structure and facilities of existing institutions: they were generally directly responsive to local needs and conditions. By the final decade of the century, however, as increasing numbers of American architects were receiving training at the Ecole des Beaux-Arts, some of whom themselves became teachers in American schools, the influence of the French school became far stronger in American education. Many young Americans, after study and work at home, went on to study in France. In 1893, some Americans who had attended the French school organized the Society of Beaux-Arts Architects "to cultivate and perpetuate the principles and associations of the Ecole des Beaux-Arts." Earlier, about 1885, Ware, who had not himself studied in France, was instrumental in organizing support among Americans who had studied at the Ecole, including Hunt, for an "American Prize" open only to French Beaux-Arts students as a gift in return for the generous treatment the Americans had received there. During the first quarter of the twentieth century, the neoclassical Beaux-Arts training, with a modified atelier system, was clearly dominant in American architectural education. The focus on the study of historical styles, development of elaborate formal designs, and work on big competitive projects, with little attention to practical social needs or economic considerations, became characteristic of American collegiate training. Although this tradition inculcated a high standard of training and draftsmanship and a sense of discipline and order, much of the architectural work was grandiose, tied to the past, and plainly irrelevant to American problems. In time, the Beaux-Arts tradition in education was repudiated.[25]

Hunt had led the way in the American trek to the Ecole des Beaux-Arts, and he had tried to transmit something of the Beaux-Arts atmosphere and principles to his own students on Tenth Street. What he started on a small scale in his atelier was the beginning of a major tradition in American architectural education, which gained considerable momentum by the final years of the nineteenth century. Hunt's first two or three years in architectural practice in New York were of importance, however, not only because of his impact on architectural education but also because of what he actually designed. The Rossiter house echoed contemporary French design and provided in its façade details something New Yorkers had not seen before. The Studio Building became the working and social center of artistic activity in New York City. For a young man who had hoped to do something significant to promote the fine arts in the United States, he had quickly achieved a great deal. His work was being noticed and he was becoming known.

8

THE AMERICAN INSTITUTE OF ARCHITECTS

Much more important than the Studio Building in advancing the arts in general and architecture in particular was a new organization, the American Institute of Architects. The Institute was one of many new professional societies formed in the mid- and late nineteenth century to promote the interests of those doing similar work, to improve the quality of the services they provided, and to foster public recognition and esteem of a particular group. Hunt played a leading role in developing the structure and in formulating the activities of the new association. For almost four decades, through the Institute and in other ways, he did as much as any other single person to improve the status of his own profession in the United States.

The position of the architect in America at the midpoint of the nineteenth century was in many ways an uncertain one. To the public at large there was little distinction between an architect and a carpenter-builder. Both seemed to do the same kind of work, and many people apparently thought that the term "architect" was only a fancy name for a carpenter. Even among those who did design buildings, moreover, little feeling of community existed. They could have little sense of having gone through a common training and preparation, for architectural education consisted of not much more than a few courses here and there attached to engineering study and apprenticeship work in architects' offices. No reference libraries were available to them, and there were no important national publications focusing on architecture. Nor could building designers expect to find others working in the field who accepted agreed-upon building standards, similar ways of dealing with clients, or common schedules of fees and charges. Before the American Institute of Architects was established, as Henry Van Brunt, Hunt's former pupil, recounted toward the end of the century, "community of thought [and] mutual friendship hardly existed among architects. The hand of each was turned with jealousy and suspicion against his brother. His processes of design and his business methods were personal secrets. Each concealed his drawings from the rest as if they were pages of a private diary. Even books and prints were carefully secluded from inspection by any rival. . . . There were no ethics of practice, no common ground of mutual protection, no unity of action or thought, no national literature of architecture." Van Brunt believed that the formation of the American Institute of Architects was a Declaration of Independence from the old conditions, and in this "most memorable emancipation," he asserted, "Hunt's influence was the most potent."[1]

The number of architectural associations established before the American Institute of Architects was not large. The French Académie

Royale d'Architecture, founded in 1671, held regular meetings, attempted to codify technical knowledge, and established classes, but it was limited to an exclusive group of royally appointed architects. Short-lived architectural societies were established in London in 1791 and 1806 and in Paris in 1812, and a permanent national organization was founded in Holland in 1819. In 1840, the Société Centrale des Architectes was established in Paris. More germane to the American experience, however, was the Institute of British Architects, formed in 1834 and chartered in 1837, which became the Royal Institute of British Architects in 1866. At its inception the British group was composed of London architects, who met to discuss common problems of practice and education; provincial societies also soon appeared, but the Royal Institute remained the dominant and most prestigious national organization. In 1861, nonetheless, of 3,843 architects in Britain only 338 were members of the Institute of British Architects.[2]

The Brethren of the Workshop of Vitrivius, a little-known group that existed in New York in 1803, was probably the first architectural society in the United States. Undoubtedly the Brethren consisted of only a few members, and probably most of them were builders or carpenters. The New York directory for 1803, in fact, listed only four architects, and two of them were named as builders and one was a builder and architect.[3]

The first substantial professional architectural organization in the United States was the American Institution of Architects, formed by eleven architects who met at the Astor House in New York on December 6, 1836. Alexander Jackson Davis was chairman of the group, and Thomas U. Walter acted as secretary. The founding members invited other architects to join them in an association to work for improvement in architectural education and better recognition of the profession. The Institution met at the Pennsylvania Academy of Fine Arts on May 2, 1837, to adopt bylaws and a constitution and to elect officers. William Strickland of Philadelphia was chosen president. Davis believed that a society of architects probably could not contribute to "a birth of genius for the profession" in America, but it could, he hoped, "discourage mediocrity and put down pretension" and, above all, educate and instruct the public "for the proper appreciation of this noble art." A library and an exhibition room open to the public as well as free lectures appealing to a general taste were essential, he felt, to gain public acceptance of the profession. Both Philadelphia and New York should be centers to disseminate the values of good architecture; and, Davis wrote facetiously, perhaps the meetings might be held between the two centers "in a Camden and Amboy [railroad] car" since this "would place us at once in a *train* for *advancing* the interests of our art." Despite the hopeful intentions of the founders, meetings of the Institution were held only irregularly, and within a few years of its inception the society had lapsed.[4]

But the need for renewed activity to improve the state of the profession continued to be felt by many architects. Richard Upjohn, who had known Hunt as a small boy in New Haven years earlier, took the lead in founding a new organization. About the middle of February 1857, Upjohn sent out invitations to fellow architects in New York to come to his office for the purpose of forming a new professional society. Although Hunt had been in New York for a relatively short time, he was one of those invited to the meeting. On February 23, 1857, twelve architects, among them Hunt, joined Upjohn in his office in the Trinity Building at 111 Broadway. Upjohn proposed to the group that a new professional association be established, to meet regularly for discussion of common problems and to provide fellowship. His proposal was received enthusiastically. Committees were named to draw up bylaws and a constitution. The organizers decided that the new organization should attempt to acquire national membership and that twelve other practitioners should be invited at once by the secretary to attend the next meeting, among them Davis and Walter. Walter subsequently turned over to the new society the records of the old Institution.[5]

At the second meeting, held on March 10, 1857, the bylaws and the constitution were presented for consideration in draft form. Thomas U. Walter, who had come to New York from Philadelphia for this gathering, suggested that the new organization be called American Institute of Architects rather than the New York Society of Architects as had originally been suggested, since the name would be more appropriate for a truly national group. Later the society was denominated *The* American Institute of Architects. In its earliest years, nevertheless, the group remained essentially local and provided a cohesive element mainly among New York architects.[6]

A third meeting followed on March 13 for continued discussion and revision of the bylaws and the constitution. The purpose of the Institute, according to the constitution, was to advance the interests of the profession and its members through regular meetings, lectures, and the establishment of a library. Meetings were to be held twice a month in winter and once a month in summer, and political and religious matters were not to be brought up in the meetings. Provision was made for probationary members, who would be termed "associates." At a fourth meeting, probably held on March 26, nine trustees, including Hunt, were elected, and they met a few days later to prepare for formal incorporation.[7]

Monday, April 13, 1857, was an important day for the new organization. At noon, Hunt and the other trustees met at Delmonico's restaurant at the corner of Beaver and William streets, where they first enjoyed an excellent luncheon and then proceeded to City Hall to take care of the official business of incorporation. Judge James I. Roosevelt of the New York State Supreme Court received them "in a most courteous manner" and gave his consent and approbation to their petition for incorporation. Hunt, serving as secretary, kept an account of the proceedings and recorded that Judge Roosevelt, in a short speech, "stated that he feared not that our Institute would fail, for we were above all others aware of the necessity of a solid foundation whereupon to construct an edifice and that consequently he felt assured that we had laid our cornerstone as on a rock." The trustees then filed the necessary incorporation papers in the office of the county clerk.[8]

Two days later, on April 15, Richard Upjohn, who had conceived the Institute, proudly presided over the first regular evening meeting of the newly incorporated organization, at 8:00 P.M. in the small chapel of the University Building. At this time the charter members signed a fair copy of the constitution prepared on parchment and handsomely lettered. Walter announced that *The Crayon* would be pleased to serve as the official organ in reporting the activities of the Institute; Hunt, who was elected secretary, thereafter sent regular notices to *The Crayon*. Walter also helped give the new organization direction by urging that, the organization having been instituted, the moment had arrived "to act": he proposed that members prepare papers to be delivered at the meetings in order to exchange knowledge and to acquaint the public with the nature of good architecture, for, above all, he stressed, education of the public at large was needed. The group decided to rent quarters at New York University, where Hunt was then a tenant; the Institute first took space in the small house just to the northeast of the University Building, but in March 1858 it moved to larger quarters in room 3 of the main building, taking room 5 as well in 1859.[9]

The new professional society was now under way, and Hunt, who had been in New York City for only a year and a half, was not yet thirty years old, and had done very little designing, was as trustee, secretary, and librarian, already accepted as a leader among New York architects. During the next three years or so Hunt was very active in Institute affairs, helping Upjohn arrange meetings, collecting books, and publicizing the programs. In the first four years of the Institute, the papers on architectural topics prepared by members were the focus of the meetings. At first, members volunteered to give papers, but when the supply of volunteers ran low, topics had to be assigned.[10]

At the next meeting, on May 5, President Upjohn gave an inspirational talk on the themes of truth in architecture and of architectural functionalism. Upjohn was certain that members, through association in the A.I.A., could promote their individual welfare, work for truth in their designs, and improve public taste. That the United States had few examples of good building design from the past was, he said, obvious. But, Upjohn felt, "this paucity of examples will oblige us to think more intently on our work, to deepen our thought to a more close and thorough investigation and search after truth, to purify our conception in our designs, and to a nobler development of the talent committed to us." He then went on to express an idea that was already gaining acceptance in America: "These convictions of our calling only can make us capable of working out with a true and clear understanding, the unity and perfection of any work intrusted to our care. The purpose of every structure we build should be marked so as to need no other inscription than what it truly presents. Its exterior and interior expression ought to make plain the uses for which it is erected. Let these principles be well studied, and the more careful thought we apply to them, the greater variety and beauty will be manifest in our works."[11]

In the first year others also exhorted their fellow members to promote understanding of the architect's occupation and to try to elevate public taste. Charles Babcock's paper, entitled "The Ways and Means of Accomplishing the Elevation of the Architects' Profession," which was presented on October 20, was strongly defensive in tone about the status of architects compared to that of other professionals in America and about public misunderstanding of what they were trying to do. An architect, Babcock pointed out, required extensive training, must acquire considerable technical knowledge, and had to develop an artistic taste. "But all this is, in our day, not appreciated by the public. They recognize as freely qualified members of the profession any full grown boys or aspiring carpenters, who hang out their signs and proclaim themselves architects. . . . In fact, the public are lamentably ignorant of what architecture is, and cannot tell good from bad. . . . Their taste is utterly undeveloped." The solution, Babcock asserted, lay in a regular course of study, regulated competitions, and high standards in both.[12]

A paper read by Calvert Vaux at the June 2, 1857, meeting concerned "the adaptation of houses *à la française* to this country." Hunt transmitted this piece to *The Crayon*, believing that it would be of general interest. Since Hunt himself in a few years would build the first example of "French flats" in the United States, his interest in Vaux's statement is of especial importance. Vaux, of course, was talking about multiple family dwellings, with separate apartments for the several families, a practice which, he considered, possessed many advantages. Up to this time multiple dwellings in New York had been confined to "what are known as tenement houses," and people of means and fashion had heretofore not accepted such inadequate quarters as suitable. Vaux believed that New York property owners should consider such buildings for housing, provided that the structures were no more than four stories in height (otherwise an inferior class of persons would come in, for the floors above the fourth would have to have low rents to attract anyone), and provided that the buildings included flats that faced on the street and not on an inner courtyard and were approached by an attractive general entrance and an elegant staircase.[13]

Two early papers debated the question of architectural competitions, a subject that would come up at A.I.A. meetings again and again. At the September 1 meeting, one speaker supported the need for architectural competitions as a means of developing new ideas, provided competent judges were selected, while another opposed competitions because they encouraged young and inexperienced architects to try what they were not yet prepared to master. After the papers were read, a general discussion ensued and Hunt reported that a majority of the members favored competitions, provided that they were "established on a good footing," that prizes were offered, and that the judges included both architects and trustees acting for the building in question. Competitions again came up for discussion at the November 17 and December 15 meetings. Hunt himself later entered many competitions and sometimes served as a competition judge.[14]

Although Hunt did his part in these early meetings and read a paper on the history of architecture on November 3, his somewhat pedantic scholarship apparently was of less interest to the members than his work as librarian. On February 2, 1858, Hunt reported his success in obtaining works of interest for the library of the Institute: "Both private associations and public corporations had manifested a deep interest in the welfare of the Institute," Hunt wrote, "and he was confident that before the expiration of another year, the collection of books belonging to the Institute, if not in every sense worthy of it, would, at least, be of sufficient importance to make the librarian feel proud of the charge intrusted to his care." Since Hunt had been building up his own private architectural library for a number of years, he was a good person to collect books for the Institute.[15]

The first annual dinner of the American Institute of Architects was held on Washington's birthday, February 22, 1858, at Delmonico's, with twenty members present. The occasion was one for celebration and self-congratulation. President Upjohn emphasized once more the continuing work of educating the public as to what real architectural practice involved. United, he exhorted, the members could best advance their common interests. Leopold Eidlitz, in an emotional address, urged his fellow practitioners always to regard their individual interests as "secondary to the interests of the art, and to those of the profession." Not only must architects improve themselves and their profession, but they must work to improve the public's knowledge of architecture. The exchange of ideas, the reading of papers, the accumulation of a library of drawings and models, the founding of an architectural school would all help to improve the profession. "The improvement of the public is to be accomplished by the publication of matters instructive to them, by lectures, and by the admission, as honorary members, of those who are true amateurs of art." The opportunities for architectural advancement in the United States, Eidlitz asserted, "are unparalleled in the history of Art, and it is, in a great measure, dependent upon ourselves whether or not this shall be the commencement of an epoch in architecture greater than any which has preceded it." A round of toasts followed the speeches. When Frederick Peterson offered a toast to Hunt as secretary, Hunt responded by saying that he had once been a great talker at dinners but had learned more in a year of recording for the A.I.A. than during all his former years of talking. He repeated the theme of a forthcoming brilliant era in American art, when it would be a source of pride for any man to say: "I am a member of the American Institute of Architects."[16]

In the second year the meetings of the Institute were less exhortative in tone and focused more on stylistic concerns. Eidlitz read a paper, "On Style," at the meeting of March 16, 1858, and Detlef Lienau gave a talk entitled, "On Romantic and Classic Architecture" on May 4. Henry Van Brunt's paper of December 7, "Cast Iron in Decorative Architecture," dealt approvingly with the possible uses of cast iron in tracery and decorative detailing. Eidlitz, responding to Van Brunt at the following meeting on December 21 in "Cast Iron and Architecture," argued that the material was unsuitable for primary walls and altogether without significant utility. In the discussion that followed Eidlitz's paper, Hunt expressed his view that cast iron could be especially useful in shop fronts in a closed-in area where considerable light was needed. Hunt's two later Broadway storefronts would carry out his ideas.[17]

A paper given by Coleman Hart on February 15, 1859, entitled "Unity in Architecture," affirmed the appropriateness of the Gothic style for religious structures and rejected the idea that any other style would be suitable. After Eidlitz had concurred with Hart and denounced Renaissance usage as a blind return to the classical, Hunt took the floor to differ strongly with both of them. History had shown, Hunt asserted, that with the brilliant epoch of the Renaissance "the architecture of the Dark Ages was supplanted by one more in accordance with the enlightenment of the age." In Protestant countries at least, "*a new style of architecture* was necessary to express the *change in religion*" which came with the Reformation as "ignorance and superstition no longer held full sway." Although he professed himself "a great admirer of Gothic architecture," he thought St. Peter's and St. Paul's were as impressive as any other monuments of Christian art. Hunt's remarks on this occasion were based on a theme to which he would often return: A new architecture was needed for new conditions.[18]

The second annual dinner, on February 22, 1859, was another spirited affair at Delmonico's restaurant. Joseph C. Wells, who had briefly assisted Hunt on the Rossiter house, presided at the festivities, calling on Richard Upjohn, Henry Van Brunt, and Frederick Peterson for speeches. Toasts followed, and the wine flowed freely. When Hunt as secretary was toasted, he responded by comparing his duties as scribe to those of the architect, who is himself "a recording secretary of the public mind." Before the invention of printing, Hunt went on, "architects may be considered the principal recorders of historical events," and even today "each structure must have peculiarities of its own, [and] thereby the history of each epoch is written in stone." Building designs must relate to the needs and the spirit of the times.[19]

While the Institute meetings of the first year had centered on the status of the profession and the need to improve public understanding of architects' work and those of the second year had dealt largely with historical styles, the meetings of the third year focused on technical matters and professional problems. At their gatherings the members dealt with such topics as the organization of competitions, auditorium acoustics, laws concerning unsafe buildings, and consideration of an academy for architectural education. The members decided that architectural working drawings must remain the property of the architect, to be used as his tools, and were not to be acquired by a client who paid a fee for a building design, a point which concerned Hunt a few years later, when the Union League Club attempted to retain his drawings for a clubhouse that was not built. On August 2, 1859, the members proposed a series of public lectures on types of architecture—church, public, civil, city residential, country residential, monumental, and street— each lecture to be read to the Institute before being given in public. Hunt was chosen by ballot to deliver a lecture on street architecture. But the full series apparently did not come off, since, it was reported, the committee was unable to find suitable pictorial material. Early in March 1860, Hunt, together with James Renwick and John W. Ritch, went to Albany to appear as spokesmen for an act pending in the New York State Assembly providing protection against unsafe buildings in New York City. The highlight of the third year, once more, was the annual banquet at Delmonico's, held on Washington's birthday. The claret was excellent, the speeches and poetry were suitably inspiring, the toasts were numerous, and the conviviality was well sustained. "Songs, English, French, and German, succeeded each other in rapid succession," it was reported. Several guests were present at the dinner, including J. Durand, editor of *The Crayon,* and Alexander Harthill, editor of the newly founded *Architects' and Mechanics' Journal,* both of whom reported on the evening's proceedings. Harthill was especially enthusiastic about the professional society; membership in the Institute, he felt, should involve strict requirements and be a badge of social and professional standing. "Architectural fraternity—in this country—was, to us," Harthill wrote, "until this evening . . . we are half ashamed to confess, a perfect myth. . . . [But] when we looked around us and saw many of those distinguished men whose tasteful pencils have done so much, in past years, towards enhancing the beauty of our cities, and rooting a taste for the fine arts among us, we confess that we saw, in such an assemblage, a noble dawn for the career of architecture in the United States."[20]

By the fourth year, however, the members' interest in the Institute was clearly waning. Hunt's activity in the organization diminished, perhaps in part because of illness, and sometime in 1860 he stepped down as secretary to be replaced by his pupil Henry Van Brunt. He resigned from the Institute on February 5, 1861. The outbreak of the Civil War severely disrupted architectural work, and attendance at meetings fell off markedly. For the Institute, dues fell in arrears and bills piled up. To save money, the society gave up part of its space in the University Building, but as the overdue rent mounted, the university headquarters was closed on June 2, 1861, and the furniture sold in order to pay the back rent. The books of the Institute library were placed in Upjohn's office, and the records were stored. The Institute continued to struggle along, with meetings in members' offices, until finally, on February 2, 1862, the members voted to suspend Institute activities until after the war had ended.[21]

At this point the American Institute of Architects seemed to be following the course of the earlier Institution of the 1830s. Although the members of the Institute had discussed common problems and interests and had tried to encourage a sense of a professional community, the organization during these five years was little more than a social club, limited to a small group, almost all of whom practiced in New York. The meetings and the dinners had stimulated fellowship and had given the members some sense of being involved in a common endeavor that was socially useful and intrinsically rewarding, but the fledgling organization had done little to improve building practices, encourage codes of ethics, establish legal standards, educate the public, or elevate public taste. A program of public lectures had not been instituted; the Institute library was little more than a few shelves of books; contact with architects outside New York was very limited, as was communication with foreign associations; and nothing had been done to provide formal, systematic architectural education. Yet the Institute was following a pattern of newly organized professional societies in the United States in its local beginnings, with outstanding figures as members, many of whom had a sustained vision of the needs and the possibilities of the profession, and in its tentative efforts at education. In a few years the organization would be reconstituted, but it would be some time before it would have a significant impact on American architectural practice. Hunt's role in its founding and early activities had been an important one. In later years he would be even more closely associated with the Institute in important positions of leadership.[22]

9

A NEWPORT
ENCOUNTER

Even though Hunt's commissions had been few in four years of professional practice, the Rossiter house and the Tenth Street Studios were recognized as important new buildings, and with them and his work in the Institute he had achieved a position of prominence in New York City, the respect of his colleagues, and a reputation as one of the city's leading architects. His social life was full; because of his fun-loving nature and his sense of humor he was sought out by others. George Templeton Strong, whose extended diary provides perhaps the fullest picture we have of midcentury New York social life, recorded, after welcoming the young architect to his home to dine in January 1859, "And a very jolly session we had—decidedly a roystering evening." Richard and his brother Leavitt attended a dancing party given by the Strongs in November 1859, and Richard once more joined the Strongs for a dinner party in early January 1860.[1]

There is little information concerning the lesser works Hunt carried on in these early years of his practice. One commission, which he probably acquired in 1859, was for a group of three houses in Boston. Built in 1860 for a Dr. Williams, the houses at 13, 14, and 15 Arlington Street faced the Public Garden, on the present site of the Ritz-Carlton hotel. The Williams houses (figure 12) were conceived as a unit, with the façade of the middle house, three bays wide, slightly recessed from the two side residences, two bays wide. The houses were four stories in height and were topped by a boldly projecting cornice and a crested mansard attic. The ornamentation featured round-arched windows and decorative rosettes at the street-level story, prominent stringcourses below the second and third stories, carved panels above and below the high-ceilinged second-story windows, and curved and triangular pediments above the third-story windows, with the story heights progressively diminished from the second story upward. The three houses formed an impressive free-standing block with a decided Gallic flavor in the arrangements of the windows and the fashionable Second Empire mansard.[2]

There were several other projects. In 1860, Hunt began plans for minor alterations to the Central Park Arsenal, originally designed by Martin E. Thompson and built in 1847 to house rifles and ammunition for the state. Hunt's alterations were probably completed early in 1861. By the summer of 1860, he also had projects in Newport, Rhode Island, designing alterations to the houses of William Beech Lawrence and of Edward Willing and planning a new house on Ocean Drive for Arthur Bronson. In 1860–1861 he worked on a picture gallery for W. P. Wright of Hoboken, New Jersey. In 1861, Hunt also submitted designs, in com-

Figure 12
Dr. H. H. Williams
houses, Boston (1860).
Courtesy The American
Institute of Architects
Foundation/Prints and
Drawings Collection,
Washington, D.C. Re-
production by James
Garrison.

petition with Leopold Eidlitz, Jacob Wrey Mould, Henry Van Brunt, and Peter B. Wight, for the National Academy of Design. Wight's Venetian Gothic structure, with elaborate stone tracery and brick polychrome, reflecting Ruskinian ideas, won the day and was built between 1862 and 1865.[3]

The Newport commissions were particularly important to Hunt, for his brother William was already well established in the community and he himself had a wide circle of friends there. It was in Newport that Richard would meet his bride-to-be, make his second home, and do some of his most important and impressive work, helping to shape the physical form of the community and to fix a part of its historic and symbolic meaning. In Newport, more than anywhere else, Hunt's work would establish his later conventional reputation.

By 1860, Newport was becoming one of the principal American summer resorts. Although its most glorious days as a summer retreat would come later in the century, for some twenty years the town had increasingly been a favorite place for summer sojourn, mainly for New Englanders but also for Southerners and New Yorkers. In the 1840s and 1850s its formerly quiescent economy had been revived by the erection of several substantial hotels to house the visitors. The Ocean House (1841) and the Atlantic House (1844) were Greek Revival in style; the second Ocean House (1845) was Gothic in inspiration. Built along the ridge rising behind the old town and looking out on the beach and the sea to the east, these and other new hotels provided comforts and amenities for those attracted by the pleasant summer climate, the charm of the eighteenth-century ambience in the old town, and the picturesque, rugged shoreline.[4]

In the pre-Revolutionary eighteenth century, Newport had been among the most important urban settlements of America, its prosperity fueled by extensive trade and commerce. But national independence had brought a breakdown of old trade patterns, and Newport had never recovered its earlier position in commercial activity. The beginnings of industrialization had bypassed the community, moreover, and for decades it remained almost dormant, removed from the main currents of early national development. The still elegant State House, lovely Trinity Church, Touro Synagogue, many decaying mansions, and extensive docks falling into disuse were reminders to visitors in the mid–nineteenth century of the city's earlier prosperity and importance.[5]

Throughout the latter part of the eighteenth century, Newport did attract summer visitors, especially plantation families from the American South and from the Caribbean Islands who were drawn by its salubrious climate. Visitors from Southern areas continued to frequent the city in the first half of the nineteenth century, renting houses or rooms for extended periods. After the large new hotels were built in the 1840s and more visitors came, Newport expanded considerably. Land values shot upward as many new streets were laid out to create building lots for new summer cottages. In 1852, Bellevue Avenue was extended southward to Bailey's Beach, and a large new area was opened up for land speculation and eventual development. Land values along Bellevue Avenue rose from $7 an acre in 1845 to $450 an acre in 1865. By 1858, Newport had eleven good-sized hotels as well as a great many rooming houses, and the influx of summer visitors and new home-owning residents had greatly stimulated the economy.[6]

Local builders by and large relied on well-illustrated plan books in constructing the new "villas." Many of the new cottages in the 1850s were built of wood and designed in the fashionable Italianate bracketed style, while others, in brick, stone, and stucco, were more rigid and symmetrical in design and topped by French-style roofs. The Wetmore house, constructed in 1851–1852, was the grandest of the new houses; built of rough Fall River granite, the mansion's exterior was an interplay of variously shaped masses, topped by a French-inspired semi-hipped roof. Twenty years later Hunt enlarged the Wetmore house, considerably expanding its scale. The eminent historians of Newport architecture Antoinette F. Downing and Vincent F. Scully, Jr., have concluded that the most significant development in Newport architecture in the 1850s was the growth of a more complex articulation of exterior parts in wooden cottages. The new trend, which would culminate in the high "stick style" of the post–Civil War years, provided greater integration of the building with its site and designs characterized by exterior decorative expression of elements of the exposed structural skeleton. The new building forms brought a movement away from imposed, abstract designs toward a more natural, "organic" development.[7]

During the 1850s, many visitors from Boston and Cambridge came to spend the summer season in Newport. Indeed, during this decade, Newport became something of a temporary seasonal center of American intellectual and artistic life. Henry Wadsworth Longfellow, Charles Eliot Norton, Louis Agassiz, and George William Curtis and their families were regular visitors, along with Appletons, Coolidges, and other prominent Bay-Staters. With a population of about ten thousand permanent residents, Newport was still a rather quiet place, not touched by the scars of industrialism or by the bustle and pressures of urban crowding. Its outlying areas had an almost rural atmosphere. Many people who had traveled in Europe came to stay for a time in Newport as a sort of place of transition to their rapidly changing homeland. Henry James, looking back some years later, thought Newport "the one right residence, in all our great country, for those tainted, under whatever attenuations, with the quality and the effect of detachment."[8]

William Morris Hunt was one of those Americans who found the transition from Europe to America difficult, and because of "the right kind of society, climate, and geographical position," he thought that Newport was "the most suitable place . . . to choose as a residence." After his return to the United States in 1855 and his marriage to Louisa Perkins, the granddaughter of the prominent Boston merchant Colonel Thomas Handasyd Perkins, William Hunt spent some months with his bride in the old Hunt family house in Brattleboro and then went to Newport late in 1856. There they found for sale, on the top of the hill behind the State House and almost opposite the Touro Synagogue and Cemetery, "an old-fashioned, bluish gray house placed back in the yard some distance from the road, with several trees about it." Hill Top Cottage, as it was called, was well built and in excellent condition and seemed to William "both a pleasant summer and winter home."[9]

William and Louisa left Newport for the winter of 1857–1858 to travel to Fayal in the Azores, and after their return the painter had a two-story studio built in the rear garden. The lower floor of the studio included carriage space and stalls for horses and part was fitted out as a classroom, while a painting room was set up on the second floor. At Richard's suggestion, John La Farge came to study with William in the Newport studio in 1859. Edward Wheelwright, William Hunt's Harvard classmate and compiler of the class of 1844 record, also came to study with Hunt, as did some young ladies. And late in 1860 William James, then eighteen, having decided that he wished to become a painter and wanted to study with Hunt, whom he had met sometime before, entered the Newport studio.[10]

William James's desire to study painting with William Morris Hunt in Newport brought a major change in the lives of the entire James family, who had been living in Europe when William made his decision. His younger brother Henry was dismayed when their father, Henry James, Sr., decided to take the entire family back to the United States in order to be near William; he was mortified because when he explained to his friends abroad that his family was leaving Europe so that William could learn to paint, they laughed or stared. But William Hunt was "then the most distinguished of our painters as well as one of the most original and delightful of men," and William James had made his choice. For six months or so, William "daily and devotedly" haunted Hunt's studio, and Henry "under the irresistible contagion" also sketched and painted under Hunt's supervision. Henry soon discovered, however, that his skills in life drawing were far inferior to William's, and he abandoned serious study. He remained, nonetheless, much taken with "the vivid and whimsical master," who had created in the studio a "world so beautifully valid," and with the talented and hard-working La Farge. Henry James's youthful experience in William Hunt's studio provided him with impressions of the painter's work and point of view that permeated his later imaginative and critical writings. After several months, William James decided against a career in art, and in the fall of 1861, he entered Harvard College.[11]

Before proceeding we might consider the relationship of the two Hunts—the most accomplished brothers in nineteenth-century American art—in contrast to that of the somewhat younger Jameses—possibly the most accomplished of all brothers in nineteenth-century America. The not always suppressed rivalry and not so hidden hostility between William and Henry James is well known. Henry James's envy and emulation of his older brother, only fifteen months his senior, was recurrent in their youth; the "irresistible contagion" of William's interests frequently affected Henry, who seemed to want to resist his brother's influence. In their youth and young adulthood the always more dynamic, outgoing, and socially attractive William easily outshone the more passive and inward-looking Henry; and their closeness in age led to considerable competitiveness and tension. The greater age difference between Richard and William Hunt—some three and one-half years—seemed to prevent this sort of rivalry or hostility. Richard was probably influenced to some degree in the choice of an artistic career by the example of his older brother, but he chose a different vocation. They shared many personality traits, moreover, both giving an impression of polish and sophistication, both sensitive and passionate about their art. William Hunt was more gentle in dealing with others, without Richard's gruff and to-the-point manner. Although William Hunt was accorded considerable public recognition in his lifetime, Richard was given far more acclaim, and William seems sometimes to have felt lonely and unrecognized and thought that his art was not understood. In some ways, then, William had something of the same relationship to his younger brother that Henry, the younger James, had to his older brother. Richard Hunt, like William James in his maturity, was a practical, highly successful man, who adapted himself well to the demands of American life. Henry James, dissatisfied with what America could offer to him, abandoned the country as an expatriate, cutting himself off, his brother felt, from his nourishing roots. William Hunt was also embittered with America, though he stuck it out for almost a quarter of a century.[12]

In the spring of 1860, feeling in need of a respite from work, Richard Hunt accepted an invitation from a friend, David Duncan, to visit the Duncan family in Providence, Rhode Island. Hunt made the trip from New York on Duncan's yacht, and while in Providence he planned some alterations to the large house that Duncan's wife had inherited from her father. Soon after his return to New York, Hunt fell ill with dysentery. The attack was debilitating, and after the worst of it, his physician, Dr. George Elliot, advised that he get away from the city, his office, and his atelier for convalescence and a long holiday, suggesting that he might spend the summer in Newport. It turned out to be an eventful convalescence.[13]

During the summer visit, Hunt met Catharine Clinton Howland, who had just returned from a visit to Scotland with a sister of Hunt's friend David Duncan. Eighteen years old that summer, she was the youngest daughter of Joanna Esther Hone and Samuel Shaw Howland. Her mother, who had died when Catharine was less than a year old, was a niece of Philip Hone, former mayor of New York and an indefatigable diarist; her father, who had died in 1853, had been a highly successful merchant. Samuel Shaw Howland and his brother Gardiner Greene Howland had inherited a prosperous shipping firm from their father, Joseph Howland, a shipowner and merchant who sometime after 1800 had moved his business from Norwich, Connecticut, to New York City. The brothers had formed the firm of G. G. and S. Howland in 1816 and had become very active in the Latin American trade. They both retired from active direction of the business in 1834. Gardiner's son, William Edgar Howland, and his nephew, William H. Aspinwall, then reorganized the firm as Howland & Aspinwall, which continued dominance of the Latin American trade, expanded with the Pacific Mail Line into shipping to Panama and California, and moved into merchant banking. They helped develop the routes through the Isthmus of Panama. In 1845, Samuel Shaw Howland's fortune was estimated to be around $250,000.[14]

One morning that summer in Newport Catharine and her brother-in-law Hamilton Hoppin encountered Hunt in front of the Bellevue Hotel. When Hoppin introduced Richard to her, she invited him to call on her: "The moment's interview must have been satisfactory, for he came the same afternoon." The next evening she saw him again at a reception at Oaklawn, the home of her eldest sister, Carrie (Mrs. Charles H. Russell). She and Richard remained so long away from the others, walking about in the carriage drive, that she was sent for and asked to return to the party. From then on until their engagement, except when he was ill for a few days, Richard and Catharine saw each other every day.[15]

On the afternoon of September 9, Hunt joined Catharine and Fanny Russell, her sister's stepdaughter, for tea at Oaklawn. "He came . . . early in the day and convinced me in the long summer afternoon, where our happiness lay," Catharine wrote many years later. Although young Fanny Russell was sympathetic to the proposed union, Catharine's family and her guardian, William Aspinwall, were adamantly opposed to the match. Not only did Hunt have an artistic vocation, which was still considered not quite proper in their social circle, but his "independence and unusual way of talking, meant to them only eccentricity." Hunt was unquestionably a gentleman, however, and this was important. In writing about her engagement, almost half a century later, Catharine did not mention the disparity of their ages (he was almost thirty-three). They did persuade Catharine's wealthy brother-in-law Charles H. Russell to take their side, and his support probably was important in swaying the rest of the family; moreover, Russell and his wife, Carrie, provided an example of a couple who were far apart in age and had a notably happy marriage. Hunt wished to go ahead with the wedding at once, but Catharine could obtain the consent of her guardian only by agreeing to delay the marriage for six months. Her family continued to be cool to the proposed union, though Richard's friends were enthusiastic.[16]

That autumn Richard went to Newport as often as he could get away from New York to visit his fiancée and to look over his work in progress, the alterations to the Lawrence and Willing houses and the construction of the Bronson house. When Catharine returned to New York on a Fall River steamer, the vessel was badly delayed by a severe snowstorm; she was delighted to find Richard awaiting her at the pier, although he was very anxious. She stayed with Charles and Carrie Russell in their large stone townhouse on the corner of Broadway and Great Jones Street. The couple's first appearance together in public in New York came at a ball honoring the Prince of Wales at the Academy of Music. The ball almost turned into a disaster, for when the Court Quadrille commenced, the rush of the crowd to see the dance was so great that a part of the balcony floor collapsed, and several spectators fell into the orchestra below. Catharine and Richard were fortunately standing to the side of the collapsed section and escaped injury.[17]

On April 2, 1861, the couple was married at the Church of the Ascension, at Fifth Avenue and Tenth Street, with Episcopal Bishop Bedell and Rev. John Cotton Smith officiating. The night before his marriage, Hunt had been honored at a bachelor's dinner held in the two front parlors of the Brevoort House, on Fifth Avenue at Eighth Street. The high point of the evening's festivities had come when a miniature castle, an architectural marvel made of nougat candy, adorning the table, was broken open and a pair of turtle doves flew out. Later the entire party walked around the block to Louisa and Hamilton Hoppin's house on Ninth Street near University Place, where Catharine was then staying, to serenade the bride-to-be. The wedding was lavish, with eight bridesmaids and eight groomsmen assisting in the ceremony. William Aspinwall, Catharine's cousin and guardian, gave away the bride, who wore a low-necked, white satin dress, covered with Brussels lace and with a long train. Afterward, her sister and brother-in-law Emily and Henry Chauncey gave a reception for the newlyweds at their home at 25 Washington Square North. A short honeymoon at Niagara Falls was somewhat marred because no hotels were open at the falls and they had to stay in a ramshackle place in Buffalo. Still they enjoyed excursions to the falls and in the evenings read aloud Oliver Wendell Holmes's new work, *Elsie Venner*. On their return to New York, the couple stayed at the Brevoort House, which was conveniently close to Hunt's office in the Studio Building.[18]

Just at this time the secession crisis was drawing the country into war. Shortly before the wedding, a bridesmaids' dinner planned for Catharine had been abruptly canceled with the excuse that the hostess was "not in spirits to give it" because of the military call-ups. The firing on Fort Sumter on April 12 was followed by President Lincoln's declaration of a state of insurrection on April 15, and the Civil War had begun. That evening the Hunts returned to New York. On April 19 at a reception and ball given by William Aspinwall for the newlyweds, Major Robert Anderson, who had just come to New York the day before, following the surrender of Fort Sumter, was also a guest and, as it turned out, much more the object of attention than the recently married couple. Major Anderson brought a flag from Sumter riddled with bullet holes, and it was hung prominently above the door of Aspinwall's picture gallery. The New York Seventh Regiment had left for the south earlier that day, its departure casting gloom on the party since so many friends and relatives of the guests had been summoned.[19]

In the next few days Hunt attempted to organize a regiment from among Century Club members along with a subscription to obtain the "largest flag in New York" to raise over the Century clubhouse. When his physician, Dr. Elliot, advised Hunt that because of his dysentery of the previous summer he would be quickly incapacitated in military action, a clause was inserted in the Century Club call that members not enlisting might pay for a substitute, which Hunt then proceeded to do. Thus, as in the years that followed, he was relatively untouched by the most important public event of his time. He made the gesture of serving the Union, was rather easily dissuaded from taking positive action, and a few days later removed himself completely from the problem of service. At noon, on April 27, 1861, Richard and Catharine Hunt, accompanied by his mother, sailed on the American steamship *Fulton* for Le Havre. They would be gone for a year and a half.[20]

The transatlantic crossing was a pleasant voyage. The *Fulton*, advertised as "unsurpassed for safety and comfort," carried 283 passengers on this trip, among them several American consuls and secretaries of legation and the United States ministers proceeding to their posts in Paris, Vienna, Rome, and the Hague. The newly appointed minister to France, W. L. Dayton, was friendly with the Hunts on shipboard, and soon after their arrival in Paris he gave a dinner in their honor. An elderly French gentleman aboard ship was so struck by young Catharine that he even announced his infatuation to her, and when they got to Paris he sent flowers repeatedly. One day he casually invited the couple to his country place at St. Germain, but the Hunts postponed their visit to the next day. When they arrived, they discovered that their host on the day before had organized a grand party in their honor, inviting officers from a nearby garrison and a military band. He was, to say the least, hurt by their lack of consideration.[21]

That Mrs. Hunt should have accompanied Richard and his bride on their wedding journey to Europe is not surprising. She was going to France to join her daughter Jane, who was already there, and to see her son John, who was practicing medicine in Paris. She would also see her son Leavitt and his new bride, the former Catherine Jarvis of Weathersfield, Connecticut. But of all her children, Mrs. Hunt was particularly close to Richard, and to make the trip to Europe together once more probably seemed quite natural to both mother and son. Richard's closeness to his mother had always been a significant part of his life. Since her husband's death, Jane Maria Hunt had devoted herself completely to her children, moving to Boston so that she might be near William at Harvard, settling close to her sons in Paris, returning to America to be there when Richard and William returned, going with Richard to Washington, D.C., and then establishing herself in New York when Richard settled there, encouraging Richard to take over her house on Thirty-Fifth Street later on. Perhaps she did not wish to give up her son to a rival, and the journey to Europe was an attempt to maintain her hold. To the young wife the presence of her mother-in-law may well have been less acceptable than it was to Richard; in her manuscript biography of her husband, Catharine was always reticent about her mother-in-law. One senses some tension in their relationship, although Catharine's remarkably placid temperament and her worship of her husband probably kept the strain from coming into the open. That Catharine came from a background of greater wealth and in some ways a more elevated social position than Richard probably gave her a security in her marital as in other relationships; she did not have to fear the older woman's rivalry since she knew who and what she was, even though quite young, and what she brought to the marriage.

In Paris, Richard and Catharine stopped first at the Hôtel des Trois Empereurs, close to Hunt's Pavillon de la Bibliothèque on the Rue de Rivoli, and then moved to an apartment just off the Champs Elysées. They saw a good deal of Richard's sister Jane and his brother John, both of whom came to like Catharine immensely. Richard was naturally eager to have his Parisian friends meet his bride, and he arranged visits with old schoolmates and colleagues. On May 27, Richard and Catharine "called at [the] Louvre and saw M. Lefuel" and the next day had him as a dinner guest. Altercations with dishonest servants led them after only a month to vacate the apartment they had taken,whereupon they moved in briefly with Mr. and Mrs. J. N. A. Griswold. At this time the Griswolds concluded arrangements with Hunt for the design and construction of a summer house in Newport the following year.[22]

At the end of July 1861, Richard and Catharine crossed the Channel to England, stopping first in London and then visiting for a day or two with Leavitt and his new wife and their newly born baby at Matlock, a watering place in Derbyshire. This was the first time that Richard and Leavitt had met each others' wives, and in the short time they were together a certain tension developed. Jane Hunt had been with Leavitt and his wife, Kate, and William and his wife, Louisa, the previous winter at Pisa, and she had taken an intense dislike to Kate Jarvis Hunt. In her journal, Richard's sister contrasted Leavitt's wife in negative terms with Richard's bride, whom she characterized as "a very amiable straightforward person," having "a happy disposition," a person with whom one was "not obliged to be constantly on your guard." Jane Hunt felt that Richard's wife, alone among her sisters-in-law, had a "proper respect" and "affection" for her own mother. Jane always remained close to Richard and Catharine, and the family papers she gathered were later handed in trust to Richard and Catharine's older daughter.[23]

The reunion of the Hunt brothers in England was brief, and Richard and Catharine soon continued their journey. At Chatsworth, the Palladian mansion of the Duke of Devonshire, they encountered Charlotte Cushman, the actress, who, like the Griswolds, would employ Hunt to design a Newport cottage. At Kenilworth in Warwickshire, made famous by Sir Walter Scott's romance, Hunt sketched the twelfth-century priory and churchyard. Then for a very happy month the couple shared a cottage with W. P. W. Dana, an American painter, and his family at Bonchurch near Ventnor on the Isle of Wight. They took many excursions around the island, where Hunt as elsewhere filled his sketchbook with watercolors and pencil drawings. In late September, after touring Hastings, they returned to France by way of Folkestone, where, before crossing the Channel, they had to wait several days for a calm sea.[24]

Back in Paris in the fall of 1861, the Hunts took over an apartment at 21 Champs Elysées, where they settled for the winter to await the birth of their first child. Both Richard and Catharine received regular remittances from home, and they lived comfortably with "excellent and devoted servants" to care for the apartment and cook their meals. Occasionally the Hunts provided financial help to some of the less fortunate American artists they encountered in Paris. They frequented painting sales and often went to the theater. Away from his work, Hunt was restless, however, and he tried other creative outlets. He sketched a good deal in Paris and on short excursions they took in the environs of the city, and in the apartment he drew his wife (figure 13) and their rooms. At the zoological section of the Jardin des Plantes he modeled an ocelot, which he had cast in bronze at Barye's atelier.[25]

For a brief time, Hunt even took singing lessons, perhaps thinking of emulating his brother William, who had notable musical talent. The incident is a good illustration of a certain elevated self-confidence and even arrogance of manner occasionally characteristic of Hunt. He started out by getting the name of the "best teacher in Paris," but when he went to see the professor the only thing he could think of to sing was a popular song of the day. The singing master was not impressed, and he bluntly informed Hunt that both of them would be wasting their time if he continued but suggested that Hunt might study with one of his pupils if he wished. A few days later the young pupil-teacher came to the apartment, but Hunt quickly became annoyed with his corrections: "Why, I never knew such presumption; he thinks he knows more than I do, and I am old enough to be his father!" The singing lessons were ended.[26]

On March 14, 1862, Catharine gave birth to a son, who was named

21 Champs Elysée 1861

Figure 13
Sketch of Catharine
Hunt by Richard Morris
Hunt, Paris, 1861. Cour-
tesy The American Insti-
tute of Architects
Foundation/Prints and
Drawings Collection,
Washington, D.C. Photo
by Wm. Edmund Bar-
rett.

Richard Howland Hunt, after both parents. Characteristically, they had obtained the services of "the foremost accoucheur in Paris," who had "brought the Prince Imperial into the world," although Dr. John Hunt, taking time from his regular medical practice, also attended the mother. A nurse was added to the household staff to care for the baby. For Richard the birth of his first child was a profoundly moving experience, and it was probably at this time that he copied down a statement of belief:

My motto is to forgive
  each other, to hold each
  other innocent and practice it.

Be not offended nor dismayed
  With these true sayings of your friend,
  For only truth on me is layed
To trust all who on him depend.

Let others serve their fighting rulers, but as for
  this new born child, his only duty is to obey the
  truth, and do it whatever the consequence may be.

Whatever human kind may
  do to me, I am determined to be
  peaceful, merciful, and
  forgiving to them.

I know of no rebels but those who rebel
  against the truth and they are
  equally the same both North & South.[27]

After many weeks of inactivity, Hunt was eager to move about. Blois fascinated him, and he spent time there in July sketching. By midsummer Catharine had recovered sufficiently to undertake a long excursion to the Pyrenees, although she was far less eager to go than was Richard. The baby's regular nurse and a maid traveled with them. Catharine was still weak, and at Biarritz in late July she fell ill and a Basque fishwife had to be hired to take over as wet nurse. From Biarritz, Hunt had a bed rigged up in a large carriage for the Pyrenees excursion; fortunately the baby was a placid child and the trip was not unduly difficult. At Lourdes, Hunt was fascinated by the shrines and the peasant worshipers, some of whom he sketched.[28]

Following their return once again to Paris, they went in late August for a few days' stay at Fontainebleau, enjoying the gardens and the forest. At Barbizon they visited William's old teacher and friend Jean-François Millet and his wife, who welcomed them with great affection into their simple house. Accompanied by Richard's mother, they later

visited Vichy for the water cure. But by early autumn they were eager to
get back to the United States and arranged for passage. Catharine's
guardian considered it necessary for her to be in New York when she
reached her twenty-first birthday in November so that an inheritance
settlement might be arranged. Richard was very anxious to get back to
work. Taking a nurse with them, they sailed from Liverpool on the
recently launched, 3,871-ton steamship *Scotia* on October 25, arriving in
New York on November 7, 1862.[29]

The Hunts returned from Europe in November 1862 to a nation severed by war, but they remained largely insulated from the conflict. Many of their friends and Richard's brother Leavitt were directly involved, and Hunt contributed his artistic talents both during and after the war to commemorate some heroes of the Union while Catharine worked in support of the U.S. Sanitary Commission; yet the Civil War was peripheral to their lives. Of most importance for Hunt's professional development during the war years was a major design for a Newport house, which opened a significant line of artistic endeavor for him.

Shortly after arriving in New York, Richard, Catharine, and the baby were comfortably settled in a house of their own. Since Richard's mother continued to travel extensively, she had been anxious about the care of her house at 49 West Thirty-Fifth Street, which she had purchased in 1859. Immediately after Catharine reached her twenty-first birthday, at which time she had apparently received money from her inheritance, Richard and Catharine purchased the house from Jane Maria Hunt for $16,000. They had the rooms redecorated and were established there before Christmas 1862. This house remained their New York home until 1885; later they lived at 2 Washington Square North, facing the square, only a few steps from Hunt's first permanent home in New York in the University Building and a short distance from Catharine's birthplace.[1]

For almost a quarter of a century after 1862, the Hunt residence on West Thirty-Fifth Street was the center of a rich and varied social life, enjoyed by a closely knit family joined by ties of affection and common interests. The Hunts liked entertaining guests in their home, and visitors enjoyed going there. Painters, sculptors, writers, musicians, actors, scholars, lawyers, and businessmen as well as architects shared the Hunts' hospitality. Their Sunday dinners became features of New York artistic and literary life. Hunt maintained a well-stocked wine and liquor cellar and collected recipes for burgundy and champagne punch for their larger receptions. Henry T. Tuckerman, the chronicler of American art, was a friend particularly close to the family who spent much time at the house. William J. Hoppin, an art critic and diplomat, was also there often, almost considered a family member. Catharine's temperament was serene and gentle, providing a complement to Richard's fiery, exuberant nature. Their lawyer friend Joseph H. Choate thought that "together they were a simply perfect couple."[2]

Four more children were born to the Hunts. Catharine Howland Hunt, known to her family and friends as Kitty, was born on May 22, 1868. She was followed by Joseph Howland Hunt, called Joe or Dody, born on March 6, 1870. A few years later came the two youngest: Esther

Morris Hunt, on September 9, 1875, and Herbert Leavitt Hunt, on August 6, 1877.

Although he retained his old studio-office in the Tenth Street Building, Hunt had set up a new office at 128 Broadway, and after his return to New York took into his employ two draftsmen, E. D. Lindsay and Maurice Fornachon. Fornachon remained as Hunt's chief assistant throughout the remainder of Hunt's career. Hunt and his men were soon at work on the house that J. N. A. Griswold had commissioned for Newport.[3]

For his summer cottage, Griswold had obtained a very prominent Newport site, directly across Bellevue Avenue from Touro Park, across Old Beach Road from the Redwood Library, and only a short distance south along Bellevue Avenue from William Hunt's Hill Top Cottage. The two-and-a-half-story Griswold house, first sketched out in 1861 (figure 14), revised and elaborated on in 1862, and completed in 1863 (figure 15), and still standing, was remarkably different from Hunt's earlier conceptions for the Rossiter house and the Studio Building. In this first major Newport commission, he abandoned the formal, symmetrical exterior composition of his two earlier New York buildings to emphasize the picturesque massing of a seemingly sprawling structure articulated into numerous projecting pavilions, bays, gables, verandas, porches, and dormers. Despite the variety of forms as well as the varied materials and colors, the house was given an exterior unity by the sheltering, multi-pitched roof with its repeated pattern of shingles and by the exterior tying skeleton—even though a sham framework—of posts, plates, brackets, and braces.[4]

The interior arrangement of the Griswold house, with the symmetry of the principal-floor rooms, belies the picturesque irregularities of the exterior. Entering through a porte cochere on the north side, one moves up a flight of steps to the central hall, into which the main rooms open. The staircase ascends to a landing above the porte cochere with access to upper rooms; above the staircase and central hall rises a high, multi-planed, timber-framed ceiling, which gives a feeling of openness and airiness to the core of the house, most appropriate for a summer resort "cottage." Directly opposite the entrance staircase, to the south, is a brightly lighted alcove facing onto the inviting veranda surrounding the house on the south and west sides. A reception room opens on a side hallway to the left and the formal drawing room opens directly into the central hall on the right. Ahead, angled at the sides of the hall, doorways give access to the dining room to the left and the library to the right. The openness of plan invites one to wander from one room to another. The many bays in the several principal rooms, as well as the octagonal shape of the dining room and library and the broken octagonal shape of the hall, give a sense of discovery in each area, and with the rich paneling and the varied timbered members the interior spaces provide a fascinating play of light and shadow. In a rather informal manner, Hunt had adapted well the Beaux-Arts lesson of the importance of relationships and the flow of interior spaces to a dwelling.[5]

With its suggestion of half-timbering and the overhang of the upper stories, the Griswold house faintly echoes medieval construction. More relevant as antecedents, however, as Downing and Scully point out, were the self-conscious rustic designs being built in France in the early 1850s and the vernacular American wood-frame buildings in which, by the early 1860s, the visual skeleton was increasingly expressed, with posts, plates, and diagonal braces emphasized. The Griswold house is thus an important example in the development of the American stick style, which reached a high point by the early 1870s.[6]

In 1916, the Griswold house was remodeled for the Newport Art Association, which after its founding in 1912 had leased the old William Morris Hunt studio below Hill Top Cottage on Church Street. The eastern part of the Griswold house, which had included stables, was rebuilt and expanded into a large gallery and studio. Other rooms were adapted as exhibition galleries, studios, offices, and storage rooms, and the former library became the new Art Association library. The Griswold house remains today a well used structure, a key part of the flourishing cultural life of Newport.[7]

Meanwhile, in the spring of 1863, as the Griswold house was moving toward completion, Richard and Catharine arranged to rent Hill Top Cottage from William and Louisa Hunt for the summer of 1863. William had decided by this time that Newport did not offer him the opportunities for portrait work and for teaching that he might find in a larger center. He had recently completed a portrait of Chief Justice Lemuel Shaw of Massachusetts, which had been widely acclaimed, and its good reception undoubtedly helped influence his decision. He settled briefly in Milton, Massachusetts, and then moved to Boston, taking a studio on Tremont Street. Boston was his wife's original home, and the presence of her family probably also helped decide the move.[8]

William and Louisa returned to Newport early in the autumn of 1863 to spend a month's holiday with Richard and Catharine. At this time William began a portrait of Catharine, a striking picture of the young mother carrying her son high in her arms (figure 16). Richard had commissioned the painting of his wife and child, paying his brother a fee of

Figure 14
J.N.A. Griswold house,
Newport, Rhode Island,
sketch (1861). Courtesy
The American Institute
of Architects Foun-
dation/Prints and
Drawings Collection,
Washington, D.C. Photo
by James Garrison.

Figure 15
J. N. A. Griswold house.
Photo by James Garrison.

$1,000. In the three-quarters length, life-size portrait, Catharine is shown in profile as if walking, and Richard Howland Hunt (Dickie) is in full front view. A year and a half later, in April 1865, Catharine went to Boston so that William might complete the portrait, which was subsequently exhibited at the National Academy in New York in 1866. William also apparently painted his brother's likeness; one of William Morris Hunt's biographers has recorded that his large painting entitled *Hamlet* was said to be an idealized portrait of Richard. William's artistic talent was becoming widely recognized, and, though he had left college before taking his degree, Harvard awarded him an honorary A.M. in 1864.[9]

Richard and Catharine enjoyed their summer stay in Hill Top Cottage so much that they arranged to purchase the house from William. Catharine's former guardian and business adviser, William Aspinwall, opposed their buying the house, since it was believed to be in an unsafe sanitary condition, two fatal cases of diphtheria having occurred there earlier. But the house suited their needs: it was substantial in size and centrally located, and the large property included the two-story studio. Moreover, the Hunts had ties of family in Newport; Catharine's sister, Caroline Russell, had died in 1863, but she had left behind six children, and two of Catharine's other sisters had houses in nearby Middletown. They acquired the cottage in the spring of 1864. Hill Top Cottage and the adjacent studio soon became centers of Newport social and cultural life. At the studio in September 1865, Julia Ward Howe gave a lecture entitled "Duality of Character" and read "Battle Hymn of the Republic" to a very responsive audience. From this time onward, then, Newport was the Hunts' second home, and they customarily spent several months each year at the resort, usually going in midsummer and staying until well into the autumn. Richard often returned to New York for brief periods of work, while the rest of the family remained in Newport, but he always was eager to get back.[10]

During the summers of 1863 and 1864 in Newport, the Hunts were very detached from the turmoil of the Civil War. They were far removed from the draft riots that swept through the streets of New York in July 1863. But when they returned to the city each year after their quiet summer, the impact of the war was evident—furloughed soldiers on the streets, military supplies awaiting shipment to the south, continuing tensions over the draft, incessant reports of battles and casualties, the building mania stimulated by army contractors putting some of their large profits into new building projects. Hunt had only a small amount of work in his office during the wartime years, however, and, more than

Figure 16
Mother and Child
(Catharine Clinton How-
land Hunt holding
Richard Howland Hunt)
by William Morris Hunt
(1865). Courtesy
Museum of Fine Arts,
Boston.

later on, he could devote himself to his favorite pastime of sketching. In the winter of 1864, he entered a drawing class that focused on a study of human anatomy, attending a series of lectures given by Dr. William Rimmer at the Cooper Union.[11]

Rimmer's father was a cobbler who had been born in France and taken to England as a very small child. William Rimmer was born in England and came with his family to New England. As a young man, he became interested in sculpture and, though untrained, he carved one of the first nude figures in American art. Through his interests in sculpture and painting, he turned to anatomy and then to medicine, and eventually took a medical degree. When he was in his mid-forties, he began serious work in sculpture and carved a few pieces, both naturalistic and allegorical, completely at variance in their anatomical precision with the mainstream of nineteenth-century American sculpture. In 1861, Rimmer began giving anatomy lessons in Boston, which William Morris Hunt, John La Farge, Daniel Chester French, and others attended, and he set up his own art school, providing the first art instruction in the country based on the human figure. He published books of drawing instruction and was invited to lecture at the Lowell Institute in Boston. In 1864, when Rimmer came to New York to lecture to art students, he was probably the best qualified art teacher in the United States respecting a knowledge of human anatomy.[12]

Hunt regularly attended Dr. Rimmer's anatomy lectures (figure 17) and copied some of the teacher's blackboard drawings into his own sketchbooks. In one sketchbook, three heads illustrated Rimmer's ideas, Hunt noted, of the "degenerate class—heavy jaw, accompanied by retreating forehead, pointed nose, flat mouth, projecting chin, muscle projecting under the eye." Catharine Hunt was intrigued by the "simple and interesting, but entirely unconventional" Dr. Rimmer, who one evening while dining with them used his fork to trace the bones and veins on her neck in order to illustrate the anatomical point he was making. Rimmer was a forceful, remarkable teacher, and Hunt, himself a teacher of experience, obviously was open to learn what he could.[13]

The art-anatomy lectures so impressed Peter Cooper that he invited Dr. Rimmer to come to New York to direct the School of Design for Women at the Cooper Union. Rimmer accepted and remained at the Cooper Union from 1866 to 1870, but his administrative ineptitude, personal eccentricities, and volcanic temper led to his dismissal, and he returned to Boston. Still later, in 1871, he lectured at the National Academy of Design in New York. He died in 1879, just three

Figure 17
Sketch of Dr. William
Rimmer lecturing, by
Richard Morris Hunt.
Courtesy The American
Institute of Architects
Foundation/Prints and
Drawings Collection,
Washington, D.C. Photo
by the author.

weeks before the death of his friend and former pupil William Hunt, with whom he had at one time discussed setting up a new school of art.[14]

One minor way in which the Civil War did touch Hunt was through the Union League Club, of which he was an organizing member. Professor Wolcott Gibbs, a member of the Executive Committee of the United States Sanitary Commission, which had been formed in 1861 to advise the War Department on sanitary conditions in military camps, proposed the idea of the Union League as a rallying center for unconditional loyalty to the Union in the midst of the war. Gibbs hoped that the new association might support the humanitarian and social ideas on which the Sanitary Commission was based. Before the new organization was formed, Gibbs exchanged ideas on the proposed society with Frederick Law Olmsted, then serving as the executive secretary of the Sanitary Commission in Washington, D.C. Although Olmsted did not participate in the preparatory meetings and took little part in Union League activities, he did suggest highly selective membership standards, which were largely followed. In a letter to Gibbs, Olmsted proposed that the Unionist club should include the natural aristocracy of the country: men of substance, high social position, good stock, or remarkably high character, those with established reputations in science or letters, those with "old colonial names well brought down," wits and artists who had made a mark, and rich young men who did not feel they had a place in American society. By Olmsted's criteria, Hunt was a good choice. He attended the organizing meeting on February 12, 1863. For the new organization's "inaugural" festivities on May 12, 1863, Hunt took charge of decorating the rooms of the Union League in a house on Union Square. Like other founders, Hunt proposed additional members, including his brother-in-law Joseph Howland, and in 1864 he served on the League Executive Committee. For a time Hunt was very active in Union League activities. When the Oxford University professor Goldwin Smith, who supported the Union cause, visited Newport in 1864, he was entertained by the historian George Bancroft, who invited Hunt to meet the Englishman. A short while later, Hunt, assisted by Catharine, helped arrange a dinner for the prominent Englishman at the Union League rooms. Hunt also drew up plans in 1867 for a proposed League clubhouse, though his design was not adopted. When the Club attempted to retain his sketches and plans, having paid him a fee of one percent of the proposed cost, Hunt responded vigorously that the drawings and designs for the unbuilt structure belonged to him, just as a lawyer's brief was his own property, and were to be returned to him.

His strong and successful stand on this occasion helped to establish this important principle for the profession. After the League ceased to play a significant political role, Hunt lost interest in it.[15]

More immediately related to the war effort was the Metropolitan Fair, held in April 1864, for the benefit of the United States Sanitary Commission. Henry W. Bellows, the president of the commission and a founder of the Union League, headed the early organizational work for the fair, beginning at a meeting held in the large chapel of the University Building on December 11, 1863. At this time Catharine Hunt was named to the Executive Committee of the Ladies Committee, headed by Mrs. Hamilton Fish. The women were asked to contact businessmen to solicit for contributions in money or goods. Catharine was assigned the bakers of the city, and she saw or communicated with more than three hundred of them.[16]

The fair opened on April 4, 1864, with appropriate military ceremonies, musical entertainment, and a speech by Hunt's longtime friend Joseph H. Choate, now a New York attorney. For three weeks a wide variety of objects was exhibited, including many curios and art objects from abroad. The art exhibit encompassed three hundred sixty American and European paintings, among them Leutze's *Washington Crossing the Delaware* and large canvases by Albert Bierstadt and Frederic Church. Private art collectors donated one hundred ninety-six canvases for sale at an auction. Numerous booths were set up for the sale of the contributed articles. Catharine Hunt was placed in charge of the International Booth, where goods from abroad were sold. Her brother-in-law, Dr. John Hunt, sent a large shipment of gloves and other articles from Paris for this booth. The *Tribune* reported that Mrs. Hunt netted $16,000 in her department during the fair. The main exhibition and sales areas were located in a national guard armory on Fourteenth Street near Sixth Avenue. Other buildings were located to the east, including a large auxiliary building on the north side of Union Square, extending to Seventeenth Street. Richard Hunt supervised construction of the Union Square annex and designed and decorated the interior of the large building. The art critic Russell Sturgis was greatly impressed by the way that Hunt had displayed flags in the Annex Building, "the most effective flag display" he had ever seen, he later wrote.[17]

After the close of the fair, when the Ladies Committee handed over the proceeds to the Sanitary Commission, Catharine Hunt was given the honor of writing a check for one million dollars. At the age of twenty-two, she was the youngest member of the committee and considered the person most likely to remember the event the longest.[18]

A by-product of the 1864 Metropolitan Fair was the reconstitution of the American Institute of Architects, which had been inactive for two years. Like other professional and artistic groups in the city, the architects had felt a duty to contribute to the fair. A meeting of the Institute was called to arrange for an exhibit of drawings, engravings, and photographs, and thereafter meetings were held regularly. To get a new start, all old unpaid dues were canceled, and new quarters were rented in the Trinity Building at 111 Broadway, just to the north of Trinity Church. Once more, the collecting of books for a library was undertaken, lectures were resumed, and the members concerned themselves as a group with common professional matters.[19]

The news of Lee's surrender on April 9, 1865, brought jubilation to the Union; Lincoln's death on April 15 changed the joy to sorrow. Catharine Hunt was in Boston, where William was completing her portrait, when word came of the president's assassination. The Union League Club took charge of arrangements for the funeral procession and ceremonies for the slain president in New York, and, for the League, Hunt supervised placement of decorations and the erection of a temporary monument in Union Square, a large white marble pedestal standing on a black dais and surmounted by a bust of Lincoln. Hunt and his friend Franklin Delano also fenced off a spot in Union Square for the League, where a permanent statue of the martyred president sculpted by Henry Kirke Brown was erected in 1868. For days the city was in mourning; houses were draped in black crepe and almost everyone wore black armbands or bows. On April 24, Hunt joined the League contingent in the long procession to City Hall, where the bier of the president was placed for public viewing.[20]

Late in 1865, Hunt designed a monument for a Civil War hero. That year the Vestry of Trinity Church on lower Broadway granted permission to Alexander Hamilton, Jr., and John Jacob Astor, Jr., to place within the church a monument to the memory of Captain Percival Drayton, who died on August 4, 1865. A United States naval officer for thirty-eight years, Drayton had distinguished himself during the Civil War as commander of a frigate at Port Royal and of a monitor at Fort Sumter, as a fleet captain at Mobile Bay, and as commander of the flagship *Hartford*, and he had served as the chief of the Naval Bureau of Navigation. Hunt was asked by Hamilton and Astor to design the monument, which was executed by a sculptor named Larmande. Placed on the interior rear wall of the church, immediately to the right as one comes through the main entrance, the blueish-gray stone monument is about fourteen feet high and extends some six feet in width and about two feet in depth. Two piers rise from a low base and carry a sarcophagus-like form, marked by the letters alpha and omega, which surmounts a low iron gate, as of a tomb. The battles of Port Royal, Fort Sumter, and Mobile Bay are commemorated on the piers, below decorative laurel wreaths centered by spar heads. On the upper part of the monument, two lateral columns of pink marble support a terminal pediment, marked by a shield, below which on a slab of black marble Drayton's name and principal achievements are listed. The Drayton Monument was in place in the church by early May 1867.[21]

A second and far more visible Civil War memorial was the impressive Seventh Regiment Monument, the result of Hunt's collaboration with John Quincy Adams Ward, erected on the west side of Central Park close to Sixty-Ninth Street. Hunt's design for the pedestal was undoubtedly completed considerably before Ward's statue was cast in 1869. The larger-than-life-size figure of a Union soldier, dressed in a heavy overcoat and with a short cape, is standing at ease, his hands resting on his rifle barrel. Hunt's granite base, rising some fifteen feet in height, is elegantly restrained. On the upper part of the artfully molded plinth is a simple circular device on each side containing the motto "Pro Patria et Gloria." The die includes thirteen-star shields at the center and double incised grooves at the edges of each face, and inscriptions identifying this as "The Seventh Regiment Memorial of 1861–1865, Erected by the Seventh Regiment National Guards, N.Y., 1873, In Honor of the Members of the Seventh Regiment, N.G.S.N.Y., Fifty Eight in Number Who Gave Their Lives in Defense of the Union, 1861–1865." Like so much civic art the target of vandals, the monument is now chipped and scarred and defaced by graffiti.[22]

Hunt thus contributed his artistic talents to the city of New York in helping to provide home-front support for the war and in commemorating its heroes. While the conflict was going on, Hunt was involved in a minor skirmish of his own, in which he was defeated. The rejection of his Central Park gateway designs was a lifetime disappointment to him.

II

THE CENTRAL PARK GATEWAYS

The movement to establish a large public park in New York City had begun as early as the 1840s, and by 1856 land in the center of Manhattan Island far to the north of the heart of the city was designated for the purpose. This area, situated north of Fifty-Ninth Street and between Fifth and Eighth Avenues, was at the time mostly a wasteland of rocky outcroppings and swamps. A large number of squatters had built shanties there, and a few slaughterhouses, rendering mills, and bone works were scattered about. A competition for the park's design was set up by the Board of Park Commissioners, and thirty-three designs were entered.

The prize-winning design was submitted by Calvert Vaux and Frederick Law Olmsted, whose "Greensward" provided for a picturesque landscaping of the eight hundred and forty-three acres into meadows, glades, copses, and lakes, taking into account the natural features of the topography and providing access by footpaths, carriage roads, and bridle paths. The park was to be surrounded by a low stone wall and simple iron gateways. The "natural" design for Central Park attempted to bring to the city something of the soothing qualities thought to be associated with the natural rural scene, from which city residents were increasingly cut off, and was an important attempt to reconcile the growing rural-urban dichotomy in American life. Olmsted had even greater hopes that the rural park might be an antidote to the restless habits of the city dwellers and that it might help relieve social discontent and improve community feeling. The Greensward design was highly influential in the American parks movement of the second half of the nineteenth century.[1]

The question of gateways for the southern entrances to the park—those facing the heart of the city—was a repeated topic of business of the Board of Commissioners of Central Park in the 1860s. On November 23, 1860, Andrew H. Green, a member, submitted to the full board general proposals for designs for iron gateways and stone walls for the park; Green's suggestions were turned over for consideration to the Committee on Statuary, Fountains, and Architectural Structures. Subsequently, on January 26, 1863, Green submitted designs for the four southern gateways to the park; the commissioners also referred these proposals to the Committee on Statuary, Fountains, and Architectural Structures, while directing the committee to consult with architects about the gateways. Significantly, one of the Central Park commissioners and a member of the Statuary Committee was Hunt's wealthy brother-in-law, Charles H. Russell, and it was Hunt whom the Statuary Committee consulted. Hunt, however, had definitely been involved with work on the Central Park gateways as early as February 19, 1861, as is shown by entries in his 1861 Daybook. Sometime early in 1863, Hunt formally submitted drawings to the Board of Commissioners but suggested that the board should also obtain other designs. The board advertised for gateway designs in June 1863. On September 2, the commissioners considered the various designs that had been submitted, but they refused to accept any of them; however, they did unanimously approve the general features of Hunt's designs and authorized the Statuary Committee to employ Hunt "and to proceed with the erection of these gates, with such modifications in their details as the said committee may approve." Green, who at first voted to proceed with Hunt's designs, nevertheless came to oppose Hunt's plans; and nothing was done to carry out the resolutions. Some seven months later, on April 19, 1864, the park commissioners, at the instigation of Russell, passed another resolution that the comptroller of the park should proceed with the erection of the gateways following Hunt's designs. Still nothing was done. Finally, on May 11, 1865, the Board of Commissioners, on Green's initiative, directed that work on the gateways be deferred until further orders were given and that compensation for Hunt for his work on the gateways and for alterations he had undertaken on the old Arsenal Building be referred to the Auditing Committee. Implementation of the design proceeded no further.[2]

Hunt was greatly disappointed that no action was taken. In the spring of 1865 he put the plans and elevations of his works for the park on exhibit at the National Academy of Design, and the following year published a little book which included the plans, illustrations of the gateways, and an extended favorable analysis of the works by his friend William J. Hoppin (who signed himself "Civis"), a critique that had originally appeared in the *New York Evening Post*. The Hunt designs were also shown in various shop windows and showcases in the city, and reproductions of the drawings were sold. The public exhibition of the gateway designs and the booklet brought the discussion even more into the local press. Although Catharine Hunt believed that the opposition of Andrew Green, a Democrat, came primarily from political differences with Hunt, who was an outspoken Republican, it is evident that this was more than a political quarrel and involved important social and aesthetic issues. Moreover, it is evident that the newspaper commentary was orchestrated from behind the scenes.[3]

Of the four proposed gateways to Central Park on Fifty-Ninth Street, Hunt designed the entrance to be built at Fifth Avenue, "The Gate of Peace" (figure 18), as the principal one. For this architectural complex,

Hunt designed a good-sized plaza around a large circular fountain as an approach to five entryways on the north side and a terrace on the west side. The two outer entryways were to serve pedestrians; the center one and that to its west would be respectively for the entrance and exit of carriages; and the one to the east of the central entry would open into the bridal path. Between the ironwork gates, Hunt proposed substantial posts of stone, which would serve as pedestals for statuary, including two equestrian pieces. The semicircular terrace on the west side of the plaza would center on a monumental group honoring Henry Hudson. Below the parapet wall to the west of the terrace, Hunt planned an elaborate double-stepped waterfall opening into a circular basin, with a statuary group honoring Columbus on a lower-level terrace.[4]

The Sixth Avenue Gateway (figure 19), which was to be called "The Gate of Commerce," led to a pedestrian path only. It included a single gateway supported by posts which were surmounted by lamps and tall fluted columns; to the sides and the rear of the gateway were three massive paired pedestals with molded bases and cornices and sunken panels on the sides for bas reliefs, each carrying colossal seated statues, possibly representing the mechanical arts. Each pedestal pair enclosed a semicircular stone seat. At Seventh Avenue, "The Artists' Gate" (figure 20), also leading to a footpath, was an ironwork grill placed between two high, square pedestals supporting colossal busts. A column inside the entrance held a winged "Genius of the Arts," and on the sides, paired pedestals held statues of the muses with small naked boys; low, curved seats were placed between each pair of pedestals. The Eighth Avenue corner, "The Warriors' Gate" (figure 21), also included a plaza centering on a large circular fountain, with double gates leading on the north and east sides into the park and a quarter circular terrace forming a large curved seat with seven statues rising above the rear parapet. The gateways proper at the two park entrances were centered by lofty pedestals, perhaps fifteen feet high, surmounted by equestrian statues. Gate posts directly on each side of the roadway as well as two additional on each end were formed of clustered parts of columns and had globes topped by eagles as decorative elements.[5]

The public response to the proposed gateways was largely negative. A writer in the *New York Weekly Review* roundly denounced Hunt's designs as completely inappropriate for "our lovely, rural, *natural* Central Park." They might be suitable in France, he opined, but if they were to be erected here, "the southern end of our beautiful Central Park will be *ruined!*" Calvert Vaux, the codesigner of the park, wrote an open letter to the park commissioners that did not attack the gateways directly but rather focused criticism on the fountains and terrace adjoining the Fifty-Ninth Street plaza. They would, he said, take away land from the park itself for an extension of the entrance by intruding into the rural treatment of the lower section. Letters printed in the New York *Evening Post* supported Vaux's objections, one writer stating that many New York painters opposed the Hunt designs. Another critic attacked the gateway art as irrelevant to American tradition, jarring with the rural, natural character of the park, and, everything considered, "lamentably out of date and out of place."[6]

Both Vaux and Olmsted worked to prevent Hunt's proposed gateways from being erected. Olmsted, who in the collaboration with Vaux had focused on social elements of park design and who admitted that he did not "feel strong on the art side," used his position as a founder and editor of *The Nation* to fight against the Hunt gateways. Although articles in *The Nation* in 1865 judged the Eighth Avenue design as "simple and well adapted to the purposes of the entrance," they were critical of the other entrances. Supporting Vaux, one writer denounced the terrace off Fifth Avenue as "an accessory of no value at all." Many of the details of the gateways were characterized as "feeble and worthless," often as meaningless, the statues and columns "clumsy" and "badly designed," and the art irrelevant to popular experience. New Yorkers deserved far better for their park. In 1866, coming back to the attack, *The Nation* again focused on the "feeble" quality of the designs and the "weak" character of the conception. Only truly noble statuary, it was suggested, might save the designs and such was not likely to be found.[7]

For his part in the maneuvers to discredit Hunt's designs, Calvert Vaux wrote a long letter to the critic Clarence Cook, who was planning an article for the *New-York Daily Tribune,* providing Cook with some rough memos for a letter Vaux had himself planned to send to Hunt. Vaux not only included several arguments concerning the nature of the park and objections to the gateways, but he also advised Cook as to how he thought Hunt's designs might best be defeated. Vaux wanted to avoid any implication of professional jealousy, he wrote, and he suggested that Cook might "say what good you can for the designs," as well as hint that Hunt was capable of better work. Hunt, Vaux recognized, had avoided the "nepotism insinuation"—probably referring to his relationship to Charles H. Russell—"by boldly exhibiting his work and demanding judgment on art grounds solely." But Hunt had been "bitten by this 'display' manner," this obviously inappropriate "imperial style." The heart of the matter was that the designs "are not American and the Park is." The "object of the Park primarily as art is to

Figure 18
Design for Central Park
Gateway, Fifth Avenue
at Fifty-Ninth Street,
New York (1863). From
R. M. Hunt, *Designs for
the Gateways of the
Southern Entrances to the
Central Park* (1866).

Figure 19
Design for Central Park
Gateway, Sixth Avenue
at Fifty-Ninth Street
(1863). From R. M. Hunt,
*Designs for the Gateways
of the Southern Entrances
to the Central Park* (1866).

Figure 20
Design for Central Park
Gateway, Seventh Av-
enue at Fifty-Ninth
Street (1863). From R. M.
Hunt, *Designs for the
Gateways of the Southern
Entrances to the Central
Park* (1866).

Figure 21
Design for Central Park
Gateway, Eighth Av-
enue at Fifty-Ninth
Street (1863). From R. M.
Hunt, *Designs for the
Gateways of the Southern
Entrances to the Central
Park* (1866).

translate Democrat[ic] ideas into trees and dirt." Hunt's gateway designs, however, had no regard or feeling for the landscape, which in the
park "is everything, the architecture nothing—till you get to the terrace"
which Vaux had designed and which he felt gave him encouragement to
believe that he had some architectural talent himself. In planning the
park, Olmsted and he had not intended "architectural demonstrations"
at the entrances; they had aimed at an instantaneous change from city to
country when a visitor came to the park. Hunt, by contrast, wanted a
gradual transition from the city to the rural park, a place where people
might be induced to linger before entering. Hunt, too, Vaux feared,
wanted to cut down trees which had been planted at the park edge
purposefully "to secure an umbrageous skyline all round the Park."
Moreover, Hunt's elaborate architectural work would lend itself to muti-
lation in that "poor and unfinished" neighborhood: "If expenditures are
made on appropriate scale—wild Irishmen may shilelagh in 10 minutes
the mouldings and noses to an extent that would be alarming. . . .
Unwise to risk when risk is unnecessary. . . . Everything is in a chaotic
state in the territory surrounding the locality."[8]

Clarence Cook's *Tribune* article was bitingly critical of the Hunt project. No one, he found, approved of the gateways, and the general disapproval could only be deemed an improvement of public taste. Following
Vaux, Cook condemned the gates as "as un-American as it would be
possible to make them." Central Park was "an American park" based on
"the purest and most elevated democratic ideas," while the gateways
were only "ugly and unsuitable" copies of modern French work, a "barren spawn of French imperialism," unrelated to American conditions.
"The spirit that inspired [the Tenth Street Studio Building] has really no
place in our American Central Park." Cook also echoed Vaux in defend-
ing the emphasis on nature and a rural landscape in the park. To construct these designs would mean altering the contours of the land and
departing drastically from the original plans. The gates, Cook concluded, must not be constructed.[9]

Another critic, Richard Grant White, writing in *The Galaxy*, was
more understanding of what Hunt was trying to do in providing a transition from the city streets to the park. Particularly at the lower end of
the park on Fifty-Ninth Street, the entrances, White suggested, should
be significant, and for the two principal entrances, Hunt's designs were
"real works of imagination," the gateway at Fifth Avenue having especially "an air of nobility and elegance." Nonetheless they were overly
French in conception and little related to the needs and character of the
American people. The American heritage was basically English, White

declared, not French, and English buildings had a closed appearance. The gateways, therefore, should "look as if they could shut out as well as let in." White also objected to the proposed statuary as unsuitable and as taking away green space.[10]

William J. Hoppin's "Civis" articles in the *New York Evening Post*, which replied to Vaux, Cook, and other critics, were incorporated in the book Hunt published to make his designs known. Hoppin related the chronology of events in the choice of Hunt's compositions, went over the architect's training and qualifications, and deplored the continuing indecision and lack of action respecting the gateways. "The Central Park," he wrote, "is now in the condition of a picture without a frame."[11]

Hoppin faced the rural landscape issue head on and echoed Hunt's own views on the matter. With the growth of the city and the development of the area surrounding Central Park, it was "unavoidable and inevitable" that the park would become "more artificial and less rural; more of a garden and less of a park." Obviously, the park had already been shaped by art in its roadways and bridges, its vistas, and its plantings. "To say even now that we forget art—that we fancy ourselves in the quiet solitudes of nature—is absurd. And in the future, when this shall be the resort of two millions of people, when the roar of traffic through the transverse roads shall drown the singing of the birds—when the restaurants and summer houses, and music halls, and conservatories, and winter gardens and museums shall be greatly multiplied—when statues and busts, and monuments and columns shall crowd the avenues, the Central Park will become one great open air gallery of Art, instead of being, as some dreamers fancy it, a silent sketch [sic] of rural landscape caught up and enclosed within the raging tumult of a vast metropolis." As the pleasure ground of the people, the park, therefore, "must call out the highest efforts of American genius." The park must have an appropriate framework in boundaries and entrances. But even if it remained comparatively rural, the gateway designs would need to be "extremely elegant and appropriate," particularly since they must be related to the architecture of the surrounding streets and suitable for the large crowds which would use these entrances. Hoppin also dealt with the criticism that the Hunt designs were too French and with the attempt to arouse against the gateways some of the hostility felt toward the French emperor for his venture into Mexico. The latter criticism was, he asserted, "extravagant and puerile"; as to the former, "it is a matter of no sort of consequence whether Mr. Hunt's plans are French in their character or not, provided they are elegant and appropriate to the purpose for which they were made." Hunt's proposals, Hoppin felt, were indeed appropriate for the future development and character of the park and would be a welcome addition to the city.[12]

The battle over the Hunt gateways was one of the earliest skirmishes in the controversy, continuing even to the present, over the character of Central Park. Vaux and Olmsted and their followers adamantly opposed the intrusion of nonlandscape, architectural elements into the park. They were determined that the area should remain rural, an oasis of greenery and "natural" land contours in the center of the island city. Others wanted the park to be more integrated into the city's design and available to fulfill more varied recreational needs of the citizens. This pleasure ground idea would welcome architectural additions for museums, music halls, restaurants, and conservatories. Hunt's gateways and his later work with and for the Metropolitan Museum of Art put him squarely in the pleasure ground tradition. A design he prepared in the winter of 1864–1865 for the New-York Historical Society Museum building (figure 22), French in conception, was contemplated for a park site but was not executed. Montgomery Schuyler, the foremost American architectural critic at the turn of the century, expressed disappointment that the Hunt gateways had not been built, since, he felt, they still "vindicate[d] themselves as appropriate and decorative entrances to a public pleasure ground."[13]

The park commissioners recognized the professional work that Hunt had done on the gateway project, and a special committee was appointed to determine compensation for his endeavors. Charles Russell did not sit on the special committee. The committee was empowered by the full Board of Commissioners on November 30, 1868, to pay Hunt up to $10,000 (the sum recommended by the special committee) for his work in preparing the plans for the gateways and for the alterations of the old Arsenal.[14]

Despite the thrust of the Greensward Plan, Central Park has evolved to a great extent over the years into a multiple-use pleasure ground, with many architectural and sculptural additions; only in limited areas has the rural quality been retained. The "umbrageous skyline" from the park interior was largely an impossibility from the beginning, for even three- and four-story houses lining the sides of the park could not be fully hidden by artful plantings. Today the south entrances of the park are neither well-defined portals, as Hunt envisioned, nor casual entrances bringing the visitor directly into a rural landscape, as Vaux and Olmsted had wanted. Massive architectural-sculptural pieces at Fifth Avenue (at Grand Army Plaza), at Sixth Avenue, and particularly at

Figure 22
Design for the New-
York Historical Society
Museum, New York
(1866). Courtesy of the
New-York Historical So-
ciety, New York City.

Eighth Avenue (on Columbus Circle) certainly do not blend into the landscape, nor do the terminal elements assist much in defining entryways. Hunt's two corner gateway-plaza conceptions seem quaint today, indeed delicately conceived, in contrast to the Sherman Statue, on Grand Army Plaza at Fifth Avenue, and the National Maine Monument, on Columbus Circle at Eighth Avenue; but surely his designs still give a far better terminal sense and are more inviting of entry than what eventually was built at these two locations. Nonetheless, the Hunt corner gateway conceptions are awkward and unsatisfying, not right for what the park was and what it has become. The two intermediate gateway designs are even more awkward, crude, and on a jarring scale, and the relationship among the elements is highly contrived. In all four cases, most of the statuary looks inept and inappropriate. Undoubtedly, it was fortunate for Hunt's reputation in the subsequent thirty years that the Central Park gateways he designed were not executed, for they were among the most graceless conceptions of his career. That the gateways were not built, however, perhaps added to his reputation as a figure who had striven to serve the city and to enhance its beauty even though in this instance he had gone down to defeat.

While the controversy over the gateway designs was intensifying, Richard and Catharine Hunt, as became their custom, spent much of the summer and early autumn in Newport in 1865 and again in 1866. In the winter of 1866 they were invited by the wealthy former New York governor, Senator Edwin D. Morgan, to visit him at his Washington, D.C., residence. A decade before, Hunt had left Washington after his very brief period of work for Thomas U. Walter on the Capitol extension, and this was his first extended visit since then. Later he would spend much time in the national capital working on his Naval Observatory buildings. The Hunts enjoyed a reception at the White House during their stay, and, since the Morgans entertained often and lavishly, they met a wide circle of celebrated people in Washington. General Philip Sheridan seemed to Catharine the most striking—"ugly, stocky and anything but distinguished looking, he impressed you with his great power, while his ready smile and quick wit made him a charming companion."[15]

The year 1867 brought another European journey for the Hunts. The main purpose of this trip was a visit to the Paris Exposition, to which Hunt and his friend William J. Hoppin, the defender of the Central Park gateways, had been named commissioners and jurors on the Committee of Fine Arts. The Hunts left New York on March 5, 1867, on the Cunard steamship *Java*, and after a very stormy passage of almost two weeks, they docked at Liverpool. In London, the Earl of Airlie, a Scottish peer, whom they had entertained in Newport and New York, met them on their arrival and was their host at an elaborate dinner in the town house which had been occupied by Lord Macaulay. Possibly the Earl of Salisbury, who was Catharine's dinner partner, was only trying to make conversation when he inquired how close to New York City the buffalo came, but she found his question characteristic of the lack of knowledge among the English about her own country. Mrs. Charles Francis Adams, the wife of the American minister, offered to have Catharine presented to the queen, but she did not participate in that ritual. The Hunts did attend one large evening party at which many of the guests had just come from Buckingham Palace. This occasion was awkward, Catharine found, since the men chatted together and "left the women to shift for themselves," although she enjoyed "quite a long talk with Robert Browning."[16]

In Paris, Richard's brother John had rented an apartment at 5 Rue Neuve and engaged servants for them. William Morris Hunt, his wife, and their daughters, who had come to Europe the summer before and had spent the winter in Rome, were living in London and in Paris that year. William was working on a portrait of Charles Francis Adams and placed two of his canvases in the American exhibit in the Fine Arts Department of the Paris Exposition; however, he failed to win an award. Catharine's sister Emily and her husband Henry Chauncey were also in Paris for the fair. Richard renewed his friendships with Lefuel, Couture, Barye, and others, and saw something of Delacroix and Viollet-le-Duc. He promised to visit the Chateau of Pierrefonds with Viollet-le-Duc, although he did not manage to see the medieval restoration project on this visit. Charles Garnier took Hunt over the new Opéra, then under construction, which Hunt found altogether a "grand work," though he seemed envious of Garnier's fee of 750,000 francs for the project. Hunt also called on Monsieur Ballou, the architect of the city, and, never tiring of the French capital, he noted in his sketchbooks his visits to places he already knew well—the Sorbonne, the Panthéon, the Hôtel Cluny, Notre Dame Cathedral.[17]

But Hunt had come to Paris to do work at the Exposition, and for some days he was kept occupied with his tasks as one of the jurors. The Paris Exposition opened on April 1, 1867, in the Champs de Mars on the left bank of the Seine, where the Eiffel Tower now stands. It continued for seven months and attracted millions of visitors. The exposition was a gaudy affair, summing up the progress of industry and technology, celebrating the material glories of France under the Second Empire, and exhibiting the optimism Europeans generally felt about the future.

Napoleon III's eleven-year-old son, the Prince Imperial, presided at the inauguration, and the Emperor and Empress spent many hours touring the grounds and the buildings. Most of the exhibits were housed in an enormous iron and glass building, oval in plan, in a display which almost overwhelmed with its countless items. Mark Twain on his visit realized that weeks, even months, would be necessary to comprehend everything; so he stayed for only two hours. But other visitors lingered over the electric dynamos, the photographs and relief maps of the Suez Canal work, or the contemporary paintings.[18]

Critics complained that the American exhibit was poorly displayed and, in any case, did not represent the best that the country had to offer. The exhibit was a strange miscellany: five Corliss steam engines, a great locomotive, a streetcar, reapers and mowers, a foghorn, surgical instruments, pianos, a three-ton lump of coal, "an apparatus to cure stammering," a dental "saliva pump," wallpaper, beehives, coffee pots, and artificial legs, among other things. The American art exhibit was small, less than a hundred items all told, including some paintings now considered national treasures. One of Albert Bierstadt's Rocky Mountain views, Frederic Church's *Niagara Falls*, John F. Weir's *Cannon Foundry*, William Morris Hunt's *Lincoln*, and Winslow Homer's *Confederate Prisoners from the Front* were shown, along with several large pieces of sculpture, some Rogers statuettes, and examples of bill engraving. Only one American was awarded a prize: Church was given a second-class medal for *Niagara Falls*. The United States was not represented in the architectural exhibit. The Paris Exposition was, however, the first foreign exhibition that the American government had supported by paying the expense of transporting goods and the cost of supervisory personnel.[19]

Although Hunt's days in Paris were mainly occupied with his work for the exposition, the evenings frequently brought elaborate fetes, as various ministers and ambassadors in Paris vied with one another in lavishing entertainment on the foreign representatives attending the fair. The Hunts often attended the theater as well. During a visit backstage with the Italian tragedienne, Adelaide Ristori, whom they had come to know in New York on a social basis, Ristori introduced Catharine to Alexandre Dumas père. The celebrated author was charming and gracious, declaring to Catharine that she was the first young American lady he had met, and he asked her many questions about her country, which she did her best to answer. Her husband, whose command of French was far better than hers, was amused by her discomfort during the interview. The social high point of the visit, however, was an imperial ball in June, honoring the Czar of Russia. The Hunts were invited, as one of two couples representing the United States, to be presented to Louis Napoleon and Eugénie. At the Tuileries the reception rooms were crowded with elegantly gowned women and with men in court dress and in uniform; a constant stream of guests moved out to the gardens, which were brilliantly illuminated for the festivities. On their entry, the Emperor simply bowed to the guests, but the Empress stopped to speak with each one. The occasion was marred, though, by an attempt on the Czar's life that had taken place earlier in the day at a formal review.[20]

An International Congress of Architects was held in Paris in conjunction with the fair at the end of July and the beginning of August, but Hunt did not participate in the gathering, for he and his family left Paris soon after the imperial ball. With the Chaunceys, and taking Dickie and a nurse, they visited Aix-la-Chapelle and then went on to Holland. Parting from the Chaunceys, the Hunts then traveled to Copenhagen by way of Hamburg, and thence by ship to Oslo (Christiania), Norway. In excursions here, Hunt became acquainted at first hand with Scandinavian wooden "stave" design, which he would adapt later in St. Mark's Episcopal Church at Islip, Long Island. In the first days of August, they traveled by ship to Göteborg and then by way of Trollhättan to Stockholm. From the Swedish capital they took a three-day voyage eastward across the Baltic Sea, stopping briefly at Helsinki and Vyborg and going on to St. Petersburg.[21]

The travelers remained in St. Petersburg for several days in mid-August, delighting in visiting the many churches and palaces. Hunt was especially impressed by St. Isaacs, with its huge cast-iron dome (a prototype for Walter's United States Capitol design) and its massive columns. He also noted the "great veneration of people taking off hats and crossing [themselves] in [the] street . . . people outside paying devotion to [the] Virgin." And, as they always did, the Hunts bought souvenirs and art objects here—"silver bas relief crucifix—20 francs, 3 snuff boxes, 2 jasper boxes, 1 book on architecture, 2 oval medallions." Later on in Moscow they purchased more silver crosses, medallions, another snuff box, and a "Russian costume with hat and boots for 34 Rubles." Eventually they had seven heavy boxes to manage as well as a great amount of luggage.[22]

"Moscow was full of barbaric color; it was as though one were transported into the heart of the Middle Ages," Catharine wrote later. The clothing of the Russian men was spectacularly colorful, and the gypsy encampments in the city were highly picturesque. The Kremlin, of course, drew them as the leading architectural attraction of Moscow; Hunt noted the variety of design elements in the towers of the palace and commented on the superb view from there of the city. An elderly Russian prince, whom they encountered each day in their hotel dining room, took a fancy to Hunt and escorted him to a political meeting one evening; later they learned that the Russian was under police surveillance.[23]

Their Russian trip was brought to an abrupt end by a bizarre incident which occurred in Moscow. Five years earlier, when Dickie was a baby of four months, the Hunts had stopped in Biarritz while on their way to the Pyrenees. Catharine had then become ill and had remained in her hotel room while their nurse took the baby for outings at the beach. Each day when she returned the nurse reported that she had been followed by two men and a woman. One day a woman with a Russian name came to see Catharine at the hotel and announced that she represented a cousin of the Czar. The visitor informed Catharine that her mistress was a childless woman who had to have an heir for her huge estates and that the Czar himself had told her to go to Europe and then to come back to Russia with a child. No questions would be asked. Her mistress, she said, had caught sight of the Hunt baby and had found out who the parents were and where they were staying. She was prepared to offer them whatever they might ask if they would turn over the child. Catharine naturally was very indignant at the proposal, and the outings for the baby were immediately stopped. Five years later in Moscow, a week or so after their arrival, Richard and Catharine took an overnight trip to Nijni Novgorod, leaving Dickie with his young German nurse. On their return the nurse reported that she had been followed in the street by some wild-looking men. When Richard went to his banker's office, the German-Russian banker asked him if he and his wife had been to Nijni Novgorod and had left their little boy in the charge of a nurse while they were gone. He then told Hunt that he had received certain information from a high authority that Hunt must not let the boy out of his sight for one moment while he remained in Russia. The banker could give no further explanation, but he advised Hunt to leave the country as soon as was convenient. That afternoon the Hunts left Moscow for St. Petersburg and transferred there at once to a train for Berlin. A companion on this leg of their journey was Professor Charles Dodgson (Lewis Carroll), the mathematician and writer, who told stories to Dickie, though none stranger, Catharine reported, than what they had just experienced. From Berlin they traveled to Dresden, where they visited their old friend George Bancroft, now serving as United

States minister to Prussia, and then on to Salzburg in early September. After gathering together their possessions in Paris, they sailed for home in the fall of 1867.[24]

At the time of his return from Europe, Hunt was just turning forty. He had done much and yet, in a way, very little in his profession. His position as a leading architect of New York City was firmly established, and his buildings had been generally well received, but he had completed only four major projects by this time—the Rossiter house, the Studio Building, the Williams houses, and the Griswold house—and three of them were already several years back. He had failed to gain important commissions for the Historical Society Museum or the Union League clubhouse. His Central Park gateway designs had attracted much attention, but were in fact of little credit to him. Had he died at this time he would have been remembered only as a figure of considerable promise but of minor accomplishment.

Soon after his return to New York late in 1867, however, Hunt's career gathered momentum, and his office produced a remarkable number of major designs. The next few years would see Hunt working in a variety of styles and dealing with many different types of buildings. He possessed a decided ability to adjust himself to new demands, and by and large he made his adaptations with considerable skill and a refined taste. Sure of his ability and firm in his ideas, he would meet his clients' needs while serving as an instructor to the larger society. One might say that during these next years of work the man later characterized as "an ambassador of art from the . . . old world to . . . the new" was moving up to ministerial rank.

I2

PROFESSIONAL CONCERNS

On returning to the United States late in 1867, Hunt was eager to get back to work and highly confident of what he might do. In a very short time he was involved in several major projects, including some of the most significant buildings of the Gilded Age. Except briefly during the depression of the 1870s, he was for the rest of his life always busy with as many projects as he could handle. He enjoyed the press of work immensely, and indeed much of his own energy and vitality was evident in his designs.

Undoubtedly Hunt's appearance as he entered his forties inspired confidence in those dealing with him. Of medium height, he was firmly built and carried himself with something of a military air. He was considered a handsome man, with his deep-set eyes, moustache and goatee, and full head of graying hair. Although he worked at the drafting board in shirt sleeves, usually with a big black cigar in his mouth, outside the office he was rigorously correct in his attire. On a visit in Baltimore on an extremely hot and humid day, he was reluctant to shed his coat and vest until he was assured that there were no ladies in the house. He was said to be partial to red neckties.[1]

Hunt's manner was vivacious, his talk pungent, and his enthusiasm contagious. Many considered him to be very French in demeanor. At social gatherings, he attracted others to him by his strong views and picturesque manner of expression. With colleagues, he set forth his opinions forcefully and prevailed on others to accept his views. In his office and in the company of other men, he punctuated his comments with violent expletives: "How he could swear—like all the armies in Flanders!" one friend exclaimed. But his swearing was without anger or malice and was tempered by humor, and, despite an often abrupt way, he almost always impressed others as genial and charming.[2]

Although Hunt was usually affable with colleagues and clients, he dealt candidly with everyone. Montgomery Schuyler concluded that his directness was "the expression of a perfectly unaffected simplicity and of a perfectly transparent honesty." He was, Schuyler felt, capable only of "the most direct and straightforward way to his objects," incapable of disguising his beliefs and his feelings. And his practice of architecture manifested his personal qualities, for in his work he approached problems in a practical way. For another critic, the aesthetics of Hunt's designs developed inevitably and logically out of the construction: "Their beauty is, we might say, organic . . . and not dependent upon ornament, or upon meretricious effect." To a later age, much of Hunt's building design would seem indirect, illogical, and full of meretricious effect, but the doctrinaire perspectives and assumptions of later times have perhaps clouded perceptions of his aims and accomplishments.[3]

Honesty compounded with kindness characterized his relations with his office staff, which remained small, usually a handful of assistants, until his final years of practice. With an increase in work in the 1890s, the staff was expanded but it never reached anything like the size of the work force that a firm such as Burnham and Root maintained in Chicago or McKim, Mead & White employed in New York. Several of those who worked for Hunt left reminiscences of their employer, in which feelings of respect and affection are apparent.[4]

Hunt's first office was, in effect, his room in the University Building. As already noted, he moved into the Tenth Street Studio Building when it was completed in 1858, but he changed his working office to 128 Broadway shortly before going to Europe in 1861, while retaining the studio. Then in 1869 he moved to the Trinity Building at 111 Broadway, overlooking Trinity Churchyard. The Trinity Building housed several architectural firms in the nineteenth century, and here the American Institute of Architects was located after its revival in 1864. In 1871, Hunt transferred his office and working studio to 28 East Twenty-First Street, a house which he had purchased that year; he remained there until May 1877, when he moved into his own newly constructed Delaware and Hudson Canal Company Building at 21 Cortlandt Street. In 1881 the office was moved into the Tribune Building at 154 Nassau Street, where he stayed until 1893, when the firm moved to larger quarters in the Metropolitan Building at 1 Madison Avenue at the corner of Twenty-Third Street. At the Madison Avenue location, Catharine Hunt arranged a library, bringing together Hunt's many architectural books from the Tribune Building office, from the Hunts' New York residence at 2 Washington Square North, and from Hill Top Cottage and the studio in Newport.[5]

The office assistants, working a nine-to-five day with early closing on Saturday afternoons, helped prepare preliminary sketches of new projects and the countless working drawings needed for each new structure. Hunt himself provided the general design conceptions, made cost estimates, and drew up the specific contractual agreements with clients. His estimates not infrequently proved low, and some of his buildings far exceeded the original sums agreed upon. Hunt also arranged for specialists in other firms to design and install plumbing, heating, lighting, and ventilating apparatus in his buildings and often consulted with engineers concerning the strength and other characteristics of building materials. His firm provided construction superintendence for most of the buildings he designed.[6]

Hunt was fatherly toward his employees; he was very interested in their families and their welfare, though always demanding absolute loyalty and professional competence of them. Frank E. Wallis, at a time of family crisis, found that Hunt cheered and encouraged him by his kindness and was "more like a father than an employer." Frank Furness felt that Hunt was like a father to him professionally, and he retained a deep and genuine affection for his former master and employer. E. L. Marsh, who entered Hunt's office as a young man, bringing an introduction from Hunt's former pupil George B. Post, considered Hunt sympathetic and understanding, though impatient with anyone who did not give his best efforts to his work. When Marsh arrived at the Studio Building office early on the morning of his first day of work, he encountered Hunt still in his nightshirt, busy at the drawing board. Hunt was always intensely involved in his work and demanded the highest standards from those whom he employed, Marsh noted. Hunt kept a close eye on the work the draftsmen were doing and always wanted them to understand how the details they were drawing fitted into the larger design. He was insistent upon absolute accuracy in measurements and upon using materials of proper strength. He felt that many younger men learning architecture did not appreciate that the technological aspects of building design were as important as the artistic aspects, and he drummed in this truth again and again. He was noted for his meticulous attention to details in working arrangements and even gave his men lessons in how to roll up drawings.[7]

As the head of a busy office, Hunt was often impatient with interruptions of his work and was sometimes brusque with salesmen and others who called on him; when their business was concluded he wanted the conversation to end, and not infrequently he was openly impatient with those who lingered on. He prided himself on his punctuality and his adherence to obligation. He objected to any time wasted in the office, and, though he emphasized the need for rest and recreation, he was on occasion even critical of the time that the draftsmen took for lunch. As Marsh recalled, Hunt would sometimes announce that he was going out for lunch, "which usually meant two chicken sandwiches and one cup of tea. Coming back puffing like an express train, [Hunt reported], 'Did it in eight minutes, Great Caesar! It don't take me as long to eat my lunch as it does you fellows,' adding with sarcasm, 'I s'pose you've been up for a drive in the park; I haven't time to do that.'"[8]

But, by contrast, he willingly gave of his time to young men seriously interested in architecture who came to see him, although his fatherly manner did not always sit well with them. Sixteen-year-old Louis Sullivan, on his way to Philadelphia after he had studied with Ware at M.I.T. for a year, called on Hunt without an appointment. In later years Sullivan gave a sarcastic account of visiting "the architectural lion" of New York City "in his den." Sullivan said he had to listen to the "mighty man's tale of his life in Paris with Lefuel" and "was patted on the back and encouraged as an enterprising youngster" before being turned over to Hunt's assistant Sydney Stratton, who talked about the Ecole des Beaux-Arts. Joy Wheeler Dow also was derisive in his account of his early visit with Hunt, who, he wrote, sat him "upon a high stool in his private office, and related about twelve chapters of his memoirs . . . all of which I have no doubt was intended for my good." But Hunt did help aspiring architects by giving them practical advice about finding employment and providing letters of introduction to other established professionals who might assist them.[9]

Frank Wallis, who worked for Hunt for more than eight years, provided the fullest account of the office and of Hunt as an employer. When Wallis first called by appointment at the office, Hunt greeted him with a characteristic: "Well! What in hell do you want?" But Wallis greatly admired "the big chief," and considered it "a fortunate day" when " 'Pop' Ware" sent him to see Hunt. More than anyone else, Wallis wrote much later, Hunt "was truly the father of the profession in this country." He was "a source of inspiration to other architects," one who "always stood for the importance of his art" and demanded "the respect and recognition which the responsibilities of the profession required."[10]

In Wallis's view, Hunt brought to his work exceptional architectural knowledge and a remarkable gift for design. Wallis believed that Hunt solved architectural problems with great efficiency and that his criticisms were always "masterly and brilliant." The older architect conceived of buildings as architectonic wholes; details and the parts evolved as the total scheme was developed. For Hunt the parts always had to be appropriate to the whole. When a draftsman had failed to sketch a big molding suitable for a large structure, Wallis related, Hunt attacked him angrily: "God damn it, man, if I asked you to get me a huge animal, would you give me a big rat or an elephant?" In Wallis's view, no other modern architect "had such a complete control of mass and of a problem as a whole as did Hunt." Hunt regularly asked the men in the office for their suggestions and criticisms on the buildings they were working on, and, according to Wallis, invited frankness in their comments. A new job was always a delight, and Hunt's excitement would intensify as he developed his ideas on what might be done. Traveling with his boss to a project under construction was a memorable experience for Wallis, for then especially he would be a party to Hunt's masterly discourse on architectural problems and to his rich fund of anecdotes about his travels in Europe and the Levant and his days at the Ecole. From all evidence available, Hunt seems to have been a heroic figure to his employees.[11]

Following his return from Europe in 1867, except for a brief lull in the great slump of the mid-1870s, Hunt had no difficulty in attracting clients. As he advanced in age and as his reputation grew, more and more work came to him. He often complained that he had more work than he could conveniently take care of, and at times he referred potential clients to other architects. In providing general superintendence over most of his projects, he spent an extraordinary amount of time traveling to one job or another. After his son Dick (Richard Howland Hunt) joined him in the firm in 1887 the burdens of business travel were somewhat lessened. All in all, Hunt completed a remarkable volume of work in his years of practice, the bulk of it after he had passed the age of forty.[12]

The firm obtained clients in several ways. Obviously, Hunt's completed buildings were important in showing what he could do and in bringing to him new patrons who wanted something similar for themselves. Most important, his large houses helped establish his reputation for handling a particular building type in a characteristic manner. Some jobs undoubtedly came to him because of his general reputation, the frequent mention of his name in the public press both as a well-known architect and as a participant in A.I.A. activities. Exhibitions of his drawings at the A.I.A. and elsewhere helped give exposure to his works. The publication of sketches and photographs of many of his projects in specialized architectural journals surely enhanced his reputation and possibly attracted some clients as well. Although Hunt was by and large unsuccessful in competitions, the contests brought exposure and increased awareness of the range of his abilities. Most important of all for Hunt, however, were the client contacts that came through his own social circles. The largest number of his commissions came from people whom he knew socially and with whose needs and tastes he was familiar.

Hunt has sometimes been accused of pandering to the materialism and ostentation of his clientele. And a remark he made to his son has often been repeated: On one occasion, Richard Howland Hunt came to his father perturbed by what he considered a total lack of taste in a client. Hunt reportedly told his son that he must remember, above all, that "it's your clients' money you're spending. Your business is to get the best results you can, following their wishes. If they want you to build a house upside down, standing on its chimney, it is up to you to do it and still get the best possible result." Such a seemingly overly accommodating position might be contrasted with that of very few others in his and related professions in the nineteenth century. Frederick Law Olmsted and Calvert Vaux, in landscape design, were perhaps most noteworthy for their insistence on artistic integrity; if a client could not be persuaded to their point of view or if they could not accept his, they refused the job.[13]

No doubt on occasion Hunt was adroit in adapting his ideas to those of clients, yet by and large, throughout his career, he functioned as a teacher and a guide to those who employed him. He was, in fact, always something of a teacher in architectural work, often instructing his clients as to what was appropriate, sharpening their perceptions of architectural values, and helping to raise the contemporary level of taste. In no way was he a mechanical copier of styles and decorative details of the past. Hunt used historical architectural elements in his own manner and for his own conscious artistic purposes. As an ambassador of art from the old world to the new, he would fulfill his diplomatic mission in the ways he believed were best. Moreover, he had clients of great wealth who allowed him to develop his ideas and in some instances spend almost unlimited sums to carry them out. By doing the best that he was capable of doing, he would not only create works of art but would also, as he saw it, advance the state of his profession.[14]

In more direct ways also Hunt worked to elevate his profession. In the reconstituted American Institute of Architects, following the Civil War, he played an active role in dealing with issues of concern to architects. The question of fees for professional services continued to be a major topic of discussion, and in June 1866 Institute members reaffirmed the schedule which had become customary: for one percent of the building's value, the architect would provide preliminary studies; for two and one-half percent, preliminary studies and general drawings and specifications; for three and one-half percent, preliminary studies, general drawings, and detailed working drawings and specifications; and an additional one and one-half percent would be charged for construction supervision. The precise meaning of "preliminary studies" was vague, however, and this continued to be a subject of debate. In the years to come, the scope of "construction supervision" also had to be defined precisely, and the fee schedule was later revised to include provision for alterations in plans, consultation fees, and traveling time as well as definitions of total building cost. A gathering at the Studio Building on November 23, 1866, billed as "the first annual reception," was attended by the principal architects of the city. Upjohn, Vaux, Lienau, Gambrill, Post, Van Brunt, and Hunt, who was then vice-president of the Institute, all contributed to the exhibit of nearly two hundred architectural designs. Visiting in London at the beginning of 1867, William R. Ware, Hunt's former pupil, could report to the Royal Institute of British Architects that the new American Institute was now well established. He brought photographs of recent American work, and he paid the Royal Institute the compliment of telling the members that the American society had been modeled on their own—which it had. Ware's report was highly optimistic about the progress of the American group in its work to elevate the profession, advance its standards, and influence public opinion.[15]

Within a few weeks of Ware's talk in London, the structure of the American Institute was changed. Following its revival in 1864, the group had become increasingly aware that the growth of the organization was limited by its local nature, even though it included some members from other cities. By early 1867, the association agreed that a truly national society must be established and that the first step would be to form a local chapter. Architects in other cities were urged to form chapters, which would then be joined in a federated national body. On the evening of March 19, 1867, the Institute members met at the Everett House on Union Square to reorganize as the New York Chapter of the American Institute of Architects. Richard Morris Hunt was chosen the first president of the New York Chapter, Leopold Eidlitz and James Renwick, vice-presidents, and Charles Gambrill, secretary. Hunt had left for Europe a fortnight before the meeting, on his visit to the Paris Exposition, and when he learned of his election he offered to resign the office. His resignation was not accepted. Calvert Vaux was subsequently elected a vice-president, and A. J. Bloor replaced Gambrill as secretary. Rooms were rented in a building on Fourteenth Street facing Union Square. That same year publication of the annual proceedings of the Institute was begun.[16]

Other chapters were organized in other cities in the next few years. In Philadelphia a group of architects who had been meeting periodically since 1861 as the Pennsylvania Institute of Architects set up the second branch of the national Institute in 1869, followed that same year by a third branch in Chicago. New chapters were founded in Boston and Cincinnati in 1870; Baltimore, 1871; Albany, 1873; Rhode Island, 1875;

San Francisco, 1881; St. Louis and Indianapolis, 1884; and Washington, D.C., 1887. By the turn of the century there were twenty-three chapters in the Institute. Richard Upjohn was president of the federated A.I.A. through 1876, when he was succeeded by Thomas U. Walter. Hunt served as vice-president for many years.[17]

Beginning in 1867, the federated Institute held regular annual meetings, in addition to the meetings on the local level. The first three annual conventions took place in New York City, and thereafter they were rotated among cities having local chapters. At the first annual convention held on October 22 and 23 in the New York Chapter offices, President Upjohn reported on William Ware's visit to the Royal Institute of British Architects the previous January and the exchange of courtesies that had taken place between the two societies. As vice-president of the federated Institute, Hunt presided at the second annual convention on December 8, 1868, in the absence of Upjohn; and he again presided at some of the sessions of the third convention, November 16–17, 1869. Hunt also served as chairman of the national Committee on Library and Publications, which published the annual proceedings and copies of the Institute schedule of architectural fees, and chaired a Special Committee on Professional Practice. When Hunt retired late in 1870 as president of the New York Chapter after three and one-half years in the office, A. J. Bloor, the chapter secretary, reported to the federated organization that the New York group owed "most of its outside success to his [Hunt's] liberal and catholic spirit, and his untiring energy and enthusiasm."[18]

Architectural education was a continuing concern of the federated Institute. In 1867 the Committee on Education looked into the possibility of setting up an architectural school in New York City, which would encompass a preparatory division, an academic course, and an evening program, as well as a polytechnic school with a focus on architecture. But the plan was far too ambitious and had to be abandoned. By the final years of the century the A.I.A. was taking the position of encouraging new collegiate departments or schools of architecture rather than attempting to establish a school directly under the Institute. As new collegiate courses were set up, the Committee on Education served in an advisory role respecting curriculum and school policies. The educational thrust of the Institute, however, was wider than merely the support of formal instruction. The whole purpose of the organization was educational in the sense of preparing architects better technically, artistically, and in their relations both with clients and the general public. Lectures, publicity, and the library were all aimed to educate.[19]

In these early years of the federated Institute, Hunt's most active participation was as chairman of the Committee on Library and Publications of the New York Chapter. On May 17, 1868, the committee asked for subscriptions from chapter members for a library fund, and soon thereafter made a general public appeal for contributions. The New York Chapter arranged to grant an honorary membership "for life" to a non-member contributing $100 and an honorary membership "in perpetuity" to someone contributing $500. By 1870, twenty-eight life memberships and one membership in perpetuity (Henry G. Marquand) had been granted, and along with the contributions from regular members the library fund grew to a substantial sum. With this money, the chapter established the Architectural Library of the City of New York, a collection that was to be free and open to all draftsmen and architectural students. It was hoped that the New York collection would at some time form a part of an architectural school and that similar libraries would be established in other cities. The opening of the New York Chapter library at a reception on October 19, 1869, attracted considerable favorable attention in the press. This event, Hunt suggested, "instituted . . . a new phase in the history of our Society."[20]

The architects' stands on architectural competitions were less optimistic than their hopes for the library and its role in the future. The controversy over the way competitions were organized and fees awarded came to a head over three major projects: on the national level, the War Department Building; on the state level, the Albany Capitol; and, on the local level, the New York City Post Office, a federal building. In November and December 1866, the War Department published an announcement of a competition for a new fireproof headquarters for the department and called for plans and specifications. An award of $3,000 was offered for the most acceptable plans and specifications, with the sums of $2,000 and $1,000 to be given for those deemed next best. The War Department reserved the right to withhold awards if no entry was judged suitable and to retain any or all of the plans submitted. On December 6, 1866, Hunt and other prominent architects in New York and elsewhere in the country joined in signing a protest against the War Department competition, affirming that they would not participate under the conditions set forth. The architects objected that the government gave no assurance that the award-winning architect would be employed to provide working drawings or to superintend the construction. "No architect of established reputation," the cosigners maintained, "will suffer his name to be attached to any building as designer, unless he has such a controlling influence over the execution of the work that the design cannot be altered or amended without his approval."

Nor did the War Department make any provision for the recognized two and one-half percent compensation for plans and specifications and five percent for full services. Moreover, the protestors were firm that drawings remained the property of the architect who made them.[21]

A similar situation occurred with the Albany Capitol competition; architects were invited to submit plans and specifications in return for small fixed sums, but since no assurance was given that the successful competitor would be employed to superintend the work or receive the customary compensation, many leading architects publicly refused to become involved. A further objection to the competitions was that the plans and specifications entered went to a judging committee composed largely of governmental officials and businessmen who knew little about architecture. Critics suggested that it would be far better to have non-competing architects participate in judging the submitted designs. The *New York Evening Post* and *The Nation* condemned the federal and state governmental procedures: ignoring "established rules of professional practice" would only lead to more badly designed public buildings, since the most reputable professionals refused to have anything to do with such competitions. Second-raters not caring about the integrity of their designs or the good of the profession would get the commissions. *The Nation,* however, also attacked the Institute schedule for basing architectural fees on total building costs; this, it suggested, was unwise, since exact costs were difficult to compute in advance, and an architect might also be suspected of trying to increase building costs in order to enlarge his fee. Whatever sum were given, nonetheless, had to be adequate remuneration for the work that was done. Governmental bodies were obviously not doing what they might to get the best designs for public buildings.[22]

Because of the problem of attracting reputable architects to the "open competitions" for the proposed War Department Building and New York State Capitol, federal commissioners who were arranging for a New York City Post Office attempted to get local architects to suggest ways of proceeding to obtain suitable designs. Institute members thereupon advised the commissioners that a small group of architects should be invited to participate in the competition, each to be guaranteed $2,000 for his plans and preliminary designs and the winner to be paid five percent of the building's cost on the first $500,000 and three percent over that amount for detailed working drawings. They also suggested that others besides those specifically invited who wished to enter the competition might submit designs for other prizes. The Post Office commissioners did not, however, follow the architects' advice and instead went back to an "open" competition. Of the fifty-two designs submitted, the commissioners did not find any worthy of being built, although they distributed the available prize money to the authors of the fifteen designs they considered best. They then asked a committee of architects, under the chairmanship of Hunt, to consider all the entries and draw up a new plan incorporating the best parts of each. Assisting Hunt in this collaborative endeavor were the firms of Renwick and Sands, Napoleon Le Brun, J. Correja, and Schulze and Schoen. By February of 1868, the architects had finished their work, and their elaborate Second-Empire design for the Post Office was approved in Washington. Alfred B. Mullett, the Supervising Architect of the Treasury, who was in charge of governmental work, thereupon apparently modified the committee work to make his own design. Construction was begun the following year on a site at the south end of City Hall Park, but when the building was finally completed in 1875, it was already inadequate for the needs of the city. Designed with a myriad of superimposed columns, the façades broken by the excrescences of jutting balconies and pediments, the mansard roof line jagged and topped by an awkward cupola, the Post Office Building was nervous and unsettling and considered remarkably ugly even at the time. Hunt can scarcely be held responsible for the endeavor—and failure.[23]

Finally, Hunt, as a professional in an artistic field, was committed to promoting the arts generally, and he was closely involved in the founding of the Metropolitan Museum of Art in New York from its earliest formal organization. This new institution interested him greatly; it was obviously a potential means to educate and elevate public taste and in other ways fulfill the mission that he saw as his own. Over a quarter of a century, he supported the museum with financial contributions, loans of paintings and other art objects, and donations of works of art, and he remained connected with its administration during the remainder of his lifetime. Hunt's design for the Fifth Avenue front and entrance of the museum, along with his plan for the future expansion of the building, was one of the most significant achievements of his career.

The Metropolitan Museum of Art had its origins, in a way, in Paris. While attending the Independence Day celebrations in Paris on July 4, 1866, John Jay, grandson of the jurist and United States minister to Austria, suggested to a group of Americans that "it was time for the American people to lay the foundation of a National Institution and Gallery of Art." In this suggestion he was voicing an idea that was already widespread. By the close of the Civil War, renewed national sentiment was creating interest in new national cultural institutions. Jay

urged those present in Paris to take the lead, and following his suggestions a committee was formed which sent to the Union League Club of
New York a request that that group begin organizational work to found
"a permanent national gallery of art and museum of historical relics."
Some time later, Jay, who had returned to the United States and had
been elected president of the Union League Club, received in his capacity as president the communication sent from Paris. He referred it to the
League's Art Committee, which recommended a meeting of club members and others to deal with the matter. Hunt, as president of the New
York Chapter of the A.I.A., was invited to join a planning meeting and
serve as one of nine vice-presidents under William Cullen Bryant, the
acknowledged first citizen of New York, as president. Hunt willingly
accepted the invitation.[24]

More than three hundred New Yorkers prominent in business, the
law, education, and the arts came to the theater of the Union League
Clubhouse on November 23, 1869, for a planning meeting. The elderly
Bryant gave the principal address of the evening, and Hunt in his capacity as president of the New York A.I.A. Chapter pledged the support of
the city's architects in erecting a building for the proposed museum. In
his talk at this planning meeting, Hunt also related how the Institute had
for many years wanted to see a national museum established and had
recently set up an architectural library, which the members hoped
would be the nucleus of a large loan collection of art books. Artistic
masterpieces, he went on, were becoming more and more difficult to
acquire; he himself had hoped a few years earlier to have a collection of
antiquities brought to New York but had failed. The time was ripe for a
national museum.[25]

The project was entrusted to a Provisional Committee of fifty men.
Hunt was named to this committee along with such men as his patrons
Rutherfurd Stuyvesant, John Taylor Johnston, James Lenox, and Henry
G. Marquand, his friend, the lawyer Joseph H. Choate, and such col-
leagues as Calvert Vaux, Russell Sturgis, Jr., Frederick Law Olmsted,
John La Farge, and Frederic Church. In the months that followed, the
Provisional Committee, later enlarged from fifty to one hundred sixteen
men, met frequently. A subcommittee was selected to work on the actual
organization of the museum and to nominate a list of officers, and on
January 31, 1870, the first officers were chosen. John Taylor Johnston,
Hunt's client for the Tenth Street Studios and the possessor of probably
the finest private collection of paintings in the city at this time, was
named president of the museum, and Hunt, among others, was named
to the executive committee. The museum was incorporated by an act of

the state legislature on April 13, 1870, and on May 24, 1870, Hunt was elected a trustee. He served in these earliest days on a committee to prepare a seal for the museum, on the loan exhibition committee, on the committee for contributions, and on the architectural committee. When the canvass for the first subscription to support the new institution was made in 1871, Hunt contributed $1,000, a sum considerably less than John Taylor Johnston's $10,000 and William B. Astor's $2,500 but one matching the amounts given by J. Pierpont Morgan, Henry G. Marquand, and Hunt's friend Theodore Roosevelt. Hunt was regularly reelected as a trustee of the museum and served in that capacity until his death.[26]

Three different sites were considered for the permanent building of the museum. Several of the executive committee members favored locating the galleries on Reservoir Square, now Bryant Park, on Forty-Second Street between Fifth and Sixth avenues; as the city center moved northward, this site would become more and more central and convenient. For a time, working with the trustees of the newly chartered American Museum of Natural History, the Metropolitan Museum trustees considered a site for both organizations on Manhattan Square at the western edge of Central Park between Seventy-Seventh and Eighty-First streets. Hunt was named to a committee to prepare preliminary recommendations on designs for the two buildings. But a location within Central Park in the area known as "Deer Park," which bordered Fifth Avenue between Seventy-Ninth and Eighty-Fourth streets, was eventually decided upon by the Department of Public Parks in March 1872. It is ironic that both Frederick Law Olmsted and Calvert Vaux, who had constantly defended Central Park from physical encroachments, were themselves very active in establishing the Metropolitan Museum, which as much as anything violated the "rural" character of the park.[27]

The design of the museum building was entrusted to Calvert Vaux and Jacob Wrey Mould. Since the first plans presented were considered much too elaborate, the museum's architectural committee, including Hunt, James Renwick, and Russell Sturgis, suggested major changes, among them a large court roofed with glass surrounded by galleries on two levels. The plans were altered, and ground was broken in 1874. Hunt was himself still not satisfied with the plans, and when the shell of the building was already up the trustees directed further changes in order to make the structure as appropriate as possible for exhibition purposes. The result, a red brick building in a Ruskinian Gothic design, costing less than half a million dollars, was not very well received.[28]

Meanwhile, temporary exhibition space had been found at 681 Fifth Avenue in the Dodworth Building, formerly a private residence that had been remodeled as a dancing academy, and the first exhibit was opened to public view there on February 20, 1872. The following spring the collection was shifted to larger quarters in the Douglas mansion on West Fourteenth Street between Sixth and Seventh avenues. A primary reason for the move was the acquisition of a collection of Cypriot antiquities and the need for more space. Johnston had acquired the objects from General Louis Palma di Cesnola, an Italian nobleman and soldier, who had carried on extensive archaeological excavations in Cyprus while serving there as United States consul. Some years earlier, in 1858 or 1860, Cesnola had settled in New York, where he gave lessons in Italian and French and where he set up a military school at the outbreak of the Civil War. He had then served with considerable distinction in the Civil War and was even captured and held in Libby Prison for several months. After the war he had been sent as United States consul to Cyprus. In eleven years there Cesnola collected more than 35,000 antique objects, which he arranged to have smuggled off the island. The first part of the Cesnola Collection was installed in the Douglas mansion in 1873, and the second part arrived in 1877. In the latter year, after his return to the United States, Cesnola was named secretary of the museum, and two years later he became manager or director. In arranging the antiquities, Cesnola sought out Hunt's advice on appropriate pedestals for display of Cypriot, Egyptian, and Assyrian statues, writing to Hunt that he knew of no one in the country better able to assist him in this matter. Cesnola subsequently undertook the transfer of the art collection to the new building in Central Park.[29]

The first permanent building of the Metropolitan Museum—that designed by Vaux and Mould—was dedicated on March 30, 1880, after a private viewing of the first exhibition there the day before. President Rutherford B. Hayes announced the opening of the museum. The head of the Department of Public Parks officially presented the building to the museum trustees, and President John Taylor Johnston formally accepted it. Joseph H. Choate gave the principal address for the ceremonies, emphasizing in his talk that the museum was not to be a refuge for aristocratic connoisseurship but was rather to provide standards from the past for the present and to instruct and elevate the people. The opening exhibition included a large loan exhibit, mostly gathered from wealthy collectors in the city, and a special showing of works of William Morris Hunt, including many from a then recent retrospective show at the Boston Museum of Fine Arts. Richard Hunt owned several of his brother's paintings, which he contributed along with other pictures and art objects for this opening exhibition.[30]

Hunt's activities to promote the arts in general and architecture in particular were to him an important part of his professional life. He was decidedly a man who was involved in a great many of the mainstream concerns of his time, and in the late 1860s and the early and mid-1870s he produced a truly remarkable body of work—public, commercial, and domestic buildings.

By the end of the 1860s, Hunt was simultaneously involved in a number of major projects, work on some of which continued well into the 1870s. Several of his commissions were for buildings for public use: academic, church, hospital, library, and club buildings. They revealed Hunt's considerable talents, as well as some of his weaknesses as a designer. At least one of these buildings—the Lenox Library—was a grand structure, not unlike a project that a Beaux-Arts student might have worked on in a *concours*. Others, though, were not at all types of buildings that Hunt would have come upon in his student days; and yet others were quite modest, the first building for the Hampton Institute being little more than a serviceable shell. The range of Hunt's work, in this period from around 1867 to 1874 as at other times, was exceptionally broad, and the resulting buildings show his talents in accommodating himself to very different circumstances.

Soon after his return from Europe in 1867, Hunt became friendly with James Lenox, philanthropist, bibliophile, and art collector, one of the wealthiest residents of New York City. Lenox was a dour, reserved person, not noted for his hospitality; the large collection of paintings, books, manuscripts, and art objects he kept in his fortresslike, crenelated Gothic Revival mansion on Fifth Avenue at Twelfth Street was inaccessible to the public or to scholars. Almost no one outside his immediate family entered the Lenox residence. But Lenox took a liking to Hunt, and both at his summer cottage in Newport and at his home in New York, he and Hunt visited frequently. The wealthy collector soon became Hunt's patron, employing him for some major projects.[1]

James Lenox had been born in New York in 1800, the son of a wealthy Scottish importer who invested well in New York City real estate. After graduating from Columbia College in 1818, the son toured Europe and subsequently joined his father's firm as a partner. On the death of his father, James Lenox took over the firm but retired early to devote himself to managing the substantial property holdings he had inherited and collecting books, manuscripts, paintings, sculpture, and other art objects. Included in his inheritance was a farm of some three hundred acres in upper Manhattan, part of which he sold around 1865 but some of which he kept to be used for philanthropic purposes.[2]

Lenox and others had long believed that the hospital facilities in New York needed to be expanded to provide more adequate health care for the sick and disabled in the rapidly growing city. At the beginning of January 1868, Lenox sent a circular letter to several prominent Presbyterian laymen in New York, inviting them to join with him as managers in establishing a new hospital under the auspices of the Presbyterian

13

SERVING THE PUBLIC

Church. Lenox promised to contribute an appropriate site for the new facility and a sum of $100,000 toward the erection of a hospital building. An organizational meeting was called for January 13, 1868, at the First Presbyterian Church, and on February 28, 1868, the New York State Legislature passed an act incorporating the hospital. The next month the board of managers met to choose officers and elected Lenox as president. Subsequently, on June 17, 1868, Lenox turned over to the managers the full block of land from Seventieth to Seventy-First streets and from Madison Avenue to Fourth Avenue, valued at $250,000, along with the promised sum of $100,000. He later made an additional contribution of some $250,000 to the hospital. Hunt was engaged to draw up plans. Construction was begun in 1869, and the hospital was opened on October 10, 1872.[3]

Although the new facility was to be operated under the patronage of the Presbyterian Church, it was considered nonsectarian. A tablet placed on the Administration Building identified the building as the "Presbyterian Hospital for the Poor of New York, without regard to Race, Creed, or Color, Supported by Voluntary Contributions." Funds were solicited not only from church members but also from the general public. In appealing for support for the new institution, the board of managers emphasized both the benefits that would result for the populace and the good that would come to the donors. "The proposed Institution is needed to properly care for the sick of the rapidly increasing population of our City. . . . [And] as long as there is room, its doors will be open to every one who may need its aid. . . . [Moreover,] it is needed for the benefit of a large Christian denomination to awaken a new interest in Hospital labors [and promote] . . . the spiritual growth and prosperity of Christians."[4]

In its origins, support, and purpose, the Presbyterian Hospital was typical of such nineteenth-century American institutions, which were largely voluntary endeavors, set up by private citizens, financed by individual bequests and subscriptions, and intended for use by the poor. Hospitals were in fact considered to be institutions where sick poor people could be taken care of more efficiently than at home. Generally, the voluntary hospitals took in those with acute illnesses and any whose stay was not anticipated as lasting for a long time, while public hospitals accepted chronic cases, the incurables, the insane, and those with communicable diseases. Since hospitals were almost exclusively intended for the indigent, they were few in number. In 1873, there were only one hundred forty-nine hospitals and similar institutions in the United States, and perhaps one third of these were for the mentally ill.[5]

Hunt's plan for the Presbyterian Hospital (figure 23) incorporated new nineteenth-century concepts of hospital design. He was particularly influenced by the plan used in the Hôpital Lariboisière in Paris, which had been erected from 1846 to 1854, at the time he was studying at the Ecole des Beaux-Arts. The Lariboisière hospital made use of ideas developed earlier at the Royal Naval Hospital in Plymouth, England, in the 1760s and subsequently considered but not carried out for the rebuilding of the huge, chaotic, disease-ridden Hôtel-Dieu hospital in Paris. At the Lariboisière, in contrast to the indiscriminate crowding in large rooms in earlier hospitals, patients were segregated according to type of illness and placed in relatively small open wards in detached pavilions, where large windows provided adequate light and ventilation. Service rooms, bathing facilities, and toilets were separated from the wards at the ends of the pavilions, which were connected to one another by covered corridors. Behind this arrangement was a theory that infections and diseases were spread by miasmas or gases generated by organic waste. Florence Nightingale, writing in 1859, supported the concept of long, narrow ward rooms, with the beds placed against opposite walls, and tall windows to bring in an abundance of sunlight and to provide cross ventilation. Toward the end of the nineteenth century, as the miasma theory was superseded by the germ theory of disease and infection, antiseptic procedures rather than fresh air and ventilation were emphasized, and hospital design reflected the new ideas in a change from separated pavilions to monoblock structures.[6]

When the Presbyterian Hospital (figure 24) was opened in 1872, it consisted of the Administration Building on Seventieth Street, a north ward pavilion south of Seventy-First Street, and a boiler house and laundry between the two larger structures. These first sections had reputedly cost $750,000. Later on, other pavilions were added on the west and east sides of the original buildings. The various structures were connected at the basement and first-floor levels by covered corridors, which could be used above at the second-floor level as open-air passageways. The Administration Building, entered from a projecting portico for carriages, included a pharmacy, a directors' room, a waiting room, and a kitchen and storerooms, as well as private rooms for the hospital superintendent and for interns. The upper part of the central section was designed as a Gothic Revival chapel, though the room was later used for other purposes. Like the Administration Building, the north pavilion was three stories in height with an attic and a basement; it accommodated about one hundred patients and, as *Harper's Weekly* stated, "introduce[d] all the latest improvements in structures of this

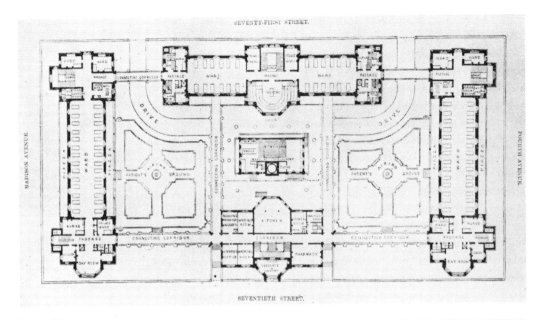

Figure 23
Plan, Presbyterian Hospital, Madison to Fourth Avenue between Seventieth and Seventy-First streets, New York (1872). From D. B. Delavan, *Early Days of the Presbyterian Hospital* (1926).

Figure 24
Presbyterian Hospital (1872). Museum of the City of New York.

kind." Each floor of the pavilion contained two wards, with service facilities, bathrooms, toilets, and nurses' rooms at the ends of the building. Staircases, private rooms, and a large surgical operating room were placed in the central part of the pavilion. The ceilings were high and the windows very large, with double sashes to prevent drafts. Between the double outer walls ventilating and heating flues were installed, and from a fan room in the basement air brought from the top of the building was circulated throughout the rooms. After a fire largely destroyed the north pavilion in 1889, it was rebuilt in a different style with fireproof materials.[7]

By the time of the completion of the first parts of the Presbyterian Hospital, it was evident that the architectonic integrity of Hunt's composition was considerably weakened by two components: First, the tall and massive chimney shaft rising above the boiler house higher than the adjacent roof ridges intruded disturbingly on the other structures, a dominating and jarring element. Second, the lavish use of decorative exterior trim of Lockport limestone so sharply and obtrusively contrasted with the red, smooth-faced Philadelphia brick that the primary massing and the primary lines of the two principal buildings were almost obscured. On the Administration Building, the first story was striped with alternate courses of this gleaming white stone; the sills and lintels of the windows above and the lower and upper jamb stones at the window corners were given the same treatment; higher yet, the glaring white stone appeared in panels, in a subcornice course, in gable ends, and even in quoins splotched on the chimneys. A. J. Bloor, Hunt's colleague in the A.I.A., thought that "the top and bottom jamb-stones of the windows" gave a viewer the impression, from a distance, "of so many little white flags being distractedly waved." Montgomery Schuyler found that because of the dressings the façade had "a confused and 'spotty' aspect which is unfavorable to repose"; the composition was successful, he believed, but the design would have been far better in monochrome. Perhaps the most interesting feature of the Hunt design were the picturesque rooflines, especially of the Administration Building, crowned by a flèche, and the central section of the north pavilion, topped by a belvedere-like element, possibly for ventilation. Hunt would later focus on such rooflines in his buildings again and again. The Presbyterian Hospital buildings were demolished late in the 1920s, when the hospital moved to a new location at Broadway and One Hundred Sixty-Eighth Street.[8]

The second major commission from James Lenox was for a library. By

1870, Lenox had collected some twenty thousand books and manuscripts. He had purchased books on such a lavish scale that most of the rooms of his large town house were filled from floor to ceiling with the collection. His purchases included rare early editions of the works of Shakespeare, Milton, and Bunyan, and the first copy of the Gutenberg Bible brought to the United States. The Lenox collection of Bibles alone eventually numbered some four thousand volumes. He also owned many paintings, including canvases by Bierstadt, Church, Durand, Copley, Peale, Stuart, and Vanderlyn, as well as Reynolds, Constable, Gainsborough, and Turner. For some time he had been considering establishing a scholarly library, and in 1870 he incorporated and endowed a public library, as a gift to the city of New York, to make his books, manuscripts, and works of art available to special students and scholars. He invited Hunt to design the building. Among the nine trustees named to direct the Lenox Library was William H. Aspinwall, Catharine Hunt's cousin and former guardian. Lenox chose the tract of land facing Fifth Avenue between Seventieth and Seventy-First streets as the site for his library; this plot, a part of the farm that he had inherited, was at that time far to the north of the heart of the city, and even for many years after the library was put up, cows were pastured beside the building and market gardening was carried on across the street.[9]

By May 1871 the foundations for the Lenox Library were laid, and by the end of that year the first-story walls were up. Construction thereafter proceeded very slowly, however, and by the close of 1872, though the north wing walls were erected and the iron framework of the roof was in place, the south wing was much less complete. The following year saw the exterior walls and the interior staircases completed, while interior construction continued throughout 1874 and 1875. On January 15, 1875, writing to Hunt, who was then in Europe, Lenox complained about the progress of the building and expressed the hope of having a superintendent living there by the first of July to "restrain the peripatetic wanderings of the workmen and eventually kick them all out." Most of Lenox's books, paintings, and statuary were placed in the library during 1876, and on January 15, 1877, the first rooms were opened for the exhibition of paintings and statues. At the end of 1877 the manuscript and rare book rooms were opened. The south-wing reading room was opened in 1880 but only for exhibits; finally, in 1882, the Lenox Library books were made available to scholars for consultation. Until 1887, access to the library collections was limited to those who had applied for and received admission cards. The restricted admissions policies led to considerable criticism of the library trustees, since in effect this was not a public library as had originally been intended.[10]

The principal facade of the Lenox Library, facing westward, extended 192 feet parallel to Fifth Avenue, with the secondary façades reaching 114 feet on each side street. On the front, a courtyard, forming a recess 42 feet deep between the two flanking wings projecting on the north and south ends, gave access to the main entrance portal reached by a wide staircase (figure 25). The front door opened directly into a large vestibule, 24 feet wide and 96 feet in length. At each end the vestibule opened into large rooms, the main reading room in the south wing and the rare book room in the north wing; each reading room was 108 feet long and 30 feet wide, with a 24-foot ceiling. In the central section behind the vestibule, offices and lavatory rooms were located on the ground floor and the superintendent's apartment on the mezzanine above, between two great staircases rising to the upper floors. The second story contained above the vestibule a picture gallery of the same dimensions, 24 feet in width and 96 feet in length, with a shallow balcony overlooking the courtyard, Fifth Avenue, and Central Park beyond. To the rear of the picture gallery was a second exhibition gallery, 40 feet by 56 feet, lighted from a skylight above. Each second-story wing contained a reading room, 108 feet by 30 feet, the ceilings vaulted and rising to a height of 40 feet in the middle. Very large windows brought a good amount of outside light into these reading rooms, the walls of which were lined with elaborately carved bookshelves. The partial third story contained another exhibition gallery, 96 feet by 24 feet. The interior spaces of the Lenox Library were very impressive, certainly among the grandest interiors in the city.[11]

The exterior of the library (figure 26) was classical in inspiration and monumental in conception. The walls, faced by gray-colored Lockport limestone, were treated at the first story with a flat rustication; above, a well-defined stringcourse established the base of the principal story. The primary decorative element was the fenestration, which helped to establish the scale of the building and provided a relieving lightness to an otherwise overly heavy structure. On the elevated second story, the large, deeply recessed round-arched windows were ornamented by rosettes. Over the front entrance, the triple arcade of windows was divided by columns of dark pink granite, with Ionic capitals and bases of white marble, while in the attic, the triple paired openings were divided by composite columns of gray granite. Each projecting wing of the main

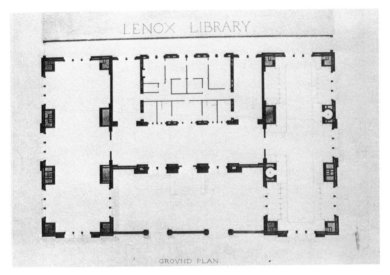

Figure 25
Ground floor plan (ca.
1870), Lenox Library,
Fifth Avenue between
Seventieth and
Seventy-First streets,
New York. Courtesy The
American Institute of
Architects Foundation/
Prints and Drawings
Collection, Washington,
D.C. Photo by
James Garrison.

Figure 26
Lenox Library (com-
pleted 1877). From *The
New-York Sketch Book of
Architecture* (April 1876).

façade was surmounted by an elaborate pediment, the tympanum on the north bearing in a garland the bust of Apollo and that on the south the garland-circled head of Minerva. Pediments also surmounted the north and south façades. Beneath the two Fifth Avenue pediments and repeated below the entablature topping the second story in the central section, broad, squat, and deeply incised pilasters provided a characteristic Néo-Grec ornamentation. For some years the use of simplified, derivative Greek elements had been fashionable in France, and Hunt utilized Néo-Grec details on some of his buildings, one of the first architects to do so in the United States. Contemporary observers often commented on the dignity of the Lenox Library, although Alexander Jackson Davis, who disliked most of what was being built in the 1870s, judged the building a "hideous deformity." Montgomery Schuyler approved of the relationship of the elements of the library, which he termed "perhaps the most monumental public building in New York."[12]

The life span of this remarkable edifice was pitifully short. When in 1895 the Lenox Library was consolidated with the Astor Library and the Tilden Trust to form the New York Public Library, a large new centrally located building was planned for the united collection. On the former site of the Croton Reservoir the monumental Beaux-Arts Public Library Building designed by the firm of Carrère & Hastings was built between 1898 and 1911. The Lenox Library building and site were purchased by Henry Clay Frick, the steel maker, in 1906 after lengthy negotiations. Many New Yorkers wanted the Lenox building to be preserved, and Frick offered to turn it over to the city and even to underwrite the cost of moving it to another location, suggesting the site of the Arsenal in Central Park. But Frick's offer was rejected. Considerable opposition came from people who objected to the intrusion of the large building in Central Park; it was argued that re-erecting the Lenox structure in the park would create a precedent for placing other buildings there, which, by destroying greenery, would gradually change the "rural" character of the park completely. Frick, in fact, had not made his offer of the building dependent on its being placed on the Arsenal site; the rejection was, the *American Architect* editorialized, "shabby" treatment. By June of 1912 the Lenox Library was vacated, and by November demolition was complete. The firm of Carrère & Hastings designed a mansion with gallery facilities for the site, and Frick moved into his new residence in the spring of 1915. After Hunt's death in 1895, the site facing the Lenox Library was selected for the Hunt Memorial, since it seemed particularly appropriate. Within a few years, though, the Lenox Library was gone. The Hunt Memorial remains but not, it would seem, fully at home where it stands.[13]

Curiously, the association of Hunt with the library did linger on in another way—through a small globe, which became one of the prized treasures of the New York Public Library. Henry Stevens, who was for years employed by James Lenox in collecting books and manuscripts, recounted how one evening while dining with the Hunts he happened to notice a small copper globe, about five and one-half inches in diameter, rolling about on the floor. When Stevens asked about it, Hunt told him that he had picked it up "for a song" while he was a student in France, and that the children, finding that it was hollow and opened at the equator, had taken it for their plaything. Stevens saw immediately that the globe was old, and he urged Hunt to take care of it, for he thought that "it would some day make a noise in the geographical world." Stevens subsequently borrowed the globe and took it to several scholars and also had a draftsman project it on a flat surface. Returning the globe to Hunt, Stevens informed him that it probably dated from 1505 to 1510 "and was in historical and geographical interest second to hardly any other globe." He suggested that "when he and his children had done playing with it," he present it to the Lenox Library; and, soon after, Hunt did give it to the library. It became known as the Hunt-Lenox Globe and passed into the collection of the New York Public Library.[14]

Simultaneously with his early work for James Lenox, Hunt was involved in one major and two minor commissions at Yale College, the first of a considerable number of collegiate buildings he designed throughout his architectural career. Later on he did major work at Princeton, Harvard, and the United States Military Academy, and minor work at other institutions. At Yale he tried out what were for him new styles of design.

The Divinity School had been opened as an autonomous branch of Yale in 1822. For many years the activities of the school were carried on in what was later called Old Divinity Hall, erected in 1835–1836. But new facilities were needed some years later, and in 1868 planning for a new "Theology Building" was begun. By July 1869 it was reported to the Yale Corporation that $75,000 had already been subscribed, "a sum sufficient to put up the walls and enclose the building," and that the "prospects for obtaining the necessary funds to complete the building were favorable." Contracts were already let by this time. Numerous donors promised funds for the Divinity School addition, including Samuel F. B. Morse of New York, who gave $10,000. Ground was broken at the northwest corner of Elm and College streets on July 13, 1869, and the cornerstone of what came to be named East Divinity Hall was laid on

September 22, 1869. Hunt designed the building and superintended construction. The work was largely finished in 1870, and students occupied the building beginning in the fall term of that year. The structure cost $125,000.[15]

A multipurpose building originally intended to form one side of a quadrangle, East Divinity Hall (figure 27) was arranged with classrooms and a library on the first floor and dormitory rooms on upper floors. The building extended about 164 feet along College Street and 46 feet on Elm Street. It rose four stories above a basement, with a fifth-story mansard terminating each end of a fourth-story mansard in the center of the structure. From the principal entrance on Elm Street a broad corridor extended almost the full length of the building, giving access to a library and reading room at the southeast corner and three adjacent classrooms, each thirty by thirty feet. Large windows lined one side of the brick-walled corridor, flooding it with light. At either end of the building staircases led to the upper floors. A secondary entrance on College Street, a janitor's apartment, and a service corridor opening onto the street were also included at the first level. On the upper floors, accommodations were provided for about thirty Divinity School students, a private study and a separate bedroom available for each, with common bathrooms and toilets located on each floor.[16]

The Divinity School Building was one of Hunt's least successful designs. Above the stone foundation walls, the exterior was faced with red brick, with decorative geometrical insets of black brick and Nova Scotia stone trimming at the doorways, the windows, and the corner balcony. Brick buttresses marked the division of the classrooms on the lower floor, while trefoil arches above some of the fourth-story windows and iron fleur-de-lis set into the walls above the second story provided additional ornamentation. The building silhouette presented a variety of elements; numerous substantial chimneys, the elevated end mansards topped by a low parapet, and, penetrating the mansards, large, boldly pedimented dormers interspersed in the central segment with much smaller corbeled, trefoil-headed dormers. The principal decorative element of East Divinity Hall was the small balcony extending at an angle outside a small alcove at the southeast corner of the library-reading room; the balcony was supported by a central pier forming a buttress having a space for a statue, and it was covered at the sides by a double canopy. Projecting above the balcony through the upper stories was a corner pavilion surmounted by a steep hipped roof, broken by a large pointed-arch dormer, and topped by cresting and finials. The angled pavilion faced directly toward a diagonal path of the green opposite and

Figure 27
East Divinity Hall and
Marquand Chapel, Yale
Divinity School, New
Haven, Conn. (1870,
1871). Yale University
Archives.

Figure 28
Perspective, Marquand
Chapel (early version,
1870), Yale Divinity
School, New Haven,
Conn. Courtesy The
American Institute of
Architects Foundation/
Prints and Drawings
Collection, Washington,
D.C. Photo by
James Garrison.

was obviously designed to be viewed from that perspective face on. With the numerous long narrow windows breaking the principal façade, the asymmetry of the composition, the curious placement of the entryways, and the rather cluttered elaboration at the corner, East Divinity Hall had an inappropriate, restless quality and is not a particularly appealing design. Montgomery Schuyler in 1895 considered that the building had been composed in "a too staccato style," although a few years later, in 1909, he thought that it had "the mark of good Gothic, . . . the straightforward expression of the actual facts of construction" and was characteristic of Hunt's "own particular and personal variety of French Gothic." Henry-Russell Hitchcock much later termed the Divinity School building "frenzied" and contrasted Hunt's "stridency" here with Russell Sturgis's contemporary Farnam Hall, also at Yale, a far simpler and more sophisticated design.[17]

Immediately adjoining and connecting with the Elm Street end of East Divinity Hall, Marquand Chapel (figure 28) was soon erected. The cornerstone for the chapel was laid on April 12, 1870, and by September 1871 the building was ready for use. A gift of Frederick Marquand of Southport, Connecticut, the chapel cost a little more than $27,000 and had a seating capacity of two hundred and fifty. Hunt designed the chapel to harmonize with the much larger hall: the same brick and stone trim were used, similar buttresses were placed on the façade, somewhat similar trefoil window heads were utilized, and the main roof line, with cresting and finials, repeated the lines of the corner pavilion of East Divinity Hall. From directly in front of the chapel, the end gable of the nave backed by the high crested hipped roof over the center of the church clearly echoed the composition of the dormer and the crested hipped roof at the corner of the larger building. Yet the design of the chapel had an elegance somehow lacking in the larger structure. On the entry front, the simple latticed windows formed a superb frame for the steeply angled pediment above the entryway with its trefoil design. Above this grouping, the circular hexamerous openings brought a delicacy of design to the gable of the nave and provided a harmonious climax to the façade composition. Overshadowed by the larger adjacent building, the Marquand Chapel was relatively simple and unpretentious but with a jewellike quality.[18]

Hunt's other commission at Yale College was Scroll and Key Hall (figure 29), a clubhouse built in 1869 at College and Wall streets for a student secret society. A highly unusual building, the hall recalls Moorish compositions in its dark striped masonry, banded columns, richly decorated impost band, and deep-set, stilted arches. Blind ar-

Figure 29
Scroll and Key Society
clubhouse, Yale Univer-
sity, New Haven, Conn.
(1869). Courtesy E.
Teitelman.

cades, a parapet set with rosettes and octagonal posts topped with striated cones, and a stair railing repeating the parapet design provide the remaining major ornamentation. The large areas of blank wall seem intended to conceal what may be transpiring within; indeed, the exterior design of the hall proclaims that the activities it houses are to be kept secret, while the weighty, almost impregnable structure implies that they must be of great importance.[19]

In addition to his work at Yale, during this period Hunt undertook another commission for an educational institution—the first academic building for the newly founded Hampton Normal and Agricultural Institute at Hampton, Virginia. Sponsored by the American Missionary Association and by the Freedmen's Bureau, the new school was organized to provide a program of manual labor education and teacher training for freedmen and Indians, aiming both to furnish male and female students with skills to make them self-sufficient and to develop character. The students' work while at the Institute was intended to provide for their support and the cost of their education. General Samuel C. Armstrong, who had commanded black troops in the Peninsular Campaign and had served immediately after the Civil War in Virginia as a superintendent of the Freedmen's Bureau, was the primary founder and first principal of the Hampton Institute. The son of missionary parents, Armstrong had grown up in the Hawaiian Islands, where his father was at one time the minister of public instruction, and he was familiar with the work of the Hilo Manual Labor School for native Hawaiians. General Armstrong strongly believed that an appropriate physical environment could do much to build character and morals, and he was determined that the architecture of the Institute would be in accord with his vision of what might be accomplished. Accordingly, he carefully selected the architects for the Institute buildings, choosing men who would, he felt, create buildings that would be symbols of taste and respectability and have a suitable impact on the students using them.[20]

In 1869, Armstrong invited Hunt to design the first permanent building at Hampton Institute, feeling, apparently, that the New York architect would provide the "tasteful" building he wanted. Moreover, having a well-known architect design this first building, would, he hoped, help give prestige and respectability to the Institute and the work it was doing. Even before Hunt was commissioned, Armstrong had selected the site for the academic building on a sandy knoll about two miles from Fortress Monroe overlooking Hampton Roads, where the *Monitor* and the *Merrimac* had battled in March 1862; and some of the young blacks who had come to be students were already at work making bricks. Hunt was acquainted with the area, having visited it on his vacation trip in 1848. Under the superintendence of Stephen D. Laune of New York City, whom Hunt recommended, construction of Academic Hall (figure 30) began in September 1869, and the building was completed by November 1870. The hall cost about $50,000, most of which was contributed by the Freedmen's Bureau. It was a three-story building in the general shape of a Greek cross, measuring 110 feet by 85 feet, built of heavy timbers covered by red brick and devoid of almost any decoration except buttresses at the corners and black brick trim around the windows. The projecting roof had a very shallow pitch. Academic Hall included an assembly room, a library and reading room, a small museum, several recitation rooms, a print shop, and several offices, as well as dormitory accommodations for forty male students. The many tall and relatively narrow windows gave the building a somewhat busy look, although one contemporary observer believed that it looked "less fussy" than its picture indicated. The Hampton students were reported to be very proud of their new academic building. With this commission, General Armstrong became friendly with Hunt and on several occasions visited him in Newport.[21]

Unfortunately, on November 9, 1879, Academic Hall was completely destroyed by fire. A month later the executive committee of the Hampton trustees approved construction of a new building on the same site. General Armstrong again asked Hunt to provide plans and specifications, this time stressing the need for fireproofing in so far as was possible. Armstrong had disliked the decorative buttresses on the first hall, and he requested Hunt to make the replacement plain and with no ornament. Second Academic Hall was completed in May 1881, at a cost of about $37,500. Slightly smaller in dimensions (110 by 75 feet), the new building had three stories and a large attic, which provided dormitory space for thirty-five students. Basically a brick structure, with some stucco surfaces, a low sloping roof, and slightly inclined first-story walls, the Second Academic Hall has a much more ordered and solid look, achieved by the fewer and larger windows, eight broad, low chimneys, and horizontal bands which counter the many vertical lines. Again, classrooms for recitation, offices, and an assembly room were included. Second Academic Hall was restored and renovated in 1967–1968 for use as an art building and museum. These two early Hampton buildings were simple, unostentatious, utilitarian structures, the second particularly successful in providing the "tasteful" surroundings that Armstrong wanted his students to experience.[22]

Hunt's other commission for the Hampton Institute was considera-

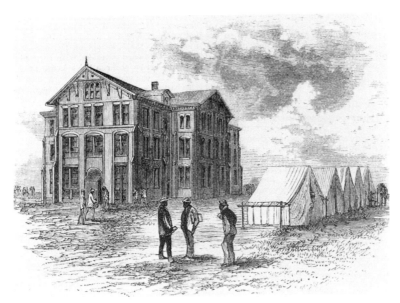

Figure 30
First Academic Hall,
Hampton Institute,
Hampton, Virginia
(1870). From *Harper's
New Monthly Magazine*
(October 1873).

Figure 31
Virginia Hall, Hampton
Institute, Hampton, Vir-
ginia (1874). Courtesy E.
Teitelman.

bly more elaborate. Virginia Hall was a much larger building containing rooms for one hundred twenty girls, quarters for ten teachers, a two-story chapel, students' and teachers' dining rooms, kitchens, a laundry, study rooms, and workrooms. Plans for the building were authorized in September 1872, and Hunt's design was exhibited to and approved by the trustees on January 23, 1873. Even though funds for the new building were not yet available, Armstrong authorized the work to begin, and by April 1873 the foundations were in place. The cornerstone of Virginia Hall was laid on June 12, 1873, at the time of the annual commencement exercises when many visitors who might give financial help were on the campus. As with the other buildings at the Institute, the students worked at the brick kiln and did some of the work of construction. A year later, on June 11, 1874, Virginia Hall was dedicated, even though it was far from complete on the inside. Through the depression years of the mid-1870s Armstrong spent much of his time trying to raise funds so that the building might be finished, and only in 1879 was the interior finally completed. In 1885, a two-story porch was added to the east end of the hall. Hunt took considerable interest in the construction work at Hampton and paid a visit there in the spring of 1874. He probably did not provide working drawings for the building, nor did his firm supervise the construction.[23]

Virginia Hall (figure 31) is a large, symmetrical, three-story structure, surmounted by a two-story mansard regularly punctuated by chalet-gable dormers. The mass of the T-shaped building, which embodies both Second Empire and Victorian Gothic elements of style, is dominated by a central projecting pavilion, fronted, in turn, by its own central projecting pavilion, which is covered by a steeply rising, crested, French-style hipped roof. The lower and smaller framing, two-story pavilion segments give an emphasis to the main motif, while each provides an intermediate form leading to symmetrical one-story projecting lateral entrances. These combine with the high central section to form the base of a triangular composition. At each end of Virginia Hall there rises a slightly projecting pavilion topped by a hipped and crested roof set at right angles to the main roof axis. The steep, high roofs of the pavilions, the tall piers rising from buttresses, and the high, narrow windows at the first story all make a vertical emphasis which plays against the accentuated horizontals of the cornice and the double line of dormers. The walls of red brick with black brick and painted wood trim are typical Victorian polychromy of the post–Civil War period. From the mid-1870s, Virginia Hall dominated the river front of the Hampton Institute.[24]

Not only was Hunt working on new public buildings for New York City and new academic buildings for Yale College and the Hampton Institute in the early 1870s, but he also put his stamp on the village of Matteawan in Dutchess County, New York. For his wealthy brother-in-law Joseph Howland, whom he had known since his bachelor days at the University Building, Hunt erected a library and a church in Matteawan (now Beacon) and provided a striking addition to Howland's own residence, which was situated in the town of Fishkill. In 1868, Joseph Howland, Catharine's brother, and his wife, Eliza Woolsey Howland, after an extended wedding trip to Europe and the Near East, purchased a farm fronting on Fishkill Creek and began transforming it into an elegant country seat. The Howland place was named Tioranda, meaning "the meeting of the waters," referring to the junction of Fishkill Creek with the Hudson River. When the Civil War broke out the Howlands had been living at Tioranda only a short time. Joseph enlisted as adjutant of the Sixteenth Regiment of New York State Volunteers. Later, after he had been made an adjutant general and chief of brigade, he was wounded at the Battle of Gaines Mill on June 27, 1862, and for gallantry in action was brevetted brigadier-general. Returning to Tioranda to recuperate, Howland continued to improve the property, landscaping the grounds and bringing in specimens of rare trees and shrubs. He served as Treasurer of the State of New York for two years, and devoted himself to banking and philanthropic activities. The Howland Circulating Library and the Presbyterian Church in Beacon were only two of his many benefactions. Howland died in France in 1886. After the death of his widow many years later, Tioranda was renamed Craig House and transformed into a private sanitarium, which it remains today.[25]

The main part of Tioranda was built in 1859, and its design has been attributed to Frederick Withers. Faced with variegated glazed brick and trimmed with wood and stone, the main body of the house is asymmetrical, and highly picturesque, with large bargeboard gables, irregularly placed roof dormers, bays and oriels, a heavy stone porte cochere, and a large veranda overlooking a great sweep of well-tended lawn and the Hudson River in the distance. The textured contrasts of the brick, stone, and wood elements are enhanced by the covering of ivy and the artfully placed trees and shrubbery. The southern segment of the house is a large music-room wing (figure 32) added by Hunt in 1873. A flagstone terrace surrounded by a low balustrade ties this end of the house to the lawn and gardens. Projecting outward from the main mass, the high-ceilinged music-room wing blends in well with the neo-Gothic of the rest of the mansion and yet is distinctive and has a French character. The steeply pitched hipped roof dominates the composition of the wing. Rising higher than the wall space beneath, the roof is like a party hat topped with all sorts of fanciful embellishments. The tall, narrow, sharply pointed dormers with their bowed and pierced bargeboards, the massive broad chimney stack with its polychrome decorations, and the array of finials and cresting provide a joyous if somewhat cluttered design. Inside, the large space still serves as a music room for staff and patients of the sanitarium. The music-room addition clearly shows its character as a large space for pleasure and recreational usage.[26]

At his own expense Joseph Howland erected the Howland Circulating Library in Matteawan Village, donating the land, the building, the furniture, and money for book purchases. The gift of the library was made as a benefaction to the local community, with the aim, as John J. Monell, a trustee, said at the dedication on August 5, 1872, "to enlighten and elevate the people, and . . . mark their onward progress in their career of improvement." The library was organized on a subscription basis, at an original rate of fifty cents for each quarter year.[27]

When the Howland Library (figure 33) was nearly completed, a local newspaper commented on the new addition to the community as follows: "What a beautiful building, how tasty and neat its plan and appearance! The elevation or exterior of the edifice has a rather peculiar look to the casual observer, yet when the outlines are scanned over with an eye to symmetry and proportion, admiration supplants a momentary perplexity." The official history of the library characterizes the design as in the "Norwegian style," and the multi-gable, timber-framed upper story rising over a richly variegated patterned brick lower story does indeed have something of a Scandinavian feel. Hunt had, of course, visited Norway and Sweden a few years earlier on his 1867 trip to Europe. The building, which still stands at the corner of Main Street and Tioranda Road in Beacon, is rather small, its dimensions some sixty-five feet in depth and forty feet in width, but it somehow appears larger than these dimensions would indicate. Rising on a base of rough granite and blue stone ashlar, the lower exterior walls are of red and black Croton brick, with light buff Jersey brick around the doorway and in the patterning below the cornice. The upper walls are covered by patterned red and gray slate shingles. The roof contour is formed by four major gables and two secondary gables; the original bargeboards have been removed from the larger gables. Large sash windows on the sides and back of the library flood the reading room with light. The posts and braces of the front porch support the projecting bay and balcony above, although the original balustrade has been removed, giving the balcony an incomplete

Figure 32
Music room addition,
Tioranda, Beacon, New
York (1873). Photo by
Janet K. Staats.

Figure 33
Howland Library, Bea-
con, New York (1872).
Photo by Robert Barnett.

look. The half-timbering in the central pavilion is clearly structural. Entering the building, a visitor passes through a hallway with workrooms on either side and a staircase leading to a private apartment above and moves into the reading room surrounded by a gallery added in 1895. The reading room ceiling rising to a height of about thirty-four feet is an elaborate network of timbering, an interplay of columns, braces, hammerbeams, and arches. Originally one hundred and forty bookcases with wire paneled doors lined the walls of this spectacular room. From 1929 to 1976, the Howland Library served as the public library of Beacon and has since been converted into the Howland Center for Cultural Exchange.[28]

The second benefaction of Joseph Howland in which Hunt was involved was a gift providing for more than one half of the cost of a new Presbyterian Church for Matteawan. A Presbyterian Church had been organized there in 1833 and a church building erected soon after; however, by about 1870, it was quite evident that the old building no longer was large enough for the congregation, and Hunt was invited to prepare plans for a new church to be erected on the site. As chairman of the building committee as well as the principal donor, Howland worked with his brother-in-law and with the builders in superintending the design and construction of the new church on Leonard Street. The dedication took place on July 17, 1872.[29]

The Matteawan Presbyterian Church was described at the time of dedication as being "Norwegian and French mixed" style. Built entirely of wood above foundations and lower walls of granite masonry, the church had a nave covered by a steeply pitched roof of slate, perforated by five high dormers on each side, with a lean-to on each side of the central mass lighted by five correspondingly placed lower windows. Considerable exterior bracing was laced on the building. From near the center of the roof a spire topped by a crested hipped roof rose over one hundred feet high. A porch and vestibule on the west end led into the main room of the church, which could accommodate five hundred people. At the east end of the nave stood the choir gallery and the pulpit. A lecture room seating two hundred eighty people and a Sunday school room adjoined the main part of the church on the east, an open arch over the choir gallery connecting into the lecture room. A pastor's study and Bible classroom were located on the north side of the lecture room in the lean-to, while a library and childrens' room were in the south lean-to. The Hunt-designed Presbyterian Church was destroyed by fire on February 17, 1943, and replaced by a new building.[30]

Finally, the account of Hunt's public, academic, and ecclesiastical

Figure 34
Elevation, Trinity
Church, Boston (1872).
From *The New-York
Sketch Book of Architec-
ture* (March 1879).

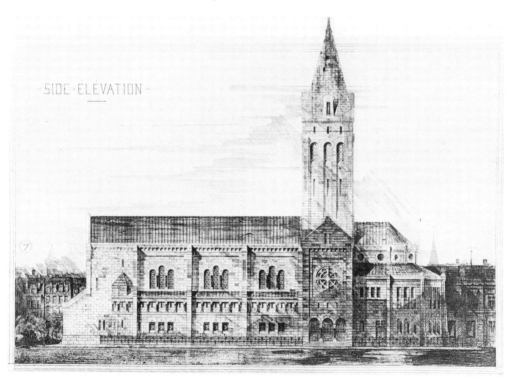

Figure 35
Perspective, Union
League Clubhouse, New
York (1879). From *American Architect and Building
News* (July 5, 1879).

buildings in the 1870s must include mention of two important commissions that he failed to obtain. In the winter of 1871–1872, Hunt was invited, along with the firms of Ware & Van Brunt, Sturgis & Brigham, and Peabody & Stearns of Boston and Gambrill and Richardson of New York, to submit designs by May 1, 1872, in a limited competition for the new Trinity Church in Boston. The work of the invited competitors as well as a few other unsolicited drawings were put on public display and were viewed by hundreds. The church building committee decided on H. H. Richardson's Romanesque designs for the new edifice to be built on Copley Square. The commission was a significant one, and more than any other building established Richardson's reputation as a leading architect of his time. Richardson's Trinity Church, in fact, became the most admired building of his generation. Hunt's design (figure 34) was Byzantine in inspiration, with a graceful tower and spire rising over the crossing, an imposing building, beautifully proportioned and much more restrained than Richardson's church. Although Hunt built a handful of small ecclesiastical structures, he never had the opportunity to try his hand with a large church. Late in the 1870s Hunt also submitted a design for a Union League Clubhouse in New York City, a commission that he had tried to get once before in 1867. His unsuccessful 1879 competition entry (figure 35) was a sober, formal design, skillfully conceived in the massing and the varied fenestration but ultimately conventional.[31]

In his public work during the years following his return from Europe in 1867, Hunt seems to have been testing himself by trying out different styles to see what he could do in different modes. The variety of his work is remarkable. Yet, one senses, he had not found himself fully. And in his commercial buildings and his domestic projects, while again his range was enormous, there is also a tentativeness and an almost experimental quality.

I4

FULFILLING COMMERCIAL NEEDS

Not only in his public buildings but also in several commercial commissions, Hunt's versatility in design and his ability to deal with a variety of needs were evident throughout the highly productive period of the early 1870s. In these commercial buildings, as in his work generally, Hunt was able to adapt his ideas to the requirements of his clients while putting his own stamp on what he did. Gilded Age clients and critics and commentators usually liked his designs, and by the mid-1870s he was becoming more and more widely recognized as an outstanding architect.

Following his return from Europe in 1867, the first of Hunt's major commercial commissions was for a building of "French flats." Large, comfortable buildings of several stories with rooms providing attractive accommodations for each family were common in Paris and other French cities, and interest in multidwelling buildings for "respectable" middle-class families had been growing in the United States for some time. In 1857, for example, Calvert Vaux, as we have seen, gave a talk at an early meeting of the American Institute of Architects on the need for good multifamily housing in New York City and the suitability of the French mode. But the concept was not carried out in the United States until Rutherfurd Stuyvesant ventured to try out the new idea in 1869–1870. The Stuyvesant Building was the first American apartment house, and it established an important precedent for a whole new class of structures in American cities.[1]

During the Civil War new housing construction had declined, and in the immediate postwar years private houses had become increasingly expensive to build and to maintain. Traditionally, middle-income American families lived in single-family houses, though some favored boarding houses or hotels for their homes. From about 1850, low-cost tenement housing had been constructed in Manhattan on a large scale, and the idea of several families living in the same building was commonly associated with the congested and unsanitary conditions of the tenements, into which foreign immigrants were crowding. The prejudice of "respectable" people against this mode of living, therefore, was strong, for to move into multiple-family housing seemed to mean a lowering of one's social position. Critics of the new idea predicted that even expensively constructed, spacious, and well-lighted flats would inevitably degenerate into slums, like the tenement houses. Some critics suggested that the French flats were indeed appropriate only to foreigners whose morals were not so elevated as those of Americans. Moving into such a building, it was felt, might also mean a lowering of moral standards. Before this mode of housing could be widely accepted, therefore, it was necessary to make the multiple-family dwelling respectable—or better yet, fashionable. When Rutherfurd Stuyvesant began his apartment house, some termed it "Stuyvesant's folly."[2]

Stuyvesant, born in 1840 and originally named Stuyvesant Rutherfurd, had the wealth and the social standing, however, to guarantee that a building he constructed and bearing his name would be impeccably respectable. A descendant of Peter Stuyvesant, he had inherited large property holdings from his mother's great-uncle, Peter Gerard Stuyvesant, and to comply with the terms of his inheritance he had been required to change his name from Rutherfurd to Stuyvesant. In France, he had met Hunt and had been impressed with the architect's work on the Louvre extension; and there he had also become acquainted with French flats, which, both he and Hunt recognized, could serve the housing needs of many New Yorkers. After Stuyvesant had purchased land at 142 East Eighteenth Street, a site on the south side of the street one hundred feet west of Third Avenue toward Irving Place, Hunt was commissioned to draw up the plans. Work commenced in May 1869, and by the end of February 1870 the building was completed.[3]

Before the Stuyvesant Apartments were finished, several prominent people had subscribed for flats there, many of them young couples with small families who considered the apartments particularly suited to their needs. Among the earliest tenants were Worthington Whittredge, the painter who had lived in the Tenth Street Studios, Colonel W. C. Church, editor of *The Galaxy*, and G. P. Putnam, the publisher. Bayard Taylor, the travel writer, lived there for many years, and even Calvert Vaux, who had taken the lead in opposing Hunt's Central Park gateways, occupied an apartment. Through the years, many writers, painters, and theatrical figures were attracted to the Stuyvesant Apartments.[4]

Hunt designed the five-story apartment house as a structure of two separate sections (figure 36), each served by a broad staircase rising from a spacious, Romanesque-style lobby decorated with tiles. Fronting on Eighteenth Street for a little over 112 feet, the main part of the building extended 37 feet in depth, while two wings, each 36 feet wide and 50 feet deep, reached to the rear, with inner courts on both sides providing light and ventilation to the rooms away from the street. Four suites of apartments were located on each of the first four stories—two in each section of the building—while the mansarded fifth story contained four high-ceilinged studios. On the first floor one apartment had nine rooms, one had seven rooms, and two had four rooms; the upper-story apartments included seven rooms and the studios six rooms. To the rear of the main staircase in each section, a separate service staircase provided

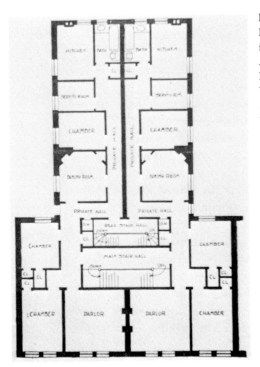

Figure 36
Plan of one-half of a typical floor, Stuyvesant Apartments, 142 East Eighteenth Street, New York (1870). From *Architectural Record* (July 1901).

Figure 37
Stuyvesant Apartments (1870). Museum of the City of New York.

access to the upper floors for servants and tradesmen. A concierge in an office by the lobby gave the entryway a Parisian flavor. Rents averaged about $1,200 a year and remained at approximately that level until well into the twentieth century. The turnover was very low and the building was always full.[5]

The exterior decoration of the Stuyvesant Apartments (figure 37) was limited to the front on Eighteenth Street. Although the various elements of the façade were reasonably well tied together, the composition was nonetheless awkward because of the overbalance of the mansard story, towering above a boldly bracketed cornice, out of scale with the rest of the structure, like a heavy crown much too large for the wearer. The twenty-three foot ceilings in the top-floor studios were almost twice as high as those in the lower stories, and while the high windows provided needed north light, their very height seemed to press heavily on the elements below. A symmetrical, balanced composition, centered upon the double entryways, the façade was overly fussy, with an abundance of stonework ornamentation, some aspects of which seemed poorly placed. The four segmental variegated arches set in over the third-story windows were especially superfluous. The stonework course at the upper part of the third-story windows was also inept, since on first glance it seemed to indicate the story delimitation but on further inspection was obviously placed somewhat below that structural terminus. Similarly, the stringcourse near the base of the fourth-story windows seemed misplaced. The trefoil arches over the third-story windows gave a Gothic touch to the building, as did the gables over the studio windows. Six iron fleur-de-lis applied to the wall surfaces between the second and third stories specifically tied the building to the French neo-Gothic tradition.[6]

The Stuyvesant Building had considerable impact on building practices in New York City, for the apartment as a mode of living quickly caught on. The immediate demand for the suites in this building made builders realize that "French flats" could be profitable investments, and within a short time many new apartment houses were constructed and many existing structures were converted into apartments. In 1871, Dr. David H. Haight rebuilt a mansion at Fifteenth Street on Fifth Avenue into the first elevator apartment house in New York City, with rentals running from $2,000 to $3,000 a year. The most luxurious of the early buildings was the Dakota Apartments on Central Park West between Seventy-Second and Seventy-Third streets, designed by Henry J. Hardenbergh and completed in 1884. Some of the new apartment buildings had a central kitchen or restaurant, but most were variants of Hunt's designs, though with the addition of elevators. By the turn of the century, it was estimated that there were some forty thousand apartment houses in New York City alone. No longer did middle-class families feel that they must undertake the expense and do the work of maintaining private houses; the convenience of apartment house living was obvious. The Stuyvesant Building was torn down in 1959 to make way for a considerably larger but architecturally undistinguished apartment house.[7]

A far more ambitious commission than the Stuyvesant Apartments was the Stevens House in New York City, a project that involved Hunt once more in litigation. Paran Stevens, known as "The Napoleon of Hotel Keepers," was the most notable hotel man of his time. Some twenty-six years older than Hunt, he came, like Hunt, of old New England stock; his grandfather had been a justice of the peace and his father a storekeeper, a postmaster, and an innkeeper in Claremont, New Hampshire. After his father's death, Paran Stevens joined his brothers in operating the inn at Claremont, and his success there called him to the attention of Boston entrepreneurs who asked him in 1843 to come to the Bay City to manage the New England Coffee House. Four years later Stevens was named proprietor of the Revere House in Boston, a hotel that became widely known for its comforts and hospitality. Soon he branched into other hotel operations, adding the Continental Hotel in Philadelphia and the old Fifth Avenue Hotel in New York to his holdings. The Stevens House apartments were projected with a Parisian flair as elegant "French flats," but the structure was later transformed into the Victoria Hotel, a general commercial establishment.[8]

Even before it was completed in 1872, *The New York Illustrated* called the Stevens House "the most truly picturesque architectural pile in the city." Occupying the short block from Broadway to Fifth Avenue, with primary frontage of 254 feet on the south side of Twenty-Seventh Street, 100 feet on Broadway, but only 28 feet on Fifth Avenue, the Stevens House (figure 38) rose an impressive eight stories, including a high two-story mansard. The roof line silhouette, an interesting composition of finial-topped hipped pavilions, variously shaped dormers, and massed chimneys, foreshadowed work that Hunt would do later on some of his large private houses. The walls were set with pressed red brick, trimmed with Nova Scotia stone, and the mansard roof was constructed of iron, tin, and slate. At street level, there was space for five stores with large divided windows. Three luxurious apartments of five large principal rooms were located on each of the next six stories, while the upper attic story included servants' rooms, two allocated to each of the several

Figure 38
Stevens House (Victoria
Hotel), Broadway and
Twenty-Seventh Street,
New York (1872). From
Appleton's Journal
(November 18, 1871).

apartments below. Every effort was undertaken to make the building fireproof; iron beams were used at the lower levels, the staircases were built of iron and marble, and the main hallways were covered with ceramic tile. Montgomery Schuyler judged this building "regular and grandiose in composition, ingenious and clever in detail, especially . . . in the iron-work and masonry . . . and perhaps the most Parisian in effect of anything of its period or of its author."[9]

An outstanding feature of the Stevens House was the installation of passenger elevators, thus making the upper-floor apartment suites as desirable as the lower ones. In the multilevel French apartment houses the upper floors had customarily been limited to more modest accommodations than those on the floors just above the street level, which were easier to walk up to. The Stevens House was the first large American apartment house with elevator service, although lifts had been utilized in different types of buildings for various purposes for nearly thirty years.[10]

Well received in the press, the Stevens House nonetheless was something of a problem in building, and its construction led to considerable trouble for Hunt. It had some major flaws, and Hunt's agreed-upon commission was not fully paid. Eventually Hunt was forced to sue the Stevens estate to obtain the money he claimed was due him. The case of *Hunt* v. *Stevens* was to be far more clear-cut than the earlier Parmly case had been, for the architect's duties and responsibilities had been spelled out in some detail in his arrangements with Stevens.

On July 27, 1870, Paran Stevens and Richard Morris Hunt signed a written contract in which, in return for Hunt's designs, specifications, drawings, and general superintendence, Stevens agreed to pay Hunt a fee of $15,000 in three installments of $5,000 each on October 1, 1870, on May 1, 1871, and on completion of the work. The parties further agreed that rather than Hunt, William Paul, the builder, was to be building superintendent and clerk of the works. Hunt's fee was set at three percent of the total estimated building cost of $500,000; in actuality the building was to cost about $800,000. In June 1871, Stevens also contracted with Hunt to provide the working drawings for, and to superintend construction of another, much smaller store and workshop building at 1160 Broadway (figure 39), for which Hunt was given a partial payment of $300 on October 20, 1871.[11]

Before the Stevens House was completed in March 1872, many problems had already arisen. During the winter of 1871–1872 almost all the water pipes, which had been placed in the exterior walls, had frozen. Some of the heating equipment had failed to function. Street-level

Figure 39
Store and loft, 1160
Broadway, New York
(1872). Courtesy The
American Institute of
Architects Foundation/
Prints and Drawings
Collection, Washington,
D.C. Reproduction by
James Garrison.

arches had bulged and had to be given new supports. This last problem was due in part to the settling of the building when foundation piles were driven for an adjacent structure on the Fifth Avenue side, and the party wall was not shored up.

After Stevens's death on April 27, 1872, Hunt submitted to the Stevens executors a statement of the fees owed him. He maintained that he had not been paid the final installment of his commission on the Stevens House, or the $1,020 due him as a fee for his work on 1160 Broadway. When the payments were not forthcoming, Hunt, on November 25, 1873, sued the Stevens estate for the money he claimed was due him on the two building projects, plus interest for the period of delinquency and payment of the costs of the suit. The suit did not come to trial, however, until January 9, 1878, at which time Hunt was represented by his longtime friend Joseph Choate, by that time one of the most renowned American lawyers, who eloquently argued the justice of Hunt's claims and dealt vigorously with the counterclaims of the defense. Hunt maintained in the trial that he had "faithfully performed and fulfilled all his undertakings in the premises," and he asserted that he was in no way responsible for the alterations and the equipment which Paran Stevens himself had ordered. Hunt denied that he had assured Stevens that the apartment house would cost under $500,000, and he rejected all allegations of negligence, wastefulness, and extravagance leveled at him. Other architects testified to his professional competence.[12]

The Stevens defense claimed that Hunt, "the most busily employed architect in the city of New York," had not given the personal superintendence he had agreed to provide for the building. A draftsman in Hunt's office had carried out the specifics of the plans, and Hunt had not given the attention to details expected of him. Nor had he given good professional advice during construction. Many of the materials that went into the building were unsuitable, the defense claimed, and some of the work had been done carelessly and had to be redone. Hunt was charged with the improper location of the water pipes, the bulging of exterior arches, and the weakness and instability of the party wall on the Fifth Avenue side of the building. Because of the architect's negligence, it was charged, the building had cost far more than was originally contemplated. If Hunt had given the care and attention he had agreed to, the defense asserted, he would have been paid long since. The defense also maintained that Hunt had agreed to do the architectural work for 1160 Broadway for no charge but as a part of his work for the Stevens House.[13]

The plaintiff's argument was based on customary architects' fees. For full services including superintendence of a project the architect regularly received five percent of the building cost. In this case, there was no dispute that Hunt and Stevens had agreed on a fee of three percent of the building's cost for the architect, or $15,000, rather than five percent, or $25,000, and that William Paul was to be paid $10,000, or two percent of the anticipated building cost. Hunt was to be saved the time and trouble of superintendence, and Paul was to be responsible for overseeing the actual construction. Hunt's suit maintained that he could not therefore be held responsible for errors in construction, since he was not being paid the superintendent's fee. Moreover, it was brought out that Hunt had protested about the piles being driven and the party wall being used for support of the adjacent structure without the foundations being shored up, but that Stevens had gone ahead contrary to Hunt's advice. Stevens himself had selected the heating apparatus, and Hunt had had no say in this matter; and Stevens had agreed to Hunt's plans on the location of the water pipes, though the architect's instructions about boxing and felting the pipes had been ignored. Choate concluded his argument by stressing the insincerity of the defense in the case, and took a vigorous satirical jab at *Mrs.* Paran Stevens, Stevens' widow and executrix, a "queen" of New York and Newport society who had left many unpaid bills behind her in her social ascent.[14]

Judge Charles F. Sanford instructed the jury that Hunt was entitled to receive full claim for work done on 1160 Broadway; there was nothing set forth to support the contention that Hunt had agreed to do this job as a part of his work on Stevens House. Moreover, since the usual full fee had been cut by forty percent on the Stevens House project, Hunt was released from the obligation of personal superintendence of the work, the judge ruled. If the architect's neglect, however, had caused the damage to the arches of the building, then the defendant might claim damages from him. The close of the trial came on January 17, 1878. The jury deliberated for only ten minutes and brought in a unanimous verdict in favor of Hunt, awarding him damages of $8,438.14. Not only was Hunt's victory complete, but also the American Institute of Architects' fee schedule and guidelines had been reaffirmed.[15]

Besides the two apartment houses, Hunt completed commissions for other types of commercial structures, including two iron-front stores. Hunt had long been interested in using cast iron. It will be recalled that on December 21, 1858, at one of the early meetings of the Institute, following a paper by Leopold Eidlitz which rejected the use of cast iron as a decorative material in building, Hunt took the opposing view. In many instances, such as for storefronts, he asserted, cast iron was, in fact, "the *most appropriate material* that could be used." In places where land was so valuable that the entire lot had to be built upon, the street façade of a building must become an immense window for the interior. Cast iron was better than stone on such fronts in combining beauty and utility. He thought that better ways might be found to preserve cast iron than had been used in the past; in addition, the material could be particularly effective when used with color, thus providing "an opportunity of developing one of the greatest beauties of architecture." That cast iron had so far not been widely used was no proof, he believed, that it could not be used successfully. "The Civilization of to-day demands an architectural honor peculiar to itself. . . . Educated architects [must] . . . keep pace with the spirit and requirements of the age." Here was "a broad field for the true artist to distinguish himself."[16]

By the time Hunt designed his first iron-front building over a dozen years later in 1871, cast iron for exterior facing had already been in use for several years. The Laing Stores, erected by James Bogardus at the corner of Washington and Murray streets in New York in 1848, were an early example of the new prefabricated cast-iron unit construction. Even earlier, in 1829–1830, John Haviland's Farmers' and Mechanics' Bank in Pottsville, Pennsylvania, had a façade made entirely of the material. The Astor Library, begun in 1849, had many cast-iron fittings. Bogardus had set up a factory in 1849 to produce cast-iron building units. The elegant Haughwout Building on Broadway at Broome Street, modeled by John P. Gaynor on Sansovino's Library of St. Mark in Venice and built in 1857, was probably the outstanding New York cast-iron building, but many others of striking design were built in the same neighborhood. The SoHo Cast-Iron Historic District, increasingly today a center for creation and dissemination of art, embodies one of the most fascinating complexes of historically important architecture in the United States.[17]

For his brother-in-law, Alexander Van Rensselaer, Hunt designed a five-story iron-front store at 474–476 Broadway between Grand and Broome streets, just a few yards from the Haughwout Building. The structure, built in 1871–1872, was first occupied by Rice, Goodwin, Walker and Co., a dry goods and notions firm, and later by Lee, Tweedy & Company. The façade of the store was one of Hunt's most fantastic creations and surely the brightly colored Moorish design (figure 40) stood out as one of the most unusual in New York City. Painted in black, yellow, white, blue, and red—"the colors of the rainbow, startlingly and yet not unpleasingly blended"—the fifty-foot façade was divided into six narrow bays, the four inner bays combined into two by cusped horseshoe arches over the second-story windows. Cusped horseshoe arches over the inner fourth-story windows, as well as smaller smooth horseshoe arches over the outer second- through fourth-story windows, and trefoil arches above the fifth story, along with single and grouped colonnettes, a first-story lintel course of molded rosettes, and a patterned frieze made for a lively assortment of elements. Despite the variety, the many units were tied together by narrow piers rising from the base to the top of the building and bracketed to the soaring, cantilevered cornice. The piers and the cornice clearly framed and ordered the fanciful elements of the front. It was a playful design, which must have been especially effective with its polychrome finish. The material was not disguised and did not pretend to be something it was not: clearly this was a metallic construction—not stone or brick or wood—shaped and decorated to call attention to itself and serve as an advertisement for the store it housed.[18]

Hunt's second iron-front store, at 478–482 Broadway, rose on the adjacent lot directly north of the Moorish design and was completed in 1874. Still standing and still known today as the Roosevelt Building (figure 41), it was built for investment purposes by Roosevelt Hospital, established from the proceeds of the estate left by James H. Roosevelt, who had lived and practiced law on this site. The building long housed Hammerslough Brothers Store. The façade is simpler and more restrained—and drabber too—than that of its onetime neighbor, but it is undoubtedly bolder and more powerful as well. Again, the structure is five stories high, with the street floor treated as a base in the façade design, the middle three stories as a unit, and the top floor as an attic. The horizontal composition is tripartite, the primary divisions defined by terminal pilasters and two central colossal columns, all with Ionic capitals. Néo-Grec piers define the base of the primary vertical elements at the street level. A filigree arch of ironwork spans the top of each of the three primary bays above the fourth level, while delicate colonnettes divide the windows within the larger bays. The short, squat attic pilasters echo similar units on the upper parts of the Lenox Library wings. The cornice is bracketed outward over a wide, slightly concave frieze marked by vertical banding. Again, the materials bespeak themselves, and the ironwork makes no pretense of disguising itself at all. This is clearly a decorative pierced screen framing large areas of glass and designed to admit as much light as possible. The iron front building at 478–482 Broadway extends to an exterior rear wall of a single bay of three windows at 40 Crosby Street; here the motifs of the main façade are repeated on a smaller scale. Despite the success of this building, Hunt was not fully satisfied with his own designs in ironwork and with

Figure 40
Perspective, iron-front
store, 474–476 Broad-
way, New York (1872).
From *American Architect
and Building News* (July
15, 1876).

Fig. 41
Roosevelt Building,
478–482 Broadway,
New York (1874).
Museum of the City of
New York.

the use of prefabricated cast-iron units generally, for late in his life he declared publicly that the problem had "never yet [been] altogether satisfactorily solved" and "much yet remains to be accomplished before the artistic mind will be satisfied."[19]

Montgomery Schuyler, who seems to have observed most of the Hunt buildings he discussed, apparently did not look at the Roosevelt Building iron front before writing his description and estimate. Rather curiously, he based his acquaintance with the structure on a sketch which appeared in the *American Architect and Building News* on June 10, 1876, and was subsequently published in James Fergusson's *History of the Modern Styles of Architecture*, as revised by Professor Robert Kerr. This sketch was probably an early version of the design, which was altered before being built. The sketch shows a vertical division into lower openings of two stories each, surmounted by the attic story as built. In the sketch the iron fretwork arches above the middle division were repeated at the top of the lowest division. Moreover, the decorative scheme of colossal columns and pilasters and Néo-Grec piers at the street and attic levels is missing from the sketch. The attenuated columns have Corinthian capitals rather than the Ionic capitals which were placed at the middle level of the building. The design in the sketch is much more delicate and less forceful than the vigorously composed structure which was actually built. Kerr called the composition "sufficiently characteristically designed as well as pleasingly proportioned and modelled" and, all in all, "decidedly unobjectionable." Schuyler supported Kerr's estimate, but he believed ultimately that although Hunt's iron fronts were as good as any, the whole problem of using cast-iron units in building design was "not really soluble."[20]

Another of Hunt's major commercial commissions of this period was the Delaware and Hudson Canal Company Building, later known as the Coal and Iron Exchange, located at 17–21 Cortlandt Street at the southeast corner of Church Street in lower Manhattan. This was an office building, considered by *King's Handbook* to be one of the finest in the city. The Delaware and Hudson Canal Company had been founded early in the century to transport coal from the fields of northeastern Pennsylvania to New York City and for this purpose had constructed a canal from the Delaware River near Port Jervis to the Hudson River, as well as connecting railway lines. The company prospered in the manipulations of the Erie ring and built its nine-story headquarters from Hunt's design between 1873 and 1876 at an estimated cost of $820,000.[21]

The principal façade (figure 42) was on Cortlandt Street, with a secondary front rising above the elevated railway on Church Street. The

Figure 42
Delaware and Hudson
Canal Company Build-
ing, 17–21 Cortlandt
Street, New York (1876).
From *King's Photographic
Views of New York* (1895).

base of the structure at street level was treated with cyclopean rusticated Dorchester stone, while above this the walls were faced with brick and with light stone trim at the windows, the main entrance, the stringcourses, and the primary cornice over the fifth story. Above the cornice rose a two-story mansard roof and corner mansard pavilions with an additional attic story. Besides the contrasts of brick and stone, the major ornamentation was found in the treatment of the entrance portal and in the dormer posts, lintels, and pediments placed in the mansard section at the top floors. Next to the entrance, two heavy polished columns, carried on high corbelled piers, rose through the second story and supported an elaborate, archlike entablature, which had a decidedly pasted-on and nonessential look. The vertical bays of the front and side were clearly delineated through double and triple window groupings under arches at the second- and fourth-story levels and pediments at the sixth level. All in all, the Delaware and Hudson Canal Company Building presented a solid and dignified appearance, though somewhat heavy and overly sober. For a time, soon after it was opened, Hunt maintained his own office in this structure.[22]

The Tribune Building was the most notable of Hunt's commercial structures. Built to house the *New York Tribune,* which had been founded by Horace Greeley in 1841, this newspaper building was an outstanding contribution to New York City commercial architecture and to the city's skyline. For a time the Tribune Building was the tallest edifice in the city except for the spire of Trinity Church and was, by some definitions, one of the first skyscrapers ever built. Obviously this landmark brought Hunt considerable general recognition, although some critics severely attacked the design. For many years the Tribune Building was undoubtedly his best-known creation.

Greeley had been nominated for the presidency of the United States in 1872 by both the Liberal Republicans and the Democrats, but he had died suddenly in late November just after losing the election to Grant. This substantial new building, therefore, was not only "the largest and most imposing newspaper office in the world" but also an eye-catching monument to the newspaper's founder. After an earlier Tribune Building was demolished in May 1873, construction was begun in June on an irregularly shaped site facing Printing House Square opposite City Hall, with frontage on Spruce and Nassau streets. The new building (figure 43) was formally opened on April 10, 1875, and fully completed just a year later. The newspaper printing presses were placed in the basement, while the editorial offices were first located on the eighth floor and the composing room on the ninth floor; the accounting department was

Figure 43
Tribune Building, Nassau and Spruce streets, New York (1876, 1883). Courtesy The American Institute of Architects Foundation/Prints and Drawings Collection, Washington, D.C. Reproduction by James Garrison.

placed on the first floor at street level. Much of the building was rented to professional tenants, and the *Tribune* declared that "the best lawyers' offices in the city" were to be found there. Two public elevators and one private elevator provided access to the upper floors.[23]

Rising eight principal stories above a subcellar and basement and crowned by a two-story attic and tower, the Tribune Building was promised to be "absolutely fire-proof in every part and built to last forever." The massive walls of stone and brick were load-bearing, with iron beams supporting the tiled floors; the iron staircases had slate treads. An iron framework tied to the granite courses below supported the slate-covered spire, and the roof of the main building was iron-framed with slate covering. The corbeled clock tower, which vaguely recalled that of the Palazzo Vecchio in Florence, was topped by a spire rising 260 feet above the sidewalk level and 285 feet above the base of the foundation. In 1881–1883, a narrow wing was built, extending north to Frankfort Street and designed by Edward Raht according to Hunt's plans, so that the enlarged *Tribune* headquarters extended in an L-shape around two sides of the old Sun Building. In 1905, in a remarkable engineering project, the main building was greatly enlarged by the addition of nine more stories; at this time the tower was rebuilt following the former design above the new, higher roof line. The Tribune Building was razed in 1966 to make way for the expansion of Pace College.[24]

Hunt designed the Tribune Building with a well-defined base of light-colored granite. Above, he had the walls faced with deep red Baltimore brick with geometrical designs in black, white, and red brick, and the windows, the cornices, and the tower trimmed with the same light-colored granite. The tower rising over the main entrance was corbeled on piers from the upper part of the fourth-story level and was a sharply defined unit, narrower than the other three triply fenestrated bays. The tower unit served as a means of transition, also, between the slightly different planes of the corner bay and the other two bays to the north of the entrance. The double planes of the principal façade were well disguised. Rising from the granite base, the second through fourth stories were treated as a unit with brick segmental arches over the bays and lateral brick piers. Above, the fifth and sixth stories were also grouped as a single unit, while the seventh floor topped by a massive cornice featuring dentil-like brackets formed another unit. The three upper stories, two of them at the mansard roof level, were tied together by the granite window trim, the vertical elements of which rose to heavy dormer pediments capping the vertical bays beside the tower. Thus the ten stories were treated as five units, which tended to de-emphasize the height of the building, while the tower itself accentuated the height. Two columns of highly polished dark Quincy granite flanked the entrance and supported a balcony of granite, and a row of smaller polished granite columns divided the windows on the seventh floor. The corbeled clock tower, terminating in a high spire with narrow dormers, rose over a curious attic-level balcony, placed much too high above the street to be used as a speaking platform but included perhaps as a symbol of a building from which public announcements and news were sent out to the city.[25]

When the Tribune Building was enlarged in 1905, the composition of Hunt's façade was essentially maintained. The ninth through the twelfth stories repeated the arched bay pattern of the second through the fourth stories. Large consoles gave an upward thrust at the thirteenth-story level, above which two high floors led to a three-story mansard roof. When the additional stories were added to the structure, however, the rebuilt tower was disproportionately small for the new building height, and the total effect, though much more massive, was less harmonious.[26]

Like that of the Presbyterian Hospital, the visual impact of the Tribune Building was immensely weakened, for modern eyes, by the awkward use of the stone trimwork. The light-colored granite trim contrasted so sharply with the background of the red brick walls that all of the stone elements were accentuated. Excessive use of the stone in lintel and sill courses, along the cornices, on the pediments, and elsewhere gave the façades a rather haphazard look. Although the upper part of the tower was admirably composed, it seemed to rest on an insubstantial base. The latticework of horizontal and vertical lines on the building surfaces did not always appear to be reasoned out, and some of the secondary features of the structure were more strongly accented than some primary ones. The design was unsettled, lacking in repose, which was especially unfortunate in a building of such size and height and importance, located in the heart of the city and providing better housing than any newspaper had ever had before. It was a pity that the strength and solidity of the building were to a great degree disguised by the design.[27]

Whether the Tribune Building was in fact one of the very first skyscrapers has been a matter of extended discussion among architectural historians. When it was completed in 1875, it was the tallest commercial structure in the country. Although as early as 1849 the Jayne Building in Philadelphia, designed by William Johnston, rose to eight stories with an additional two-story tower, most structures before the early 1870s had been limited to five stories, since few people were willing to walk up more than four flights of stairs. The invention and improvement of the elevator made additional floors readily usable, and with more light, less street noise, and better air, the upper floors were considered desirable. A tall building could be a symbol of prestige for a company as well. Hunt's Tribune Building and George Post's Western Union Telegraph Building, also begun in 1873 and completed in 1875, both had passenger elevators and, rising to new heights of 260 feet and 230 feet respectively, they were much higher than any earlier commercial buildings. Post's edifice, above the rustication of the first two stories and beneath the differentiated topmost stories and tower, had a general uniformity of design in the midstories, and serves as an early example of the concept of the tall building as an analogue to a column, with a clearly defined base, shaft, and capital. This became the characteristic tripartite styling for most tall buildings in the years to come. Both the Western Union and the Tribune buildings were basically masonry structures with load-bearing walls, and although taller than any other earlier office buildings and making use of passenger elevators, they did not have metallic skeletons with curtain walls, which some historians consider to be the essence of the true skyscraper. Although awkward in many ways and uncertain in scale, these two tall buildings of 1873–1875 nonetheless moved toward an entirely new architectural conception. A decade later, iron and steel construction would make even greater heights feasible, and, especially in Chicago, a new aesthetic would be formulated in conjunction with the technical advances.[28]

A few years later, in 1881–1882, Hunt completed the Guernsey Office Building at 160–164 Broadway in New York City for Henry G. Marquand. This was a commonplace structure, much smaller and simpler than the landmark Tribune Tower, much less interesting in detail than the iron-front Roosevelt Building, and much less pleasing in appearance than most of Hunt's other large buildings. Consisting of seven stories and having only a street-front design, the Guernsey Building (figure 44) was divided into three units, both vertically and horizontally. A stonework base of two floors supported five upper stories. The topmost story was treated as an attic with colonnettes around the windows and a heavy, bracketed cornice above, while the third through the sixth stories were composed in a basically similar manner, with piers and colonnettes dividing the windows. In the horizontal division, the left and center bays were treated identically, each with two large windows at the first two stories and four smaller windows in the stories above, the two units separated by a broad wall pier. On the right above the two-story main

Figure 44
Guernsey Building,
160–164 Broadway, New
York (1882). Courtesy
The American Institute
of Architects Foundation/
Prints and Drawings
Collection, Washington,
D.C. Reproduction by
James Garrison.

entrance rose a slender tower which was accentuated by a slight projection commencing at the base of the fifth story. The tower contained an additional story and terminated in a steeply sloped roof. The most pleasing decorative feature were the delicate colonnettes framing the upper-story windows. As in the Presbyterian Hospital and the Tribune Building, Hunt made use of light-colored stone in lintels and sills and set in additional stones above and below the piers and colonnettes and as jamb stones at the outer edges of the window banks making a broken horizontal line, which contrasted sharply with the brick of the upper wall. The decorative stonework once more gave a somewhat agitated appearance to the façade.[29]

Hunt's commercial work of the early 1870s, along with the later Guernsey Building, provided some outstanding buildings for New York City. The precedent-making Stuyvesant Apartment Building was soon widely copied, while the prototype itself was long recognized as one of the city's most comfortable and attractive multiple residences. Hunt's iron-front designs were unpretentious and strikingly original and among the most remarkable examples of this type of work. The Tribune Tower, like the Lenox Library and the Presbyterian Hospital, was an important commission that brought him widespread notice. Although there were many awkward features in these designs, they stood out among the general run of commercial buildings of the day and helped contribute to Hunt's reputation.[30]

15

VENTURES IN HOUSE DESIGN

The commissions Hunt undertook at the end of the 1860s and in the early 1870s kept him and his small staff very busy. When in 1871 he was requested by John F. Weir, director of the Yale School of Fine Arts, to contribute drawings for an exhibit of architectural designs, Hunt responded that he had been "so pressed with work for the last two years that no time could be spared to provide finished drawings." His available working drawings, he believed, would be of no interest to the public. He also was asked that year to lecture on architecture at Yale, but he declined the invitation not only because he had so little time available to prepare a lecture but also because he found distasteful the idea of speaking before an academic audience. Although Hunt was noted for his fluent and pungent speech, he had great difficulty in putting his ideas on paper, and he intensely disliked speaking in public. Whenever he had to give a public talk, he agonized over the preparations for days. His few published speeches are generally commonplace in ideas and expression.[1]

Perhaps Hunt was attempting to avoid a drain on his time or possibly he was just being candid when he was called for jury duty in connection with the trial of Boss Tweed in 1872. The *New York Times* reported that Hunt, a member of the Union League Club but not identified as an architect, was the first person questioned by the lawyers. Hunt expressed the opinion that "if the charges against Tweed were true, they were infamous swindles. He [Hunt] was in the habit of reading the *New York Times* and he disbelieves half he reads." Needless to say, he was given a peremptory challenge by the defense and did not have to serve on the jury.[2]

Hunt's work brought him good earnings, though undoubtedly a substantial share of the family's income came from Catharine's inheritance. The *New York Herald* reported in the spring of 1869 that Hunt's taxable income for 1868, as filed under the internal revenue laws, was $13,286. With the many large commissions he undertook in the early 1870s, Hunt must have had a considerably larger income in the succeeding years. Taxable income figures, however, belied the couple's financial resources. Catharine recalled in her biographical memoir that on September 2, 1869, they purchased a stable at 17 East Twenty-Seventh Street for $25,000, and leased half of it while retaining the other half for their own use. Richard continued to look after his own investments and those of his family in Western real estate, which his father had acquired, and in 1873 he traveled to Chicago and Detroit to check on these properties.[3]

In New York the Hunts lived comfortably though not lavishly or ostentatiously, entertaining often in their town house and going out often. George Templeton Strong noted in his diary that at a small dinner party he attended at the home of the John Astors in December 1868, the Hunts were present, and at Strong's own house "Dick Hunt and his exuberant Sultana of a Mrs. Hunt" joined John Hay and others for an evening in March 1873. "Hunt," Strong commented, "would put life into the dullest Fifth Avenue dinner party or into *convivium mortuorum*." One observer of the New York social scene in the 1870s characterized the Hunts' home as "one of the early strongholds of taste and culture" in New York. There people of wealth and fashion mingled with artists and writers. In Newport, a noted house guest of the Hunts was Christine Nilsson, a Swedish soprano, who toured the United States in the early 1870s. She and Richard, who still enjoyed singing but was not noted for his musical talent, had fun planning a possible joint concert tour: customers would pay to hear Nilsson sing, then after her selections the doors would be locked and when Richard began the customers would have to pay to get out. Hunt was given the opportunity to indulge his musical interests one year when Jim Fisk, the financial manipulator and a fellow migrant from Brattleboro, sent him and Catharine free passes good for a year at the Eighth Avenue Grand Opera House after Hunt had strengthened the building and remodeled the Erie Railroad offices there.[4]

Hunt's remarkable output of work during these years was accomplished despite frequent illness. In 1868 he suffered his first attack of gout, which would plague him and often incapacitate him for days at a time during the rest of his life. Seeking relief from his ailment, the Hunts visited Saratoga that June so that Richard might take the water cure. They subsequently went regularly to Saratoga, for Hunt thought that the waters there helped him a great deal. (They were at the United States Hotel in Saratoga on July 4, 1868, when it caught fire and burned to the ground. The Hunts had a ground-floor room and managed to save all their belongings, and Richard helped rescue several women from the burning building.) In the summer of 1873, Hunt was taken severely ill with what his doctor called "neuralgia of the heart." He was denied tobacco, wine, and tea and had to spend much of the time resting.[5]

Hunt's domestic buildings of the late 1860s and the early and mid-1870s included city dwellings in Boston, New York, and Chicago and summer cottages in Newport, and a country house in Peekskill. Hunt designed these houses in two very different modes, mostly following French inspiration for the city residences but turning to domestic vernacular and stick style for the Newport and Peekskill houses.[6]

In 1869, Hunt designed for his long-time friend Martin L. Brimmer at 47–48 Beacon Street in Boston a double house, French in inspiration and decidedly picturesque. A wealthy Boston aristocrat, a fellow of the Harvard Corporation, a vestryman of Trinity Church, and a trustee of the Boston Athenaeum and of the Massachusetts General Hospital, Brimmer stood at the apex of Boston social life. He was noted for his brilliant conversation and his sociability and wit, and he was also admired as a philanthropist and patron of the arts, serving from its founding until his death as president of the Boston Museum of Fine Arts. Brimmer was very impressed with the work of William Morris Hunt and purchased several of his paintings. Richard and Catharine Hunt and Brimmer remained close friends; the Hunts often visited Brimmer and his wife in Boston, and Brimmer saw the Hunts frequently in New York.[7]

The three- and four-story Brimmer houses (figure 45) were faced with red brick and Nova Scotia buff stone and included a spire-topped tower at the south corner, rising over the upper mansard story. In various decorative details, the Brimmer houses prefigured Hunt's later use of French Renaissance elements, which became such an important characteristic of his later major domestic work. A tier of bay windows trimmed in carved Dorchester stone extending upward from the second story was the principal feature of the front of the upper house, which the Brimmers occupied, while the lower house, which was rented, had a tier of bay windows trimmed mainly in brick. The upper window moldings, the pilasters and capitals, the ironwork finials, and the corner tower gave the façades, one critic thought, something of the appearance of a château of the time of Francis I. Hunt lavished particular care on the enframement of the dormers in the two-story mansard roof of the upper house. Elsewhere, here and there on the lower wall surfaces, the window jambs, and the middle-level spandrels, he used Néo-Grec detailing. To Montgomery Schuyler, the Brimmer houses were "restless" and "animated" and Gothic in feeling, though not at all Gothic in detail or form; they were, he judged, a highly individual rendering of French romantic architecture.[8]

Little information is available on the first of Hunt's New York commissions following his return from Europe in 1867. In 1868 he executed designs for two one-family houses for John Quincy Adams Ward, the sculptor and Hunt's long-time collaborator. These were located at 7 and 9 West Forty-Ninth Street, part of the future site of Rockefeller Center. The twin houses were tall and narrow, rising sixty-nine feet but extending only thirteen and one-half feet in width. Faced with Ohio ashlar and

Figure 45
Martin Brimmer houses,
Boston (1870). Courtesy
The American Institute
of Architects Foun-
dation/Prints and
Drawings Collection,
Washington, D.C. Re-
production by James
Garrison.

decorated with Néo-Grec linear incised panels and small rosettes, the houses were topped by a slate and tin mansard roof. To the rear, a large studio for the sculptor extended the full width of both houses.[9]

The next year, 1869, Hunt designed twin houses for William H. Osborn and Jonathan Sturges (figure 46) on the west side of Park Avenue south of Thirty-Sixth Street. Built of brick and faced with stone, the two houses, rising three stories and topped by an elaborated mansard roof, were treated as a unit. The façade of the larger house to the south was dominated by a three-story tier of bay windows, which was echoed by a second-story oriel on the house to the north. Somewhat more restrained than the Brimmer complex, the Park Avenue houses nonetheless also prefigured, in the window placement, the dormer enframement, and the rich profusion of carved stone surfaces, some of the architect's major work twenty years later.[10]

Toward the end of the 1870s, Hunt designed yet another pair of twin houses in New York City at the northwest corner of Madison Avenue and Thirty-Third Street. The adjoining houses for Egerton L. Winthrop and Frederic Bronson, built in 1878–1879, were sober, formal structures of four stories topped by a mansard attic. The principal, or Madison Avenue, front was divided into a triple and a double bay, clearly delineating the two houses, the inner half again as wide as the corner residence. Recalling the Williams houses in Boston of nearly two decades earlier, these New York houses were decorated by little more than molded window and door frames topped by paneled lintels and small cornices and by small dormer pediments and rooftop cresting. The Winthrop-Bronson houses were substantial but commonplace in their Second Empire–derived design.[11]

A group of four adjacent four-story, single-family town houses at 219, 221, 223, and 225 East Sixty-Second Street in New York City was begun in the fall of 1873 and completed the following spring for Thomas and John D. Crimmins, building contractors, at an estimated cost of $9,000 each. Like other houses on both sides of this same block between Second and Third avenues and on the adjoining Sixty-First Street block, these were brownstone dwellings designed in the Second Empire style. Of these four extant houses, the façade of number 219 today remains least altered of the group. Only two windows wide, the façade is decorated by moldings, a stringcourse, and a cornice that are quite unpretentious. The property here had been a part of a twenty-four-acre farm owned by Adam Treadwell, a wealthy merchant and landowner. When the farm was purchased from the Treadwell heirs in the late 1860s, the new owners voluntarily joined in a protective covenant establishing

Figure 46
William Osborn and
Jonathan Sturges houses,
32 and 34 Park Avenue,
New York (1870).
Museum of the City
of New York.

certain standards for the size and construction of their houses, providing for a general uniformity in architectural design and excluding specific types of businesses and activities from the neighborhood. Today the area forms the Treadwell Farm Historic District, two streets of charming houses notable for the uniformity and the excellence of their design. Seven other dwellings designed by Hunt in this immediate neighborhood have been demolished; one multiple residence remains at 201 East Sixty-First Street.[12]

Hunt's Chicago house of the early 1870s was a mansion built for Marshall Field, who had made a vast fortune in merchandising and was continuing to enrich himself in real estate ventures. The house at 1905 Prairie Avenue was under construction when the great Chicago fire broke out in 1871, but the fire did not reach it and work went ahead. Nothing was spared to make the Field residence luxurious and elegant; it was the first private house in Chicago to be lighted by electricity. Completed by 1873 at a cost of some $250,000, the mansion was long pointed out by proud Chicagoans as one of the principal embellishments of the city. Here Mrs. Marshall Field reigned for some twenty years as the queen of Chicago society. The Field's "Mikado" costume ball, which more than five hundred guests attended in January 1886, was a high point of Chicago social life—the Midwestern answer to the famous Vanderbilt ball of 1883 in New York—and provided a spectacular display of richly decorated costumes in the ivory and gold ballroom of the mansion. Field's widow, his second wife, occupied the house until her death in 1937, after which it was turned over to the Association of Arts and Industries, which opened The New Bauhaus, American School of Design, to be used as a school of industrial art. At that time the dwelling was extensively remodeled. The New Bauhaus, which was directed by Laszlo Moholy-Nagy, who had been on the faculty of the original Bauhaus in Weimar, Germany, in the 1920s, was plagued with financial troubles and closed after a short time. The Field mansion was demolished after World War II.[13]

A three-story structure, raised above a high basement, the Field mansion (figure 47) was faced in red brick trimmed with light-colored sandstone and decorated on the principal façade by attenuated Néo-Grec pilasters, a heavy stringcourse set between the first and second stories, an even heavier cornice above the second story with a high frieze of geometrical design, and second-story balconies having an intricate intertwining of ironwork. From directly in front on Prairie Avenue, the Field mansion's tall, shingled mansard resting on the prominent cornice below, and topped by a conspicuous cornice above, looked like

Figure 47
Marshall Field mansion,
1905 Prairie Avenue,
Chicago (1873). Chicago
Historical Society.

an overly large hat planted firmly on the boxlike form beneath. But this street façade was unsettlingly asymmetrical: the right-hand dormer was diminished in size and awkwardly placed, and the large first- and second-story windows below on the right were moved to the terminus of the wall, with two small secondary windows interjected like after-thoughts between the central bay and the right terminal bay. The reason for the seemingly awkward fenestration on the west front of the house was that the house was intended to be viewed mainly from the angle to the right side, where the corner was cut diagonally to provide a transition to the varied planes of the garden front. Like Yale's East Divinity Hall, the Field mansion was best seen from the angle. Viewed thus, the formality of the street front to the left contrasted markedly with the more informal elements facing the garden to the right. Most prominent on the garden side was the gently bowed hemicycle of the conservatory windows. An ornate ironwork fence surrounded the property.

Hunt's most significant domestic work of the 1870s, however, was in Newport, which continued to draw the Hunt family for the summer and early fall months each year. The family was now enlarged by Kitty (Catharine), born in 1868, and Joe, born in 1870, besides young Dickie. For the adults as well as the three children, Hill Top Cottage provided space which they did not have in New York, and undoubtedly the move each summer to Newport gave them all a sense of greater freedom than they had in the city. Like his own family during his childhood, Hunt and his wife and their children were very close, and especially in Newport they could share many activities.

An incident that seemed to reflect badly on the Hunts' family relations and their integrity brought them considerable distress. In 1868, John La Farge, William Hunt's former pupil, did a sketch of Dickie, still in curls, which was incorporated in a painting with a greyhound. The Hunts did not consider the portrait satisfactory and refused to accept it, even though Richard sent La Farge three hundred dollars to compensate him for his time and expense. They understood that La Farge was not satisfied with the painting either. Several years later, La Farge reworked the portrait, exhibited it, and put it up for sale on various occasions, bringing about newspaper criticism of Hunt for allowing what was said to be an unpaid-for picture of his son to be "hawked about the city." This personal attack particularly offended Catharine, who demanded and got a newspaper correction and an apology from the critic.[14]

In 1869, Hunt began to enlarge Hill Top Cottage with alterations, which went on intermittently for a full year. He also acquired adjoining property on Church Street, incorporating the grounds with his own. In

June 1871, it was reported in the local press that Hunt, who had just arrived in Newport for the summer season, now had "the most attractive lawn in Newport." Although a large house, Hill Top was not pretentious, but it was centrally located and became a Newport landmark.[15]

The Hunts entertained frequently and were very much involved in Newport social affairs. When President Grant and his family came to the resort, Mrs. Hunt was honored one evening by being seated next to the general at dinner. The president and his wife, Catharine reminisced, were simple and unpretentious people, though their children, she thought, were just the opposite. When the Grant children went to a tea party with the offspring of Charles H. Russell, Catharine's brother-in-law, at Oaklawn, one of the Russell children exclaimed over the beauty of the table decorations, only to be cut short by a young Grant who replied: "We only drink out of gold cups at home." For intellectual stimulation, Hunt joined the Town and Country Club of Newport, which Julia Ward Howe founded in the summer of 1871. Members met regularly for lectures on such subjects as natural history or philosophy or for a performance by a visiting musician or dance group. By 1881 the new Casino, designed by McKim, Mead & White, was the focus of Newport social life, and the Hunts were often seen there. But Richard's life in Newport was by no means just a round of luncheons, dinners, balls, and drives in fashionable society or the more cerebral pleasures of lecture attendance or musical and dance recitals, for Hunt was occupied in his summer studio with his creative endeavors. His Newport commissions of these early and mid-1870s years are rather similar and yet show an inventiveness and originality that the architect seldom again equaled.[16]

Hunt's freedom and inventiveness in his Newport dwellings of this period were in keeping with much Newport building in the post–Civil War years. The "eclectic extravagance" which broke away from the older fashions of Gothic Revival and Italian bracketed was due in large part to the availability of new machine-made, standardized building elements, which could be assembled by workmen with limited skills. The growing impact of industrialization brought new products and new ways of dealing with materials, while at the same time it meant a breaking up of traditional work relationships and a rejection of many old standards. In domestic design, this led to considerable experimentation and usually a new openness and informality. Although many standards of building design and construction seemed to be lowered, particularly in the judgment of a later time which contemptuously rejected the elaboration of detail and the often unfocused fussiness of Victorian clutter, much of the architecture from this period possesses many charms for us today and affords us considerable aesthetic pleasure. By the 1870s the stick style, emphasizing skeletal articulation and primary organic relationships, was, as Antoinette Downing and Vincent Scully have suggested, developing into a more elaborate "full bloom stick baroque." At the same time, with land prices shooting upward in Newport, there was a movement toward greater opulence and luxury, which would continue to new heights in the 1890s. Other than the Griswold house, Hunt's early Newport houses have largely been forgotten, but they embodied some of the most interesting work he ever did.[17]

Following the Griswold house, which was discussed in chapter 10, Hunt's next domestic commission in Newport was a Swiss chalet for Mrs. Colford Jones on Halidon Avenue. Drawings in the Hunt Collection indicate the architect was at work on this dwelling by 1866, and it was probably finished the next spring. Composed as a rectangular block with a projecting porch on the rear side, the two-and-one-half story chalet (figure 48) included a distinctive second-story projecting balcony extending around three sides of the house, sheltered on the two principal faces of the dwelling by the roof overhang and the outer edges of the attic story. Below the windows at the first-story level on the front and one side other small balconies were placed. The Jones chalet presented a fascinating interplay of vertical, horizontal, and diagonal sticks, and the patterns of light and shadow on the wall surfaces were made all the more complex by the scroll saw-cut balustrades, the carving on the braces, and the scalloped lower ends of the vertical sheathing on the attic. In later years, the Hunt-designed cottage was largely enclosed by massive additions on the back and at one end.[18]

In 1870 the Hunts purchased a small cottage standing between Hill Top Cottage and the corner of Church Street as well as a triangle of land located a few hundred feet to the east, at the southeast corner of the intersection of Greenough Place and Catherine Street, to which they had the building moved. By the fall of 1870, Hunt was working on the redesign of the cottage, and in 1871 he turned over this dwelling at 33 Greenough Place to Colonel George E. Waring, Jr., a dairyman, author, and sanitary engineer, who was active in the Town and Country Club. The cottage was called The Hypothenuse, since it was built diagonally at the corner and faced the angle at the juncture of the two streets, with a triangular lawn in front. The small house was widely admired, one early commentator calling it "a model of the union of exterior architectural beauty and substantial interior convenience and refined comfort."[19]

A largely symmetrical, two-story structure, topped by a small attic, the Waring cottage (figure 49) successfully combines somewhat dispa-

Figure 48
Perspective, Mrs. Colford Jones chalet, Newport, Rhode Island (1866). Courtesy The American Institute of Architects Foundation/Prints and Drawings Collection, Washington, D.C. Photo by James Garrison.

Figure 49
The Hypothenuse, the Col. George Waring house, Newport, Rhode Island (1871). Courtesy Wayne Andrews and the Newport Historical Society.

rate elements into a picturesque whole. The heavy roof, which is both hipped and gambrel, with the lower part of the gambrel treated as a mansard, pushes the house toward the ground, while the roof overhang and the bracketed cornice over the first story reinforce the earth-hugging, horizontal feel. A portico of Doric columns screens the entrance, while above this rises the central feature of the façade—a rustic, alpine gable containing a bargeboard arch of perforated wood, above a large, flower-filled, corbeled window box. Double-window dormers in the mansard roof frame the central gable element and form side bays with the first-story windows, giving the cottage a slight colonial revival appearance. Although the Hill Top Cottage estate has long since disappeared, the Waring cottage still stands on the site where it was rebuilt.

More pretentious, more picturesque, and more important at the time was Villa Cushman (figure 50), also known as The Corners. It stood just a few steps from Colonel Waring's cottage at 49 Catherine Street, at the corner of Rhode Island Avenue, on a small knoll overlooking the Atlantic. Hunt designed this rambling, stick-style house in 1870–1871 for the famous actress Charlotte Cushman, who remained a close friend and frequent correspondent of the Hunts for the rest of her life. Although the architect apparently ignored most of Miss Cushman's instructions for her dwelling, making it "so much more than a cottage and almost like a château," she nonetheless found it "pretty, and much admired," and a very comfortable place to return to from her frequent tours. The towering chimneys and the peaked roofs, topped by cresting and finials, the high windows, the sharply hooded dormers, and the dramatically corbelled little balcony in the attic all contributed to the vertical thrust of the two-and-one-half-story structure. The posts of the enveloping porches echoed the verticality of the main mass, while the broad, low porch roofs provided a sort of spreading skirt that tied the building to the ground. Many elements of the structural frame were clearly indicated in the exterior design. Villa Cushman was destroyed by fire in the 1920s.[20]

In 1871, Hunt also worked on a cottage on Catherine Street for Thomas G. Appleton of Boston, whom he as a youth had known in Europe, and on the adjoining lot a summer residence for George C. Richardson of New York. Both men were bachelors and wanted summer residences where they could entertain guests. Little information has been found concerning the Richardson house other than that it was painted "in deeply contrasting colors, the trimmings scarlet" and was said to have cost some $50,000. Tom Appleton, like so many of Hunt's clients, was a close friend of Richard and Catharine, although the latter

Figure 50
Elevations, Charlotte
Cushman house, New-
port, Rhode Island (early
version, 1870). Courtesy
The American Institute
of Architects Founda-
tion/Prints and
Drawings Collection,
Washington, D.C. Photo
by James Garrison.

sometimes wished that the "immensely original" conversationalist and wit would not drop by at Hill Top Cottage in the morning and stay all day, as he often did. Like Villa Cushman, Appleton's house (figure 51) was highly picturesque, with balconies and variously shaped dormers popping out at different levels, a multisurfaced painted shingle roof, and a profusion of posts, brackets, and diagonal braces. The exterior wall surfaces involved a complex interplay of varied textures: the ground story was faced with rubblestone, while the second story included both wood and colored slates laid in patterns. The central gable feature of the Waring cottage was here enlarged to form substantial, timberwork balconies at two levels arranged beneath a gable-enveloped arch. A broad veranda surrounded a good part of this animated house, pulling it to the ground and helping tie the parts together, while at the same time adding to the complex interplay of voids and solids in the design.[21]

Just a short distance from Villa Cushman and the Appleton and Richardson houses on the north side of Old Beach Road at 140 Rhode Island Avenue was Linden Gate, the summer residence of Henry G. Marquand, a long-time friend and patron of Hunt. Marquand was a railroad financier and philanthropist who became president of the Board of Trustees of the Metropolitan Museum of Art. Linden Gate, built in 1872, was considerably larger and more elegant than Colonel Waring's cottage, Charlotte Cushman's house, or Tom Appleton's place, and it was attractively situated in the middle of good-sized grounds. The three-and-one-half-story house became so jammed with art objects Marquand had collected that it became known as "Bric-a-brac Hall" in the neighborhood. More sober and restrained than the Cushman and Appleton houses, Linden Gate (figure 52) gave an impression of great strength and solidity. The first story was faced with random coursed ashlar, the second story with patterned red and black brick, and the third and attic stories primarily with wood. The central gable element of the Waring and Appleton houses was here transformed into a great, soaring, timber-framed gable enclosing as a bargeboard a lancet arch, the whole resting on a corbeled balcony. The lively play of light and shadow within the central gable was echoed on a smaller scale in the dormer gables set into the very steep roof. The upward thrust of the higher elements gave the building a Gothic feel. The posts and beams set in the upper exterior surfaces were clearly applied decoratively rather than being organically united to the framework, somewhat like the Queen Anne designs of Philip Webb and Richard Norman Shaw of about the same time in England. A porte cochere was placed on the west side of the dwelling, offices were located on the north side, and the most important lower-floor rooms faced the east and the south. Analyzing Linden Gate in 1895, Montgomery Schuyler saw it as transitional to the larger "palaces" of Newport, and he emphasized its "unity and repose in spite of its comparatively complicated disposition and its variety of material." This was, Schuyler judged, truly "a sober . . . vigorous and individual piece of work." Like many of the large residences of Newport, Linden Gate eventually suffered the indignity of being converted into apartments in its old age. This splendid house was destroyed by fire on February 18, 1973.[22]

At the same time that Linden Gate was being built, Hunt was involved in the enlargement of the then grandest house of Newport, Château-sur-Mer (figure 53). Constructed twenty years earlier, in 1851–1852, for William Shepard Wetmore, a prosperous merchant in the China trade, Château-sur-Mer was designed by Seth Bradford, a local Newport builder, for a site in the midst of large grounds on the east side of Bellevue Avenue. Bradford's mansion was austere and heavy, built of rugged Fall River granite ashlar, three stories high, with an entrance tower rising an additional story, and covered by a hipped gambrel roof having a gentle concave lower slope over the upper story. Although a large veranda extended around much of three sides of the house, giving a feeling of some openness at the ground level, the mansion contrasted markedly with the greater openness and delicacy of detail of Hunt's contemporary Newport houses.[23]

George Peabody Wetmore, who had inherited Château-sur-Mer after the death of his father in 1862, decided at the time of his marriage in 1869 to remodel his dwelling, and he commissioned Hunt to make the changes. The first remodeling was completed by 1873. Subsequently, in the 1880s, Hunt was once more called upon by Wetmore for further alterations and enlargement of the mansion, which became an important center of political activity when Wetmore served as governor of Rhode Island (1885–1889) and U.S. senator from that state (1895–1913). As well as making many exterior and interior structural changes, Hunt provided for elaborate interior paneling, carvings, and painted decorations and even suggested furniture for the principal rooms. The walnut-paneled library, designed by the Florentine decorator Luigi Frullini, received in its many carved surfaces perhaps the most extensive elaboration in the house. Winslow Ames, in his important detailed study of the alterations of this building, has characterized Hunt's work as the "transformation" of Château-sur-Mer. At the termination of Hunt's labors, this was indeed a very different building from the original.[24]

In the first alteration Hunt rebuilt and slightly enlarged a service

Figure 51
Thomas G. Appleton
house, Newport, Rhode
Island (1871). Courtesy
The American Institute
of Architects Foun-
dation/Prints and
Drawings Collection,
Washington, D.C.
Reproduction by James
Garrison.

Figure 52
Linden Gate, the Henry
G. Marquand house,
Newport, Rhode Island
(1873). Courtesy The
American Institute of
Architects Foundation/
Prints and Drawings
Collection, Washington,
D.C. Reproduction by
James Garrison.

Figure 53
Château-sur-Mer, the
George Peabody Wet-
more mansion, New-
Port, Rhode Island
(1872+). The Preserva-
tion Society of Newport
County Photos.

wing on the north side of the mansion into a large billiard room, adding to the east of this a magnificent stairhall entered from a vestibule and porte cochere with Néo-Grec detail; a new service block was erected with butler's pantry, a china room, other service rooms, a service staircase, and, on the second floor, a two-room nursery and a bedroom. On the east side of the original house, Hunt gutted a large area to build a balconied three-story hall, topped by a skylight. At the same time he raised the roof of the dwelling and transformed it into a mansard structure with a steep lower slope and a pointed tower over the new entrance. Eastlake woodwork was installed in the new center hall, the billiard room, and the stairhall. The former drawing room was redesigned as a French ballroom. The former entrance hall, paved with marble, was refurbished with a new ceiling; later, the old front door was made into a long window. In Hunt's second "campaign" on the mansion, he raised the dining room and service wings by an additional story and lifted the skylight into a higher mansard roof over the central hall well. By the 1890s, Château-sur-Mer had been enlarged to a grand scale indeed.[25]

A small commercial building, looking very much like a group of picturesque adjoining houses, completes the record of Hunt's major Newport commissions of the early and mid-1870s. The Travers Block (figure 54), dating from 1870–1871 and still standing and very much in use on Bellevue Avenue, is a long structure, built of rich, deep-red brick, with decorative nonstructural half-timbering and bracketed eaves, housing a row of small shops. Above the street-level stores were bachelor apartments in the second story and in the mansard-roofed attic. The Travers Block has a quaint and cozy pseudo-medieval appearance so often echoed in the 1920s and the 1930s in similar shop complexes built elsewhere in the United States.[26]

Later, in 1881–1883, Hunt designed yet another Newport cottage in a similar picturesque mode, recalling his domestic work of the early 1870s. The three-story house for Professor Charles W. Shields (figure 55) at Ochre Point and Ruggles avenues was built on an intricate timberwork frame resting upon a basement of roughly dressed stone, which rose into the walls in some areas of the first and second stories. Projecting bays on the principal fronts were capped by hipped gables connected by a large loggia at the third-story level. Somewhat awkward in the treatment of the surface planes, yet vigorously assertive in the bold expression of inner volumes and structural materials, the Shields house was a highly individualized building. In later years the house was converted into apartments and extensively remodeled within and altered without. At this time much of the exterior detailing was removed, new rooms

Figure 54
Travers Block, Bellevue
Avenue, Newport,
Rhode Island (1871).
Courtesy Newport His-
torical Society.

Figure 55
Charles W. Shields
house, Newport, Rhode
Island (1883). Courtesy
The American Institute
of Architects Founda-
tion/Prints and
Drawings Collection,
Washington, D.C. Re-
production by James
Garrison.

were added, the loggia was enclosed, and the exterior walls were uniformly covered by stucco. In its contemporary bland disguise, the piling and interpenetration of the basic elements of Hunt's house are still evident, but the force and vigor of the design have largely been wiped away.[27]

The picturesque mode of design was also evident in a country house that Hunt worked on for Henry Ward Beecher in the 1870s. By this time Beecher was the best-known preacher in the United States. From his pulpit at Plymouth Church in Brooklyn he articulated the American pieties for his contemporaries probably better than anyone else in the nation. Although Beecher had some years earlier written that ideally men should design their own houses and not rely on architects and their "conventional" plans, he nonetheless had accepted the need for architects, considering what he saw as the low level of national taste. At that time Beecher had expressed his own preference for a "mazy diversity, that most unlooked-for intricacy in a dwelling, and the utter variation of lines in the extreme which pleases the eye." A house, he suggested, should grow piecemeal, reflecting the changes in the lives of the owner and his family. By the 1870s, Beecher regarded Hunt "as one of the few men in his profession who are artists rather than artizans" and he made it known that he was most eager to have the pleasure of being able to say: " 'I live in one of Hunt's houses.' " Although by 1874 Beecher was consulting with Hunt about his house and although Hunt provided him with plans by the middle of the decade, it was a few years before the cottage was built, and as completed in 1878 the residence may not have followed Hunt's plans. The Peekskill house, however, fulfilled the clergyman's architectural ideals, for it was a ramble of projecting bays and pavilions, assorted gables and dormers, oddly placed chimneys, and a large stick-style wraparound porch. The structure had very much an added-to and lived-in look but less coherence than most of Hunt's domestic designs of the 1870s.[28]

Hunt's prodigious activity of the early seventies took its toll. In the late winter of 1874, he returned exhausted on a wet and snowy day from a trip to Peekskill to look over the site for Beecher's house. On the following Sunday in church, he came down with a chill. A severe siege of double pneumonia ensued, and for nearly three months the architect was completely incapacitated, "out of his head a great deal." At the same time he was again plagued by boils. Catharine, who was herself very ill with a high fever for several weeks, was given the power of attorney to attend to the business of the office, and during the time that Richard was recuperating she acted as an intermediary between her husband and his office staff. By early spring Hunt's doctor ordered him to take a six months' break from all professional work. On May 5, 1874, therefore, Richard and Catharine, with their three children and two servants, once more sailed for Europe. Once again Hunt would find his inspiration renewed by the art and the architecture of the Old World. When he returned home, he was to move in new directions in his work.[29]

The European visit of 1874–1875 provided an intermission in Hunt's professional career, removing him for a year almost entirely from the pressures of creative work and the demands of a busy office. By early May 1874, when the Hunts left for Europe, most of the public, commercial, and domestic commissions of the previous few years had been completed, although a few large projects such as the Lenox Library and the Tribune Building were still under way. The panic of 1873 and the severe depression it set off had largely brought new construction to a halt, and for much of the seventies, after Hunt's return from abroad, the architect had few new projects. His health had been weakened by the overwork of the early seventies, and probably the three months' illness in the winter of 1874, coming as it did in his mid-forties, precipitated something of a middle-age crisis for Hunt. Commonly in such midlife crises, an individual becomes acutely aware of his own limitations, of the constricting boundaries of his life, and of his own mortality. And the sense of transiency and of the passage of time was surely intensified by family tragedies that occurred during this period. Hunt seemed to draw into himself during the mid–1870s, reassessing his work and reintegrating his ideas. On a few occasions late in the decade he spoke in public about his views on architecture, giving indication of some of his most basic standards and beliefs. By the end of the seventies, when he once more undertook several new and important projects, Hunt began work in what were for him new styles, with a mastery of design that he had seldom achieved earlier.

When they arrived in England, the Hunts went directly to London, where they remained for a few weeks with Catharine's sister and her husband, Emily and Henry Chauncey. In London, the Irishwoman who had come with them from New York as nursemaid to four-year-old Joe was sent back to her home in Ireland when it was discovered that she suffered from an incurable illness; she was replaced by an English governness hired to care for all three youngsters. Their other servant, Joseph, a French Canadian, acted as majordomo and took care of their travel arrangements.

In the middle of June, the family moved on to Cologne by way of Brussels. They had planned to continue traveling at a leisurely pace but were obliged to stop in Cologne for several weeks when Joe fell desperately ill with scarlet fever. For a time, Richard, Catharine, and the manservant were put under quarantine at their hotel with the little boy, separated from the two older children and their governness, who stayed in a private home. Fortunately, the Hotel du Nord overlooked the Rhine, and during their long confinement they could watch the vessels

16

CLOUDS OVER THE SEVENTIES

on the river from their rooms. Often Catharine saw the sun rise over the river after sleepless hours with her sick child. While Joe recuperated they stayed on in Cologne, often visiting the cathedral, the city fortifications, and the zoological park. Hunt was acquainted with the architect in charge of maintaining the cathedral, and he frequently went there to sketch. The child's illness was a terrible physical and emotional drain on them, especially on Catharine, who was his constant nurse for six weeks.[1]

To add to the strain, the Hunts were shocked by receiving news at the end of June that Richard's older brother John had taken his own life in Paris. While Catharine remained with the two younger children in Cologne, Richard hurried to Paris to try to settle his brother's affairs and took twelve-year-old Dick with him to enroll him there in a school. For years, John had been the black sheep of the Hunt family. Trained as a physician, he had settled in Paris, where he had for some twenty years had a liaison with a woman, Célestine Matheu, who was, as Catharine gently put it, "not of his own class." The couple had a daughter, Jeanne, who became hopelessly insane; Catharine believed that this had occurred because the girl had been brutally teased at school about being illegitimate. For years, John had led a double life, keeping knowledge of the fact that he had a mistress and a child from his own family and from most of his friends in Paris. On a short visit to New York a few years before, John had finally told Catharine his secret, and she had begged him to marry Célestine and return with her to the United States to practice medicine in his own country. Célestine later informed Catharine that when John had returned to Paris and had proposed that they marry, she had refused because she felt that she would hinder him professionally. As it was, his position had made impossible even in Paris a medical practice of the sort Catharine felt he ought to have; instead he ministered to working people and the poor. In the summer of 1874, long weeks of severe illness, worry about his daughter, and chronic insomnia had brought on a deepening depression. One day, overwhelmed by his situation, he sent Célestine to an apothecary for a purgative and while she was gone he slashed his throat with a razor. John, Catharine wrote, had "a hopeless inconsequent nature, but a warm heart, which made all love him, who were brought into contact with him." Richard arranged for his brother's burial at Père-Lachaise cemetery in Paris and employed a friend from Lefuel's atelier to erect a monument at the gravesite. He also helped Célestine find a cottage in the country, but young Jeanne had to be confined at an asylum at Charenton. John's paintings and his library were sent to the United

States; his medical books were subsequently presented to the Presbyterian Hospital in New York.[2]

After the tension of the weeks in Cologne and the shock of the tragedy in Paris, the Hunts greatly needed rest, and for a month they stopped at the watering place of Schwalbach in Germany. Here Catharine took a cure of twenty-one baths, while Hunt devoted his days to sketching. Catharine characteristically was delighted that another visitor at Schwalbach, the Queen of Naples, was much taken by young Joe and gave him several presents of toys. Late in August they went south to the Italian lakes region for a long driving tour. They were in Switzerland in September, visiting Lucerne, sketching at the Castle of Chillon, and then relaxing in Geneva.[3]

Once again that year, however, family troubles disturbed their extended holiday. At Geneva they were abruptly asked to return to London to assist the Chaunceys. The panic of 1873 had hit Henry Chauncey hard, and in his worry over his financial situation he had become seriously ill. For some weeks in the fall Catharine remained with her sister, while Chauncey recuperated. Finally, when he was able, Chauncey returned to the United States, while his wife and daughter went on to Paris with the Hunts. By this time, Richard was very restless and wanted to return home to work. Keeping in regular touch with his office staff, who sent him periodic reports on the progress of the Lenox Library, the Tribune Building, and other jobs, he wrote that he was ready to return if he were needed but reported that his doctors had advised him to stay away from regular work until the following spring. He confessed that he was still far from well: at times he had difficulty getting his breath and he was plagued by weak ankles and by problems with one hand.[4]

So the Hunts remained in Europe. Lingering in Paris in November, they frequently saw Theodore Roosevelt, Hunt's friend, the father of the future president. Hunt renewed his friendship with Viollet-le-Duc on this visit and enjoyed a few days with the architect-writer at the Château of Pierrefonds, which the Frenchman had restored—overrestored, some felt. When Henry Chauncey came back from the United States to his wife and daughter in Paris, the Hunts went south to Nice, where they spent the Christmas season. There Kitty came down with the scarlet fever that earlier had struck her little brother, but her bout with the illness was much less severe. Dick, who had been at school in Paris since October, had been so bothered by trouble with his eyes that he was allowed to leave school and join them in Nice. Along the country roads around Nice, Richard made ink and wash and watercolor sketches of the scenery, and indoors he captured his children in moments of joy and delight in holiday merrymaking.[5]

Early in 1875 they traveled to Italy. In Genoa, Richard fell ill with pleurisy, but despite his discomfort they went directly on to Rome, where they stayed at the Hotel Grand Bretagne. He gradually recovered, and in Rome they saw many American acquaintances who were wintering or living permanently there. The younger children enjoyed the Pincian Gardens, where they could see Punch and Judy shows, while Dick accompanied his father to sketch at several of the major monuments and churches.[6]

In March, the family started north, stopping at Siena and Florence, and then went on to Bologna and Venice. By April they were back in Paris, and they sailed from Liverpool at the end of May. But their troubles continued; late in their year of travel, Joseph, their manservant, was arrested for a misdemeanor, and Hunt became embroiled with lawyers and the courts in trying, though without success, to get him released. Then on the ship, just before landing in New York, a man entered their stateroom at night and attempted to rob them. Richard chased him from the cabin, whereupon the intruder drew a knife and was only subdued after other passengers came to Hunt's rescue. The year abroad had been a difficult and troubled time, and they were all happy to return home.[7]

During the months after their arrival in June 1875, Richard and Catharine devoted themselves in large part to preparations for the Centennial Exhibition at Philadelphia. Hunt was invited to serve as a juror for the architectural exhibits, and he also was instrumental in getting the American Institute of Architects to cooperate with the Centennial officials. At the ninth convention of the Institute, held in Baltimore in November 1875, Hunt offered a resolution "that the several chapters of the American Institute of Architects be requested to take such measures as may be necessary to have the professional work of their members properly represented at the Centennial Exhibition." The A.I.A. chapters contributed, but not generously.[8]

In New York City, Catharine was named to a committee set up to stimulate interest in the Centennial both in the city and the state. The group arranged for an evening of *tableaux vivants* at the Union League Club and presented scenes from one hundred years of American life to 1875. Such tableaux had long been popular at informal social gatherings among the Hunts' friends; posing in elaborate costumes against carefully detailed backdrops was considered not only entertaining and amusing but also instructive and morally elevating. Richard, who immensely enjoyed this sort of thing, posed in a tableau of "The Nations," while Catharine represented "Asia" in another scene, loaded down with borrowed Astor jewels; "barbaric in pearl and gold, motionless and calm, she stood leaning on the back of a tiger" (figure 56).[9]

Planning for the Centennial Exhibition had begun some years earlier. On March 3, 1871, Congress had passed "an act for celebrating the one hundredth anniversary of American independence, by holding an international exhibition of arts, manufactures, and products of the soil and mine" in Philadelphia, and a Centennial Commission was set up to supervise the work of preparation. By the spring of 1873 a tract of 450 acres in west Fairmount Park had been selected as the site, and toward the end of that year Hermann Joseph Schwarzmann, a Bavarian immigrant, was named engineer of the exhibition grounds and later architect-in-chief. More than anyone else, Schwarzmann was responsible for the design of the fair: he landscaped the grounds, arranged the building sites, and designed thirty-four of the two hundred and forty-nine structures. Thirty-six nations took part in the Centennial. On May 10, 1876, President Ulysses S. Grant and Emperor Pedro II of Brazil were the honored guests at the opening ceremonies, which were attended by over a hundred thousand people. Although the Philadelphia Exhibition has often been pilloried for the undiscriminating eclecticism of much of the architecture and for the extravagance of design of many of the products shown, foreign visitors by and large responded favorably to what they saw, admiring the grounds and lavishing praise on the American-made products. The outstanding attraction of the fair was the giant Corliss steam engine, which provided power for hundreds of machines in Machinery Hall. The exhibition was an obvious success in providing Americans with a visual display of their material accomplishments in one hundred years of nationhood.[10]

The architectural entries for the fair were shown in two groups, some under the category of "Architecture and Engineering" and others under "Art." Building plans, drawings and sketches, and specimens of building materials were included. Hunt and a Danish architect were the only architects among the judges, but men from other, related, professions also served as judges of these exhibits. There were some two hundred seventy American entries as well as a few from abroad. For a good part of a very hot June, Hunt was occupied with his work at the exhibition, and Catharine came to Philadelphia twice to see the exhibits. The following year Hunt was awarded "a special bronze medal" by the United States Centennial Commission "in recognition of valuable services rendered to the Administration of the International Exhibition of 1876."[11]

Figure 56
Catharine Hunt as
"Asia" (1875). From an
old photograph, Hunt
Papers.

On October 11 and 12, the American Institute of Architects held its tenth annual convention in Philadelphia in conjunction with the fair. At this meeting the long-time president, Richard Upjohn, was replaced by Thomas U. Walter, the architect of the United States Capitol extension and Hunt's one-time employer. Hunt's talk to his colleagues on the architectural work at the exhibition was a major contribution to the Institute program.

Although in his speech Hunt mainly described the buildings and the exhibits at the fair, he did make some telling comments on the state of American architecture in the Centennial year, and his talk provided the fullest estimate he ever gave of the profession's standing at a time when he had himself contributed to American building for over two decades. The tone of his talk was decidedly defensive and apologetic.[12]

Hunt found considerable evidence of change and progress during the preceding decades in the materials shown at the Philadelphia Exhibition. He was hopeful that the display of industrial arts would help to educate and cultivate laymen as well as to instruct professional students and specialists. The exhibits, he believed, provided impressive evidence of the new care that both public bodies and private corporations were taking to improve health conditions and make life easier and more pleasant. In America, as in Europe, he affirmed, the spirit of progress was clear.

Although American architects had accomplished a great deal in adapting modern improvements to the requirements of American culture, still the architectural profession in this country had manifestly not attained "the elevated position" it had in Europe. Architects, he felt, must have the sympathy and the understanding of the general public, but they would not get this response in any meaningful way until art education had become more general. He expressed the hope that the Centennial Exhibition would stimulate and improve the industrial arts in the United States as had the London Exhibition of 1851 in England.

Hunt was impressed by the "striking natural advantage" of the site of the fair, and the grounds, he thought, had been "tastefully laid out as a landscape garden." He judged that with few exceptions the main exhibition buildings were "well adapted to their various purposes . . ., appropriate in design, and neatly executed." The huge, twenty-acre Main Exhibition Building, constructed of iron, glass, and brick, had, he suggested, a "light and pleasing" interior, which, however, was "wanting in effect and variety." All in all, he thought the "general effect of the building . . . satisfactory, considering its temporary character." Machinery Hall, though somewhat smaller, was more substantial looking than the main building, while Agricultural Hall had "a very satisfactory feature" in its great arches, springing directly from the ground. Memorial Hall, "by far the most pretentious structure on the Exhibition grounds," which would be used as a permanent museum, had, however, a poor scale, he felt, and commonplace and meager ornamentation. The several smaller buildings housing the state exhibits and the special exhibits were, Hunt judged, mostly "beneath criticism, architecturally considered."

Although some of the large temporary buildings were impressive, architecture had fared badly in the Centennial exhibits, "the designs being few in number and mostly of minor importance." Foreign drawings were limited and disappointing in execution. The American drawings brought to the exhibition struck Hunt by their "ambitious pretense . . . overloaded as they too often are with meretricious ornament." Characteristic of the American entries and of American architecture generally was "a certain insane desire to carry up some portion of a building to an excessive height." Moreover, many of the designs attempted "to produce novelty of effect, often resulting in a want of harmony and repose so essential to good work." All in all,

the [architectural] Exhibition is wanting in much that would render it interesting and instructive, not only to the profession, but to a large class of the public, who would certainly appreciate a thoroughness both in architectural design and construction, which prevails abroad, and which is wanting with us; due to a more scientific and judicious use of the various building materials, and to the higher standard of taste, which naturally exists in the Old World.

Hunt's 1855 view of Old World achievements and of American deficiencies had changed little in two decades of practice. His emphasis on "harmony and repose so essential to good work" nonetheless provides an important key to his later endeavors.

While Hunt worked in Philadelphia at the Centennial in the early summer of 1876, Catharine and the children, who now included Esther, born on September 5, 1875, took a cottage at Fishkill, close to Tioranda, the mansion owned by her brother, Joseph Howland. As usual, the family spent the latter part of the summer at Newport. Their close friend Charlotte Cushman, whom they had often visited in Newport the summer before, had died in February; Catharine felt that the actress was "the most brilliant talker" she had ever listened to, and she was greatly missed. In the fall Dick was entered at St. Paul's School in Concord, New Hampshire; some time later, after a severe injury suffered in a sledding accident, he was taken out of school and privately tutored until he entered the Massachusetts Institute of Technology in 1879. For several years Dick worked during summers in the office for his father. Subsequently, he studied in Paris at the Ecole des Beaux-Arts, and in 1887 he joined his father as a partner in the firm.[13]

Despite his dislike of speaking in public, Hunt agreed to give an address on October 30, 1877, before the Fourth Church Congress of the Protestant Episcopal Church, meeting at Chickering Hall in New York, on the topic, "The Church Architecture That We Need." Hunt was becoming increasingly interested in church building, and this was obviously a subject that he had been thinking about. His talk was historical and scholarly; it showed well his absorption in the development of historical styles and his wish to glean general truths and architectural principles from the best work of the past. Whatever might be done in the present, he asserted, had to be done with knowledge of and sensitivity toward the developments of the past. And yet he emphasized that architecture must never be servile copying: as he put it, "Real progress can be hoped for only in originality of ideas. . . . Our architecture should be true rather than traditional."[14]

In this talk, Hunt attempted to define the most suitable architectural style for the Protestant Episcopal Church of his own day by first looking over the styles of church architecture of the past and reviewing what were different needs in relation to various building types. He then summarized what he believed were the requirements of the Protestant Episcopal Church: a building must be adapted to both worship and instruction; it should embody "dignity" and "repose" and appeal to the sense of awe; it "should be truthful throughout in its arrangement, its construction, and decoration"; and it should provide appropriate facilities for the officiating clergy and be so arranged that all the congregation might see and hear. Well-adapted materials should be employed and the construction should be sound. Painting and sculpture should be utilized to intensify the monumental effect and to stimulate religious emotions.[15]

After these general considerations, Hunt got down to specifics. He concluded that attempts to adapt the basilica form to the Protestant Church had generally failed: this type of building, with its long nave and aisles, subdividing piers, and an altar widely separated from the congregation, was unsuitable for Protestant worship. Circular buildings, he contended, were also inappropriate since they usually had bad acoustics. Oblong churches without aisles were not objectionable if of moderate size, but they tended to be monotonous. But most appropriate for Protestant services, he affirmed, was the cruciform shape, with transepts and a nave of relatively short length. "The nearer we approach to the Byzantine type, where the church becomes square in plan, and the Greek cross replaces the Latin, the more nearly we arrive at the desired solution." The Greek cross form, he said, had the advantages of a variety of perspective effects and the possibility of various treatments of the arms of the cross; deep recessed galleries could be utilized above the crossing; and a lantern or dome could accentuate the crossing and produce a monumental effect. "In fact, the Byzantine church [the Greek cross form], without doubt, presents superior advantages over all other types for Protestant worship."[16]

Hunt's address, largely echoing Viollet-le-Duc in his principles but not in his choice of style, indicated the direction of some of his work to come; but the speech was generally technical, pedantic, and tedious. At the close, Reverend Henry C. Potter of Grace Church in New York, who was presiding, responded that "the excellent essay we have just listened to reminds me of a remark once made by a Bishop at the consecration of a very costly church. When asked how he liked the church, he said that he had only two little faults to speak of: one was, you could not see, and the second was, you could not hear." Laughter ensued, the *Church Journal* reported. Probably this weak witticism provided a real sense of relief for the audience after Hunt's long and dry commentary on architectural styles.[17]

As a leader of the profession, Hunt increasingly was called upon to give his views not only before private groups but also before governmental bodies. In subsequent years he would spend considerable time providing expert Congressional testimony in Washington, D.C. In New York he soon became involved in the long and bitterly contested problem of the state capitol building at Albany. Designed principally by Thomas S. Fuller (with contributions by Arthur Gilman and Augustus Laver) in what was described as an Italian Renaissance style, the massive new capitol was begun in 1871. Originally the cost of the building had been put at $4 million, but by 1875, when it was not even completed to the third story, some $7 million had already been spent. By then the mounting costs and the questionable suitability of the design had aroused so much criticism that the state legislature established a new Capitol Commission to investigate the work and see what if any changes might be made in the original plans. The Commission appointed an architectural advisory board consisting of Henry Hobson Richardson, Frederick Law Olmsted, and Leopold Eidlitz, who recommended various changes from the original plans in the interior and urged as well that the original style be abandoned and that the uncompleted portion of the building be designed in a Romanesque style. Their report was submitted to the state senate, and on request the advisory architects submitted full drawings and obtained contractors' estimates of costs. Richardson and Eidlitz were shortly employed to continue the capitol construction on the basis of their recommended changes, while Olmsted served as a general adviser.[18]

When work on the capitol following the new plans and designs began in 1876, however, criticism built up over the changes, and soon a large segment of the architectural community was involved in the controversy. Fuller, the original architect, was understandably upset, and in public statements he objected to the style of the exterior modifications as completely out of character with what had already been built. He also contended that many of the interior features that had been criticized and altered had originally been determined by state authorities and had not been his doing. To support his position, Fuller published in *The American Architect and Building News* a letter he had received from Hunt, Henry Dudley, and Detlef Lienau, condemning the major alterations and the change in style. Even more important, though, was a formal remonstrance presented to the state legislature by the New York City Chapter of the A.I.A., protesting the new plans and design. While disclaiming any endorsement of Fuller's original design, the memorial asserted that the new design was "an agglomeration of incongruous forms," highly inharmonious in detail, and that changing the building's style while retaining what had already been done "must inevitably result in a disastrous failure." If the existing work was so objectionable that any addition could not be made in harmony with it, "the façades should be removed and sold, and the work commenced anew." Other chapters of the Institute also put out public statements denouncing the changes in design and the mixing of styles. Richardson was aggrieved by the New York Chapter's public attack on his work, particularly since the group had not given him any opportunity to present his side of the case. Olmsted too was upset by the public criticism and wrote Hunt to protest the remonstrance. Various architects and others as well objected to the position that the Institute chapters had taken. The editors of *The American Architect and Building News* supported the proposed interior alterations, but objected strongly to the exterior stylistic changes; the old and the new elements obviously clashed and certainly did not lead to a desirable "unity, repose, and dignity."[19]

Despite the many objections, work on the Albany capitol continued in accord with the revised plans. But criticism of the new work was so intense that the Finance and Ways and Means Committees of the New

York legislature jointly invited five New York City architects to testify early in March 1877 on the propriety of the changes. The five—Hunt, George B. Post, Napoleon Le Brun, Henry Dudley, and Detlef Lienau—condemned the changes in no uncertain terms. Subsequently, in a letter addressed to several New York newspapers and republished in *The American Architect and Building News*, Hunt and the other four experts reiterated the points they had made in their testimony. They denied that they had spoken as advocates of the Renaissance style, as some had charged, and asserted that they were familiar with the published plans and the work that already had been executed according to the revised plans. They maintained that for a civic building they advocated combining practical convenience with artistic excellence, without regard to style, but they absolutely objected to utilizing two radically different styles which, if they were to be carried out, "would be totally wanting in unity, and consequently an architectural failure." Such a large structure with its incongruent elements "would vitiate instead of educating the taste of the people." If the building were to be erected according to the plans of the advisory board "it would be a perpetual reflection upon the architectural skill of the generation in whose time it was erected."[20]

The problem of the alterations was subsequently referred to the Finance Committee, which soon decided in a majority report that the legislature had not intended that the style of the capitol be "materially changed," and that the advisory board's project was "radically defective" both in the design and in the treatment of the building material. When the full legislature, however, then voted that work on the capitol be carried on in accord with the original plans, the governor vetoed the bill. The bill was soon repassed over the veto but without reference to the question of style, and in June 1877 the board of architects was instructed to proceed. After Richardson and Eidlitz had built up the north side of the building in a Romanesque style, the legislature again expressly ordered a return to the Renaissance style, which was done on the south side. Hunt's position as a leading critic of the revised plans and the opinions he expressed in his letter, as a member of the New York Chapter of the Institute, and in legislative testimony undoubtedly helped influence the final action. His position was, in a sense, very narrow, based on a commitment to maintain the purity of historical precedents and not mix what he saw as clashing stylistic elements. His stance was the customary one among architects of the day, who believed that Richardson and Eidlitz, supported by Olmsted, had violated a major canon of taste, and that their supposed solecism would fail to provide a "correctness" necessary for educating the public taste. It was assumed that a large public building, above all others, not only must serve practical governmental functions but also must educate and elevate public taste. To this belief Hunt was passionately committed.[21]

At home that year, Hunt's concerns were mainly for his new son, Herbert, who was born in August 1877. The newborn baby was sickly, so much so that it was considered risky to take him to New York in the fall, and so the entire family spent the winter in Newport. During the winter Hunt extensively remodeled Hill Top Cottage, adding a story to the main part of the house and a three-story wing on the rear, as well as having large bays put in some of the older rooms. Catharine later remembered this Newport winter as a very happy time, with at-home classes for Kitty and Joe given by a Swiss governness, private theatricals for the adults, pony rides for the children, and Richard working close by in the studio below the main house. The Newport sojourn was darkened, however, by the death on December 30, 1877, of Jane Maria Hunt, who had always been especially close to Richard among her sons, and by concern over the Stevens house litigation, which came to trial in New York in January 1878. In later years the Hunts once again became friendly with Mrs. Paran Stevens, who said that she harbored no resentment over the lawsuit she lost and that Hunt was the most honest man she had ever dealt with. There was also considerable family concern over Richard's brother Leavitt, who for years had been in financial trouble. He had lost money in one bad investment after another, most importantly in a Hartford silverware factory, and had gone deeply in debt. He often borrowed money from other members of the family, who became reluctant to assist him any longer.[22]

High quality in architecture and the elevation of public taste was the subject of another talk Hunt gave on February 21, 1878, at a Harvard Club dinner in New York City. Hunt stressed that as the American population and American cities expanded, more and more construction was taking place, and proper architectural training was obviously essential. "That the public taste needs cultivating is hardly to be questioned," he also emphasized. He went on to deplore the fact that so much work of an unstudied and untrained nature was being turned out, particularly "the unsightly piles which demoralize the national standard," the buildings being erected by the federal government. Good, long-lasting architecture must embody the ideas of the age, and to accomplish this required well-directed study for the practitioners. Hunt urged that architectural study be established at Harvard College as it had already been at the Massachusetts Institute of Technology. Proper training would mean proper building, which would in turn raise the standards of public taste. But several years would pass before Harvard would follow the lead of its Cambridge neighbor.[23]

In another public statement the following year, Hunt directed himself to a more pressing problem—housing for the urban poor. The need for better housing for the mass of the urban populace was becoming more and more apparent. Housing conditions had deteriorated so badly with the huge influx of newcomers into the cities that several of the New York churches arranged to call attention to the problem by observing a Tenement House Sunday on February 23, 1879. Subsequently, Mayor Edward Cooper appointed a committee of nine men, including the great landlord William Waldorf Astor, to investigate the housing conditions in the city. The committee issued a call for model tenement plans, and a jury awarded the prizes to three of those submitted that provided for interior rooms that were completely dark. Many architects concerned with housing, and others interested in public health and welfare, were outraged at this turn of events. Among others Hunt spoke out against the intolerable dark bedrooms and the horrendous ventilating shafts, which served to spread fires and gave little air, while others on his office staff attacked the rapacity of landlords and praised the Parisian system, which provided that tenements could not cover more than two-thirds of the land area available. The competition and the public discussion did lead to the development that same year of the "dumbbell" tenement, with minuscule side courts, which became the standard mode of tenement housing for the remainder of the century, but which, in fact, failed to solve the problems of crowding, foul air, and unhealthful conditions. In the latter part of the 1880s, Hunt himself designed at least five New York City tenements, all five stories high and housing from nine to twenty families each. There is no evidence that Hunt's tenements were any better or any worse than the thousands of others being erected.[24]

But the Hunts' private life was far removed from the problems of the urban poor. Although they went regularly each summer and fall to Hill Top Cottage, some years they also took holidays at such places as Saratoga, Lakewood in New Jersey, or the Delaware Water Gap, where they sought to rest and recover from their frequent illnesses. The children ran through the usual childhood diseases: one winter the younger ones had no sooner recovered from the measles than they all came down with the whooping cough. Richard's gout, moreover, had become a chronic condition, flaring up more intensely from time to time. One winter Catharine was laid prostrate with typhoid fever and did not fully recover until the following April. The summer of 1879 brought more theatrical entertainments, when Catharine and her friend Mrs. Robert

Cushing presented two plays for their acquaintances at the Masonic Temple in Newport. In August, Hunt went alone on his doctor's orders to take a water cure at Richfield Springs, but he was suddenly recalled in early September by yet another family tragedy—the suicide of his brother William Morris Hunt.[25]

Many years earlier, in 1862, William had moved from Newport to Boston, taking space in the Studio Building on Tremont Street for his workrooms and then later renting a large studio in the Mercantile Library Building on Summer Street. His Boston workrooms were filled with a rich collection of French paintings, engravings, plaster casts, and art objects, which rivaled Richard's own cache in New York. In his studio William hosted frequent parties and artists' receptions, exhibited his own paintings, including the large portrait of Catharine with young Dick in her arms, introduced to Bostonians many works of contemporary French painters, and gave lessons to young ladies. In his maturity as in his youth, William was witty and energetic, a magnetic person, usually dominating whatever group he was in. With his dark skin, his long, flowing, silvery white beard, his prominent nose and piercing gray eyes, he cut a striking figure. He still liked to sing, play the banjo, the guitar, and the violin, and act out charades. His fellow painter Thomas Ball, who also had a studio in the Mercantile Library Building, thought that the "boyish vein in his disposition was very charming."[26]

As a teacher, William Hunt stimulated great enthusiasm among his pupils. He deeply believed in his responsibility to teach: "It is the duty of an artist to teach; it will do good. Every artist ought to teach; that is the greatest need of art in this country. There is too much talking about art. The talkers are busy, the workers should be busier still." While he demonstrated elements of technique and style and attempted, above all, to shape his students' visual perception, he kept up a continuous outpouring of ideas. One of his students, who later assisted him in his classes, Helen M. Knowlton, took notes on Hunt's remarks, and he helped her prepare these notes for two volumes published as *Talks on Art*. His teachings were democratic: each artist, he felt, must seek out truth and express that truth, and to find the truth each one must learn to see clearly, while trusting his own instincts and impulses. William Hunt distrusted systems, any form of regimentation, always stressing simplicity. But he also emphasized that art students must study and get to know well the best art works of the past; an emphasis on high quality was at the heart of his educational ideas. His criticisms of his pupils' endeavors were considered helpful; though, on the other hand, he probably did not receive enough serious criticism of his own work, and, despite his sociability, he claimed that he always felt a sense of isolation and loneliness as an artist in America.[27]

The 1870s were turbulent for him. When his Summer Street studio was ravaged by the great Boston fire of 1872, all his own paintings and sketches not in others' hands were destroyed as well as the many French paintings he owned. The following year he was separated from his wife, who broke off relations between him and his children. His wife became mentally unbalanced and for some time was placed in an asylum. His health declined, and he rented a succession of unsatisfactory studios until he built himself a new one in a building on Boylston Street near Park Square. He also converted an old barn and carpenter's shop into a summer studio at Magnolia, Massachusetts, and purchased a movable painting van in which to travel about the countryside.[28]

In June 1878, while painting at Niagara Falls, William received an invitation from Leopold Eidlitz to execute two large mural paintings for the assembly chamber of the Albany capitol. At first William declined to undertake the work because of his poor health, but Richard persuaded him to undertake the commission, basing the murals on cartoons he had in his studio. The allegorical murals, titled *The Discoverer* and *The Flight of Night*, were to be large, and the time available for their completion was very limited. By mid-October the scaffolding was in place, and William began his difficult work some forty feet above the floor, painting directly on stone, and under great pressure to finish before Christmas. During these two months he exerted himself to his utmost, working nine or more hours a day on the scaffold, paying little heed to fatigue, and even taking his midday dinner on the scaffold. He was in a continuous state of excitement about his work. Richard came to Albany several times to observe the progress of the murals and to encourage his brother, and their sister Jane joined William during the final days of the work. Richard also came to Albany on January 27, 1879, when the murals were dedicated.[29]

As soon as the paintings had been completed, William began to feel the strain of the pace of work of the previous months, and he returned to Boston exhausted. He was disappointed when a bill providing for further decoration of the Albany capitol was vetoed and work which he had hoped to get would not be forthcoming, and became upset when an exhibit of his own paintings in Boston turned out to be a financial disaster. Apparently very depressed, he closed his studio and went to Vermont in the spring to stay with his brother Leavitt. In the summer of 1879, still out of spirits and worried about his health, he joined friends at Appledore Island in the Isles of Shoals off the New Hampshire coast, where he had often visited before. On September 8, he suddenly walked away from his friends, exclaiming that he wished he were dead, and a few hours later his body was discovered nearby floating face downward in a shallow reservoir. It was not absolutely clear whether he had become dizzy, lost his balance, and fallen into the water, or had deliberately taken his life. The early accounts indicated suicide, though some of his close friends were convinced that his death had been accidental. From Paris, Marian Hooper Adams wrote to her father how shocked she and Henry Adams were to learn that William Hunt had "put an end to his wild, restless, unhappy life. Perhaps," she went on, "it has saved him years of insanity, which his temperament pointed to." Six years later, Mrs. Adams would take her own life.[30]

Since Richard had shared so much with his oldest brother, not only in family ties and experiences, but also in their commitment to art and their hopes and work to advance artistic taste in the United States, William's death was a terrible blow that brought him intense grief. Undoubtedly, William's death hit him much harder than John's suicide five years before or his mother's death two years earlier, for the two had remained very close. Richard helped arrange a memorial exhibition of William's work at the Museum of Fine Arts in Boston, supplying some items from his own collection. After being on exhibit in Boston in November and December 1879, some of the paintings were shown at the inaugural exhibit of the first permanent building of the Metropolitan Museum of Art in New York in the spring of 1880. Although a few of William's paintings were judged uneven, the portraits, landscapes, genre, historical, and other works were generally acclaimed, and *The New York Times* pointed out that "probably no single American artist has ever had more pictures on exhibition at any one time, or has attempted greater variety in subject and treatment." In 1914, the Boston Museum of Fine Arts opened a William Morris Hunt Gallery as a memorial "eminently fitting to a man, who, more than any other of his time, brought America into touch with Europe in matters artistic."[31]

The decade of the seventies had been a difficult time for Richard Hunt. He and others in his family had suffered frequent and severe illness; he had seen the death of his mother and the suicides of two brothers; and he had endured the interruption of his work by the long European stay and the economic downturn. The mid-seventies brought a hiatus in his career between the commissions of the early years and new and important projects he undertook at the close of the decade. In much of his new work, Hunt seemed to be surer of what he wanted to do than he had been earlier. And while his artistic vision matured, he became ever more prominent as a leader of his profession and one making contributions of national significance to American art.

17

A CHATEAU FOR
FIFTH AVENUE

The first of Hunt's new projects of the late 1870s and the first of a group of commissions in Princeton, New Jersey, was the Lenox Library at the Princeton Theological Seminary, a gift of James Lenox, Hunt's long-time friend and patron and a leading philanthropist. For many years, Lenox, who had built the Lenox Library and the Presbyterian Hospital in New York, had maintained ties with Princeton both as a trustee of the college and a trustee and director of the separate Princeton Theological Seminary. Many years earlier he had contributed funds and arranged for the construction of a seminary library, which was built in 1842–1843 on a site close to Library Place and Mercer Street, where the Speer Library of the seminary now stands. This battlemented early Gothic Revival building proved inadequate for the needs of the seminary, however, and in 1877 Lenox made another gift of $65,000 to be used for a new library building. He also donated $35,000 for two houses for professors which were to be erected to the north of the new library building. The Lenox Library at the Princeton Seminary was completed in the spring of 1879 on a site at Library Place and Stockton streets, adjoining the old library, which then became known as the Lenox Reference Library. Both Lenox libraries were demolished in the 1950s.[1]

The Lenox or New Seminary Library (figure 57), faced with red and black brick and Nova Scotia, Newark, and blue stone, was rectangular in shape, seventy six by sixty feet, rising to a height of seventy feet, with a round tower at one corner housing a ventilating shaft and a smokestack, which rose to ninety-six feet. Hunt designed the lower two stories as a lean-to against the high and spacious central area, which was lighted by twenty large windows ranged in a massive clerestory. The core area was buttressed at the corners and was surmounted by a graceful hipped roof. An elegantly proportioned gabled porch helped define the principal entrance on the main-floor level above the sloped, heavy stone basement. Inside, piers and arches separated the central room from the surrounding alcoves on the main floor and the galleries above, where most of the bookshelves were located. In the corners were placed librarians' offices and workrooms as well as staircases providing access to the lean-to galleries and to the clerestory and tower. The New Seminary Library was a solid, dignified structure, its broad, gently curving segmental window arches and the tower vaguely Romanesque in inspiration and all the elements combined in an original way, well-proportioned and very handsome.[2]

Hunt's most significant Princeton commission was the Marquand Chapel at the college (figures 58, 59). As with the Lenox Library at the seminary, the donor chose the architect for the building he was giving.

Figure 58
Marquand Chapel,
Princeton University,
Princeton, New Jersey
(1882). Courtesy Prince-
ton University Archives.

Figure 59
Marquand Chapel interior. Courtesy Princeton University Archives.

Henry G. Marquand, for whom Hunt had already built Linden Gate in Newport, employed Hunt to prepare plans for a campus chapel. By November 11, 1880, a site was chosen, and on June 21, 1881, the cornerstone was laid. At the time the building was dedicated, on June 18, 1882, it was presented to the college with the proviso that it "should be used for no other purpose than for the worship of God." From its completion until it was destroyed by fire on the night of May 14, 1920, the Marquand Chapel served the Princeton collegiate community. When it was subsequently replaced by the large, high Gothic University Chapel, dedicated in 1928, the old church was recalled by naming the north transept the Marquand Chapel.[3]

For the Marquand Chapel plan, Hunt followed up the ideas he had presented to the Episcopal Church Congress in 1877. He created a Greek cross plan, with a shallow apse, and the interior so arranged (figure 59) that the entire congregation might be seated conveniently close to the pulpit. The lower part of the apse extended outward to a greater radius than the upper area, making a sort of exterior lean-to. Inside, over the apse, a series of pointed arches rose above columns with intricately carved capitals, supporting a drum pierced by small windows and, above, an upper half-dome decorated with massive Byzantine-style figures. The richly embellished apse established an appropriate visual center for the church. Large rose windows, set above five vertical windows in the transepts, and triple vertical fenestration in the nave provided diffused light through the stained glass for the interior. A huge, circular chandelier, hanging low in the auditorium, reminiscent of similar pieces in Greek Orthodox churches, and the rich timberwork of arched ribbing, which supported the ceiling, furnished other elements of visual interest in the interior.

The exterior walls of the Marquand Chapel were constructed of roughly dressed stone, which gave the building an interesting surface texture and a rugged appearance, almost as if it had been built up from a mound of rocks. On the principal façade, a low triple gable rose over the three openings of the porch, while, in the steeply sloped gable above, three tall windows indicated the high-ceilinged nave within. At the right stood a campanile, the delicate, open, and rounded belfry of which rested upon a high, multistory, square base; the bell tower was balanced at the left by a low, rounded corner tower, housing stairs giving access to an interior gallery. The upper portion of the campanile was treated very much like the upper section of the Lenox Library tower at the seminary. Like the seminary library, the Marquand Chapel was an elegant and well-proportioned building, which was given particular visual interest by an artful use of varying surface textures, both outside and within. It suited well Hunt's call for buildings embodying harmony, dignity, and repose.[4]

Sharply contrasting with the aesthetic success of the Marquand Chapel was the plain and aesthetically mediocre Princeton Chemical Laboratory, planned in 1885 but built a few years later, at the southeast corner of Nassau Street and Washington Road. The Chemical Laboratory was completed in 1891. A three-story rectangular structure of brick with stone trim, set upon a high, inclined base of rough-dressed stone, the Chemical Laboratory (figure 60) was decorated primarily by a curious crenellated parapet and by heavy stone lintel courses and more delicate sill courses at the upper levels. For no discernible reason, the main entrance was placed off center on the principal front, while the window heights were shortened and the sill courses raised part way across the street fronts toward the corner nearest the street intersection. The still-standing Chemical Laboratory was very much a plain sister to the shorter-lived Marquand Chapel.[5]

Hunt also returned to domestic work late in the seventies and at that time began his long and significant association with the Vanderbilt family. His first Vanderbilt project was a large and rambling, shingle-covered, Queen Anne-style country residence (figure 61) called Idlehour, for William Kissam Vanderbilt at Oakdale, Long Island, begun in 1878. In subsequent years Hunt added to the mansion itself as well as designing numerous dependencies to the estate, including a gardener's cottage, greenhouses, stables, and an entrance gate and two gatehouses. Idlehour was destroyed by fire in 1899 and replaced by a very large mansion designed by Richard Howland Hunt.[6]

While his country home was still being erected, William K. Vanderbilt commissioned Hunt to design a church for Islip, Long Island. A small building, about ninety feet in length and somewhat over fifty feet in width, St. Mark's Church (figure 62) was fashioned in a Scandinavian timberwork style, characterized by numerous high-pitched, projecting gables, surmounted by carvings, exposed framing, and decorative timberwork, and by shingled wall surfaces. The vigorous framing of this building, which is still standing, echoes some of Hunt's earlier Newport houses, while the variety of surface planes and textures make it one of the liveliest of Hunt's designs. The protruding porch at the narthex originally was open but was later enclosed. Montgomery Schuyler judged that "in invention, freedom and picturesqueness" no building of Hunt's was superior to this small church. An adjoining rectory and other dependencies were styled in the same manner.[7]

Figure 60
Chemical Laboratory,
Princeton University,
Princeton, New Jersey
(1891). Courtesy Prince-
ton University Archives.

Figure 61
Idlehour, the W. K.
Vanderbilt mansion,
Oakdale, Long Island
(1880+). Courtesy The
American Institute of
Architects Foundation/
Prints and Drawings
Collection, Washington,
D.C. Reproduction by
James Garrison.

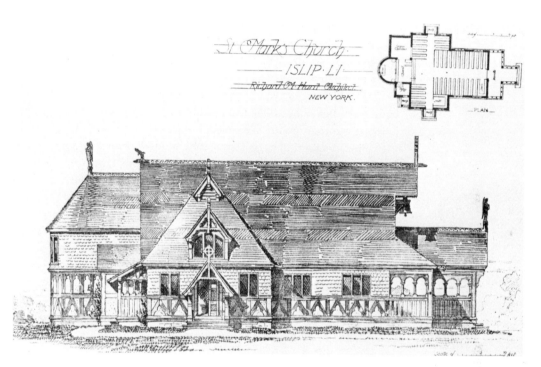

Figure 62
Elevation and plan, St.
Mark's Church, Islip,
Long Island (1880). From
*American Architect and
Building News* (February
14, 1880).

By the end of the seventies, Hunt was also at work on a third project for William Vanderbilt, one of the most important commissions of his entire career: a château for Fifth Avenue. The William Kissam Vanderbilt house brought considerable popular recognition and critical acclaim to Hunt and also initiated his use of a new mode of design, as he increasingly looked back to the late Gothic–early French Renaissance for inspiration for his domestic buildings. The significance of the W. K. Vanderbilt house, however, has sometimes been distorted, as some critics have viewed this building as *the* turning point which set the course for the remainder of Hunt's career. Hunt's full body of work in the years to come continued to be varied both in building types and in styles, and was certainly not devoted just to providing variations on the themes set forth at this time.

Probably in 1878, W. K. Vanderbilt employed Hunt to design the large town house he wished to build on land he had acquired on the northwest corner of Fifth Avenue and Fifty-Second Street in New York City. Since Vanderbilt suggested that he wanted a house set off from its neighbors, "with air and breathing space around it," Hunt urged him to assemble the entire Fifth Avenue block frontage between Fifty-Second and Fifty-Third streets and place the residence in the middle of the site. But Vanderbilt, who had already obtained a hundred-foot frontage on the avenue and one hundred twenty-five feet on the side street, refused to do this, since the land was so expensive. He later regretted that he had not tried to purchase the larger site. Hunt sketched out several ideas before Vanderbilt and his wife settled on the one to be built in the French Renaissance style of the time of Francis I. Construction of the mansion began at the end of 1879 and was basically completed at the end of 1882, although the interior details and decoration were not fully executed until 1883.[8]

William Kissam Vanderbilt was a grandson of Commodore Cornelius Vanderbilt, who had accumulated millions of dollars in his shipping and railroad enterprises, and the second son of William Henry Vanderbilt, who had shrewdly parlayed his inheritance of more than $100 million to about $200 million during his lifetime. Like his grandfather, William K. Vanderbilt found routine work unsatisfying; he enjoyed dashing into ventures and taking risks in the stock market. Although "W. K." came to head a vast railroad empire and ostensibly made trains move, it was his wife, Alva Smith Vanderbilt, who dominated the family and directed their social life. As their daughter, Consuelo, put it, using railroad lingo, "It seemed to us he [W. K. V.] was always shunted or sidetracked from our occupations."[9]

Clearly Alva Smith Vanderbilt undertook to direct the design of the new Fifth Avenue château, as she did to establish her own social position and to dominate the destinies of her children. While her husband was a risk-taker, his temperament was gentle and he hated strife. Alva Vanderbilt, by contrast, "loved a fight" and "her combative nature rejoiced in conquest." Southern-born, the daughter of a Mobile, Alabama, cotton merchant, she had grown up in New York City and had lived briefly in Paris following the Civil War. She was married to Vanderbilt in 1875. Although Alva always felt a disdain for what she saw as the mercenary spirit of Northerners, she acquired through her marriage the resources to fulfill her own "towering ambition." Alva's ambition for her children, as for herself, was enormous, and their upbringing was carefully planned. They had French and German governesses. Consuelo recalled that she and her brothers customarily spoke French with their parents, their father having been sent to school in Geneva, and that she had learned to read and write in French and in German before she had mastered English. Consuelo thought her parents completely unsuited to each other, and she wondered why they had ever married. Her violent-tempered, domineering mother, who on occasion whipped the children with a riding whip and manipulated their lives like pawns in a chess game, later married off Consuelo to become the Duchess of Marlborough in one of the most spectacular unions of the nineteenth century. But some years afterward, Alva seemed to regret what she had done to her daughter, and perhaps her own subsequent activities as one of the most ardent feminists of the early twentieth century, working to help all American women have more control over their own lives, was something of an act of penance.[10]

The stories told of Alva Vanderbilt were frequently unkind, for as "a born dictator," as her daughter termed her, she made many enemies. One of her acquaintances once wrote that Alva had told Hunt that he might choose any style he wanted for the new Fifth Avenue mansion just so long as it was medieval; when the designs for the residence were shown her, she reportedly exclaimed that the house was lovely and exactly what she wanted: "A real Venetian palace like the Doges had." That she reacted to the drawings with such a solecism must be doubted, for along with her ambition and her relentless drive, she was knowledgeable about architecture and decoration and intelligent. Hunt himself, as Catharine later wrote, "had the greatest admiration for Mrs. William K. Vanderbilt's intellect and broad grasp of architecture and he often said: 'She's a wonder!'" For their new home on what would become "Vanderbilt Row," Alva and her husband obviously wanted the best they could get. What they did get was for many years the most remarkable house in New York City.[11]

As the Vanderbilt house took shape, it quickly attracted attention. To some critics, a château for Fifth Avenue seemed irrelevant to American life, but almost everyone agreed on the beauty of the structure and on Hunt's skill in creating a dwelling of such elegance and refinement. Set back slightly from the sidewalks, the Vanderbilt house (figure 63) occupied most of the available site and rose to three and four stories in height. The exterior facing was of gray Indiana limestone, which soon became the most fashionable building material in the city. The mansion was covered by a steeply hipped, blue slate roof, topped by high, ornate copper cresting and finials, and the chimney stacks were high, massive, and richly carved. At the principal entrance on Fifth Avenue, reached by a short flight of wide steps, the front doors were arranged to slide sidewise into pockets; the inner vestibule doors were fashioned of wrought steel. On the avenue façade, a graceful, elliptical-arched opening, flanked by pilasters, outlined the doorway and was surmounted by a deep, recessed balcony with lateral canopied niches on the splayed sides and an intricately carved solid balustrade on the front. Additional balustrades at the upper levels and a dormer window topped by a cusped round arch below a pediment supported by flying buttresses further accentuated the asymmetrically placed entrance pavilion. Increasingly from this time Hunt emphasized entrances on his houses.

Attached to the left of this elaborated entrance was the most striking detail of the mansion, a delicately proportioned corbelled tourelle, topped by a sharply pointed conical roof and finial marking the highest point of the building. The tourelle had a finely wrought surface design of fleur-de-lis, stringcourses, thin pilasters, and applied tracery, and it was locked firmly to the main structure by the attic-story balcony balustrade. A single bay of windows rose to dormers on either side of the entrance pavilion. The left, or southern, bay rose one story higher than the northern bay. The windows were ornamented with carved jambs and hood-molds, and the dormer to the left was decorated by a molded double-curved ogee opening set in a gable and flanked by pinnacles. The richness of detail of the entrance pavilion and tourelle was effectively set off on the left by the substantial areas of plain wall surface broken only by the molded stringcourses. Montgomery Schuyler suggested that the flanking area of unbroken wall gave the house an impression of "power and massiveness" and helped establish that the heavy walls were pierced by the openings and were not just enframing them.

On the Fifty-Second Street front, a three-sided protruding bay rose

Figure 63
William K. Vanderbilt
mansion, Fifth Avenue
(660) at Fifty-Second
Street, New York (1882).
Museum of the City of
New York.

Figure 64
Oriel, William K. Van-
derbilt mansion. From
John V. Van Pelt, *Mono-
graph of the William K.
Vanderbilt House* (1925).

through the first two stories near the corner and was balanced by a broader and heavier protruding bay at the first-story level toward the rear. In between, at the second-story level, was a rounded, richly carved corbelled oriel (figure 64). Above the three-sided bay and the oriel, two large dormer windows with ogee openings, flanked by pinnacles, repeated the design of the left-hand dormer on the avenue façade. The ogee motif was further repeated as a hoodmold both over three of the large first-story windows and over four of the small second-story and a pair of upper-story openings. The profusion of rich carving and decorative sculpture on the exterior and the interior of the mansion reportedly took some forty workmen many months to complete.[12]

Viewed from the diagonal at the southeast corner, the Vanderbilt house was more impressive than when seen from face on, opposite the main entry. In the latter position, as Schuyler pointed out, the several roof levels were disconcerting; and the pyramiding of roof levels up to the corner segment was broken by the placement of the tourelle. The three-story treatment of the segment to the right of the entrance pavilion, when contrasted with the four-story treatment to the left, made the building look truncated and lopsided. From the avenue, the house appeared to be almost unfinished, as if the Vanderbilt purse had been so emptied by the expense of the entrance pavilion decorations that one story had to be lopped off the right section. The lower roof level here made the topmost parts of the central pavilion look awkward from this angle, also, and the two chimney stacks on this side seemed badly positioned. However, from farther south along Fifth Avenue with the two street fronts in view, this problem was not apparent.[13]

A pair of statues perched high on the roof gave a handsome flourish to the Vanderbilt house. One was a figure of a small, chubby boy placed on top of the pediment of the dormer window in the entrance pavilion. The other, erected on the topmost roof crest, was a statue representing Richard Morris Hunt himself (figure 65), slightly smaller than life size, dressed as a stonemason wearing a cap and apron and holding a chisel and mallet. The story was later told that Hunt had failed to instruct the stone contractors about the figure planned for the high rooftop. Receiving no instructions, the stone contractors proceeded to set up a cloth-enclosed booth in the dining hall where for some time, unbeknown to the architect, a sculptor worked on the portrait statue, catching glimpses of his subject through a peephole cut in the cloth. At first Hunt paid little heed to the booth, but the activity and occasional talking and laughter there aroused his curiosity, and when he ordered the booth taken out he discovered what had been going on. The inclusion of a sculptured por-

Figure 65
Statue of Richard Morris
Hunt as a stonemason,
William K. Vanderbilt
mansion. From John V.
Van Pelt, *Monograph of
the William K. Vanderbilt
House* (1925).

trait of the architect was not at all unusual in European public buildings, and, according to his son, though Hunt had not considered the idea of having his own portrait used on the house, he was, apparently, not displeased and allowed the statue to be placed on the roof. He later used a pictorial representation of it as his personal bookplate.[14]

Inside the front entrance, (figure 66), the vestibule led into the main hall (figure 67), a large room, sixty feet long and twenty feet wide, with a beamed and paneled oak ceiling and a dado of carved Caen stone, a fine limestone imported from France, rising seven feet high on the walls. Half way down the hall on the right, opposite a huge stone fireplace, the grand staircase of richly carved Caen stone gave access to the second story. The French Renaissance library with ebony woodwork and the tiled Moorish billiard room were placed on either side of the staircase; across the main hall were the parlor, a dark room paneled in French walnut, and the salon, a white-paneled Régence–Louis XV room with Boucher tapestries and a circular ceiling panel painted by Hunt's old friend Paul Baudry. To the west of the salon was a small breakfast room, which had a painted beamed ceiling and was decorated with Flemish tapestries and a Rembrandt portrait, and beyond this the butler's pantry. The largest and most elaborate room of the mansion was the dining hall (figure 68) at the back of the house, fifty feet long, thirty-five feet wide, and rising through two stories. In the style of the period of Henry II, the room was paneled by a seven-foot wainscoting in quartered oak; above it, tapestries were hung over walls faced in Caen stone. At one end of the room stood huge double fireplaces of red sandstone with caryatids holding the great oak overmantel, and at the other end a musicians' balcony projected into the hall. On the side, a large, mullioned, stained-glass window depicted the meeting of Francis I and Henry VIII at the Field of the Cloth of Gold.[15]

On the second floor were children's rooms and bedrooms, and, at the southeast, the Fifth Avenue corner, Alva Vanderbilt's bedroom, which was connected by a small circular staircase in the tourelle with her husband's room above. The principal room on the third floor was a large gymnasium and children's playroom located over the two-story dining hall. This room was large enough so that the three Vanderbilt children could roller skate and ride their bicycles here.

Alva Vanderbilt wanted a house that would make everyone, particularly those on the uppermost reaches of New York society, take notice of her and her family. The people who counted most for Alva realized that a powerful new force had entered New York social life when she made known her plans for her housewarming costume ball, to be held on the

Figure 66
Plan, William K. Van-
derbilt mansion. From
*American Architect and
Building News* (August
29, 1891).

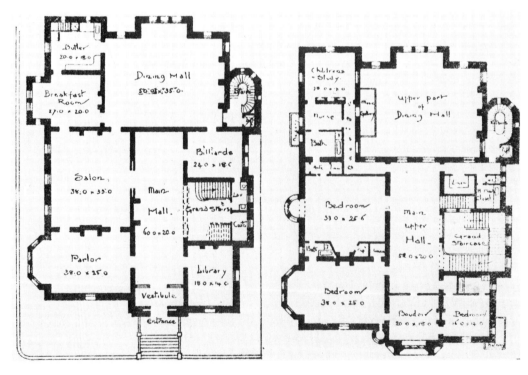

Figure 67
Hall, William K. Van-
derbilt mansion. From
Architecture, V (March
15, 1902). Reproduction
by James Garrison.

Figure 68
Dining hall, William K.
Vanderbilt mansion.
From *Architecture*, V
(March 15, 1902). Repro-
duction by James Garri-
son.

night of March 26, 1883. Soon young people of fashion were busying themselves preparing quadrilles for the party. Carrie Astor, the daughter of Mrs. William Astor, acknowledged queen of New York society, and some friends set about practicing a "Star Quadrille." It is said that when Alva Vanderbilt made it known, however, that the Astors could not possibly be issued invitations to her ball since Mrs. Astor had never called on her, the queen promptly left her card at the door of the new house. Over one thousand guests were invited, including the Astors. Alva Vanderbilt's social eminence was clearly established.[16]

"Like an Oriental Dream/The Scene in Mr. W. K. Vanderbilt's Beautiful House Last Evening/. . . The Wealth and the Grace of New York in Varied and Brilliant Array" was the headline the next day in the *New York Herald*. The fancy-dress ball presented a scene "probably never rivalled in republican America and never outdone by the gayest court of Europe," the newspaper article went on. It was "a gladsome night of such merrymaking as all the resources of the world, easily commanded, could afford." The party began at 11:00 P.M. William K. Vanderbilt, dressed as the Duc de Guise in a suit of yellow satin, and his wife as a Venetian princess, in cream-colored brocade and heavily bejeweled, greeted their guests on a dais in the French salon. Cornelius Vanderbilt II came as Louis XVI, while his wife was an "Electric Light." Mrs. Paran Stevens, not to be outdone, was Queen Elizabeth. Catharine Hunt appeared as a courtier of the time of Francis I, wearing a "velvet dress of a singular shade of brown trimmed with jewels," while Richard Hunt, perhaps wryly, came as Cimabue, the painter whom Dante chose to symbolize the transience of fame (figure 69). Dancing began around midnight in the great dining hall, the guests watching and joining in the several quadrilles, including a "Mother Goose Quadrille," a "Hobby Horse Quadrille," and a "Go-as-You-Please Quadrille," the latter reported as particularly lively. Dick Hunt, wearing knee britches and a coat and hat of mouse color, joined Mrs. James Brown Potter to lead one quadrille. Unfortunately, Carrie Astor's "Star Quadrille" could not be given because of the failure of the young ladies' lighting apparatus. Upstairs, a supper room was set up to satisfy the guests' hunger after their exertions in the ballroom. Flowers were everywhere; over ten thousand were used in the decorations.[17]

And as the guests wandered through the rooms and halls no doubt many of them realized that something new was being signaled on Fifth Avenue that night: wealth and fashion could be united to good taste, derived from the past, albeit with ostentatious display. For those with adequate means and awareness of the new fashion, the era of com-

Figure 69
Richard Morris Hunt as
"Cimabue" (1883). From
an old photograph, Hunt
Papers.

monplace, nearly identical brownstone houses and of cluttered, over-furnished Victorian rooms would soon be replaced by one of ever more luxurious mansions, usually designed in period styles, the rooms of which would be filled with treasures from the past coordinated in selection and placement. Alva Vanderbilt herself would assume something of the role of an arbiter of elegance for New York and Newport society, ransacking the treasure troves of Europe to adorn her mansions and offering instruction in the art of costly elegance to her contemporaries.

Within a few years many people of wealth and fashion paid the W. K. Vanderbilt house the compliment of trying to reproduce it. A veritable "châteauesque" revival took place in the United States, although most of the houses it produced were less lavish than and inferior in detail to the American prototype. In Boston, for example, the Oliver Ames house of 1882 and the Burrage mansion of 1889 emulated Hunt's French Renaissance design. Cornelius Vanderbilt II's residence on Fifth Avenue and Fifty-Seventh Street, designed by George B. Post, followed the château style. Another descendant appeared immediately adjacent to the north of the original mansion, when in 1905–1907 McKim, Mead & White built a house there for W. K. Vanderbilt, Jr. In the same general style and rising to the same height approximately, the new dwelling had five stories rather than four, which necessitated somewhat smaller proportions. Looking back to a later phase of French Renaissance architecture, it also included far less ornamentation. Moreover, since the newer Vanderbilt residence occupied a fairly narrow lot, it did not have the massive unbroken wall areas that the older dwelling had and lacked something of the strength and solidity of the older house.[18]

Not only did people of wealth and fashion seek to imitate Hunt's Vanderbilt house, but also many architects and architectural critics lavishly praised the building. Charles F. McKim recalled that he used to like to stroll past the mansion in the evening after finishing his work of the day, saying that he was refreshed just by looking at it. Montgomery Schuyler was largely positive and enthusiastic in his judgment and thought that Hunt had found "his proper and congenial architectural environment" in this house. The critic Royal Cortissoz could barely contain himself, finding the house "a tour de force. . . . a lyric inspiration. . . . an isolated triumph of lightness and vivacious beauty. . . . It stands alone in all America, for that matter." In this instance, he wrote, Richard Hunt had "been a poet as well as an architect." The critic "J. A. S.," writing in 1916, found the house "a wonderful, scholarly, exquisite, and original piece of work. . . . the finest work of architecture in this country." Barr Ferree, another critic, praised Hunt's success in providing rich and abundant detail but without a "sense of overloading," with results that were "beautiful, stately and harmonious." Herbert Croly, the eminent social and architectural critic, judged the Vanderbilt house somewhat antiquarian and pedantic, but the avenue façade, he decided, was thoroughly composed and serene; the best of Hunt's houses, this was a building of "ease . . . grace and . . . urbanity." Of all Hunt's works, it was the most highly praised.[19]

Almost alone in criticism of the Vanderbilt house was Hunt's old antagonist on the Central Park gateways, Clarence Cook, essayist and critic and for a time editor of *The Studio* magazine. Cook had in 1867 objected to Hunt's Central Park gateways for their "Frenchness," and in 1882 he renewed his attack on the architect once more for plundering the styles of the past. Cook's critique was a general one on the course of contemporary architecture, but it was apparently occasioned by the completion of the Vanderbilt residence. Cook asserted that American architects had come to neglect the essentials of "comfort and convenience and hospitality" in their works, and, seeking fantastic variations on clear and simple old themes, they had achieved only "universal self-indulgence and love of ostentatious display." American architecture had fallen into the control of "a set of clever, accomplished but overcultivated young men," who had brought back from Europe ideas alien to the life and needs of their countrymen. The United States was being defaced by architectural blunders, and Hunt had "certainly loaded earth with some of the most ungainly among all the ungainly structures that make our streets such a misery to any one who cares for good building." Hunt, Cook charged, had spoiled Beacon Street by the Brimmer houses, "the ugliest that . . . [have] ever been built this side of the Atlantic." The Lenox Library "with its silly pediments and blank monotony of wall [was] a very fit tomb . . . for the mummied treasures that are hermetically sealed within." And now Hunt had produced in the Vanderbilt house a "pretentious, fussy building . . . a patch-work made up of bits," just a "slavish" copy of Francis I architecture, giving "a hash of French Renaissance detail." Seldom had "the art of architecture . . . received many worse blows in this country" than it had here on Fifth Avenue.[20]

After the death of William Kissam Vanderbilt in 1920, the Fifth Avenue mansion was closed. An unsuccessful attempt was made to preserve it as a museum, and it was used in the early 1920s as a setting for a motion picture; but the prime location made it an exceptionally valuable property, and in 1925 the house and property were sold for $3,750,000. The house was torn down in February and March 1926 to make way for a large office building. At the time some voices were raised deploring the destruction of what many considered Hunt's "masterpiece," but commentators also recognized that the building could no longer serve as a private house on the site and that the course of events leading to its passing was "as irresistible as the commercial spirit that is reducing even our fine architecture to a simple matter of dollars and cents."[21]

Within a few years of the completion of the Fifth Avenue mansion, Hunt rather closely repeated some of the features of this dwelling for a client in Chicago. The William Borden house was a smaller and less ornate and perhaps better integrated version of the New York mansion. Located at 1020 Lake Shore Drive at the corner of Bellevue Place, the Borden residence soon became something of a showplace in Chicago, like the Marshall Field house, which Hunt had built there several years before.

William Borden was a lawyer and mining engineer who had amassed a considerable fortune in mining ventures at Leadville, Colorado, and had subsequently become involved in Chicago real estate transactions. Borden was a difficult client who demanded innumerable changes in the plans and the design as they were being worked out. Much of the architectural preparation for his house went on while Hunt was absent in Europe in 1885, and Borden was irritated that Holland C. Anthony, from Hunt's office, was completing the work on the project. At one point Borden objected that the basement was too high and the first and second stories were too low. Another time, having seen a photograph of the W. K. Vanderbilt house, he demanded that all work be stopped on his house since it was becoming too elaborate and he wanted it decidedly more modest than the New York mansion. Eventually he was reassured that he was not in competition with the Vanderbilts, and once more work went ahead on the drawings. But another crisis arose when Borden did not receive the large-scale working drawings at the time he expected them, and he put off starting construction for nearly a year. Then, a few months after this decision, the erratic Borden demanded that the plans be drastically altered: the front steps, the size of some rooms, and the size and shape of many of the windows did not satisfy him, and a full set of new drawings had to be made. From Europe, Hunt urged that Borden be dealt with firmly—although he also made some modifications in the drawings—and the office staff eventually ignored some of the Chicagoan's requests. Work finally began on the Borden house in the spring of 1886, and it was completed in 1889.[22]

Constructed of gray stone, resting on a high, sloped basement and rising three and one-half stories, the Borden house (figure 70) gave an

Figure 70
William Borden mansion, Chicago (1889).
From *Inland Architect and News Record,* X (October 1887). Reproduction by James Garrison.

impression of forceful dignity and strength, particularly on the southern front, which was somewhat less broken than the eastern face. Like the Vanderbilt house, the Borden dwelling presented a variety of cornice levels below the multiplaned hipped roof of slate, which was broken by high, gabled dormers, small dormer windows (lucarnes), and massive chimney stacks. Copper cresting and finials topped the upper roof edges. The house was entered through an elliptically arched portal on the side street. The treatment of the openings was varied and picturesque, with windows of several shapes and sizes, some carved jambs, and several ogee hoodmolds. A corbelled center bay on the eastern façade recalled the upper part of the entrance pavilion of the Vanderbilt house, while a three-quarter-round corbelled tourelle, delicately carved and with a sharply peaked cone roof, also echoed the New York house, although here this picturesque feature was placed at the salient angle of the walls, so that it formed an element of both principal fronts, rather than of just one. The Borden house was demolished in 1960.[23]

Hunt's projects for the Vanderbilts in the early and mid-1880s also included a mausoleum. William H. Vanderbilt, who recognized that his son's Fifth Avenue dwelling was considerably more impressive than his own in the next block to the south, selected Hunt as the architect for the family tomb, and early in December 1884 he and his sons accompanied Hunt to look over the site that had been chosen. A year or so earlier W. H. Vanderbilt had tried to acquire an acre plot in the Moravian Cemetery at New Dorp, Staten Island, near where his father, the Commodore, was buried. But the owners of the gravesites in this plot demanded such exorbitant amounts for their land that Vanderbilt gave up on the idea and instead bought a plot of several wooded acres on higher ground behind the cemetery proper, which he proceeded to have prepared for the mausoleum. Construction began on the Vanderbilt Mausoleum in 1885, and it was completed by 1889. Placed at the apex of a high knoll, it had a splendid location with a view for miles around of Staten Island and New York Harbor. Frederick Law Olmsted, with whom Hunt had clashed two decades earlier over his Central Park gateway designs and a decade before on the Albany capitol, was employed to landscape the private cemetery. Hunt and Olmsted got along well on this collaboration as they did on their later, considerably more important, shared commissions.[24]

W. H. Vanderbilt wanted a structure that was appropriate to the family's fortune and position but also a place that was secure, apparently fearful that bodies of family members might be stolen and held for ransom as had happened a few years earlier to the remains of A. T.

Stewart, which were taken from the graveyard of St. Mark's Church in the Bowery. Hunt's first design for the tomb struck Vanderbilt as much too "showy" for the "plain, quiet unostentatious" Vanderbilts. He preferred something "roomy and solid and rich," but without any "unnecessary fancy-work on it." Vanderbilt died on December 8, 1885, before the mausoleum was completed, but he appeared to be satisfied with the new design that Hunt had made. After his death his youngest son, George W. Vanderbilt, directed the work on the mausoleum; this was Hunt's first collaboration with one of his most important clients. In Hunt's absence in Europe in 1885–1886, his staff did much of the detailed work on the tomb.[25]

In styling the Vanderbilt Mausoleum (figure 71), Hunt turned to Romanesque architecture of the twelfth century for a model. He selected the Church of St. Gilles near Arles in France as the inspiration for his own work, constructing the building of Quincy granite on the exterior and facing the interior with Indiana limestone. Hunt created a symmetrical façade with three semicircular-arched portals. Each portal and the set of doors it enclosed was of identical dimensions. The central portal, however, was framed by a massive pavilion that projected well forward from the wall plane. This monumental porch rose the full height of the structure to a gable whose profile was superimposed on the gable line of the mausoleum roof. Above the great central archway, the architect placed a bracketed cornice whose shadow repeated the horizontal line of the belt course below that ran across the building at the springing line of the three portal arches. Above the cornice stood a range of seven narrow and deeply recessed windows, their arched heads conforming to the rise and fall of the gable line.

To the sides of the main doorway, reached by broad, semicircular steps, were the side doorways, reached by steps with straight treads. The central wall surfaces were carved in regularly aligned squares; this design was somewhat "hard and rigid," Hunt himself felt. Two decorative cupolas rose on the roof of the large tomb, which was set directly into the hillside. The Vanderbilt Mausoleum remains today an impressively monumental and dignified structure.[26]

As the work on the mausoleum progressed, Hunt's acquaintance ripened into friendship with George W. Vanderbilt, who in 1886 commissioned Hunt to make alterations on his house at 9 West Fifty-Third Street and in 1887–1889 to design new farm buildings at the old Vanderbilt homestead at New Dorp. In 1887, George Vanderbilt also employed Hunt to design a small public library building at 251 West Thirteenth Street near Horatio Street. The lot, the building, and the books were all

Figure 71
Vanderbilt Mausoleum,
New Dorp, Staten Is-
land, New York (1889).
Staten Island Advance
photo.

gifts of Vanderbilt to the people of New York City. The new structure became the Jackson Square Branch of the New York Free Circulating Library. The building (figure 72) was mostly constructed in 1887 and was opened for general use on July 6, 1888. The Flemish-style brick façade is simple, with triple bays on the two lower stories and a double bay on the upper story, the openings all surmounted by delicate trefoils set in arches. The façade is terminated by a shaped gable with multicurved sides rising to a central, finial-topped arched section that repeats the rhythm of the arches below. All in all, the unpretentious front—the street-level openings now altered somewhat from the original work—stands out as a little gem in the drab residential and commercial street.[27]

Different in style from the Vanderbilt château on Fifth Avenue but also looking back to the French Renaissance was the New York mansion Hunt conceived in 1881 for Henry G. Marquand, for whom he had already designed Linden Gate in Newport and for whom he was presently working on the Chapel at Princeton and the Guernsey Building at 160–164 Broadway. Marquand, who had long been active in real estate and banking in New York, was also associated with Hunt at the Metropolitan Museum of Art, of which he later became president. The Marquand house, erected on the northwest corner of East Sixty-Eighth Street and Madison Avenue, and two smaller houses immediately adjacent to the north on Madison Avenue, were completed in 1884.[28]

In the Marquand houses (figure 73) Hunt again turned to the French Renaissance of the early sixteenth century for inspiration, finding in the stylistic mixture of classical and Gothic elements the richness of detail he sought. The four-story complex was a decidedly elegant addition to upper Madison Avenue, which, like other streets of the area, was then being lined with nearly identical, drab brownstone fronts. The principal Marquand house, facing south on Sixty-Eighth Street, rose high above the street on a heavy, rusticated basement, which was carried along at the same line in the two smaller houses on Madison Avenue; the rise in street level was recognized by the lifting in succession of the rooflines and of the cornice of the uppermost house. Above the basement the houses were faced with brick and sandstone trim. The fourth story in all three houses was treated with a mansard roof, which at each top level enclosed an attic story.

The two street façades provided an interplay of variously shaped forms of wall and roof, penetrated by complex and varied fenestration and animated by an array of balconies, projecting pavilions and bays, a richly worked cornice, high, pedimented dormer gables, roof cresting,

Figure 72
Perspective, New York
Free Library, 251 West
Thirteenth Street, New
York (1887). Courtesy
The American Institute
of Architects Founda-
tion/Prints and
Drawings Collection,
Washington, D.C. Photo
by James Garrison.

and massive grouped chimneys. An iron and glass conservatory on the first floor of the principal house added an additional interesting element. Yet the many and varied features were harmoniously composed. Hunt brought the various details together particularly through the common facing materials, the uniform line of the basement, and the similar treatment of the windows at the third story and in the mansard roof. Like so many houses of the 1870s and the 1880s, the main house especially seemed by the very exterior complexity to invite exploration within; the viewer would like to go inside and see just how the exterior forms relate to interior spaces.[29]

Marquand's house soon became one of the showplaces of New York, a veritable museum of precious objects and of interior design. Leading painters, wood and stone carvers, and makers of stained glass, furniture, and mosaics were brought in to decorate the mansion. John La Farge, Louis C. Tiffany, Sir Frederick Leighton, and Sir Lawrence Alma-Tadema created some of the appointments of the house. Inside the principal entrance (figure 74), a vestibule led into the great central hall, lighted by a skylight from above and surrounded on the upper floors by balustraded galleries, reached by a large double staircase. To the right of the main hall was a Pompeian drawing room, off which opened a Moorish den and the conservatory. To the left were the Japanese-style living room and a Spanish dining room, with oak-paneled and embossed leatherwork walls. The Japanese living room became especially well known; work on it took some three years to complete and reputedly cost some $150,000. Manly N. Cutter, the designer, used lacquerwood panels and embroidered silk on the upper walls, while below he arranged small shelves for display of some of the choicest pieces of Marquand's extensive collection of Oriental porcelains. The library and upstairs bedrooms were also filled with precious objects and furnishings.[30]

On the diagonally opposite corner of the same block as the Marquand house and constructed between 1885 and 1887 was another Hunt-designed New York town house. For Ogden Mills, the son of D. O. Mills, a millionaire who had become rich in the California Gold Rush, Hunt created a three-and-one-half story brick and stone residence on the southeast corner of Fifth Avenue and Sixty-Ninth Street. In various respects, the Mills house (figure 75) was a throwback to Hunt's work of the 1870s, for its Victorian Gothic style echoed some of the earlier buildings, though here the character was decidedly Venetian or Ruskinian Gothic. The distinctive second-story arcades, with their high, stone-arched windows and blind arches, separated by delicate columns, repeated a theme established at the first-story level in the large, well-separated

Figure 73
Henry G. Marquand
mansion and two adjoin-
ing houses, Madison
Avenue at Sixty-Eighth
Street, New York (1884).
From *King's Photographic
Views of New York* (1895).

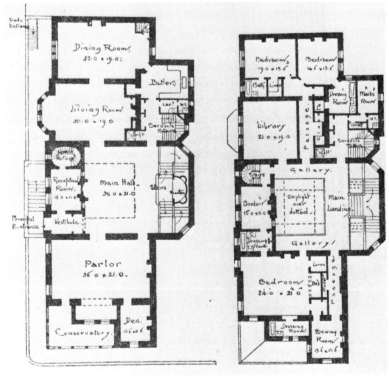

Figure 74
Plan, Henry G. Mar-
quand mansion, Madi-
son Avenue at Sixty-
Eighth Street, New York
(1884). From *American
Architect and Building
News* (August 29, 1891).

Figure 75
Ogden Mills mansion,
Fifth Avenue at Sixty-
Ninth Street, New York
(1887). Museum of the
City of New York.

Figure 76
Association Residence,
Amsterdam Avenue at
One Hundred Fourth
Street, New York (1883).
Photo by James Garri-
son.

openings. A deep-set, higher, arched opening defined the main entrance on the side street. A sill course at the third story in effect marked off the large reception rooms on the two lower floors and defined on the exterior the lower-ceilinged private apartments on the third and the attic stories. An attractive, ample cornice terminated the main façade above the third story, above which a less felicitous attic story rose. Identical massive chimney stacks on the avenue and street fronts displayed blind decorative arches and were buttressed by a gable which formed a pediment embracing the attic-level double windows on each side of each stack. The building was far more restrained than the Marquand house, but dignified and impressive, and certainly not the tour de force that the W. K. Vanderbilt house was. Mrs. Ogden Mills was one of the leading figures of fashionable New York society—some placed her just below Mrs. William B. Astor—and this "really handsome house," as one of her friends called it, furnished in the styles of Louis XV and Louis XVI, was much admired.[31]

Finally, at the beginning of the eighties, in sharp contrast to the opulent town house commissions but important in showing Hunt's attention to varying needs of his day, was the architect's most significant venture into housing for the poor. This was the Association Residence for Respectable Aged Indigent Females, located in New York City on Amsterdam Avenue at One Hundred Fourth Street. The Association had been founded in 1814 to provide relief and support for widows and orphans of soldiers who had served in the War of Independence and in the War of 1812; it had built its first asylum on East Twentieth Street. The new Association home, designed by Hunt, was begun in September 1881 and completed at the end of June 1883, built on land donated some years earlier by James Lenox. In 1903 the building was extended southward to One Hundred Third Street, following Hunt's design, and in 1908 a Gothic-style chapel was added.[32]

Faced in rich red brick above a rough-dressed stone basement, the four-story Association Residence (figure 76) blends both French and Gothic Revival elements. The chief features of the exterior design are the two (later, three) central, slightly projecting pavilions rising into steeply peaked gables, which, with the corner peaked-roof pavilions, provide a rhythmical accent to the line of dormer gables pushing outward from the mansard roof. Well-defined stringcourses and a graceful porch make an interesting horizontal counterrhythm in this main façade.

A major renovation of the Residence was undertaken in 1965 to meet new sanitary standards, but as nursing home requirements were tightened, the building—renamed the Association Residence for Women—

was declared a fire hazard and unsafe and was condemned. In the late 1970s the still handsome building stood empty and vandalized, while an active preservationist campaign sought to save it from demolition.[33]

The dominant achievements in this miscellany of commissions at the close of the seventies and in the early eighties adumbrate one of the most characteristic features of Hunt's work in the years that followed— his great houses in the grand manner, many of them inspired by the style of the early French Renaissance. The W. K. Vanderbilt château, the Borden house, and the Marquand and the Mills mansions all proclaim a mode of building in which Hunt was well prepared to work and that he obviously enjoyed. And yet in this same period, the Princeton Seminary library, the Marquand Chapel, St. Mark's Church, and the Association Residence show his continuing response to different needs and his use of varying styles. The work of the remainder of his career would continue to be richly varied. The ambassador of art had many different missions still to come.

I8

MONUMENTS AND MEMORIALS

As a leading architect, Hunt was increasingly called upon by the early 1880s to design both public monuments and private memorials. In a few instances, such work brought him greater recognition nationally, although he felt that in some of these commissions he did not receive the attention he deserved. In an age that believed in the importance of statuary monuments for civic embellishment and moral inspiration, his contributions were among the most important of their time. In a few of these commissions, such as his collaborations on the statue of George Washington at the New York Subtreasury Building, the Yorktown Monument, and the Statue of Liberty, Hunt created highly significant symbols of shared nationality that could help bind the nation together after the division of the Civil War and the bitter experiences of Reconstruction.

The architect's civic and national monuments were all collaborative endeavors, most of them undertaken with the sculptor John Quincy Adams Ward. Hunt and Ward worked closely together for a quarter of a century, and though they had some disagreements their relationship was generally amiable and was certainly fruitful. The two men were frequently associated as well in civic and artistic organizations, and Hunt designed two houses and a studio on West Forty-Ninth Street in 1868 and a studio-home on West Fifty-Second Street in 1882 for his partner. In their work together, Hunt usually sketched out the general ideas of the design, planned the inscriptions, and furnished drawings of the pedestal, while Ward created the sculptured figures.[1]

One of the more prominent American sculptors of the second half of the nineteenth century, Ward worked primarily in a popular, naturalistic vein, rejecting the neoclassical idealism which had earlier dominated American sculpture. He was born on a farm near Urbana, Ohio, in 1830, and as a child he liked to model small figures in clay in a potter's workshop. On a visit to New York City, he became acquainted with Henry Kirke Brown, with whom William Hunt had studied briefly in Rome in 1844. Brown took him on as a pupil and later hired him as his assistant. After working with him for seven years, Ward left Brown in 1856 to set up his own studio, first making portrait busts in Washington, D.C., and after 1861 working in New York. His *Indian Hunter* for Central Park gave him widespread recognition. Ward was noted for his self-conscious Americanism and was strongly opposed to an American artist's undertaking a career abroad. He did advise young sculptors to study draftsmanship in Europe, perhaps in Paris, and also to visit Rome, but to live abroad, he believed, was a bad mistake, since a modern person must take his inspiration from modern times, not from the past. "An

American sculptor," he insisted, "would serve himself and his age best by working at home." In his work he favored a straightforward realism, which Americans could easily understand and accept. According to Wayne Craven, a leading present-day historian of American sculpture, "Ward removed the banalities from naturalism in American sculpture and ended up with a sharp character-defining naturalism." The frequently derivative character of Hunt's work apparently did not bother Ward, who found himself in special sympathy with the architect's "noble designs." The Seventh Regiment Monument, designed in 1867–1868 and erected in 1873 in Central Park, discussed earlier in connection with Hunt and the Civil War, was only the first of several collaborative commissions of the two artists in New York City and was conceived at the same time the two men were also working on a monument for Newport.[2]

In 1865, August Belmont, the wealthy banker who represented the Rothschild interests in the United States, saw the plaster cast of Ward's *Indian Hunter* in a New York gallery and was so impressed that he sought out the sculptor for a statue commemorating his wife's father. Ward and Hunt worked together, then, on the monument to Commodore Matthew Calbraith Perry, the naval hero remembered particularly for opening ports of Japan to the Western world, whose daughter was married to Belmont, and who had been born in Newport in 1794. The memorial figure of Perry was first destined for the Newport Island Cemetery, but Belmont was prevailed upon to have it set up in Touro Park on a prominent site just opposite the Griswold house.[3]

Perry's statue, cast in bronze, rose eight feet from a pedestal of Quincy granite, also eight feet high. The figure was portrayed in an attitude of repose, the body weight thrown on the left foot and the left hand resting lightly on a sword. The rounded pedestal was simple, not detracting in any way from the figure, and included on a lower belt Perry's name and date and age at death, and, on an upper belt, "Africa, 1843; Mexico, 1846; Treaty with Japan, 1854." The central feature of the pedestal was a group of curved, bas-relief panels, about two feet high, one depicting Perry in Africa, one of Perry in Mexico, and two of the naval hero in Japan. On the plinth of the pedestal were cut an American ensign and anchors and a notation of the donors and the date the statue was erected.[4]

At the dedication of the statue on the morning of October 1, 1868, some one thousand school children sang "America" as Mrs. Caroline Belmont drew a covering from the figure. Following the ceremonies, a large reception was held at the Ocean House Hotel, with many toasts and speeches.

Some Newporters felt, however, that the wrong Perry had been honored and that Matthew's brother Oliver Hazard Perry, the hero of the Battle of Lake Erie in 1813 ("We have met the enemy and they are ours"), was more worthy of remembrance by the city. A subscription was subsequently raised for another statue to the second Perry, which was placed in 1885 on the Newport Parade Ground.[5]

The early 1880s brought another collaboration with Ward and Hunt's first commission from the federal government—the Yorktown Monument. One hundred years before, on October 29, 1781, the Congress of the United States had ordered a marble column erected at Yorktown in Virginia to commemorate the victory of General Washington over Lord Cornwallis, but nothing had come of this directive. With the centennial of the victory approaching, Congress, on December 19, 1879, appointed a joint committee to look into the question of an appropriate monument at Yorktown, and on June 7, 1880, a sum of up to $100,000 was appropriated for the monument. Under the act of 1880, the Secretary of War appointed Hunt, his former pupil Henry Van Brunt, and John Quincy Adams Ward as a commission of artists to select a suitable design for the "Monument to the Alliance and Victory." The three men submitted a design to the Joint Congressional Commission created on March 3, 1881, to oversee construction of the monument and administer a centennial celebration, and after they had made some minor changes their design was approved.[6]

The centennial exercises at Yorktown in October 1881 lasted four days and were very impressive. The ceremonies began with the laying of the cornerstone of the monument in a Masonic rite on October 18. The governor of Virginia welcomed the guests and the chairman of the Congressional Commission made introductory remarks, while a band concert and fireworks added to the festivities. The following day, President Chester A. Arthur gave the principal address, while Robert C. Winthrop presented a centennial oration to the assemblage. A military parade and review took place on October 20, and a naval drill and review on the day after. Ex-presidents Ulysses Grant and Rutherford Hayes, three former vice-presidents, state governors, Supreme Court justices, and members of Congress were present at the exercises.[7]

Hunt, who served as chairman of the monument commission, and his two colleagues oversaw the bidding on the work for the monument and made recommendations on the materials to be used. For their work they charged the usual A.I.A.-recommended fee for monumental work of ten percent of the total estimated cost, which in this case was $100,000, less two percent since the actual superintendence of construction was carried out by the War Department. For their preliminary designs and sketches they were paid $3,000, or three percent, and for their detailed working drawings and models they received an additional $5,000, or five percent. Both Hunt and Ward traveled to Virginia to inspect the progress of the work at Yorktown, and both were there when the crowning figure was set in place on August 12, 1884. At this time Hunt drew a sketch of the monument, still largely enclosed by the scaffolding (figure 77). Hunt attended the unveiling on October 10, 1884, the anniversary of Cornwallis's surrender, but Catharine was ill and could not accompany him to Virginia.[8]

The Yorktown Monument (figure 78) was designed as a statue-topped column celebrating both in sculptured image and word the military victory of 1781, which terminated the Revolutionary War. The monument soared above a terrace which carried a base (stylobate and pediments) that rose thirty-seven feet. A sculptured drum, some twenty-five and one-half feet high, stood atop the base. Then the eye rose another sixty feet to the top of the memorial column. There, standing on her own base, was a figure of Liberty, her arms outstretched. The total height of the monument was about one hundred fifty feet. Extensive inscriptions on the four sides of the base dedicated the monument as a memorial to the Yorktown victory, gave a short narrative of the siege of Yorktown, recounted the treaty of alliance with France, and described the treaty of peace with England. Above these inscriptions, reliefs were placed in the pediments, respectively of the emblems of nationality, war, alliance, and peace. Encircling the drum or podium, Ward sculpted thirteen female figures, representing the original states, hand in hand, above the inscription "One Country, One Constitution, One Destiny." The shaft consisted of several drums joined by bands of laurel leaves with stars in high relief, while the capital of the column displayed boldly articulated eagles on each of the four faces. The sculptor and the architects devised the monument with graceful proportions, the many details not detracting from the unity and impressive scale of the composition as a whole. Hunt was very proud of the Yorktown Monument, which he realized was "little seen and known," but which he believed was "really a good thing." On July 29, 1942, the Liberty figure was decapitated by lightning; a new figure was completed by the sculptor Oskar J. W. Hansen and installed in 1957.[9]

Simultaneously with their work on the Yorktown Monument, Hunt and Ward were engaged on some other projects. The two men worked together on a statue of Lafayette set up at the University of Vermont in Burlington, Vermont; Lafayette himself had come to the college during

Figure 77
Yorktown Monument
under construction,
Yorktown, Virginia,
sketch by R. M. Hunt
(1884). Courtesy The
American Institute of
Architects Foundation/
Prints and Drawings
Collection, Washington,
D.C. Photo by Wm. Ed-
mund Barrett.

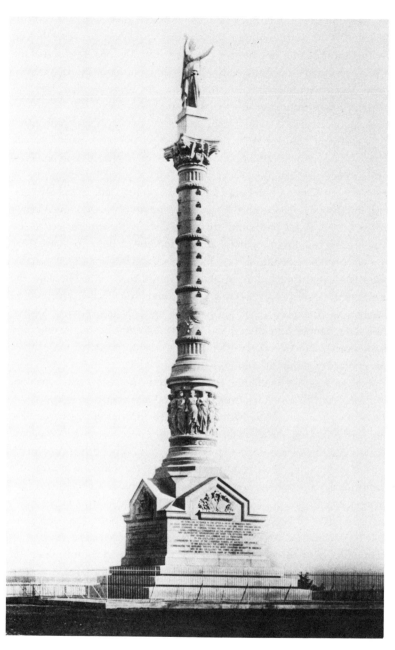

Figure 78
Yorktown Monument,
Yorktown, Virginia
(1884). Courtesy The
American Institute of
Architects Foundation/
Prints and Drawings
Collection, Washington,
D.C. Reproduction by
James Garrison.

his visit to the United States in 1824–1825 and had then laid the cornerstone of the main building. When Hunt and Ward attended the unveiling of the heroic-size bronze statue on June 27, 1883, they heard the college president extoll the statue pedestal as "a work of art," which, since it had been standing on the campus for some months, had "already called forth our earnest thanks to the designer."[10]

A more celebrated statue by the collaborators was unveiled later that same year, on November 26, 1883. Placed on the New York City site where George Washington first took the oath of office as president of the United States in 1789, the Washington Statue (figure 79) was erected by the New York State Chamber of Commerce on the steps of the Subtreasury Building (now Federal Hall National Memorial) on Wall Street facing Broad Street. Ward had submitted two models for the project to the supervisory committee, which had selected one of them in March 1882 and contracted with him to provide a bronze statue for $33,000, while Hunt was commissioned to supply the granite base for $8,000. Like the centennial exercises at Yorktown, the unveiling of the Washington Statue was conceived of as an event of national importance. Several thousand people attended, including President Chester Arthur and Governor Grover Cleveland of New York. Hunt and Ward both sat on the platform among the dignitaries.[11]

For the Washington Statue, Hunt placed the pedestal on a rostrum or abutment, which rose flush from the sidewalk for about seven feet above the base of the steps. The rostrum extended in front of the statue base and formed a platform that might be used for public events. The pedestal was crafted five feet, six and one-half inches high, with simple moldings at the top and near the bottom, and formed a solid and appropriate statue base, harmonizing well with the Greek Revival architecture of the Subtreasury Building. Dignity was the keynote of Ward's larger-than-life-size figure of Washington. Relying considerably in dress and position on Jean-Antoine Houdon's statue in the Virginia Capitol at Richmond, the figure stands beside a truncated fluted column shaft and is shown in the act of taking the oath of office, the right arm somewhat extended. Ward depicted the tall figure in the dress of Washington's day, with a large cloak hanging over the left shoulder and draping the back in full folds.[12]

A year and a half later, on June 6, 1885, the day that the Hunts once more sailed for Europe, another New York civic monument by the two artists was unveiled by Ward. The Pilgrim Statue, set up at the juncture of East Drive and the Seventy-Second Street Roadway in Central Park, was a gift to the city from the New England Society. Here Hunt's pedes-

Figure 79
George Washington
(sculpted by J. Q. A.
Ward), Wall Street, New
York (1883). From *King's
Photographic Views of
New York* (1895).

tal, rising nearly eight feet, was more elaborate than the Washington base: three large granite blocks superimposed on one another with roughly dressed side panels topped with transitional moldings recalled Plymouth Rock in the rugged stone mass. Ward modeled four bronze panels in low relief for the pedestal, placing them in a frieze and flanking them by Doric triglyphs. The front panel represented the emblems of the New England Society, a Bible lying closed on a rock with a sword between the pages. On the rear face, the panel depicted the *Mayflower* under sail, while the two side panels showed an allegory of industry and education and a representation of American Indian objects. An inscription on the front of the pedestal recorded that the statue had been erected "To Commemorate the Landing of the Pilgrim Fathers on Plymouth Rock, December 21, 1620." The bronze statue, nine feet tall, portrayed a stern-visaged Pilgrim dressed in a doublet and wearing a broad-rimmed hat, holding in his right hand the muzzle of a flintlock musket, the butt resting on the plinth of the statue.[13]

Relations between the architect and the sculptor became somewhat strained during the course of their next joint project, the Soldiers' and Sailors' Monument in Brooklyn. The problem was that more than once newspaper stories about their works attributed the civic monuments solely to the sculptor. Hunt was particularly aggrieved that in publicity concerning the large commission for Brooklyn his name had been omitted from one newspaper account and Ward's photograph had been included in another story, while there had been no picture of him. Hunt wanted it made clear in public accounts of their work that he had designed the "ensemble" of the monuments, was responsible for the architectural work, and had shared with the sculptor the preparation of the models. Early in 1886 the model for the Brooklyn Soldiers' and Sailors' Monument was completed; it included four equestrian statues and a crowning group representing peace. Hunt and Ward had been apprised of a limit of $250,000 for the monument, but they went ahead with a design which it was estimated would cost more than twice that figure. The project was stopped, and the costly work was never built.[14]

Yet another joint endeavor of the two artists was the Garfield Monument (figure 80), erected near the western edge of the United States Capitol grounds in Washington, D.C., and unveiled on May 12, 1887. The Society of the Army of the Cumberland commissioned the monument, and by an act of Congress in 1884, $30,000 was appropriated for preparation of the site and erection of the pedestal. The site was selected on December 1, 1884, and by the spring of 1885 Hunt's and Ward's designs for the model of the monument had been completed. There was

Figure 80
James Garfield Monument (sculpted by J. Q. A. Ward), Washington, D.C. (1887). Photo by the author.

then little progress, for some reason, until March 1887, when work moved ahead rapidly. The pedestal was completed by the end of April, and the bronze figures were in place in early May.[15]

A somewhat conventional representation of the heavily garbed president stood atop a fourteen-and-one-half-foot circular pedestal of Quincy granite, decorated by three panels in low relief and an encircling swag of garlands. At the projecting base, Ward placed three reclining allegorical figures, reminiscent of Michelangelo's Medici Chapel figures, representing Garfield as the student, the warrior, and the statesman. The idealized figures below are in sharp contrast with the naturalistic figure above, though the difference in treatment does not jar the viewer but rather adds a further dimension in visual impact. Hunt's pedestal is nicely subordinated to and seems an appropriate resting place for the figures.[16]

Hunt's long association with Ward included two more major works early in the 1890s. The statues of Horace Greeley and Henry Ward Beecher honored two prominent citizens of New York and Brooklyn who for years had been civic leaders and molders of public opinion and who both articulated for their contemporaries nationwide many of the ideals and attitudes of the Gilded Age.

Greeley, who had founded the *New York Tribune*, long espoused reformist causes through his newspaper. A move to raise a statue to him began almost immediately after his death in 1872 and was renewed somewhat later when Hunt's new Tribune Building was completed, but little was done for some years, until in 1881 Whitelaw Reid, the subsequent editor of the *Tribune*, invited Ward to create a statue. An awkward site was chosen for the statue in a sidewalk niche in front of the Tribune Building directly before a large window.[17]

The Greeley Statue was unveiled in a dignified ceremony on September 20, 1890. Colonel John Hay gave a brief address, and Chauncey M. Depew, one of the foremost speakers of his times, delivered the oration of the day; then, as the Seventh Regiment band played, Miss Gabrielle Greeley, a daughter of the journalist, pulled aside the enveloping draperies to reveal the seated bronze figure. Ward had portrayed the newspaperman in a characteristic pose, seated in a low, fringed, upholstered armchair, leaning forward and looking up from a copy of the *Tribune* resting on his right knee with his left arm placed on the arm of the chair. The figure was shown dressed in a suit of rough cloth, the vest cut low, and a cravat loosely tied under his chin whiskers. The pose is contemplative, as if Greeley were listening to a visitor who had interrupted his reading. Ward said of the work that he had attempted to give "the features the expression of childlike simplicity, together with the strength of a philosopher, which was peculiar to him." The portrait was both highly realistic and very penetrating. Hunt's austere, slightly sloped pedestal of polished dark Quincy granite stood about six and one-half feet high and included the single inscription "Horace Greeley Founder of The New York Tribune." In 1916, the Greeley Statue was moved a short distance to City Hall Park, where it is located today.[18]

The Beecher Statue was considerably more elaborate, more costly, and more carefully planned. As the noted preacher of Brooklyn's Plymouth Church lay dying, plans were already being made for a death mask to be taken, and within an hour of Beecher's death on March 8, 1887, Ward was summoned to make the facial likeness. Within three days, arrangements were started for a subscription and a Statue Fund Committee was set up. By the end of July 1887, some $25,000 had already been collected from about six thousand subscribers. An additional $10,000 was subscribed for the statue in the months that followed.[19]

The Beecher Statue Fund Committee signed Articles of Agreement with Ward on April 6, 1888, to provide the statue for a payment of $35,000. Ward in turn arranged for the pedestal with Hunt and paid for the materials, the casting, and the work of erection. Hunt's pedestal design was a simple, splayed-edge block with upper moldings and set upon two steps; but the preparation of the statue actually involved the continuing attention of the architect, and his small fee of $310 was not commensurate with the work involved.[20]

Ward completed the plaster model of the Beecher Statue in the winter of 1889, and the figures were cast in May of 1890. Originally a site in Prospect Park in Brooklyn was chosen, but subsequently a more prominent location in front of Brooklyn City Hall (later Borough Hall) was selected. The statue was unveiled on June 24, 1891, in ceremonies presided over by the mayor and attended by an estimated 15,000 spectators. After the invocation and selections by a military band, while several hundred children sang Beecher's favorite hymn, the minister's granddaughter, aided by the sculptor, pulled the cord allowing the cloth covering the statue to fall. Seth Low, the president of Columbia College, provided the customary oration, an extended eulogy of the controversial preacher, and the ceremonies concluded with everyone singing "America" followed by a final prayer. Like most of the other unveiling ceremonies, this was looked upon as a solemn and significant civic occasion in which an object having important symbolic meanings was presented to the public for their instruction and moral elevation.[21]

In the view of Lewis I. Sharp, a noted historian of American sculpture, "the Beecher Monument epitomizes 19th-century public statuary at its best." Here (figure 81) Ward presented a realistic image of a stern-faced Beecher (the expression taken from the death mask) standing as if poised to deliver an address. The nine-foot figure is decidedly monumental in conception, with the details of dress simplified by a large enveloping cape, and it forms the apex of a triangle with the secondary figures at the two sides of the base. The lower genre figures placed on the narrower faces of the pedestal have an intimate and informal character much in contrast to the rather awesome figure above them: on the left, a young black girl kneels on the pedestal steps and reaches up to place a palm leaf at the clergyman's feet, symbolizing Beecher's abolitionist role, while on the right, a small boy assists a little girl, who reaches up to lay a garland of flowers on the plinth, indicating Beecher's love for children. The Beecher Statue, like that of Greeley and like most public statuary in America, is little regarded today in Cadman Plaza Park, but it remains an outstanding example of late nineteenth-century realistic portrait statuary and as such an important part of our national artistic inheritance.[22]

Decidedly different from Hunt's other monument projects and one that Ward did not share was an 1887 commission for the village of Geneseo, New York. William Austin Wadsworth and Herbert Wadsworth wished to honor the memory of their mother with a civic monument, and they invited Hunt to design a fountain to be erected at the prominent intersection of Main and Center streets. The Wadsworth Memorial Fountain was erected and dedicated in 1888. It was modeled on a street fountain Hunt had seen in Bern, Switzerland, during his visits there in 1844 and 1885. The basin of the fountain was carved in Maine from a single piece of Bay of Fundy red granite. It was twelve feet in diameter and weighed fifteen tons, and its transportation to Geneseo was a difficult engineering feat that attracted much local attention. The most arresting feature of the fountain was a metal statue of a bear sitting upright on its haunches and holding a lamp standard in its forepaws. The pedestal on which the bear sat was the capital of a high shaft that rose from the center of the basin. Originally a steady stream of piped-in spring water poured into the granite basin from each of four arms extending outward from the lower part of the shaft. Later, the fountain was altered so that the arms might support electric lights and water might flow from piping encircling the shaft. For years, the Wadsworth Memorial Fountain served both an aesthetic function and one of utility for the residents of Geneseo. When a traffic signal was attached, it even played a role as a silent policeman at the busy intersection. In 1976, the traffic

Figure 81
Henry Ward Beecher
Monument (sculpted by
J. Q. A. Ward), Brook-
lyn, New York (1891).
Photo by the author.

paraphenalia was removed and the fountain was restored to its original state.[23]

Besides public monuments, Hunt designed several private cemetery memorials, the most important of these being the memorial to August Belmont and his wife, for whom Hunt had created the Perry Monument. Located at the east end of Perry Circle in the Newport Island Cemetery, just a few steps from the Romanesque Belmont Chapel, which Hunt remodeled, the Belmont tomb was erected in 1890–1891, commissioned by O. H. P. Belmont to honor his parents. Ward's life-size portrait statue of August Belmont placed some yards distant in front of the chapel contemplates the tomb and enlarges the composition physically as well as deepens it spiritually. Once more, Hunt and Ward worked successfully together.

Classical Greek in inspiration, the Belmont tomb (figure 82) is essentially a large, curved, stone bench backed by a high railing terminating in piers and centered upon a sarcophagus covered by a small, temple-like shrine. This architectural conceit has a gabled roof, carried by Ionic columns. A round arch at its front is supported at each end by a graceful caryatid. An elevated sarcophagus is placed in front of the central element. The lines and forms of the monument are simple and straightforward, giving the composition an impressive dignity.[24]

The most important of Hunt's statuary collaborations came not with John Quincy Adams Ward but with an Alsatian who had conceived a monument on a colossal scale. Frédéric Auguste Bartholdi's Statue of Liberty in New York Harbor is surely the most significant work of monumental sculpture in the United States and an object that has become central among national symbolic images. A gift from the people of France to the people of the United States, the statue was bestowed to celebrate the friendship of the two countries and to serve as a memorial to the idea of liberty. Subsequently, it became widely recognized as a symbol of America as a refuge for immigrants and later yet as a personification of the nation and a symbol of its ideals.

Like the founding of the Metropolitan Museum of Art, the original impulse for the Statue of Liberty came from a gathering held in France. Several years passed before the idea took hold and work was begun, however, and several more years went by before the monument was completed. The project was a vast undertaking, involving many people and many complicated transactions. Hunt's work on it came in the early 1880s when his creative energies were at a peak.

The idea of commemorating the centennial of American independence and Franco-American friendship by the gift of a sculptural memo-

rial to the United States first came up in the summer of 1865 at a dinner at the home near Versailles of Edouard de Laboulaye, a professor and historian and an interpreter of American politics to the French. Laboulaye was a steadfast opponent of the Second Empire and later would become a principal supporter of the Third Republic. He and other republicans envisioned the monumental gift as an affirmation of French ideals of freedom and independence—submerged under Napoleon III—and as a means, therefore, to strengthen their own cause of republican liberty in France. One of the guests at the 1865 dinner, Bartholdi, an Alsatian sculptor, was excited by the idea of this international gift, which he kept in mind for some years. In the summer of 1870 he began work in his studio on a preliminary model for the project. Following the close of the Franco-Prussian War, Bartholdi in 1871 visited the United States, where he spent five months studying the land and the people. Later, he recounted that when he first entered New York Harbor he had a vision of a colossal statue of the goddess of liberty holding a torch of freedom. Bartholdi's suggestions were received enthusiastically both in the United States and in France; and in 1874 a Franco-American Union was formed, headed by Laboulaye, to organize and arrange financing for the project. Bartholdi was employed to build the statue in France, while the French Committee worked to raise funds for it through public entertainments, a lottery, and donations. An American Committee was established to raise funds for erection of a suitable pedestal for the statue.[25]

By 1875, Bartholdi had settled on the final form of the statue in a clay model, and the next year the right arm and torch were built and were sent for exhibit at the Philadelphia Centennial. Subsequently the arm and torch were placed on exhibit in Madison Square in New York City, and the colossal head was shown at the Paris Exposition of 1878. Meanwhile, in the United States, contributions for the pedestal were lagging. A new committee under the Union League Club and headed by John Jay was set up in September 1876 to collect funds, while yet another committee worked in Philadelphia to make collections. But despite the exhibit at the Centennial and the exposure in Madison Square there was general apathy toward the project and apparent disbelief that the statue would ever be completed. Americans outside New York City were generally uninterested. Moreover, cost projections for the pedestal shot up to twice the original estimate of $125,000. Matters were not helped when word got out that Bartholdi, on his visit to the United States in 1876, had brought with him as his mistress his model for the statue. However, *that* problem was resolved by their marriage in Newport at the end of the year. Although a new pedestal committee of four hundred prominent citizens was formed in January 1877 under William M. Evarts, soon to become U.S. Secretary of State, public indifference continued.[26]

By a joint resolution of Congress, on March 3, 1877, the president was authorized to designate and set apart a site for the statue and provide for its maintenance and preservation. President Rutherford B. Hayes quickly authorized General William T. Sherman to choose a site, and Sherman, supporting Bartholdi's preference, fixed on Bedloes Island, though for some time a jurisdictional dispute went on between the War and the Treasury Departments respecting the facilities already there. Fort Wood, a small installation in the shape of an eleven-point star, built as protection for New York Harbor and garrisoned from 1811 to 1877, was located on the small island. Later, when construction began, control of the island was turned over to the executive committee of the general American Committee of the Franco-American Union, which named Hunt as architect in chief of the project. On November 25, 1881, Hunt requested a survey of Bedloes Island, showing the size and dimensions of the fort and parapet, along with the ground plan and sections; about the same time he also wrote to Bartholdi asking for information about the pedestal. In reply to Hunt, Bartholdi attempted to impress on the architect the importance of getting competent engineering advice on anchoring the statue to the pedestal. By this time, of course, the design for the statue had long been fixed and much of it had already been built, and the French Committee had as early as October 1875 made preliminary determinations about the size, shape, and decorations of the pedestal. Bartholdi's early pedestal designs, with a high, narrow massing provided the basic forms that Hunt subsequently elaborated upon. Hunt, however, had his own ideas, and the completed design was his.[27]

By early 1883, the engineers on the project, headed by General Charles P. Stone, an army engineer, had decided that the most feasible site for the statue foundation was "all the space enclosed by the parapet wall of Fort Wood." The fort itself would become a part of the statue base, with the interior filled in, thus providing the statue a wide surrounding esplanade. In the months that followed, the concrete foundation placed within the fort was built up as a hollow, truncated pyramid, ninety-one feet square at the base, sixty-six feet seven inches square at the top, and sixty-five feet, ten inches high. The foundation was completed on May 17, 1884, and the cornerstone of the pedestal was laid on August 5, 1884. The pedestal, another hollow truncated pyramid of concrete, faced by granite from Leete's Island, Connecticut, rose eighty-nine feet above the foundation to a square forty-three feet six inches at the top. The statue itself stood one hundred fifty-one feet one inch above the pedestal.[28]

As the foundation was being built up, work on the statue itself continued in France. By 1882 the funds necessary for constructing and transporting the figure had been fully raised in France. But American donations for the pedestal continued to lag, and it was even feared that construction might have to be abandoned. On July 4, 1884, the completed statue, *Liberty Enlightening the World,* was officially presented to the United States minister in Paris, Levi P. Morton, Hunt's friend and patron. At Bedloes Island, work on the pedestal moved along into the fall of 1884, but then had to stop since funds had run out.

Joseph Pulitzer, the owner and editor of the *New York World,* came to the rescue. In March 1885, Pulitzer undertook to publicize the campaign for additional funds—some $100,000 was still needed—emphasizing that this was not a local project but a truly national endeavor, which had significance for all Americans. Theatrical benefits, cake sales, sporting events, and dances were organized to raise funds. School children were asked to contribute their pennies. Emma Lazarus's poem ("Give me your tired, your poor, . . .") helped arouse interest in the statue. For months, Pulitzer printed the names of contributors on the front page of the *World;* as the campaign continued, the circulation of the newspaper soared. On May 11, work was resumed on the pedestal, and by August it was completed. On August 11, Pulitzer presented to the American Committee more than $100,000 sent to the *World* by some 120,000 people. The disassembled statue sections, made from thin sheets of beaten copper, arrived at Bedloes Island on June 19 and were stored in warehouses there until the figure was erected in 1886.[29]

Gustave Eiffel designed and built the supporting frame for the statue, which was tied into Hunt's pedestal base. At the twenty-nine-foot level of the pedestal, four huge steel girders were built into the walls forming a square across the inner core; fifty-five feet higher, near the top of the pedestal, another such square of girders was placed in the core. Four tie posts connected the two squares and extended upward to form the main posts of the framework of the statue itself. In this way the statue was securely tied to the pedestal. Horizontal struts joined the four inward leaning main posts, and two diagonals were used as braces in each of the panels formed by the struts and posts. An elaborate trusswork extended out from the frame and to it the copper sheathing of statue was attached. The smaller framework of the arm and the head were supported by the main frame.[30]

In designing the pedestal for *Liberty*, Hunt faced the same challenge as in his other, less ambitious statuary collaborations: he had to provide a base that was proportionate in size and that harmonized with the statue, though not so massive or bulky nor so elaborate as to call attention to itself and turn the viewer's eye from the figure placed upon it. In this case, in addition, the great statue had to be situated so as to dominate upper New York Harbor. Using the star-shaped fort to form a wide, terraced base, into which the foundation was fixed, was an excellent conception, since this solid, spreading base helped give a strong impression that the colossus was securely anchored to the ground.

Hunt made his first tentative designs for the pedestal in 1882 and 1883. As Marvin Trachtenberg has pointed out in his thorough study of the Statue of Liberty, Hunt soon realized the need for a strong vertical emphasis in the pedestal to counter the outward thrust of the star-shaped fort as well as a rough textured surface to complement the strong stonework of the fort. His first elaborated model, known as "Pharos I," executed in 1883, was a one hundred-fourteen-foot high shaft of textured stone with projecting blocks emphasizing the rough surface and a triple loggia set high in each face and a Doric frieze in the socle. In a second version, "Pharos II," made in 1883–1884, Hunt removed the Doric frieze and integrated the loggia into a heavy cornice directly above, thus more sharply defining the loggia and tightening the composition. But criticism of the projected height of the pedestal and the shortage of funds led him to scale down the height to eighty-nine feet and rework the design. The definitive pedestal project (figure 83) was ready by August 7, 1884.[31]

In the executed pedestal (figure 84), the roughly dressed cyclopean stonework in the plinth gives an impression of great strength and solidity, which is emphasized as well by the contrasting openings. Pedimented openings are centered low on each side above the terrace level, while higher up the tall loggia openings accent the verticality of the monument and lead the eye upward to the figure. A heavy, parapeted cornice serving as a balcony surrounding the upper portion of the pedestal appears to provide a secondary plinth for the statue and gives it a yet firmer resting place; smaller pedimented openings here lead to the interior. The panels, the pilasters, the shields, and other decorations on the faces of the pedestal are characteristically Néo-Grec. In the scale of the forms and in the subordination of decorative detail as well as in the emphasis on solidity and vertical thrust, the Statue of Liberty pedestal was highly successful.[32]

Inaugural ceremonies were held on October 28, 1886. Following a

Figure 83
Pedestal design (1884)
for the Statue of Liberty,
New York (1886). Cour-
tesy of American
Museum of Immigra-
tion, Statue of Liberty
N.M.; National Park Ser-
vice, U.S. Department of
the Interior.

Figure 84
Statue of Liberty. Cour-
tesy The American Insti-
tute of Architects
Foundation/Prints and
Drawings Collection,
Washington, D.C. Photo
by Edward Bierstadt.

parade in Manhattan, the participants proceeded by ship to Bedloes Island, where the main events were held in front of the statue. After an opening prayer, Count Ferdinand de Lesseps spoke on behalf of the Franco-American Union, and then William Evarts, now senator from New York, gave the presentation address. During his rather florid oration, Evarts took special notice of "the genius of the architect" in designing "a pedestal not unworthy of the statue." While the speeches were going on, Bartholdi was waiting high up in the torch holding a rope to release a huge tricolor flag covering the statue's face at the moment of acceptance. Unfortunately, from his high perch Bartholdi could neither hear the words of the speaker below nor see what was happening. Suddenly, hearing applause, he pulled the rope and the flag fell; at this signal the bands began to play and ships' whistles blew. But Senator Evarts had not in fact completed what he had come to say, and he directed the music to be stopped. He then went on speaking. The whistles from ships around the harbor nonetheless continued. Finally, when Evarts concluded, President Cleveland was able to accept the monument. Next on this day of speechmaking came a commemorative address by Chauncey M. Depew, in which he extolled the friendship of the French and American peoples, focused on Lafayette's part in the American Revolution, and dealt with the statue's symbolic meaning of freedom for the individual in the United States. In this year of the Haymarket Massacre, however, he also inveighed against anarchists and bombings and those aliens and enemies who would disturb the peace and dethrone the laws. Music, more prayers, and salutes from the men-of-war in the harbor terminated the ceremonies. All in all, the speeches and the celebration provided a comforting re-affirmation of generally held values.[33]

The following May, the French government sent to Hunt a blue Sèvres vase, which Bartholdi had selected. Inside an inscription on paper recorded that the vase was presented in appreciation of all that he had done for the work of the Franco-American Union. Some time later Catharine came upon her husband washing out the vase with soap and water, and the inscription had disappeared. When she asked him what he was doing, Hunt replied indifferently that he just "wanted to get rid of that dirty piece of paper."[34]

With the design for the Statue of Liberty pedestal settled and the work finally moving along toward completion, the Hunts with their four younger children once again sailed for Europe on June 6, 1885. It was another return to the font, going back once more for renewal of their physical energies and a sharpening of their aesthetic perceptions. This time there was an additional reason: Dick Hunt had preceded his parents to Europe the previous October to prepare to enter the Ecole des Beaux-Arts, and they naturally were eager to see him. Richard Morris Hunt was to remain for a full year on this visit, while his wife stayed four months longer.[1]

The trip on the *Etruria* began inauspiciously. Fifteen-year-old Joe came down with the mumps aboard ship, and when they arrived at Liverpool, eight days after leaving New York, Joe and his mother had to remain in quarantine for a few days. But their discomforts were soon behind them. In London, as usual, the elder Hunts quickly plunged into a round of dinner parties, theater going, and sightseeing. MacVickar Anderson, president of the Royal Institute of British Architects, gave a dinner in Hunt's honor. Sir Frederick Leighton, president of the Royal Academy, entertained them at dinner as well as at an Academy opening, where he was dressed in "scarlet velvet robes with a great jeweled collar." Sir Lawrence Alma-Tadema, the painter and decorator, Russell Sturgis, the American architect and critic, and Junius Spencer Morgan, the American banker, all invited the Hunts to dine. After a busy fortnight in London, they went on to Paris, arriving just in time to learn of Dick Hunt's engagement to Pearl Carley from Louisville, Kentucky— and for his younger sister Kitty to come down with the mumps. In Paris, Bartholdi was most anxious to meet with Hunt and discuss the work on the Statue of Liberty pedestal. Hunt apparently wanted to put the cares of his work completely behind him, however, and failed to get in touch with the sculptor, much to the Frenchman's disappointment. Hunt preferred spending time with his children, taking them to places that he had known so well over the years.[2]

In late July the family went on to Germany. For a time Richard took the waters at Bad Homburg, near Frankfurt, while the rest of the family remained in Schwalbach, where they had stayed on their last European trip. The spa was "a delightfully lazy resting place," where they could sit listening to the bands on long sunny afternoons. Esther and Kitty took music lessons there, and Kitty and Joe studied German. Subsequently, in Frankfurt, they were joined by the parents of their son's fiancée, and they soon went by way of Holland and Belgium back to England, where, in the rustic village of Sonning-on-Thames, Dick Hunt and Pearl Carley were married on September 16, 1885. A few friends came for the wedding as well as several people from the village. Local choirboys and ten bell ringers provided music for the occasion. The wedding festivities precipitated a severe attack of gout for Hunt, however, and for two weeks the family stayed on in the village at a small inn overlooking the river, where the local vicar amused them with ghost stories. After the wedding, Joe returned to the United States to re-enter St. Marks School.[3]

In October, the Hunts went on to Lucerne, Bern, and Lugano in Switzerland. The two youngest children, Esther and Herbert, were placed in a boarding school in Switzerland, while their parents and the older daughter Kitty traveled to Italy. Richard returned once more to his sketchbooks, recording many church fronts and architectural details, though by 1885 his hand seemed much less sure than it had been ten years earlier. Still very much the collector, he delighted in scouring antique shops, picking up carved panels and other objects. A high point of the Italian visit was the day that Hunt took his daughter to the Charterhouse at Pavia for several hours of sketching. Catharine, with Kitty, joined her brother Joseph Howland and his wife Eliza for a brief tour of the Italian lake country. And there was Venice too: on every return Hunt was greatly moved by the beauty of the island city. As his daughter noted in her journal, her father was "as wild about Saint Marks as if he had seen it for the first time."[4]

But Paris always remained their European home, and they returned to settle there for the winter, hiring governesses and teachers of French, German, music, and painting for the three children. Dick Hunt was now studying at the Ecole, and his father regularly attended dinners held by the school. Hunt also participated in a reception of the Institut de France, of which he had been elected a corresponding member in the Beaux-Arts section. "It was so nice," his daughter wrote in her journal, "to see the dear father amongst the great men of France in embroidered coats." Richard went to the château at Chantilly to have breakfast one day with his long-time acquaintance, the Duc d'Aumale, a son of Louis Philippe, and he regularly saw such old friends as the painters Adolphe William Bouguereau and Paul Baudry. Baudry, who had been Hunt's traveling companion in Venice in 1852 and who had recently painted the salon ceiling in the W. K. Vanderbilt House, died while they were in Paris and a particularly elaborate funeral was held for him in his painting studio. Hunt helped out his friend the painter Carolus-Duran as an intermediary in a controversy the Frenchman had become involved in with a Brooklyn brewer. On a visit to Paris the brewer had purchased a Carolus-Duran painting of "an exceedingly nude lady, lying upon a couch." When he got the picture to the New York Customs House, his sense of propriety reasserted itself and he refused to pay the duties and had the picture sent back to the artist. After considerable transatlantic correspondence, Hunt made an arrangement whereby the artist agreed to drape the lady to meet the brewer's requirements, and the painting went off to America once again. When the Hunts visited César Daly, the art publisher, at his country house, one of the sons of the family proposed marriage to seventeen-year-old Kitty, whom he had just met, a proposal that was reiterated a short time later by Madame Daly, who formally requested Kitty's hand for her son.[5]

As during the sojourn in Europe a decade earlier, the Hunts again experienced many family troubles. In Paris, Richard once more was immobilized with the gout, Herbert contracted the chicken pox, and Kitty fell very ill with the flu. Then Richard had an eye infection. Catharine was called to Menton to be with her brother, Joseph Howland, who had become critically ill and who died there in March 1886. Later, while Catharine remained in Paris with her sister-in-law, Richard made a three weeks' trip to Spain, in part to see the Holy Week ceremonies in Seville. There he especially admired the Giralda Tower, later copied by Stanford White at the old Madison Square Garden in 1890. Near Ávila, Hunt's train was attacked by brigands, but he escaped unharmed and returned to Paris with a trunkful of souvenirs. In June, he sailed for the United States to return to work. Catharine, who suffered chronic problems with one arm, went back to Schwalbach, where Joe joined them, coming from school in the United States; subsequently, she and the children visited Heidelberg, Baden-Baden, Vevey, Interlaken, and Geneva, while she awaited the birth of her first grandchild. On August 27, 1886, in Paris, Richard Howland and Pearl Carley Hunt became the parents of a son, whom they named Richard Carley Hunt. Catharine and her younger children stayed on for a month longer in France and a few days in London, before sailing on the *Etruria* in October. Still suffering from the gout, Hunt met the ship in New York, and they all went directly to Newport for the autumn.[6]

Hunt's life thus had fallen into a pattern of years of intensive work preceded and followed by extended sojourns abroad. Somehow Hunt needed the European interludes, even though in America he was not confined to the city and did considerable travel and had extended holidays. Europe afforded much that America did not and much that he found essential. The ambassador of art from the Old World to the New had in a sense to return from time to time to renew his mandate.

The Hunts had sold their New York town house at 49 West Thirty-

Fifth Street before going abroad in 1885. On their return to New York, after the autumn months in Newport, they rented furnished number 2 Washington Square North, and were established in this Greek Revival house by early 1887. The house was a substantial row house dating from the early 1830s, with large rooms, elegant plaster moldings, a delicate, curved staircase, and a comfortable library. Hunt had now returned almost to the spot where he had made his first home in New York City in 1856; the old University Building stood diagonally just across the street. And Catharine, who had lived as a child at 12 Washington Square North, was also returning to a street she knew well. This house would be their New York residence for the remainder of Hunt's life.[7]

With the three younger children at home, there always was much going on in the large house. And the Hunts, as in their old house, frequently entertained at home and were sought-after dinner guests. Hunt continued to enjoy his clubs and often dined at the University and the Century. At the latter he occasionally spent an evening with his engaging and witty patron Martin Brimmer, visiting from Boston, or his flamboyant colleague Stanford White.[8]

In 1887, while a student at St. Marks, Joe was plagued by ill health; when he fell sick with pneumonia, his mother went to stay with him at school for several weeks. Later he came down with pleurisy and then peritonitis and on recovery was sent by his doctor to Bermuda for recuperation. Anxiety over his son's condition brought on an especially severe attack of the gout for Hunt. Despite Joe's loss of school time, he continued to be an outstanding student, and at his graduation in June 1888, he was named the class valedictorian and the winner of several prizes. His father was invited to speak to the graduating class, and though he refused to prepare a formal address, he did make some "ringing" impromptu remarks to the graduates. Joe subsequently studied at Harvard College and worked in his father's office, later following his older brother to the Ecole des Beaux-Arts. He later yet entered into architectural practice with his brother.[9]

Despite his dislike of speechmaking, Hunt did continue to make public appearances for which a speech was in order. When honored by the Vermont Association in 1887 by a dinner in Boston, he responded with a prepared talk, which, his widow later recorded, "seems to have left an indelible impression upon all who heard it." He was also honored by the members of the Architectural League of New York, a society of young professionals established in 1881, which gave a reception for him on December 17, 1887, at the opening of an exhibition of drawings at the Fifth Avenue Art Galleries. The most prominent display area in the galleries was given over to drawings that Hunt had made as a student at the Ecole and while he had worked with Lefuel on the Pavillon de la Bibliothèque. Hunt responded with informal remarks. On another occasion when he spoke before the Architectural League, his announced topic was "Vistas," but in his informal and rambling fashion he managed to avoid the stated subject completely.[10]

The architect was obliged to make several public appearances in the next few years, after he had agreed at the annual meeting of the American Institute of Architects held in Chicago in 1887 to serve as the third president, following Richard Upjohn and Thomas U. Walter in that position. Hunt assumed office on January 1, 1888, and as presiding officer made the opening address at the twenty-second annual convention, which met in Buffalo in October 1888. He always agonized over his speeches—and this one was no exception—although even in large meetings he sometimes ended by discarding the address he had prepared and speaking extemporaneously.[11]

By the time Hunt became president, one of the principal questions before the Institute was the question of communications and liaison with the newly formed Western Association of Architects. Separated by considerable distance from the Eastern seaboard and feeling themselves neglected by the Institute, a group of more than one hundred Midwestern architects had come together in Chicago on November 12, 1884, to form the Western Association. The founding of *The Inland Architect and Builder* the previous year had intensified the self-consciousness of the Midwesterners, and Robert Craik McLean, the editor, had taken a leading part in organizing the new group. The membership expanded very rapidly; by the time of the 1888 Institute meeting, the Western Association was already considerably larger than the much older Institute, and consolidation between the two organizations had been under discussion for some months. One sticking point was the fact that the Institute maintained two classes of membership—fellows and associates—while the Western Association had no such distinction.[12]

Hunt presided over the important November 1889 meeting of the Institute—the twenty-third annual convention—held in Cincinnati. In greeting the delegates, Hunt reviewed the Institute's history and dwelt especially on the importance of the chapter system of organization for promoting the interchange of ideas and experiences and making a strong association. "The Institute," Hunt affirmed, "depends upon its chapters for its very life blood." Every architect as a "self-protective duty" should belong to one of the Institute chapters. Too often, Hunt stated, young men beginning to practice architecture were "eager to establish new leagues, associations, societies and clubs, rather than affiliate with established institutions and reap the profit of proved effort." But "a little reflection" would show them that "the insistent and persistent course of the Institute for the rights, for the dignity, and for the position of architecture as a fine art, so long ignored in this country" had created important precedents and had "elevated the profession in America to its present honorable standing."[13]

In the business meeting, a special committee on consolidation, which had been set up in conjunction with the Western Association, submitted recommendations for the proposed merger. Hunt supported consolidation. The discussions were stormy, and Hunt worked long hours behind the scenes to effect compromises. During the meeting the two groups agreed to consolidate under the name of the older association, with a revised constitution that enlarged the board of directors and abolished the category of "associate" member. Architects in the Western Association entered the Institute as fellows, while the former associates of the Institute also became fellows of the restructured Institute. The chapter system was retained.[14]

Before nominations for officers were opened, a letter was read from Dankmar Adler, chairman of the Western Association consolidation committee, who expressed his regret at not being able to be present at the meeting and his wish that the name of Richard Morris Hunt would be placed in nomination as president of the reorganized Institute. Adler's praise of Hunt was so well phrased and so widely shared that the reading of his letter was interrupted by bursts of applause. It was then moved and seconded that Hunt be elected by acclamation, and this was done. Hunt was so affected by the unanimous vote that when he rose to speak his voice broke and tears streamed down his cheeks, and he was obliged to sit down. When he stood up a second time, more composed, he thanked the members and promised to do all he could to carry out the work of the Institute. He was re-elected the next year and served through 1891, a two-year limit on presidential office having been placed in the revised bylaws.[15]

Hunt's unanimous selection by his fellow professionals to head the newly unified national organization was a formal recognition of his position as the leading architect in the United States. As a skilled designer, he had been highly productive, and his body of completed buildings was impressive. His work with his colleagues in the Institute during three decades had greatly helped to build and strengthen professional ties. His public statements had consistently been aimed at

improving the position of the profession. He had conscientiously worked
to elevate the public taste.

Yet just as important as his record of achievement was his character.
At the 1889 convention, a young architect, Glenn Brown, got his first
look at a number of well-known practitioners, including Hunt. To
Brown, "the newly elected president, Richard Morris Hunt, active, aggressive, intelligent, with high social and professional standing, was in
every way fitted for a good executive." He was, Brown thought, "affable
and charming in his personality, enthusiastic and persistent in all that
pertained to the advancement of architecture and the allied arts," and
decidedly a "virile man" who could put vigor into the consolidated
association. In the view of Montgomery Schuyler, "the good sense, the
moderation and the judicial temper" of the architect "so impressed
themselves upon all who came to know him that they esteemed him as
an eminently safe counsellor." Already for years, with "his unselfish
devotion to the interest of [his] profession," Hunt had been regarded
"as the *doyen* and representative of his profession" and now "he had
attained that place by seniority of years [and] service." He was, another
commentator wrote, "perhaps the most beloved by the greatest number
of his own profession."[16]

The reorganized and enlarged Institute met in Washington, D.C., the
following year in October. Just two weeks before the 1890 meeting, Hunt
penned a frantic note to John Wellborn Root, the secretary, asking Root
to send him any information he might have to help him in preparing his
presidential address. He was uncertain as to what he should talk about.
But Hunt, who was then already working on George W. Vanderbilt's
estate in North Carolina, fell ill with a bad cold, was confined to his
room, and could not attend the convention. He sent his presidential
address to be read.[17]

In the speech, Hunt touched on subjects that were central to his
preoccupations. He commended the delegates for meeting in the nation's capital, where they might particularly enjoy several works of
Thomas U. Walter, which, by contrast to the mixture "of every conceivable style of building to be found in this metropolis," were characterized
by "dignity and repose," the two qualities which he most often positively emphasized as architectural values. A spectator, indeed, might
have "a certain feeling of rest while contemplating [Walter's] work."
Hunt went on to discuss the situation of architectural design for governmental buildings. In his opinion the Supervising Architect of the
Treasury, who was generally responsible for the design and superinten-

dence of new federal buildings, could not do the necessary work. These responsibilities would much better be placed in the hands of competent, well-selected architects, with the federal Supervising Architect providing overall supervision. In the years that followed, the Institute would work toward this goal. Finally, Hunt dealt with professional standards and responsibilities, a favorite theme. Architects, he asserted, should eschew criticism of their fellow architects' work and try to avoid professional jealousy. They should avoid any gratuitous offering of professional services. Above all, as architects,

we should be most conscientious in our endeavors to faithfully serve the interests of our clients to the best of our ability; to do so even should it at times be necessary to sacrifice some of our artistic preferences. As trustees we should carefully avoid incurring any useless expense, and we should do all in our power to rightfully gain confidence and well deserved esteem from our clients. We should satisfy them that any structure in experienced hands can be given an architectural excellence without necessarily increasing its cost.

As usual, he seasoned his idealism with great practicality. Obviously, professionals must deal with the world as they found it, and, accepting this reality, try to make it better.[18]

Hunt's farewell address as president of the Institute was delivered in Boston at the twenty-fifth annual meeting in 1891, held in the new, still unfinished, public library. As usual Hunt was very nervous about making a formal speech, and it "loomed up as a dragon to be met and overcome." Like many of his public statements, this one was in large part a summary of recent events and current problems. He spoke about architectural competitions and urged that they be better regulated to insure fair play; he commended the design of Charles F. McKim's new library; and he objected to the excessively high buildings being constructed in American cities as injurious to nearby property and dangerous to public health in their obstruction of fresh air and sunlight. He also touched on the selection of the architects and the preparation of the site for the World's Columbian Exposition in Chicago. The uniform classical style chosen for the Court of Honor would, he believed, "be of benefit to the public and to the profession [as] a practical illustration of that dignity and repose so lost sight of in the search for originality, not to say eccentricity." Hunt concluded that "marked progress in our art, both in design and construction, is everywhere observable," and "with the growing culture of our people," architectural opportunities were "likewise great and ever improving." But, he went on, "eminence in our profession can alone be gained by a thorough study of the works of the past." The architectural student must be as well acquainted with classical architecture as the literary man is conversant with the work of classical writers. The outgoing president was obviously still very much the practical man, involved in the important work of the day, but committed to the standards established in the past.[19]

Three events highlighted the close of the eighties for the Hunts. In March 1889 the inauguration of Benjamin Harrison drew them to Washington, D.C., as guests of the newly elected vice-president, Levi P. Morton, Hunt's client and friend. They had spent election day and evening the previous November with Morton at his country home, Ellerslie, sharing the excitement of receiving the returns over a private wire. During inaugural week in Washington, a group of friends, including Archibald Rogers of Hyde Park, New York, another Hunt patron, joined together to act as "political bridesmaids and groomsmen" for the Mortons, enjoying special accommodations and special treatment, and accompanying the Mortons everywhere "as guard of honor." For the post-inaugural parade, the Hunts and the other Morton guests were seated in a pavilion adjoining the presidential box, where, under dripping skies, they could observe both the long procession and the new president and his wife. Catharine Hunt was amused to see "thrifty Mrs. Harrison tie her handkerchief over her best bonnet to protect it from the wet."[20]

At the end of April 1889, the Hunts joined in the celebrations of the centennial of George Washington's inauguration. A temporary arch had been erected over Fifth Avenue immediately to the north of Washington Square, and viewing platforms were built in front of the houses on the north side of Washington Square for the commemorative parade. Hunt was invited to meet President Harrison on his visit to New York, and he was one of eight hundred prominent guests at a banquet held at the Metropolitan Opera House on the evening of April 30. Each day of the celebration the Hunts opened their house on Washington Square to guests, and their housekeeper served an average of fifty people a day for lunch and tea. A permanent arch was planned as a suitable memorial to the Washington Centennial. Henry G. Marquand, Hunt's long-time patron, was named chairman of the Committee to Erect a Memorial Arch, while Hunt served as chairman of the subcommittee on building and contributed $100 to the arch fund. Stanford White was chosen to design the permanent arch in Washington Square, the cornerstone of which was laid on May 30, 1890.[21]

A short trip to Europe, lasting less than two months, was another high point of the year 1889. This was a different sort of visit than any of their previous transatlantic journeys. George W. Vanderbilt, for whom

Hunt had already made preliminary sketches for the great mansion he planned to build near Asheville, North Carolina, invited Richard and his wife to accompany him on a trip having the double purpose of visiting historic houses and châteaux in order to get architectural ideas for the projected dwelling and of collecting funishings and art objects destined for the huge residence. When the party left New York on May 15, 1889, Hunt was suffering so badly from the gout that he had to be carried aboard ship. But he soon recovered and was in high spirits during "the pleasantest voyage" the Hunts ever made. No doubt young Vanderbilt paid most of the expenses on this trip.[22]

In London the travelers stopped at the Grand Hotel on Trafalgar Square, and the three of them spent several days searching shops for objects appropriate for the new house and visiting some of the great English country houses. On one morning, Vanderbilt purchased from a pleasantly astonished carpet merchant some three hundred Oriental rugs for his new residence. Vanderbilt was, Catharine remembered, "insatiable in his desire to see beautiful interiors and pictures," and he delighted in comparing rooms they visited with what was being planned for Biltmore. The three spent one lovely spring day at the huge pile of Knole as guests of Lord Sackville, who invited them to lunch. Hatfield House, with its Elizabethan rooms and gardens, "was another joy." Richard and Vanderbilt visited Haddon Hall one Sunday, while Catharine remained in London to rest. In these same days, Hunt was sitting for a sculptured bust which Vanderbilt had commissioned for his house. While Catharine remained in London for a few more days with George Vanderbilt, Richard went on to Paris to meet with the William K. Vanderbilts about the work at Marble House in Newport.[23]

Hunt had scarcely arrived in Paris when William K. and Alva Vanderbilt insisted that he join them for the Sunday horse races at Chantilly. At the racecourse, as the Vanderbilts' four-in-hand drove into the grounds, the Duc d'Aumale in the royal box recognized Hunt in the coach and sent his equerry to bring Hunt to his side, remarking at the same time that though Hunt called himself an American he was in truth "un général français," so French in manner and appearance and so military in bearing was he. When Catharine and George Vanderbilt joined Hunt in Paris, the Duke invited them all to breakfast with him at his great château at Chantilly. The occasion was a grand one. Henri Eugène Philippe Louis d'Orléans, Duc d'Aumale, the fourth son of King Louis Philippe, had had a distinguished career with the French forces in Algeria and had been governor there. He had rebuilt the château at Chantilly, and in 1886 had donated it and its collection to the Institut de

France. Gilded royal carriages were awaiting the Hunts at the railway station when they got to Chantilly, and various aides received them in the audience chamber of the château. Presently, from the adjoining library, the duke entered the room, followed by his house guests, the Duc and Duchesse de Montpensier, to greet the new arrivals and usher them to the lavish breakfast awaiting them. There were some two dozen persons at the table. Richard had previously visited the duke at Chantilly, but this was the first time that Catharine had seen the château, with its great staircase, its fountains and moats, and its large and well-cultivated gardens. The duke gave them the use of his box at the theater in Paris for the remainder of their stay.[24]

From Paris, the three travelers continued to visit great houses and to look for furnishings and works of art. The Paris Exposition was in progress during their stay, and Catharine paid a visit there. The International Congress of Architects was meeting in Paris at this time, and Hunt, as a member of the Ecole des Beaux-Arts and of the congress, was invited to make an address and present the *récompenses* (awards) at a session held on June 21 at the Ecole. We can only imagine Hunt's agonies while preparing his remarks, though, since he apparently had little advance notice, the short talk probably was less of a trial for him than many other speeches he gave. When their business of looking at great houses and buying furnishings and art objects was concluded, the Hunts returned to New York. They were home by the middle of July. Although architectural exploration had been a primary purpose of this visit to Europe and Hunt did some sketching while on the trip, there is little to indicate that he was inspired by what he found on this short return; rather he went to collect specific architectural details and interior furnishings for immediate use.[25]

On arriving home, Hunt was immediately immersed in a flood of large and varied commissions. The number of projects he was able to undertake and complete in the next six years is most remarkable. As best he could, and as he had been doing for most of his professional life, he took seriously his own exhortation to his students in the Tenth Street Studio Building years before: "You have not got long to live. . . . You have got to work at day, and you have got to work at night." But the accelerated pace took its toll, and more and more often he was temporarily incapacitated by illness. Approaching sixty-two years of age, he knew well that the time he had left for his work was rapidly passing, but he also knew that he still had much to do. What he did was spectacular indeed.

20

THE GRAND MANNER

Following his return from Europe in 1886 and increasingly after the 1889 trip, Hunt was involved with work on large domestic commissions. These large residences were among his most noteworthy work, and today he is probably best remembered for the lavish mansions he designed for plutocrats of the Gilded Age. By the mid-1880s Hunt had become the most fashionable architect of his time, and some undoubtedly considered a house designed by him to be a badge of high social position. All these large houses, of course, were created with a particular life style in mind, which Hunt himself readily entered into and enjoyed, even though he did not fully share it. Of all the building types he employed, the architect seemed to find the designing of large private houses most congenial. He could provide his very wealthy clients what they wanted and what they needed, indulging their whims and satisfying their vanity, while giving himself the satisfaction of creating elegant buildings in different architectural styles and with a decorative richness that few other architects were able to achieve.

The very large private houses built in the United States in ever greater numbers during the final years of the nineteenth century and the opening years of the twentieth have frequently been characterized as vehicles of ostentation and conspicuous consumption, erected by newly rich owners who were insecure in their social position and who hoped to gain self-satisfaction and recognition by impressing others with their material wealth. No doubt much of the building of great houses did have behind it a competitive drive to outshine others. With their lack of a firmly established class system and acceptance of the democratic myth of universal equality on the one hand, and their desire for achievement and individual distinction on the other, many Americans have had considerable uncertainty about who they are and where they belong. Although group identity has been fairly well established throughout the history of the nation, individual identity has been less readily fixed upon, and tension has been characteristic, and perhaps even endemic, among Americans, given the conflict between democratic uniformity and social differentiation. An exceptionally large and richly appointed dwelling probably could for some relieve insecurities about social position and satisfy personal ambition and pride. Moreover, Americans had the European tradition to emulate: English and Continental experience suggested that high social position was usually associated with elegant residences.

In the post–Civil War decades, wealth in the United States came into the hands of owner-investors at an ever increasing rate from the developing transportation system, industrial and commercial expansion, financial manipulations, and the soaring values of real estate. The many new American millionaires most often were men who came from families which had already accumulated substantial wealth—far more than the average—and who had had advantages of good education and of superior vocational opportunity. Many of them did not need to prove themselves socially in any way, since their status was already acknowledged. For some, like Alva Vanderbilt, marrying into the Vanderbilt family was not enough, however, and she made use of her new château on Fifth Avenue to solidify and even raise her own and her immediate family's position. Social competitiveness such as she displayed was not unusual.[1]

But the motivations for erecting these very large houses were more complex than pecuniary emulation and social ambition. Indeed, the reasons might be very private or philanthropic or idealistic: the big house as a gift to a loved one, or to show the owner's simple pride in being rich; or the mansion as a residence with an aura of stability and security for a large family, for generations to come; or the huge building as a project providing employment to workers for its construction and its continuing maintenance, and thus an economic benefit to a local community; or the great dwelling as itself a work of art and a means of beautification of the community; or the house and its contents as providing patronage to artists; or the American "palace" as a national treasure, bringing to the country something that Europe already had and America did not.[2]

The role of the architect in conceiving the big houses must not be underestimated. By and large, well-to-do house builders hired architects as experts who could provide a specific service, like other experts. In some cases architects possibly pushed their clients toward ever grander conceptions because their own fees were based on a percentage of total costs—the higher the expenditure, the greater the commission to the designer. And perhaps sometimes architects hoped to improve their own positions both in business, by attracting additional clients, and socially, by making their names more widely known, by erecting ever grander buildings. But another factor cannot be overlooked, and this was true in Hunt's case: the architect would work, as he felt necessary, to elevate taste by bringing beauty, as he saw it, on a substantial scale both to the inhabitants of the dwelling and to the community where the house was located. Hunt, who never had to doubt his own status, wanted to provide his American upper-class clients with a fitting ambience, one that elevated taste and conferred dignity. The large and well-conceived house, designed by one knowledgeable in the arts and acquainted with the best of the European past, could be justified as educative for its inhabitants and as serving, by its very presence, as an example to the larger society.[3]

Criticism of the great houses was not infrequent. The mansions were attacked as wasteful of resources, as conducive to selfish indulgence and sloth, as alien to the American experience and ideals, as undemocratic, and as leading to class hatreds and conflict. Obviously, the great houses contrasted sharply with the wretched places that a large part of the American populace had to exist in. To some critics, the money spent on such large and luxurious residences could be better spent in other ways, such as providing for parks, monuments, and public buildings to beautify the cities. While architectural critics often took pleasure in the great houses because of the variety of architectural ideas that were embodied in them, the attitudes of social critics generally were unfavorable.[4]

Hunt's great houses designed from the latter 1880s to the mid-1890s included buildings that expanded on architectural concepts he had used earlier as well as structures that moved in what were for him new stylistic directions. In these works he looked to the European past for general style and specific details. And in these country mansions, New York town houses, and Newport "cottages," he worked on a scale considerably grander than that of most of his earlier work.

Levi P. Morton was one of Hunt's clients for a large country house. Years earlier, in 1869, Hunt had added a ballroom to Morton's Newport house, Fairlawn, and in 1871 he had designed a stable for Morton on East Forty-Second Street in Manhattan. When Morton returned to the United States in 1885, after having served as American minister to France, he decided to sell his Newport house and purchase an estate nearer to New York City. He employed his friend Hunt in 1886 and 1887 to create a large country house, named Ellerslie, on a thousand-acre site he acquired at Rhinecliff-on-Hudson, New York. Besides the main house, Hunt and his staff also designed several auxiliary buildings for the estate, including a dairy, a laundry, stables, an engine and boiler house, and the entrance gates. In November 1888, as already noted, the Hunts were at Ellerslie on election night as the returns came in and Morton was elected vice-president on the ticket with Benjamin Harrison. The following year Hunt was asked to serve as arbitrator in a dispute between Maitland Armstrong, who prepared the glass for Ellerslie, and Morton, and between the farm superintendent and the owner. Hunt frequently was called upon to arbitrate such disputes.[5]

Ellerslie had a vaguely Elizabethan look. The massive two-and-one-half-story house (figure 85) was characterized by Tudor half-timber work at both the second-story and third-story gable levels, rising above a ground story enveloped by large verandas, various projecting bays and pavilions, and a broad porte cochere. The varied planes of the high roof, with its many gables, dormers, and chimneystacks, provided a picturesque complement to the irregularities on the side wall planes, broken not only by the half-timbering but also by the solids and voids of differently shaped projecting sections and of the verandas, balconies, and a loggia, patterned with intricate stickwork.[6]

In three other large houses, Hunt turned in a different direction, possibly influenced to some extent by the work of Henry Hobson Richardson, whose brilliant career was terminated by his early death in 1886. Grey Towers, the Milford, Pennsylvania, estate of James Wallace Pinchot, a New York businessman whose family had settled in Milford and who was associated with Hunt in several New York clubs, was also built mainly in 1885 and 1886. A large, rustic-looking structure (figure 86), having a commanding view of the Delaware River Valley, the dwelling was designed in a late French medieval style. The mansion is faced with rough-textured gray stone and is dominated by three squat, conical-roofed towers, each sixty-three feet high and twenty feet in diameter, rising at three of the corners of the building. Hunt apparently planned for a larger dwelling than Pinchot was willing to erect, and some of the dimensions of the forty-one-room house were scaled down during its construction. When the Hunts visited Grey Towers in June 1888, Catharine found it a "perfectly enchanting" place, having "a character about it quite unlike anything else in America." This very romantic dwelling, now owned by the U. S. Forest Service, houses the Pinchot Institute for Conservation Studies and is open to the public.[7]

For Archibald Rogers, Hunt worked on the estate of Crumwold at Hyde Park, New York, from 1886 to 1889, creating another impressive large country house. Faced with roughly dressed Maine granite, Crumwold Hall was erected on a knoll commanding extensive views of the Hudson River and Valley. Including servants' quarters, the kitchen, and storerooms, the two-and-one-half-story mansion has some fifty rooms, which center on a main hall, used originally at times as a ballroom. Like Grey Towers, Crumwold (figure 87) has three conical-roofed, rounded towers, rising, in this case, at the corners and center of the garden façade. On the side where the main low-arched entrance is located, the heavy rough stone and the comparatively small window openings give the mansion an almost fortress-like solidity. On the sides toward the river, the walls are pierced by considerably more and larger windows, provid-

Figure 85
Ellerslie, the Levi P.
Morton mansion,
Rhinecliff-on-Hudson,
New York (1887). From
H. W. Desmond and
Herbert Croly, *Stately
Homes in America* (1903).

Figure 86
Grey Towers, the James Pinchot mansion, Milford, Pennsylvania (1887). Courtesy Forest Service, U.S. Department of Agriculture.

Figure 87
Crumwold Hall, the Archibald Rogers mansion, Hyde Park, New York (1889). Courtesy Roosevelt Vanderbilt National Historic Sites, National Park Service, Hyde Park, New York.

ing a much more animated surface. A large, curving veranda originally extended outward from the main mass of the building toward the river, enlarging the base and emphasizing the horizontal configuration of the structure. The Eymard Preparatory Seminary was later located on the former Rogers estate.[8]

Even more ground-hugging and horizontally fixed was Indian Spring, which Hunt executed in 1889–1891 for Joseph R. Busk on Ocean Avenue in Newport. Constructed of rubble-coursed masonry so rooted to the rocky coastal site that the house almost seems to be a part of it, the two-story Busk house (figure 88) was one of the architect's most successful conceptions. The ruggedness of the walls is even more emphasized here than in Grey Towers or Crumwold. Like those houses, the Busk house has rounded, conical-roofed towers and openings with relatively spare decorative detail. Along one side of the irregularly shaped structure the broad, low-pitched roof sweeps down to envelop a deeply recessed veranda, echoing in this theme the relationship of the whole house to the site. Perhaps in no other work did Hunt achieve such an organic and "natural" quality in a building.[9]

Hunt's large New York City town houses of the early 1890s included the William V. Lawrence house, the Elbridge T. Gerry mansion, and the double residence of Mrs. William Astor. The Lawrence house (figure 89), on which Richard Howland Hunt collaborated as designer, was built in 1890 on Fifth Avenue at the southeast corner of Seventy-Eighth Street. Constructed of brick with stone trim, the long and very narrow three-and-one-half-story residence, facing on the side street, was dominated by the large, four-and-one-half-story rounded corner tower at the avenue end, a feature so characteristic of Hunt's work at this time. In a modest way, the Lawrence house recalled some of the details of the W. K. Vanderbilt house, including a high, gabled, buttressed dormer, hoodmolds in ogee shape surmounting some of the openings, and the massing of the roof planes. This was a substantial town house, but not particularly distinguished. It was eventually razed for an apartment building occupying the same long and narrow site.[10]

Far more imposing than the Lawrence house was the Elbridge T. Gerry mansion on Fifth Avenue at Sixty-First Street, one of Hunt's most important creations. In designing this home for Gerry, who was a large real-estate holder and the director of several trust companies, the architect took his inspiration from the early French Renaissance and especially from the Louis XII wing of the Château of Blois. The placement of the tower and the decorative details recalled the transitional French Renaissance work of the late fifteenth century, when considerable Gothic

Figure 88
Joseph R. Busk mansion,
Newport, Rhode Island
(1891). Courtesy The
American Institute of
Architects Foundation/
Prints and Drawings
Collection, Washington,
D.C. Reproduction by
James Garrison.

Figure 89
William V. Lawrence
mansion, Fifth Avenue
at Seventy-Eighth Street,
New York (1891). Photo-
graph by Byron, The
Byron Collection,
Museum of the City of
New York.

detail was still utilized. Like the Lawrence house, the Gerry mansion featured a corner tower, in this case an essentially square structure topped by a crested hipped roof, rising one story higher than the three-story sections along the street and the avenue. As in the W. K. Vanderbilt house, Hunt piled the masses of the building toward the corner segment. The house was meant to be viewed primarily from across the avenue diagonally opposite the tower, where the pyramiding from the sides was evident. By contrast, from face-on across the street or avenue, the bulk of the tower appeared to overpower the side structures.[11]

Hunt probably began planning the Gerry mansion in 1891; construction was begun in April 1892, and the structure was completed at the end of November 1894. Although the architect and his client got along well and were frequent social companions, Gerry had the annoying habit of approvingly quoting the views of his servants on technical matters: a minor crisis was averted when Hunt finally convinced Gerry that his own design for the butler's pantry was more convenient than the butler's revisions. By March of 1893, when the walls were up to the third-story level, it was apparent that the house would be very imposing. At the end of the following year when the work was completed, however, Gerry did not like the principal staircase that Hunt had erected, and he hired another architect to tear out Hunt's work and had the staircase rebuilt in accord with his own ideas.[12]

The exterior of the Gerry house (figure 90) was a feast of rich architectural details drawn skillfully into an integrated whole. Although abundantly ornamented with alternate-length quoins, elaborate dripstones, a paneled balustrade, and tall, pinnacled dormers, the imposing corner tower, its large mass accentuated by areas of blank wall space, provided a suitable, even necessary relief from the profuse detail of the two main ranges.

The entrance range on Sixty-First Street was itself a symmetrical structure fronted by a porte cochere of filigreed ironwork and glass, with a one-story secondary pavilion, terminated by delicate spiral columns on the left, to the east. The stonework ornamentation on this façade was far more lavish than on the corner tower, especially at the third-story level. There, pedimented dormer windows stood watch on either side of the central configuration of three windows surmounted by cusped and canopied arches. Lateral piers supported a screen containing a filigree of tracery, which was pierced by the tips of the hoodmolds rising above the three windows beneath. Soaring above all this stonework from about halfway up the height of the third-story windows was the steeply sloped hipped roof, topped by cresting and surrounded

Figure 90
Elbridge Gerry mansion,
Fifth Avenue at Sixty-
First Street, New York
(1894). Photograph by
Byron, The Byron Collec-
tion, Museum of the
City of New York.

by very high and rather awkwardly placed chimney stacks, extremely long and narrow, which again repeated the motif of the alternate-length quoins.

The Fifth Avenue range was somewhat less ornate. It featured at the second-story level a loggia with a small, semicircular, corbelled balcony and surmounted by a delicately cusped elliptical arch. The dormers on this wing had hoodmolds in ogee shape, with lateral piers all elaborately worked, much like the two dormers on the tower. Montgomery Schuyler judged the Gerry mansion to be "the most interesting and the most successful" of Hunt's later houses, "so distinctly an ornament to the city [as to be] one of the public possessions." But this "public possession" remained standing for little more than three decades. The land on which the house stood was extremely valuable, and two years after Gerry's death in 1927, the mansion was demolished to make way for the Hotel Pierre.[13]

Considerably more restrained in exterior design, but a larger building and more ornate within, was the double residence that Hunt built in the nineties for Mrs. William Astor and her son, Colonel John Jacob Astor IV, four blocks to the north of the Gerry mansion, on Fifth Avenue at Sixty-Fifth Street. For years Caroline Webster Schermerhorn Astor had dominated fashionable New York society from her large but undistinguished brownstone house at 350 Fifth Avenue at the corner of Thirty-Fourth Street. Her husband, William Backhouse Astor, Jr., a grandson of John Jacob Astor and heir to a large real estate fortune, paid the bills for his wife's lavish dinners and balls for "the Four Hundred" (said to be the number her ballroom could hold), but by and large he had no part in her social program. After the death in 1890 of his brother, John Jacob Astor III, who had lived at 340 Fifth Avenue at the corner of Thirty-Third Street, his nephew, John's son William Waldorf Astor, in a dispute with his aunt, decided to have his parents' house torn down and a large hotel built on the site. While the construction of the Waldorf Hotel increased the value of William Astor's own property next door, it also made his house virtually uninhabitable. The William Astors, therefore, decided to build another hotel, the Astoria, on the house site and to construct a new residence for themselves on then newly fashionable upper Fifth Avenue. William Astor died in 1892 while the house was still being planned, but Mrs. Astor went ahead with the large double residence. Ground was broken for the mansion in March 1893. Mrs. Astor moved into the dwelling on February 1, 1896, and two days later opened the house with a gala reception and ball. Her new ballroom could accommodate some 1,200 guests. To the south on Fifth Avenue, the connecting Waldorf and Astoria Hotels soon became the most fashionable in the city.[14]

Although executed in a French Renaissance style, the Astor mansion (figure 91) was based on later models than those for the Gerry house. Here the details dated from the reign of Henry II in the middle of the sixteenth century, when the more classical Italianate manner had largely superseded the Gothicism of the early part of the century. The outlines and the detail of the Astor mansion were less picturesque, more formalized and regular than those of the Gerry house. Curiously, the tripartite division of the Fifth Avenue façade of the Astor residence and the large, arched, triple windows echoed major themes of Hunt's Néo-Grec Lenox Library just five blocks to the north along Fifth Avenue and built nearly a quarter of a century earlier.[15]

Constructed of light gray limestone, the four-story structure presented a symmetrical design on the avenue front, with its projecting end pavilions, while the side-street face was organized into two somewhat different divisions in addition to a carriage entrance at the rear. The crisp lines of the pilasters, the window frames, the moldings and panels, and the insistent entablatures created a formalized composition up to the lower roofline, where the slate surfaces rising steeply upward, the copper cresting, the several small dormer windows, and the massive chimney stacks provided a much more picturesque expression. The Astor mansion was decidedly grand, but colder and less richly decorated, and it lacked something of the charm of most of Hunt's other large houses.[16]

Mrs. Astor occupied the north half of the double residence, and her son and his family lived in the south part. Beyond the large bronze gates at the portal was a huge entrance hall with an imposing marble staircase, which, along with the art gallery, used as a ballroom, the occupants shared. Each of the public rooms was designed in the style of a different period. The entrance hall had a German baroque character, and for its ceiling, Karl Bitter, the young Austrian immigrant sculptor who did extensive work for Hunt, carved several half-length nude female figures. Mrs. Astor's reception room boasted a peacock-tail rug, while much of the furniture was copied from pieces in the Petit Trianon. Hunt is said to have directed the decoration of the interiors and the selection of the furniture.[17]

When Mrs. Astor died in 1908, her son had the architectural firm of Carrère & Hastings remodel the house so as to serve just his family and to provide more rooms for large-scale entertainment. At this time the grand staircase was replaced by an interior court. On the death of Col-

Figure 91
Mrs. William B. Astor
mansion, Fifth Avenue
at Sixty-Fifth Street,
New York (1895). Photo-
graph by Byron, The
Byron Collection,
Museum of the City of
New York.

onel Astor, who went down on the *Titanic* in 1912, the mansion was appraised in his estate at a value of nearly two and one-half million dollars. After the dwelling and property were sold in 1926 for three and one-half million dollars, the house was torn down to make way for Temple Emanu-El.[18]

Hunt's culminating designs in the grand manner were those for his four great "palace-cottages" at Newport and for Biltmore near Asheville, North Carolina (to be discussed in a later chapter). By the 1880s, as Newport was established as the most fashionable resort in the United States, the large cottages and villas no longer sufficed for some summer residents. An era of "palace" construction began, which continued through the first years of the twentieth century. From about 1890 to the outbreak of World War I, Newport was at its height, its social life fashioned at the Casino and by wealthy hostesses who vied with one another in the appointments of their dinners and balls. The intellectuals who earlier had made Newport their summer home were long gone, and the hotels which had once attracted many short-term visitors were gone or of little importance. Hunt was by no means alone in providing such houses for the Newport elite. Other architects and architectural firms such as Peabody & Stearns, Dudley Newton, Horace Trumbauer, Cram, Goodhue & Ferguson, and McKim, Mead & White participated in the era of palace building. But Hunt's four houses in the grand manner were among the largest and the most lavish, and they clearly set standards for subsequent construction in the city.

For Ogden Goelet, a wealthy New York real estate developer, Hunt began work on a Newport mansion in 1888. This house, named Ochre Court, was completed three years later at a cost said to be four and one-half million dollars. Ochre Court, one of Hunt's largest houses, was a free adaptation of French Renaissance elements of the sixteenth century. In interior appointments, it was also one of his most sumptuous houses, although the exterior of Indiana limestone was comparatively restrained in design among his late works, and was, in certain ways, rather cold and almost austere.[19]

The entrance front (figure 92), approached along a short, straight driveway from the intricately worked iron gateway, was, Schuyler judged, "the most artistic composition that its author has produced." The principal feature of the main façade is the entrance pavilion placed toward the right along the front, with a broad, arched porte cochere positioned before the main portal. Above the doorway, a large stained-glass window marks the grand staircase, while at the third-story level an arched double window breaks into the cornice of the pavilion—set higher than the other cornices of the front—and rises into a richly decorated pedimented dormer projecting from the high, crested, hipped roof. Embossed panels and low doors opening onto the balcony over the porte cochere accentuate the large expanse of wall in this section.

To the immediate left of the principal pavilion, at the angle of recession, an angled turret was placed. The next window bay to the left corresponds with the window bay to the right of the entrance, both having slightly less ornamented dormer windows than that on the entrance pavilion. Still farther to the left a large bay, with spare decoration, rises into an angled half-cone roof, while yet another pavilion subdivided into an additional story terminates the front on the left, but this final segment is not fully integrated into the composition.

The opposite façade of the house facing the ocean (figure 93) is much more open. In the central section on the ground story a loggia opens onto a large terrace. The loggia is surmounted by a balcony. Above these, canopied dormer windows look out on an intricately carved balustrade. Projecting lateral pavilions having a higher cornice and roof crest than those of the central section repeat the elliptical-arched triple windows in the middle section at the second-story level and are topped by carved dormer windows somewhat more elaborate than the secondary dormers on the opposite side of the mansion.

The relationship of the various segments of Ochre Court, the placement of the openings, and the skyline of the mansion were well thought out, and, all in all, combine into a highly satisfying composition. The aesthetic impact of the dwelling comes not so much in the decorative detail as in the placement of the masses and the relationship of the forms. Like other Newport "palaces," the Goelet house was unfortunately erected on a parcel of land highly inadequate to set it off to good advantage. Here was a great château built on what amounted to a few city lots.[20]

Hunt directed the designing of the interiors at Ochre Court with the assistance of Karl Bitter, who did much of the sculptural work. Like other wealthy Americans, Goelet gathered many of the appointments for his house—mantelpieces, wall panels, and ceiling paintings, as well as furniture and pictures—from European residences. Inside the main entrance, the grand staircase, with carved dolphins and cupids supporting the balustrade, rises to the second story; above the landing is the large stained-glass window, brought from Germany. The great hall, which extends three stories, is Gothic in character. The lower walls of Caen stone are carved with heraldic designs; above the richly worked balcony arcades are twelve large caryatids, supporting the ceiling, which is

Figure 92
Entrance front, Ochre
Court, the Ogden Goelet
mansion, Newport,
Rhode Island (1892).
Photo by James Garri-
son.

Figure 93
Sea façade, Ochre Court.
Photo by James Garri-
son.

painted with a banquet scene of the gods. To the right of the great hall is
the ballroom, and to its rear, overlooking the ocean, is the drawing
room, both designed in the style of the period of Louis XIV. On the other
side of the great hall are the library, and, beyond, the state dining room,
paneled with richly carved wood, embellished with a painted ceiling,
and heated by a huge, double-hearth marble fireplace. The Goelet family, in their customary eight weeks of annual residence in the mansion,
ordinarily used a small family dining room, done in Louis XV style, at
the front of the house. A study designed in Tudor style completed the
main rooms of the first floor. Upstairs were sitting rooms and bedrooms,
all profusely decorated with carvings.[21]

In March 1947, Robert Goelet, the son of the builder, donated Ochre
Court to the Roman Catholic diocese of Providence, Rhode Island, to be
used for educational purposes. Salve Regina College was opened there
in the fall of 1947, and today the mansion is used for administrative
offices, a chapel (the former ballroom), and reception rooms.

In 1892, "another monument to Mr. Hunt," as one young lady
termed it, was completed not far from Ochre Court on Bellevue Avenue.
For perhaps his most demanding client, Alva Vanderbilt, Hunt built a
marble palace that reportedly cost two million dollars for the actual structure and nine million dollars for the interior decorations and the furnishings. William K. Vanderbilt had been so pleased with his château on
Fifth Avenue that he gave Hunt, in effect, carte blanche to build as a
birthday gift for his wife "the very best living accommodations that
money could provide." Alva soon began to direct the building of the
Newport mansion. Hunt started his planning work on Marble House in
1888, and construction was begun in the fall of 1889. The house was
ready for occupancy in June 1892. Adèle Sloane, a niece of William
Vanderbilt, the young lady who looked upon Marble House as a monument to the architect, went all through the mansion in August of 1892,
two days before a gala housewarming party. Her reaction surely was not
exceptional: "No description can possibly give one an idea of how mar-
vellously beautiful it is. It is far ahead of any palace I have ever seen
abroad, far ahead of any I have ever dreamed of."[22]

During the three years while her Newport cottage was under construction, Alva Vanderbilt attempted to keep her friends as well as
strangers away from the building site so that the mansion might be
viewed only when it was fully completed. High fences were erected
around the grounds, and only those working on the house were permitted to go inside. Many of the workmen on the project were foreigners,

hired, it was said, because they were less likely than American workers to talk in the outside community about what was going on there.[23]

Although she might try to keep the house a surprise until it was finished, Mrs. Vanderbilt could not conceal the fact that substantial building activity was going on. The amount of land available for Marble House was relatively small, and construction work took place only a few steps from Bellevue Avenue. As the gleaming white marble mansion took shape, modeled in part on the White House in Washington, D.C., with details taken from the Petit Trianon at Versailles, it was evident that it would be a remarkable structure.[24]

The principal front of Marble House (figure 94), facing west, is centered by a huge portico carried by four colossal Corinthian columns, which are echoed in the giant fluted Corinthian pilasters set between the bays all around the two-story house. The ocean front (figure 95), facing east, has two projecting end wings enclosing a large court opening onto a terrace. Lunette-topped windows at the first-story level and at the intermediate mezzanine level in the sea-front recession contrast with the square-headed rectangular openings at the second-story level. A large entablature and a roof-edge balustrade (figure 96) hide the almost flat roof covering the attic story. The mansion was designed to give an impression of great formality and dignity.

Sweeping up to the portico is a semicircular, inclined driveway. It is bordered by a heavy stone balustrade carrying large lamp standards. To the front of the center of the low wall containing this ramp-driveway, water pours from three carved masks into a large fountain, above which the stone balustrade is replaced by a delicate bronze railing. Although graceful in itself, the driveway was unfortunately placed so high that it hides the bases of both the portico and the pilaster fronts, and by hiding these supports it weakens the visual impact of the carefully elaborated colossal orders. In contrast, on the sea front, the balustrade does not conceal the base, which is the terrace.[25]

A notable feature of Marble House is the bronze and steel doorway grille (figure 97), measuring twenty-five feet four inches wide and sixteen feet high, set at the back of the portico and said, at the time, to be "the finest piece of work of this character ever turned out in the United States." Hunt himself designed the doorway, which was constructed of an inner and an outer layer of bronze and steel separated by a thick layer of glass. The metallic screen is divided by fluted bronze columns entwined with flowers into two framing panels fixed in place and two center panels, which swing on pivots. Each of the movable doors is ten

Figure 94
Entrance front, Marble
House, the William K.
and Alva Vanderbilt
mansion, Newport,
Rhode Island (1892).
Photo by James Garri-
son.

Figure 95
Sea façade, Marble
House. Photo by James
Garrison.

Figure 96
Marble House detail.
Photo by James Garri-
son.

Figure 97
Front entry screen, Marble House. The Preservation Society of Newport County Photos.

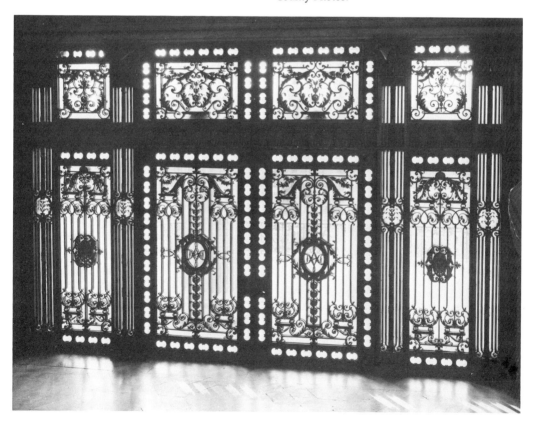

feet eight inches high and six feet one and one-half inches wide and weighs about one and one-half tons. Hunt used designs from the palace at Versailles for the grille, centering each of the gates with cartouches containing a monogram of the letters "W" and "V," adapted from Louis XIV's monogram, and placing in the side panels copies of medallions with the head of the boy Apollo giving out sun rays, the artistic "signature" of the Sun King's reign. In the spring of 1892, before the grille was installed at Marble House, it was placed on exhibit at the foundry in New York where it had been made.[26]

The grille was set up as the front wall of the entrance hall of the mansion; the inner walls of the great hall and the floor are faced and paved with yellow Siena marble brought from a quarry near Montagnola, Italy. Its ceiling is decorated with stucco relief of masks and arabesques. To the right of the entrance hall is the gold ballroom (figure 98), the most richly ornamented room of the building. Arched door and window surrounds set off the gilded walls and mirrors, the four giltwood panels carved in relief, possibly by Karl Bitter, and a marble fireplace with large bronze figures. Above an elaborately carved cornice, ceiling panels surround a central mythological painting and enframe the supports of two huge bronze chandeliers. Scallops, dolphins, and stalactites are sea motifs used in many of the carvings in the ballroom and elsewhere in the house.[27]

Behind the gold ballroom in the south wing of the mansion is the Gothic room (figure 99), arranged to display a collection of medieval and Renaissance art objects and used by the Vanderbilts as a family living room, which was given, according to Consuelo Vanderbilt Balsan, "a melancholy atmosphere" by the stained-glass windows. Originally the ribbed ceiling, centered on a large pendant, was painted in polychrome and the walls were covered in red damask above the Gothic-style paneling. The walls and ceiling are now white. The chimney-breast is covered with carved panels, niches, pinnacles, finials, and even crenelations.[28]

Opposite the ballroom at the front of the mansion is the dining room (figure 100), which is faced with dark pink Numidian marble brought from western Algeria. In this room tall pilasters with Corinthian capitals and bases of gilt bronze, along with a gilt, carved, and paneled ceiling, with a central mural, and bronze wall sconces made the room "gleam . . . like a fire." The bronze dining table chairs were so heavy that a footman had to push each diner up close to the table. To the rear of the dining room, in the north wing, the library was decorated in a rococo style. Connecting the two wings is the terrace hall, the walls and floor covered by the same yellow Siena marble used in the entrance hall.

Figure 98
Ballroom, Marble
House. The Preservation
Society of Newport
County Photos.

Figure 99
Gothic room, Marble
House. The Preservation
Society of Newport
County Photos.

Figure 100
Dining room, Marble
House. The Preservation
Society of Newport
County Photos.

Up the main staircase, on the mezzanine, are William K. Vanderbilt's office and his wife's small sitting room, both designed in the Louis XV style. Here on the landing, placed prominently above the windows, are high relief medallions by Karl Bitter of Jules Hardouin-Mansart, Louis XIV's principal architect at Versailles, and of Hunt, who did so much work for the Vanderbilt family. The architectural associations at Marble House with the *ancien régime* cannot be overlooked.[29]

Among the several rooms on the second floor is Mrs. Vanderbilt's bedroom, conceived in an elaborate rococo revival style; over the doors cherubs bear shields emblazoned with the letter "A" for Alva. Mr. Vanderbilt's bedroom is considerably smaller and simpler, decorated in the style of the time of Louis XVI. While in residence the Vanderbilts maintained twenty-five live-in servants to care for the fifty or so rooms of the mansion.

Richard and Catharine Hunt were among the guests at Marble House on the night of August 19, 1892, when the Vanderbilts opened the mansion to their friends. Although this "housewarming" was one of the most spectacular parties that Newport had ever seen, it was outshone three years later, on August 28, 1895, when the Vanderbilts opened Marble House to present their daughter Consuelo to society. On that occasion files of footmen in livery attended the guests, among them the young Duke of Marlborough, a houseguest of the Vanderbilts. A short time later Consuelo's engagement to the Duke was announced, and when the couple was married on November 6, 1895, Alva Smith Vanderbilt's social ambitions appeared to have been fully realized. Vanderbilt made a handsome settlement on the duke and his bride, who as the Duchess of Marlborough became mistress of Blenheim Palace, a rather larger place than the New York and Newport homes she had grown up in. But Consuelo had accepted the duke's proposal of marriage reluctantly, pushed on by her mother. Alva herself later admitted, when Consuelo petitioned for an annulment on grounds of having been forced into the marriage, that she had indeed compelled her daughter to marry the duke.[30]

In the meantime, Alva's own marriage to William Vanderbilt had broken up, and on January 11, 1896, she was married to Oliver Hazard Perry Belmont. In Newport, she moved from Marble House down the avenue to his home Belcourt, another Hunt mansion. She closed up Marble House, which she had owned from the first deed transfers of the property, though it was said that she continued to have her washing and ironing done there since facilities were inadequate at Belcourt. After Belmont's death in 1908, Alva moved back into Marble House, where in the summer of 1909 she opened it to the public for two days of speeches, refreshments, and tours in support of the women's suffrage movement.

Hunt's sons, Richard and Joseph Hunt, in 1913 built a Chinese teahouse on the cliffs overlooking the ocean at Marble House. When the United States entered World War I, Alva closed Marble House, and she spent the final years of her life in France. She sold the mansion to Frederick H. Prince of Boston in 1932. The Prince family in turn sold it from his trust to the Preservation Society of Newport County, and it is now open to the public. When Alva Vanderbilt Belmont died in 1933, a suffragette banner displayed at her funeral carried the motto "Failure Is Impossible." Somehow the motto seemed just right for the former mistress of Marble House.[31]

Belcourt, known also as Belcourt Castle, which Belmont deeded to Alva as a wedding present, was a very different sort of place from Marble House. "A most singular house," Julia Ward Howe called it after she had gone there to lunch with Belmont. "The first floor is all stable, with stalls for some thirteen or more horses, all filled and everything elaborate and elegant! . . . The residential part of the house is on the next story, designed by Hunt and palatial in its character." Belmont's horses not only had very elegant living quarters but also morning, afternoon, and evening clothes—"the finest 'horse clothing' ever seen"—most emblazoned with the Belmont crest. Upstairs in the living quarters, Belmont kept two stuffed horses, old-time favorites of his, mounted by figures of men in armor. Belmont was a very popular man about town in Newport, but his greatest love apparently was for his horses, and his home was designed as a magnificent stable and as a carriage house, with living quarters attached.[32]

The son of August Belmont, the banker, O. H. P. Belmont had the sixty-room summer home built in 1891–1893 at a reputed cost of three million dollars. After his marriage to Alva Vanderbilt in 1896, the house became the scene of frequent lavish dinners and balls. The Belmonts entertained in style: even at lunch, the table servants were dressed in red plush breeches and silk stockings and wore powdered wigs. Guests arriving for an evening party might find themselves climbing up the grand staircase between rows of footmen arranged on the steps and holding candelabra.[33]

The principal wing of Belcourt containing the large public rooms abuts on an inner courtyard, which is enclosed on the other three sides by the secondary wings. On the ground story, what later became a reception room was originally a passageway, open to the outside so that carriages might be driven directly into the house up to the foot of the grand staircase. Next to this area is a large banquet hall, with a marble mosaic floor, capable of accommodating as many as three hundred guests. On the second story is a French Gothic ballroom—seventy-five feet long—with ribbed vaulting and containing a musicians' gallery and an organ loft, large stained-glass windows, and a playfully fanciful castellated fireplace. Nearby are the master bedroom, the music room, an oval neoclassical dining room, and a loggia, at one time open to the inner courtyard below. Alva commissioned certain structural alterations and refurbishing even before she married Belmont.

The exterior of the roughly dressed stone and brick mansion provides a curious combination of French, Italian, and English elements. The main concept was a hunting lodge of the time of Louis XIII. The principal façade (figure 101) was conceived as a mixture of French motifs with Victorian polychromy of variegated brick and stone. Two slightly projecting lateral pavilions frame an arcaded central section. The high mansard roof on this side is punctuated by small round dormers (lucarnes), copied from popular usage in France. Although the inner courtyard was Italian in inspiration, the half-timbered work there was probably derived from sixteenth-century England. The large expanse of slate roof helped draw together the somewhat disparate elements of the great house.[34]

The splendors of Ochre Court, Marble House, and Belcourt were soon to be outdone, however, by The Breakers. For William K. Vanderbilt's older brother, Cornelius Vanderbilt II, Hunt designed the largest and most lavish of the Newport "cottages."

In October 1885, Cornelius Vanderbilt had purchased from Pierre Lorillard, who was developing Tuxedo Park in New York State, a rambling brick and frame residence with an observation tower on Ochre Point overlooking the ocean. Lorillard had erected this house, which he named The Breakers, in 1877 following designs by Peabody & Stearns of Boston. The new owner enlarged the house, adding a wing on the north side, and built greenhouses and a children's playhouse on the grounds. For several years, the Cornelius Vanderbilt family came each summer to The Breakers, closing up their huge town house on Fifth Avenue north of Fifty-Seventh Street, which George B. Post had designed and which was completed in its original form in December 1882. In November 1892, the first Breakers was completely destroyed by fire.[35]

Almost at once Cornelius Vanderbilt began planning a new summer home on the same site, and he requested Hunt to provide a design. Vanderbilt was said to have wanted a relatively modest residence, and Hunt's first design—like "a tent wrought in marble"—was for a simpler

Figure 101
Belcourt, the O. H. P.
Belmont mansion, New-
port, Rhode Island
(1894). Courtesy The
American Institute of
Architects Foundation/
Prints and Drawings
Collection, Washington,
D.C. Reproduction by
James Garrison.

and much lower building than the house that was ultimately built. But their ideas burgeoned, and they soon undertook what became the greatest house in Newport. Construction began in the spring of 1893, and in August 1895 the mansion was "inaugurated" with a ball celebrating its completion. The speed with which the complex plans were drawn up, the materials were acquired, and the building was constructed is remarkable. Over two hundred workmen were employed at times, solely for the carving and setting of the stonework. Very grand in scale and sumptuous in decor, The Breakers was the culmination of Hunt's work in the grand manner in Newport and was rivaled in size among his houses elsewhere only by Biltmore.[36]

Almost everything about this house was lavishly conceived. Containing more than seventy rooms, the house measures approximately two hundred and fifty feet by one hundred and fifty feet. It occupies two basement levels and an attic besides the three principal stories. Almost half of the rooms comprise facilities for the servants and staff. In so far as was possible, The Breakers was built to be fireproof, and no wood was used in the construction. The lighting fixtures were both wired for electricity and piped for gas, while in the principal bathrooms, hot and cold running salt water were made available as well as hot and cold fresh water. Because of the relatively limited land available for the dwelling—some eleven acres—the stables were erected on another property about half a mile distant. They contained accommodations for nearly thirty horses, along with many sleeping rooms for grooms, and a living room, a dining room, and even a library.[37]

Prototypes for The Breakers were the large, sixteenth-century Italian *palazzi* of Genoa. Here in Newport, Hunt constructed the American equivalent of a Genoese seaside palace of the Renaissance. The dwelling was a summer place, and the loggias, terraces, and arcades for outdoor activities were made an integral part of the plan and the design. Moreover, with the high ceilings, especially that of the two-story dining room and the great hall, and the very large rooms, some flowing one into another, the mansion, despite its balanced formality of design, was given an open and airy character, appropriate to summer living and summer weather conditions.

Hunt arranged each façade of the building in a distinctive way, while superbly integrating them into a harmonious whole. Here indeed is a structure embodying Hunt's favorite architectural qualities of "harmony, dignity, and repose." Set on a terrace overlooking the sweep of lawns and the ocean, the house appears to rise in three stories, the attic fenestration being artfully concealed among the elaborate consoles of the heavy cornice and the substantial roof overhang.[38]

The tripartite sea (east) façade (figure 102) is the most impressive. Two projecting wings rise the full height of the house and enclose a double-level loggia, in which the openings of the large triple arcade at the ground level are doubled and strikingly lightened and refined at the second story. Terminal arcades provide an expanding base for the mass of the building on this side and help give a pleasing, balanced relationship among the primary forms. Heavy, rusticated quoins impart a feeling of strength to the wings and to the lateral arcades, while the decorative application of double-level attached columns and balustrades, inset panels, and large carved figures in the spandrels gives an interesting variety to the ocean face.

On the south side (figure 103) the arcade on the right is balanced by the library alcove on the left. The central section of this façade is a two-story balustrade-topped hemicycle, embraced at the base by a peristyle of paired columns. Here, as on the other faces of the mansion, the division between the first and second stories and between the second and third stories is well defined by full entablatures, balustrades, and stringcourses.

The west or entrance front is marked by a tripartite division, general symmetry, a large porte cochere, and similar ornamentation and story divisions. To the left, the kitchen wing is attached somewhat awkwardly to the main block of the house. The north façade projects in its center into a rectangular pavilion which rises the full height of the building and is considerably heavier than the two-story hemicycle at the south end. The north façade is the least successful, but it is also the least observable face of the dwelling.

Hunt centered the plan for The Breakers on the great hall (figure 104), which rises over forty-five feet and is surrounded by galleries on three sides at the second-floor level. To the left on entering the house, the skylighted grand staircase rises to a landing and then divides to rise to the second story. Directly ahead one approaches a wall with large windows opening out onto the lower loggia, with a fine view of the ocean beyond. The great hall is faced with carved Caen stone inlaid with marble panels of various colors and topped by a painted sky ceiling. In the arcade opposite the grand staircase and facing into the great hall is a huge Caen stone fireplace, which was decorated by Karl Bitter. Four massive chandeliers hang from the ceiling of the great hall. Along the walls rising from high bases, colossal pilasters support the gilded and

Figure 102
Sea façade, The Breakers, the Cornelius Vanderbilt II mansion, Newport, Rhode Island (1895). Photo by James Garrison.

Figure 103
South façade, The Breakers. Photo by James Garrison.

garlanded cornice, with alternate marble and alabaster piers and columns in the gallery bays.[39]

The state dining room terminates the main axis of the house on the north, and the grand salon or music room closes the axis on the south. The state dining room (figure 105), designed for Hunt by Richard Bouwens van der Boijen in Paris, is the most lavishly decorated room of the mansion, forty-two by fifty-eight feet and rising two full stories to a ceiling painting entitled *Aurora at Dawn*. Twelve massive monolithic columns of red alabaster surmounted by gilded bronze Corinthian capitals carry the gilded cornice, above which are life-size figures in the ceiling arches. On the walls are low relief medallions.

The grand salon, also by Bouwens, with its graceful semicircular bay, was used for concerts and for dancing and is embellished by wall paneling in gray and gold and huge freestanding Ionic columns, with an elaborate coffered ceiling in silver and gold surrounding an allegorical ceiling painting. A morning room and a billiard room occupy the two sea-front wings enclosing the loggia, while the library, a breakfast room, two reception rooms, the entrance hall, and the butler's pantry are located on the entrance side of the mansion. Although various other architects and decorators created the appointments of most of the rooms, Hunt himself designed the library and the billiard room.

The library and library alcove have walls paneled in Circassian walnut and Spanish leather, and a coffered ceiling. A large sixteenth-century French fireplace with a high, carved chimney breast dominates the library. On it in old French is an inscription, which might be translated as follows: "Little do I care for riches, and do not miss them, since only cleverness prevails in the end." The walls of the billiard room are faced with pale gray-green Cippolino marble; alabaster is placed as trimming for insets of colored marble pieces and for a mosaic picture set in the ceiling. The mosaic pavement of the room contains a pattern of dolphins and acorns, Vanderbilt family symbols, which are repeated throughout the mansion. Bedrooms were placed on the second and third floors, and the attic story was given over to servants' rooms.

Like the other Hunt "palaces" and other mansions in Newport, The Breakers provided richly ornate and theatrical settings for the lavish dinner parties, the costume balls, and the other entertainments that became so characteristic of fashionable society during the summer season in the years around the turn of the century. The ambience was singularly appropriate for the display of costly furniture and art objects, expensive dress and jewelry, and servants in livery that some Newporters de-

Figure 105
Dining room, The
Breakers. The Preserva-
tion Society of Newport
County Photos.

lighted in. To many social critics, however, the extravagant display was simply appalling.

European visitors sometimes commented that they had never known anything at home comparable to the luxury they found in Newport. For example, Paul Bourget, a French journalist and novelist, thought that the Newport pleasure house display typified American excess in general, and he concluded that rich Americans just could not understand moderation, a judgment his friends Henry James and Edith Wharton agreed with. Most things about American life were excessive, he found, from the height of American skyscrapers to the spending of large sums of money. But these "senseless prodigalities of high life," Bourget concluded, exemplified as well the American people's energy and vigor, which had brought about the tremendous development of the country and the accumulation of huge fortunes, and so were very much in accord with the character of the people. To the Irish-born journalist E. L. Godkin, the building of the great houses was a slavish imitation by wealthy Americans of "the most conspicuous European mode of asserting social supremacy"; however, the American rich, he thought, did not have the polish and the cultivation to use their vast possessions to good advantage. They had, Godkin felt, a great deal to learn.[40]

The rich might have a great deal to learn about proper modes of living, but Hunt could do little more to teach them, for in these great houses he had provided clear lessons in the taste and the elegance he believed the country needed. In a way, here and there, he was making parts of America into the Europe that meant so much to him. More than anything else that he created, the great houses would be his way of providing something that was lacking in his native land. They would be more than private houses; inspired by the European past, these buildings would become national treasures which would, he hoped, serve as examples to elevate American aesthetic standards.

At the beginning of the nineties, while Hunt was creating the several great houses in the grand manner, he was also working on several other large projects, including a collaborative sculptural endeavor, two designs for academic institutions, and two substantial governmental jobs. Unlike the work on the great houses, which generally went smoothly, Hunt's employment for the United States Naval Observatory in Washington, D.C., and for the United States Military Academy at West Point involved many problems and subjected him to a great deal of stress. The academic projects, by contrast, proceeded well, although one of them, when completed, was so commonplace as to bring little credit to the designer and the other was harshly criticized. The sculptural project, which Hunt planned and supervised, was unquestionably a superb achievement, although for the work Hunt must share the credit with his protégé Karl Bitter, who also worked with him on Ochre Court, Marble House, The Breakers, Biltmore, and the Chicago fair.

Hunt had met Bitter the year after the sculptor had arrived in the United States in 1889, at the age of twenty-one. Bitter had come from a middle-class family living in a suburb of Vienna and had studied sculpture during his youth in the School of Art and Industry in Vienna and worked in the Imperial Academy of Fine Arts. When he was drafted into the imperial army and found that he was facing three years of service rather than one year as he had anticipated, he deserted after one year, fled to Germany, and then shipped to the United States, bringing with him little more than a dictionary, a few dollars, and a pack of sculptor's tools. When Hunt met Bitter, he realized that the young sculptor desperately needed help, and since he was very impressed by what he saw of Bitter's work and needed a great deal of architectural sculpture for several of his projects, he employed the young Austrian almost immediately. Hunt's "encouragement and recognition" gave the immigrant sculptor a start for what became a distinguished career, which was tragically cut short in 1915, when he was struck down and killed by an automobile.[1]

In March 1890, William Waldorf Astor, the son of John Jacob Astor III, offered to donate funds for bronze doors for the main entrance and the two principal side entrances of Trinity Church on lower Broadway in New York City, as a memorial to his father, who had recently died. The church vestry accepted his gift, and Hunt was invited to provide general designs and direct the work on the portals. Hunt accepted the commission, and at first he hoped to have Bitter, whom he had recently come to know, undertake the entire project. Realizing, however, that the Austrian could not manage the full commission along with other work he had begun, Hunt set up a competition, asking the entrants to model a panel showing the expulsion of Adam and Eve from Paradise. He was astounded when he learned that the Reverend Morgan Dix, rector of Trinity Church, had some qualms about exhibiting a naked woman on the Broadway entrance to his church and had sent word that the architect should pray carefully over the matter. Hunt's gleeful response was characteristic: "He'd be God-damned if he would!" And he went ahead and used the Adam and Eve theme for the competition. On March 18, 1891, it was announced that Bitter had been chosen to execute the portals for the main entrance. The south doors were awarded to Charles Henry Niehaus, a Cincinnati sculptor, while the north doors went to J. Massey Rhind, a Scotsman who had come to New York in 1889. Hunt continued to oversee the work on the doors. Most of the sculpting was done in 1893, the doors were cast in June 1894, and the work was completely set in place by 1896.[2]

Bitter's two large bronze doors (figure 106) at the principal entrance to the church were placed under a carved tympanum showing Christ opening the Kingdom of Heaven, and set in niches below were highly individualized figures of the twelve apostles, seated under small cusped arches and pointed gables and separated by miniature columns. The Gothic reference of the tympanum was repeated at the sides of each door with standing figures of prophets and saints set on pedestals, under canopies and recessed in niches. In contrast, the six panels of the two doors were early Italian Renaissance in inspiration, echoing Ghiberti's second set of gates for the baptistry in Florence. Above and below the panels are reclining allegorical figures flanking the emblems of the four evangelists. The style of the panel sculpture, as James Dennis points out in his definitive biography of Bitter, is basically baroque: the reliefs are well modeled, with considerable fluidity and circularity of movement and a sense of recession and return in the individual panels. Alternating on the edges with the figures of the prophets and saints are small, beautifully modeled portrait heads, including that of the sculptor himself in the lower right-hand corner of the right door and, above, that of Hunt. The principal doorway is a magnificent work, and the architect is well honored in the portrait head.[3]

Hunt's national reputation led to his selection for two collegiate commissions in the early 1890s. For the College for Women of Adelbert College in Cleveland, Ohio, Hunt designed Clark Hall, the main academic building of the small college, which was later incorporated into what eventually became Case Western Reserve University. At Harvard College, Hunt designed the Fogg Museum, which would become

Figure 106
Trinity Church entrance
doors (sculpted by Karl
Bitter), Broadway at Wall
Street, New York (1894).
From *King's Photographic
Views of New York* (1895).

one of the most controversial of his structures. Added to his other commissions at Yale, Princeton, the Princeton Seminary, the Hampton Institute, and the United States Military Academy, Hunt's academic work was diverse and extensive.

In 1888 the small, coeducational Adelbert College in Cleveland was turned into a school for men, and a separate associated College for Women was established, staffed by the Adelbert faculty. A gift on March 6, 1889, of $50,000 by Mrs. Eliza Clark to build a structure to house the classrooms, library, gymnasium, and offices of the College for Women was a decisive factor in the survival of the new college. The Building Committee was delighted with its "good fortune to secure the services of that great architect, Mr. Richard M. Hunt, of New York City, generally considered . . . to be at the head of his profession in the country." Clark Hall was completed late in 1892 at a cost of $54,419.[4]

Although the Building Committee found the evidences of Hunt's "taste and skill in designing a building to meet all [its] requirements," what they got (figure 107) was decidedly commonplace. The three-story, asymmetrical, multigabled building of sandstone and buff brick, resting on a slightly inclined basement of rugged, roughly dressed stone, included Victorian Gothic and archaeological Gothic elements. Two large and steep gables define the main axes and indicate the principal rooms of Clark Hall. The pointed Gothic arch of the entrance façade, approached by heavy stone steps, however, now somehow seems out of keeping with the other elements on that front. To the side a large, traceried window of the assembly room nearly fills the gable wall, which is supported by pairs of cornering buttresses. The largest room of the upper floor served as the gymnasium, "well equipped with appliances carefully selected and adapted for the use of young ladies." The interior also contains a variety of other rooms of varying sizes, shapes, and heights, including originally a library and studies, classrooms, offices, a lounge and a lunchroom, a faculty room, a cloakroom, a reception room, and baths and dressing rooms. The exterior arrangement of the forms and details is rather agitated. The intrusive secondary gables, including at least two with pierced bargeboards, the awkwardly placed dormers, the overly heavy lintels, and the nervous little attic windows and finials all weakened the impact of Clark Hall, which was one of the lesser works to come from Hunt's office.[5]

In contrast to Clark Hall, the William Hayes Fogg Art Museum of Harvard University was stylistically more integrated but was accorded an emphatically negative reception. Funds for the museum were bequeathed by Mrs. Elizabeth Fogg of New York City in memory of her

Figure 107
Clark Hall, Adelbert College, Cleveland, Ohio (1892). Courtesy The American Institute of Architects Foundation/ Prints and Drawings Collection, Washington, D.C. Reproduction by James Garrison.

Figure 108
Fogg Museum, Harvard University, Cambridge, Massachusetts (1895). Courtesy The American Institute of Architects Foundation/Prints and Drawings Collection, Washington, D.C. Reproduction by James Garrison.

husband, and on her death in 1891, some $218,000 was given to Harvard, of which not more than $150,000 was to be spent on the building with the remainder to be used for maintenance. The Harvard Building Committee, headed by Edward W. Hooper and including Hunt's long-time friend and former client Martin Brimmer, invited the New York architect to execute the building. Since Hunt received an honorary doctoral degree from Harvard in June 1892, his selection was especially appropriate. A site in the Harvard Yard behind Appleton Chapel was selected in November 1892, and the building was completed by early 1895.[6]

Hunt faced some difficult problems in the Fogg Museum. The site chosen for the building was an awkward one, a small plot crowded close to Appleton Chapel but facing away from it toward the street. Close by stood other collegiate structures built in a variety of styles—Richardson's Sever Hall in neo-Romanesque, Bulfinch's University Hall in Federal style, Ware & Van Brunt's massive Memorial Hall in a polychrome Victorian Gothic, and Matthews Hall in a Gothic and Jacobean design, as well as the earlier Georgian buildings. Among the Harvard buildings there was no general style to conform to. Perhaps, as Schuyler suggested, Hunt chose a classic mode because in the midst of the many different styles he wanted to aim for the "utmost purity," so that the new museum could best stand on its own merits. Another problem was that the Building Committee wanted both a place to store and exhibit the Harvard art collection and a large lecture hall. Hunt tried to provide for both needs, but he maintained that the money available was insufficient for the double purpose. After the museum had been finished, moreover, it was reported that while it was being designed the architect had never been fully and precisely informed as to exactly how the building would be used or how many people would occupy it.[7]

Hunt's neoclassical design was simple (figure 108). Facing the street he erected a flat-roofed, two-story, symmetrical, rectangular building, housing, on the first floor, the main exhibition hall, two small exhibit rooms, a lecture room, and two offices, while attached at the rear was an elongate apsidal extension, containing a large lecture room. The street façade incorporated two projecting end wings and a recessed central section decorated by attached Ionic columns. The low-ceilinged upper story was clearly delineated on the exterior by a full entablature rising over the high first story, while the lower wall was rusticated under the leaded windows. Rather plain pilasters were placed at the corners of the end pavilions and at intervals around the hemicycle to the rear. Although invisible from a position directly in front of the building, a pediment terminated the rear section hemicycle roof at the place where its upper portion joined the roof of the forward rectangular section. A griffin rested on acroteria at each end of the pediment. All in all, the Fogg Museum was straightforward and unpretentious, if decidedly cold and formal and even mausoleum-like. The light-colored stone contrasted sharply with the rich red brick and the brown stone of most of the other Harvard buildings.[8]

Even as the Fogg Museum was nearing completion, complaints began. Critics charged that the building was too low and squat in appearance, that the proportions were awkward, and that the detail was not artistic. It was argued that the exhibition space was far too limited for adequate display of the Harvard art collection. *The Springfield* (Mass.) *Republican* presented a common judgment: "The Fogg Museum is a great disappointment to every one; it is a dismal, inartistic example of architecture, and far from what the giver intended to bestow upon the university."[9]

The most outspoken critic of the building was Charles Eliot Norton, the eminent professor of fine arts and a leading purveyor of "culture" in America. Norton, it should be pointed out, found little to like in any of the buildings erected at Harvard in the previous half century. Although the large lecture hall in the Fogg Museum had been in part designed for his use, Norton soon refused to lecture there, having discovered that the acoustics were so deplorable that he could not be heard halfway across the room and that the sight lines were so bad that many students could not see objects displayed on the platform. Norton was unrestrained in his condemnation and characterized Hunt's building as "beneath contempt" and unfit for its purposes, while declaring that it showed the "lack of civilization" in the United States. Indeed, he ranted, "Had it been intended as an example of what such a building should not be, it could hardly be better fitted for the purpose." On one occasion, Norton suggested that it was "the duty of the graduates to remove this impediment." A year or so after the museum had been opened, while Norton's censure continued, students responded by painting "Norton's Pride" in large red letters on the building. Catharine Hunt suggested that Norton's voice was not strong enough to fill a large lecture room. She reported that he had once admitted his real cause of complaint to be that there was no good place in the building to leave his rubbers and umbrella![10]

The poor acoustics in the large lecture hall were a problem, however, to many others besides Professor Norton. To try to improve the matter, acoustical experiments were carried on in the hall in the late 1890s, and in 1912 the hall was remodeled by closing off the rear of the room to form a smaller lecture room and a new exhibition gallery behind it. Later, offices and other rooms were built into the semicircular gallery area. Further endeavors to improve the acoustics were made in 1967 and 1972, with the installation of fiberboard panels, floor carpeting, and even a sound-reflecting canopy over the lecturer's position. In 1913, the roof on the front section was raised to provide a higher ceiling and better lighting for a rebuilt and enlarged second-story exhibition gallery.

When the new Fogg Museum building on Quincy Street was completed in 1927, Hunt's building became known as the Robinson Hall Annex, serving the Graduate School of Design for classrooms and offices. Then in 1935, the old Fogg Museum was renamed Hunt Hall, honoring an architect whose work would have little meaning in the Bauhaus-dominated school. The departments of architecture, landscape architecture, and city planning used the space. Finally, in the summer of 1973, Hunt Hall was torn down. Even though the old Fogg Museum was a minor work of the architect and a building that was in many respects awkward and inefficient and that presented continuing acoustical problems, its destruction removed an interesting segment of the rich and varied architectural legacy of Harvard.[11]

Beginning a few years earlier, Hunt's work for the federal government included two major commissions in the late eighties and the early nineties. The first of these was a group of buildings for the United States Naval Observatory, which were authorized in 1886–1889. As early as 1881, the Navy had selected a seventy-acre site for the new observatory buildings close to Massachusetts Avenue in Georgetown Heights in Washington, D.C. Hunt was at work on the observatory buildings by the spring of 1887; construction got under way the next year and continued into 1892. The observatory was officially completed on May 13, 1893.[12]

Hunt ran into considerable trouble with the observatory project. Part of it was due to the inferior quality of the stone furnished by government contractors, which the architect refused to accept, while clashes between workmen on the job and inspectors who were superintending the work led to further problems. At one point the contractor failed to do his work, and the Navy Department took over construction. Both Hunt and his principal associate, Maurice Fornachon, made frequent trips to Washington to oversee the job. On one occasion Hunt appealed to high naval officers and to the Secretary of the Navy, W. C. Whitney, with whom he was personally acquainted, to bypass bureaucratic red tape and get the project moving. He was successful.[13]

At the Georgetown Heights site, besides a building for the offices of the several observatory departments and a clock house, Hunt planned domed structures to house special astronomical instruments—transit circles, a great equatorial, and a prime vertical instrument—as well as a boiler house, a dynamo building, and stables. Because of the highly utilitarian nature of the buildings, architectural treatment was limited mainly to the office building and the large telescope building housing the twenty-one-inch equatorial instrument. The latter structure was faced by rough-dressed marble; and a projecting balcony encircling it threw strong shadows on the stone below the forty-eight-foot hemispherical dome. The long, two-story office building (figure 109), set on a low base, included at the east end a circular library extension with a conical roof and at the west end a telescope tower "having a decided Egyptian leaning." The main section of the office building and the library were covered by dressed stone with Néo-Grec details and the telescope end by rock-face stone. Several of the instrument buildings were covered by corrugated sheet iron and looked like temporary sheds. In the view of one critic, the architect Glenn Brown, the architectural effects of the Naval Observatory were frankly "disappointing both as a whole and in detail." The structures were placed indiscriminately and little related to one another. While possibly convenient for astronomical requirements, the grouping of buildings, Brown judged, was completely lacking in harmony and in pleasing effect.[14]

At the United States Military Academy, Hunt designed a gymnasium, a new Academic Building, and a guardhouse for the south entrance to the post, and made renovations for the old library. Early in 1889, Congress appropriated $100,000 for a new gymnasium and $490,000 for the Academic Building, and on September 14 Hunt was invited by the superintendent of the Academy, Colonel John M. Wilson, to prepare drawings, specifications, detailed plans, and estimates for the two structures, working with an Academic Board of the Academy. Wilson no doubt flattered Hunt by writing in his letter of invitation that the distinguished position the architect occupied "before the country, as a man eminent in your profession" had led to his being nominated to design the proposed buildings. Wilson hoped to have work begun immediately on the gymnasium, followed by the construction of the Academic Building. When Hunt accepted the job it was agreed that the architect would receive a five percent fee based on total costs of the work for his designs and specifications, plus traveling expenses, but that someone else would actually superintend construction under his overall direction. Subsequently, Colonel Wilson advised Hunt that the actual

Figure 109
Main (Office) Building,
The United States Naval
Observatory (1892).
Official U.S. Naval Ob-
servatory Photograph.

cost of the gymnasium must not exceed $88,000 and of the Academic Building $431,000, so that twelve percent might be allowed for contingencies and for Hunt's compensation. Contracts would be let after advertising, and Hunt was to furnish blueprints. Wilson also notified Hunt that the Academic Board retained the right of general supervision over the work.[15]

Correspondence about the gymnasium and the Academic Building, now in the Archives of the United States Military Academy, provides an exceptionally full record of Hunt's relations with a client, albeit the United States government. Colonel Wilson was most cooperative and sent to Hunt the suggestions of various instructors at the Academy about the gymnasium facilities needed, and he directed the fencing and gymnastics instructors to go to New York City to consult with Hunt about their proposals. Wilson also continued to remind the architect that the cost of the building must not under any conditions exceed $88,000. Within three months of his initial invitation, Hunt's office had the plans, sections, and elevations ready, proposing two bowling alleys, a swimming pool and dressing rooms, and reading rooms on the first floor, a fencing room and a running track on the second floor, and storerooms in the towers. Later a shooting gallery was placed in the basement, and the tower rooms were converted into dressing and locker rooms. Hunt's plans and designs were inspected by the Academic Board, whose members made some suggestions concerning details.[16]

But the architect soon ran into difficulties. The first contractors' estimates sent by Hunt exceeded the sum allotted for the building. Colonel Wilson did not disguise his irritation both at the figures and the fact that the estimates had not been made in detail. When Hunt then sent detailed estimates as requested, the total came to about $107,000, instead of the $88,000 allotted. At this time Hunt suggested ways that costs might be cut, particularly by reducing the size of the building and cutting out the bowling alleys. Colonel Wilson's annoyance increased when he went over the figures Hunt had sent him and discovered arithmetical errors of about $7,000, so that the total cost estimate was in fact about $114,000. "When these facts were reported to the Board," Wilson wrote, "its confidence in the accuracy of the estimates was somewhat shaken." He reported that the board wanted to retain the original building dimensions and felt that the cost might best be reduced by omitting the swimming pool and some exterior ornamentation. Wilson also admonished Hunt that it would be useless to spend time on plans for the projected Academic Building unless it were certain that it could be built for the allocated $431,000. Hunt was apologetic over the errors in his estimate, but he defended the increase in costs since the instructors had wanted more facilities included.[17]

The architect then revised the plans for the gymnasium, eliminating some of the facilities. Perhaps by this time Colonel Wilson wished that he had selected someone less eminent in the profession for the job, since in the newly revised specifications he found several more errors. For example, "on page 8 the floor of the shooting gallery is finished with a layer of best imported cement, while on page 16 it is paved with one heavy coat of . . . asphalt." Moreover, "a discrepancy exists between the elevation submitted and the specifications for brick construction; the drawing shows the walls from water table down to be of brick, while the specifications call for stone."[18]

When the specifications for the gymnasium were put out for bids, only two contractors responded and both bids were in excess of the funds available. The Academic Board thereupon sought out new bids, and by early June 1890 the contract had been awarded within the allocated sum. Colonel Wilson was anxious to get the building started, and he pushed Hunt hard to have the detailed working drawings sent to the Academy. When the drawings arrived, it was discovered that on the drawings the building was one foot shorter than on the specifications.[19]

Wilson had already requested Hunt to recommend a superintendent of works, and Hunt's nominee was hired. After construction had been started, however, Hunt was not satisfied with the man, who, he decided, had not inspected the job "with sufficient diligence, care, and efficiency." This superintendent was thereupon dismissed and another was hired. The exterior masonry work had to be suspended during the winter because of the cold, but construction was resumed in the spring, whereupon trouble broke out almost at once. The contractor, John Sheehan, refused to follow the new superintendent's orders. Moreover, Hunt and the contractor got into a quarrel over stone that had been paid for but not used and which Hunt ordered not be disposed of without Colonel Wilson's orders. By the end of May 1891, the contractor had stopped all work on the gymnasium. Wilson blamed the impasse on the new works superintendent, who was, he believed, "too domineering," a "nagging man," who talked too much and lacked tact. Yet another superintendent-inspector was thereupon found, and work started up once again. The contract had called for completion of the gymnasium by June 15, 1891, but at that time it was far from finished. By August, relations between the contractor and the architect had deteriorated again, and once more the contractor stopped work. John Sheehan's telegram to Colonel Wilson was right to the point: "Impossible for me to work under Mr. Hunt's office and there is no use of me trying again."[20]

Friction had continued to build up, and when the newest superintendent condemned some lintel stones in one of the towers, Sheehan had refused to go on with the work. Sheehan stated that the architect's office had "baffled and delayed" him "by condemning cut stones every day, and at the tantalizing time, after they [had] been placed in position in the Building." This "humbugging" had gone on "continually" until his patience was "completely worn out." He felt that there was some motive behind their treatment of him. Abandoning the contract was a terrible hardship for Sheehan since he claimed that he had invested "all the earnings" of his life in the building. Maurice Fornachon from Hunt's office suggested that the contractor was in financial difficulties with his subcontractors and that this was the real reason for the stoppage of work. In any case, the contract was declared forfeited and the contractor paid for what he had done.[21]

By October 1891, a new contractor willing to finish the gymnasium had been found, and the date of completion was extended to July 15, 1892. A year after the replacement had been hired, however, the building was still not completed. Colonel Wilson was adamant that the Academy must have possession by November 1, 1892, even if it were not finally finished. Maurice Fornachon and the works superintendent carefully inspected the building at the end of October to record everything that still had to be done before the second contractor was fully paid. But then still another impasse developed when this contractor refused to correct many small defects. Not until a year later were the details finally finished. On November 13, 1893, almost two and one-half years behind schedule, the gymnasium was at last reported completed. It stood until 1923, when it was razed to make way for Washington Hall.[22]

At the Military Academy, Hunt faced the challenge of relating his new buildings to existing structures. This was a problem, of course, that he had faced at Yale, Princeton, and even on city streets, but in many cases he had largely ignored the relationship of a new building to others already standing. At West Point, nevertheless, he endeavored to harmonize the new structures with the buildings around them especially the massive Central Barracks, which extended between the new gymnasium and the Academic Building, and the old Gothic-style library as well. Most of the Academy buildings were heavy stone structures, crenellated and fortress-like, presenting a solid, traditional, military appearance. In his Academy buildings, Hunt turned to a castellated Gothic design, reverting to a style that had been fashionable a half-century earlier.

Using roughly dressed granite from Chester, Massachusetts, Hunt made his new large buildings solid and imposing. The gymnasium (figure 110), with two principal stories, was dominated on the façade by twin towers, with bracket-supported cone-shaped roofs, which rose laterally beside the broad arch of the portico. The arcade of windows above the portico led to a series of embrasures beneath a small battlement. Small, corbelled turrets projected at the recession of the towers. The sides of the building were provided with a series of decorative buttresses. The iron and glass roof was certainly not military, but it did provide good light for the principal exercise room.[23]

Hunt ran into more problems with the much larger Academic Building. At the outset the architect was given precise instructions about what facilities were needed in the building, its outside dimensions, and the total cost. As soon as he began to work on the plans, however, Hunt concluded that if the requirements imposed on him were carried out, the cost would necessarily be more than twice the appropriation that had been made. But he went ahead anyway, and his first designs provided for a building twice as large as that originally contemplated. They were rejected outright by the Academic Board. Hunt then proceeded to scale down his plans and suggested ways of cutting costs. But his ideas obviously were still too grandiose, and he had to be reminded once more of the dimensions and the cost that had been established. Charles W. Larned, the professor of drawing at the Academy, was particularly upset by Hunt's seemingly cavalier attitude toward the work at West Point, believing that the architect had not given "that serious study to the design to which we are entitled and which the subject merits." Inasmuch as the work "after so much discussion and such exact illustration has resulted in such unsatisfactory condition," Larned suggested that Hunt be requested to meet with the Academic Board before proceeding further. Hunt apparently did not meet with the committee, but by mid-April 1890, he had prepared a new set of plans for the Academic Building, which the Board at first found suitable, although soon various Academy professors suggested many detailed changes.[24]

In June 1890, Hunt was asked to prepare further general drawings and specifications, along with alternative plans for reducing the building cost. Two and one-half months later, with nothing yet received, Colonel Wilson inquired where the plans were. It was mid-October before revised regular and alternative designs were ready. In these plans, in order to cut costs, Hunt had not included a tower on the

Figure 110
Gymnasium, United
States Military
Academy, West Point
New York (1893). U.S.
Military Academy Ar-
chives.

Academic Building, and he informed Professor Larned of this change. Once more Colonel Wilson was patently annoyed with Hunt, since a simple arithmetical error appeared in the accompanying estimate; in addition, he had expected the tower to be included, and although Hunt had communicated with Larned, his subordinate, about not including it, he had not informed Wilson.[25]

More changes were then made in the design—the corner tower was put back—and by mid-February 1891, the plans finally met with the approval of the Academic Board and of the War Department. Colonel Wilson hoped to have the north wing completed by December 1892 and the entire building ready for use by August 1893. In early May 1891, the building contract was awarded and construction was begun. Richard Howland Hunt took over general supervision of the work. Colonel Wilson relinquished command of the Military Academy in March 1893, and when he left he graciously thanked Hunt for his "uniform courtesy and patience in our official intercourse," and, keeping silent about the many problems they had encountered, he expressed his appreciation of the "eminent talent and ability shown by you and yours" in the work on the new buildings.[26]

Wilson's successor, Colonel Oswald H. Ernst, had difficulties with the architect also. With the Academic Building well under way, Hunt's ambiguous specifications for a roof covering came to light and led to major changes at considerable additional expense. Work on this large structure continued for four years, and only in mid–1895, about two years late, was it eventually completed. The building was subsequently renamed West Academic Building and later Pershing Barracks and is still in use.[27]

The Academic Building (figure 111) built of the same Massachusetts granite as the gymnasium with stone trim of a lighter tint, was a more elaborately finished building than the athletic pavilion and a much larger edifice. Four stories high, with a U-shaped floor plan, the Academic Building formed, at the rear, a part of a quadrangle with the Central Barracks. The main masses of the primary façade are symmetrically arranged, broken only by the clock tower rising at the northeast corner. The central pavilion surmounts the Gothic-arched sally port, topped by crenellations. High, lateral, crenellated turrets with gargoyles help emphasize the central section. At the first-story level, Tudor arches with deep reveals are set over both the windows and the secondary entrances, while most of the second- and third-story windows are set under basket arches. The most striking features of the design, though, are the machicolated cornice, with small arches between the corbels, and the crenellated parapet topping the corner tower as well as the other segments of the façade. At one time the building walls were covered by vines, although they have been removed and the spectator can now take delight in the texture of the stone.[28]

Despite some problems, Colonel Ernst was satisfied with Hunt's work on the two buildings, for he asked the architect to undertake two additional commissions, and Hunt, despite his many troubles at the Academy, readily accepted. The two works were completed posthumously. Renovations were to be undertaken on the old library building, built in 1841, and on March 7, 1895, Ernst invited Hunt to furnish plans for a fee of $1,250. Within six weeks, his office had plans ready, and with some changes they were approved by May 20. After Hunt's death, a few further alterations were made by Richard Howland Hunt, and the work was carried out.[29]

The second of the posthumous works was a small guardhouse, which Ernst wanted to have built at the south entrance to the post. On September 11, 1894, Ernst invited Hunt to provide "one of your original designs" for the small, one-story granite building, to cost $4,000 or $5,000. "Though small," Colonel Ernst wrote, "the building will be the first one seen by a person entering the Post, and should be carefully designed." Hunt immediately accepted the commission, and by September 26 Ernst had received a proposed plan, providing for a guard waiting room, two smaller sleeping rooms, and a washroom. A month later, the plans, sections, and elevations were delivered to Ernst. Subsequently a basement was added to provide space for a furnace and a coal room. Hunt's death the next year and the lack of an appropriation brought a halt to this project.[30]

A military appropriation bill for 1897, however, allotted $7,500 for construction of the south gate guardhouse. Colonel Ernst wanted to go ahead with construction based on Hunt's plans, utilizing Academy personnel to prepare specifications and working drawings, and he inquired of Richard Howland Hunt whether there were objections to using his father's designs. Hunt at first responded that the Hunt office had never permitted "any designs prepared by it to be carried out by others," but shortly he acquiesced to having the permanent force at West Point do this work in order to keep the costs down to the allotted sum. A contract was let on March 16, 1897, for construction of the guardhouse and the gates at the southern entrance to the post, and they were completed later that year.

The little guardhouse (figure 112), built of coursed rubble masonry, echoed Hunt's two grander West Point commissions. The rugged stones

Figure 111
Academic Building,
United States Military
Academy (1895). U.S.
Military Academy Ar-
chives.

Figure 112
Guardhouse, United
States Military Academy
(1897). Stockbridge Col-
lection, U.S. Military
Academy Archives.

provided an attractive, rough-textured surface. The bracketed cornice, topped by battlements, served notice to anyone arriving at the gate that this was a military post. Within ten years, planning had already begun for a new guardhouse. Additional construction at the south end of the post, beyond the Hunt-designed gatehouse, had made it necessary to relocate the guardhouse. There was some discussion of moving the Hunt building farther to the south, but this was never carried through. The Hunt guardhouse was demolished by the middle of the 1920s and possibly earlier.[31]

Despite their visibility, these various public commissions—church, academic, and governmental—were decidedly secondary projects for Hunt, whose primary energies in the early 1890s were directed to his great houses, the World's Columbian Exposition, the estate at Biltmore, and the plans for the Metropolitan Museum of Art. Nonetheless these works do point up some important characteristics of the architect and his ways of working. Above all, the buildings demonstrate the architect's flexibility and adaptability to differing needs and conditions, showing his willingness to take on very different kinds of work for very different clients. Possibly Hunt felt a certain responsibility because of his position to do work asked of him in places such as the Harvard Yard or at Georgetown Heights or at West Point which could have a national meaning because of the institutions involved.

That Hunt and his staff set high standards for the materials used led to some of his problems in the governmental work. Blame for the errors in the firm's computations and specifications might be placed on the staff members working on the buildings, though the responsibility must rest ultimately with Hunt. The architect who had erred on his computations on the Rossiter house at the beginning of his career was still not above making simple careless mistakes. Hunt's difficulty in keeping within cost estimates had not infrequently caused troubles with his clients.

Possibly, in this very prolific period of work, Hunt was trying to do too much and trying to satisfy too many people. It would seem that he had difficulty in refusing jobs offered to him, and considering that he was deeply immersed at the time in several of the largest projects of his career, it might have been better for him to have undertaken less work.

22

THE CHICAGO
FAIR

The activity that brought Hunt the greatest notice during his lifetime was his work at Chicago on the World's Columbian Exposition, the culminating American public cultural event of the nineteenth century. Hunt's selection as president of the Board of Architects and the award to him of the design for the Administration Building, the focal point of the exposition, were testimonies to his position as the leading figure of his profession in the United States, and the success of his leadership in developing the architecture of the fair and the appropriateness of his design for the Administration Building justified the respect and judgment of his fellow professionals.

During the latter part of the 1880s, there was growing interest in the approaching quatercentenary of the discovery of America. In 1886, the American Historical Association set up a special committee under the chairmanship of George Bancroft to encourage Congressional interest in celebrating the four hundredth anniversary of Columbus's first voyage, while that same year Senator George F. Hoar of Massachusetts presented to the Senate a New England promotion board's suggestion for a world's fair in 1892 to be held in the national capital. By the summer of 1889, interested citizens in Washington, New York, Chicago, and St. Louis had established committees working to have an international Columbian exposition in their cities.[1]

In New York, Mayor Hugh J. Grant called for a preliminary meeting in his office on July 25, 1889, to set up a committee to procure the proposed fair for his city. The commemorative exposition, it was suggested, would be "the opportunity of a century": it would increase commerce, elevate property values, provide considerable employment for three years, and make New York "more than ever the pride of the whole country, [and] secure her in the lasting respect and admiration of the world." Hunt and Frederick Law Olmsted were among the many prominent citizens who sat on the New York Committee for the International Exposition of 1892. As the group was organized, Hunt was elected to the Executive Committee and was chosen a member of the Committee on Site and Buildings and its Sub-Committee on Buildings as well as the representative of the city's architects for the general committee. A drive to raise $200,000 to be used as an expense fund was begun immediately, while the general committee also sought to ensure a guarantee fund of $5,000,000. Helping with the fund raising, Hunt undertook to solicit contributions from the members of the New York Chapter of the A.I.A. He subscribed $500 himself.[2]

Several sites in the greater New York area were proposed to the New York Committee. Some favored locating the exposition in Central Park, making use of the Metropolitan Museum building and the Museum of Natural History adjacent to the west side of the park, but there was also considerable opposition to any encroachment on Central Park. Others suggested locating the Columbian fair in Riverside and Morningside parks. Sites on Staten Island, on Governor's Island, at Coney Island, in Washington Heights, and in the Bronx also had their advocates. The pressures on the Committee on Site and Buildings were very strong, and Hunt as a member received several letters urging him to vote for one location or another. Even William Waldorf Astor had a favored site and wrote Hunt urging him to consider Pelham Park for the exposition, adding parenthetically, though, that the Astors owned no property in that vicinity. Hunt was very conscientious in going out to look over proposed sites. Before the end of 1889, the Committee on Site and Buildings recommended to the general committee that a location be chosen in the area between Ninety-Seventh and One Hundred Twenty-Seventh streets from Fourth Avenue to the Hudson River, which encompassed Riverside and Morningside parks and Central Park north of the large reservoir as well as adjacent lands. The committee also recommended that most of the exposition buildings be erected outside Central Park. A bill to organize a legal corporation for the fair was introduced in the legislature at Albany, but a factional fight ensued and the bill was stalled. Hunt was active in trying to keep the New York endeavors nonpartisan. Early in January 1890, the New York Committee presented their case for the fair to a Senate committee in Washington.[3]

Although New Yorkers were working hard to get the Columbian Exposition for their city, the proponents of a Chicago site had been working even harder. A large Chicago committee had been appointed in July 1889. Chicago businessmen rallied to the support of the project, heartily convinced that they would win the prize, and within a few months a five-million-dollar subscription was arranged. A group of Chicagoans traveled to Paris to examine and report on the 1889 French Universal Exposition. And a committee was chosen to report on sites in and around Chicago. John Wellborn Root of the firm of Burnham and Root was hired to plan general layouts for possible Chicago sites. Another group of citizens went to Washington, D.C., to present the case for a Chicago location. Unlike the New York delegation, they were able to convince the legislators that if the fair were placed in Chicago it would be kept out of politics.[4]

On February 24, 1890, the House of Representatives passed a bill awarding the prize to Chicago and setting up a national World's Columbian Commission, with two representatives from each state and territory and eight commissioners at large, to oversee the exposition. The Senate subsequently passed the bill, and it was signed into law by President Benjamin Harrison on April 25, 1890. An early decision was made to open the Chicago fair on May 1, 1893, so that it might run through the summer months, though the formal dedication ceremonies were scheduled for October 1892, commemorating the centenary of Columbus's landing. An Illinois corporation, fully established by April 9, 1890, was charged with providing a site, preparing the grounds, designing and construction the exposition, and operating the enterprise. The national commission was to approve the site, the general plans, and the allotment of space, to appoint judges, and to dedicate the buildings. The existence of the two supervisory organizations proved to be awkward, and they did not always work in full harmony.[5]

The World's Columbian Exposition of 1893 was the fifteenth of the great international expositions held during the second half of the nineteenth century. Prince Albert had conceived of the Crystal Palace Exhibition in London in 1851, which had led the way in celebrating, like the fairs that followed, the material wealth of the age. The New York Exposition of 1853, though on a smaller scale, emulated the British example, while the Philadelphia Centennial Exhibition of 1876 was both a commemoration of the birth of the American republic and a celebration of the material progress of the American nation. The Chicago fair was envisioned on a far grander scale than the two earlier American expositions but like them was also a paean to progress. At Chicago considerably more attention was given to architectural planning and design than had been the case at the Centennial Exhibition.[6]

During the summer of 1890, the directors of the Illinois corporation considered various sites in the Chicago area. In July, James Ellsworth, then president of the South Parks Board, invited Frederick Law Olmsted and his associate Henry Sargent Codman to Chicago to give an expert opinion on sites. The two landscape architects looked over seven possible locations in August, and though they were not fully satisfied with any of them, they settled on two possible lakeshore areas: one, wooded lands near Buena Park, on the north side of the city, and the other on the south side in the sand and marshes of Jackson Park. The north shore location was soon judged to be inconvenient to railroad transportation, and by late in the year the Jackson Park location had been agreed upon, along with a small secondary section on the downtown lake front where a fine arts building, a music hall, and a liberal arts building were planned. Consideration of the downtown section was subsequently abandoned. Olmsted was already well acquainted with the Jackson Park

area, since nineteen years earlier he and Calvert Vaux had surveyed the
south side parks of Chicago and had designed a plan for their future
development. Almost nothing of this earlier plan, which called for a
chain of lagoons, dredged out with higher ridges between, a shore
drive, and a long pier, had been carried out, however. But Olmsted
believed that the fundamentals of the original design might be adapted
for the exposition.[7]

Meanwhile, the Committee on Grounds and Buildings, established
under the Illinois corporation on August 20, 1890, invited F. L. Olmsted
& Co. to be consulting landscape architects for the fair. That same day,
the *Chicago Tribune* reported that Richard Morris Hunt—"an intimate
friend of Mr. Olmsted"—would be named consulting architect for the
exposition. The *Chicago Inter-Ocean* also indicated that Hunt would be
chosen as consulting architect and reported testimony from leading
Chicago architects endorsing Hunt's selection. To William Le Baron Jenney, the choice of Hunt as consulting architect would be "the best selection that could possibly be made." Dankmar Adler supported Hunt, too,
stating that Hunt stood at the top of the profession in the United States.
To S. S. Beman, this would be "a good choice, the best in the country
. . . because Richard M. Hunt unquestionably stands at the head of his
profession as an artistic, educated architect." The following day, however, the Committee named John Wellborn Root as consulting architect.
One wonders how Root must have felt knowing of the accolades fellow
Chicago architects had given Hunt. On September 2, Abraham Gottlieb
was appointed consulting engineer, and on September 4, Daniel Burnham was also named as joint consulting architect. In October, in an
administrative shift, Root and Burnham both resigned as consulting
architects, whereupon Root was immediately reappointed to that position and Burnham was named chief of construction.[8]

Preliminary plans for the fair were drawn up in early September.
Olmsted's original Jackson Park plan suggested the general scheme of
land and water areas. Like Olmsted, Root had also considered making
use of the lagoons and waterways in the design of the grounds. Root
worked closely with Henry Codman, who devised the arrangement of
terraces, bridges, and landings, while Root and Burnham decided on the
placement and the shape of the buildings. By one account, Codman was
said to have suggested the great central court—which had been used in
Paris—while Olmsted wanted the principal architectural feature of the
fair placed at the head of the court. Daniel Burnham later dismissed any
idea that the preliminary plan was particularly original, except for the
inclusion of the lagoons, the canal, and the wooded island. The early

design, he asserted, was thought out logically a step at a time, keeping in mind the character of the exposition and the ultimate use of the grounds afterwards as a public park. At this early point, nothing had yet been decided about architectural style, although Root was leaning toward a "variety in style and color for the buildings." On September 11, the plans were well enough along so that Root and Codman could present them to the Grounds and Buildings Committee. They were soon presented to and adopted by the directors of the Illinois corporation, and by the national commission by the beginning of December.[9]

At this time a decision had to be made regarding the designing of the various buildings. Burnham was becoming anxious and felt that a force of architects had to be got together quickly to begin work. After all, the fair was scheduled to open in a little over two years. On December 9, 1890, Burnham gave to the Committee on Grounds and Buildings a memorandum, which he and Root had drawn up, suggesting various ways of selecting designers. He pointed out that one man might be chosen to design all the exposition buildings, that an open competition or a selected competition might be held, or that a direct selection of individual architects by invitation might be made. For reasons of speed and efficiency, Burnham opted for the direct selection of a few prominent architects. Root had already suggested this course some time earlier, and Olmsted, Codman, and Gottlieb favored it as well. After a lively discussion, the Committee on Grounds and Buildings accepted Burnham's recommendations.[10]

Following the committee's approval, Burnham on December 13 sent letters to the architectural firms of Richard Hunt, George B. Post, and McKim, Mead & White, in New York City; to Peabody & Stearns in Boston; and to Van Brunt & Howe in Kansas City, inviting them to design the principal buildings around the Court of Honor. Henry Van Brunt responded quickly and accepted the invitation. The Eastern architects, however, were hesitant and wanted to meet to talk the matter over. Hunt had earlier decided that he would have nothing to do with the Chicago fair, primarily because of his weakened condition with the gout. But George Post persuaded him to reconsider his decision, arguing that none of the other New York architects would serve unless he did. Hunt therefore presided at a mid-December meeting held in the offices of McKim, Mead & White. Charles F. McKim took the lead in the discussions, advocating the use of classical motives, at least in the buildings around the central court, which Root had laid out. The use of classical modules, he pointed out, would make the buildings easier to design and more efficient to construct than would the adoption of other styles and would provide for a harmonious uniformity. When McKim went on at excessive length about what might be done in Chicago, Hunt became impatient and cut him off with a characteristic remark: "Damn your preambles; get down to facts!" The conference terminated in unanimous agreement that the use of classical motives for the exposition would be appropriate and imposing as well as efficient and manageable.[11]

On December 22, Burnham came to New York City to dine with Hunt, Post, Peabody, and William Rutherford Mead at the Player's Club. Although Peabody had by this time decided to accept the invitation to work on the fair, the other three men were still lukewarm about the project. But Burnham's enthusiasm was convincing; arguing that what would be done in Chicago would be "the measure by which America, and especially Chicago, must expect to be judged by the world," he persuaded them to serve. Even so, when in early January Root also visited New York to attend as secretary a board meeting of the American Institute of Architects and talked with the Easterners about the general plan for the grounds, he found them still apathetic and hesitant. Back in Chicago, Burnham invited five Chicago architectural firms—Burling & Whitehouse, William Le Baron Jenney, Henry Ives Cobb, S. S. Beman, and Adler & Sullivan—to design the other large buildings planned for the exposition.[12]

Burnham's choice of leading non-Chicago architects to create the principal buildings of the fair, was, needless to say, vigorously criticized in Chicago. Wounded civic pride was involved. Burnham justified his selection by arguing that the exposition was a national endeavor and had to include the best qualified men from all over the country. Later, his choices helped make the myth of "the lost cause": it was argued that the Easterners, whom Burnham had selected, had by settling upon a classical style for the fair, destroyed the burgeoning new Chicago style; the great "White City" of classical buildings undermined the new, original work being done in Chicago and fastened an inappropriate neoclassicism upon the country that would not be shaken off for decades. Burnham's choices of designers were confirmed by the Committee on Grounds and Buildings on January 5, 1891, after which formal invitations were issued to the architects. Root himself would have been an obvious person to design a major building for the central Court of Honor, but as consulting architect he felt that he should not participate, probably foreseeing a possible conflict of interest were he to do so. Perhaps, too, the praises earlier bestowed on Hunt by his fellow Chicago architects made him step back.[13]

Early in January 1891, the Board of Architects, including both the out-of-towners and the Chicagoans, met in Chicago along with Olmsted and Codman to discuss their ideas. When Hunt and his colleagues from the East arrived in the city on Saturday, January 10 and were taken by Burnham to look over the site in Jackson Park, they were all disheartened by what they saw. The site was a dreary waste of sand dunes and marshes, covered by dry grass, low bushes, and stunted trees, seemingly inhospitable as a location for a great new city which had to be completed by the spring of 1893. A splendid banquet that evening, hosted by the Committee on Grounds and Buildings, raised their spirits, however. When Lyman Gage, the Chicago banker who headed the Illinois corporation, and Burnham gave pep talks stressing teamwork and the need for the "highest qualities of artistic expression," the architects were apparently encouraged about what might be accomplished in so short a time.[14]

At the first formal meeting of the Board of Architects on Monday, January 12, in the library of Burnham & Root's offices, Hunt was elected chairman of the board and Louis Sullivan was chosen secretary. Henry Van Brunt, whose affection for his old teacher was especially great, later described Hunt's selection in this way: "The natural dominance of the master again asserted itself without pretension and we once more became his willing and happy pupils." Louis Sullivan, to whom Hunt represented much that he despised about American architectural practice, was less charitable in his account, written much later. Sullivan related that when Burnham rose to welcome the visitors he appeared to be grossly apologetic about the presence of the Western men. Eventually, Hunt cut him short in a typical burst: "Hell, we haven't come out here on a missionary expedition. Let's get to work." But Sullivan felt that Hunt had done Burnham a favor by coming.[15]

The work got off to an inauspicious start. After the first day, Hunt was once again incapacitated by gout and confined to his hotel room; Post served as acting chairman in Hunt's absence. Mead, Peabody, and Van Brunt, who represented their firms, refused to commit their partners to any major decisions without consulting them. Root gave a tea and reception for the visiting architects at his home on Sunday afternoon, and Harriet Monroe, the poet and Root's sister-in-law, who also attended, "was amazed at their listless and hopeless attitude toward the great undertaking which brought them to Chicago." As his guests were leaving, Root accompanied them to their carriages without putting on an overcoat and caught a bad cold. His condition rapidly grew worse. When pneumonia developed, Burnham absented himself from the conferences in order to remain with his partner. On Thursday, January 15, Root died.[16]

Root's death at the age of forty-one was a terrible shock to Burnham, who had relied on him as the chief designer of the firm, and it was manifestly a loss both to the fair and to American architecture generally, for in his years of association with Burnham since 1873 Root had created a remarkable body of work and had shown himself to be one of the most accomplished of American architects. Harriet Monroe believed that if Root had lived, he would have battled for the progressive ideals of the Chicago architects and resisted the return to a style of the past. She felt that he would have persuaded the architects to use color in their works and surely would have fought for structures that frankly expressed their purpose and materials, rather than going back to what she saw as an irrelevant past. But Root had much earlier decided that the architects should design as they wished, and he had already learned that the Easterners had decided on a classical style. At the time of his death he seemed to be going along with what the others were doing, and there is no evidence that the fair would have been much different had he lived.[17]

In their several meetings, the Board of Architects reaffirmed the preliminary plan accepted earlier and decided upon the exact size and location for the various buildings as well as for the Court of Honor and the canal. They also agreed as a full group upon the use of the classical style for the Court of Honor buildings, utilizing common modules and a uniform cornice line to make the structures harmonious with one another. No contrary style was proposed. In reviewing the preliminary plans, the architects decided to detach the Administration Building from the railway station behind it and make it "the most important architectural feature of the Exposition," with a large dome to give it added prominence. When Burnham assigned the buildings to the architects, he awarded the Administration Building to Hunt. Like the other architects, Hunt was required to provide only a general design and one set of full working drawings, along with the necessary description and instructions. The engineering work and actual construction would be undertaken by the Bureau of Construction of the exposition. A second conference was planned for the following month when the building plans would be presented to the Board of Architects for criticism and correction if necessary. Each architectural firm would be paid $10,000 for its work along with traveling expenses for the designing architects.[18]

While the conferences were taking place, several of the other architects regularly visited Hunt in his hotel room to talk over their ideas and get his views. Henry Van Brunt and George B. Post, Hunt's former

pupils, who always had a great affection for him, were especially so-
licitous. Hunt fully supported the idea of a uniformity of design in the
Court of Honor.[19]

Frederick Law Olmsted, who always favored landscape design in
harmony with the natural features of the land, found the work on the
Chicago fair a considerable challenge. The difficulties of building up the
land for the exposition out of sand dunes and swamps in order to provide a suitable lake view seemed to him to present a parallel with the
building of Chicago itself. Later, Olmsted concluded that the formal
stateliness of the site that the architects were determined to have had
been reconciled with the need for "a picturesque motive of natural
scenery"—at least to the satisfaction of the architects. And apparently
largely to his own satisfaction as well, for Olmsted felt that at Chicago he
was able to work with "these men of the enemy [who were concerned
primarily with architectural rather than with natural beauty] . . . in
hearty, active, friendly cooperation."[20]

When on February 22, 1891, the Board of Architects assembled in
Chicago for a second series of meetings, they brought with them their
preliminary sketches for the buildings they had been assigned. William
R. Mead was replaced by Charles F. McKim, who brought along Augustus Saint-Gaudens, the sculptor. The landscape architects had prepared
a detailed plan of the grounds. With Hunt presiding, each designer
submitted his work to the group for comment and criticism. In the
opinion of the Chicago architect S. S. Beman, every member of the
board viewed Hunt "with the greatest respect and confidence" and
looked to him "to harmonize the conflicting personalities in the various
styles of architecture" and bring them into unity. More than any one
else, Beman believed, Hunt should be credited for the ultimate conception of the Court of Honor. He not only freely advised the others about
their plans and sketches, often correcting proportions for them, but he
also "fired the laggards with some of his own ceaseless energy and
enthusiasm." Robert S. Peabody echoed Beman's view in suggesting
that Hunt had "formed from all the varied elements, the happiest working body of architects and other artists" that he had ever known in
his career.[21]

Although the architects had considered utilizing iron, glass, and tiles
for the temporary exhibition buildings—which were to be essentially
sheds for the display of goods and artifacts—Hunt and his colleagues
agreed that a suitable ironwork and glass style had not been found so
far. They wanted the exposition to have a "monumental look" about it,
and so they concluded that what was needed was a material that could

be easily and quickly worked for temporary buildings but that resembled stone. They hoped, moreover, that the exposition buildings would be "an object lesson for the United States Government," which put up so many public buildings. The architects therefore decided upon a combination of plaster of Paris and fibers or straw called "staff" as the primary building material for the wood- and iron-framed structures, both for the exterior walls and for decorative elements. It was inexpensive, easily produced, sufficiently durable, and readily worked into various forms and shapes. When painted white, the color Burnham and the Board of Architects decided upon, the material presented a marble-like appearance. The uniform whiteness of the staff walls of most of the structures made the neoclassical style all the more effective. A visitor might well imagine himself transported back to the gleaming marble Forum of ancient Rome. Among the main halls at the fair, only Louis Sullivan's Transportation Building and Henry Ives Cobb's Fisheries Building, both located away from the Court of Honor, were not neoclassical in design.[22]

On February 24 in the library at Burnham's offices in the Rookery, the Board of Architects presented their sketches to the members of the Committee on Grounds and Buildings and to Lyman Gage, the president of the Illinois Board of Directors. Although Hunt was suffering badly from the gout, he presided throughout the day as each man put his drawings on the wall and talked about his building. From all accounts, those present in the library felt, as the drawings were shown, that this was a truly historic occasion. Here was a group of highly talented artists who were working closely together, subordinating when necessary their own ideas to further the collaborative endeavor, integrating the arts of painting and sculpture into their works, creating an ensemble which seemed to them a vision of ideal beauty.[23]

Looking back to that meeting, Daniel Burnham thought that the artistic collaboration, the sense of interdependence and mutual confidence, made this "the most notable event in the history of Art in this country." As the winter day went on, the architects, sculptors, painters, and landscape designers present became aware that the drawings they were seeing gave promise of something "far more grand and beautiful" than any of them had previously imagined might be possible. Some of the architects recognized that aspects of their designs might have to be changed in order to accord better with the total scheme, and they willingly altered their plans for the sake of unity. As the afternoon drew to a close and the last drawing had been displayed, Lyman Gage stood up and broke into the low murmur of voices to exclaim: "You are dreaming, gentlemen. May your visions only be realized." Saint-Gaudens, who had been sitting quietly throughout the day, then came over to Burnham and, taking both of his hands, said: "Look here, old fellow, do you realize that this is the greatest meeting of artists since the Fifteenth Century?"[24]

Despite the enthusiasm for the exposition which the February meetings had stimulated, Hunt did not move ahead with his work on the Administration Building as rapidly as Burnham felt that he should. A month later, the chief of construction urged Hunt to press on with his work "with utmost speed" so that his own office could begin the necessary structural drawings. "The elaboration of exact artistic detail should not make us wait," he chided Hunt. Delay was hurting the fund raising. "The main thing is to get started." When three months later Hunt's office sent a watercolor of the projected Administration Building to Burnham, he found it of no use whatsoever. Francis Hopkinson Smith, who had made the rendering, had placed the building in "an imaginary environment" having no relation to the actual setting. Burnham was sardonic at this *lèse-majesté:* "There is not to be a vista of eastern domes, towers and minarets, back of your building toward the railway. On the contrary, there will be a railway station, and this should be shown." Nor had the artist depicted the agreed-upon placement of the building in relation to the lagoon. Burnham had wanted a publishable view, but to publish this picture would be "to invite derision, and to undoubtedly get it."[25]

In spite of this awkward beginning, Hunt devoted a great deal of time to the fair. His drawings were finally sent, and construction was well under way by the autumn. In late November 1891, the Board of Architects again met in Chicago to inspect the works and decide on questions of lighting and decoration. Meeting with the Grounds and Buildings Committee, Hunt expressed his satisfaction with the appearance of the "staff" and his confidence that the exposition would be "dignified and magnificent." Hunt's daughter Kitty accompanied him on this trip, and they visited Niagara Falls on the way back to New York. In an early December interview with a reporter from the *New-York Daily Tribune,* Hunt said he was certain that the buildings would be ready for the dedication scheduled for the following October. Late in April 1892, Hunt joined Charles McKim, George Post, Karl Bitter, and others for yet another visit to Chicago. Hunt was apparently considered obdurate in some of his ideas about decoration, for just after this visit McKim was urged in a confidential memorandum from Francis D. Millet, who did decorative painting for the fair, to hint to Hunt that a concentric and

radial brick pattern would be preferable to the plain cement floor originally planned for the Administration Building rotunda. The change was
made. Once more in September, Hunt returned to Chicago to check on
the progress of his building, this time accompanied by George Vanderbilt, who was on his way to Japan.[26]

The World's Columbian Exposition dedication ceremonies were held
on October 21, 1892. McKim, always an efficient organizer, arranged for
two private railway cars to convey him and the Hunts and several of
their friends as guests to Chicago on the 19th. As co-host Hunt paid for
half of the cost of the transportation. Unfortunately, he was once again
laid low by the gout and was confined to his small compartment for the
rail trip westward. A week earlier, when a Columbian quatercentenary
celebration had been held in New York, Hunt had also been incapacitated with the gout and had not been able to participate in the ceremonies, for which he had helped prepare the decorations, collaborating
with Stanford White and Augustus Saint-Gaudens. The relaxation of the
train ride, however, did wonders, and he recovered sufficiently to participate in the Chicago ceremonies. Arriving in Chicago on the 20th, the
party had great difficulty getting to their hotel because of a large labor
procession, which seemed to Catharine Hunt's "Eastern eyes" to consist
"almost entirely of Russian and Polish Jews."[27]

On the 21st, the McKim-Hunt group, including, among others,
Daniel Coit Gilman, the president of the Johns Hopkins University, and
Richard Harding Davis and Charles Dudley Warner, the novelists, on
arriving at the fairgrounds were taken by a steamer launch placed at
their disposal to the dedication ceremonies at the Manufactures and
Liberal Arts Building. A hundred thousand people were estimated to be
present, and with the noise of the crowd and the vast expanse of the
building, Catharine Hunt complained, they could scarcely hear the
speeches, including the principal dedicatory address by their long-time
friend Vice-President Levi P. Morton. The music was provided by a
large orchestra led by Theodore Thomas and by a chorus of 5,500 voices,
along with the United States Marine Corps Band and a Mexican band.
For the Hunts the high point of the ceremonies was the award of medals
to the master artists who had created the exposition. One wonders how
well Hunt, pained by gout, managed when he and his colleagues, surrounded by representatives of the diplomatic corps in full dress and
military and naval officers in uniform, descended a long flight of crimson carpeted steps to receive the medals. "The general effect," Hunt's
wife found, "was immensely impressive."[28]

Karl Bitter, Hunt's sculptor-collaborator on the Administration

Building, spoke later about his patron, who, he felt, revealed that day a great deal about "his unspoiled character":

We had come early and listened until late to speeches and odes we could not hear, and everybody was thoroughly weary and tired, in rather a bad humor, like the weather outside. Finally Messrs. Burnham and Morton presented the medals. Shortly after the weary crowd of artists made its way across the grounds, I well remember what a bedraggled lot we were. I heard Mr. Hunt exclaim, just as we reached the Court of Honor, and his tone brought us to a sudden standstill: "Look around you," he said, and he became eloquent in a manner I shall never forget. There he stood, erect with his bushy eyebrows slightly contracted, and his outstretched arm beckoning us to survey the surrounding structures. "Here we stand in the midst of what we have done, and have a cause to be proud of doing so much in so short a time! Why don't you hold up your heads in appreciation of the honor you have just received, like men, instead of crawling along in this dejected manner." And he swore right roundly. "Artists you are, and like artists you should live, full of life and merriness." As he continued speaking his eyes shone brighter, and he spoke with the enthusiasm of a young man, brimming over with the joy of success. He spoke about the work, of art, and many other things. He also spoke about his country and what it had done, with a fire that warmed the heart of each listener. If we felt tired before, we felt tired no longer. The great enthusiasm of the speaker had kindled our own, and we cheered and cheered. A joyous band adjourned to the Island to make merry in the good old way, as only artists can, and all because Mr. Hunt, the oldest in age, was, in spirit, the most youthful.[29]

Obviously there was a strong seasoning of self-congratulation in what Hunt said to his friends and colleagues that afternoon, stimulated as he must have been by the events of the day. And yet the anecdote demonstrates once again Hunt's feelings of dedication to his art and to the cause of artistic achievement in his country. Here in Jackson Park was a large-scale collaborative artistic endeavor such as had never before been attempted in the United States. The outer shells of the buildings had been raised and the architectural character of the fair was now evident, even though the opening of the exposition was still more than six months away. Next to Burnham, Olmsted, and Root, Hunt had been as responsible for the conception as anyone else. In a short space of time, architects, landscape architects, painters, sculptors, and others, working closely together, had created a spectacular new city. They had provided an example for possible future collaborative endeavors. Hunt had reason to be excited and proud.

This feeling of artistic achievement inspired a testimonial dinner for Daniel Burnham, held on March 25, 1893, in the Madison Square Concert Hall in New York. McKim suggested the banquet honoring Burnham, "in recognition of the incalculable benefits that have resulted from his service to Painting, Sculpture, and Architecture throughout the country from his connection with the Fair." McKim took charge of the arrangements, but he wrote Hunt that there was "a universal feeling" that Hunt was the man to preside over the evening. Hunt readily agreed to do so and, as representative of the architectural profession, he also joined in issuing the many invitations sent to architects, painters, sculptors, men of letters, and other prominent citizens.[30]

The banquet was a lavish affair. Evergreens and palm trees decorated the hall. From the ceiling hung three banners, one labeled "Painting," another "Sculpture," and the third "Architecture," each decorated with a wreath of gilded laurel. While the women guests looked down from the gallery, the more than two hundred male invitees were served a sumptuous dinner, which lasted for over two hours. Then, with the coffee and cigars, the guests were treated to stereoscopic views of the buildings of the exposition projected on a large screen. With the guest of honor at his right and Professor Charles Eliot Norton of Harvard at his left, Hunt served as master of ceremonies.

Many of the custodians of culture were in attendance: William Dean Howells, Charles Dudley Warner, Joseph H. Choate, Henry Villard, Parke Godwin, and Henry G. Marquand, among others, were also at the principal table. As Hunt started the speechmaking he drew from a cluster of American Beauty roses a large silver loving cup, which McKim had had engraved, and presented it to Burnham "in phrases so complimentary and appreciative that they evoked unbounded enthusiasm." The Chicagoan poured the contents of a bottle of claret into the cup, took a drink, and passed it back to Hunt, who drank from it and sent it around the room, "each distinguished man being warmly cheered as he drank." When he was toasted, Burnham responded generously, saying that the honors of the evening should more rightly have been given to Frederick Law Olmsted than to himself, and he paid tribute to John Root and Henry Codman, both of whom had died before the exposition was finished, and to his friend Hunt. Among the toasts of the evening was Norton's presentation to "Architecture, Sculpture, and Painting." When Norton called the exposition "the height of the attainment of American artists," he was only echoing the common sentiment of the occasion. The tone of the evening was again one of self-congratulation for the great cooperative endeavor that was almost completed and that would shortly be shown to the public.[31]

After the dedication ceremonies and the Burnham dinner, the opening of the World's Columbian Exposition on May 1, 1893, was almost anticlimactic for those who had been involved for so long in the undertaking. The final push to get everything ready had set a hectic pace for weeks. Just over a fortnight before the opening, Olmsted found "the greatest imaginable outward confusion" on the grounds, though he supposed "order in most essential respects" would be achieved by the time of the opening. On the first of May, more than half a million people, it was estimated, crowded into the western end of the Court of Honor, where a large platform had been erected in front of the Administration Building to accommodate the many notables and special guests, led by President Grover Cleveland. As the prayers and the speeches went on, many spectators were injured in the crush of the mob. During the ceremonies, Olmsted wandered around the outskirts of the crowd with McKim and Post; he considered the occasion "a notable success." Hunt, who was shortly to go to Europe once more, did not attend.[32]

Six months later, in October 1893, as the exposition neared its close, Richard and Catharine, with their daughter Esther, traveled to Chicago, meeting their son Joe there. This was the first time that Hunt had visited the grounds since the dedication ceremonies a year earlier. Burnham placed an electric launch at their disposal, provided the Hunts with quarters in one of the pavilions of the Administration Building, and arranged for meals to be sent in to them from the exposition hospital kitchen. Frank R. Stockton, the author, and his wife regularly took meals with them. Hunt was again suffering badly from the gout, but Joe remained with his parents and pushed Hunt around the grounds from one exhibit to another in a rolling chair. The Hunts themselves had loaned *Boy with Butterfly,* which was displayed along with others of William Hunt's paintings as part of the "Exhibition of American Retrospective Art." The Hunts apparently decided not to pay a call on Little Egypt, the famed belly dancer, but they did go one day to see Buffalo Bill and his "Wild West" act on the Midway Plaisance. One moonlit night, when the Court of Honor was illuminated, "the beauty surpassed anything seen before or since," Catharine later remembered, and she was enormously proud of what Richard "had done to bring about the conception and unity of those wonderful buildings." John F. Weir, the painter, who was visiting the fair at the same time, encountered Hunt in his rolling chair inside the Administration Building. He reported that the architect, "then an invalid, . . . commented freely on the architectural effect and detail as if it were the work of another than himself," an objectivity respecting his own work that was characteristic of Hunt throughout his career.[33]

The Administration Building was the dominating architectural feature of the exposition. Rising at the head of the Court of Honor, reflected in the great basin, its gleaming gold and white dome visible from all over the grounds, this huge, monumental, neoclassical structure set the tone of stately formality for the exposition buildings. In the view of the influential contemporary art critic Royal Cortissoz, Hunt here "struck the note that was peculiarly his, the grandiose note of a kind of formal magnificence, of academic and official dignity. There was no building at the fair more precisely adapted in its position and purpose, more perfect in its field. . . . Its proportions were good, its details were good, it fell judiciously into its given space, and yet it dominated, as was intended, everything that surrounded it."[34]

From the Administration Building on the west end, the Court of Honor stretched some two thousand feet to the east toward Lake Michigan and some seven hundred feet from north to south. Lined on the broad sides by double-walled terraces backed by exhibition halls, the court was centered on a large water basin, containing at the west end a statuary group of an antique galley, with eight huge rowers, preceded by eight couriers riding marine horses, conceived by Frederick MacMonnies. At the east end of the basin stood Daniel Chester French's colossal statue *The Republic*. The court itself was terminated on the east by a peristyle or covered colonnade in two ranges separated by a triumphal arch. A canal gave access on the north side of the basin to the lagoon, around which several of the other principal exhibition buildings were located. Small launches and gondolas plied the waters of the basin and the lagoon to carry visitors from one part of the fair to another.

Visitors mostly arrived at the grounds by train; on entering they passed directly from the railway shed across a small open court and through the Administration Building. The structure designed by Hunt thus served as a vestibule to the exposition, and as such it was the only major building given an interior finish. Most visitors saw the interior before they could view the building as a whole from the outside. The interior space was octagonal in shape, in effect a shell one hundred and twenty feet in diameter, which was placed about twenty-four feet inside an outer shell. Each of the eight sides of the interior contained an archway framing a series of doors and bronze grilles surmounted by panels filled with inscriptions and sculpture. Over these a large cornice served as an interior viewing balcony, over which, supported by an order of pilasters, rose the one-hundred-ninety-foot-high inner dome decorated with panels. The inner dome had a fifty-foot-wide circular opening at its apex. Unlike the plain white exterior, the interior walls were embel-

lished with color. The interior space was large and imposing and provided an appropriate introduction to what lay beyond.[35]

With its spreading base and high outer dome, the Administration
Building (figure 113) was best viewed from a distance. Only from a
perspective many yards away could a viewer see the relationship among
the main elements of the building and experience the monumentality of
the structure, its strength and stability emphasized by the overall
pyramidal composition. No doubt the viewer would first let his gaze rest
on the great, shining, gold and white dome, ornamented by panels and
vertical springing ribs, which were outlined at night by electric lights.
Rising two hundred seventy-five feet, the dome was some fifty-seven
feet higher than that on the United States Capitol, not including the
lantern, and thus, although a temporary structure, briefly rivaled and
even surpassed the masterpiece of Thomas U. Walter, Hunt's one-time
employer.

The dome rested upon a low, octagonal drum, which in turn rose out
of a forty-foot-high Ionic colonnade topped by a gallery decorated by
flambeaux. The colonnade was splayed at the corners, where small
domed staircase pavilions were set between heavy piers. The entire
upper section rested upon the octagonal base, which was pierced by
four main portals on the primary faces. The building extended from the
alternate diagonal inner faces out into four flat-roofed, square wings,
making a quatrefoil ground plan. These four-story corner pavilions
housed administrative offices and service facilities and were faced with
large areas of glass, giving the effect, with the attached giant Doric
columns and the central portal openings, of a great closed loggia base.
The corner pavilions were raised to the same upper cornice level as the
other buildings situated around the Court of Honor.[36]

An integral part of the Administration Building were the colossal
allegorical sculptural groups conceived by Karl Bitter and executed in the
same plaster and straw material as were the buildings. Hunt had the
statuary placed flanking each major recessed portal at the ground level,
as final pieces terminating the three corner piers of each pavilion, and
topping the eight piers rising at the corners of the outside gallery above
the colonnade. The theme of the sculpture was the evolution of man
from barbarism to civilization. The repose of the lower figures accentuated the solidity of the architectural design, while the animation of the
uppermost groups provided a transition from the vertical emphasis of
the lower part of the building to the curved lines above, reinforcing the
spring of the dome.[37]

Critics and commentators writing about the fair usually had some-

Figure 113
Administration Build-
ing, World's Columbian
Exposition, Chicago
(1893). From *Photographs
of the World's Fair* (1894).

thing to say about the Administration Building. Schuyler was very enthusiastic and termed the structure "triumphantly successful for its purpose . . . [and] in its kind not only the crowning achievement of its architect, but one of the chief triumphs of modern academic architecture." The dome itself compared favorably with that of Brunelleschi in Florence. Schuyler's only qualification was that the first-level pavilions were not solid enough to provide a fully appropriate mass for the superstructure to rest upon. Other commentators were more restrained, some even negative in their judgments. C. Howard Walker, writing in the new Boston *Architectural Review,* found the dome "thoroughly unsatisfactory" in scale and awkward without a lantern and judged the building as a whole "grandiose . . . [and] all out of scale with everything else." Foreign critics usually singled out the Administration Building for special mention, partly because it was the best known building at the exposition and partly because the most eminent American architect had designed it. Several characterized it as majestically calm and tastefully composed and yet pointed out that it was not very original. Jacques Hermant, a French visitor, felt that Hunt's building was embarrassing because of the overelaboration of the base pavilions and the lack of a lantern on the dome. By and large, however, critics usually judged the Administration Building in terms such as "the crown of the Columbian Exposition" and responded positively to it as they did to the fair as a whole.[38]

For most of those working at the fair in an artistic capacity and for countless Americans who came to visit the grounds in Jackson Park, the White City brought an experience never before encountered. The unity of architectural design wrought on a truly grand scale, the careful attention to the placement and relationship of the structures, and the harmonizing with architecture of the other arts produced a vision of beauty that provided standards to judge the present and that gave inspiration for the future. For its brief moment, the Chicago exposition approached more closely the Gilded Age–Genteel Tradition ideal of beauty than had anything else in the American experience.

From the White City some took away a lesson in coordination and planning, while others were impressed by the use of the classical revival style. Out of the fair, on the one hand, came the "City Beautiful" movement and a whole generation of city planners led by Chief of Construction Daniel Burnham. On the other hand, the exposition gave a strong stimulus to the Beaux-Arts neoclassical revival (begun considerably earlier), which came to dominate much of American building for three or four decades thereafter. Schuyler and others commended the builders of the fair for their skill in creating an architecture of illusion that was eminently successful for recreational and entertainment purposes, but they also warned that real, permanent architecture would have to be very different. Although the influence of the fair was certainly not so pernicious as Louis Sullivan thought it to be, the work at Chicago did help bring a turning nationally to a dominant architectural fashion.[39]

Henry Adams, ever questioning the meaning of the course of historical change in the nineteenth century, pondered "on the steps beneath Richard Hunt's dome" what the fair actually meant. It seemed to him that this "sharp and conscious twist towards ideals" at Chicago obviously had brought "a breach of continuity" with what had been the mainstream course of American development, dominated by business and politics. But was this "rupture in historical sequence . . . real, or only apparent?" Would creative artists be honored and art ideals implemented in the future? The architects and artists at the fair, he suggested, "offered little encouragement" that art would flourish since artistic ideals were not integrated into Americans' lives. And the artists whom Adams knew, though they had tried to raise standards, did not feel that they had achieved much success. "The effort," Adams wrote, "had been for the older generation, exhausting, as one could see in the Hunts." The effort to raise standards, no matter how exhausting, would nonetheless continue to occupy Richard Hunt for the brief time remaining in his life.[40]

23

BILTMORE

The commission that in some ways culminated Hunt's body of creative work was yet another Vanderbilt residence—the mansion of Biltmore, near Asheville, North Carolina. The project was originally conceived as a country seat for winter and spring occupancy away from the cold of New York City, but gradually developed into something else—a great château and an increasingly enlarged estate on which was carried out the first significant endeavor at systematic scientific forest management and education in the United States. Although Hunt's principal concern was with the house itself, his architectural work was an integral part of the fashioning of the estate, which was directed by Frederick Law Olmsted. During the final six years of his life, Biltmore occupied Hunt more than any other of his several projects.[1]

Biltmore House, a French château set in some 125,000 acres of land, in an area largely occupied by poor dirt farmers, was a curious venture even in the 1890s. Requiring the services of scores of house servants, stablemen, and gardeners to maintain the establishment, as well as large crews for the greenhouses, the dairy, the arboretum, and the forestry work, the estate was, on the one hand, a monument to Gilded Age extravagance. Yet programs of scientific forest management, dairy farming, rural road building, and collecting of botanical specimens gave the project substantial social importance. Hunt's opportunity to erect a great house in appropriate surroundings—unlike the cramped conditions of New York and of Newport—and his chance to design almost without limitations on expenditure allowed him here more than anywhere else to indulge his grandest architectural ideals and satisfy most fully his creative energies and aesthetic requirements. In time the château came to seem to be married to its site, perfectly in place in the midst of its gardens, grounds, farms, and forests.

George Washington Vanderbilt, Hunt's client, was the younger brother of Cornelius and William Kissam Vanderbilt. When his father, William Henry Vanderbilt, died in 1885, George was left as his share of the paternal estate his parents' house at 640 Fifth Avenue and a sum of $10,000,000, far less than the $67,000,000 that Cornelius inherited or the $65,000,000 that William received. For some years George lived with his mother in the Fifth Avenue mansion and concerned himself with philanthropy, the arts, and education. He provided the funds for the library on West Thirteenth Street, which Hunt designed, and he purchased the property of the Bloomingdale Asylum in Morningside Heights, which he donated to Columbia University for a new campus for Teachers College. Hunt had already done considerable work for George Vanderbilt at the family farm at New Dorp on Staten Island and at the family mausoleum near by. He also remodeled for him a house on West Fifty-Third Street and built a new picture gallery and conservatory in the house at 640 Fifth Avenue.[2]

George Vanderbilt was remarkably different in appearance and temperament from his brothers Cornelius and William, who shared their father's and their grandfather's involvement in business. His interests, by contrast, were mainly artistic and literary. He loved landscape architecture and interior decoration. With his dark hair and black eyes, a black moustache, and his narrow sensitive face, he looked vaguely foreign. He was shy as a young man, and Gifford Pinchot when he first met him thought him rather simpleminded. Perhaps more than his brothers and sisters he felt a personal sense of social responsibility and was eager to use his money well rather than in idle pleasure. Those working with him at Biltmore always wrote of him with affection and respect. Hunt considered George Vanderbilt as close to him as one of his own children; he always enjoyed visiting him at Biltmore because of the "atmosphere of affection and attention" he found and the "perfect harmony" they shared. Olmsted judged Vanderbilt "a delicate, refined and bookish man; with considerable humor, but shrewd, sharp, exacting and resolute in matters of business." The house and estate of Biltmore became the passion of Vanderbilt's life, and into them he sank most of his fortune.[3]

Sometime in the mid-1880s, George Vanderbilt and his mother first visited Asheville, which had long been a resort popular among Northerners for its pleasant climate. The young man enjoyed taking long walks and horseback rides in the invigorating air. On one ride, some three miles from Asheville, he came upon a spot overlooking the French Broad River close to its junction with the Swannanoa River, and was especially impressed by the view. He almost immediately decided that he would like to have a house there.

The area was of broken, hilly land bordering on the two river bottoms and was held by small farmers who had long since cut much of the timber for fuel, fences, and lumber. Vanderbilt soon acquired a few acres of land at a low price. He then decided that he did not want to risk having uncongenial neighbors close by, and so he sent an agent to buy out the nearest farms but kept his name out of the negotiations to prevent the residents from holding out for "Vanderbilt prices." Later, as he enlarged his holdings and his identity became known, one black farmer held out and refused to sell his nine acres in the heart of the Vanderbilt acquisition, declaring that he had "no objection to George Vanderbilt as a neighbor." But he too finally sold his land.[4]

In 1888, when he had purchased some two thousand acres of land and was considering making a large park around his projected house, Vanderbilt asked Frederick Law Olmsted, who had landscaped the family mausoleum, to look over the property and advise him as to how it might best be developed. Visiting the site with young Vanderbilt, Olmsted was greatly disappointed with what he found. The air was indeed mild and invigorating and the prospect was lovely, but the soil was poor, the woods were in a deplorable condition, and the topography, Olmsted believed, was not suitable for a large park. But even though he considered it "a generally poor and vagabondish region," he did think that the site had potential. He advised Vanderbilt to have gardens and a small park developed near the house. The river bottoms, he suggested, should be used for farming and grazing, and the rest of the land turned into a forest, planting old fields with trees and improving the existing woods, with the ultimate aim of producing timber. As Olmsted later recalled his conversation, he told Vanderbilt: "That would be a suitable and dignified business for you to engage in: it would, in the long run, be probably a fair investment of capital and it would be of great value to the country to have a thoroughly well organized and systematically conducted attempt in forestry made on a large scale." Vanderbilt responded positively to Olmsted's advice, and after a few months decided to go ahead with the project. He engaged the landscape architect to oversee the development of the estate, while Hunt was employed to design the house. Vanderbilt continued to acquire additional land, so that he had more than six thousand acres by the beginning of 1891. In the meantime, Olmsted had arranged for a thorough inventory of the land, set up a nursery for trees and shrubs, planted seedling trees in some of the old fields, and begun preparations for removal of the trees that were in poor condition.[5]

Although George Vanderbilt's early ideas for his country house were fairly modest and conventional, he soon changed his mind about the dwelling, apparently largely influenced by Hunt, who urged him to build on a scale commensurate with the size of the holdings and the natural features of the property. (Later on, as the mansion took shape, Hunt wrote to Catharine elatedly that "the mountains are just the right size and scale for the chateau!") On various European trips—including the short 1889 visit with the Hunts—Vanderbilt had accumulated art objects, furnishings, and architectural elements for his dwelling, and it soon became evident that a very large house would be needed to accommodate his collections. Already by early March 1889, Hunt had re-

Rybczynski, Witold. <u>A Clearing in the Distance: Frederick Law Olmsted and America in the Nineteenth Century.</u> New York: Scribner, 1999. print

The book is mainly about Olmsted and his achievements as a horticulturist. Rybczynski goes into detail about the Biltmore and the processes that went into building it and the gardens surrounding it. Vanderbilt actually had slowly bought the land slowly through the years and had finally amassed 2,000 acres (379). Olmsted looked at the soil and it was of poor quality but he was able to build a grand garden non-the less. The house is a combination of different châteaux's from the French region, along with the French-renaissance architecture. Olmsted then fixed the gardens around the style of the house combining both French and English landscaping into one (383). The book describes what type of plants where planted and the general layout out of the grounds.

vised his first designs for the residence and had created a new set of plans on a very grand scale.[6]

Olmsted was enthusiastic about these revised plans for the mansion, which Hunt had prepared, although he felt that the precise placement of the structure still had to be worked out. Since Hunt had not yet visited Asheville in March 1889, Olmsted, who had been there the year before, stressed to him the bleakness of the place and the lack of any special picturesqueness at the site, the only attraction being the spectacular view to the west. It was essential, Olmsted believed, that the house be given the best possible position in terms of the natural situation as well as in relation to the approaches, the gardens, and the other features which were being planned. The wind from the northwest, which hit the rise where the house was to be built, could be very bitter, Olmsted pointed out. He suggested to Hunt that the stables and offices be located with walled courts in front, stretching east from the north end of the mansion so as to form a windbreak and protect from the wind the esplanade, which Olmsted was planning to extend eastward in front of the house. He also suggested a sheltered glen for walks in the area to the southeast shielded by the house from the northwest wind. He pointed out that a terrace adjoining the dwelling on the south could provide a promenade and viewing place overlooking the valley as well as shield the ramble to the southeast, and he advised that the greenhouses be located farther down the slope below the ramble. Olmsted was anxious to get Hunt's agreement on these matters, but he assured the architect that he did not want to "cross [his] views."[7]

Preliminary construction work got under way in 1889. Hunt and Olmsted quickly agreed on the positioning of the house and the adjacent service buildings and gardens, and by midsummer 1889 the outlines of the mansion were marked by stakes; however, in January 1890, to provide a more secure foundation, the position of the house was moved twenty-five feet to the east and the grading of the esplanade was altered. A road was built to provide access to the building site; a small but substantial residence nearby called Brick House was made over into a temporary residence for Vanderbilt, Olmsted, Hunt, and others to use on their visits; a three-mile railway spur was begun for hauling in building materials; and a village for estate employees was started. The name "Biltmore," which Vanderbilt chose for his estate, was derived from the Dutch town of Bildt, from which the Vanderbilt ancestors had come, and "more," an Old English word for rolling upland country.[8]

When Hunt paid his first visit to Biltmore early in 1890, work was going on throughout the estate. He returned again in the late spring and brought along his son, Dick, who would supervise much of the architectural work. On this occasion they traveled with George Vanderbilt in his private railway car, which was pulled to the esplanade on the first train running on the newly completed spur. By this time several hundred workmen were already engaged in grading the land and clearing the forests, building roads and drainage works, and planting trees. A brick kiln was turning out 32,000 bricks a day. The mansion foundations had been dug but awaited the stone to be brought in from Indiana on the railroad spur. Hunt believed that everything was progressing rapidly and well—"nothing being spared by G. W. V. If it is not a success the fault will lie with us, who are called upon to do our best," he wrote to his wife. By this time public interest in Biltmore was beginning to grow as press reports came out on the progress of the works. Vanderbilt, however, like his sister-in-law at Marble House, attempted to keep newspapermen and strangers out of the grounds before the mansion was finished so that it could be first shown publicly in its full splendor.[9]

Olmsted felt "a good deal of ardor" about the work at Biltmore. The estate, he believed, was of great public interest and significance and, next to the Boston parks system, was the most important project his firm was engaged in. Indeed, he wrote to his partners, Biltmore "is the most permanently important public work and the most critical with reference to the future of our professions of all those we have. The most critical and the most difficult." In another letter to his partners, Olmsted referred to Biltmore as "the most distinguished private place, not only of America, but of the world, forming at this *period*."[10]

Over the next five years, Hunt regularly visited Asheville, while his son Dick remained there for long periods. Richard Hunt often traveled there with Vanderbilt in his private railway car, sometimes in the company of other members of the Vanderbilt family. At times, Olmsted, his associate Henry Codman, or his son John Olmsted were also at Biltmore when Hunt was making one of his visits. Brick House, used to accommodate the visitors, though not luxurious, was comfortable; when Vanderbilt was in residence the guests were especially well cared for. During the days, supervision and inspection of the works alternated with drives, horseback rides, and shooting. Dick Hunt liked to take excursions on horseback and shoot small game and birds when he stayed at Biltmore. His father, who had "a genuine fear" of horses, refused to ride horseback around the estate and always used a buckboard instead. When ladies were in residence at Brick House, there were long evenings of card games, charades, and candy pulls. Catharine Hunt, who came occasionally, was a lively addition to these house parties, and if Hunt was feeling well and, as Gifford Pinchot put it, "at concert pitch," those at Brick House had "his delightful noise all the time." Visiting the estate in October 1890, Hunt fell ill with influenza, which Olmsted, who was already suffering from lumbago, then caught. Both were confined to their rooms. Hunt recovered too late to get to the annual convention of the American Institute of Architects in Washington and, as noted earlier, had to send his presidential address to be read in absentia. After Hunt had left for the north with Vanderbilt following this visit, Olmsted reported to his own son that Hunt appeared to be feebler than he himself was. Both men were feeling their age; each had only five more working years.[11]

Late in 1891, Vanderbilt hired Gifford Pinchot to direct the forestry operations on the Biltmore estate. Pinchot, who came from the wealthy family for whom Hunt had designed Grey Towers in Milford, Pennsylvania, had taken a bachelor's degree at Yale College only two years earlier. Eager to learn forestry management, he had then studied for a year in France at the Ecole Nationale Forestière at Nancy and had traveled widely in France, Switzerland, and Germany, studying silviculture and becoming acquainted with Dietrich Brandis, who was widely considered to be the leading forestry expert of Europe. Olmsted, like Hunt, an old friend of Pinchot's father, invited the young forester to visit Biltmore in October 1891. Arriving there he "was amazed and charmed by [the] situation and scale of [the] new place." Pinchot had known the Hunt family for some time. He saw Hunt at Biltmore on this first visit and had long talks with Olmsted about the landscape architect's plans for the estate. The following month, after he had further discussed the situation at Biltmore with Olmsted in Boston, he accepted the position of director of forestry operations and returned to Asheville on New Year's Day with Olmsted, Hunt, Vanderbilt, and Dick Hunt. During the week of their stay, Olmsted took Pinchot over the entire estate and instructed him carefully on the work that was proposed. They discussed the possibility of establishing a school of forestry management at Biltmore.[12]

Pinchot began work as chief Biltmore forester in February 1892. He set out to inventory the forest land with a very precise topographical survey, and he expanded on Olmsted's program of thinning, cutting, and planting. From the first, harvesting was carried on simultaneously with planting and improvement. By the end of his first year, Pinchot's selective lumbering operations showed a small profit. He also prepared a photographic exhibit and pamphlet on Biltmore Forest for the World's

Columbian Exposition. Both drew considerable public attention to this first program of comprehensive practical forest management in the United States. Meanwhile, George Vanderbilt, on Pinchot's recommendation, was enlarging his land holdings. Eventually the estate was expanded to some 125,000 acres.[13]

On Pinchot's recommendation also, Carl Alvin Schenck of the University of Darmstadt in Germany came to work at Biltmore in 1895 as resident forester, at which time Pinchot himself became a nonresident consultant. In 1898, Schenck set up the Biltmore School of Forestry, which operated until the outbreak of World War I. The forestry work at Biltmore had implications far beyond the work carried on at the estate itself. A whole generation of foresters was trained at the Biltmore School, and the techniques of forestry management practiced and taught at Biltmore were widely adopted elsewhere. Even earlier, before the school was set up, J. Sterling Morton, the United States Secretary of Agriculture, commended Vanderbilt for his interest in forestry, while saying regretfully that "Mr. Vanderbilt has more workers and a larger budget for his forestry projects than I have at my disposal for the whole Department of Agriculture."[14]

In both the forestry work and the erection of the mansion and the preparation of the gardens, Vanderbilt employed a force of several hundred workmen, and with the large labor force building went on at an impressive pace. During 1892, the understructure of the dwelling, with its complex of boiler rooms, storerooms, dynamo rooms, a laundry, a swimming pool, dressing rooms, and food preparation areas, was largely completed. Steel beams were used for floor joists, and by the end of 1893, the second story had mostly been finished. In 1894, most of the steel rafters and the stonework of the upper parts of the mansion were set in place (figure 114). By Christmas 1895, five months after Hunt's death, the estate was a going concern, and Vanderbilt, his mother, and many relatives and friends celebrated the formal opening of the house.[15]

As the Biltmore work advanced, Hunt and Olmsted maintained a harmonious collaboration, disagreeing only for a time about a pergola which Olmsted wanted placed at the outer end of the terrace that extended south from the library wing and about the arrangement of the streets in Biltmore Village. Hunt came around to Olmsted's view on the suitability of the pergola and acquiesced in Olmsted's platting of the village in an English rather than a French manner. Olmsted was pleased that he and Hunt had been able to reconcile their requirements for an appropriate setting for the mansion with "a generally picturesque natural character in the approaches and in the main landscape features."

Figure 114
Biltmore House under
construction (looking
southwest), Asheville,
North Carolina (March
1894). Courtesy of
Biltmore House & Gar-
dens.

Hunt had, indeed, "aided in marrying the two motives" to Olmsted's full satisfaction, and each man had accepted the other's suggestions. At Biltmore, as well as at the Chicago fair, the two men worked well together. "There has not been," Olmsted wrote, "the slightest lack of harmony between us."[16]

In his landscape design, Olmsted wished to retain an effect of naturalness and picturesqueness in all areas away from the immediate vicinity of the mansion. The landscaping was artfully adapted to the topography and the various natural features. Roads, paths, bridges, ditches, and walls were constructed of stones found nearby which related most readily to the natural scenery. The trees and shrubs planted came from the region around Asheville as well as from other American areas and abroad. Originally Olmsted had conceived of the plantings on the road borders, including a road encircling the entire property, as forming a comprehensive arboretum, "in effect an Experiment Station and Museum of living trees," which, with its thousands of species and varieties, would, he hoped, prove of national horticultural value. But the large-scale arboretum he envisioned was not carried out. Nonetheless, a great many species were planted, and the variety of trees and shrubs on the estate is still exceptionally large today.[17]

From the lodge gate in Biltmore Village to the mansion the entrance road traverses a picturesque winding course of three miles through plantings of pines, hemlocks, hardwoods, rhododendrons, mountain laurel, and azaleas. Olmsted planned the landscaping along the entrance drive to enhance the natural setting and, in a sense, remove a visitor from the outside world before he came to the final approach to the mansion, which he envisioned as both a surprise and the climax of the long rustic drive. Hunt was particularly impressed by Olmsted's work along the approach road, where he thought his collaborator had "done wonders." At the terminus of this drive, the visitor enters through large, wrought-iron gates into a rectangular graveled area close to the east end of the esplanade, which extends westward to the mansion itself. The house, then, appears suddenly after the long drive, and the visitor first sees the dwelling with the long sward of the esplanade stretching before it. In the area close to the mansion, Olmsted adapted his landscaping to the style of Hunt's château, the various subsidiary structures, and the other features required for the owner and his guests, making the landscaping here, in effect, an extension of the architectonic features. The Biltmore landscaping, eclectic and architecturally conceived in the vicinity of the mansion, was characteristic of American professional landscape design of the next quarter century.[18]

Hunt and Olmsted positioned the dwelling close to the edge of a steep, wooded slope above the French Broad River. The entrance façade faced approximately east and looked over the esplanade, lined with tulip trees, terminating at the far end in a double set of low-rising *rampes* leading to a vista. As Olmsted had urged, the stables and two service courts were placed at a slightly lower level to the north of the esplanade, while to the south were located the Italian Garden, with three large pools, and below, the Shrub Garden. At yet a lower level was the four-acre Walled Garden, including the rose garden, adjacent to the large conservatory and greenhouses. Still farther removed from the mansion was the Vernal Garden, which later became the experimental azalea station. On the library terrace extending to the south of the mansion a bowling green was built, but it was later replaced by an outdoor swimming pool. The surroundings and accessories were commensurate in arrangements and in size with the 255-room mansion itself. Here was a dwelling on a truly "royal scale."[19]

In exterior design, Biltmore House is reminiscent of Ochre Court, but on a considerably larger scale. Once again, as in Ochre Court, the Gerry and the W. K. Vanderbilt town houses, and other commissions, Hunt turned back to French architecture of the early French Renaissance for his inspiration. Once more he boldly adapted, artfully massed, and richly embellished early Renaissance forms for his own purposes. The style allowed him a freedom and inventiveness that he found very congenial; and at Biltmore it seemed especially appropriate to the surroundings, particularly as the new plantings matured. The three-story structure is faced with a light-colored Indiana limestone; with its steeply peaked roofs, crestings, massive grouped chimneys, richly decorated dormers, loggia and arcade, and spectacular staircase, it is a highly romantic building, evoking much beyond what immediately strikes the eye.

Although the primary massing on the entrance façade is essentially balanced, there are considerable variety and asymmetry in forms and details (figure 115). Small, recessed courts extend to each side of the richly detailed entrance pavilion, to which the grand staircase is attached on the left. The staircase is modeled on that of the Château of Blois, though differing from the prototype in that the spiral is in the opposite direction. Lateral projecting wings, varying in fenestration and decoration (figure 116), terminate the main front, with the service wing and accessory structures attached on the right. A large, arched window, divided vertically into three parts by heavy mullions and horizontally into three parts by equally heavy transoms, and topped by an ogee hood

Figure 115
Entrance front, Biltmore
House (1895). Photo by
James Garrison.

Figure 116
Library wing roof detail,
Biltmore House. Photo
by James Garrison.

molding, dominates the lower part of the right pavilion. Its French Gothic motif is repeated as a theme with variations on the other façade of the mansion.

From the west, the massiveness of the masonry revetment underpinning the house and the terrace is readily apparent. The retaining wall is some seventeen and one-half feet thick at the base and is underlaid by a concrete foundation twenty feet wide. The rugged, undressed gneiss contrasts effectively with the texture of the smoothly worked limestone facing on the house itself and provides an eminently suitable foundation, strong and stable, for the intricate, interlocking forms above. On the west front (figure 117) two towers accent the center of the composition, which includes a loggia and the library wing to the right, balanced by the lower service wing and stables to the left. The great expanse of roof, said to be the largest on a private house in the United States, helps mold together the many varied forms and rich decorative elements of the mansion, while providing a highly picturesque silhouette.[20]

Although the design of the exterior of Biltmore has a basic uniformity of style, the interior of the residence is much more diversified and, in this respect, typical of Hunt's great houses. To the right of the marble-paved entrance hall is the palm court (figure 118), a polygonal sunken area filled with light from an intricately ribbed glass domed ceiling. Potted flowers, ferns, and palms surround the central fountain with a statue of a boy and two struggling geese carved by Karl Bitter. The oak drawing room, the Norwegian oak panels of which are covered with engravings of paintings, served as an informal living room for the Vanderbilts.

The banquet hall, like that of The Breakers, was designed as the grandest room of the house (figure 119). The ribbed timber ceiling, an arched vault, rises seventy-five feet above the forty-two-by-seventy-two-foot expanse beneath. Designed and decorated in a vaguely medieval style, the banquet hall is dominated at one end by a huge triple fireplace, over which Karl Bitter carved a twenty-five-foot frieze entitled *The Return from the Chase*. Bitter also carved for the banquet hall five oak panel relief scenes of Wagnerian operas, placed on the organ gallery balustrade, along with two large statues of Joan of Arc and St. Louis, in full battle dress, placed over the entrance to the hall. Copies of these two statues were also mounted outside along the staircase under canopies. Five large sixteenth-century Flemish tapestries on the lower walls of the banquet hall depict the intrigues of Venus, Mars, and Vulcan.

The dining room, a more intimate place where the family regularly took its meals, has walls of red marble and tooled Spanish leather and a

Figure 117
West facade, Biltmore
House (1895). Photo by
James Garrison.

Figure 118
Palm court, Biltmore
House. Courtesy of
Biltmore House & Gardens.

Figure 119
Banquet hall, Biltmore
House. Courtesy of
Biltmore House & Gar-
dens.

fireplace mantel of jasperware. From the entrance hall, one enters the ninety-foot-long tapestry gallery, dominated by a series of early-sixteenth-century Brussels tapestries. The adjoining tapestry gallery loggia provides an open yet covered area which takes good advantage of the spectacular views of the distant hills to the west.

The library (figure 120), paneled with Circassian walnut, is the most richly decorated room of the house and was the favorite room of the scholarly Vanderbilt. Here he brought together over twenty thousand volumes, mainly on art, architecture, history, landscape gardening, and forestry. On the overmantel above the Italian black marble fireplace stand large female figures carved from wood in a baroque manner by Karl Bitter and flanking a late-seventeenth-century tapestry. Bitter also created the small, polished steel figures of Venus and Vulcan on the library andirons. An allegorical painting, which Vanderbilt acquired in Europe, covers the ceiling. It was once attributed to Tiepolo but is now thought to have been painted by Giovanni Antonio Pellegrini. A delicate spiral staircase provides access to the gallery and the upper-level bookshelves of the library.[21]

Upstairs, in the large first hall are, among other paintings, full-length portraits of Hunt and Olmsted painted by John Singer Sargent. George Vanderbilt had wanted both portraits to honor and memorialize the two men most responsible for Biltmore, and he arranged to have Sargent come to Biltmore for a stay of two or three weeks to paint the two portraits. Vanderbilt was certain that Sargent would "feel en rapport with his sitters" and would create "two masterpieces." On May 15, 1895, in New York, Richard and Catharine joined Sargent as Vanderbilt's guests in his private railway car for the journey south. Olmsted was already at Biltmore, and Sargent set to work on the portraits soon after their arrival. Although he pictured Hunt standing in the front court beside the marble well head near the spiral staircase (figure 121), most of the posing had to be done indoors before a fire, as the spring days were still very chilly. This house party at Biltmore was a pleasant one for the Hunts, and with the mansion and the adjacent landscape preparations nearly completed, Hunt could experience what he and Olmsted had created. At the time, Hunt's physical condition had seemed no more than of usual concern to his wife, but Sargent's portrait of him depicted a gaunt and worn man. Catharine later realized how perceptively the painter had depicted her husband, who was obviously far more ill than the others had realized. When Hunt's friend and attorney Joseph Choate saw the painting on a visit to Biltmore a few years later, he found it "a ghastly thing, exhibiting in most glaring way the dreadful disease of

Figure 120
Library, Biltmore
House. Courtesy of
Biltmore House & Gardens.

Figure 121
Portrait of Richard Morris Hunt by John Singer Sargent (1895). Courtesy of Biltmore House & Gardens.

which he was dying." Some time after completing the painting, Sargent offered to make Catharine a copy, but she had no wish for the portrait, as it lacked all the "fire" and "vigor" of her husband's personality.[22]

Contemporary response to Biltmore was by and large highly favorable. A description of the estate published in *The Chautauquan*, no doubt keyed to the upward-striving middle-class reader, was typically enthusiastic: Biltmore was "the finest, largest, and most magnificent private estate on this continent," which, when everything was completed, would be "unexcelled in the civilized world." Joseph Choate, who was used to the luxuries of life, felt, on his visit in 1901, that the mansion "constantly grows upon one and is truly a great affair—a worthy monument to Richard Hunt as his last work." Another visitor found the house "one long tale of delight. . . . the proportions and scale, combined with the details, fill one with the kind of peace which comes from artistic perfection."[23]

One who did not like Biltmore was Henry James, who visited the estate on his American tour in February 1905. Having fled from the icy winter of New York City, James arrived in the middle of a snowstorm to find the southern retreat insufferably cold. His caustic remarks were possibly influenced in part by the state of his health: he was suffering from the gout and had lost a front tooth. The place was imposing, James opined, but "utterly unaddressed to any possible arrangement of life, or state of society." It was, he decided, only "a phenomenon of brute achievement." His own room, "a glacial phantasy," was located about half a mile from the "mile-long library. . . . We measure by leagues and we sit in Cathedrals," he wrote a friend. James stayed nearly a week, but confined indoors in the largely empty house with little social stimulation he felt cooped up and wanted only to leave. He went on to Charleston and Palm Beach, where warmth and flowers restored his spirits.[24]

George Vanderbilt used Biltmore as his principal home and was often in residence there after his marriage to Edith Stuyvesant Dresser in 1898. Following Vanderbilt's death in 1914, an area of over eighty thousand acres was deeded to the federal government and became part of Pisgah National Forest. Further acreage was developed into the town of Biltmore Forest, and some was sold for the Blue Ridge Parkway. The Vanderbilt's only child, a daughter, Cornelia, who married John Francis Amherst Cecil, inherited the property, and Mr. and Mrs. Cecil made it their home. In 1930, the Cecils opened Biltmore house and gardens to the public. Today the estate, including some eleven thousand acres of land, is both a prominent tourist attraction and an active business engaged in dairy farming and sustained-yield forestry operations.[25]

The collaborative endeavor that created the multiuse estate had been eminently successful. Working closely with Olmsted and others, Hunt had created a great house that fitted perfectly into the surroundings and was highly appropriate to the entertainment and recreational uses for which it was mainly intended. Ostentatious, indulgent, grandiose—the house was all of these, and it was irrelevant to much of American life. Yet the varied forms and decorative elements of the building were superbly integrated into an architectonic whole that remains a greatly pleasing and distinctive work of art.

The 1890s brought many important honors to Hunt. The Chicago fair, of course, was an international exposition, and Hunt's presidency of the Board of Architects and his Administration Building design led to considerable international recognition. However, he had begun to receive international honors several years earlier. In 1882, he was made an honorary and corresponding member of the Académie des Beaux-Arts of the Institut de France. In 1884, he was decorated as a chevalier of the Légion d'Honneur of France, and two years later he was elected a member of the Société Centrale des Architectes Français and named an honorary and corresponding member of the Royal Institute of British Architects. The year 1887 brought him honorary and corresponding membership in the Engineers' and Architects' Society of Vienna, and the succeeding year, as we have seen, he was honored by being chosen president of the American Institute of Architects. In 1892, he became an academician of the Society of St. Luke in Rome, and the next year was named an honorary member of the Society of Architects in Amsterdam.

An honorary doctorate of laws from Harvard University, awarded on June 29, 1892, was particularly gratifying to Hunt. Years before, in 1864, Richard's brother William had been awarded an honorary master's degree by Harvard; now, just as Richard was about to design the new Fogg Museum for the Harvard Yard, he was himself honored. Hunt's degree was the first honorary doctorate awarded by the university to an architect. The 1892 ceremony was the two hundred and fiftieth anniversary of the first Harvard commencement and was solemnly impressive. Upon receiving the degree, Hunt spoke extemporaneously, putting into his talk "all the fire and rush of words of which he was such a master." The honor paid him, he felt, was not personal but rather "a tribute to the profession he loved."[1]

An even greater honor, professionally, was the award to him in 1893 of the Queen's Gold Medal by the Royal Institute of British Architects. Hunt was the first American to receive this award. He was notified of his selection by MacVickar Anderson, the president of the Royal Institute, after the Council of the Institute had met in February and nominated him and the members had voted to award him the medal. With Esther and Joe, the Hunts sailed for England on June 3 so that Richard might receive the award in person. This was Hunt's last and his shortest trip to Europe. As usual on their arrival in London, the Hunts were sought out by friends and had a full schedule of luncheon and dinner parties. With their sightseeing and official engagements, they had "as strenuous a life as it was possible to lead."[2]

The presentation ceremony on the evening of June 19 was held in conjunction with the annual meeting of the Royal Institute. Following dinner with Anderson and a reception, the members and their guests, including many ladies, moved into the meeting room. Charles Garnier, who had created the Paris Opéra, and Baron von Geymüller, representing the Institut de France, had come to London especially for the presentation. In a graceful tribute to Hunt, President Anderson reminded those present of the American's many ties to England and of his significant work at the Chicago fair, which he characterized as "the most wondrous development that international exhibitions have ever reached, or, perhaps, are ever likely to attain." He further observed that it was indeed fortunate that the development of American architecture had "been inspired by one possessing the refined taste, the educated judgment, and the cosmopolitan experience of Richard Morris Hunt." Anderson then touched on high points of Hunt's life and works and rejoiced that among the "first masters" of American art, there was "an architect with such a delicate taste." While presenting the gold medal, the highest award of the Royal Institute, Anderson said that he hoped that "our American brethren" would recognize in this royal gift "to their most eminent representative, the embodiment of the hearty good-will, the sincere respect, and the ardent admiration with which they are regarded by the architects of the Old World." In the view of the British professionals, American architecture had now come of age and was being recognized as of international significance.[3]

Hunt's reply, which he had prepared beforehand, was both effusively sincere and tediously pedantic. He felt himself, he said, at a loss for words to express his gratification to the Royal Institute, and he accepted the award not just as a personal tribute "but as an honor conferred upon the whole profession in the United States." He would, nonetheless, subdivide the honor with France, because to the Ecole des Beaux-Arts "he owed everything." He then launched into a discussion of the orders used on the Pavillon de la Bibliothèque, eventually drawing back, fearful that he was "becoming too tedious with these historical points." He then went on at some length about the selection of the site for the Chicago fair and the method of choosing the architects who worked there. The architects of the fair hoped, he emphasized, that it would be "an object lesson to the United States government," which allocated millions of dollars each year for public buildings. Hunt concluded by thanking the Institute members for himself and for his colleagues in the United States. Baron von Geymüller briefly commended Hunt and reported how pleased his colleagues in France were by this important recognition of one who had introduced fine design in his own country and might be aptly called "the Brunelleschi of the United States." Thereafter the company adjourned to the lower galleries for further refreshments and light musical entertainment.[4]

Two days after the awards ceremony, the Hunts moved on to Paris, where Richard met with Ogden Goelet and Cornelius Vanderbilt and assisted them with purchases of interiors for Ochre Court and The Breakers. A dinner at the Institut de France and a subsequent head cold brought on a very bad attack of Hunt's gout, and on the advice of a Parisian doctor, the family went to Saint-Germain-en-Laye—"it was a drive of great suffering"—where Richard might recuperate. But his recovery was slow, and Catharine had to arrange for a tramcar to get him back to Paris without the jolting discomfort of a carriage. After a few days at the Hotel Continental in Paris and at the Barclay in London, they sailed for the United States on July 23, going directly to Newport. A course of sulfur baths at Sharon Springs, New York, did little to relieve his pain. They moved back to their house on Washington Square in late September so that Richard might remain in close touch with the business at his office. A few days later they went to Chicago to see the fair.[5]

On December 23, 1893, yet another important honor was conferred on Hunt. The Académie des Beaux-Arts of the Institut de France, of which Hunt had been an honorary and corresponding member since 1882, chose him as one of only ten foreign associate members. Hunt was the second American-born artist—coming after Benjamin West—and the first American-born architect to be named a foreign associate in fine arts. Only five other Americans in addition to West had ever been elected foreign associates of one of the academies under the Institut, the others being Thomas Jefferson, Edward Livingston, Louis Agassiz (who was not American-born), John L. Motley, and Ralph Waldo Emerson. Here was distinguished company indeed![6]

Invitations to speak or serve his profession in other ways continued to arrive in the early nineties. John F. Weir was again trying to get Hunt to talk at the Art School at Yale. Alfred Stone wanted him to prepare a paper for the next A.I.A. convention. Charles W. Eliot invited him to lecture at Harvard College. But burdened by the pressures of his work, often unable to move because of the gout, and still hating to prepare public addresses, Hunt had little hesitation in refusing. On various occasions he was called to Washington to testify before Congressional committees. And there were also special conferences he felt obligated to attend, among them a White House conference on the metric system in January 1891 and a meeting in May 1892 sponsored by the newly organized National Art Association to consider the abolition of duties on imported art works. He found difficulty in refusing requests to serve as a judge in architectural competitions or as a consulting architect. In July 1895 he acted as a consultant for a new city hall for Worcester, Massachusetts, and had two meetings with the mayor at Hill Top Cottage. He does not appear to have accepted a February 1895 request by the New York Board of Parks Commissioners to serve on a supervisory committee to oversee the landscape and architectural work on the Harlem River Driveway.[7]

Probably the most important aspect of Hunt's work in the early nineties, outside his own commissions, was his support of the arts. First through two new associations, the Municipal Art Society and the National Sculpture Society, Hunt, joining with others, endeavored to advance the development of the arts in the United States. The Municipal Art Society, founded in 1892, with the aim of beautifying the streets and public places of New York City by providing sculptural and mural decorations for parks and public buildings, chose Hunt as its first president. Pursuant to its aims, the society donated as a first gift three allegorical mural paintings by Edward Simmons for the Criminal Courts Building. Subsequently, members of the society collaborated with other arts organizations in erecting the Hunt Memorial and in founding the Municipal Art Commission (1898), the City Improvement Commission (1902), the Commission on City Planning (1914), and the Landmarks Preservation Commission (1962). In many different ways, members of the society have worked to protect the city parks, to beautify the streets, to preserve landmark structures, and to improve public design. The Municipal Art Society has had a splendid record of achievement. As its president, Hunt was given a walking stick that had once belonged to Benjamin Franklin, and the stick has been passed down from one president to the next. The other group, the National Sculpture Society, was founded in 1893, and Hunt was chosen the first vice-president of the new organization. This society also aimed to beautify public buildings, squares, and parks with sculpture as well as to encourage the taste for and the production of good sculpture, to promote sculpture in industry, and to provide for the exhibition of sculpture.[8]

In another way, also, in the nineties, Hunt attempted to raise artistic standards as he continued to try to improve the quality of architecture in new buildings erected by the federal government. Well-designed public buildings, he always believed, could have an important ramifying effect. For nearly two decades architects had called for changes in the manner by which federal building designs were decided upon, and Hunt provided active support of several bills aimed at opening the way for competent and experienced professionals to design public buildings instead of undistinguished assistants in the Office of the Supervising Architect in the Treasury Department. Hunt himself had been approached about the position of Supervising Architect in 1886, but he had turned the job down since it would have meant the loss of his own practice. Bills to effect changes were introduced in Congress in 1874, 1884, 1886, 1888, and 1890, but none was enacted. In February 1892, Hunt testified before a House committee regarding his support of the Windrim bill, introduced in 1891, to open up governmental work to professionals, but this bill also failed. Finally, with the full and well-publicized support of the American Institute of Architects, yet another bill, introduced by Representative John C. Tarsney of Missouri, and designed to ensure competitive selection of architects for federal buildings, was passed by both houses of Congress and approved by President Benjamin Harrison before he left office in 1893. Hunt spoke out in support of this bill and sent notices about it to New York newspapers.[9]

By the terms of the Tarsney Act, the Secretary of the Treasury was authorized to obtain plans, drawings, and specifications for federal buildings by competition among invited architects, the winning designer to be awarded the commission. Overall supervision would remain with the Supervising Architect. Hunt was distressed that all those invited to participate in a competition were not assured of some compensation, but the new law, he realized, was obviously better than nothing. A problem arose at once, however: the Tarsney Act provided for the implementation of the law at the discretion of the Secretary of the Treasury. Although Hunt and other Institute leaders had met with the new secretary, John G. Carlisle, soon after he entered office in March 1893 under Grover Cleveland, and he had assured them of his cooperation, he refused to put the act into operation. When early in 1894 a sketch was published of a new federal building in Buffalo designed by the Supervising Architect, the response of the Institute leaders, headed by Daniel Burnham as president, was outrage. An acrimonious correspondence followed, which was eventually made public. Secretary Carlisle considered one letter from Burnham highly offensive in tone and he had the Supervising Architect, Jeremiah O'Rourke, write Hunt and the other directors individually that the letter was so contrary to professional standards of courtesy that he could scarcely believe it was legitimate. Matters soon became even more strained, and Secretary Carlisle informed Burnham that he would have no further correspondence with him on any subject whatsoever. Charles McKim, who talked over the situation with Hunt, Burnham, and others, asked Attorney General

Richard Olney if he would intervene with Carlisle on behalf of the Institute. Olney refused to become involved. The press largely supported the A.I.A. position, and Carlisle finally agreed to enforce the Tarsney Act if reinforcing legislation were passed. A new bill was thereupon introduced in the House to provide for the *mandatory* apportioning of public works designs. Once more Hunt appeared before a House committee to support the claims of the profession. This bill passed the House, but failed to get through the Senate before Congress adjourned. In 1897, however, when William McKinley took office, his Secretary of the Treasury, Lyman J. Gage, who had presided over the Illinois Corporation at the Chicago fair and was sympathetic to the architects' position, began to implement the Tarsney Act. The *Inland Architect* stated that this was "the most important reform in architectural practice that has been sought for by the profession." Hunt had taken an important part in getting the legislation approved, so that the way was finally opened for competitive design of federal buildings.[10]

Of long-run importance in furthering the arts in America was another institution to which Hunt gave his active support—a school of architecture in Rome to which young Americans might go for further training in their craft and for the inspiration of European art, especially that of ancient and Renaissance Rome. The American Academy in Rome with its School of Architecture was envisioned as providing a similar opportunity to that which the Prix de Rôme had long offered French nationals who had been trained at the Ecole des Beaux-Arts. With this opportunity for study in Rome and for travel throughout Europe, young American architects in the future might be better able to carry on the tradition to which Hunt and others had been so committed.

Although Hunt played a leading part in establishing the new school in Rome in 1894 and 1895, his role was subordinate to that of Charles F. McKim, who was most responsible. McKim, like so many others, had been tremendously impressed by what he and the other architects had accomplished at the Chicago fair. The revival of classical forms at Chicago, McKim believed, had been a turning point in American architecture, for he felt strongly that only by returning to the principles of classical design could a truly great architecture arise in the United States. Neoclassicism would rid the country of the excesses and idiosyncrasies of romantic revivalism and picturesque eccentricity and bring a return to basic architectural principles. To McKim an academy in Rome for American architectural students would help ensure the continuity of the American neoclassical revival.[11]

McKim had enrolled at the Ecole des Beaux-Arts in 1867 and there, like Hunt, had faced the fact that he as a non-French national was not eligible to compete for the highest award of the school, the Prix de Rôme, which provided fellowship support for a stay at the French Academy, located in the Villa Medici. A similar American Academy, McKim now asserted in an informal prospectus, could provide the "same support and encouragement that is afforded by other nations to their sons." For McKim, Rome was the ideal location for such a school: "No other city offers such a field for study or an atmosphere so replete with the best precedents. . . . The value of constant and long-continued study in proximity with the best examples of architecture cannot be over estimated, and is of incalculable advantage to the student before entering upon his professional career." A few years earlier, McKim had donated funds to Columbia to set up a traveling scholarship in architecture, for which Hunt and Thomas Hastings had served as jurors. The new program would go considerably further in advancing students' acquaintance with the great architectural work of the European past.[12]

At a dinner party for a few friends on March 31, 1894, McKim first broached his ideas for establishing an advanced school, modeled on the French Academy, for American architectural students in Rome. He suggested that the American students from different universities receiving traveling architectural fellowships be sent there and that an American prize competition be set up. Living together at the school, the students would engage in supervised travel and a supervised course of study focusing on the great architectural works of the past. The response to McKim's proposal was enthusiastic, and Austin W. Lord, one of the draftsmen from his firm and a former holder of the Rotch Traveling Fellowship, agreed to take charge of the projected school. To formulate plans and set up an organizing committee, McKim gave another dinner on May 23, 1894, to which he invited several interested men, including Hunt, Daniel Burnham, the president of the American Society of Beaux-Arts Architects, and representatives from Columbia, the University of Pennsylvania, and the Rotch Scholarship Committee of Boston. Although Professor William Ware of Columbia, Hunt's former student, was chosen chairman of the Managing Committee for what would first be named the American School of Architecture, McKim himself dominated the undertaking. Within a short time, Hunt was actively working for the Roman school, first heading a nominating committee to bring other prominent men into the endeavor—he enlisted Henry G. Marquand and Martin Brimmer—and later succeeding Ware as chairman. The three current recipients of American fellowships agreed to enter the new atelier, and McKim rushed ahead to prepare for its opening in the fall. By September 8, rules of organization had been adopted, and on November 1, 1894, the American School of Architecture was formally opened in rooms on the upper story of the Palazzo Torlonia on the Via Bocca di Leone. The three initial students and their instructor were soon engaged in making measurements of various Roman antiquities.[13]

Problems arose almost at once respecting the Roman school. Although the members of the American Society of Beaux-Arts Architects had at first approved of the new undertaking, the group subsequently reversed itself to register disapproval, mainly on the grounds that Paris, not Rome, was the center of modern architectural work. But their opposition was weak, and some members of the society nonetheless continued to support the new school. Ware incited another controversy when he strenuously objected to the idea of a formal course of study at the academy. McKim and others believed, in contrast, that some systematic instruction was essential to keep the school from becoming merely a club to which traveling fellows came as the spirit moved them. In a tempestuous outburst, Ware resigned the chairmanship of the Managing Committee and refused to be considered for the position as permanent chairman. McKim thereupon successfully prevailed upon Hunt to take Ware's place. In McKim's view, Hunt's leadership would "give the School a support which . . . no other name could give it."[14]

At a meeting on March 9, 1895, at the University Club, Hunt presided over the reorganized Managing Committee, at which time it was reaffirmed that the students in the School of Architecture would follow a formal course of study but also that transients would be welcome to use the library and to attend lectures. Already it was reported that news about the competition for the Prize of Rome, which the school would offer, had aroused great interest among American architectural students and recent graduates. McKim had managed to get the various groups offering traveling fellowships to agree to conduct their competitions on the same problem, the winning designs to be used for the Roman prize competition. Departments of Archaeology, Painting, and Sculpture were being planned for the future.[15]

The next month Hunt and two other committee members, William Kendall and Frank M. Day, served as judges of the entries for the competition, awarding the first prize of a $1,500 scholarship to John Russell Pope, who many years later would design the National Gallery of Art in Washington. Shortly after the prize was awarded, Hunt was annoyed when he learned that Ware had counseled Pope to postpone going to Rome for a year so that he might better prepare himself. Hunt was adamant that such a postponement was an impossible precedent and would interfere with the regularity of the Roman prize. Pope did go to Rome on schedule in September 1895.[16]

In April 1895, Hunt agreed to underwrite with McKim the leasing of more spacious quarters for the American School in the Casino dell'Aurora on the grounds of the Villa Ludoviso on the Pincian Hill. When permanent officers were chosen on May 11, Hunt was elected president, Ware vice-president, and McKim, treasurer. A formal incorporation of the American School of Architecture in Rome was also instituted, partly in order to raise funds: Hunt and McKim each held two shares in the new corporation, and six others held one share each. Hunt did a great deal to try to get financial support for the school.[17]

After the transfer to the new quarters, new departments of archaeology and sculpture were soon added. In 1897, the school was renamed the American Academy in Rome, and the following year the corporation of the School of Architecture was dissolved. For several years McKim substantially supported the academy from his own funds, but the students were few in number and the scope of academy activities was limited. Following a reorganization in 1904 and incorporation by an act of Congress in 1905, the academy became more solidly established and has since played an important role in providing opportunities for work, study, and travel for young American artists. Hunt's assistance in starting the Roman school, while secondary to McKim's work, did help to implement his deeply held commitment to acquaint Americans with the greatest art of the past.[18]

Even more significant in forwarding the cause of the arts in the United States was Hunt's final major commission. Although Biltmore was the undertaking of Hunt's last years which he found personally most satisfying, the work that would become the most widely viewed of all he did was the Fifth Avenue wing of the Metropolitan Museum of Art, completed posthumously. The great interior spaces and the monumental façade provided not only new exhibition space but also an impressive entry to the museum collections. Further, Hunt's design established the character of the subsequent museum extensions along Fifth Avenue. In this work, perhaps more than in any other he did, Hunt was able to provide to a large public an embodiment of his artistic ideals that could help to mold public taste. Hunt once said that he wanted the museum to be considered his monument, and it is surely a worthy monument to this first American trained at the Ecole des Beaux-Arts.[19]

The need for more space for the display of museum objects was apparent soon after the original building, designed by Calvert Vaux and

J. Wrey Mould, had been opened in 1880. The first addition was a wing to the south of the original building designed by Theodore Weston. Hunt, who had been named advisory architect to the museum on December 22, 1881, along with James Renwick and Weston, did not like the plans for the south-wing addition, but when asked to correct them he said it was too late to do so, and the museum trustees went ahead with the design. The south wing was opened on December 18, 1888. The additional space in the new area was still not adequate, however, and within six months the state legislature, at the instigation of the trustees, authorized the City of New York to appropriate money for another extension. Arthur L. Tuckerman was the original architect selected for this new north wing, and on his death he was succeeded by Joseph Wolf. Although Hunt was mentioned as a candidate for the design of the north wing in 1890, he was not selected. The north wing was opened on November 5, 1894.[20]

Hunt had long felt a certain uneasiness about his position at the Metropolitan Museum. Although he had been closely connected with the museum for many years as a founder, a patron, a trustee, a donor, and a periodic member of the Building Committee, he frequently found that his own work and his absences from the city prevented him from attending to museum duties. On more than one occasion he considered tendering his resignation as a trustee. Moreover, in the eighties, Hunt had frequently loaned paintings and art objects from his own collection as well as plaster casts of architectural elements, but General Cesnola, the museum director, had been reluctant to display the casts. Part of Hunt's equivocal feelings about the museum arose quite naturally, too, from the fact that he had not been asked to design the original building in Central Park nor the two extensions. He believed that his professional advice had been consistently ignored when the original building was erected—though this was not fully the case—and when the first addition was decided upon. Hunt and Cesnola had a sometimes strained relationship over the years, and at Hunt's death Cesnola admitted that though he admired Hunt's work he did not care for the man himself.[21]

Even before the north-wing extension was opened it was again apparent that yet more exhibition space was needed. As a third addition on the east side along Fifth Avenue began to be considered, Joseph Wolf, who completed the work on the north extension, was asked to prepare preliminary designs for the new entrance section. However, Henry G. Marquand, Hunt's long-time friend and patron and now president of the Metropolitan Museum, wanted Hunt to design the new wing and late in 1894 authorized him to move ahead with preliminary sketches and to prepare a plan for the future enlargement of the museum. By April 5, 1895, Hunt had his first drawings (figure 122) ready to show to Marquand and Cesnola at a meeting of the Building Committee, held in Hunt's offices. The three men agreed to submit the plans to the trustees of the museum at their next meeting.[22]

On April 16, 1895, the New York State legislature passed the requisite law authorizing the City of New York to raise a sum of one million dollars to pay for the new extension, to be constructed by the Department of Public Parks. A few days later, Hunt informally showed his sketches to the Museum Executive Committee, going over the details of his plans and responding to questions about them, and on May 20, while Hunt was absent at Biltmore having his portrait painted, Richard Howland Hunt presented the plans to the Board of Trustees. Consideration of the Hunt plans was in abeyance, when Hunt's unexpected death on July 31 made the situation problematic. When General Cesnola learned of Hunt's death, he immediately expressed concern to Marquand about what might be done about the projected wing. Cesnola wanted to go ahead with the building on the basis of Hunt's plans, provided that Richard Howland Hunt and Maurice Fornachon, the chief draftsman of the firm, could complete the work as the deceased architect had originally intended; otherwise, Cesnola foresaw various trustees pushing their favorite architects to do the work and considerable delay in completing the new wing. Although Marquand also wished to move ahead with the work on the basis of Hunt's designs, allowing no one else "to come in and snatch his monument," some of the other trustees apparently felt that an older and more experienced architect than Richard Howland Hunt should complete the work. By the terms of Hunt's will, however, he had left all his possessions including his plans and drawings to his wife, and Catharine Hunt resolutely refused to release the plans of the new wing except on the condition that her eldest son would be employed to do the remaining architectural work. She soon won her point. The reconstituted Building Committee, the Executive Committee, and finally the Trustees on October 30, 1895, approved Hunt's designs, and Richard Howland Hunt was named architect. After approval by the Commissioners of Public Parks and the Board of Estimate and Apportionment, work was begun. The new wing was completed and opened in 1902. The wings flanking Hunt's work on Fifth Avenue, subsequently erected, were entrusted to Charles F. McKim.[23]

As the east wing of the Metropolitan Museum took shape, it became evident to New Yorkers that Hunt had conceived of something very different from the old red-brick building, with its similar extensions, to

Figure 122
Elevation, Metropolitan
Museum of Art, New
York, sketch (1895).
Courtesy The American
Institute of Architects
Foundation/Prints
and Drawings
Collection, Washington,
D.C. Photo by James
Garrison.

the rear. He had discarded any attempt to harmonize the new with the old, since the new building and the projected avenue extensions would hide the old structure from the avenue side, while the further planned extensions would eventually surround the old building and remove it completely from view. The scale of the new wing was grand and in keeping with Hunt's vision of the greatly enlarged future museum. Hunt's projections suggested a palace of art that would eventually cover eighteen and one-half acres of ground (figure 123). Since the new wing would include the principal entrance to the enormous building that was envisioned, it had to be of a suitable scale and set the tone for the whole structure. Both on the façade and in the interior space, Hunt succeeded admirably in establishing a character of dignified monumentality for what would become one of the front-ranking museums of the world.[24]

The design for the Metropolitan Museum was Hunt's, but the conception behind it owed much to the Beaux-Arts tradition that had already come to characterize museum design in the United States. As John Maass has pointed out in his study of the Philadelphia exhibition, Memorial Hall, built for the 1876 fair, was only the first of many American museums in a Beaux-Arts manner. In the decades that followed, one museum after another was fashioned as a symmetrical edifice, divided into a center section and corner pavilions, and characterized by triple portals, paired columns, and niches and statuary; some were provided with domes, others were not. Art museums in Chicago, Milwaukee, Brooklyn, and Detroit all shared much with Hunt's design. Surely Hunt's work, especially in the plan for the projected expansion, also looked back to Leo von Klenze's Glyptothek in Munich (1816–1830), based on conceptions by J.-N.-L. Durand as given in architectural lessons at the Ecole Polytechnique at the beginning of the nineteenth century. The Metropolitan Museum of Art as Hunt conceived it was in an established tradition and unmistakably announced that it was a museum of art.[25]

The interior of Hunt's Fifth Avenue wing is largely occupied by the grand entrance hall, some 166 feet in length, 48 feet in width, and two stories in height. A vast space like a great Roman bath, the hall was used at first for the display of large works of sculpture but it was as well, and remains today, a vestibule for the entire museum. Three saucer domes not visible from the exterior cap the hall.

Outside, from a distance, the exterior of the central part of the east wing is effectively framed as a vista of East Eighty-Second Street, one of the few architectural vistas in New York City. The Beaux-Arts classical design (figure 124) puts into permanent form some of the ideas of the

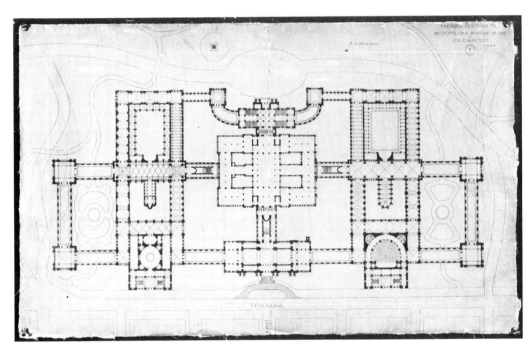

Figure 123
Plan by Richard Morris
Hunt for the expansion
of the Metropolitan
Museum of Art (1895).
The Metropolitan
Museum of Art.

Figure 124
Metropolitan Museum of
Art, Fifth Avenue at
Eighty-Second Street,
New York (1902).
Museum of the City of
New York.

Chicago fair. Set upon a high rusticated base, which is pierced by a few window openings, the structure consists of an elaborated central section, with three high, round-arched bays flanked by pairs of colossal Corinthian columns, and lower and simpler wings on each side. Originally, a crescent-shaped driveway led to a rather steep stairway, which rose to a small porch and somewhat incongruent bronze doors set in the lower half of the central arched bay. In recent years, the old driveway, staircase, and bronze doors were replaced; the new entrance doors are now reached by a very broad stairway extending far forward from the front of the building.

Each of the three bays of the central section contains a triple window within the arch, below which on the two side bays is a rusticated wall divided by two attached columns. The four pairs of colossal columns stand on projecting bases and support on the broken entablature massive blocks of rough stone, which Hunt originally had intended to have carved into sculptural groups representing the arts of four great epochs. Hunt also planned to have reproductions of great works of sculpture representing each of the four major artistic periods placed in the niches at the base of the columns. A high attic over the central section carries above the cornice a cresting of female masks joined by swags of fruit. Six medallion portraits of great artists by Karl Bitter are located in the spandrels of the three arches. Bitter also carved large heads for the keystones of the arches and four caryatids, representing architecture, sculpture, painting, and music, which adorn the attic of the two lateral wings. Each of the caryatids is flanked by a plain panel placed directly above a large pedimented window at the first-story level.[26]

As a composition that catches and holds the eye of a person walking along or standing on the street below, Hunt's Metropolitan Museum façade is remarkably successful. The variety of architectural and sculptural elements—the powerful columns, the jagged stone masses, the graceful arches, the portrait heads and the roof-edge masks, the convoluted caryatids, the rough-hewn base, the severe projecting triangular pediments over the lateral windows, the simple panels—gives the front an intrinsic interest. Moreover, although the building scale is grand, the spectator does not feel overwhelmed, for the dimensions and the many architectural elements are readily comprehensible. The effective balancing of the primary masses of the central section and the wings and of the secondary masses of the column plinths, the staircase, and the great stone blocks gives an impression of strength and stability to the building. At the same time, there is a certain tension between the central segment, with the upward thrust of the columns, the arches, and the pyramidal blocks, and the two wings, which, with dominating horizontals, restrain the thrust of the central part. The play of light and shadow, especially around the projecting columns but also over the receding arches of the bays, the projecting window pediments, and the many carvings provides a continual change, a most vital quality, to the structure. Here, then, is a building that has variety in unity, vitality in stability, and humanity in monumentality.

Organizing and working for institutions that would serve the cause of art had been an important concern for Hunt from his earliest endeavors in establishing the American Institute of Architects. Only with many institutions working vigorously to promote art, he believed, would the level of national taste be raised. And in Hunt's view, with the several new associations, the success of the world's fair, and the new architectural work going on, there was good reason to be optimistic. As one who had done and was continuing to do a great deal in the field, he hoped to do yet more. At a dinner of the members of the Architectural League early in 1893, inspired at the time by his work in Chicago, he gave a rousing talk proclaiming a new era for the arts in America. His conviction was unmistakable: "By the Great Caesar, if this country doesn't take up art, we'll make it, we'll educate it, we'll show it what a great and glorious thing it is."[27]

25

THE AMBASSADOR OF ART

The pace of Hunt's life after the return from the short summer trip to England and France in 1893 and the October visit to the Chicago fair was exhausting. And the state of his health had clearly declined. Catharine felt that "he was never the same man after his return from the Chicago Fair: the wonderful vitality had lessened." On one occasion, when one of his employees suggested he needed a rest, Hunt countered with, "Work, work, keep on going; that is the best rest you can have." And work he did.[1]

Carrying on several large commissions simultaneously necessitated traveling a great deal. Frequently Hunt had to be gone for days at a time from his New York office and home to supervise the progress of the projects at Newport, Cambridge, Washington, Asheville, West Point, and Cleveland. To take care of much of the necessary drafting for the great houses in Newport, Hunt sent Holland C. Anthony, a draftsman from the New York office, to work full time in the studio at Hill Top Cottage (figure 125), and he often went to consult with Anthony. On one trip to Washington, while inspecting the work at the Naval Observatory, he joined Commodore George Dewey and Captain Alfred Thayer Mahan for lunch; on another Washington visit, he enjoyed an evening with Secretary of State James G. Blaine.[2]

The close-knit family was becoming scattered. Dick Hunt, back from his studies at the Ecole des Beaux-Arts, had been working with his father since 1887; however, he was away from New York much of the time supervising jobs for the office. He and his own family lived in Tuxedo, New York. Joseph Hunt graduated from Harvard College in June 1892 and then went on to special classes in architecture at Columbia University before leaving for Paris and his turn at the Ecole. Richard and Catharine's daughter Kitty (Catharine Howland Hunt) was married on July 7, 1892, to Livingston Hunt of the United States Navy in Trinity Church in Newport; she and her husband settled in Washington, D.C. Herbert was enrolled at St. Marks and later at the Pomfret School. Esther lived with her parents.[3]

During part of the summer of 1894 the Hunts were at Newport, where Richard was caught up in the details of the work going on at Ochre Court and The Breakers and was often made miserable by the demands of Mrs. Ogden Goelet and Mrs. Cornelius Vanderbilt, the ladies of the two mansions. A visit to Cambridge to assess the work at the Fogg Museum in November—he had also been there in April—brought on a bad cold and a severe siege of the gout so that on his return to New York he had to remain in bed until the end of December. But shortly after Christmas Hunt set out for Biltmore, and then immediately

Figure 125
Hunt's studio, Newport,
Rhode Island (ca. 1890).
Courtesy The American
Institute of Architects
Foundation/Prints and
Drawings Collection,
Washington, D.C. Re-
production by James
Garrison.

on coming back to New York he went to Cambridge once again, followed by another visit to The Breakers in Newport. In New York, the house for Mrs. Astor and her son was nearing completion and needed his attention, and there were several conferences with Charles McKim about the school in Rome. In March 1895, the Hunts traveled to Washington to pay a short visit to their daughter Kitty and her new son, born the previous August in Newport. But Hunt caught cold there and then was laid up with lumbago. In April, the opening of McKim's Boston Public Library brought him back to Boston and Cambridge, where he also spent a day at Harvard with President Charles W. Eliot. Then in May came the trip to Biltmore so that Sargent could paint his portrait. Returning from Biltmore, Richard and George Vanderbilt stopped over in Washington, where he saw Secretary Carlisle once more. Early in July, the Hunts went to Lenox, Massachusetts, for the wedding of Adèle Sloane, a niece of George Vanderbilt, to James A. Burden. Hunt got very wet leaving Lenox and had to return to New York in damp clothing. The next day, on his way to Newport, he came down with another severe attack of gout. For nearly two years, the pressures of his work had been exceptionally grueling. Hunt was very tired—and very ill. Confined to the sofa in the morning room at Hill Top Cottage, he was able to transact some business, but he was weak and in constant pain.[4]

Late in July, Hunt's Newport physician decided that a consultation was in order, and a Philadelphia doctor was summoned. The consulting doctor was reassuring about Hunt's condition and gave the opinion that the architect had many years of creative life ahead of him. But suddenly, early on July 30, Hunt began to fail rapidly. Catharine had Dick summoned from New York by telegraph, and he got to Newport by late evening, in time to spend a few hours with his father. Hunt died about noon on July 31, 1895.[5]

The funeral, held in Newport's Trinity Church, was well attended. Relatives, friends, Newport neighbors, professional colleagues, and associates from various societies and organizations were present. Floral tributes were piled high in the front of the church, and "a special musical programme" was presented. Martin Brimmer, Henry G. Marquand, Charles F. McKim, Joseph H. Choate, George B. Post, Sidney Webster, and Maurice Fornachon served as pallbearers.[6]

Burial was in the Island Cemetery at Newport, not far from the Belmont Chapel and the Belmont Memorial as well as the Ledyard, Russell, and Marquand monuments, all of which Hunt had designed. The grave marker selected for Hunt was austere: a large, flat slab of highly polished dark granite. On it was incised "Richard Morris Hunt / October 31, 1827 /

July 31, 1895 / 'Laborare est Orare.'" Fourteen years later Catharine Hunt was buried beside her husband, her inscription reflecting her generous and good-willed nature: "Catharine Clinton Howland Hunt / November 25, 1841 / February 10, 1909 / 'Thou Shall Love Thy Neighbor as Thyself.'" Four of their children and other family members were also buried near by.

Hunt's will, which had been drawn up on June 5, 1885, the day before they had sailed for Europe, was filed for probate in New York City on August 8. It left his entire estate, estimated at $50,000 in real estate and $450,000 in personal property, to Catharine Hunt, on her death to be divided among the surviving children in equal shares. Catharine Hunt and her son Richard Howland Hunt were named as executors. No public or charitable bequests were made. Several newspaper obituaries suggested that Hunt was making an income of about $150,000 annually at the time of his death. The *Boston Herald* commented that Hunt's will seemed to demonstrate "that genius is sometimes rewarded in this world."[7]

A deluge of tributes to Hunt poured forth. Almost always he was characterized as the leading architect in the United States and a person widely recognized throughout the world. He was praised for his many important buildings, but most especially for the Administration Building at Chicago. He was commended for his fine taste, for his exacting standards, for his work for the profession, for his contributions to the cause of the arts in America, and for his qualities as a man. At the annual convention of the A.I.A., held in St. Louis in October 1895, several of the speakers extolled their former colleague who had done so much for American architects. Edward H. Kendall related that even in Hunt's final days, the dying man had urged that the Institute must be built up "so that it may remain an influence for good, forever and forever!" To Henry Van Brunt, Hunt "more than any other, had by personal force and high training secured for the architecture of our time and country a standing adequate at last to represent our civilization in terms of art." *The Inland Architect and News Record* published a "Richard Morris Hunt Memorial edition" in August 1895, and the October–December 1895 number of *Architectural Record* was largely devoted to Hunt.[8]

The various organizations and societies Hunt had been associated with issued tributes to him. The Board of Trustees of the Metropolitan Museum of Art framed a resolution stating that they had learned of Hunt's death with "a profound sense of personal loss." Hunt's "natural gifts and taste" had made him "a valuable counsellor" concerning all that related to the collections of the museum. In his advice on museum policy, "the firmness and decision of tone . . . exhibited the courage and independence" which always characterized him. The Century Club tribute suggested that though Hunt's work would leave an impress on the nation for all time, showing his taste, learning, and artistic spirit, those who knew Hunt best would remember him most "by the ambitions that he excited in others, by the wonderful vitality that he imparted to the whole art movement about him, and by his absolutely unselfish devotion to the best interests of the profession that he adorned."[9]

At Biltmore, workers representing the various crafts drew up resolutions to send to Catharine Hunt. Because of Hunt's "generosity, sympathy, and services in behalf of the worthy laboring men of all classes," and deeming it appropriate to send their "love for and appreciation of him," they had resolved "that to him more than any other man of our time all the representative workmen of this country are indebted for the elevation of their trades and arts to the position which they now hold in the ranks of the great army of skilled workmen." In Hunt not only had the country lost "its greatest architect," but they had lost "a kind, considerate and constant friend; for neither his great fame nor his wealth ever caused him to be forgetful, indifferent, or careless of the rights and feelings of his fellowmen and laborers."[10]

European critics also lavished tributes on Hunt. His European reputation had depended in part on his many contacts abroad and his membership in honorary societies. Probably H. H. Richardson had been more respected as a designer in European professional circles and his work better known. But Hunt's W. K. Vanderbilt house and his world's fair building were well known abroad and usually admired, and in the tributes coming after his death he was frequently praised for having done work that was "refined and knowledgeable" though, some felt, uneven. He was commonly characterized as the preeminent American architect of his time.[11]

A memorial exhibit of some of Hunt's work was quickly organized in late December 1895. More than one hundred fifty drawings and photographs were placed on display at the Philadelphia Academy of Fine Arts. Some of the architect's student drawings from his days at the Ecole were shown, along with early studies for the Louvre addition, drawings for the Central Park gateways, and photographs of several of his more important works. A somewhat less extensive exhibit of his work was held at the Rhode Island School of Design in March 1897.[12]

At Biltmore Village, George Vanderbilt had a stained-glass window honoring Hunt placed in the Church of All Souls. The subject of the window, which was first shown on December 25, 1898, is the building of the temple. Solomon and Hiram of Tyre are pictured consulting a parchment scroll relating to the unfinished temple standing on the hill behind them. "For Glory and For Beauty" is the text at the base of the window, with a memorial inscription to Richard Morris Hunt.[13]

The most important memorial undertaking honoring Hunt was the project for a civic monument in New York City. The Municipal Art Society, of which Hunt had been the first president, took the initiative, soon joined by the Metropolitan Museum of Art, the Century Association, and other societies. Although the erection of Hunt's Fifth Avenue gateway at Fifty-Ninth Street was suggested, this proposal aroused little support. A monumental seat, to be located possibly at Fifth Avenue and Eighty-Third Street, was then considered, and by April 1896, Daniel Chester French had been placed in charge of creating the memorial. By February 1897, French, working with the architect Bruce Price, had prepared a model, which the Municipal Art Society accepted. A site opposite the Lenox Library between Seventieth and Seventy-First streets was chosen that summer, and the work was well under way in the winter of 1897–1898. When the monument was ready for dedication, the two allegorical figures planned for it had not yet been cast; they were set in place in 1901. Eventually about $20,000 was raised to pay for the monument.[14]

The unveiling took place on October 31, 1898—"a changeful afternoon, banks of grey clouds above blue sky with small white clouds—and the trees in the park warm brown and golden," Kitty Hunt noted in her diary. She, her mother, and her sister Esther sat on the balcony of the Lenox Library watching the late afternoon proceedings. Representatives from the several sponsoring societies gathered in the lower hall of the Lenox Library, and at four o'clock they walked across the avenue where a crowd of several hundred persons had gathered. George B. Post, president of the Institute and of the Fine Arts Federation and chairman of the Memorial Committee, spoke briefly of Hunt's works and his many honors, and he then presented the memorial to the city. While Post was speaking, Richard Carley Hunt, Hunt's oldest grandson, drew the cord, removing a white silk banner and a flag from the bust of the architect, and two wreaths of laurel were laid on the pedestal. Randolph Guggenheimer, president of the City Council, accepted the memorial for the city and then turned it over to the president of the Parks Board, who accepted it for Central Park. The rector of Grace Church concluded the ceremonies with a prayer and a benediction. Many of Hunt's friends came to the library to speak to Catharine Hunt, "who bore herself very well." The family was very pleased by the tribute.[15]

Within the Hunt family, interest in family history and especially in Richard Hunt's life and work grew as the nineteenth century drew to a close. Catharine Hunt, devoted to the memory of her husband, began to write a biography of Richard, and there was a flurry of letters back and forth to his sister Jane and his brother Leavitt, as Catharine sought information on her husband's early life. Jane Hunt, living in California, at this time wrote several short sketches of family biography and gathered together a great many family letters and other materials. Catharine attempted to establish the facts for her adoring account from contemporary documents insofar as she could, but she did not see everything her sister-in-law had collected, nor did she get everything right. She apparently worked on this biographical account for some years, probably completing it in 1907. She also compiled scrapbooks of clippings and other memorabilia, and for her children she arranged a book of clippings and other materials relating to Richard, which she presented to them in 1900 on the fifth anniversary of their father's death.[16]

Catharine herself was not well in the years following her husband's death. She had been partially lame since an illness many years earlier, and her right arm and hand were almost useless. In addition she suffered from a weak heart, and exertion quickly tired her. Nonetheless, she continued working with the Society of Decorative Art of which she had been a founder and provided support for an art colony at Tannersville, New York. She remained active in Grace Church, which she had for many years intermittently attended. On a trip to Egypt in 1909, she fell ill, contracted pneumonia, and died at Luxor on February 10 in her sixty-eighth year.[17]

Richard Howland Hunt continued to operate his father's office under his own name from 1895 until 1901, when he was joined by his brother Joseph Howland Hunt. They formed the partnership of Hunt and Hunt. The firm completed the work on the central section of the Metropolitan Museum, which their father had designed, and executed many palatial urban and country residences. Richard Howland Hunt also designed halls at Vanderbilt and Sewanee universities. Both brothers followed their father in serving as presidents of the Municipal Art Society, while Richard also was president of the Architectural League of New York and the New York Chapter of the A.I.A. Joseph Hunt died in 1924 and Richard Howland Hunt in 1931. Their library and memorabilia of their father, along with thousands of plans and sketches, formed the heart of the Hunt Collection donated to the American Institute of Architects. Esther Morris Hunt married George M. Woolsey, but she died in London in 1901, when she was only twenty-six years old; her mother presented a stained-glass window to Grace Church in her memory. Herbert Leavitt Hunt, the youngest of Richard and Catharine's children, died in France in 1960. Catharine Howland Hunt—Kitty—lived until June 28, 1963.[18]

When Richard Morris Hunt returned to the United States in 1855, he settled in an America whose architecture was largely undisciplined, uneducated, and lacking in taste. He saw his social role as creating needed structures that would be dignified and tasteful and that would apply ideas taken from traditions of the past to the construction problems at hand. This always remained for him a fundamental purpose of his work. In a country where architecture was by and large undistinguished, he attempted to create attractive and impressive buildings and at the same time provide materials that might help raise the public taste.

As an artist—and Hunt always saw himself above all as an artist— Hunt covered a remarkable range in his work: a few modest private houses and numerous mansions and palatial dwellings, apartment houses, tenement houses, office buildings, classroom buildings, a gymnasium, churches, libraries, a hospital, a retirement home, warehouses, artists' studios, scientific laboratories, observatories, stores, mausoleums and graveyard monuments, statuary pedestals, a guardhouse, two museums, and a temporary exposition structure. Hunt's body of works included structures for a great many of the needs of Americans in the latter half of the nineteenth century. He was very much a man of his times.

And to do this work he always kept himself conversant with the technological side of his art/craft. Hunt consistently emphasized the importance of technical knowledge, paid close attention to technological developments in the building trades, and knew when and where to seek out specialized advice; and he was respected for his competence by construction engineers. At the time of his death, *The Boston Transcript* stated that Hunt would long be remembered as "the foremost advocate in this country of a thorough knowledge of engineering principles among architects."[19]

Trained in the academic tradition, which emphasized classical prototypes and adaptations of classical elements, Hunt was committed to the great architectural traditions of the European past, especially those of antiquity and the Renaissance. Yet he attended the Ecole des Beaux-

Arts at a time of ferment, when new structural and design ideas were in the air and when new attention was being paid even among professors at the Ecole to the picturesque. And Hunt was strikingly attracted to the picturesque. His sketchbooks, both from his student years and from his later European journeys, are filled with drawings of medieval castles, old town houses on narrow streets, and ancient churches and cathedrals. Montgomery Schuyler believed that if Hunt had not studied at the Ecole des Beaux-Arts but had remained in America during his formative years, he would have become one of the leaders of the Gothic Revival, for he was so obviously drawn to romantic elements of design. Certainly much of Hunt's work throughout his career was permeated by picturesque evocative elements, and such romantic tendencies appear in various forms and in several types of structures. To say that because he used neoclassical designs for the world's fair Administration Building, Marble House, and the Fogg Museum at the end of his career, he had settled on neoclassicism, is to neglect the highly romantic Biltmore, in which the late-Gothic-derived elements season the Renaissance-inspired whole, or his work at the Military Academy, or other works. Hunt's temperament favored restrained use of romantic forms, but he strenuously objected to individual expression that was undisciplined. He always believed an architect should do his work guided by the established traditions of the past; eccentricity in design was abhorrent to him. Yet he was willing to adapt his work to the needs and the wishes of his clients, while attempting all the while to do the best he could to educate and sensitize the taste of those for whom he worked.[20]

In many of his commissions, this was relatively easy to do, since so many of his clients were already his social acquaintances and close friends, people who liked him and respected his judgment. Especially in his domestic work, but also in many of his commercial and public buildings, moreover, he worked not only with personal friends but also with people of considerable wealth. The often expressed view that Hunt raised his clients' status by providing them with elaborate housing is not true of most of his large domestic commissions, for most of Hunt's patrons for the very large houses already had well-recognized social positions. With their large resources to work with, Hunt was often in the fortunate situation of being able to carry out fully the ideas which seemed most appropriate to him, and them, for the particular projects. More than any other architect in the Gilded Age, he could realize fully his own artistic vision.

Perhaps one reason that he settled on no one style, though much of his domestic work did look back to the early French Renaissance, was that he could achieve greater satisfaction by mastering different modes of design. His opportunities to do largely as he wished were great, and his method of design was eclectic both in choosing from past traditions and in selecting stylistic elements. Yet he utilized great works from the past solely for inspiration, adapting their forms and elements for his own purposes. He did not attempt to reproduce the past.

As an architect, he had no followers, other than his sons; he created no school, although other American architects did make use of early French Renaissance forms after Hunt had first done so. He did not, like Richardson, develop in an original way one special style that became closely identified with him and that others then attempted to assimilate. Hunt's importance as an architect, therefore, came not so much directly through his specific works as through his example as a well-trained, knowledgeable, sensitive artist and through the pupils from his studio who were thoroughly grounded in the fundamentals of artistic design through acquaintance with the greatest achievements of the European past. The sense of order and discipline, a feeling for proportion, balance, the relationship of parts to the whole, dominance and subordination, the flow of space—these his pupils learned and could pass on in their turn to others.

Hunt, then, did a great deal in his own atelier in helping to establish a tradition of systematic training that subsequently had considerable impact on American architectural education, especially through William Robert Ware. Hunt's widespread reputation as "dean" of the profession, coming when he was still fairly young, probably arose, however, more from his association with the American Institute of Architects and his commitment to the profession than from his activity as an educator. In his work for his colleagues he helped gain public recognition of the architect's function, thus elevating the status of architects and helping to make architecture a respected profession in the United States. As much as any other figure in the latter part of the nineteenth century he was recognized as a spokesman for his profession. During many years, Frank Wallis later reported, "his personality so dominated the profession," that even several years after his death, when his name was mentioned at a dinner by a speaker, "the entire body of two hundred men [rose] on their feet, shouting 'Hunt! Hunt! Hunt!'"[21]

Not only did his colleagues respect him for his professional activity and loyalty, for his knowledge, taste, and judgment, and for the buildings he had created, but they also almost universally liked him as a man. His directness and forthrightness, his air of authority, his self-esteem and self-possession, his commitment to his ideals all helped inspire confidence. Moreover, as Karl Bitter said, "He had the power of kindling enthusiasm in others." No doubt, as well, some admired him for his social position; in a society where status often seemed so unclear, Hunt was firmly established. His family was long a respected one, his social connections were excellent, and his wealth was adequate to support a very comfortable life style.[22]

With his many associations in organizations and societies—both professional groups and social clubs—Hunt was at the center of a web of relationships whereby he could make his ideas known to and influence other influential persons. To the extent that there was an artistic "establishment" toward the end of the nineteenth century in the United States, Hunt stood close to the center of the group of men who made the most important decisions, as in the thrust of the activities of the American Institute of Architects, the Metropolitan Museum of Art, the American Academy in Rome, and other organizations, the design of the Chicago fair, the placement of public monuments and memorials, and the artistic causes that would be supported. In such activities, as a central figure of influence, Hunt always worked to educate and to raise the public taste.

Hunt was unconcerned with trying to develop an original or distinctively American architectural style. He firmly believed that architectural designs must be adapted to the specific purposes and needs of the situation at hand. But this did not mean the use of something new and different that rejected the past. Rather, he felt, tradition must be the source, for the highest architectural achievements of the past had expressed most fully the principles of beauty in form, relationship of elements, and the application of ornament. The architect must learn from the best of the past and then sensitively and sensibly apply what he had learned to the problems of the present. In a time of uncertain artistic standards, he had the authority of his own convictions as to what good taste meant. He had the air of knowing what was good. Like poets, novelists, and painters within the Genteel Tradition, he had a vision of an ideal and he attempted to realize that vision in varying circumstances. To Hunt, the best architecture meant above all a realization of his ideals of dignity, harmony, order, and repose.

As with few other artists of his time, however, Hunt's vision was not a moral one. He did not aim to provide moral elevation through his works. Nor did he wish to use his art for purposes of social reform or social engineering. Rather, his viewpoint was aesthetic. In an atmosphere of beauty, the individual might be most fully realized. Possibly there was some element of "social control" in his thinking: an attempt to bring coherence and order to an often incoherent and disordered society through the harmony and repose of art. For Hunt, art could have an elevating impact on the human spirit and enrich peoples' lives, perhaps, then, serving to diminish social turbulence and certainly to reduce the crassness and roughness of American life. But Hunt was in no way a social theorist or a speculative philosopher. He would deal with practical building needs to bring more beauty to Americans' lives because this was good in itself. Yet even before Hunt died, men who *were* social theorists were moving to the fore in art and architecture. Committed to the ideology of art as a means of social engineering and to the ideal of the communal artist, they had begun to shape a new aesthetic for the coming century.[23]

The United States was still a young nation and, compared with Europe, had but a short past. "In this country, where everything is of yesterday, [Americans] hunger and thirst for the long ago," the French critic Paul Bourget wrote in 1895. Just as countless Americans—Hunt among them—had visited Europe and found there a sense of history in the remnants of a rich past that they had never known at home, so also the poet, the novelist, the painter, and the architect might bring back to Americans at home something of that sense of the extension of time and a realization of aesthetic values in their own artistic creations. Hunt himself had the need to return to Europe for long periods again and again, steeping himself in the atmosphere of art and experiencing a sense of the past that he could not find at home. The artistic values of the past brought a sense of perspective and a richness to his own life. He had tried to help others experience this richness.[24]

INTRODUCTION

1. The Hunt Memorial was designed by Bruce Price, architect, and Daniel Chester French, sculptor, and was originally dedicated on Oct. 31, 1898. On the theft of the bronzes, see *New York Times*, Feb. 18, 1962, p. 76, and Nathalie Dana, "The Municipal Art Society: Seventy-Five Years of Service to New York," *New-York Historical Society Quarterly*, LI (Apr. 1967), 160, 164, 176.

2. For descriptions of the Hunt Memorial, see Anon., "The Richard M. Hunt Memorial," *Engineering Record*, XXXVIII (Nov. 5, 1898), 493–494; William Francklyn Paris, "Richard Morris Hunt: First Secretary and Third President of the Institute," *Journal of the American Institute of Architects*, XXV (Feb. 1956), 80; Lewis I. Sharp, *New York City Public Sculpture by 19th-Century American Artists* (New York, 1974), p. 49; Wayne Craven, *Sculpture in America* (New York, 1968), p. 400.

3. Charles De Kay, "The Memorial to Richard M. Hunt," *New York Times Magazine*, June 12, 1898, p. 3.

4. Charles De Kay's estimate that Hunt was "New York's foremost architect" (ibid.) was typical of the 1890s, while the view of John Burchard and Albert Bush-Brown, who label Hunt a leader of "the arrogant would-be tastemakers . . . who denied their day altogether," is characteristic of mid-twentieth-century estimates (*The Architecture of America: A Social and Cultural History* [Boston, 1961], p. 184).

5. Russell Lynes, "Chateau Builder to Fifth Avenue," *American Heritage*, VI (Feb. 1955), 22.

6. See the brief but important reassessment of the state of American architecture in Ada Louise Huxtable, "The Gospel According to Giedion and Gropius is under Attack," *New York Times*, June 27, 1976, Sec. II, pp. 1, 29.

7. Arthur Drexler, ed., *The Architecture of the Ecole des Beaux-Arts* (New York, 1977), including essays by Arthur Drexler, Richard Chafee, David Van Zanten, and Neil Levine. An earlier indication of reassessment of the Beaux-Arts training and tradition came in Vincent Scully, *American Architecture and Urbanism* (New York, 1969), in which the author suggested that "the French school had served America well" (p. 136).

8. A survey conducted by *The American Architect and Building News* in 1885 asked American architects to select the ten best American buildings. Richardson's work easily dominated the poll, with five of his buildings among the top ten choices. Only one of Hunt's designs, the William K. Vanderbilt house, placed among the top ten. See "The Ten Best Buildings in the United States," *American Architect and Building News*, XVII (June 13, 1885), 282–283.

CHAPTER 1

1. The date of the birth of Richard Morris Hunt (hereafter RMH) has been variously given as Oct. 31, 1827, and Oct. 31, 1828. According to Catharine Clinton Howland Hunt (CCHH), the widow of RMH, in an unpublished biography of her husband (CCHH, Hunt Papers [HP], p. 1), when the Leavitt family Bible was presented to a church, Jane Maria Leavitt Hunt, the mother of RMH, tore out the pages on which births and deaths had been re-

corded, and these pages were later mislaid. CCHH believed that her husband had been born on Oct. 31, 1828, though she wrote that the exact date was "not positively known." The sketch of RMH in Mary R. Cabot, ed., *Annals of Brattleboro, 1681–1895* (Brattleboro, 1922), II, 726–728, also gives Oct. 31, 1828, as did most of the RMH obituaries in 1895, and this date was used on the Hunt Memorial in New York City, erected in 1898. Most historians have accepted this date.

The sketch of RMH by John V. Van Pelt in the *Dictionary of American Biography* (New York, 1927–1936), IX, 389–391, however, gives Oct. 31, 1827, for RMH's birth, following some obituary accounts and the biographical sketch in the same author's *Monograph of the William K. Vanderbilt House, Richard Morris Hunt, Architect* (New York, 1925). The office of the Brattleboro Town Clerk has no official record of the birth of RMH, nor has a certificate of baptism been located.

The confirming evidence for Oct. 31, 1827 is that RMH consistently accepted Oct. 31, 1827, as the date of this birth. (1) In a letter that RMH wrote to his mother from Geneva, on Jan. 3, 1845, regarding his possible admission to the United States Military Academy, which he then sought: "The only thing that might be an obstacle is my age, but this be as it may, I was 17 yrs. old October / 44" (Jane Hunt, 1832–1874, HP, VI). (2) RMH's dossier at the Ecole des Beaux-Arts (AJ–52–369) includes three mentions of his birth date, all Oct. 31, 1827. (3) In his journal for Oct. 31, 1846, RMH wrote: "Aujourd'hui: 19 ans. Turn over a new leaf." (RMH, Journal, 1844–1848, HP). (4) In court testimony at the Parmly Trial in 1861, RMH stated: "I went to Europe at the age of 15 and returned at 27 . . . in September 1855." The Hunt family sailed for Europe on Oct. 9, 1843, so that the statement is consistent with Oct. 31, 1827, as his birth date (Anon., "Important Trial: Compensation of Architects," *Architects' and Mechanics' Journal*, III [Mar. 9, 1861], 222). (5) In an interview with a reporter for the *Cincinnati Times Star*, dated Nov. 22, 1889, RMH stated: "I am a Vermonter, born in Brattleboro sixty-two years ago" (CCHH, HP, p. 227). Additional evidence is as follows: (6) RMH's sister Jane Hunt in her rough notes on the family history wrote that Richard was born in Oct. 1826 and "was 3 weeks old when Father went to W[ashington]." She then wrote that Jonathan Hunt first went to Washington, D.C., for the First Session of the Twentieth Congress, in 1828. Actually, Hunt left Brattleboro on Nov. 25, 1827, for the opening of Congress on Dec. 3, 1827, which confirms Jane Hunt's statement that RMH was three weeks old when her father left home (Jane Hunt, 1832–1874, HP, VI). (7) Jane Hunt's own Bible has the Oct. 31, 1827, date for RMH's birth in the list of family dates (HP). (8) The Hunt family had the date Oct. 31, 1827, carved on RMH's gravestone, which is located in the Island Cemetery, Newport, R.I. Barring discovery of an official contemporary record giving another birth date, the evidence for Oct. 31, 1827, is persuasive.

2. Jonathan Hunt's sister Ellen (1781–1865) was the third wife of General Lewis Richard Morris (1760–1825), who was a delegate to the Vermont Convention of 1791, called to ratify the Constitution, and a Federalist member of the

House of Representatives in the Fifth, Sixth, and Seventh Congresses, *Dictionary of American Biography*, VII, 215–216; *Biographical Directory of the American Congress, 1774–1949* (Washington, D.C., 1950), p. 1591; a letter from Lieut. Richard Hunt Morris to Jonathan Hunt, Dec. 25, 1825, is preserved in Jonathan Hunt I–V, 1610–1823, HP, I.

3. Jane Maria Hunt, Aug. 31, 1822; William Morris Hunt, Mar. 31, 1824; Jonathan Hunt, June 15, 1826; Leavitt Hunt, Feb. 22, 1830. Jane was known familiarly in the family as "Jennie" or "Jenney"; William was often called "Bill"; Jonathan was known as "John" or "Jack"; Leavitt was usually called "Leav"; and RMH was sometimes known to his friends as "Dick."

4. Cabot, *Annals*, I, 289; Helen M. Knowlton, *Art-Life of William Morris Hunt* (Boston, 1899), p. 1; Henry M. Burt, *The Attractions of Brattleboro; Glimpses of The Past and Present* (Brattleboro, 1866), pp. 56–57; Journals of Jane Hunt, HP, VII, Pt. I, 1; see the description of the Hunt property in "Deed of Quit Claim: Mrs. Jane M. Hunt to Jane Hunt, Richard M. Hunt,

Leavitt Hunt, Jan. 5, 1857," Jane Hunt, 1832–1874, HP, VI; MS U.S. Census of 1830, Vermont, IV, 7, records eleven persons in the Hunt household. For an illustration of the Jonathan Hunt house in the early twentieth century, see Martha Shannon, *Boston Days of William Morris Hunt* (Boston, 1923), p. 8.

5. John N. Houpis, Jr., *Brattleboro: Selected Historical Vignettes* (Brattleboro, 1973), p. 10; Ray Bearse, ed., *Vermont: A Guide to the Green Mountain State*, 2d rev. ed. (Boston, 1966), p. 185.

6. Houpis, *Brattleboro*, pp. 17, 30, 36–38; *Biographical Directory of the American Congress, 1774–1949*, p. 1623; *Dictionary of American Biography*, VI, 414–415; XII, 473; XIII, 589–590; XIX, 95–97; Cabot, *Annals*, II, 722; *Fifth Census; Or, Enumeration of the Inhabitants of the United States, 1830* (Washington, D.C., 1832), p. 33; *Compendium of the Enumeration of the Inhabitants and Statistics of the United States . . . of the Sixth Census* (Washington, D.C., 1841), p. 18.

7. Jonathan Hunt I–V, 1610–1823, HP, I, 1–18; Thomas B. Wyman, Jr., *Genealogy of the Name

and Family of Hunt* (Charleston, S.C., 1863), pp. 183–184, 217; *Records of the Governor and Council of the State of Vermont*, E. P. Walton, ed. (Montpelier, 1873–1880), III, 228; Cabot, *Annals*, I, 289.

8. Jonathan Hunt I–V, 1610–1823, HP, I, 19–26; Wyman, *Genealogy*, pp. 218–220; Walter H. Crockett, *Vermont, the Green Mountain State* (New York, 1921), I, 482, and II, 403, 460; *Records of the Governor and Council of the State of Vermont*, III, 32, 64, 102; James B. Wilbur, *Ira Allen, Founder of Vermont, 1715–1814* (Boston, 1928), I, 514 ff. Jonathan Hunt's wife's name is sometimes given as "Lavinia," but a letter of Jan. 21, 1831, to her son Jonathan in her own handwriting establishes her name as Levinah (HP, I, 23).

9. Jonathan Hunt I–V, 1610–1823, HP, I, 22.

10. Jonathan Hunt VI, 1787–1820, HP, II, 27–41 (included in this volume of the HP are numerous compositions written by Jonathan Hunt while a student at Dartmouth College, as well as later journals, notebooks, account books, and orations); Wyman, *Genealogy*, p. 189; Cabot, *An-*

nals, I, 289, 366–367; Crockett, *Vermont*, III, 232, 253; *Biographical Directory of the American Congress, 1774–1949*, p. 1350; Samuel H. Fisher, *The Litchfield Law School, 1774–1833* (New Haven, 1946), pp. 1–3, 66; George T. Chapman, *Sketches of the Alumni of Dartmouth College* (Cambridge, Mass., 1867), p. 133.

11. Elias Loomis, *Descendants of Joseph Loomis in America* (n.p., 1875), rev. ed. by Elisha S. Loomis (n.p., 1909), p. 218; Emily Leavitt Noyes, *Leavitt, Descendants of John Leavitt* (Tilton, N.H., 1949), III, 45, 67; Jane Hunt, 1822–1903, HP., VII, Pt. II.

12. Col. S. Dunham to Col. Thaddeus Leavitt, Sept. 19, 1819, Jonathan Hunt VI, 1787–1820, HP, II, 41–42; Jane Hunt, 1822–1903, HP, VII, Pt. II, 2. The honeymoon trip of Jonathan and Jane Maria Hunt is described in Jane Maria Hunt's Diary, June 29–July 20, 1820, in Jonathan Hunt VI, 1787–1820, HP, II.

13. CCHH, HP, p. 4; Henry Van Brunt, "Richard Morris Hunt," *Proceedings of the Twenty-Ninth Annual Convention of the American Institute of Architects* (Providence, 1895), p.

73; William Francklyn Paris, "Richard Morris Hunt: First Secretary and Third President of the Institute," *Journal of the American Institute of Architects*, XXIV (Dec. 1955), 248; Edward Wheelwright, *The Class of 1844, Fifty Years after Graduation* (Cambridge, Mass., 1896), p. 133.

14. CCHH, HP, pp. 4–5; Helen M. Knowlton, "William Morris Hunt," *New England Magazine*, X, n.s. (Aug. 1894), 685. Jane Maria Leavitt as a child also expressed interest in "Tambouring Musick," but her father admonished her not to spend time "in that employment," but rather to study "the more important parts of an education" (Thaddeus Leavitt to Jane Maria Leavitt, May 31, 1813, Leavitt-Hunt, HP, IX).

15. CCHH, HP, p. 3; Cabot, *Annals*, II, 723; Knowlton, "William Morris Hunt," 687; Jane Hunt to James W. Paige, Aug. 21, 1829, Manuscript Collection, Massachusetts Historical Society.

16. CCHH, HP, pp. 1–2, 13; Jane Hunt, 1822–1903, HP, VII, Pt. I, 3; Jane Hunt, First Memoir, Jane Hunt, 1822–1903, HP, VII, Pt. II.

17. Jonathan Hunt to Jane Maria Hunt, Dec. 16, 1827, Jonathan Hunt VI, 1821–1828, HP, III.

18. Jonathan Hunt to Jane Maria Hunt, Dec. 27, 1827, Jonathan Hunt VI, 1821–1828, HP, III.

19. CCHH, HP, pp. 2–3, 7; Perry M. Goldman and James S. Young, eds., *The United States Congressional Directories, 1789–1840* (New York, 1973), p. 196.

20. CCHH, HP, pp. 2–3, 5, 7; Jonathan Hunt to Daniel Webster, Sept. 21, 1828, and Aug. 10, 1829, Webster Papers, New Hampshire Historical Society; Jane Hunt to James W. Paige, Aug. 21, 1829, Massachusetts Historical Society. See also Charles M. Wiltse, ed., *The Papers of Daniel Webster: Correspondence, 1825–1829* (Hanover, 1976), II, 362, 422. According to CCHH, HP, p. 6, Jane Maria Hunt possessed many letters from Webster, which she kept for many years but later destroyed, since she felt they were of a personal nature.

21. Jonathan Hunt to Jane Maria Hunt, Jan. 15, and Jan. 23, 1830, Jonathan Hunt VI, 1828–1832, HP, V.

22. CCHH, HP, pp. 3–4; Account Books of

Jonathan Hunt, 1830–1831, Jonathan Hunt VI, 1828–1832, HP, V.

23. Account Books of Jonathan Hunt, 1830–1831, Jonathan Hunt VI, 1828–1832, HP, V; Goldman and Young, eds., *United States Congressional Directories, 1789–1840*, pp. 229, 240.

24. CCHH, HP, pp. 2, 4–5.

25. Jonathan Hunt to Jane Maria Hunt, Mar. 31, 1831, Jonathan Hunt VI, 1828–1832, HP, V; CCHH, HP, p. 4.

26. Speech on Representation, notebooks, and letters of condolence, Jonathan Hunt VI, 1828–1832, HP, V; CCHH, HP, p. 7; *Register of Debates in Congress*, 22nd Congress, 1st sess., VIII (Washington, D.C., 1833), Pt. 1, Senate, Dec. 5, 1831–July 16, 1832, col. 931, and Pt. 3, House, May 9–July 16, 1832, cols. 3036–3037; Burt, *Attractions of Brattleboro*, p. 61.

27. CCHH, HP, p. 7; Jonathan Hunt VI, 1828–1832, HP, V.

CHAPTER 2

1. Mary R. Cabot, ed., *Annals of Brattleboro, 1681–1895* (Brattleboro, 1922), I, 368; Jonathan Hunt's account books,

listing his assets and his debts, placed his net worth at $91,000 on Nov. 10, 1829, and $107,500 on Nov. 2, 1831. The estate valuation was made following his death: Jonathan Hunt VI, 1828–1832, HP, V.

2. Cabot, *Annals*, I, 368; CCHH, HP, pp. 16–17; Pelham W. Hayward to Jane Maria Hunt, Mar. 1, Nov. 1, and Dec. 15, 1844, and Apr. 1, and July 31, 1845, Jane Hunt, HP, VI; Jane Maria Hunt to Epaphroditus Seymour, Dec. 26, 1836, Jane Hunt, 1832–1874, HP, VI.

3. CCHH, HP, pp. 9–10.

4. CCHH, HP, pp. 10, 13; Jane Hunt, 1822–1903, HP, VII, Pt. I, 5–6.

5. CCHH, HP, p. 14; Dennis Kimberly to Jane Maria Hunt, Mar. 6, 1836, Jane Hunt, 1832–1874, HP, VI.

6. Gaetano de Castillia to Jane Maria Hunt, June 12, 1837, and Eleuthere Felix Foresti to Jane Maria Hunt, Dec. 26, 1837, Jane Hunt, 1832–1874, HP, VI.

7. CCHH, HP, pp. 11–12; Helen M. Knowlton, "William Morris Hunt," *New England Magazine*, X, n.s. (Aug. 1894), 687. Gambardella is known to have worked in New

York City in 1838–1839 and exhibited at the National Academy: see *The New-York Historical Society's Dictionary of Artists in America, 1564–1860* (New Haven, 1957), p. 249. The portrait of RMH and Leavitt Hunt is now in the possession of Mrs. Carley Angell. The Hunt family recorded the painter's name as Gambadella.

8. CCHH, HP, p. 12; testimony of Richard Upjohn in the Parmly Trial, in Anon., "Important Trial: Compensation of Architects," *Architects' and Mechanics' Journal*, III (Mar. 16, 1861), 232.

9. CCHH, HP, pp. 14–15; Jane Hunt, 1832–1874, HP, VI.

10. Anon., "Important Trial," (Mar. 9, 1861), 222; quoted in CCHH, HP, pp. 15–17; the certificate of "approbation" is in Jane Hunt, 1822–1903, HP, VII, Pt. I; Eliza G. Wing to P. W. Hayward, Aug. 19, 1842, Jane Hunt, 1832–1874, HP, VI. RMH did not graduate from the Boston Latin School, although his brother John did.

11. Jane Hunt, 1822–1903, HP, VII, Pt. I.

12. Gertrude S. Cole, "Some American Cameo

Portraitists," *Antiques*, L (Sept. 1946), 171, with illus., p. 170.

13. Josiah Quincy to Jane Maria Hunt, Aug. 24, 1841, and May 29, 1843, Jane Hunt, 1822–1903, HP, VII, Pt. I, 10–11.

14. Edward Wheelwright, *The Class of 1844, Harvard College, Fifty Years after Graduation* (Cambridge, Mass., 1896), pp. 317–318, 351, 133–134; quoted in Helen M. Knowlton, *Art-Life of William Morris Hunt* (Boston, 1899), pp. 3–4; CCHH, HP, p. 17.

15. CCHH, HP, p. 18; Knowlton, *Art-Life of William Morris Hunt*, p. 4.

16. CCHH, HP, pp. 18–19; certification of Jonathan Hunt's Harvard College work by Edward Everett, Aug. 2, 1848, Jane Hunt, 1822–1903, HP, VII, Pt. I, 10–11; Knowlton, *Art-Life of William Morris Hunt*, p. 4; Anon., "Important Trial," (Mar. 9, 1861), 221.

17. CCHH, HP, p. 19; Samuel and Elizabeth Parker to Jane Maria Hunt, Sept. 15, 1843, and Daniel Webster to Jane Maria Hunt, Oct. 2, 1843, Jane Hunt, 1832–1874, HP, VI.

18. As quoted in Knowlton, "William Morris Hunt," 687–688, and in a slightly different form in Knowlton, *Art-Life of William Morris Hunt*, p. 5.

19. Paul R. Baker, *The Fortunate Pilgrims* (Cambridge, Mass., 1964).

20. Jane Hunt, Journal, 1843–1844, Oct. 9–Oct. 29, 1843, HP; CCHH, HP, pp. 19–20. Elisha Dyer was governor of Rhode Island, 1857–1859.

21. Jane Hunt, Journal, 1843–1844, Oct. 29, 1843–Feb. 20, 1844, HP; CCHH, HP, p. 20; also Jane Hunt, 1822–1903, HP, VII, Pt. I, 15.

22. RMH, Journal, 1844–1848, Feb. 28–Mar. 3, 1844, HP; Jane Hunt, Journal, 1843–1844, Feb. 20–Mar. 3, 1844, HP. CCHH indicated in HP, p. 21, that Jane Maria Hunt and the three older children went to Italy first and that RMH and Leavitt subsequently followed them, but the journals of RMH and Jane Hunt show that the entire family traveled together.

23. CCHH, HP, p. 21; letters of Pelham W. Hayward to Jane Maria Hunt, Mar. 1, Nov. 1, and Dec. 15, 1844, and Apr. 1 and July 31, 1845, provide commentary on the Hunt family activities in Europe: Jane Hunt, 1832–1874, HP, VI.

24. RMH, Journal, 1844–1848, Mar. 4–Mar. 8, 1844, HP; CCHH quoted these passages, but here as elsewhere she edited the original document, CCHH, HP, p. 21; Baker, *Fortunate Pilgrims*, pp. 198 ff.

25. RMH, Journal, 1844–1848, March 5–April 13, 1844, HP; Jane Hunt, Diary, Mar. 20–June 5, 1844, Jane Hunt, 1822–1903, HP, VII, Pt. I.

26. CCHH, HP, p. 21; Albert Ten Eyck Gardner, "A Rebel in Patagonia," *Metropolitan Museum of Art Bulletin*, III (May 1945), 224; Rose V. S. Berry, "American Painters Who Have Especially Influenced American Art: William Morris Hunt," *Art and Archaeology*, XV (May 1923), 204.

27. Mason Wade, ed., *The Journals of Francis Parkman* (New York, 1947), I, 133–139, 181, 185, 187, 188; RMH, Journal, 1844–1848, Mar. 17, 1844, HP.

28. RMH, Journal, 1844–1848, April 15–May 1, 1844, HP.

29. RMH, Journal, 1844–1848, May 4–May 29, 1844, HP.

30. RMH, Journal, 1844–1848, May 29, 1844 ff., HP; Jane Hunt, Diary, Mar. 20–June 5, 1844, Jane Hunt, 1822–1903, HP, VII, Pt. I; RMH to Jane Maria Hunt, Jan. 3, 1845, Jane Hunt, 1822–1903, HP, VII, Pt. I; Leavitt Hunt and RMH to Jane Maria Hunt, May 5, 1845, Jane Hunt, 1832–1874, HP, VI; CCHH, HP, pp. 21–22. At the time of RMH's death, an American in Whatcom County, Washington, revealed that he had known the Hunt brothers, Richard and Leavitt, fifty years before at the Geneva school and he recalled the pride they took in their Vermont origins: clipping from the *Seattle Post-Intelligencer*, Aug. 3, 1895, Obituaries Scrapbook, Hunt Collection, American Institute of Architects Foundation, Washington, D.C. (hereafter HC).

31. RMH, Journal, 1844–1848, Aug. 3–Sept. 14, 1844, HP; Jane Hunt, Diary, Aug. 4–Oct. 16, 1844, Jane Hunt, 1822–1903, HP, VII, Pt. I.

32. Jane Hunt, Diary, Feb. 22–May 20, 1845, Jane Hunt, 1822–1903, HP, VII, Pt. I; Susan Hale, ed., *Life and Letters of Thomas Gold Appleton* (New York, 1885), pp. 258–260, including T. G. Appleton to Fanny Appleton Longfellow, Apr. 17, 1845; Frederic C. Jaher, "Businessman and Gentleman: Nathan and Thomas Gold Appleton—An Exploration in Intergenerational History," *Explorations in Entrepreneurial History*, IV (1966), 19–39; see also Stephen A. Larrabee, *Hellas Observed* (New York, 1957), pp. 253–254.

33. Jane Hunt, Diary, Feb. 22–May 20, 1845, Jane Hunt, 1822–1903, HP, VII, Pt. I; Hale, ed., *Appleton*, pp. 259–264, including T. G. Appleton to Nathan Appleton, Apr. 27, 1845; Jane Hunt, Second Memoir, Jane Hunt, 1822–1903, HP, VII, Pt. II.

34. RMH to Jane Maria Hunt, Jan. 3, 1845, Jane Hunt, 1822–1903, HP, VII, Pt. I.

35. Leavitt Hunt and RMH to Jane Maria Hunt, May 5, 1845, Jane Hunt, 1832–1874, HP, VI.

36. RMH to Jane Maria Hunt, July 28, 30, 1845, Jane Hunt, 1832–1874, HP, VI; CCHH, HP, p. 22; RMH, Journal, 1844–1848, July 31 and Aug. 1, 1845, HP; Anon., "Important Trial" (Mar. 9, 1861), 222. The HC includes architectural drawings by RMH, "élève de M. Darier." In his journal, RMH did not mention his study with Darier.

37. *Ecole des Beaux-Arts: Elèves architecture*, XVII; *présences antérieures au 31 décembre 1895*, Dossier R. M. Hunt, AJ–52–369, Archives Nationales, Paris (I am indebted to Richard Chafee for a copy of the RMH dossier).

38. RMH, Journal, 1844–1848, Oct. 1, 1845 ff., HP; Gibson A. Danes, "A Biographical and Critical Study of William Morris Hunt, 1824–1879," Ph.D. Diss., Yale University, 1949, pp. 12–13; Thomas B. Wyman, Jr., *Genealogy of the Name and Family of Hunt* (Charleston, S.C., 1863), p. 198.

39. RMH, Journal, 1844–1848, Dec. 31, 1845, and Jan. 1, 1846, HP.

CHAPTER 3

1. S. C. Burchell, *Imperial Masquerade: The Paris of Napoleon III* (New York, 1971), pp. 83–84.

2. Theodore Winthrop to his mother, Nov. 22, 1849, quoted in Laura

W. Johnson, ed., *The Life and Poems of Theodore Winthrop* (New York, 1884), pp. 43–44.

3. Henry-Russell Hitchcock, *Architecture: Nineteenth and Twentieth Centuries* (Harmondsworth and Baltimore, 1958; 3d ed., 1968), pp. 48–49.

4. Ibid., pp. 52, 108–109, 49, 50.

5. Ibid., p. 51.

6. For descriptions of the Ecole des Beaux-Arts buildings and facilities see Edwin H. Denby, "The Ecole des Beaux-Arts Revisited," *Légion d'Honneur*, III (Jan. 1933), 125–139, including plans and illustrations; Eugene Muntz, "The History of the School," *Architectural Record*, X (Jan. 1901; spec. issue), 1–33; and Ernest Flagg, "The Ecole des Beaux-Arts," *Architectural Record*, III (Jan.–Mar. 1894), 302–313 (Apr.–June 1894), 419–428, and IV (July–Sept. 1894), 38–43.

7. Denby, "The Ecole des Beaux-Arts Revisited." See also David Van Zanten, "Félix Duban and the Buildings of the Ecole des Beaux-Arts, 1832–1840," *Journal of the Society of Architectural Historians*, XXXVII (Oct. 1978), 161–174. In 1860–1862,

Duban added an exhibit building to the complex, and in 1884 the eighteenth-century Hôtel de Chimay nearby was purchased for the school.

8. Paul Cret, "The Ecole des Beaux-Arts and Architectural Education," *Journal of the Society of Architectural Historians*, I (Apr. 1941), 3–5; Arthur C. Weatherhead, *The History of Collegiate Education in Architecture in the United States* (Los Angeles, 1941), pp. 15–16; Muntz, "The History of the School," 1–11; Richard Chafee, "The Teaching of Architecture at the Ecole des Beaux-Arts," in Arthur Drexler, ed., *The Architecture of the Ecole des Beaux-Arts* (New York, 1977), pp. 61–65.

9. Cret, "The Ecole des Beaux-Arts and Architectural Education," 6; Weatherhead, *History of Collegiate Education in Architecture*, pp. 15–16; Turpin C. Bannister, ed., *The Architect at Mid-Century: Evolution and Achievement*, vol. I of the Report of the Commission for the Survey of Education and Registration of the American Institute of Architects (New York, 1954), p. 87; Henry O. Avery, "The Paris School of Fine Arts," *Scribner's Magazine*, II (Oct. 1887),

387; Chafee, "The Teaching of Architecture," pp. 65–79.

10. Marianne Griswold Van Rensselaer, *Henry Hobson Richardson and His Works* (Boston, 1888), p. 141. Admissions examinations were held twice a year after 1865: see Chafee, "The Teaching of Architecture," p. 82.

11. RMH, Journal, 1844–1848, Oct. 1–Dec. 20, 1845, HP; Chafee, "The Teaching of Architecture," p. 82.

12. RMH, Journal, 1884–1848, passim, HP; *Ecole des Beaux-Arts: Elèves architecture, XVII; présences antérieures au 31 décembre 1895*, Dossier R. M. Hunt, AJ–52–369, Archives Nationales, Paris (I am indebted to Richard Chafee for a copy of the RMH dossier); E. Delaire, *Les Architectes Elèves de l'Ecole des Beaux-Arts* (Paris, 1907), 2d ed., p. 23. Descriptions of earlier *concours* are found in the HC.

13. Flagg, "The Ecole des Beaux-Arts," 313 and 38; Bannister, ed., *Architect at Mid-Century*, p. 88; Chafee, "The Teaching of Architecture," pp. 83–85.

14. Thomas Hastings, "The influence of the

Ecole des Beaux-Arts upon American Architecture," *Architectural Record*, X (Jan. 1901), 70–74; Bannister, ed., *Architect at Mid-Century*, p. 88. Systematic training in drawing was added in the late 1850s.

15. Bannister, ed., *Architect at Mid-Century*, pp. 88–89; Van Rensselaer, *Henry Hobson Richardson*, p. 141.

16. Flagg, "The Ecole des Beaux-Arts," 428. Until the reforms of 1863, all the ateliers were outside the Ecole, but at that time three free ateliers were set up in the Ecole; the *atéliers intérieurs* were considered less prestigious than the *atéliers extérieurs*.

17. Flagg, "The Ecole des Beaux-Arts," 428; Charles Moore, *The Life and Times of Charles Follen McKim* (Boston, 1929), pp. 27–29.

18. Flagg, "The Ecole des Beaux-Arts," 421; John Mead Howells, "From 'Nouveau' to 'Ancien' at the Ecole des Beaux-Arts," *Architectural Record*, X (Jan. 1901; spec. issue), 45–48; Walter Cook, "The Story of Design in the Ecole des Beaux-Arts," *Architectural Record*, X (Jan. 1901; spec. issue), 61; Avery, "The Paris School of Fine Arts,"

402–403; Jean Paul Carlhian, "Beaux Arts or 'Bozarts'?" *Architectural Record*, CLIX (Jan. 1976), 131; Chafee, "The Teaching of Architecture," pp. 83–85.

19. Flagg, "The Ecole des Beaux-Arts," 421; Avery, "The Paris School of Fine Arts," 403; Chafee, "The Teaching of Architecture," p. 83.

20. CCHH, HP, pp. 23, 26, 31.

21. James F. O'Gorman, *The Architecture of Frank Furness* (Philadelphia, 1973), p. 23.

22. Flagg, "The Ecole des Beaux-Arts," 39–40; John Burchard and Albert Bush-Brown, *The Architecture of America: A Social and Cultural History* (Boston, 1961), pp. 248–249; Leland Roth, *A Monograph of the Works of McKim, Mead & White, 1879–1915,* new ed. (New York, 1973), p. 14; Henry-Russell Hitchcock, *The Architecture of H. H. Richardson and His Times* (New York, 1936), p. 45. Louis Sullivan, who studied at the Ecole for about two years, felt that he, unlike most Americans there, had absorbed "the real principles that the school *envelops*." He further wrote in a letter to Claude Bragdon in 1904: "Because of the

teachings of the school . . . there entered my mind, or fructified in my mind, the germ of that law which later, after much observation of nature's processes, I formulated in the phrase, 'Form follows Function.' It was at the school, also, that I first grasped the concrete value of logical thinking; and it is doubtless due to this first impulse that I later developed a scientific system of thought and expression of my own." Quoted in Claude Bragdon, "Letters from Louis Sullivan," *Architecture*, LXIV (July 1931), 8. See also Hugh Morrison, *Louis Sullivan, Prophet of Functionalism* (New York, 1935), p. 46.

23. Flagg, "The Ecole des Beaux-Arts," 40; Cret, "The Ecole des Beaux-Arts and Architectural Education," 12; Anon., "Correspondence," *American Architect and Building News*, V (Jan. 11, 1879), 13.

24. A. D. F. Hamlin, "The Influence of the Ecole des Beaux-Arts on Our American Architectural Education," *Architectural Record*, XXIII (Apr. 1908), 243; Montgomery Schuyler, "The Works of the Late Richard M. Hunt," *Architectural Record*, V

(Oct.–Dec. 1895), 98; Weatherhead, *History of Collegiate Education in Architecture*, p. 21; Ralph Adams Cram, "The Case Against the Ecole des Beaux-Arts," *American Architect and Building News*, LIV (Dec. 26, 1896), 107–108; The Museum of Modern Art, New York, *The Architecture of the Ecole des Beaux-Arts,* An Exhibition Presented at the Museum of Modern Art, New York, preface by Arthur Drexler (New York, 1975), p. 9; Carlhian, "Beaux-Arts or 'Bozarts'?" 132; Franz Schulze, "The Architecture of the Beaux-Arts," *Art News,* LXXV (Jan. 1976), 86–87.

25. The exhibit on the Ecole des Beaux-Arts held at the Museum of Modern Art, New York, Oct. 29, 1975–Jan. 4, 1976, was a remarkable display of drawings, mostly Prix de Rome compositions, and of photographs of completed buildings, which aroused considerable public interest and discussion of the historical and contemporary implications of such work. Many commentators remarked on the beauty of the drawings and of formerly maligned Beaux-Arts-style buildings, which provided aesthetic satisfactions that much twentieth-century modern design did not. On Nov. 11, 1975, at the Museum of Modern Art, a panel moderated by Arthur Drexler, director of the Department of Architecture and Design, and consisting of Henry-Russell Hitchcock, Vincent Scully, Jr., David Van Zanten, Richard Chafee, and Neil Levine, discussed the Beaux-Arts work and, over all, evaluated it very positively. In conjunction with this exhibit, see the Museum of Modern Art, *The Architecture of the Ecole des Beaux-Arts* and Arthur Drexler, ed., *The Architecture of the Ecole des Beaux-Arts.* See also Ada Louise Huxtable, "Beaux-Arts—the Latest Avant-Garde," *New York Times Magazine,* Oct. 26, 1975, 76–82, and Russell Lynes, "A Grand School of Academic Design is Reexamined," *Smithsonian,* VI (Nov. 1975), 78–86.

26. Chafee, "The Teaching of Architecture," pp. 97–109; Barbara Kornfeld Silvergold, "Richard Morris Hunt and the Importation of Beaux-Arts Architecture to the United States," Ph.D. Diss., University of California, Berkeley, 1974, pp. 53–61, 71; Henry Hope Reed, *The Golden City* (New York, 1959; new ed., 1971), pp. 121–131.

27. *Ecole des Beaux-Arts: Elèves: architecture, XVII; présences antérieures au 31 décembre 1895,* Dossier R. M. Hunt, AJ–52–369, Archives Nationales, Paris; Richard Chafee, "Richardson's Record at the Ecole des Beaux-Arts," *Journal of the Society of Architectural Historians,* XXXVI (Oct. 1977), 181.

28. No recognition was given for completion of training at the Ecole des Beaux-Arts before 1867; that year a diploma was authorized for those completing the required course of study and competitions, but it was little used for twenty years: see Chafee, "The Teaching of Architecture," p. 88; James Philip Noffsinger, *The Influence of the Ecole des Beaux-Arts on the Architects of the United States,* Ph.D. Diss. (Washington, D. C., 1955), p. 17; Chafee, "Richardson's Record," 175. Agnes Foster Buchanan, in "Some Early Business Buildings of San Francisco," *Architectural Record,* XX (July 1906), 28–29, wrote that Peter Portois, a Belgian by

birth, who practiced architecture in San Francisco in 1849 and after, was trained at the Ecole des Beaux-Arts, but his name is not given in Delaire, *Les Architectes Elèves.*

29. RMH, Journal, 1844–1848, Jan. 13, 1846, and passim, HP.

30. RMH, Journal, 1844–1848, Aug. 4–Sept. 5, 1846, HP; Jane Hunt, Journal, Aug. 4–Sept. 11, 1846, Jane Hunt, 1822–1903, HP, VII, Pt. I.

31. RMH, Journal, 1844–1848, Sept. 1, 1846, HP; T. H. Bartlett, "Sketch of the Art Life of William Morris Hunt," in *Exhibition Catalogue of the Paintings and Charcoal Drawings of the Late William Morris Hunt, at His Studio, Jan. 19 . . . Jan. 31, 1880* (Boston, 1880), pp. 9–13; Frederic P. Vinton, "William Morris Hunt, Personal Reminiscences," *American Art Review,* I (1880), 49; Lloyd Goodrich, "William Morris Hunt," *Arts,* V (May 1924), 279–280; Albert Ten Eyck Gardner, "A Rebel in Patagonia," *Metropolitan Museum of Art Bulletin,* III (May 1945), 224–227; Edward Wheelwright, *The Class of 1844, Harvard College, Fifty Years after Graduation* (Cambridge, Mass.,

1896), p. 135; Helen M. Knowlton, "William Morris Hunt," *New England Magazine,* n.s. X (Aug. 1894), 688–689; Gibson A. Danes, "A Biographical and Critical Study of William Morris Hunt, 1824–1879," Ph.D. Diss., Yale University, 1949, p. 38; Henry T. Tuckerman, *Book of the Artists; American Artist Life* (New York, 1867), pp. 447–448. For the influence of Couture on William Morris Hunt, see Martha Jay Hoppin, "William Morris Hunt; Aspects of His Work," Ph.D. Diss., Harvard University, 1974, pp. 170 ff. and 190 ff.

32. CCHH, HP, pp. 23, 30, and 71; John Vredenburgh Van Pelt, *A Monograph of the William K. Vanderbilt House, Richard Morris Hunt, Architect* (New York, 1925), p. 6; Lois Fink, "American Artists in France, 1850–1870," *American Journal of Art,* V (Nov. 1973), 36.

33. Van Pelt, *Monograph of the William K. Vanderbilt House,* p. 6; CCHH, HP, pp. 25, 32. See also 1852 Sketchbook, HC.

34. RMH, Journal, 1844–1848, July 3, 1846, and passim, HP; Benjamin Champney, *Sixty Years' Memories of Art*

and Artists (Woburn, Mass., 1899), p. 51.

35. RMH, Journal, 1844–1848, passim, HP; CCHH, HP, p. 26.

36. RMH, Journal, 1844–1848, Apr. 22, 1848, HP, translated from the French with some additions by CCHH, HP, pp. 27–28. See also Jonathan Hunt to Jane Maria Hunt, Feb. 23, Apr. 26, and May 18, 1848, Jane Hunt, 1822–1903, HP, VII, Pt. I. CCHH indicated (p. 28) that John (Jack) was wounded in the 1848 uprising, but this event was not recorded in the RMH Journal, 1844–1848, from which the passage was taken. It occurred, rather, during the coup of December 1851: see L. P. Cazeaux to Jane Hunt, Nov. 25, 1895, Jane Hunt, 1822–1903, HP, VII, Pt. II.

37. Quoted in CCHH, HP, pp. 24–25.

38. Ibid., p. 23.

39. Ibid., p 30; Jane Hunt, Journal, June 13–Oct. 8, 1848, Jane Hunt, 1822–1903, HP, VII, Pt. I, 88–100; Jonathan Hunt to Jane Maria Hunt, May 18 and Dec. 26, 1848, Jane Hunt, 1822–1903, HP, VII, Pt. I; RMH to Jane Maria Hunt, Dec. 13, 1848, Jane Hunt, 1832–1874, HP, VI.

40. Quoted in Johnson, ed., *Life and Poems of Theodore Winthrop*, pp. 44–46; Elbridge Colby, *Theodore Winthrop* (New York, 1965), p. 30.

CHAPTER 4

1. CCHH indicated that RMH took this journey in 1849 (CCHH, HP, p. 30), but the sketches and notes of this trip are clearly dated in an 1850 sketchbook, preserved in the HC.

2. RMH, 1850 Sketchbook, HC.

3. Ibid.

4. RMH, 1851 Sketchbook, HC. On the Crystal Palace, see Patrick Beaver, *The Crystal Palace: 1851–1936; A Portrait of Victorian Enterprise* (London, 1970), esp. chaps. 5–8. During the winter of 1851–1852, Leavitt Hunt traveled to Egypt and the Near East, going over much of the ground that RMH covered the following year. With a sculptor friend from Cincinnati named Baker, Leavitt visited Egypt, going up the Nile, and then went on to the Levant, traveling as far east as Damascus. He took many photographs on his trip and afterward visited Berlin, where Baron Alexander von Humboldt became interested in his pictures

and showed some of them to the King of Prussia. Mary R. Cabot, ed., *Annals of Brattleboro* (Brattleboro, 1922), II, 728, dates this trip in 1850, but see Jane Hunt, undated fragment and Second Memoir in Jane Hunt, 1822–1903, HP, VII, Pt. II, with Leavitt Hunt's comments, establishing the time of his trip.

5. RMH, 1852 Sketchbook, HC.

6. CCHH, HP, p. 29; L. P. Cazeaux to Jane Hunt, Nov. 25, 1895, and fragment in Jane Hunt, 1822–1903, HP, VII, Pt. II.

7. RMH to Jane Maria Hunt, Dec. 13, 1848, Jane Hunt, 1832–1874, HP, VI; Gibson A. Danes, "A Biographical and Critical Study of William Morris Hunt, 1824–1879," Ph.D. Diss., Yale University, 1949, pp. 44–48; Helen M. Knowlton, *Art-Life of William Morris Hunt* (Boston, 1899), pp. 27–28; Susan Hale, ed., *Life and Letters of Thomas Gold Appleton* (New York, 1885), p. 280; Martha Jay Hoppin, "William Morris Hunt; Aspects of His Work," Ph.D. Diss., Harvard University, 1974, pp. 50, 291, 301–302.

8. Danes, "Biographical and Critical Study of

William Morris Hunt," pp. ii–iv, 23, 27–28; Lloyd Goodrich, "William Morris Hunt," *Arts*, V (May 1924), 280; Knowlton, *Art-Life of William Morris Hunt*, pp. 16–17, 21–22; William Morris Hunt, quoted in T. H. Bartlett, "Sketch of the Art Life of William Morris Hunt," in *Exhibition Catalogue of the Paintings and Charcoal Drawings of the Late William Morris Hunt, at his Studio, Jan. 19 . . . Jan. 31, 1880* (Boston, 1880), p. 11; Lois Fink, "American Artists in France, 1850–1870," *American Journal of Art*, V (Nov. 1973), 38–39; Hoppin, "William Morris Hunt," p. 43. RMH noted in an 1852 sketchbook (HC) that he visited his brother Bill at "Barbison" in June 1852; the two brothers traveled together during much of the latter part of that year.

9. Quoted in RMH, "Nile Diary," Foreword. The "Nile Diary" includes selections made by Alan Burnham, focusing particularly on architecture, taken from the original diary of fifty-nine pages compiled by CCHH from RMH's travel diaries. I am indebted to the American Architectural Archive and to Alan

Burnham for the use of this material. All of the original RMH diaries for this journey have not been located, although much of CCHH's version came from the RMH sketchbooks of 1852 and 1853. Where available, the original sketchbook passages were utilized rather than CCHH's often slightly altered version.

10. RMH, 1855 Sketchbook, but containing the Loire châteaux trip, dated July 1852, HC; also 1852 Sketchbook, HC. RMH recorded that he sat for his portrait by Gérôme on June 6 and 12, 1852. See also note 4, above.

11. RMH, "Nile Diary," Foreword and p. 1. See also RMH, 1852 Sketchbook, HC.

12. RMH, "Nile Diary," pp. 2–3; RMH, 1852 Sketchbook and 1853 Sketchbook, HC. Daniel Stuart Elliott was a half-brother of Martha Bulloch Roosevelt, the mother of President Theodore Roosevelt. See Joseph G. Bulloch, *A History and Genealogy of the Families of Bulloch* (Savannah, Ga., 1892), p. 160.

13. John A. Wilson, *Signs and Wonders upon Pharoah: A History of American Egyptology* (Chicago, 1964), pp. 12–13, 23, 36–41.

14. RMH, "Nile Diary," pp. 3–4.

15. Ibid., p. 3.

16. Ibid., p. 6; RMH, 1852–1853 Sketchbook and 1853 Sketchbook, HC.

17. RMH, "Nile Diary," p. 6.

18. RMH, two 1853 Sketchbooks, HC; RMH, "Nile Diary," p. 8.

19. RMH, 1853 Sketchbook, HC.

20. Ibid.; RMH, "Nile Diary," pp. 8–9. The gold ornament and the Acropolis sketches are in the possession of a descendant of RMH.

21. RMH, 1853 Sketchbook, HC; letter of Sept. 10, 1853, quoted in RMH, "Nile Diary," p.8.

22. CCHH, HP, p. 32; RMH, 1854 Sketchbook; Martin Van Buren to Richard Upjohn, Feb. 4, 1854, the American Architectural Archive; Sylvia E. Crane, *White Silence: Greenough, Powers, and Crawford, American Sculptors in Nineteenth-Century Italy* (Coral Gables, 1972), chap. 19. RMH enrolled for *concours* at the Ecole on Aug. 2, Sept. 6, and Oct. 4, 1853; his next registration was on April 4, 1854 (I am indebted to Richard Chafee for this information regarding RMH at the Ecole).

23. CCHH, HP, pp. 32–33; *New-York Daily Tribune*, Aug. 1, 1895, p. 1; "Civis" (William Hoppin), in the *New York Evening Post*, April 5, 1866, wrote that RMH was responsible for both "the original sketch and the working drawings" of the Pavillon de la Bibliothèque.

24. S. C. Burchell, *Imperial Masquerade: The Paris of Napoleon III* (New York, 1971), pp. 83–85.

25. Ibid., pp. 85, 93, 113, 195.

26. Ibid., pp. 91, 95.

27. Rosalie Thorne McKenna, "James Renwick, Jr., and the Second Empire Style in the United States," *Magazine of Art*, XLIV (Mar. 1951), 97–98; Henry-Russell Hitchcock, *The Architecture of H. H. Richardson and His Times* (New York, 1936), pp. 37–38; David H. Pinkney, *Napoleon III and the Rebuilding of Paris* (Princeton, 1958), pp. 218–219. The "Néo-Grec" movement arose in France in the second and third de-

cades of the nineteenth century in the work of leading Beaux-Arts architects, including Joseph Louis Duc, J.-F. Duban, and Henri Labrouste, who hoped to introduce something of the spirit of Greek design into French architecture. Characteristic of Néo-Grec design were incised linear ornamentation, stylized geometric and floral forms, and broad linear relief on pilasters and columns.

28. Pinkney, *Napoleon III*, pp. 80–82; Hitchcock, *Architecture of H. H. Richardson*, p. 27; Burchell, *Imperial Masquerade*, p. 195.

29. Anon., "Royal Institute of British Architects: Presentation of the Royal Gold Medal," *American Architect and Building News*, XLI (July 15, 1893), 41. RMH devoted a considerable portion of his acceptance speech for the RIBA Gold Medal in 1893, rather inappropriately, to a minute detailing of the work on the Pavillon de la Bibliothèque and Lefuel's problems because of what Visconti had begun to do there. The stylistic problems in this, Hunt's first project as a professional, had continued to bother him for nearly forty years.

30. CCHH, HP, pp. 33–34; Anon., "Death of R. M. Hunt," *American Architect and Building News*, XLIX (Aug. 3, 1895), 45; Anon., "Richard M. Hunt," *American Architect and Building News*, XLIX (Aug. 17, 1895), 70; Alan Burnham, "The New York Architecture of Richard Morris Hunt," *Journal of the Society of Architectural Historians*, XI (May 1952), 10; Lefuel, quoted in Henry Van Brunt, "Richard Morris Hunt," *Proceedings of the Twenty-Ninth Annual Convention of the American Institute of Architects* (Providence, 1895), pp. 73–74.

31. CCHH, HP, p. 34.

32. RMH to Jane Maria Hunt, Jan. 14, 1855, and RMH to Jane Hunt, Feb. 22, 1855, Jane Hunt, 1832–1874, HP, VI, 11, 12.

33. RMH to Jane Maria Hunt, Mar. 15, 1855, Jane Hunt, 1832–1874, HP, VI, 13.

34. CCHH, HP, pp. 34, 35; Anon., "Important Trial: Compensation of Architects," *Architects' and Mechanics' Journal*, III (Mar. 9, 1861), 222. Pelham Hayward misappropriated family funds and had RMH's shipment sold in public

auction when the customs duties were not paid. RMH eventually bought back many of his own things from those who had purchased them.

35. CCHH wrote that RMH spent Christmas 1855 in Paris and returned home the following mid-summer (CCHH, HP, pp. 34, 36), but RMH's own testimony in the Parmly trial indicated that he returned to the United States in September 1855 (see Anon., "Important Trial," 224). CCHH dated the letter from which she quoted (CCHH, HP, pp. 34–35) at Christmas 1855 *before* RMH's return. The letter that she quotes—the original has not been located—may have been written at Christmas 1854, when RMH was beginning to make plans for his return, or may have been written to his mother following his return.

36. Van Brunt, "Richard Morris Hunt," 74. CCHH copied this passage almost verbatim into CCHH, HP, p. 36, not attributing the statements to Van Brunt.

CHAPTER 5

1. Anon., "Important Trial: Compensation of

Architects," *Architects' and Mechanics' Journal*, III (Mar. 9, 1861), 222; Russell Lynes, *The Tastemakers* (New York, 1954), pp. 133–134; Royal Cortissoz, "The Basis of American Taste," *Creative Art*, XII (Jan. 1933), 22–24.

2. Frederic C. Jaher, "Businessman and Gentleman: Nathan and Thomas Gold Appleton—An Exploration in Intergenerational History," *Explorations in Entrepreneurial History*, IV (1966), 22–28.

3. Neil Harris, *The Artist in American Society* (New York, 1966), p. 298. See also Calvin Tompkins, *Merchants and Masterpieces: The Story of the Metropolitan Museum of Art* (New York, 1970), p. 27.

4. Rembrandt Peale, *Notes on Italy, Written During a Tour in the Years 1829 and 1830* (Philadelphia, 1831), p. 304; E. C. Wines, *Two Years and a Half in the American Navy* (London, 1833), p. 69; Orville Dewey, *The Old World and the New* (New York, 1836), II, 190–192; William Ware, *Sketches of European Capitals* (Boston, 1851), pp. 135, 139–142; Paul R. Baker, *The Fortunate Pilgrims: Americans in Italy, 1800–1860* (Cambridge, Mass., 1964), pp. 152–153.

5. Harris, *Artist in American Society*, pp. 247–251, 297–298.

6. Anon., "Important Trial," 222; CCHH, HP, p. 44; Rent Rolls, 1856–1860, Archives, New York University; Jonathan Hunt to Jane Maria Hunt, Jan. 20, 1860, Jane Hunt, 1832–1874, HP, VI. CCHH related (p. 44) that RMH occupied "the great lecture hall, with two small adjoining rooms"; however, the New York University Rent Rolls indicate that RMH occupied only the small studio, room 12. The studio rent was payable in quarterly installments, and the tenants were also charged for the use of gas piped into their rooms.

7. Arthur Scully, Jr., *James Dakin, Architect; His Career in New York and the South* (Baton Rouge, 1973), pp. 17–18; Roger Hale Newton, *Town and Davis, Architects* (New York, 1942), p. 230; James H. Dakin to Alexander Jackson Davis, Mar. 13 and 19, 1833, Alexander Jackson Davis Papers (Box 1), Manuscripts and Archives Division, The New York Public Library, Astor, Lenox and Tilden Foundations.

8. Newton, *Town and Davis*, pp. 230–231; Glenn Patton, "Chapel in the Sky: Origins and Edifices of the University of the City of New York," *Architectural Review*, CXLV (March 1969), 177–180; LeRoy E. Kimball, "The Old University Building and the Society's Years on Washington Square," *The New-York Historical Society Quarterly*, XXXII (July 1948), 159.

9. Kimball, "The Old University Building," 160–161; Theodore F. Jones, ed., *New York University: 1832–1932* (New York, 1933), p. 393.

10. Patton, "Chapel in the Sky," 178, 180; Scully, *Dakin*, pp. 17–18. The Morse painting is in the collection of the New-York Historical Society.

11. Kimball, "The Old University Building," 182–183; Edward L. Morse, *Samuel F. B. Morse, His Letters and Journals* (Boston, 1914), II, 37–38.

12. Rent Rolls, 1856–1860, Archives, New York University; Jones, ed., *New York University*, pp. 395–396.

13. Henry Van Brunt, "Richard Morris Hunt," *Proceedings of the*

Twenty-Ninth Annual Convention of the American Institute of Architects (Providence, 1895), pp. 75–76. Much of RMH's architectural library is now located in the Hunt Collection in the library at the headquarters of the American Institute of Architects in Washington, D. C. See also the sketch of room 12, University Building, in RMH, Undated Sketchbook, HC.

14. J. R. Halliday, "Statement of Janitor," September 30, 1856, and Rent Rolls, 1856–1859, Archives, New York University. While Hunt had a studio in the University Building, he had an unexpected visit from the Reverend Henry Ward Beecher, of whose identity he was unaware. The eminent preacher came right to the point: "Young man," he said, "I hear that you have just returned from Paris and are supposed to know a great deal. What do you know about acoustics? I want to build a big church in Brooklyn." "Not a d—— thing," replied Hunt, "and that is as much as anyone else knows." CCHH (HP, p. 128) commented that either RMH's blunt honesty or his language discouraged Beecher and

ended the interview. Beecher's own large and austere Plymouth Church of the Pilgrims, designed by Joseph C. Wells, had been completed just a few years earlier in 1850, and in 1857 the interior was redesigned with fixed aisle seats installed. The church was, however, inadequate in size for the congregation, and in September 1858 it was decided to build a new church large enough to accommodate six thousand persons for services. By 1861, because of insufficient funds, dissatisfaction with the site selected, and the outbreak of the Civil War and general business stagnation, the project for the new building was abandoned. The proposed size of the projected church and the problem of acoustics were discussed at the regular meeting of the American Institute of Architects on April 5, 1859. In 1862, an enlarged lecture room and Sunday school room were erected at Plymouth Church. See Noyes L. Thompson, *The History of Plymouth Church* (New York, 1873), pp. 69, 98–108, 127–128; *Crayon*, VI (May 1859), 150–151 and "Statement of Trustees of Plymouth Church to

Architects," 155–157; Glenn Brown, *1860–1930, Memories* (Washington, D.C., 1931), p. 248; Henry R. Stiles, *The Civil, Political, Professional, and Ecclesiastical History and Commercial and Industrial Record of the County of Kings and The City of Brooklyn from 1683 to 1884* (New York, 1884), II, 1018. See also George B. Post, "Richard Morris Hunt," *Proceedings of the Twenty-Ninth Annual Convention of the American Institute of Architects* (Providence, 1895), p. 88.

15. See the biographical sketch of Winthrop by George William Curtis in Theodore Winthrop, *Cecil Dreeme* (Boston, 1862), pp. 5–19; see also Elbridge Colby, *Theodore Winthrop* (New York, 1965), passim.

16. Winthrop, *Cecil Dreeme*, passim.; see also Wayne Andrews, *Architecture in New York* (New York, 1969), p. 30.

17. CCHH, HP, p. 288. A few years earlier Henry James, Sr., had lived at 21 Washington Place, adjacent to the University Building to the east, and here Henry James, Jr., was born on Apr. 15, 1843. The James family had sailed to Europe on Oct. 19, 1843, within a few days of the

Hunt family's embarkation. Returning to America, they had lived at 58 West Fourteenth Street from 1848 to 1855, when they again went to Europe. Their next return to the United States in 1858–1859 was brief, and they went back to Europe in 1859. They returned to the United States once more in the autumn of 1860 so that William James might study painting with William Morris Hunt at his Newport Studio.

18. Charles Haswell, *Reminiscences of an Octogenarian of the City of New York (1816–1860)* (New York, 1896), pp. 497–501.

19. Charles Mackay, *Life and Liberty in America; or Sketches of a Tour in the United States and Canada in 1857–8* (New York, 1859), pp. 15, 17, 18–21. See also RMH, 1861 Daybook, HP.

20. Edward Pessen, *Riches, Class, and Power Before the Civil War* (Lexington, Mass., 1973), p. 178; Anon., "New-York Daguerreotyped," *Putnam's Monthly Magazine*, I (Feb. 1853), 123. See also Charles Lockwood, *Manhattan Moves Uptown* (Boston, 1976).

21. Edith Wharton, *A Backward Glance* (New York, 1934), p. 55; John Maass, *The Victorian Home in America* (New York, 1972), p. 65.

22. Ellen W. Kramer, "Contemporary Descriptions of New York City and Its Public Architecture *ca.* 1850," *Journal of the Society of Architectural Historians*, XXVII (Dec. 1968), 280; Anon., "New-York Daguerreotyped," 132, 135–136.

23. Anon., "The Modern Architecture of New York," *New-York Quarterly*, IV (1855), 110–115.

24. Harry W. Desmond and Herbert Croly, *Stately Homes in America* (New York, 1903), p. 194; Maass, *Victorian Home*, p. 62; Talbot Hamlin, "The Rise of Eclecticism in New York," *Journal of the Society of Architectural Historians*, XI (May 1952), 3, 6, 8; A. D. F. Hamlin, "The Influence of the Ecole des Beaux-Arts on Our American Architectural Education," *Architectural Record*, XXIII (Apr. 1908), 241.

25. Anthony Trollope, *North America* (Philadelphia, 1862), I, 219–220; Maass, *Victorian Home*, p. 113; Rosalie Thorne McKenna, "James Renwick, Jr., and the Second Empire Style in the United States," *Magazine of Art*, XLIV (Mar. 1951), 97; Talbot Hamlin, "The Rise of Eclecticism in New York," 8; Henry-Russell Hitchcock, *The Architecture of H. H. Richardson and His Times* (New York, 1936), p. 27; Ellen W. Kramer, "Detlef Lienau, An Architect of the Brown Decades," *Journal of the Society of Architectural Historians*, XIV (Mar. 1955), 19. See also Ellen W. Kramer, "The Domestic Architecture of Detlef Lienau, A Conservative Victorian," Ph.D. Diss., New York University, 1957, 3 vols. Francis James Dallett, "John Notman's Mansard," *Journal of the Society of Architectural Historians*, XIX (May 1960), 81, has found that in a house for Harry Ingersoll on the northern outskirts of Philadelphia Notman used a mansard roof on a building with Italianate details in 1848.

26. Harmon H. Goldstone and Martha Dalrymple, *History Preserved: A Guide to New York City Landmarks and Historic Districts* (New York, 1974), pp. 73, 102–104.

27. Anon., "New-York Daguerreotyped," (April 1853), 358; Anon., "The Modern Architecture of New York," 118; Talbot Hamlin, "The Rise of Eclecticism in New York,"

8; Kramer, "Contemporary Descriptions of New York City," 271–272; Winston Weisman, "Commercial Palaces of New York: 1845–1875," *Art Bulletin,* XXXVI (Dec. 1954), 289–294.

28. Goldstone and Dalrymple, *History Preserved,* pp. 136, 138.

29. Kramer, "Contemporary Descriptions of New York City," 274; see also RMH, 1861 Daybook, HP.

30. Harris, *Artist in American Society,* pp. 281–282, 262–263; Pessen, *Riches, Class, and Power,* p. 275; Winifred E. Howe, *A History of the Metropolitan Museum of Art* (New York, 1913), I, passim.

31. Constitution excerpts quoted in Century Association, *The Century, 1847–1946* (New York, 1947), p. 5; Frederick G. Mather, "Club Life in New-York City," in James Wilson, ed., *The Memorial History of New-York* (New York, 1893), IV, 243–244. Although CCHH indicated in the HP (p. 87) that RMH joined the Century in 1857, Hunt is listed in the official history and in the annual lists of members as having been a member from 1855. Laura Roper, *FLO: A Biography of Frederick*

Law Olmsted (Baltimore, 1973), p. 338. In 1891 the Century Association moved to a new clubhouse, designed by McKim, Mead & White, all Centurions, at 7 West Forty-Third Street.

32. CCHH, HP, pp. 87–88; Pessen, *Riches, Class, and Power,* pp. 226–227; Century Association, *The Century,* pp. 12, 44; Henry Holt, *Garrulities of an Octogenarian Editor* (Boston, 1923), pp. 110–112; Russell Lynes, *The Art-Makers of Nineteenth-Century America* (New York, 1970), pp. 314, 410. In 1856, RMH also joined the Union Club, a purely social group having a clubhouse at Fifth Avenue and Twenty-First Street, just opened in April 1855; see also Reginald T. Townsend, *Mother of Clubs: Being the History of the First Hundred Years of the Union Club of the City of New York* (New York, 1936), p. 194.

CHAPTER 6

1. The Rossiter house was built on the north side of West Thirty-Eighth Street on a site now occupied by the Lord and Taylor department store.

2. *Crayon,* VI (May 1859), 154.

3. For discussion of the Rossiter house, see Montgomery Schuyler, "The Works of the Late Richard M. Hunt," *Architectural Record,* V (Oct.–Dec. 1895), 99; Alan Burnham, "The New York Architecture of Richard Morris Hunt," *Journal of the Society of Architectural Historians,* XI (May 1952), 11; Mildred Frances Brenner, "Richard Morris Hunt, Architect," M.A. Thesis, New York University, 1944, p. 23.

4. Anon., "Important Trial: Compensation of Architects," *Architects' and Mechanics' Journal,* III (Mar. 9, 1861), 222–224, and ibid. (Apr. 6, 1861), 9. This series of articles in five issues of the *Architects' and Mechanics' Journal* includes considerable verbatim testimony from the Parmly trial. The quoted statements are taken from these articles.

5. "Important Trial" (Mar. 9, 1861), 222.

6. Ibid. (Mar. 9, 1861), 222, and ibid. (Apr. 6, 1861), 4. In a letter from RMH to his sister Jane, Mar. 3, 1856, RMH wrote: "Mr. Parmly tells me by no means to let the opportunity pass [to assist Thomas U. Walter on the U.S. Capitol] in

case I desire accepting. He thinks that I will be able to go on with Rossiter's house at same time, especially as R. returns in June" (Jane Hunt, 1832–1874, HP, VI).

7. "Important Trial," (Mar. 9, 1861), 222, and ibid. (Mar. 23, 1861), 245.

8. Ibid. (Mar. 23, 1861), 243–245.

9. Ibid. (Mar. 9, 1861), 222, and ibid. (Mar. 23, 1861), 245. That Rossiter had some success as a painter is indicated by the fact that a sale of some of his paintings at the National Academy of Design on December 20, 1860, brought in $5,222.50 (*Crayon,* VII [Jan. 1861], 25).

10. "Important Trial" (Mar. 9, 1861), 222; ibid. (Mar. 16, 1861), 232–233; and ibid. (Apr. 6, 1861), 4, 9.

11. Ibid. (Mar. 23, 1861), 242–243.

12. Ibid.

13. Ibid., 243–244.

14. Ibid. (Mar. 16, 1861), 233–234, and ibid. (April 6, 1861), 1.

15. Ibid. (Apr. 6, 1861), 1, 9; CCHH, HP, pp. 37–43. Hobart Upjohn, "The American Institute of Architects; The Early Years, 1860–1900,"

Brunner Scholarship Award, 1941, MS, p. 97, New York chapter, A.I.A., discusses the Parmly Case but is in error on some of the most important details, including the basis of Hunt's suit and the jury verdict.

16. CCHH, HP, p. 37; "Important Trial" (Mar. 9, 1861), 222; RMH to Thomas U. Walter, Mar. 3, 1856, copy enclosed in a letter of RMH to Jane Hunt, Mar. 3, 1856, Jane Hunt, 1832–1874, HP, VI.

17. Homer T. Rosenberger, "Thomas Ustick Walter and the Completion of the United States Capitol," *Records of the Columbia Historical Society,* L (1948–1950), 285; Turpin C. Bannister, "The Genealogy of the Dome of the United States Capitol," *Journal of the Society of Architectural Historians,* VII (Jan.–June 1948), 2; William Sener Rusk, "Thomas Ustick Walter," *Dictionary of American Biography* (New York, 1927–1936), X, 397–398.

18. Bannister, "Genealogy of the Dome," 1; Rosenberger, "Thomas Ustick Walter," 283; I. T. Frary, *They Built the Capitol* (Richmond, Va., 1940), pp. 174–179.

19. Bannister, "Genealogy of the Dome," 3–4.

20. Ibid., 4; Rosenberger, "Thomas Ustick Walter," 298, 313–317.

21. Bannister, "Genealogy of the Dome," 5.

22. Quoted in ibid., 2–3.

23. Capt. M. C. Meigs, "Reports on the Capitol Extension, Reconstruction of the Dome, and Post Office Extension," in the *Report of the Secretary of War,* in 34th Cong., 2d Sess., Senate Ex. Doc. 6 (Washington, D.C., 1857), pp. 217–227. The report is summarized in Glenn Brown, *History of the United States Capitol* (Washington, D.C., 1902), II, 130, and in Frary, *They Built the Capitol,* p. 298. See also John R. Kerwood, compiler and editor, *The United States Capitol: An Annotated Bibliography* (Norman, Okla., 1973).

24. Quoted in "Important Trial," (Mar. 9, 1861), 223. CCHH, in the HP, p. 37, wrote that RMH received $50 a week.

25. Bannister, "Genealogy of the Dome," 18, 19, 25, 29–30; P. B. Wight, "Richard Morris Hunt," *Inland Architect and News Record,* XXVI

(Aug. 1895), 2. The quotations come from Schoenborn's previously unpublished autobiographical sketches, included in Bannister, "Genealogy of the Dome," as Appendix A and Appendix B, entitled "Sketch of My Education and Connection with the Extension of the United States Capitol, Washington, D.C." (17–23) and "Contribution to the History of the Building of the Capitol Extension, New Dome, Stone Terrace, Etc., with the Particular Object to Show the Services of the Different Men who were Employed in this Work . . . by an Eye-Witness" (23–30).

26. U.S. Capt. of Engineers in Charge of the U.S. Capitol Extension.—To the Secretary of War, in *Capitol and Post Office Extensions; Message from the President of the United States Transmitting a Report from the Secretary of War, in Relation to the Capitol and Post Office Extensions*, 34th Cong., 1st Sess., House Ex. Doc. 139 (Washington, D.C., 1856), p. 68. The line on p. 68 with the information about RMH contains an obvious misprint, for though the entire table clearly deals with the period Jan. 1 to

July 1, 1856, and the other entries explicitly concern that period (except for one other transmutation of 1856 into 1850), RMH is listed as working in Apr. and May 1853. This date is obviously incorrect. Brown, *History of the United States Capitol*, II, 204, includes a table of workers and their compensation, which includes several obvious errors respecting both Schoenborn and RMH. See also Kerwood, *The United States Capitol*, p. 196, and "Important Trial" (Mar. 30, 1861), 254.

27. RMH, 1856 Sketchbook, HC; William and Frank Furness, quoted in CCHH, HP, pp. 37–38; James F. O'Gorman, *The Architecture of Frank Furness* (Philadelphia, 1973), p. 18.

CHAPTER 7

1. Emily Johnston de Forest, *John Johnston of New York, Merchant* (New York, 1909), passim. Research by Annette Blaugrund indicates that James Boorman Johnston was initially the sole client for the Tenth Street Studios.

2. CCHH, HP, pp. 43–44; Montgomery Schuyler, "The Works

of the Late Richard M. Hunt," *Architectural Record*, V (Oct.–Dec. 1895), 99; Wayne Andrews, *Architecture in New York* (New York, 1969), p. 74; Nathan Silver, *Lost New York* (Boston, 1967), p. 142; J. Owen Grundy, " 'This Vanishing Village,' No. 10 in Series," *Greenwich Village News* (Nov. 18, 1960), 5. The Studio Building at 51 West Tenth Street (originally numbered 15 West Tenth Street) was razed in the mid-1950s to make way for the Peter Warren Apartment House. Hunt was also engaged on two or three minor jobs in the winter of 1857: see Anon., "Important Trial: Compensation of Architects," *Architects' and Mechanics' Journal*, III (Mar. 16, 1861), 232.

3. Thomas Bailey Aldrich, "Among the Studios," *Our Young Folks*, I (Sept. 1865), 594–598, and ibid. (December 1865), 775–778; *Crayon*, V (Feb. 1858), 55; Grundy, " 'This Vanishing Village,' " 8.

4. *Crayon*, V (Feb. 1858), 55.

5. Grundy, " 'This Vanishing Village,' " 5, 8; J. Owen Grundy, "10th St. Studios," *The Villager* (Oct. 3, 1946), 7; Aldrich, "Among the Studios,"

775–778; Anon., "Sketchings," *Crayon*, VI (Nov. 1859), 349; Garnett McCoy, "Visits, Parties, and Cats in the Hall: The Tenth Street Studio Building and its Intimates in the Nineteenth Century," *Journal of the Archives of American Art* (Jan. 1966), 1–2; Theodore Sizer, ed., *The Recollections of John Ferguson Weir* (New York and New Haven, 1957), p. 60; William A. Coles, "Richard Morris Hunt and his Library as Revealed in the Studio Sketchbook of Henry Van Brunt," *Art Quarterly*, XXX (Fall–Winter 1967), 224, 227, 232, established through a sketch by Henry Van Brunt of the chimneypiece in Hunt's studio that RMH was there by Apr. 1858. See also William A. Coles, ed., *Architecture and Society: Selected Essays of Henry Van Brunt* (Cambridge, Mass., 1969), p. 12. CCHH, in the HP (p. 44), was in error in writing that RMH set up his studio in the building on Tenth Street in 1859.

6. McCoy, "Visits, Parties, and Cats," 2; Grace M. Mayer, *Once Upon a City* (New York, 1958), p. 422; Elizabeth G. Martin, *Homer Martin: A Reminiscence* (New York, 1904), p. 14; Helene Barbara Weinberg, "John La Farge: The Relation of His Illustrations to His Ideal Art," *American Art Journal*, V (May 1973), 59; Royal Cortissoz, *John La Farge* (New York and Boston, 1911), pp. 109–110; Mary Sayre Haverstock, "The Tenth Street Studio," *Art in America*, LIV (Sept.–Oct. 1966), 49.

7. Aldrich, "Among the Studios," 775–778; quoted in Haverstock, "The Tenth Street Studio," 56; Neil Harris, *The Artist in American Society* (New York, 1966), p. 263; John I. H. Baur, ed., "The Autobiography of Worthington Whittredge," *Brooklyn Museum Journal*, I (1942), 57–58; Sizer, ed., *Recollections of John Ferguson Weir*, pp. 41–65.

8. Mrs. Thomas Bailey Aldrich, *Crowding Memories* (Boston, 1920), p. 57; Anon., "Sketchings," *Crayon*, V (Jan. 1858), 24; Harris, *Artist in American Society*, pp. 268–269.

9. Katharine Metcalf Roof, *The Life and Art of William Merritt Chase* (New York, 1917), pp. 56, 86; Russell Lynes, *The Art-Makers of Nineteenth-Century America* (New York, 1970), pp. 408–409; Haverstock, "The Tenth Street Studio," 54; Mary French, *Memories of a Sculptor's Wife* (Boston, 1928), pp. 161–162; McCoy, "Visits, Parties, and Cats," 8.

10. Helen Mary Knowlton, *Art-Life of William Morris Hunt* (Boston, 1899), p. 125; Martha A. S. Shannon, *Boston Days of William Morris Hunt* (Boston, 1923), pp. 94–95.

11. Turpin C. Bannister, ed., *The Architect at Mid-Century: Evolution and Achievement*, vol. I of the Report of the Commission for the Survey of Education and Registration of the American Institute of Architects (New York, 1954), p. 94; Talbot Hamlin, *Greek Revival Architecture in America* (New York, 1944; new ed., 1964), pp. 43, 66, and passim; H. M. Pierce Gallagher, *Robert Mills, Architect of the Washington Monument, 1781–1855* (New York, 1935), pp. 6–9; Roger Hale Newton, *Town and Davis, Architects* (New York, 1942), p. 27.

12. Bannister, *Architect at Mid-Century*, pp. 94–95; Homer T. Rosenberger, "Thomas Ustick Walter and the Completion of the United States Capitol," *Records of the*

Columbia Historical Society, L (1948–1950), 285; Gallagher, *Robert Mills*, p. 21. Douglass's course on architecture and civil engineering at the University of the City of New York included the study of the nature and use of materials, elements of construction, principles of design, and the planning and construction of public works: see University of the City of New York, *Bulletin* (New York, 1836), p. 13, Archives, New York University.

13. James Wynne, *Private Libraries of New York* (New York, 1860), pp. 269–280; Coles, "Richard Morris Hunt and His Library," 231, 235; CCHH, HP, p. 60; Henry Van Brunt, "Richard Morris Hunt," *Proceedings of the Twenty-Ninth Annual Convention of the American Institute of Architects* (Providence, 1895), p. 76. The Hunt Collection at the headquarters of the American Institute of Architects, The Octagon, Washington, D.C., donated in 1925, includes books from the libraries of Richard Morris Hunt and his sons, Richard Howland Hunt and Joseph Howland Hunt.

14. In 1895, Van Brunt placed the establishment of the atelier in the autumn of 1858 (Van Brunt, "Richard Morris Hunt," p. 75); however, the testimony of George Bradbury at the Parmly Trial (Anon., "Important Trial" [Mar. 16, 1861], 231–232) and the evidence presented by Coles, *Architecture and Society* (above, n. 5) place the beginnings of the atelier in the University Building in 1857. The Redwood Library, Newport, R.I., possesses a letter written by Douglas Smyth, architect, to RMH, May 12, 1883, in which Smyth refers to a newspaper article that had mentioned him as Hunt's "favorite pupil," and he expresses his pride in being known as one of Hunt's students but is not so presumptuous to think that he was Hunt's favorite. The quotation is from A. J. Bloor, "Annual Address," *Proceedings of the Tenth Annual Convention of the American Institute of Architects* (Boston, 1877), p. 29. See also Russell Sturgis, "A Review of the Work of George B. Post," *Architectural Record*, spec. issue (June 1898), 3.

15. George B. Post et al. "Richard Morris Hunt,' *Proceedings of the Twenty-Ninth Annual Convention of the American Institute of Architects* (Providence, 1895), p. 87; Bloor, "Annual Address," p. 29; CCHH, HP, pp. 54–55; James F. O'Gorman, *The Architecture of Frank Furness* (Philadelphia, 1973), pp. 24–25.

16. Quoted in CCHH, HP, p. 46.

17. Quoted in Post, "Richard Morris Hunt," p. 87. The second of these mottos was carved on RMH's gravestone at Island Cemetery, Newport, R.I.

18. William Robert Ware, "On the Condition of Architecture and of Architectural Education in the United States," *Papers Read at the Royal Institute of British Architects*, Jan. 28, 1867 (London, 1867), p. 86; letter of Ware quoted in CCHH, HP, pp. 56–57; obituary account from Buffalo, N.Y. *Courier*, Aug. 3, 1895, Obituaries Scrapbook, HC.

19. Quoted in CCHH, HP, pp. 54–55; Van Brunt, "Richard Morris Hunt," pp. 76–77; William Francklyn Paris, "Richard Morris Hunt: First Secretary and Third President of the Institute," *Journal of the American Institute of Architects*, XXV (Jan. 1956), 15–18.

20. Neil A. Levine, "The Idea of Frank Furness' Buildings," M.A. Thesis, Yale University, 1967, p. 91. Levine quotes the unpublished letter of RMH to William Henry Furness, 1858, on p. 92 and discusses the important influence of Hunt on Furness on p. 33 and passim. See also O'Gorman, *Architecture of Frank Furness*, pp. 18–19, and William Campbell, "Frank Furness: An American Pioneer," *Architectural Review*, CX (July–Dec. 1951), 311–315.

21. Quoted in CCHH, HP, pp. 47–48.

22. Quoted in ibid., p. 50.

23. Ware, "On the Condition of Architecture and Architectural Education," 86; Arthur C. Weatherhead, *The History of Collegiate Education in Architecture in the United States* (Los Angeles, 1941), passim; Henry H. Saylor, *The A.I.A.'s First Hundred Years* (Washington, D.C., 1957), p. 110; Henry-Russell Hitchcock, "Ruskin and American Architecture, or Regeneration Long Delayed," in *Concerning Architecture*, ed. John Summerson (London, 1968), 173 n. 3; A. D. F. Hamlin, "William Robert Ware," *Journal of the American Institute of Architects*, III (Sept. 1915), 384–385; CCHH, HP, pp. 57, 161–162; Ware, quoted in O'Gorman, *Frank Furness*, p. 24. See also C. Howard Walker, "William Robert Ware, 1832–1915," *Harvard Graduates' Magazine*, XXIV (Sept. 24, 1915), 38–40.

24. Hamlin, "William Robert Ware," 384–385.

25. James Philip Noffsinger, *The Influence of the Ecole des Beaux-Arts on the Architects of the United States* (Washington, D.C., 1955), pp. 17 ff.; Weatherhead, *History of Collegiate Education in Architecture*, pp. 2–3, 33–59, 246–248; Ernest Flagg, "Influence of the French School on Architecture in the United States," *Architectural Record*, IV (Oct.–Dec. 1894), 223; letter of Holland Anthony to RMH, ca. 1885, HC; Anon., "The History and Aims of the Society of Beaux-Arts Architects," *American Architect*, XCV (Mar. 24, 1909), 101–102; for a negative estimate of the impact of the Beaux-Arts tradition on American architectural education and practice, see Claude Bragdon, "Made-in-France Architecture," *Architectural Record*, XVI (Dec. 1904), 561–568.

CHAPTER 8

1. Glenn Brown, "The American Institute of Architects, 1857–1907," *American Institute of Architects Bulletin*, VIII (Apr. 1907), 7; Leigh Hunt, "Outline History of the American Institute of Architects," *Michigan Society of Architects Bulletin*, XVI (June 23, 1942), 29; Henry Van Brunt, "Richard Morris Hunt," *Proceedings of the Twenty-Ninth Annual Convention of the American Institute of Architects* (Providence, 1895), 78.

2. Turpin C. Bannister, ed., *The Architect at Mid-Century: Evolution and Achievement*, vol. I of the Report of the Commission for the Survey of Education and Registration of the American Institute of Architects (New York, 1954), pp. 71–72; Barrington Kaye, *The Development of the Architectural Profession in Britain: A Sociological Study* (London, 1960), p. 175.

3. Rawson W. Haddon, "The First Architectural Society in America," *Architectural Record*, XXXVIII (Aug. 1915), 287–288.

4. Bannister, ed., *Architect at Mid-Century*, p. 72; Alfred Stone, "The Early History of the American Institute of

Architects," *Proceedings of the Fortieth Annual Convention of the American Institute of Architects* (Washington, D.C., 1907), 171–172; Alexander J. Davis to Thomas U. Walter, 1841, A. J. Davis Letterbook, 1821–1890, pp. 363–366, Alexander Jackson Davis Papers, Manuscript and Archives Division, The New York Public Library, Astor, Lenox and Tilden Foundations.

5. Everard M. Upjohn, *Richard Upjohn, Architect and Churchman* (New York, 1939), pp. 159–160; Henry H. Saylor, *The A.I.A.'s First Hundred Years* (Washington, D.C., 1957), pp. 4–5; CCHH, HP, pp. 223–224B; William Francklyn Paris, "Richard Morris Hunt: First Secretary and Third President of the Institute," *Journal of the American Institute of Architects*, XXV (Jan. 1956), 16. The thirteen founding members of the A.I.A. were Charles Babcock, H. W. Cleaveland, Leopold Eidlitz, Henry Dudley, Edward Gardiner, R. M. Hunt, J. Wrey Mould, Frederick A. Peterson, J. W. Priest, Richard Upjohn, Richard M. Upjohn, Joseph C. Wells, and John Welch. See also Meyer Berger, "About New York," *New York Times*, Feb. 22, 1957, p. 22.

6. E. M. Upjohn, *Richard Upjohn*, p. 161.

7. Ibid.

8. Quoted in ibid., p. 162; Hobart Upjohn, "The American Institute of Architects: The Early Years, 1860–1900," MS, New York City chapter, American Institute of Architects, p. 28; Leigh Hunt, "Outline History," 29. The nine members taking care of the business on April 13, 1857, included, besides Hunt, who was secretary and librarian, Richard Upjohn, president; Thomas U. Walter, first vice-president; Frederick A. Peterson, second vice-president; Alexander J. Davis; Henry Dudley; John W. Ritch, treasurer; Joseph C. Wells; and Frederick Diaper.

9. Hobart Upjohn, "American Institute of Architects," pp. 28–30, 54–55; E. M. Upjohn, *Richard Upjohn*, p. 162; *Crayon*, IV (May 1857), 151, including the constitution; RMH to Alexander J. Davis, Apr. 11, 1857, Alexander Jackson Davis Papers (Box 1), Manuscripts and Archives Division, The New York Public Library; Rent Rolls, 1857–1859, Archives, New York University. In late 1859, the *Architects' and Mechanics' Journal* became the official public organ of the A.I.A. in place of *The Crayon*.

10. E. M. Upjohn, *Richard Upjohn*, p. 164.

11. Quoted in *Crayon*, IV (June 1857), 183. See also Anon., "The Modern Architecture of New York," *New-York Quarterly*, IV (1855), 105–123, for canons of architectural criticism that are decidedly functional.

12. Quoted in *Crayon*, IV (Dec. 1857), 371–372.

13. Quoted in ibid., (July 1857), 218; see also Calvert Vaux, "Parisian Buildings for City Residents," *Harper's Weekly*, I (Dec. 19, 1857), 809–810, and in *Architects' and Mechanics' Journal*, II (July 21, 1860), 154–157.

14. *Crayon*, IV (Nov. 1857), 339, and V (Feb. 1858), 20, 53; RMH to J. Durand, Sept. 1857, Miscellaneous Manuscripts, Manuscript and Archives Division, The New York Public Library. By 1876, the A.I.A. was considering a full statement to be entitled "How Competitions Had Best Be Conducted": see A.I.A., *Pro-*

ceedings of the Tenth Annual Convention (Boston, 1877), pp. 63–66.

15. *Crayon,* V (Jan. 1858), 20; ibid. (Feb. 1858), 53; and quoted in ibid. (March 1858), 79; RMH to J. Durand, February 9, 1858, Miscellaneous Manuscripts, Manuscript and Archives Division, The New York Public Library.

16. Quoted in *Crayon,* V (Apr. 1858), 109–111.

17. *Crayon,* V (May 1858), 139; ibid. (June 1858), 168; and ibid., VI (January 1859), 15–24.

18. Quoted in ibid., VI (March 1859), 88.

19. Quoted in ibid., 100.

20. Ibid. (April 1859), 122; ibid. (May 1859), 150; ibid. (June 1859), 182; ibid. (Sept. 1859), 278; and ibid., VII (Feb. 1860), 52; quoted in Alexander Harthill, "American Institute of Architects," *Architects' and Mechanics' Journal,* I (Mar. 3, 1860), 169, 172, and ibid. (Mar. 17, 1860), 192. Alfred J. Bloor recorded in his Diary that the 1860 banquet was "a very nice dinner at five dollars a head & kept up till about 12½ o'clock with the usual speechifying,

toasts, songs, etc.": see Alfred J. Bloor, Diary, Feb. 22, 1860, Manuscript Collection, New-York Historical Society.

21. Hobart Upjohn, "The American Institute of Architects," pp. 46–47; E. M. Upjohn, *Richard Upjohn,* p. 167; RMH, 1861 Daybook, Feb. 5, 1861, HP.

22. Bannister, ed., *Architect at Mid-Century,* I, 70.

CHAPTER 9

1. George T. Strong, *The Diary of George Templeton Strong,* Allan Nevins and M. H. Thomas, eds. (New York, 1952), II, 431, 469, and III, 3.

2. Bainbridge Bunting, *Houses of Boston's Back Bay* (Cambridge, Mass., 1967), pp. 86–87, 469; Montgomery Schuyler, "The Works of the Late Richard M. Hunt," *Architectural Record,* V (Oct.–Dec. 1895), 112.

3. CCHH, HP, pp. 65–66; *Minutes of Proceedings of the Board of Commissioners of Central Park, for the Year Ending April 30, 1861* (New York, 1861), pp. 147, 157; ibid., *for the Year Ending April 30, 1866* (New York, 1866), pp. 15, 69; ibid., *for the Year Ending April 30, 1867* (New

York, 1867), p. 99; ibid., *for the Year Ending April 30, 1869* (New York, 1869), pp. 55–56; Alan Burnham, ed., *New York Landmarks: A Study and Index of Architecturally Notable Structures in Greater New York* (Middletown, Conn., 1963), p. 360; Henry-Russell Hitchcock, "Ruskin and American Architecture, or Regeneration Long Delayed," in John Summerson, ed., *Concerning Architecture* (London, 1968), pp. 190–192; RMH, 1861 Daybook, Feb. 22, 1861, HP.

4. Antoinette F. Downing, "The Kay Street–Catherine Street–Old Beach Road Neighborhood, Newport, R.I.," Statewide Preservation Report—N–N–1, Rhode Island Historical Preservation Commission (Jan. 1974), p. 14; Henry-Russell Hitchcock, *Architecture: Nineteenth and Twentieth Centuries* (Harmondsworth and Baltimore, 1958; 3d ed., 1968), pp. 88, 104–105.

5. Downing, "The Kay Street–Catherine Street–Old Beach Road Neighborhood," p. 13; George W. Curtis, "Newport—Historical and Social," *Harper's New Monthly Magazine,* IX (Aug. 1854), 289–319.

6. Downing, "The Kay Street–Catherine Street–Old Beach Road Neighborhood," passim.; Harold Hurst, "The Elite Class of Newport, Rhode Island: 1830–1860," Ph.D. Diss., New York University, 1975, pp. 18–19.

7. Roger Hale Newton, "Our Summer Resort Architecture—an American Phenomenon and Social Document," *The Art Quarterly*, IV (Fall 1941), 297–321; Antoinette F. Downing and Vincent F. Scully, Jr., *The Architectural Heritage of Newport, Rhode Island, 1640–1915* (Cambridge, Mass., 1952; rev. ed., New York, 1967), pp. 130–131, 137, 140–141.

8. Gibson A. Danes, "A Biographical and Critical Study of William Morris Hunt, 1824–1879," Ph.D. Diss., Yale University, 1949, p. 89; Gibson A. Danes, "William Morris Hunt and His Newport Circle," *Magazine of Art*, XLIII (Apr. 1950), 144–150; Henry James, *Notes of a Son and Brother* (London, 1914), p. 63.

9. William Morris Hunt to Jane Maria Hunt, Nov. 1856, quoted in Martha A. Shannon, *Boston Days of William Morris Hunt* (Boston, 1923), p. 43. Hill Top Cottage was located on a large lot at the point where Touro Street comes into Bellevue Avenue. It was built by Henry Schroeder of Baltimore as a one-story house; his son-in-law, a Mr. Gilliatt, from whom William Hunt purchased the house, had the original building lifted up and a new lower story added. During his ownership, Richard Hunt altered the house considerably. In 1915, it was further enlarged and altered to become the Hilltop Inn. In 1923, it was razed and the Viking Hotel was built on the site (*Newport Daily News*, Sept. 7, 1923, p. 13). The Viking Motor Inn now occupies most of the site.

10. Danes, "Biographical and Critical Study of William Morris Hunt," pp. 95–96; Edward Wheelwright, *The Class of 1844, Harvard College, Fifty Years After Graduation* (Cambridge, Mass., 1896), p. 133; CCHH, HP, p. 63. The painting studio was later used as headquarters by the Newport Art Association; it was torn down in 1951: see Bruce Howe, "Early Days of the Art Association," *Newport History*, No. 110 (Apr. 1963), with a photograph of the studio.

11. James, *Notes of a Son and Brother*, pp. 57, 59, 74–75, 77–78; Henry James, *A Small Boy and Others* (New York, 1913), p. 341; Leon Edel, *Henry James: The Untried Years, 1843–1870* (Philadelphia, 1953), pp. 159–166; Downing, "The Kay Street–Catherine Street–Old Beach Road Neighborhood," p. 26. Edward Waldo Emerson recalled visiting the James family in Newport at this time and going to see William Hunt's studio where William James and John La Farge were working; Hunt invited the young boy to see his studio quarters upstairs and brought out paintings and sketches for him to look at: see Edward Waldo Emerson, *The Early Years of the Saturday Club, 1855–1870* (Boston, 1918), p. 467.

12. Edel, *Henry James: The Untried Years*, esp. pp. 55–66; Burton White, *The First Three Years of Life* (Englewood Cliffs, N.J.), pp. 233–236; Maud Howe Elliott, *This Was My Newport* (Cambridge, Mass., 1944), p. 117; M. A. DeWolfe Howe, *Memories of a Hostess* (Boston, 1922), p. 98; Elihu Vedder, *Digressions of V.* (Boston,

1910), pp. 257–258; CCHH, HP, p. 281.

13. CCHH, HP, pp. 62–63.

14. Ibid., obituary clippings concerning CCHH, Charles H. Russell Scrapbook, Manuscript Collection, Newport Historical Society; Robert G. Albion, *The Rise of New York Port, 1815–1860* (New York, 1939), pp. 201, 246, 264, 365; Moses Yale Beach, *Wealth and Biography of the Wealthy Citizens of New York City* (New York, 1845), p. 15. CCHH was born on November 25, 1841 (some obituaries placed her birth date wrongly in 1844) at the Howland home, 12 Washington Square North. Her much older sister Caroline (Carrie), born in 1821, became the wife of Charles H. Russell, a wealthy merchant, who owned the large Newport house "Oaklawn," designed by Richard Upjohn. Her other sisters were Joanna, married to George B. Dorr, Louisa, married to Hamilton Hoppin, Emily, married to Henry Chauncey, and Mary, married to Alexander Van Rensselaer. Joseph Howland was her older brother. See Franklyn Howland, *A Brief Genealogical and Biographical History of Arthur, Henry, and John Howland and Their Descendants of the United States and Canada* (New Bedford, 1885), II, 357.

15. CCHH, HP, pp. 63–64.

16. Ibid., pp. 64–65, 224; Louis S. Auchincloss, "Oaklawn," *Newport History*, XLIV, No. 141, Pt. 1 (Winter 1971), 19–24; Ethel Smith Dana, *Young in New York* (Garden City, 1963), pp. 92–93.

17. CCHH, HP, pp. 65–66.

18. Ibid., pp. 67–68; RMH, 1861 Daybook, Apr. 2, 1861, HP; *Newport Mercury*, Apr. 6, 1861, p. 3; *New York Times*, Apr. 4, 1861, p. 5.

19. RMH, 1861 Daybook, Apr. 12–27, 1861, HP; Jane Stuart Woolsey to Margaret Hodge, Apr. 1861, quoted in Georgeanna Muirson Bacon, *Letters of a Family During the War for the Union* (privately printed, 1899), I, 50; CCHH, HP, pp. 68–69; *New-York Daily Tribune*, Apr. 28, 1861, p. 8; *New York Times*, Apr. 28, 1861, p. 5. Major Anderson stayed at the Brevoort House with his family and dined with William H. Aspinwall on his first evening in New York, April 18: *New York Tribune*, Apr. 19, 1861, p. 8.

20. CCHH, HP, p. 69. Richard's brother Leavitt, who had been married in July 1860, did become involved in the Civil War. He was abroad on his wedding trip when the fighting broke out, but on his return he was commissioned a colonel in the adjutant general's department and served both in Washington, D.C., and with forces in Virginia: see Mary R. Cabot, ed., *Annals of Brattleboro, 1681–1895* (Brattleboro, 1922), II, 728.

21. CCHH, HP, pp. 69–70; RMH, 1861 Daybook, passim, HP; *New-York Daily Tribune*, Apr. 27, 1861, p. 3; N. R. P. Bonsor, *North Atlantic Seaway* (Preston, England, 1955), p. 61.

22. CCHH, HP, p. 70; RMH, 1861 Daybook, May 27, 28, 1861, HP; Jane Hunt, 1822–1903, HP, VII, Pt. II.

23. RMH, 1861 Daybook, Aug. 10–11, 1861, HP; Jane Hunt, 1822–1903, HP, VII, Pt. II, pp. 102–103.

24. CCHH, HP, pp. 70–71; RMH, 1861 Day-

book, Aug. 12–Sept. 25, 1861, HP; 1861 and 1862 Sketchbooks and Account Book, HC.

25. CCHH, HP, pp. 71, 74; RMH, 1861 Daybook, Sept. 27–Dec. 31, 1861, HP; 1861 and 1862 Sketchbooks, HC.

26. Quoted in CCHH, HP, 72–73.

27. CCHH, HP, p. 74; "Water Colours" Sketchbook, HC. CCHH wrote "Probably Yorktown 1884" on this poetic motto, but 1862, soon after Richard Howland Hunt's birth and during the Civil War, seems a more probable date.

28. CCHH, HP, pp. 75–76; 1861 and 1862 Sketchbooks, HC.

29. CCHH, HP, pp. 76–77; *New York Times*, Nov. 9, 1862, p. 8; Bonsor, *North Atlantic Seaway*, p. 38.

CHAPTER 10

1. CCHH, HP, pp. 77, 173. The Collingwood Hotel now stands on the site of the Hunt residence on West Thirty-Fifth Street. RMH never lived in a house of his own design, although he extensively remodeled Hill Top Cottage in Newport.

2. CCHH, HP, p. 86; clippings, Charles H. Russell Scrapbook, Manuscript Collection, Newport Historical Society; RMH, Account Book, 1861–1862, HC, includes besides recipes for punch a "very good" recipe for diarrhea syrup.

3. CCHH, HP, pp. 78, 104.

4. Antoinette F. Downing, "The Kay Street–Catherine Street–Old Beach Road Neighborhood, Newport, R.I.," Statewide Preservation Report—N–N–1. Rhode Island Historical Preservation Commission (Jan. 1974), p. 28. An ink and wash elevation and a plan from the HC are erroneously identified in David Gebhard and Deborah Nevins, *200 Years of American Architectural Drawing* (New York, 1977), pp. 134–135, as an early version of the Griswold house.

5. Antoinette F. Downing and Vincent F. Scully, Jr., *The Architectural Heritage of Newport, Rhode Island, 1640–1915* (Cambridge, Mass., 1952; 2d ed., New York, 1967), pp. 145–146, provides an excellent description of the Griswold house, terming it "Hunt's most American creation" and "perhaps Hunt's best

building." Montgomery Schuyler, who found that the Griswold house "lacks unity and tends to straggle," did admire the carriage porch, "in which the treatment of the material is as idiomatic as it is artistic" and in which the small mansard roof contributed to "a successful and piquant composition." See Montgomery Schuyler, "The Works of the Late Richard M. Hunt," *Architectural Record*, V (Oct.–Dec. 1895), 101.

6. Downing and Scully, *Architectural Heritage of Newport*, p. 145; Vincent Scully, Jr., "Romantic Rationalism and the Expression of Structure in Wood: Downing, Wheeler, Gardner, and the 'Stick Style,' 1840–1876," *Art Bulletin*, XXXV (June 1953), 139, included in Vincent Scully, Jr., *The Shingle Style and the Stick Style: Architectural Theory and Design from Richardson to the Origins of Wright*, rev. ed. (New Haven, 1971), liii–liv; Vincent Scully, Jr., *American Architecture and Urbanism* (New York, 1969), p. 91. Downing and Scully point out (*Architectural Heritage of Newport*, pp. 141, 145, and plates 171 and 172) that Richard Upjohn's Hamilton

Hoppin house of 1856–1857 at Middletown, R.I., had used exterior structural articulation and that the Alexander Van Rensselaer house build next to it subsequently had included some degree of skeletal articulation; since both houses had been built by husbands of Catharine Hunt's sisters, RMH was obviously familiar with them. Hunt later made alterations on the Van Rensselaer house.

7. Maud Howe Elliott, *This Was My Newport* (Cambridge, Mass., 1944), p. 127; see also Bruce Howe, "Early Days of the Art Association," *Newport History*, No. 110 (Apr. 1963).

8. CCHH, HP, p. 78.

9. Helen Mary Knowlton, *Art-Life of William Morris Hunt* (Boston, 1899), pp. 36–37, 47; Gibson A. Danes, "A Biographical and Critical Study of William Morris Hunt, 1824–1879," Ph.D. Diss., Yale University, 1949, p. 148; Martha A. S. Shannon, *Boston Days of William Morris Hunt* (Boston, 1923), illus. on p. 72. Two versions of this painting exist, one held by the Museum of Fine Arts, Boston, and the other by a descendant of RMH; a similar

sketch also exists. See Martha Jay Hoppin, "William Morris Hunt: Aspects of His Work," Ph.D. Diss., Harvard University, 1974, pp. 97–99, 277–278.

10. CCHH, HP, pp. 81–82; Elliott, *This Was My Newport*, pp. 87, 119.

11. Anon., "Looking Ahead," *The Architectural Review and Builders' Journal*, II (June 1870), 689. The painter John Ferguson Weir was living at the Tenth Street Studio Building and was in New York City at the time of the draft riots; his impressions are recorded in Theodore Sizer, ed., *The Recollections of John Ferguson Weir* (New York and New Haven, 1957), p. 37.

12. Wayne Craven, *Sculpture in America* (New York, 1968), pp. 347, 351; Lincoln Kirstein, *William Rimmer, 1816–1879*, Catalogue of Exhibition at Whitney Museum of American Art, Nov. 5–27, 1946 (New York, 1946), pp. 17–24; Lincoln Kirstein, "The Rediscovery of William Rimmer," *Magazine of Art*, XL (Mar. 1947), 94; Truman H. Bartlett, *The Art Life of William Rimmer* (Boston, 1882), pp. 59, 140–141.

13. RMH, 1861 Sketchbook (including drawings from different years), HC; CCHH, HP, p. 86.

14. See above, note 12.

15. CCHH, HP, pp. 83, 89, 107; Henry W. Bellows, *Historical Sketch of the Union League Club of New York* (New York, 1879), pp. 12–15, 39, 43, 63; Laura Roper, *FLO: A Biography of Frederick Law Olmsted* (Baltimore, 1973), p. 215; George T. Strong, *The Diary of George Templeton Strong*, Allan Nevins and M. H. Thomas, eds. (New York, 1952), III, 307, 321. Hunt also was unsuccessful in an 1879 competition for a new Union League clubhouse.

16. CCHH, HP, pp. 83–84; *New-York Daily Tribune*, Apr. 5, 1864, p. 1.

17. *New-York Daily Tribune*, Apr. 5, 1864, p. 1, and Apr. 27, 1864, p. 8; Winifred E. Howe, *A History of the Metropolitan Museum of Art* (New York, 1913), I, 90–91; Strong, *Diary*, III, 427; Georgeanna Muirson (Woolsey) Bacon, *Letters of a Family During the War for the Union* (privately printed, 1894), II, 570; Russell Sturgis, *The Artists' Way of Working in the Various Handicrafts*

and Arts of Design (New York, 1910), II, 605–606.

18. CCHH, HP, pp. 84–85.

19. Hobart Upjohn, "The American Institute of Architects: The Early Years, 1860–1900," MS, New York chapter, American Institute of Architects, pp. 180, 195.

20. CCHH, HP, pp. 86–87.

21. Vestry minutes and M. Fornachon to Alexander Hamilton, Jr., May 7, 1867, Archives, Trinity Church, New York; CCHH, HP, p. 232; Anon., *Churchyards of Trinity Parish, 1697–1947* (New York, 1948), p. 23. "R. M. Hunt, Architect" is incised at the base of the pier on the left of the Drayton Monument. Earlier, after the death in 1863 of Caroline Russell, Catharine's sister, Hunt had designed a monument for the Russell family for Island Cemetery, Newport.

22. For discussion of Hunt's long collaboration with John Quincy Adams Ward, see chapter 18, this volume.

CHAPTER 11

1. Geoffrey Blodgett, "Frederick Law Olmsted: Landscape Ar-

chitecture as Conservative Reform," *Journal of American History*, LXII (Mar. 1976), 877–878; Henry Hope Reed and Sophia Duckworth, *Central Park: A History and a Guide* (New York, 1967), pp. 15–37; Laura Roper, *FLO: A Biography of Frederick Law Olmsted* (Baltimore, 1973), esp. pp. 124–145; Thomas Bender, *Toward an Urban Vision* (Lexington, Ky., 1975), pp. 169–181.

2. RMH, 1861 Daybook, Jan. 8 and 16, Feb. 19, and Apr. 22, 1861, HP; CCHH, HP, pp. 78–81; *Minutes of Proceedings of the Board of Commissioners of Central Park, for the Year Ending April 30, 1861* (New York, 1861), p. 137; ibid., *for the Year Ending April 30, 1864* (New York, 1864), pp. 11, 25; ibid., *for the Year Ending April 30, 1866* (New York, 1866), p. 15; Richard Morris Hunt, *Designs for the Gateways of the Southern Entrances to the Central Park* (New York, 1866); quoted in "Civis" [William J. Hoppin], "Monumental Art in the Central Park: Mr. Hunt's Gateways," *New York Evening Post,* Mar. 29, 1866, p. 1. On later occasions discussion of carrying out Hunt's designs came up, most seriously after his death in 1895, when a

committee of the Architectural League of New York suggested, before the memorial on Fifth Avenue was decided upon, that the gateways would be a highly fitting memorial to Hunt: see *New York Times,* Feb. 15, 1896, p. 5.

3. CCHH, HP, pp. 80–81.

4. See Hunt, *Designs For the Gateways* for plans.

5. Ibid.; Anon., "The Proposed Designs for the Central Park Gates," *Nation,* I (Aug. 10, 1865), 186–188. The names of the gateways varied from one article to another and from time to time; the names in the text are those that Hunt used in his book.

6. *New York Weekly Review,* May 27, 1865, letters to the *New York Evening Post,* and Calvert Vaux to President of the Board of Commissioners of the Central Park, May 1, 1865, all in Central Park Scrapbook, HC.

7. Frederick Law Olmsted to Calvert Vaux, Aug. 1, 1865, quoted in Roper, *FLO,* p. 292; Ibid., 298; Anon., "The Proposed Designs," 186–188; letter of "C.P." and reply in *Nation,* I

(Sept. 28, 1865), 410–412; Anon., "The Central Park Gates," *Nation*, III (Sept. 27, 1866), 255–256.

8. Calvert Vaux to Clarence Cook, June 6, [1865] and undated fragment, Central Park, Box 36, Olmsted Papers, Manuscript Division, Library of Congress. See also Albert Fein, *Frederick Law Olmsted and the American Environmental Tradition* (New York, 1972), pp. 11–13.

9. [Clarence Cook], "Mr. Hunt's Designs for the Gates of the Central Park," *New-York Daily Tribune*, Aug. 2, 1865, p. 8. Clarence Cook in *A Description of the New York Central Park* (New York, 1869; reissued 1972), pp. 156–157, presented many of the same arguments and suggested that Hunt's designs had been too hastily accepted by the commissioners in response "to a pressure from within, for the erection of these gates in particular."

10. Richard Grant White, "Gateways of the Central Park," *Galaxy*, I (Aug. 1866), 650–656.

11. "Civis" [William J. Hoppin], "Monumental Art in the Central Park: Mr. Hunt's Gateways," *New York Evening Post*,

Mar. 29 and Apr. 5, 1866, reprinted in Hunt, *Designs*, pp. 11–29.

12. Ibid. Other positive commentary on the gateway designs was published in the *New York World*, May 9, 1866, and the *New York Evening Mail*, Oct. 6, 1869: see Central Park Scrapbook, HC.

13. Jay E. Cantor, "Museum in the Park," *Metropolitan Museum Bulletin*, XXVI (Apr. 1968), 333–340; Fein, *Frederick Law Olmsted*, p. 11; Montgomery Schuyler, "The Works of the Late Richard M. Hunt," *Architectural Record*, V (Oct.–Dec. 1895), 104.

14. *Minutes of Proceedings of the Board of Commissioners of Central Park, for the Year Ending April 30, 1867* (New York, 1867), p. 99, and ibid., *for the Year Ending April 30, 1869* (New York, 1869), pp. 55–56. Probably Hunt was paid the sum authorized, since the matter disappeared from the Commissioners' minutes.

15. CCHH, HP, pp. 89–90; Harry J. Carman, "Edwin Denison Morgan," *Dictionary of American Biography*, XIII (New York, 1934), 168–169.

16. CCHH, HP, pp. 92, 94–96; N. R. P. Bonsor, *North Atlantic Seaway* (Preston, England, 1955), p. 38.

17. CCHH, HP, p. 96; RMH, two 1867 Sketchbooks, HC; Frederick P. Vinton, "William Morris Hunt, Personal Reminiscences," *American Art Review*, I (1880), 52.

18. CCHH, HP, pp. 96–97; S. C. Burchell, *Imperial Masquerade: The Paris of Napoleon III* (New York, 1971), pp. 124, 128, 136–137; Samuel L. Clemens (Mark Twain), *The Innocents Abroad, or The New Pilgrims' Progress* (New York, 1911), I, 170.

19. "G. A. T.," "The Paris Exhibition," *New-York Daily Tribune*, May 2, 1867, pp. 1, 5; United States Commissioners to the Paris Universal Exposition, 1867, *Reports* (Washington, D.C., 1870), I, 116, 184, and included in Vol. I, Frank Leslie, *Report on the Fine Arts* (Washington, D.C., 1868), 8–16, 38–40; Lois Fink, "American Artists in France, 1850–1870," *American Journal of Art*, V (Nov. 1973), 41.

20. CCHH, HP, pp. 91–92, 97–98.

21. Ibid., pp. 98–100;

RMH, 1867 Sketchbook, HC.

22. RMH, 1867 Sketchbook, HC.

23. CCHH, HP, pp. 101, 103–104; RMH, 1867 Sketchbook, HC.

24. CCHH, HP, pp. 101–104. In 1867, it was announced that Hunt was associated with the firm of Donald G. Mitchell and William H. Grant, landscape architects and rural architecture and engineering specialists, as "advising architect." See advertisement following the text in Donald Grant Mitchell, *Rural Studies, with Hints for Country Places* (New York, 1867), and William B. Rhoads, "Donald G. Mitchell and the Colonial Revival Before 1876," *19c: Nineteenth Century*, IV (Autumn 1978), 80.

CHAPTER 12

1. Royal Cortissoz, "Leaders in American Architecture," *Art and Common Sense* (New York, 1913), p. 391; Anon. [Royal Cortissoz], "Richard M. Hunt," *American Architect and Building News*, XLIX (Aug. 17, 1895), 70; *New York Sun*, Aug. 2, 1895, and *Newport Daily News*, Aug. 5, 1895, p. 6, both Obituaries Scrapbook,

HC; CCHH, HP, p. 125, 257; Henry D. Bates, "The Inside Story of the Founding of the Architectural Review," *Architectural Review and Builders' Journal*, V (Nov. 1917), 255.

2. CCHH, HP, pp. 60–61, 88; Cortissoz, *Art and Common Sense*, p. 391–392; Royal Cortissoz, "The Basis of American Taste," *Creative Art*, XII (Jan. 1933), 23–24; Charles Moore, *Daniel H. Burnham* (Boston and New York, 1921), I, 54, 116; Royal Cortissoz, "Richard Morris Hunt," *New-York Daily Tribune*, Aug. 4, 1895, p. 23. Frank Furness, who intensely admired Hunt, acquired something of his teacher's proficiency in swearing: see Hugh Morrison, *Louis Sullivan* (New York, 1935), p. 36, and CCHH, HP, pp. 52–53.

3. Montgomery Schuyler, "The Works of the Late Richard M. Hunt," *Architectural Record*, V (Oct.–Dec. 1895), 180; Anon., "Richard Morris Hunt," *Critic*, XXVII (Aug. 10, 1895), 90; Henry Van Brunt, "Richard Morris Hunt," *Proceedings of the Twenty-Ninth Annual Convention of the American Institute of Architects* (Providence, 1895), pp.

71–72; Anon. [Royal Cortissoz], "Richard M. Hunt," 70.

4. At their offices in the Rookery in Chicago after 1888, Daniel Burnham and John W. Root employed eighteen regular draftsmen, as well as specialists for plumbing, heating, and ventilation, and as many as sixty draftsmen might be employed for special jobs: see Donald Hoffman, *The Architecture of John Wellborn Root* (Baltimore, 1973), pp. 88–89. Richard Upjohn in the mid-nineteenth century had a more modest office: he kept four draftsmen employed in addition to himself and his son: see Everard M. Upjohn, *Richard Upjohn, Architect and Churchman* (New York, 1939), p. 154.

5. See the annual A.I.A. *Proceedings* for addresses; CCHH, HP, pp. 104, 125, 151, 209, 268; Jane Hunt, 1822–1902, HP, VII, Pt. II; Royal Cortissoz, "Richard Morris Hunt: The Life and Work of a Distinguished Architect," *New-York Daily Tribune*, Aug. 1, 1895, p. 1.

6. For many years Hunt's office staff was headed by Maurice Fornachon, to whom Hunt

frequently referred clients for information on building details. Some of the others working at one time or another on Hunt's office staff were E. D. Lindsay, Frank Furness, E. E. Raht, E. L. Masqueray, Alexander F. Oakey, Sydney V. Stratton, Holland C. Anthony, E. L. Marsh, Frank E. Wallis, Warrington G. Lawrence, Henry Ogden Avery, and Joseph Morrill Wells, who later joined the staff of McKim, Mead & White. William Schickel, a German immigrant who later designed several Roman Catholic churches in New York City, found work in Hunt's office the very day after he had arrived in America.

7. Frank W. Wallis, "A Tribute to Hunt," *American Architect and Building News,* XLIX (Aug. 17, 1895), 72; CCHH, HP, pp. 52–53, 58, 60–62.

8. Quoted in CCHH, HP, p. 59.

9. Louis Sullivan, *The Autobiography of an Idea* (New York, 1924, new ed., 1956), p. 190; Joy Wheeler Dow, *The American Renaissance* (New York, 1904), pp. 120–121; William Francklyn Paris,

"Richard Morris Hunt: First Secretary and Third President of the Institute," *Journal of the American Institute of Architects,* XXIV (Dec. 1955), 247; Frank E. Wallis, "Richard M. Hunt, Master Architect and Man," *Architectural Review,* n.s. V (Nov. 1917), 240. RMH to W. R. Ware, Sept. 18, 1872, General Collection, Houghton Library, Harvard University, is one such letter of introduction.

10. Quoted in Wallis, "Richard M. Hunt," 239–240.

11. Quoted in ibid.; Wallis, "A Tribute to Hunt," 72.

12. D. W. Willard to RMH, April 14, 1883, Manuscript Collection, Redwood Library, Newport, R.I., thanks RMH for sending him another client.

13. Quoted in John V. Van Pelt, *A Monograph of the William K. Vanderbilt House, Richard Morris Hunt, Architect* (New York, 1925), p. 10; Laura W. Roper, *FLO: A Biography of Frederick Law Olmsted* (Baltimore, 1973), pp. 333–334.

14. J. A. S., "Richard Morris Hunt, A Reminiscence and an Ap-

preciation," *Architectural Record,* XXXIX (Mar. 1916), 296.

15. Hobart Upjohn, "The American Institute of Architects: The Early Years, 1860–1890," MS, New York Chapter, American Institute of Architects, esp. Chap. 9; William Robert Ware, "On the Condition of Architecture and of Architectural Education in the United States," *Journal of the Royal Institute of British Architects,* XVII (Jan. 28, 1867), 81–90. The question of architects' fees remained a continuing problem for the A.I.A. in the 1870s and 1880s. In 1879, the Institute published a detailed schedule of professional charges, which was made available for members to provide to clients (see Anon., "Professional Charges," *American Architect and Building News,* VI [July 5, 1879], 8). In the years following, the *American Architect* often carried stories of architects who sued to collect payment of the standard fees and were awarded the customary amounts (see, e.g., *American Architect and Building News,* XXIII [May 19, 1888], 231).

16. Hobart Upjohn, "The American Institute of Architects," p. 198; E.

James Gambaro, "Early Days of the Institute," *Journal of the American Institute of Architects,* XVII (Apr. 1952), 165; Henry H. Saylor, *The A.I.A.'s First Hundred Years* (Washington, D.C., 1957), p. 7; A. J. Bloor, Diary, Mar. 19, 1867, Manuscript Collection, New-York Historical Society.

17. Leigh Hunt, "Outline History of the American Institute of Architects," *Michigan Society of Architects Bulletin,* XVI (June 23, 1942), 31; Turpin C. Bannister, ed., *The Architect at Mid-Century: Evolution and Achievement* (New York, 1954), I, 73; Saylor, *A.I.A.'s First Hundred Years,* p. 15.

18. Gambaro, "Early Days of the Institute," 162; American Institute of Architects, *Proceedings of the Annual Convention . . . 1867* (New York, 1867), p. 8; A.I.A., *Proceedings of the Second Annual Convention . . . 1868* (New York, 1869), pp. 50, 52; A.I.A., *Proceedings of the Third Annual Convention . . . 1869* (New York, 1870), pp. 7, 16–20; A.I.A., *Proceedings of the Fourth Annual Convention . . . 1870* (New York, 1871), p. 26.

19. Arthur C. Weatherhead, *The History of Collegiate Education in Architecture in the United States* (Los Angeles, 1941), pp. 14–15; Hobart Upjohn, "The American Institute of Architects," p. 54; Gambaro, "Early Days of the Institute," 165–166.

20. A.I.A., *Proceedings of the Second Annual Convention . . . 1868,* pp. 10–14; A.I.A., *Proceedings of the Third Annual Convention . . . 1869,* pp. 23, 25–26; A.I.A., *Proceedings of the Fourth Annual Convention . . . 1870,* pp. 24–26; A.I.A., *Proceedings of the Fifth Annual Convention . . . 1871* (New York, 1872), pp. 15–17; Hobart Upjohn, "The American Institute of Architects," p. 82; Anon., "Architectural Libraries, *Architectural Review and Builders' Journal,* I (May 1869), 680–681.

21. Anon., "The New War Offices: Protest of the Architects," *New York Evening Post,* Jan. 9, 1867, p. 3.

22. Anon., "Architectural Competitions for Government Buildings," *New York Evening Post,* Editorial, Jan. 10, 1867, p. 2; Anon., "Payment for Professional Services," *Nation,* IV (Feb. 7, 1867), 111–112.

23. Anon., "The Architects and the Post-Office Commissioners," *New-York Daily Tribune,* Feb. 19, 1867, p. 4; Anon., "Architectural Cheese-Parings," *New-York Daily Tribune,* Feb. 28, 1868, p. 4; I. N. Phelps Stokes, *Iconography of Manhattan Island, 1498–1909* (New York, 1915–1928), V, 1928, 1929, 1931; Rosalie Thorne McKenna, "James Renwick, Jr., and the Second Empire Style in the United States," *Magazine of Art,* XLIV (March 1951), 101; George T. Strong, *The Diary of George Templeton Strong* (New York, 1952), IV, 251, 535; Lawrence Wodehouse, "Alfred B. Mullett and His French Style Government Buildings," *Journal of the Society of Architectural Historians,* XXXI (Mar. 1972), 27; Anon., "The New York City Post-Office," *Builder* XXIX (Nov. 25, 1871), 924, 927; Anon., "New Post Office," *Real Estate Record and Builders Guide,* X (Sept. 28, 1872), 109.

24. Quoted in Winifred E. Howe, *A History of the Metropolitan Museum of Art* (New York, 1913), I, 100–101; RMH to George P. Putnam, Nov. 13, 1869 (H 913), Archives, Metropolitan Museum of Art (MMA), New York.

25. Miscellaneous clippings, Metropolitan Museum Scrapbook, HC; Howe, *History of the Metropolitan Museum*, I, 113.

26. Trustees' Minutes, T1:24, T1:56, T1:65, T1:114, T1:117, T1:257; Corporation Minutes, C1:2, C1:5; and R. M. Hunt, H:913, in Archives, MMA; MMA, *Annual Reports*, 1871–1902; Howe, *History of the Metropolitan Museum*, I, viii, 115–116, 119; Calvin Tompkins, *Merchants and Masterpieces: The Story of the Metropolitan Museum of Art* (New York, 1970), pp. 29–34; *New York Herald*, March 15, 1871, p. 4.

27. Jay E. Cantor, "Museum in the Park," *Metropolitan Museum Bulletin*, XXVI (Apr. 1968), 333–340; Howe, *History of the Metropolitan Museum*, I, 138, 152; Roper, *FLO*, p. 339; Tompkins, *Merchants and Masterpieces*, p. 39; Executive Committee Minutes, May 6, 1871 (E1:97), Archives, MMA.

28. Howe, *History of the Metropolitan Museum*, I, 175–176; RMH to John Taylor Johnston, July 10, 1884, Building Committee Records (B868), Archives, MMA.

29. Howe, *History of the Metropolitan Museum*, I, 143–153; Tompkins, *Merchants and Masterpieces*, pp. 49–58; L. P. di Cesnola to RMH, July 22 and July 29, 1879, HC. See also Elizabeth McFadden, *The Glitter and the Gold* (New York, 1971), passim. "General" Cesnola had actually only attained the rank of colonel during the Civil War.

30. Tompkins, *Merchants and Masterpieces*, pp. 15–16; Howe, *History of the Metropolitan Museum*, I, 192; McFadden, *The Glitter and the Gold*, pp. 187–190; RMH to Waldo Pratt, Nov. 10, 1880, and Charles G. Loring to L. P. di Cesnola, Mar. 19, 1880, R. M. Hunt (H 913), Archives, MMA.

CHAPTER 13

1. CCHH, HP, p. 106; Lloyd Morris, *Incredible New York: High Life and Low Life of the Last Hundred Years* (New York, 1951), p. 113.

2. Franklin F. Hopper, *Three Men—Their Intellectual Contribution to America* (Princeton, 1944), p. 12; Harry Miller Lydenberg, "James Lenox," *Dictionary of American Biography* (New York, 1933), XI, 172; Henry Stevens, *Recollections of James Lenox* (New York, 1951), p. 4.

3. John Fletcher Richmond, *New York and Its Institutions, 1869–1872* (New York, 1872), pp. 364–365; David Bryson Delavan, *Early Days of the Presbyterian Hospital in the City of New York* (East Orange, N.J., 1926), pp. 17–24, 34.

4. Quoted in Delavan, *Early Days*, pp. 22–23, 56.

5. George Rosen, "The Hospital: Historical Sociology of a Community Institution," in Eliot Friedson, ed., *The Hospital in Modern Society* (Glencoe, Ill., 1963), pp. 24–25.

6. John D. Thompson and Grace Goldin, *The Hospital: A Social and Architectural History* (New Haven, 1975), esp. Chap. 5, "The Pavilion Hospital: A Designed Plan," pp. 118–169; Isadore Rosenfield, *Hospital Architecture and Beyond* (New York, 1969), pp. 24–27. James Renwick's Charity Hospital on what became Welfare Island, New York City, built in 1858–1861, was also planned with pavilions and a heating and ventilating system modeled upon Lariboisière, which Renwick had visited: see Rosalie Thorne McKenna, "James Renwick, Jr., and the Second Empire Style in the

United States," *Magazine of Art*, XLIV (Mar. 1951), 100.

7. Delavan, *Early Days*, pp. 51–53; Anon., "New Hospital," *Harper's Weekly*, XVI (Nov. 16, 1872), 901; Anon., "Opening of a Presbyterian Hospital," *New York Times*, Oct. 11, 1872, p. 2; Richmond, *New York and Its Institutions*, p. 365.

8. A. J. Bloor, "Annual Address," *Proceedings of the Tenth Annual Convention of the American Institute of Architects* (Boston, 1877), p. 23; Montgomery Schuyler, "The Works of the Late Richard M. Hunt," *Architectural Record*, V (Oct.–Dec. 1895), 104–105; Montgomery Schuyler, "The Architecture of American Colleges: Yale," *Architectural Record*, XXVI (Dec. 1909), 411–412.

9. Hopper, *Three Men*, pp. 12–14; Phyllis Dain, *The New York Public Library: A History of Its Founding and Early Years* (New York, 1972), p. 11; Anon., "The Lenox Library, New York," *The Architectural Review and American Builders' Journal*, II (Feb. 1870), 483; James G. Wilson, "The Lenox Library," in *Memorial History of the City of New York* (New York, 1893), IV, 88–96; Ethel Nathalie Dana, *Young in New York* (Garden City, 1963), p. 26.

10. Harry Miller Lydenberg, *History of the New York Public Library: Astor, Lenox, and Tilden Foundations* (New York, 1923), pp. 100–104; Dain, *New York Public Library*, p. 12; James Lenox to RMH, Jan. 15, 1875, autograph file, HP.

11. Anon., "The Lenox Library," *The New-York Sketch-Book of Architecture*, III (Apr. 1876), 1–2; Anon., "The Lenox Library," *New York Illustrated* (1891), pp. 46–47. In the Lenox Library, as in most of his other public and commercial buildings, RMH employed the firm of J. D. Clarke, 276 Water Street, New York City, for design and installation of heating and ventilating apparatus: see Anon., "Steam Heating," *Architectural Record*, V (Oct.–Dec. 1895), 196–197.

12. Wilson, "The Lenox Library," IV, 88; Anon., "New York Architecture," *New York Times*, July 5, 1873, p. 2; Montgomery Schuyler, *American Architecture and Other Writings*, ed. by William H. Jordy and Ralph Coe (Cambridge, Mass., 1961), pp. 76–77; Talbot Hamlin, *The American Spirit in Architecture* (New Haven, 1926), p. 174; M. G. Van Rensselaer, "Recent Architecture in America: Public Buildings I," *Century Magazine*, XXVIII (May 1884), 66; Herbert Croly, "The Work of Richard Morris Hunt," *Architectural Record*, LIX (Jan. 1926), 88; Miscell. Clippings, Sept. 1877, HC; A. J. Davis to James Donalson, n.d., Alexander Jackson Davis Papers (Box 1), Manuscripts and Archives Division, The New York Public Library, Astor, Lenox and Tilden Foundations; Schuyler, "The Works of the Late Richard M. Hunt," 109, 112. See chapter 4, note 27, this volume, on Néo-Grec ornamentation. Néo-Grec ornamentation became widely used on cast-iron façades in the 1870s and 1880s. See A. D. F. Hamlin, "Modern French Architecture," *Architectural Record*, X (Oct. 1900), 152; N.Y.C. Landmarks Preservation Commission, *SoHo Cast-Iron Historic District Designation Report* (New York, 1973), p. 13; Alan Burnham, ed., *New York Landmarks: A Study and Index of Notable Structures in Greater New York* (Middletown, Conn., 1963), pp. 42–43.

13. Dain, *New York Public Library*, pp. 340–341; Lydenberg, *History of the New York Public Library*, pp. 390, 398; Anon., "Lenox Library Building Controversy a Closed Incident," *American Architect*, CII (July 3, 1912), 7–8; Anon., "A Last Word on the Lenox Library," *Architectural Record*, XXXII (Dec. 1912), 580–581.

14. Stevens, *Recollections of James Lenox*, pp. 110–111; CCHH, HP, pp. 126–127; E. L. Stevenson, *Terrestrial and Celestial Globes* (New Haven, 1921), I, 73–74. The Hunt-Lenox Globe is often considered "the oldest extant post-Columbian globe" (Stevenson, I, 73). On the globe, South America is drawn as a large island, while in place of North America, there are scattered islands.

15. Anon., *Addresses at the Laying of the Corner Stone of the Divinity Hall of the Theological Department of Yale College, Sept. 22, 1869* (New Haven, 1869), passim; "Records of the Corporation at Yale," July 1869, Manuscript Division, Yale University Library; George E. Day, "The East and West Divinity Halls and The Marquand Chapel," in William L.

Kingsley, ed., *Yale College: A Sketch of Its History* (New York, 1879), II, 51–53; Anon., "The New Hall of the Theological Department of Yale College," *The College Courant*, V (Dec. 25, 1869), 381–382.

16. Anon., "The New Hall of the Theological Department," 381–382; Day, "The East and West Divinity Halls," II, 51–53; Miscellany Scrapbook, HC.

17. "Yale Old and New," XXXVIII, 106, Scrapbook, Manuscript Division, Yale University Library; Schuyler, "The Works of the Late Richard M. Hunt," 104; Schuyler, "The Architecture of American Colleges: Yale," 412; Henry-Russell Hitchcock, *Architecture: Nineteenth and Twentieth Centuries* (Harmondsworth and Baltimore, 1958; 3d ed., 1968), pp. 192–193; Henry-Russell Hitchcock, *The Architecture of H. H. Richardson and His Times* (New York, 1936), p. 94. East Divinity Hall was renamed Edwards Hall in 1909. It was razed in July 1931, and Calhoun College was erected on the site: see *Yale Alumni Weekly* (Oct. 2, 1931), 10.

18. Day, "The East and West Divinity Halls," II,

51–53. The Marquand Chapel was razed in 1931, and Calhoun College was erected on the site.

19. Schuyler, "The Works of the Late Richard M. Hunt," 112–113; Schuyler, "The Architecture of American Colleges: Yale," 416. Scroll and Key Hall is still standing and in use.

20. Thelma Robins Brown, "Memorial Chapel: The Culmination of the Development of the Campus of Hampton Institute, Hampton, Virginia, 1867–1887," M.A. Thesis, Faculty of the School of Architecture, University of Virginia, May 1971, pp. 1–13; Helen W. Ludlow, "The Hampton Normal and Agricultural Institute," *Harper's New Monthly Magazine*, XLVII (Oct. 1873), 672–685.

21. Brown, "Memorial Chapel," pp. 126–142; Ludlow, "The Hampton Normal and Agricultural Institute," 674–676; CCHH, HP, 105–106.

22. Brown, "Memorial Chapel," pp. 166–175.

23. Ibid., pp. 144–155. The total cost of Virginia Hall was $88,136.

24. Ibid., pp. 156–161.

25. Anne L. Austin, *The Woolsey Sisters of New York* (Philadelphia, 1971), pp. 22–23, 145, 161; Georgeanna Muirson (Woolsey) Bacon, *Letters of a Family during the War for the Union* (privately printed, 1894), passim; Frank Hasbrouck, ed., *History of Dutchess County, New York* (Poughkeepsie, 1909), p. 323; *Joseph Howland: In Memoriam* (n.p., n.d.); J. E. Spingarn, "Henry Winthrop Sargent and the Early History of Landscape Gardening and Ornamental Horticulture in Dutchess County, New York," *Year Book of the Dutchess County Historical Society, 1937* (n.p., 1937), XXII, 61–62.

26. CCHH, HP, p. 127; Spingarn, *loc. cit.*, and Carole Rifkind and Carol Levine, *Mansions, Mills, and Main Streets* (New York, 1975), pp. 31–32 both attribute the main body of Tioranda to RMH, but a letter of Dr. Jonathan Slocum, Physician in Charge of Craig House to the author, Dec. 2, 1976, with enclosures from Francis R. Kowsky, who discovered a notice in the *Architects' and Mechanics' Journal*, I (Mar. 17, 1860), 192, names Frederick C. Withers as architect of the mansion.

27. Quoted in *Fishkill Standard*, June 22 and Aug. 3 and 10, 1872.

28. Patricia H. McGurk "The History of the Howland Circulating Library, 1872–1971," pamphlet (n.p., n.d.), pp. 2–3; quoted in Patricia H. McGurk, "The Howland Library," in *Beacon Golden Jubilee, June 1–8, 1963, Souvenir Program* (n.p., [1963]), pp. 8–9.

29. *Joseph Howland: In Memoriam*, pp. 54–55; Hasbrouck, ed., *History of Dutchess County*, pp. 332–333.

30. *Fishkill Standard*, July 20, 1872; CCHH, HP, p. 123.

31. Clippings, Miscellany Scrapbook, HC; Schuyler, *American Architecture*, pp. 532–533.

CHAPTER 14

1. *Crayon*, IV (July 1857), 218.

2. Thomas W. Ennis, "New York's Original Apartment House: A Model of Gracious Living for 88 Years," *New York Times*, Sept. 22, 1957, Sec. VIII, pp. 1, 8; *New York Daily News*, June 30, 1957, p. 58; Robert N. Cool, "No House Big Enough for Two Families," *New York Herald Tribune*, Sept. 10, 1939, Sec. II, p. 5; Anon., "Parisian 'Flats,'" *Appletons' Journal of Literature, Science and Art*, VI (Nov. 18, 1871), 562; James H. Richardson, "New Homes of New York," *Scribner's Monthly*, VIII (May 1874), 67–68 (Richardson stated that Hunt had designed a small apartment house on Wooster Street, N.Y.C., some twenty years earlier); Lloyd Morris, *Incredible New York* (New York, 1951), pp. 109–110; miscellaneous clippings, Museum of the City of New York; E. T. Littell, "Club Chambers and Apartment Houses," *American Architect and Building News*, I (Feb. 19, 1876), 59–60.

3. New Buildings Dockets file (NBD), No. 562 of 1869, New York City Buildings Department, Municipal Building, N.Y.C.

4. Cool, "No House Big Enough," p. 5; John I. H. Baur, ed., "The Autobiography of Worthington Whittredge," *Brooklyn Museum Journal*, I (1940), 65.

5. "Annual Report of the Superintendent of Buildings for the Year 1869," *New York City, Borough of Manhattan Buildings Bureau . . .*

Reports (New York, 1862–1872), pp. 570–572; CCHH, HP, p. 114; Charles H. Israels, "New York Apartment Houses," *Architectural Record*, XI (July 1901), 477; Cool, "No House Big Enough," p. 5; Ennis, "New York's Original Apartment House," pp. 1, 8; C. D. Loring, "Stuyvesant Apartments," *American Builder and Journal of Art*, I (Dec. 1869), 232–233. The actual cost of the Stuyvesant Building was $165,858.62, and Hunt received a commission of $4,500 for his work, indicating that he did not provide full working drawings or superintendence. In 1870–1871, gross income on the apartments was $24,091.98, less $5,781.27 in repairs, bringing a net income of $18,310.71, an excellent return on the initial investment. See Rutherfurd Stuyvesant, Account Book, Avery Library, Columbia University. Hunt also remodeled a triple apartment building at 236–246 East Thirteenth Street for Rutherfurd Stuyvesant: see Rutherfurd Stuyvesant, Account Book, and Alterations Buildings Dockets file (ABD), No. 496 of 1870 and No. 775 of 1873, New York City Build-

ings Department, Municipal Building, N.Y.C.

6. "Annual Report of the Superintendent of Buildings for the Year 1869," p. 570; Montgomery Schuyler, "The Works of the Late Richard M. Hunt," *Architectural Record*, V (Oct.–Dec. 1895), 110–111, indicating erroneously that the Stuyvesant was "the first of the elevator apartment houses"; Mildred Frances Brenner, "Richard Morris Hunt, Architect," M.A. Thesis, New York University, 1944, p. 33; Alan Burnham, ed., *New York Landmarks: A Study and Index of Architecturally Notable Structures in Greater New York* (Middletown, Conn., 1963), p. 44, emphasizing the influence of Viollet-le-Duc's work on this building.

7. Cool, "No House Big Enough," p. 5; Anon., "Parisian 'Flats,'" 562; miscellaneous clippings, Museum of the City of New York; Harmon H. Goldstone and Martha Dalrymple, *History Preserved: A Guide to New York City Landmarks and Historic Districts* (New York, 1974), p. 301; Arthur Gilman, "Family Hotels," *New York

Times*, Nov. 19, 1871, p. 5.

8. Jefferson Williamson, *The American Hotel* (New York, 1930), pp. 41, 154; Israels, "New York Apartment Houses," 477; NBD, No. 811 of 1870; CCHH, HP, p. 123. Hunt also designed a four-story house for Paran Stevens on Thirty Sixth Street west of Madison Avenue, built 1870–1871, and he probably designed alterations for a stable for Stevens on East Twenty-Eighth Street in 1871: see NBD, No. 769 of 1870 and ABD, No. 573 of 1871.

9. Anon., "Parisian 'Flats,'" 562; *New York Evening Post*, Mar. 10, 1871, p. 1; Morris, *Incredible New York*, pp. 109–110; Anon., *New York Illustrated* (New York, 1870), pp. 25–27; Schuyler, "Works of the Late Richard M. Hunt," 111.

10. A lift operated by steam and capable of carrying up to six people had been installed in 1844 at the Bunker Hill Monument in Charlestown, Mass., and warehouses and factories in the 1840s and 1850s often had steam-operated lifts for moving goods and materials. A safety elevator for

passengers was demonstrated by Elisha Graves Otis at the tower at the New York Crystal Palace Exhibition in 1853. More significant was the first practical passenger elevator for public use in a store: at the Haughwout Store on Broadway in New York an elevator to carry shoppers to upper floors was installed in 1857. The Fifth Avenue Hotel had elevator service by 1859, and other hotels soon followed this example. The Equitable Life Assurance Company Building in New York, completed in 1870, was the first office building designed with elevator service to upper stories. The more substantial apartment houses constructed after the Stevens House were usually equipped with elevators. By the beginning of the 1870s the elevator was in wide use, and its impact on building heights was becoming apparent. See Henry-Russell Hitchcock, *Architecture: Nineteenth and Twentieth Centuries* (Harmondsworth and Baltimore, 1958; 3d ed., 1968), pp. 85, 239; Burnham, ed., *New York Landmarks*, p. 126; Henry-Russell Hitchcock, *The Architecture of H. H. Richardson and His*

Times (New York, 1936), pp. 14, 76; Sigfried Giedion, *Space, Time and Architecture* (Cambridge, Mass., 1967), 5th ed. rev., pp. 209–210; Winston Weisman, "Commercial Palaces of New York: 1845–1875," *Art Bulletin*, XXXVI (Dec. 1954), 297.

11. *New York Superior Court: Richard M. Hunt against Marietta R. Stevens, Executrix, etc. and others, Pleadings and Arguments* (New York, 1878), p. 2; Anon., "Hunt vs. Stevens," *American Architect and Building News*, III (Jan. 26, 1878), 25; CCHH, HP, pp. 152–153; NBD, No. 811 of 1870. The five-story brownstone building at 1160 Broadway included a street-level store and was constructed in 1871: see NBD, No. 902 of 1871.

12. *Hunt against Stevens*, pp. 1–13. For the building at 1160 Broadway, Hunt was to receive a fee of three percent of the estimated cost of $44,000, and he had already been paid $300, leaving a claim of $1,020. The projected cost of the Stevens House was $500,000 when the building permit was issued: see NBD, No. 811 of 1870.

13. *Hunt against Stevens*, passim; Joseph Hodges

Choate, *The Boyhood and Youth of Joseph Hodges Choate* (New York, 1917), pp. 178–197.

14. *Hunt against Stevens*, pp. 37–61; Anon., "Hunt vs. Stevens," *American Architect and Building News*, III (Feb. 23, 1878), 61; CCHH, HP, 153–155.

15. *Hunt against Stevens*, 61 ff.; CCHH, HP, pp. 153, 155; *New-York Daily Tribune*, Jan. 18, 1878, p. 3. The Victoria Hotel was closed in 1914 and demolished soon after: see J. A. S., "Richard Morris Hunt, A Reminiscence and an Appreciation," *Architectural Record*, XXXIX (Mar. 1916), 295.

16. Quoted in RMH, "Architecture," *Crayon*, VI (Jan. 1859), 24.

17. New York City Landmarks Preservation Commission, *SoHo Cast-Iron Historic District Designation Report* (New York, 1973).

18. RMH, Miscellany Scrapbook, HC; Anon., "An Iron Store Front on Broadway, New York," *American Architect and Building News*, I (July 15, 1876), 228, illus.; A. J. Bloor, "Annual Address," *Proceedings of the Tenth Annual Convention of the American Institute*

of Architects (Boston, 1877), pp. 15–34; Schuyler, "The Works of the Late Richard M. Hunt," 110; NBD, No. 898 of 1871.

19. New York City Landmarks Preservation Commission, *SoHo Cast-Iron Historic District,* pp. 37–38; Margot Gayle, "Cast-Iron Architecture U.S.A.," *Historic Preservation,* XXVII (Jan.–Mar. 1975), 18; Weisman, "Commercial Palaces of New York," 301; Margot Gayle and Edmund V. Gillon, *Cast-Iron Architecture in New York* (New York, 1974), pp. 86–87, 140–141; Richard M. Hunt, "Address Delivered at the 25th Annual Convention of the A.I.A. at Boston, Mass.," *Inland Architect and News Record,* XVIII (Nov. 1891), 40; NBD, No. 285 of 1873.

20. Schuyler, "The Works of the Late Richard M. Hunt," 110; Anon., "An Iron Store Front on Broadway, New York," *American Architect and Building News,* I (June 10, 1876), 188; James Fergusson, *History of the Modern Styles of Architecture* (London, 1891), 3d ed. rev. by Robert Kerr, II, 354–355.

21. Moses King, ed., *Handbook of New York City* (Boston, 1892), p. 774; George Templeton Strong, *Diary* (New York, 1952), IV, 535; undated clipping, Miscellany Scrapbook, HC; NBD, No. 287 of 1873.

22. Bloor, "Annual Address," 25; Schuyler, "The Works of the Late Richard M. Hunt," 109. The Delaware and Hudson Canal Company Building did not contain elevators.

23. Anon., "The Old and New Tribune Buildings," *New-York Daily Tribune,* May 17, 1873, p. 6, and May 27, 1873, p. 5; Anon., "The Best Lawyers' Offices in the City," *New-York Daily Tribune,* Apr. 7, 1875, p. 7; Anon., "The New 'Tribune' Building," *Frank Leslie's Illustrated Newspaper,* May 1, 1875, pp. 123–124; RMH to Whitelaw Reid, May 12, 1873, Manuscripts and Archives Division, The New York Public Library. The Tribune Building was given the place of honor on the first page of the first issue of the *New-York Sketch-Book of Architecture,* edited by H. H. Richardson (January 1874), I, 1–2; the building as illustrated, however, is one story lower and slightly different from the building as constructed. Apparently from this early sketch some historians have concluded that the Tribune Building had nine stories rather than the ten which were built. The sketch is reproduced in William A. Coles, ed., *Architecture and Society: Selected Essays of Henry Van Brunt* (Cambridge, Mass., 1965), 505. See also NBD, No. 465 of 1873.

24. Anon., "Old and New Tribune Buildings," 6; Carl W. Condit, *American Building Art— The Nineteenth Century* (New York, 1960), 285; Historic American Buildings Survey, *New York City Architecture,* no. 7 (July 1969), pp. 30–44; *New York Times,* May 20, 1966, p. 49; ABD, no. 729 of 1881.

25. Anon., "The New Tribune Building," *American Builder,* IX (Oct. 1873), 235; Bloor, "Annual Address," 24–25.

26. Brenner, "Richard Morris Hunt, Architect," pp. 42–43.

27. Bloor, "Annual Address," 24–25; Schuyler, "The Works of the Late Richard M. Hunt," 106–107; Royal Cortissoz, *The Life of Whitelaw Reid* (New York, 1921), I, 302. Whitelaw Reid,

proprietor of the *Tribune,* who was very satisfied with Hunt's building and saw it as an appropriate symbol for his newspaper, was not entirely happy with the construction superintendence of E. E. Raht from Hunt's office, and he apparently tried at one point to avoid full payment of the agreed-upon fees. The matter was turned over to Joseph Choate, Hunt's lawyer, and a compromise was reached (CCHH, HP, p. 141).

28. Some of the high points of the discussion on the early development of the skyscraper and the Tribune Building include the following: Hugh Morrison, *Louis Sullivan; Prophet of Modern Architecture* (New York, 1935), pp. 140–141, considers the Tribune Building a high building but not a true skyscraper because it had no metallic frame. Winston Weisman, "New York and the Problem of the First Skyscraper," *Journal of the Society of Architectural Historians,* XII (Mar. 1953), 13–21, focuses on the height of buildings as the chief criterion for skyscraper status. If skeleton construction were a criterion, Weisman points out, then

many low buildings would be designated as skyscrapers and many tall buildings left out. The late nineteenth-century conception of a skyscraper was an unusually tall building, and the Tribune and Western Union Buildings were thus "the first skyscrapers in the world." Weisman, in "Commercial Palaces of New York: 1845–1875," *Art Bulletin,* XXXVI (Dec. 1954), 285–302, views the Tribune Building as a skyscraper, with the emphasis on structure rather than on decoration; the building represents an important turning away from the earlier sensuous modes of the commercial buildings of New York City. Henry-Russell Hitchcock, *Architecture: Nineteenth and Twentieth Centuries,* pp. 239–240, reiterates Weisman's view of the two buildings. J. Carson Webster, "The Skyscraper: Logical and Historical Considerations," *Journal of the Society of Architectural Historians,* XVIII (Dec. 1959), 126–139, replies to Weisman, emphasizing for a true skyscraper skeleton construction, as well as height and the number of stories, and suggesting that the Tribune Building does not thus qualify to be called a

skyscraper, though it might be called an early "elevator building" or a "preskyscraper." The Tribune Building was not called a skyscraper at the time it was built. Weisman, "A New View of Skyscraper History," in Edgar Kaufman, Jr., ed., *The Rise of an American Architecture* (New York, 1970), pp. 115–160, changes his earlier position and now calls the Equitable Life Assurance Company Building, by Gilman, Kendall, and Post, 1868–1870, at 130 feet in height, the first skyscraper, since it was the first office building utilizing a passenger elevator. William H. Jordy, *American Buildings and Their Architects,* Vol. III: *Progressive and Academic Ideals at the Turn of the Century* (New York, 1972), pp. 3–5, shows that Chicagoans at the beginning of the 1890s were willing to concede the first skyscraper to New York with the Western Union Building, but that the early New York structures were merely footnotes to the significant later developments in Chicago.

29. CCHH, HP, p. 162; Schuyler, "The Works of the Late Richard M. Hunt," 107; NBD, No. 415 of 1881 and ABD,

No. 142 of 1894. The Guernsey Building is no longer extant.

30. Hunt did other commercial buildings in New York City in the early 1870s including for Royal Phelps, a five-story office building and store at 25 Union Square West, south of Sixteenth Street (NBD, No. 449 of 1872) and a warehouse on Fifteenth Street near Broadway (ABD, no. 526 of 1872); for James Lenox, a three-story store on the east side of Broadway one hundred feet south of Bleecker Street (NBD, no. 286 of 1873); and for the Trustees of Roosevelt Hospital, a warehouse at 21–23 Peck Slip at the corner of Water Street (NBD, no. 261 of 1873). The last building is still standing.

CHAPTER 15

1. RMH to J. F. Weir, June 22, 1871, J. F. Weir Papers, Manuscript Collection, Yale University; CCHH, HP, p. 122.

2. Undated clipping, *New York Times*, Architectural Cuttings Scrapbook, HC.

3. *New York Herald*, May 18, 1869, p. 10; CCHH, HP, p. 126.

4. George Templeton Strong, *Diary* (New York, 1952), IV, 237, 471; CCHH, HP, pp. 122–124; M. E. W. Sherwood, "New York in the Seventies," *Lippincotts Monthly Magazine*, LXII (Sept. 1898), 393–394; Theodore Sizer, ed., *The Recollections of John Ferguson Weir* (New York and New Haven, 1957), p. 61.

5. CCHH, HP, pp. 112–113; Jane Hunt, Journals, 1822–1903, HP, VII, Pt. II, 122.

6. The music room addition to the country house Tioranda in Beacon, N.Y., discussed in chapter 13, was French in inspiration.

7. John Jay Chapman, *Memories and Milestones* (New York, 1915), pp. 87–99; Helen M. Knowlton, *Art-Life of William Morris Hunt* (Boston, 1899), p. 28; Wayne Andrews, "Martin Brimmer: the First Gentleman of Boston," *Journal of the Archives of American Art*, IV (Oct. 1964), 1–4; Martin Brimmer to Sarah Wyman Whitman, Mar. 20, 1889, Archives of American Art (D–32), Washington, D.C., and New York.

8. Clipping from *The Boston Traveller*, 1871, in Architectural Cuttings Scrapbook, HC;

Montgomery Schuyler, "The Works of the Late Richard M. Hunt," *Architectural Record*, V (Oct.–Dec. 1895), 104; see also *American Architect and Building News*, II (Jan. 27, 1877), 28, ibid., XLIX (Sept. 7, 1895), 97, ibid., LI (Jan. 18, 1896), 26, and ibid., LXXX (May 9, 1903), 41–42. The Brimmer houses were demolished in 1903.

9. NBD, No. 579 of 1868. A watercolor elevation at the HC emphasizes the Néo-Grec detail. In 1882, RMH designed a second studio of three stories for Ward at 119 West Fifty-Second Street, N.Y.C.: NBD, No. 442 of 1882.

10. NBD, No. 858 of 1869; CCHH, HP, p. 123; the estimated cost for the Osborn houses was $35,000 and $30,000. Jonathan Sturges occupied the second Osborn house.

11. Anon., "Correspondence," *American Architect and Building News*, V (Jan. 11, 1879), 13; CCHH, HP, p. 151; NBD, No. 483 and No. 484 of 1878.

12. N.Y.C. Landmarks Preservation Commission, *Designation Report: Treadwell Farm Historic District*, Dec. 13, 1967, p. 5; Harmon H. Goldstone

and Martha Dalrymple, *History Preserved: A Guide to New York City Landmarks and Historic Districts* (New York, 1974), pp. 285–287; NBD, No. 648 of 1873. At the same time, 1873–1874, RMH designed a three-story, one-family house, also for Thomas and John D. Crimmins, building contractors, on the north side of East Sixty-First Street to the east of Third Avenue: see NBD, No. 12 of 1873. On the east side of Third Avenue south of Sixty-Second Street and north of Sixty-First Street, RMH prepared plans for the Crimmins for seven other houses, built 1872–1874. These were all five-story, four-family houses, with stores at the street level: see NBD, No. 878 of 1872 and No. 11 of 1873.

13. Anon., "Correspondence," *American Architect and Building News* I (Apr. 1, 1876), 111; David Lowe, *Lost Chicago* (Boston, 1975), pp. 26, 27, 154; John Drury, *Old Chicago Houses* (Chicago, 1941), p. 36; Anon., *Artistic Houses* (New York, 1883), II, pt. 7, pp. 43–47; Charles Moore, *Daniel H. Burnham* (Boston, 1921), I, 27.

14. CCHH, HP, pp. 110–112; *New York Herald,* July 5, 1869, p. 6; the account of the La Farge painting by Jeannette L. Gilder was published in the Boston *Gazette,* Mar. 21, 1885, clipping in HP; John La Farge to RMH, Jan. 5, 1878, RMH to John La Farge, Jan. 22, 1878, John La Farge to RMH, Nov. 10, 1878, CCHH to Jeannette L. Gilder, Apr. 9, 1885, Robert U. Johnson to RMH, Apr. 16, 1885, and Jeannette L. Gilder to CCHH, Apr. 17, 1885, HP. CCHH, writing around 1907, misremembered the chronology of the incident and put the apology by Gilder in 1868 rather than 1885, when it occurred.

15. Clippings, Margery Dean Scrapbook, June 21, 1870, and June 12, 1871, pp. 48 and 92, Manuscript Collection, Newport Historical Society. The house and property were assessed at a value of $46,800 in 1876, on which Hunt paid a tax of $402.48, and $49,800 in 1877, with a considerably lower tax of $338.64: *New York Herald,* Aug. 27, 1876, p. 6, and Aug. 23, 1877, p. 4.

16. Quoted in CCHH, HP, p. 113; Maud Howe Elliott, *This Was My Newport* (Cambridge, Mass., 1944), p. 106; Mrs. Winthrop Chanler, *Roman Spring* (Boston, 1935), p. 121; *New York Herald,* Aug. 3, 1880, p. 3, and July 16, 1881, p. 3. The classic statement about the tedium of the activities of the fashionable world of Gilded Age Newport is in Edith Wharton, *A Backward Glance* (New York, 1934), pp. 82–84.

17. Roger Hale Newton, "Our Summer Resort Architecture—an American Phenomenon and Social Document," *Art Quarterly,* IV (Fall 1941), 303, 313; Antoinette F. Downing and Vincent F. Scully, *The Architectural Heritage of Newport, Rhode Island, 1650–1915* (Cambridge, Mass., 1952; 2d rev. ed., New York, 1967), pp. 144–148; clippings, June 1, 1870, Margery Dean Scrapbook, Newport Historical Society.

18. CCHH, HP, p. 120. The original Jones house can be clearly seen in the illustrations in Downing and Scully, *Architectural Heritage of Newport,* plate 169 (see also p. 140) and in Anne L. Randall and Robert P. Foley, *Newport: A Tour Guide* (Newport, rev. ed. 1976), p. 106, which show an extant Swiss chalet on Halidon Avenue, Newport. Downing and Scully attribute the

Swiss chalet to Leopold Eidlitz in 1854. The chalet, however, clearly does not resemble the Eidlitz design for "rural house no. 4," published in John Bullock, *The American Cottage Builder* (Philadelphia, 1854), opp. pp. 222 and 224, which may have been the source of their attribution. See elevation and detailed plans in Plans File–2–10–3 and "Photograph of the work of Richard Morris Hunt" in the HC. The interesting and complex design of this house deserves further study.

Other early Newport domestic commissions include the Lewis Rutherfurd house, 1869; alterations on the house of Mrs. William F. Coles, 1869–1870; alterations on the William R. Travers (formerly the Thomas H. Hitchcock) house, 1869–1872; the large Richard Baker house, 1870; and the very large T. W. Phinney house, 1871–1872. Highly asymmetrical planning, stick-style porches and wall-surface treatment, and upper mansard stories or hipped and gambrel roofs with the lower surfaces treated as mansards characterized these houses.

19. CCHH, HP, p. 82; Anon., "Letter from Newport," Margery Dean Scrapbook, p. 54, Newport Historical Society; Antoinette F. Downing, "The Kay Street–Catherine Street–Old Beach Road Neighborhood, Newport, R.I., Statewide Preservation Report N–N–1," Rhode Island Historical Preservation Commission, Jan. 1974, p. B–3; Martha J. Lamb, ed., *The Homes of America* (New York, 1879), p. 206; Downing and Scully, *Architectural Heritage of Newport*, pp. 149–150; Schuyler, "The Works of the Late Richard M. Hunt," 111. Waring served as drainage engineer of Central Park, N.Y.C., 1857–1861, and as street-cleaning commissioner of New York City, 1895–1898; he gave a paper on ventilation at the 1877 convention of the A.I.A.

20. Lamb, ed., *Homes of America*, pp. 202–203, including a romantic illustration of the Cushman house as built; quoted in Emma Stebbins, ed., *Charlotte Cushman* (Boston, 1878), p. 234; quoted in Joseph Leach, *Bright Particular Star: The Life and Times of Charlotte Cushman* (New Haven, 1970), pp. 358–359; Elliott, *This Was My Newport*, p. 90; Downing, "Preservation Report," p. 28; *Newport Journal and Weekly News*, Aug. 10, 1901, and June 7, 1912; miscellaneous letters, Charlotte Cushman to CCHH, Autograph File, HP.

21. CCHH, HP, p. 120; Anon., "Letter from Newport," May 1, 1871, Margery Dean Scrapbook, p. 10, Newport Historical Society; Anon., "House at Newport, R.I.," *American Architect and Building News*, I (Jan. 1, 1876), 5; Lamb, ed., *Homes of America*, p. 206; Schuyler, "The Works of the Late Richard M. Hunt," 111; Downing and Scully, *Architectural Heritage of Newport*, p. 150; Vincent J. Scully, Jr., *The Shingle Style and the Stick Style: Architectural Theory and Design from Richardson to the Origins of Wright*, rev. ed. (New Haven, 1971), pp. 40–41. The Appleton house was honored by being the first house pictured in the first issue of *American Architect and Building News*. This house burned down many years ago.

22. George C. Mason, *Newport and Its Cottages* (Boston, 1878), pp. 63–64; Lamb, ed., *Homes of America*, p. 203; Wayne Andrews, *Ar-*

chitecture in New England (Brattleboro, Vt., 1973), p. 124; Downing, "Preservation Report," pp. 28, A–1, B–9; Schuyler, "The Works of the Late Richard M. Hunt," 111; Downing and Scully, *Architectural Heritage of Newport*, p. 150.

23. Winslow Ames, "The Transformation of Château-sur-Mer," *Journal of the Society of Architectural Historians*, XXIX (Dec. 1970), pp. 291–306, provides one of the best architectural accounts of any building that Hunt designed or altered.

24. Ames, "Transformation of Château-sur-Mer," passim; Lamb, ed., *Homes of America*, p. 204; John Maass, *The Victorian Home in America* (New York, 1972), p. 117; Henry-Russell Hitchcock, *Rhode Island Architecture*, 2d. ed. (Cambridge, Mass., 1968), p. 56; Downing and Scully, *Architectural Heritage of Newport*, p. 151. See also Paul L. Veeder II, "The Outbuildings and Grounds of Château-sur-Mer," *Journal of the Society of Architectural Historians*, XXIX (Dec. 1970), 307–317. The Preservation Society of Newport County acquired Château-sur-Mer in

1969, and it is now open to the public.

25. Ames, "Transformation of Château-sur-Mer," passim.

26. Schuyler, "The Works of the Late Richard M. Hunt," 112; Downing and Scully, *Architectural Heritage of Newport*, p. 150; on Dec. 22, 1870, *The Newport Journal*, p. 2, reported that the Travers Block was going up at a rapid rate and when completed would be the largest block of shops in Newport. Travers was said to have won the land on which the Travers Block was built from the owner of a gambling house just to the rear: see Frederick Platt, *America's Gilded Age: Its Architecture and Decoration* (Cranbury, N.J., and New York, 1974), p. 169. Hunt had designed a house for William R. Travers at the corner of Narragansett Avenue and Ochre Point Avenue sometime after 1864; the house was probably incorporated as a wing into the mansion called Whiteholm, which was later demolished.

27. Schuyler, "The Works of the Late Richard M. Hunt," 129.

28. RMH to G. F. Ford, Feb. 13, 1874, Manu-

scripts and Archives Division, New York Public Library; Henry Ward Beecher to RMH, July 1, 1876, Autograph File, HP; quoted in CCHH, HP, p. 129; see illus. in W. C. Beecher and Samuel Scoville, *A Biography of Rev. Henry Ward Beecher* (New York, 1888), p. 631; Beecher's 1855 essay entitled "Building a House" is discussed and partially quoted in William G. McLoughlin, *The Meaning of Henry Ward Beecher: An Essay on the Shifting Values of Mid-Victorian America, 1840–1870* (New York, 1970), pp. 111–112.

29. CCHH, HP, pp. 128–130; Jane Hunt, 1874 Journal, in Jane Hunt, 1822–1903, HP, VII, Pt. II, 135–137. Possibly Hunt also had a slight stroke during his extended illness, for he "could hardly move his hand and arm without help."

CHAPTER 16

1. CCHH, HP, pp. 130–132, 134.

2. Ibid., pp. 132, 136–138; Jane Hunt, 1874 Journal, Jane Hunt, 1822–1903, HP, VII, Pt. II, 128; RMH to Jane Maria Hunt, July 6, 1874, RMH to Jane Hunt, July 12, 1874, and Célestine

Matheu to Jane Maria Hunt, Aug. 4, 1974, Jane Hunt, 1832–1874, HP, VI, 16, 19, and 15.

3. CCHH, HP, pp. 133–134; Jane Hunt, 1874 Journal, Jane Hunt, 1822–1903, HP, VII, Pt. II, 138, 140, 141.

4. CCHH, HP, p. 134.

5. Ibid., pp. 136, 138; miscellaneous sketchbooks, 1874–1875, HC; James Lenox to RMH, Jan. 15, 1875, Autograph File, HP.

6. CCHH, HP, pp. 138–139.

7. Ibid., p. 140.

8. A.I.A., *Proceedings of the Ninth Convention*, Nov. 17, 1875 (New York, 1876), 26; Anon., "Report of the Ninth Annual Convention of the A.I.A.," *American Architect and Building News*, I (Jan. 1, 1876) 1, 3–4. Hunt, as vice-president of the national A.I.A., presided over some of the proceedings in Baltimore in the absence of the president. At this time Hunt was also president of the New York Chapter. At the ninth convention the question of adopting the metric system in the United States was discussed; Hunt spoke in favor of the metric system and stressed the ease of calculations with it, while denouncing "the stubborn resistance of the English" for hindering its use. At this convention it was decided that the new journal *The American Architect and Building News*, beginning publication in 1876, would be recognized as the "organ of publication" for the A.I.A.

9. CCHH, pp. 142–143, with quotation on p. 143, HP; Edward Pessen, *Riches, Class, and Power before the Civil War* (Lexington, Mass., 1973), p. 233.

10. John Maass, *The Glorious Enterprise: The Centennial Exhibition of 1876 and H. J. Schwarzmann, Architect-in-Chief* (Watkins Glen, N.Y., 1973), pp. 23, 28, 34, 41, 43, 85, 88.

11. Ibid., p. 116; Hunt Miscellany, HC. Hunt's friend, George E. Waring, Jr., who acquired The Hypothenuse in Newport, was also a judge at the Philadelphia Centennial.

12. The material in this and the following paragraphs is taken from RMH, "Paper on the Architectural Exhibit of the Centennial Exhibition," in American Institute of Architects, *Proceedings of the Tenth Annual Convention*, X (Boston, 1876), 34–38.

13. CCHH, HP, pp. 146–147, 195. Before the New York Chapter of the Institute on Feb. 1, 1877, Hunt presented two reports from the Committee on Examinations providing recommendations for state and city actions respecting theater safety and fire precautions. The Institute documents were endorsed by the Board of Fire Underwriters and forwarded to the state legislature: see A.I.A., *Proceedings of the Eleventh and Twelfth Annual Conventions*, XI (Boston, 1879), 50.

14. RMH, "The Church Architecture That We Need," *American Architect and Building News*, II (Nov. 24, 1877), 374–376 and ibid. (Dec. 1, 1877), 384–385; CCHH, HP, pp. 149–150.

15. RMH, "The Church Architecture That We Need," 384.

16. Ibid., 385.

17. Quoted in "The Church Architecture That We Need," *Church Journal and Gospel Messenger*, XXV (Nov. 8, 1877), 708.

18. Marianne Griswold Van Rensselaer, *Henry*

Hobson Richardson and His Works (Boston, 1888), p. 74; Henry-Russell Hitchcock, The Architecture of H. H. Richardson and His Times (New York, 1936), p. 169; Laura W. Roper, FLO: A Biography of Frederick Law Olmsted (Baltimore, 1973), pp. 367–370; Walter C. Kidney, "Triumph Over Adversity: The Albany Capitol Building," The Victorian Society in America Bulletin, II (Oct. 1968), 2–3.

19. The proposed changes were published in American Architect and Building News, I (Mar. 11, 1876), pp. 82–83; see also Anon., "Mr. Fuller's Reply," American Architect and Building News, I (Apr. 1, 1876), 106–107; quoted in Anon., "N.Y. Chapter on Albany Capitol," American Architect and Building News, I (Apr. 8, 1876), 113–115; Van Rensselaer, Henry Hobson Richardson, p. 75; Montgomery Schuyler, "The Capitol of New York," Scribner's Monthly Magazine, XIX (Dec. 1879), 166; Roper, FLO, pp. 370–371.

20. RMH et al., "The Experts and the New York Capitol," American Architect and Building News, II (Mar. 17, 1877), 85; Van Rensselaer,

Henry Hobson Richardson, pp. 75–76; Roper, FLO, p. 371.

21. Quoted in Van Rensselaer, Henry Hobson Richardson, pp. 75–76.

22. CCHH, HP, pp. 148, 150–151, 158; New York Herald, Mar. 29, 1878, p. 5; Jane Hunt, 1872–1874 Journal, Jane Hunt, 1822–1903, HP, VII, Pt. II, passim. Jane Maria Hunt was buried in the Suffield, Conn., cemetery. See chapter 14 for the account of the Stevens case.

23. Quoted in CCHH, HP, p. 152.

24. Harvey O'Connor, The Astors (New York, 1941), pp. 167–168. For Frederic Bronson, Hunt designed numbers 140 and 142 Tenth Avenue, built in 1886–1887; number 142 was called "French flats" on the first Buildings Department application and number 140 "apartments." On the second application both were called "French flats," and they were set up for 9 and 18 families respectively (NBD, Nos. 1301 and 1386 of 1886). For Peter T. O'Brien, Hunt designed numbers 226 and 228 East Thirty-Sixth Street, both called "French flats" and both housing 20 families, built

1887 (NBD, No. 458 of 1887). These buildings are extant. For Thomas Riley, Hunt designed a "French flat" for 11 families on the north side of Seventy-Eighth Street, west of Avenue A, built in 1889 (NBD, No. 301 of 1888). All these were relatively inexpensive buildings costing $15,000 or $18,000. The seven four-family houses for Thomas and John D. Crimmins on Third Avenue north of Sixty-First Street were termed second-class tenements (see NBD, Nos. 878 of 1872 and 11 of 1873).

25. CCHH, HP, pp. 159–160, 164; Newport Daily News, Aug. 9, 1879, p 2.

26. Frederic P. Vinton, "William Morris Hunt, Personal Reminiscences," American Art Review, I (1880), 51–54; Gibson Byrd "The Artist-Teacher in America," Art Journal, XXIII (Winter 1963–1964), 131; Gibson A. Danes, "A Biographical and Critical Study of William Morris Hunt, 1824–1879," Ph.D. Diss, Yale University, 1949, pp. 136–137; Thomas Ball, My Threescore Years and Ten (Boston, 1892), p. 306; Gamaliel Bradford, "Portrait of an Ar-

tist," *North American Review*, CCXVII (May 1923), 644, 649–650; Helen M. Knowlton, *Art-Life of William Morris Hunt* (Boston, 1899), pp. 71–74.

27. Albert Ten Eyck Gardner, "A Rebel in Patagonia," *Metropolitan Museum of Art Bulletin*, III (May 1945), 224–227; T. H. Bartlett, "Sketch of the Art Life of William Morris Hunt," in *Exhibition Catalogue of the Paintings and Charcoal Drawings of the Late William Morris Hunt* (Boston, 1880), quoted on p. 14; F. D. Millet, "Mr. Hunt's Teaching," *Atlantic Monthly*, XLVI (Aug. 1880), 189; *New York Times*, Sept. 14, 1879, p. 8; Helen M. Knowlton, "William Morris Hunt," *New England Magazine*, X (Aug. 1894), 697; Danes, "Biographical and Critical Study," p. 133; Lloyd Goodrich, "William Morris Hunt," *Arts*, V (May 1924), 279–283.

28. Knowlton, "William Morris Hunt," 685–705; Edward Wheelwright, *The Class of 1844, Harvard College, Fifty Years after Graduation* (Cambridge, Mass., 1896), pp. 138–141; Jane Hunt, 1873–1874 Journal, Jane Hunt, 1822–1903, HP, VII, Pt. II, 129, 137, 143.

29. Anon., "William Morris Hunt," *Art Journal*, n.s. V (Nov. 1879), 346–349; Knowlton, *Art-Life*, pp. 163–167, 176; Goodrich, "William Morris Hunt," 282; William Morris Hunt, *Talks on Art*, 2d series (Boston, 1884), pp. 85–86; CCHH, HP, p. 157. The capitol assembly roof unfortunately leaked and perhaps William Hunt had not properly prepared his paints, for within a few years large portions of the murals had flaked off. Although RMH and Jane Hunt tried to set up a subscription in 1888 to save and restore the murals, the superintendent of public buildings in Albany refused to remove them or to alter the pace of work of placing a lower ceiling in the assembly chamber, and Hunt's disintegrating murals were hidden from view. In 1937 only tattered, peeling remnants were discovered in the attic above the lowered ceiling. See *New York Times*, Sept. 7, 1888, p. 9, Sept. 9, 1888, p. 5, Sept. 16, 1888, p. 10, Sept. 20, 1888, p. 2, and Sept. 25, 1888, p. 9, and Troy, N.Y., *Times Record*, Nov. 5, 1937, on Roll P75, Archives of American Art.

30. *New-York Daily Tribune*, Sept. 9, 1879, p.

2 and Sept. 10, 1879, p. 5; *New York Times*, Sept. 9, 1879, p. 2, Sept. 10, 1879, p. 1, Sept. 13, 1879, p. 5, and Nov. 17, 1879, p. 5; Marian Hooper Adams, *Letters of Mrs. Henry Adams* (Boston, 1936), p. 181; CCHH, HP, pp. 159–160.

31. Vinton, "William Morris Hunt," 96; *New York Times*, Nov. 17, 1879, p. 5, Nov. 24, 1879, p. 3, and May 1, 1880, p. 5; *American Art News* (Mar. 21, 1914), p. 8.

CHAPTER 17

1. Minutes of the Trustees, Apr. 24, 1878, and Apr. 30, 1879, Princeton Theological Seminary, Princeton, N.J.; George T. Purves, "The Theological Seminary," *Princeton Book* (Boston, 1879), pp. 293–328; William H. Roberts, "Library of the Theological Seminary," in ibid., pp. 329–333; Varnum Lansing Collins, *Princeton: Past and Present* (Princeton, 1931), sec. 123. CCHH (HP, p. 145) believed that planning for the Lenox Library was started in 1876. The houses for professors were also completed in 1879.

2. Purves, "The Theological Seminary," pp. 312–313. One of the

seminary professors' houses still stands today at 31 Library Place. Basically cruciform, the two-and-one-half-story building, set on a rough-dressed stone base, is faced in rich, wine-red brick with courses, lintels, and sills of stone patterning the walls and subtly accentuating the fenestration.

Close to the Lenox Library, at 12 Library Place, Hunt built a house and studio in 1883–1884 for Professor William Miller Paxton. Paxton, who served as a director of the Seminary from 1866 to 1883, while pastor of the First Presbyterian Church in New York City, came to Princeton in 1883 as professor of ecclesiastical, homiletical, and pastoral theology, and served until his retirement in 1902. CCHH, HP, pp. 165 and 171; biographical information, Archives, Princeton University.

3. Minutes of the Trustees, June 23, 1880, Nov. 11, 1880, Feb. 19, 1881, June 20, 1881, June 19, 1882, Archives, Princeton University; *The Princetonian*, VI (July 1, 1881), 43–44; Miscellany Scrapbook, HC; Collins, *Princeton: Past and Present*, sec. 166.

4. Montgomery Schuyler, "The Architecture of American Colleges," *Architectural Record*, XXVII (Feb. 1910), 151–152; Montgomery Schuyler, "The Works of the Late Richard M. Hunt," *Architectural Record*, V (Oct.–Dec. 1895), 120.

5. The Chemical Laboratory, still standing, was also known as the New (later the Old) Chemical Laboratory and the Old Chemistry Building, and was used as an annex by the School of Engineering. It is now called Green Annex. See Minutes of the Trustees, June 17, 1889, and miscellaneous materials, Archives, Princeton University; CCHH, HP, p. 172.

6. Anon., " 'Idlehour,' the Estate of W. K. Vanderbilt, Oakdale, L.I.," *Architectural Record*, XIII (May 1903), 461; CCHH, HP, pp. 165, 197, 206. The RMH Idlehour gatehouses are extant: see illus. in Carole Rifkind and Carol Levine, *Mansions, Mills, and Main Streets* (New York, 1975), pp. 129–130.

7. "Program of Consecration," June 22, 1880, in Miscellany Scrapbook, HC; Schuyler, "The Works of the Late Richard M. Hunt," 120–122; Rifkind and

Levine, *Mansions, Mills, and Main Streets,* p. 128. Another church commission was the Presbyterian Church in Palatka, Florida (1880), a gift of Robert Lenox Kennedy of New York City; the Palatka Church was destroyed by a fire in 1882 and immediately rebuilt from Hunt's original plans with minor modifications (letter to author from Rev. Arthur Wilson Rideout, First Presbyterian Church, Palatka, Fla., Sept. 17, 1975). In 1891, RMH rebuilt the Belmont Chapel, Island Cemetery, Newport, R.I., in a Romanesque style utilizing roughly dressed stone richly colored in browns and buff. The Belmont Chapel, extant, has a memorial window by Eugène Oudinot. RMH also entered competitions for several churches but was unsuccessful (see also Appendix).

8. John V. Van Pelt, *A Monograph of the William K. Vanderbilt House* (New York, 1925), pp. 13–15; NBD, No. 898 of 1879 and ABD, Nos. 26 and 1250 of 1887. The house and decorations reportedly cost some $3 million. Henry-Russell Hitchcock suggests that RMH owed his use of "correct" Francis I detail

on the W. K. Vanderbilt House to Léon Palustre, *La Renaissance en France,* the first part of which had just been published in 1877. The second volume was published in 1882. Whether RMH yet had a copy of the first volume of this work in 1878 may be questioned. The copy in the HC came from the library of his son Joseph Howland Hunt and not RMH. (Henry-Russell Hitchcock, *The Architecture of H. H. Richardson and His Times* [New York, 1936], p. 182.) Hunt hit on a style in the W. K. Vanderbilt house which combined the picturesqueness popular at the time with the grandeur and elegance associated with Renaissance architecture (see Mildred Frances Brenner, "Richard Morris Hunt, Architect," M.A. thesis, N.Y.U., 1944, p. 62).

9. Frank Crowninshield, "The House of Vanderbilt: The Closing of Their Fifth Avenue Mansion Ends a Long Period of Elegance and Gala," *Vogue,* XCVIII (Nov. 15, 1941), 94; William A. Croffut, *The Vanderbilts and the Story of Their Fortune* (Chicago, 1886), pp. 264–265; Consuelo Vanderbilt Balsan, *The Glitter and the Gold* (New York, 1952), p. 11.

10. Balsan, *Glitter and the Gold,* pp. 5, 6, 8, 20.

11. Ibid., p. 6; quoted in Elizabeth D. Lehr, *King Lehr and the Gilded Age* (Philadelphia, 1935), p. 177; quoted in CCHH, HP, p. 243; Allen Churchill, *The Splendor Seekers* (New York, 1974), pp. 53–59. Just across Fifty-Second Street to the south at 640 Fifth Avenue, Christian Herter completed two houses in 1882, one for William H. Vanderbilt and the other a double house for his daughters, Mrs. Elliott F. Shepard and Mrs. William D. Sloane and their families. According to a letter of George E. Pettengill, librarian of the A.I.A., to Stapleton D. Gooch IV, Nov. 8, 1965, there is no evidence that Alva Vanderbilt was ever elected "a member or honorary member of the A.I.A.," as is often stated: see Stapleton Dabney Gooch IV, "Richard Morris Hunt and the Vanderbilts," M.A. thesis, University of Virginia, 1966, p. 30.

12. Henry Hope Reed, "The Vision Spurned: Classical New York," *Classical America,* I, 2 (1972), 10; Van Pelt, *Monograph,* passim; Arthur W. Colton, "A Monograph of the William K. Vanderbilt House," *Architectural Record,* LVIII (Sept. 1925), 295; A. A. Cox, "American Construction through British Eyes," *American Architect and Building News,* XXXIII (Aug. 29, 1891), 132; Schuyler, "The Works of the Late Richard M. Hunt," 129–131; Montgomery Schuyler, "Recent Building in New York: Part V. The Vanderbilt Houses," *American Architect and Building News,* IX (May 21, 1881), 243–244. Schuyler objected to the "needlessly tormented" aspect of the skyline of the house because of the variations in wing roof levels, and he did not like the placement of the turret hood and the vigor of its surfaces and corbel designs, the smallness of much of the exterior detail, the mixture of styles in the avenue front dormers, and the useless flying buttress decorations on the entrance pavilion. But the wealth of detail on the house was effectively subordinated to the general design, he felt, and he generally admired the mansion.

13. Schuyler, "Recent Building in New York," 243.

14. Anon., "Architect's Likeness in Stone Atop Vanderbilt Mansion,"

Gas Logic, XXXVI (Aug. 1924), 3–4; *New York Times,* July 29, 1924, p. 15, and May 31, 1925, Sec. IV, p. 9. John Burchard and Albert Bush-Brown, in *The Architecture of America: A Social and Cultural History* (Bostin, 1961), p. 165, express doubt that with RMH's careful attention to the details of design a sculptor might have surreptitiously modeled his portrait. The plaster model for the statue, 57 inches high from the bottom of the base to the top of the cap, is now stored in the basement of the Museum of the City of New York. The original statue is now located in a niche above the entrance portal of the William Kissam Vanderbilt II mansion at Centerport, L.I. The mansion, now The Vanderbilt Museum, is owned and maintained by Suffolk County.

15. Anon., "Mr. Wm. K. Vanderbilt's House," *Real Estate Record & Guide,* XXXVII (June 12, 1886), 770, and XXXVIII (July 3, 1886), 856–857; Van Pelt, *Monograph,* passim; Balsan, *Glitter and the Gold,* pp. 10–12; J. Donald Adams, "A Lamp of Architecture Disappears from the City," *New York Times,* May 31, 1925, Sec. IV. p.

9. James, Sinclair & Co. did much of the stonework on this and other large houses that RMH designed, while Ellin, Kitson & Co., stonecutters and architectural sculptors, executed most of the interior carving here. Jules Allard et Fils and Herter Brothers did most of the interior decoration of the W. K. Vanderbilt house. Léon Marcotte executed the Moorish billiard room. See Anon., "Modern Stonework," *Architectural Record,* V (Oct.–Dec. 1895), 192–193, and Anon., "Artistic Stone Carving," ibid., 190–191. The stained-glass window was designed by Eugène Oudinot, who also executed the memorial window in Hunt's Belmont Chapel, Island Cemetery, Newport, and windows for H. G. Marquand's town house in N.Y.C.

16. Balsan, *Glitter and the Gold,* p. 6; Wayne Andrews, *The Vanderbilt Legend* (New York, 1941), pp. 253–260; Andrew Tully, *Era of Elegance* (New York, 1947), pp. 39–44.

17. Anon., "Like an Oriental Dream," *New York Herald,* Mar. 27, 1883, p. 3; CCHH, HP, pp. 168–169; Grace M.

Mayer, *Once Upon a City* (New York, 1958), pp. 30–31. The *New York World* reported that the Vanderbilt Ball had cost some $250,000, not including the expense of the costumes.

18. Bainbridge Bunting, *Houses of Boston's Back Bay* (Cambridge, Mass. 1967), pp. 301–303; Anon., "An Architectural Comparison," *Architectural Record,* XXIII (May 1908), 409; Hitchcock, *Architecture of H. H. Richardson,* pp. 220, 237.

19. Charles Moore, *Daniel H. Burnham: Architect Planner of Cities* (Boston, 1921), I, 116; Montgomery Schuyler, "Richard Morris Hunt," *Harper's Weekly,* XXXIX (Aug. 10, 1895), 749; Royal Cortissoz, "Richard Morris Hunt," *New-York Daily Tribune,* Aug. 4, 1895, p. 23; Royal Cortissoz, "Leaders in American Architecture," *Art and Common Sense* (New York, 1913), p. 396; J. A. S., "Richard Morris Hunt, A Reminiscence and an Appreciation," *Architectural Record,* XXXIX (Mar. 1916), 297; Barr Ferree, "Richard Morris Hunt: His Art and Work," *Architecture and Building,* XXIII (Dec. 7, 1895), 274; Russell

Lynes, "Chateau Builder to Fifth Avenue," *American Heritage*, VI (Feb. 1955), 25; Herbert Croly, "The Work of Richard Morris Hunt," *Architectural Record*, LIX (Jan. 1926), 88–89.

20. Clarence Cook, "Architecture in America," *North American Review*, CXXXV (Sept. 1882), 243–252.

21. Anon., "Architect's Likeness," 3; Adams, "A Lamp of Architecture," 9; Jacob Landy, "The Domestic Architecture of the 'Robber Barons' in New York City," *Marsyas*, V (1947–1949), 82; I. N. Phelps Stokes, *Iconography of Manhattan Island, 1498–1909* (New York, 1915–1928), V, 1974; Anon., "Scrapping an Architectural Masterpiece—the William K. Vanderbilt House, at 5th Ave. and 52nd St.," *American Architect and Building News*, CXXIX (Apr. 20, 1926), 459–460.

22. John Drury, *Old Chicago Houses* (Chicago, 1941), pp. 132–135; correspondence from Holland C. Anthony to RMH, Aug. 22, 1885, Sept. 1, 1885, Dec. 6, 1885, Jan. 21, 1886, and Mar. 4, 1886; Holland C. Anthony to William Borden, Dec. 19, 1885; and

William Borden to H. C. Anthony, Dec. 11, 1885, HC.

22. Schuyler, "The Works of the Late Richard M. Hunt," 131; Drury, *Old Chicago Houses*, p. 133; David Lowe, *Lost Chicago* (Boston, 1975), p. 34; Montgomery Schuyler, "Glimpses of Western Architecture: Chicago," reprinted in *American Architecture and Other Writings*, ed. William H. Jordy and Ralph Coe (Cambridge, Mass., 1961), pp. 285–287. The Borden house became the home of John Borden, an Arctic explorer, whose daughter married Adlai Stevenson. The house was later used for a time as an art center and was razed for an apartment house in the early 1960s.

24. Anon., "The Tomb of the Vanderbilts," *New-York Daily Tribune*, Dec. 16, 1884, p. 2; F. L. Olmsted to George W. Vanderbilt, Aug. 7, 1886, July 16, 1887, and June 22, 1888; and F. L. Olmsted to RMH, May 5, 1887, Private Estates, Box 43, Olmsted Papers, Manuscript Division, Library of Congress. See also Robert Miraldi, "The Vanderbilt Mausoleum," *Staten Island Advance*, Sept. 24,

1978, pp. 1, 12; Sept. 25, 1978, pp. 1, 8; Sept. 26, 1978, pp. 1, 8; and April 15, 1979, p. 8.

25. Churchill, *Splendor Seekers*, p. 51; Andrews, *Vanderbilt Legend*, pp. 239, 232–233; quoted in Croffut, *Vanderbilts*, p. 213 and in Wayne Andrews, *Architecture in New York* (New York, 1969), xii; Holland C. Anthony to RMH, Sept. 1, and Oct. 2, 1885, HC; CCHH, HP, pp. 163–164.

26. Anon., "How the Rich Are Buried," *Architectural Record*, X (July 1900), 26; Schuyler, "The Works of the Late Richard M. Hunt," 114; Croffut, *Vanderbilts*, pp. 213–218; Landy, "Domestic Architecture of the Robber Barons," 77; Holland C. Anthony to RMH, Oct. 2, and Dec. 6, 1885, HC. Surrounded by a high, forbidding fence and occasionally the target of vandals, the Vanderbilt Mausoleum is hidden from the view of outsiders, and legitimate access to the grounds is closely controlled by a supervisory trust.

27. Harry Miller Lydenberg, *History of the New York Public Library: Astor, Lenox, and Tilden Foundations* (New York, 1923), pp. 208, 222;

Nathan Silver, *Lost New York* (Boston, 1967), p. 217; CCHH, HP, pp. 188, 197; ABD, No. 1296 of 1886 and NBD, No. 1536 of 1887.

28. NBD, No. 811 of 1881.

29. Schuyler, "The Works of the Late Richard M. Hunt," 131, 165; Landy, "Domestic Architecture of the Robber Barons," 72, 82. Schuyler considered that the Marquand houses were superior in design to the more widely acclaimed W. K. Vanderbilt house: see "M.S." clipping from *The Record & Guide*, Feb. 3, 1883, HC.

30. *New York Times*, Apr. 16, 1905, p. 8; Harry W. Desmond and Herbert Croly, *Stately Homes in America* (New York, 1903), pp. 99, 103, 105 illus.; Cox, "American Construction Through English Eyes," 131–132; Russell Sturgis, "The Famous Japanese Room in the Marquand House," *Architectural Record*, XVIII (Sept. 1905), 192–201. When the principal Marquand house was opened to inspection by the New York architects in 1889, RMH had the gout and could not take his colleagues through (CCHH, HP, p. 223). Early in the

twentieth century, the three Marquand houses were torn down to make way for an apartment building.

31. Alan Burnham, "The New York Architecture of Richard Morris Hunt," *Journal of the Society of Architectural Historians*, XI (May 1952), 14; Schuyler, "The Works of the Late Richard M. Hunt," 173; Holland C. Anthony to RMH, Oct. 2, Dec. 6, and Dec. 28, 1885, HC; Mrs. Winthrop Chanler, *Roman Spring* (Boston, 1935), p. 235; NBD, No. 1144 of 1885. Another, much more modest, domestic commission of the early 1880s is still standing: the Sidney Webster house at 245 East Seventeenth Street, N.Y.C., now serves as offices for Beth Israel Hospital. It was built in 1883–1885 at an estimated cost of $35,000: see NBD, No. 890 of 1883.

32. *New York Times*, Jan. 25, 1970, sec. D, p. 26; Paul Goldberger, "A Visible Anchor to Past Would be Lost in Razing," and John L. Hess, "Victorian Home for Aged to be Demolished," *New York Times*, July 19, 1974, p. 49; NBD, No. 934 of 1881.

33. In a letter to the Editor of the *New York Times*, Dec. 25, 1974, Robert A. M. Stern, President of the Architectural League of New York, characterized the Association Residence as "an outstanding example of institutional and functional architecture as well as one of the few remaining examples of nineteenth-century medical architecture in the United States . . .", a superb model of what one of America's finest architects did when faced with a problem of sociological urgency." At the time of the publication of this book, the fate of the Association Residence is still uncertain.

CHAPTER 18

1. CCHH, HP, p. 166; RMH to J. Q. A. Ward, Dec. 28, 1887, Ward Papers, New-York Historical Society.

2. Wayne Craven, *Sculpture in America* (New York, 1968), pp. 246–257; Lewis I. Sharp, "John Quincy Adams Ward: Historical and Contemporary Influences," *American Art Journal*, IV (Nov. 1972), 71–73; quoted in G. W. Sheldon, "An American Sculptor," *Harper's New Monthly Magazine*, LVII

(June 1878), 66; quoted in Adeline Adams, *John Quincy Adams Ward, An Appreciation* (New York, 1912), pp. 22–29. See chapter 10 of this volume for discussion of the Seventh Regiment Monument.

3. Sharp, "John Quincy Adams Ward," 73; miscellaneous Perry clippings, Architectural Cuttings Scrapbook, HC.

4. Miscellaneous Perry clippings, Architectural Cuttings Scrapbook, HC.

5. Maud Howe Elliott, *This Was My Newport* (Cambridge, Mass., 1944), p. 238; Anon., "The Queen of Aquidneck," *Harper's New Monthly Magazine,* XLIX (Aug. 1874), 313; George H. Richardson Scrapbook, No. 970, p. 42, Manuscript Collection, Newport Historical Society; miscellaneous Perry clippings, Architectural Cuttings Scrapbook, HC.

6. *Report of the Commission . . . Providing for the Erection of a Monument at Yorktown, Va.* (Washington, D.C., 1883), p. 11; Sharp, "John Quincy Adams Ward," 76; "Yorktown Monument," *American Architect and Building News,* X (Oct. 15, 1881), 303 illus.

7. *Report of the Commission,* p. 11; CCHH, HP, p. 163.

8. RMH to Lieut. Col. William P. Craighill, Aug. 3, 1882, General Records Division, National Archives, Washington, D.C.; *Annual Report of the Secretary of War for the Year 1883* (Washington, D.C., 1883), pp. 704–707; *Annual Report of the Secretary of War for the Year 1884* (Washington, D.C., 1884), p. 871; CCHH, HP, pp. 169–170. The total cost of the Yorktown Monument came to $94,500.

9. *Report of the Commission,* p. 11; *Appleton's Annual Cyclopedia, 1881,* n.s.VI (New York, 1882), p. 870; Montgomery Schuyler, "The Works of the Late Richard M. Hunt," *Architectural Record,* V (Oct.–Dec., 1895), 118; Sharp, "John Quincy Adams Ward," 76; quoted from the Cincinnati *Times-Star,* Nov. 22, 1889, in CCHH, HP, p. 227.

10. Clipping from Burlington, Vermont, newspaper, n.d., Ward Scrapbook, p. 148, Ward Papers, New-York Historical Society.

11. Lewis I. Sharp, *New York City Public Sculpture by 19th–Century American Artists* (New York, 1974), p. 31; clipping from *New York Herald,* Nov. 25, 1883, p. 7, Miscellany Scrapbook, HC.

12. Sharp, *New York City Public Sculpture,* p. 31; Russell Sturgis, "The Work of J. Q. A. Ward," *Scribners Magazine,* XXXII (Oct. 1902), 292–293; Craven, *Sculpture in America,* p. 252; miscellaneous items, Ward Scrapbook, Ward Papers, New-York Historical Society.

13. Miscellaneous items, Ward Scrapbooks, Fine Arts Division, New York Public Library, and New-York Historical Society; *New York Herald,* June 6, 1885, p. 3; Walter S. Wilson, "Statues and Monuments of New York," *The Memorial History of the City of New York* (New York, 1893), IV, 230.

14. J. Q. A. Ward to Alexander E. Orr, Mar. 28, 1885; J. Q. A. Ward to Seth Low, Feb. 3, 1886; RMH to J. Q. A. Ward, Mar. 3, 1886; and J. Q. A. Ward and RMH to Alexander E. Orr, Feb. 8, 1886, all in Ward Papers, New-York Historical Society. Another Soldiers' and Sailors' Monument collaboration for Indianapolis was not built either: see W. R. Ware to J. Q. A. Ward,

Aug. 17, 1887, and RMH to J. Q. A. Ward, Dec. 28, 1887, Ward Papers, New-York Historical Society.

15. RMH to J. Q. A. Ward, Mar. 3, 1886, and Ward Scrapbook, Ward Papers, New-York Historical Society; Garfield Monument files and "Cash Book for Army Medical Museum and Library," National Archives. For his work on this monument, Hunt received his usual fee of ten percent on the cost of the architectural portion of the work, not including the statuary, and apparently here, as in most other Hunt-Ward collaborations, Ward in effect subcontracted the pedestal work to Hunt.

16. Sharp, "John Quincy Adams Ward," 78; Craven, *Sculpture in America*, p. 253; CCHH, HP, p. 169. In 1887, Ward and Hunt also collaborated on a small monument for Goodale Park in Columbus, Ohio. A bronze bust of Dr. Lincoln Goodale was placed on a pedestal having an elaborated frieze and rising from a spreading, volute-decorated base, which formed the back to a basin. The monument was installed at a cost $5,000 in 1888: see Daniel F. Prugh, ed., *Goodale Park Centennial, 1851–1951* (Columbus, 1951), p. 8, and CCHH, HP, p. 189.

17. Sharp, *New York City Public Sculpture*, p. 33; Ward Scrapbook, Ward Papers, New-York Historical Society. Ward was paid a commission of $15,000 for the statue, while for the pedestal Hunt received $3,000, from which he presumably paid for the stone and its preparation.

18. Report from *New-York Daily Tribune* clipping, Sept. 21, 1890, in Ward Scrapbook, Fine Arts Division, New York Public Library; miscellaneous items in Ward Scrapbook, New-York Historical Society; Sturgis, "Work of J. Q. A. Ward," 391–392; Craven, *Sculpture in America*, p. 255. Ward's own intentions were reported in the *New York Sun*, May 10, 1890, quoted in Sharp, *New York City Public Sculpture*, p. 33.

19. Telegram of Horatio C. King to J. Q. A. Ward, Mar. 8, 1887, and Fred W. Hinricks to J. Q. A. Ward, July 27, 1887, Ward Papers, New-York Historical Society.

20. Articles of Agreement, Apr. 6, 1888; RMH to J. Q. A. Ward, Sept. 12, 1888, Dec. 6, 1889, Jan. 27, 1890, July 7, 1890, and Aug. 18, 1890; and Receipt, July 20, 1891, all in Ward Papers, New-York Historical Society. Hunt arranged for the preparation of the polished black Quincy granite pedestal at a cost of $3,200 and was himself paid $310 for his design.

21. Ward Scrapbook, Fine Arts Division, New York Public Library; Sharp, *New York City Public Sculpture*, p. 13; John Henry Barrows, *Henry Ward Beecher, The Shakespeare of the Pulpit* (New York, 1893), pp. 513–514; Craven, *Sculpture in America*, pp. 255–256.

22. Sharp, *New York City Public Sculpture*, p. 13; Sharp, "John Quincy Adams Ward," 81; John Sanford Saltus and Walter E. Tisné, *Statues of New York* (New York, 1923), p. 116.

23. Margaret E. Gilmore, "The Fountain," *Livingston County Leader*, July 10, 1958, p. 3; Schuyler, "The Works of the Late Richard M. Hunt," 116–117; Sarah Ullyette Harrington, "The Wadsworth Memorial Fountain (Geneseo, N.Y.), "*The Arts in the Genesee Valley*, Vol. V: *Art and History* (1976), 51–57, with an un-

documented attribution of the sculptured bear to Antoine Louis Barye.

24. Schuyler, "The Works of the Late Richard M. Hunt," 114; Cemetery Records, George H. Richardson Scrapbook, No. 974, p. 82, Newport Historical Society. A listing of other known tombs, sarcophaguses, and cemetery commissions is included in the Appendix.

25. Much of the general account in this and the following paragraphs is taken from the following works: Benjamin Levine and Isabelle F. Story, *The Statue of Liberty*, National Park Service Historical Handbook Series No. 11 (Washington, D.C., 1952); Barbara L. Clark, "Remembering a Forgotten Goddess," Baltimore *Sun*, July 28, 1936; Ruth McKenney and Eileen Bransten, "The Colossus," *New-York Herald Tribune Magazine*, Oct. 24, 1965, 14–17, 24, 26, 28–31; Marvin Trachtenberg, *The Statue of Liberty* (New York, 1976), chap. 1. Bartholdi is said to have met Richard and William Hunt at La Farge's New York studio in 1871: see Hertha Pauli and E. B. Ashton, *I Lift My Lamp: The Way of a Symbol* (Port

Washington, N.Y., 1948; reissued, 1969), p. 99.

26. Trachtenberg, *Statue of Liberty*, chap. 6.

27. Miscellaneous Land Papers and RMH to Robert Lincoln, Nov. 25, 1881, Land File No. 12, National Archives; Laboulaye to Editor of the *Tribune*, Oct. 15, 1875, and A. Bartholdi to Richard Butler, Dec. 23, 1881, Correspondence of the American Committee of the Statue of Liberty, Manuscript Division, New York Public Library; William Evarts et al., *An Appeal to the People of the United States in Behalf of the Great Statue, Liberty Enlightening the World* (New York, 1883); National Park Service, Department of the Interior, "The Story of the Statue of Liberty," pamphlet, p. 5. The first consulting engineer in France for the project was Viollet-le-Duc, who was succeeded by Gustave Eiffel.

28. Feb. 6, May 9, and May 10, 1883, Land File No. 13, National Archives; National Park Service, "Story of the Statue of Liberty," 5; Carl W. Condit, *American Building Art—The Nineteenth Century* (New York, 1960), p. 335.

29. See note 25, above.

30. Condit, *American Building Art*, pp. 46, 230–231; *Appleton's Annual Cyclopedia, 1886*, n.s. XI (New York, 1887), p. 323; National Park Service, "Story of the Statue of Liberty," 5.

31. Trachtenberg, *Statue of Liberty*, pp. 158 ff., with illus. of models and drawings.

32. Schuyler, "The Works of the Late Richard M. Hunt," 115–116; William Franklyn Paris, "Richard Morris Hunt: First Secretary and Third President of the Institute," *Journal of the American Institute of Architects*, XXV (Feb. 1956), 78; CCHH, HP, pp. 187–188. For his work Hunt was paid $1,000, a sum equal to his donation to the pedestal fund.

33. American Committee to Erect the Statue of Liberty, *Inauguration of the Statue of Liberty* (New York, 1887); McKenney, "The Colossus," 31; CCHH, HP, p. 188.

34. Quoted in CCHH, HP, p. 193.

CHAPTER 19

1. CCHH, HP, pp. 171, 173; Catharine Howland Hunt (CHH), known to

the family as Kitty, seventeen years old in the summer of 1885, kept a day-by-day journal recording family activities during the entire European trip of 1885–1886 (HP). Fellow passengers on the *Etruria* were Sidney Webster and his wife, whose Hunt-designed house on East Seventeenth Street had just been completed at the beginning of the year.

2. CCHH, HP, pp. 173–175; CHH, Journal, 1885–1886, HP; A. Bartholdi to Richard Butler, July 21 and July 30, 1885, Correspondence of the American Committee of the Statue of Liberty, Manuscripts and Archives Division, New York Public Library.

3. CCHH, HP, pp. 175–176; CHH, Journal, 1885–1886, HP; Holland C. Anthony to RMH, Dec. 6, 1885, HC.

4. CCHH, HP, pp. 176–177; CHH, Journal, 1885–1886, HP; 1885 Sketchbooks, HC.

5. CCHH, HP, pp. 178–181; CHH, Journal, 1885–1886, HP.

6. CCHH, HP, pp. 182–185; CHH, Journal, 1885–1886, HP; RMH to J. Q. A. Ward, Mar. 3, 1886, Ward Papers,

New-York Historical Society.

7. CCHH, HP, p. 194.

8. CCHH, HP, pp. 194–195; Martin Brimmer to Sarah Wyman Whitman, Apr. 14, 1889, Archives of American Art (D–32).

9. CCHH, HP, pp. 191–192, 200–205.

10. CCHH, HP, pp. 194, 197; *New-York Daily Tribune,* Dec. 19, 1887, p. 4; H. Van Buren Magonigle, "A Half-Century of Architecture—A Biographical Review," *Pencil Points,* XV (Jan. 1934), 10.

11. CCHH, HP, p. 208; RMH, "President's Address," *Proceedings of the Twenty-Second Annual Convention of the A.I.A.* (1888) (n.p., n.d.), pp. 3–8.

12. Donald Hoffman, *The Architecture of John Wellborn Root* (Baltimore, 1973), pp. 91–93; Thomas Hines, *Burnham of Chicago: Architect and Planner* (New York, 1974), p. 69; George C. Mason, *Architects and Their Environment, 1850–1907* (Lancaster, Pa., 1907), p. 29; Harriet Monroe, *John Wellborn Root* (Boston, 1896), p. 174. *The Inland Architect and Builder* became *The*

Inland Architect and News Record in 1888.

13. RMH, "President Hunt's Address," *Convention Proceedings of the American Institute of Architects, the Western Association of Architects, and Consolidation of the American Institute and the Western Association,* 1889 (Chicago, 1890), p. 21.

14. Alfred Stone, "The Early History of the American Institute of Architects," *Proceedings of the Fortieth Annual Convention of the American Institute of Architects* (Washington, D.C., 1907), p. 175.

15. Stone, "Early History of the American Institute of Architects," 175; Leigh Hunt, "Outline History of the American Institute of Architects," *Michigan Society of Architects Bulletin,* XVI (June 23, 1942), 29, 31; CCHH, HP, pp. 225–228, 230.

16. Glenn Brown, *1860–1930 Memories* (Washington, D.C., 1931), pp. 210, 246; Montgomery Schuyler, "The Works of the Late Richard M. Hunt," *Architectural Record,* V (Oct.–Dec. 1895), 180; Stone, "Early History of the American Institute of Architects," 174. Everett C. Hughes, "Professions," in *The*

Professions in America, ed. Kenneth S. Lynn (Boston, 1965), p. 3, stresses "commitment" to the group and its interests as perhaps the most important foundational element of professionalism.

17. CCHH, HP, p. 245; RMH to J. W. Root, Oct. 8, 1890, HC.

18. RMH, "Presidential Address," *American Institute of Architects, Proceedings, Twenty-Fourth Convention, 1890* (Chicago, 1891), pp. 9, 13. CCHH, HP, p. 206, indicated that RMH was offered the post of supervising architect in 1886.

19. RMH, "Opening Address to Twenty-Fifth Annual Convention," Oct. 28, 1891, *American Institute of Architects, Proceedings* (Chicago, 1892), pp. 9–16; RMH, "Address, Delivered at the 25th Annual Convention of the A.I.A. at Boston, Mass.," *Inland Architect and News Record,* XVIII (Nov. 1891), 39–41; CCHH, HP, p. 253.

20. CCHH, HP, p. 211.

21. Ibid., p. 211; Clarence W. Bowen, *History of the Centennial Celebration* (New York, 1892), pp. 244, 360, 408, 414.

22. CCHH, HP, p. 211.

23. Ibid., pp. 212–213. A Miss Grant was the sculptor.

24. Ibid., pp. 213–217.

25. Ibid., pp. 217, 220; undated clipping, Miscellany Scrapbook, HC.

CHAPTER 20

1. That most of the rich were not self-made but were instead largely born to wealth was already true before the Civil War, the so-called "era of the common man": see Edward Pessen, *Riches, Class, and Power Before the Civil War* (Lexington, Mass., 1973), p. 303.

2. Edward C. Kirkland, *Dream and Thought in the Business Community, 1860–1900* (Ithaca, N.Y., 1956; reprinted Chicago, 1964), pp. 33–37, 41; Jacob Landy, "The Domestic Architecture of the 'Robber Barons' in New York City," *Marsyas,* V (1947–1949), 76; Allen Churchill, *The Splendor Seekers* (New York, 1974), p. 96; Harry W. Desmond and Herbert Croly, *Stately Homes in America* (New York, 1903), pp. 12, 280, and passim.

3. Desmond and Croly, *Stately Homes,* pp. 318–323.

4. For a negative criticism, see E. L. Godkin, "The Expenditure of Rich Men," *Scribner's Magazine,* XX (Oct. 1896), 500–501.

5. CCHH, HP, pp. 186, 188, 211, 222; Robert McElroy, *Levi Parsons Morton, Banker, Diplomat and Statesman* (New York, 1930), p. 167; NBD, No. 994 of 1871.

6. Ellerslie was destroyed by fire on Oct. 27, 1950.

7. David A. Clary, Head, History Section, U.S.D.A. Forest Service, to the author, June 21, 1977; CCHH, HP, p. 200; *Pennsylvania: A Guide to the Keystone State,* compiled by workers of the Writers' Program of the Work Projects Administration (New York, 1940; 4th printing, 1950), p. 356. See also The Preservation/Design Group, *Grey Towers: Preliminary Historic Structure Report* (Albany, N.Y., 1978). Grey Towers was donated by the Pinchot family to the Conservation Foundation and then to the U.S. Department of Agriculture Forest Service as headquarters for the Pinchot Institute for Conservation Studies. In 1963 the estate was designated a registered na-

tional historic landmark.

The Hunt and James Pinchot families were close friends. The Pinchots' daughter Nettie stayed with the Hunts in Newport in the winter of 1884–1885, and she and her mother at times traveled with the Hunts in Europe in 1885 1886. Materials in the Gifford Pinchot Papers at the Library of Congress reveal a brief "engagement" in March 1885 between Gifford Pinchot and Catharine Howland Hunt (see Preservation Design Group, *Grey Towers*, pp. 10 and 31, n. 5).

8. CCHH, HP, pp. 195, 205.

9. Ibid., p. 222; Antoinette F. Downing and Vincent F. Scully, Jr., *The Architectural Heritage of Newport, Rhode Island, 1640–1915* (Cambridge, Mass., 1952; 2d rev. ed., 1967), p. 165; Montgomery Schuyler, "The Works of the Late Richard M. Hunt," *Architectural Record*, V (Oct.–Dec. 1895), 129.

10. NBD, No. 1485 of 1890.

11. Churchill, *Splendor Seekers*, p. 71; Landy, "Domestic Architecture of the 'Robber Barons,'" 73; Barr Ferree, "Richard Morris Hunt: His Art

and Work," *Architecture and Building*, XXIII (Dec. 7, 1895), 274.

12. CCHH, HP, p. 252; *New York Times*, Mar. 26, 1893, p. 11; *New York Sun*, Aug. 2, 1895, in Obituaries Scrapbook, HC; NBD, No. 537 of 1892.

13. Schuyler, "The Works of the Late Richard M. Hunt," 131; *New York Times*, Feb. 9, 1929, p. 5.

14. Harvey O'Connor, *The Astors* (New York, 1941), p. 236; *New York Times*, Mar. 3, 1893, p. 11; NBD, No. 36, of 1893.

15. Mildred Frances Brenner, "Richard Morris Hunt, Architect," M.A. thesis, New York University, 1944, p. 72.

16. Schuyler, "The Works of the Late Richard M. Hunt," 172; Ferree, "Richard Morris Hunt," 275; Landy, "Domestic Architecture of the 'Robber Barons,'" 74; Alan Burnham, "The New York Architecture of Richard Morris Hunt," *Journal of the Society of Architectural Historians*, XI (May 1952), 14.

17. Anon., "The Residence of Col. John Jacob Astor," *Architectural Record*, XXVII (June 1910), 470–482; Chur-

chill, *Splendor Seekers*, pp. 114–115.

18. Landy, "Domestic Architecture of the 'Robber Barons,'" 73; O'Connor, *The Astors*, pp. 236, 280, 333–334; Herbert Croly, "The Work of Richard Morris Hunt," *Architectural Record*, LIX (Jan. 1926), 88–89.

19. CCHH, HP, pp. 197, 221.

20. Schuyler, "The Works of the Late Richard M. Hunt," 165–168. To Schuyler, "the design of the house itself is most distinctly and triumphantly successful," and it was surely an outstanding "example of a free and romantic domestic architecture" no "less noteworthy than the châteaux of the Loire." Banister Fletcher, the British architectural historian, however, found "nothing very remarkable in [this] house" which seemed to him "rather hard in treatment": Banister Fletcher, "American Architecture through English Spectacles," *Engineering Magazine*, VII (June 1894), 315. In the twentieth century, Antoinette F. Downing and Vincent F. Scully, Jr., have judged Ochre Court an "academically

conventional" plan, "cold and barren" in execution, in reality nothing more than "a tremendous Beaux-Arts *projet,* magnificently unconcerned with reality": *Architectural Heritage of Newport,* pp. 171–172.

21. James M. Dennis, *Karl Bitter, Architectural Sculptor, 1867–1915* (Madison, Wis., 1967), p. 23; Anon., "Welcome to Ochre Court," pamphlet, n.p., n.d. The stone and wood carving and the molded plasterwork at Ochre Court were mainly executed by Ellin, Kitson & Co. of New York, the firm that did most of the carving in stone and wood on Hunt's large houses: see Anon., "Artistic Stone Carving," *Architectural Record,* V (Oct.–Dec. 1895), 190–191.

22. Florence Adèle Sloane to Gifford Pinchot, Aug. 17, 1892, General Correspondence, Gifford Pinchot Papers, Manuscript Division, Library of Congress; CCHH, HP, p. 221; Wayne Andrews, *The Vanderbilt Legend* (New York, 1941), p. 267; clipping from Newport *Observer,* May 9, 1892, Manuscript Collection, Newport Historical Society.

23. Clipping from the *New York World* (n.d.), HC.

24. The marble work at Marble House, The Breakers, Biltmore, the Astor house, and the Mills house was executed by Batterson & Eisele of New York, who acquired marble from all over the world. After Hunt's death one writer commented that "no architect knew better than he how to use [marble] to artistic effect": see Anon., "Marble Work," *Architectural Record,* V (Oct.–Dec. 1895), 194–195.

25. Desmond and Croly, *Stately Homes,* p. 426; Schuyler, "The Works of the Late Richard M. Hunt," 172.

26. *New York Times,* April 26, 1892, p. 8. The $40,000 grille was exhibited at the foundry of John Williams 544–556 West Twenty-Seventh Street, N.Y.C.

27. Henry Hope Reed, "Marble House: the William K. Vanderbilt Mansion" (Newport, 1965), pamphlet, passim.

28. Consuelo Vanderbilt Balsan, *The Glitter and the Gold* (New York, 1952), pp. 25–26.

29. Dennis, *Karl Bitter,*

p. 23; CCHH, HP, p. 232.

30. Reed, "Marble House," pp. 1–2; Andrews, *Vanderbilt Legend,* pp. 274, 277.

31. Mary Cable, "The Marble Cottages," *Horizon,* VII (autumn 1965), 18–27; Reed, "Marble House," pp. 2–3.

32. Quoted from a letter of Julia Ward Howe to Maud Howe Elliott, Oct. 15, 1895, in Maud Howe Elliott, "Newport, the Cradle of American Sports," *Bulletin of the Newport Historical Society,* No. 89 (October 1933), 8–9; Balsan, *Glitter and the Gold,* p. 50; Cleveland Amory, *The Last Resorts* (New York, 1952), p. 178.

33. Elliott, "Newport, the Cradle of American Sports," 8; Amory, *The Last Resorts,* p. 243.

34. Schuyler, "The Works of the Late Richard M. Hunt," 174. Downing and Scully find parodies of Gothic Revival work at Belcourt: see *Architectural Heritage of Newport,* p. 173. In 1956, Belcourt Castle was acquired by Harold B. Tinney, and the principal rooms are now open to the public.

35. Copies of the agreements of Sept. 22

and Oct. 12, 1885, between Pierre Lorillard and Cornelius Vanderbilt II are in the manuscript collection of the Newport Historical Society, along with many specification documents for the Hunt-designed mansion. In 1885, the land, buildings, and furniture were valued at $400,000. See also Holbert T. Smales, " 'The Breakers': An Illustrated Handbook," pamphlet (Newport, 1952), p. 11. Hunt assisted Post in resolving a critical design problem in the extensive alterations of Cornelius Vanderbilt II's Fifth Avenue house in 1892.

36. Smales, " 'The Breakers,' " p. 12; Montgomery Schuyler, "A Newport Palace," *Cosmopolitan*, XXIX (Aug. 1900), 369; Anon., "Artistic Stone Carving," 191.

37. Smales, " 'The Breakers,' " 36; Anon., "The Breakers," *Life*, XXXI (July 23, 1951), 46–52.

38. Some descriptions and critiques of The Breakers include Schuyler, "The Works of the Late Richard M. Hunt," 174; Schuyler, "A Newport Palace," 361–371; Desmond and Croly, *Stately Homes in America*, p. 425; Down-

ing and Scully, *Architectural Heritage of Newport*, p. 172; Alan Gowans, *Images of American Living: Four Centuries of Architecture and Furniture as Cultural Expression* (Philadelphia 1964), p. 368; Henry-Russell Hitchcock, Jr., *Rhode Island Architecture* (Cambridge, 1968), p. 61; Vincent Scully, Jr., "American Villas: Inventiveness in the American Suburb from Downing to Wright," *Architecural Review*, CXV (Mar. 1954), 178–179.

39. For a detailed description of The Breakers' interior, see Smales, " 'The Breakers,' " passim. Jules Allard et Fils worked with Hunt on the interiors of The Breakers and on several of his other houses: see the important discussion of Hunt as decorator in James T. Maher, *Twilight of Splendor: Chronicles of the Age of American Palaces* (Boston, 1975), pp. 279–280.

40. Paul Bourget, *Outre-Mer; Impressions of America* (New York, 1895), pp. 47–50; Godkin, "Expenditure of Rich Men," 498–501.

CHAPTER 21

1. James M. Dennis, *Karl Bitter, Architectural Sculptor, 1867–1915*

(Madison, 1967), pp. 15–23; clippings from *New York Evening Mail*, April 10, 1915, and *New York Globe*, April 10, 1915, in Karl Bitter Scrapbook, Fine Arts Division, New York Public Library; CCHH, HP, p. 233.

2. Dennis, *Karl Bitter*, pp. 40–41, 48; Anon., "The Bronze Doors of Trinity Church," pamphlet ([New York], 1972); quoted in Frank E. Wallis, "Richard M. Hunt, Master Architect and Man," *Architectural Review*, n.s. V (Nov. 1917), 240; CCHH, HP, pp. 231–232.

3. Dennis, *Karl Bitter*, pp. 48, 51, 53–55; Anon., "The Bronze Doors of Trinity Church."

4. Anon., "Emblematic Key," *Cleveland Leader*, Oct. 25, 1892, p. 6; Ruth W. Helmuth, University Archivist, Case Western Reserve University, to the author, Sept. 24, 1975.

5. Clark Hall accounts, miscellaneous memoranda, and application for the National Register of Historic Places, Archives, Case Western Reserve University; Anon., "Wisely Equipped," and Anon., "Emblematic Key," *Cleveland Leader*, Oct.

25, 1892, p. 6; Mildred Frances Brenner, "Richard Morris Hunt, Architect," M.A. thesis, N.Y.U., 1944, p. 110. In 1891, Hunt also designed a house for the president of Adelbert College, an unpretentious two-and-one-half-story wood-frame building set on a basement of roughly dressed stone.

6. "E. W. P." et al., "The William Hayes Fogg Art Museum of Harvard University," [Boston] *Museum of Fine Arts Bulletin,* VII (June 1909), 21; clipping from *Boston Globe,* Mar. 8, 1895, Archives, Harvard University.

7. Montgomery Schuyler, "The Works of the Late Richard M. Hunt," *Architectural Record,* V (Oct.–Dec. 1895), 123–125; letter from A. R. McKim, *Architecture and Building,* XXIV (Jan. 11, 1896), 22; clipping from *Boston Daily Advertiser,* Sept. 25, 1894, Archives, Harvard University. Although Schuyler thought that the Fogg Museum was a "pure" and "peaceable" building, he also found it too self-consciously executed and having the air of a "learned and competent" academic exercise.

8. Elevations of the Fogg Museum are included in the *Architectural Review,* III (Aug. 1894), 32 and plates XIX–XXII.

9. Clippings from *Boston Daily Advertiser,* Sept. 25, 1894, *Boston Globe,* Mar. 8, 1895, *Harvard Crimson,* Mar. 14, 1895, and *Springfield* [Mass.] *Republican,* Jan. 27, 1895, Archives, Harvard University.

10. Ewart A. Wetherill and Robert B. Newman, "Hunt Hall—An Historical Review," typescript, p. 2, and quoted in clippings from *Boston Daily Advertiser,* Mar. 18 and Apr. 27, 1896, Archives, Harvard University; quoted from *Harvard Graduates' Magazine* (Mar. 1904) in Charles Moore, *The Life and Times of Charles Follen McKim* (Boston, 1929), p. 111; CCHH, HP, pp. 279–280.

11. Wetherill and Newman, "Hunt Hall," passim; *Harvard University Gazette,* Nov. 8, 1912, Archives, Harvard University; *New York Times,* May 14, 1935, p. 2; Harvard University Graduate School of Design, *News,* II (Oct. 1973), 4–5; *Harvard Today* (Oct. 1973), 7.

In the early 1890s, Hunt was involved in another academic project in New York City. An

opportunity to provide a large and suitable institutional setting for Columbia University came in May 1892. Having just acquired the new site on Morningside Heights, the trustees of the university employed a committee consisting of Charles Coolidge Haight, who had designed the old Columbia campus on Madison Avenue at Forty-Ninth Street, Charles F. McKim, and Richard Hunt, to recommend a plan. When the three architects discovered that they could not agree on a common proposal, each one submitted a separate plan in April 1893. Haight's design, following English collegiate tradition, faced east. McKim's plan featured two separate platform areas with neoclassical buildings connected by courts; it faced south toward the heart of the city. Hunt favored placing the buildings around a large central courtyard with smaller courts open to the streets on the east and the west, where the principal entrance would be located. Hunt included a chapel and a library breaking into the symmetry of the interior court at the ends and suggested that the façades be treated in an Italian Renaissance manner. When the plans were received, the Columbia trustees invited William R. Ware and Frederick Law Olmsted to combine certain features of each of them into a new project. McKim's monumental placement of the buildings had impressed the trustees, and after Ware and Olmsted had made their recommendations, McKim was employed in December 1893 as architect for the new campus. Hunt's plan was solid and almost fortress-like and not especially interesting. See Francesco Passanti, "The Design of Columbia in the 1890's, McKim and His Client," *Journal of the Society of Architectural Historians*, XXXVI (May 1977), 70–73; Charles Moore, *The Life and Times of Charles Follen McKim* (Boston, 1929), p. 265; C. F. McKim to RMH, Sept. 2, 1893, Charles F. McKim Papers, Library of Congress. In May 1895, the trustees of New York University also invited Hunt to enter a limited competition for a design for the new library planned at University Heights in the Bronx, but Hunt's final illness prevented his participation.

12. "W. H.," "The New U.S. Naval Observatory," *Monthly Notices of the Royal Astronomical Society*, LIV (Feb. 1894), 261–264; Gustavus A. Weber, *The Naval Observatory: Its History, Activities and Organization* (Baltimore, 1926), p. 31; RMH to D. Greene, May 20, 1887, Historical Society of Pennsylvania, Philadelphia, Pa.

13. CCHH, HP, pp. 221, 245; miscellaneous correspondence of the Naval Observatory, 1888–1892, Rec. Group 78, National Archives, Washington, D.C.

14. Glenn Brown, "The New Naval Observatory, Washington, D.C.," *American Architect and Building News*, XXXVIII (Nov. 19, 1892), 121–122; Glenn Brown, *1860–1930 Memories* (Washington, D.C., 1931), p. 247; Captain Joseph C. Smith, USN, Superintendent, Naval Observatory, to the author, Sept. 27, 1976. Most of Hunt's Naval Observatory buildings are standing and in use today. Leon E. Dessez designed the superintendent's house, now the official residence of the vice-president of the United States, on the Naval Observatory grounds. Some of the mounting machinery at the Naval Observatory was designed and built by the firm of W. B. Warner and Ambrose Swasey of Cleveland, Ohio. Hunt designed adjoining two-and-one-half-story brick and stone-trim houses for them in Cleveland in 1891: see CCHH, HP, p. 254.

15. Col. John M. Wilson (hereafter JMW) to RMH, Sept. 14, Oct. 5, and Oct. 28, 1889, and RMH to JMW, Sept. 19, Sept. 21, Oct. 8, and Oct. 29, 1889, Superintendent's Letter Books, Archives, United States Military Academy, West Point, N.Y. (hereafter SLB–USMA). Earlier plans for the gymnasium are discussed in Consolidated Correspondence File, Apr. 4, Mar. 22, and Mar. 30, 1888, Office of the Quartermaster General, National Archives, Washington, D.C.

16. JMW to RMH, Nov. 6, Nov. 8, Nov. 11, Nov. 13, Dec. 20, and Dec. 23, 1889, and Jan. 4, and Jan. 16, 1890, and RMH to JMW, Dec. 14 and Dec. 27, 1889, and Jan. 3, 1890, SLB–USMA.

17. RMH to JMW, Jan. 25, Feb. 3, Feb. 21, and Feb. 26, 1890, and JMW to RMH, Feb. 1, Feb. 5, and Feb. 24, 1890, SLB–USMA.

18. JMW to RMH, Mar. 10, 1890, SLB–USMA.

19. JMW to RMH, Apr.

29, June 7, June 11, June 13, June 24, June 27, July 5, and July 9, 1890, and RMH to JMW, June 10, June 12, June 16, June 28, and July 7, 1890, SLB–USMA.

20. JMW to RMH, Apr. 7, May 13, and May 28, 1891; RMH to JMW, Aug. 26 and Aug. 28, 1890, Apr. 29, May 12, Aug. 17, and Aug. 19, 1891; and John Sheehan to JMW, Aug. 18, 1891, SLB–USMA.

21. John Sheehan to JMW, Aug. 17, 1891; Maurice Fornachon to JMW, Aug. 19, 1891; JMW to RMH, Aug. 14, Aug. 19, and Aug. 28, 1891; JMW to Adjutant General, Aug. 20, 1891; Adjutant General to JMW, Aug. 26, 1891, SLB–USMA.

22. JMW to John Moore, Oct. 20, 1892; JMW to RMH, Oct. 27, 1892; RMH to JMW, Oct. 31, 1892; Col. Oswald H. Ernst to RMH, Sept. 14, 1893; Col. Oswald H. Ernst to Adjutant General, Nov. 13, 1893, SLB–USMA.

23. Louis Brown to JMW, July 19, 1892, SLB–USMA; David W. Gray, "The Architectural Development of West Point," typescript, p. 5, Archives, USMA; Montgomery Schuyler, "The Architecture of

West Point," *Architectural Record,* XIV (Dec. 1903), 471. Schuyler judged that Hunt's West Point buildings bore "no traces of his architectural personality" nor was it "likely that they had much of his personal attention." While Maurice Fornachon and others in the RMH office worked on the drawings and the plans, RMH himself was very much involved, as the correspondence shows, and he made several visits to inspect the work in progress.

24. RMH to JMW, Dec. 27, 1889, and Jan. 27 and Apr. 17, 1890; memoranda of Charles W. Larned, Dec. 30, 1889, and Feb. 3 and Mar. 19, 1890; JMW to RMH, Apr. 2, Apr. 15, May 15, and May 31, 1890, SLB–USMA.

25. RMH to JMW, June 23, July 10, July 12, Oct. 14, and Oct. 29, 1890; JMW to RMH, June 17, June 25, Sept. 3, and Oct. 22, 1890; RMH to Charles W. Larned, Oct. 18, 1890, SLB–USMA.

26. RMH to JMW, Feb. 14 and May 11, 1891; JMW to RMH, Feb. 20 and Mar. 4, 1891, and Mar. 28, 1893, SLB–USMA.

27. Col. O. H. Ernst to Maurice Fornachon, Aug. 18, 1893, and RMH

to Col. O. H. Ernst, May 31, 1895, SLB–USMA.

28. Schuyler, "The Architecture of West Point," 471–472. Gray, "The Architectural Development of West Point," 6–7, sees the Academic Building as blending details from the several surrounding older buildings. To Schuyler, respecting the Academic Building, "the whole force of the design resides in the artful disposition of the masses, and in the straightforward and structural character of the treatment": see "The Works of the Late Richard M. Hunt," 122–123.

29. Col. O. H. Ernst to RMH, Mar. 7, Apr. 20, and May 20, 1895, and Col. O. H. Ernst to Richard Howland Hunt, Aug. 2, 1895, and Mar. 17, 1896, SLB–USMA.

30. Col. O. H. Ernst to RMH, Sept. 11, Sept. 13, Sept. 14, Sept. 17, Sept. 26, Oct. 22, Nov. 3, and Nov. 27, 1894, SLB–USMA.

31. Col. O. H. Ernst to Richard Howland Hunt, Feb. 26 and Mar. 7, 1896, and Richard Howland Hunt to Col. O. H. Ernst, Mar. 2 and Mar. 6, 1896, SLB–USMA; *Annual Report of the Superintendent of the United States Military*

Academy (Washington, D.C., 1897), p. 6; Stanley J. Tozeski, Chief USMA Archives, to the author, July 3, 1975.

CHAPTER 22

1. Daniel H. Burnham and Francis D. Millet, *World's Columbian Exposition: The Book of the Builders, Being the Chronicle of the Origin and Plan of the World's Fair* (Chicago and Springfield, Ohio, 1894), p. 9.

2. CCHH, HP, p. 220; Burnham and Millet, *World's Columbian Exposition*, p. 9; Hugh J. Grant to Frederick Law Olmsted, July 17, 1889, World's Fair File, Box 47, Olmsted Papers, Library of Congress; William Speer to RMH, Oct. 24, 1889, and miscellaneous Chicago World's Fair clippings, World's Columbian Exposition Scrapbook, HC; Committee for the International Exposition of 1892, "Official List of Committees and Committeemen," pamphlet (New York, 1889), HC; Joseph W. Tappin to members of the General Committee, Nov. 18, 1889, Gen. Corres., HC.

3. William Waldorf Astor to RMH, Aug. 23, 1889, HC; CCHH, HP, p. 231; various undated clippings, World's Co-lumbian Exposition Scrapbook, HC; William Earl Dodge Stokes, "How New York Lost the World's Fair. Platt and Fassett Did It!" pamphlet (New York, Oct. 10, 1891).

4. Harriet Monroe, *John Wellborn Root* (Boston, 1896), p. 218; Robert Craik McLean, "Did John Wellborn Root Design the World's Fair?" *Western Architect*, XXI (Mar. 1915), 18; Titus M. Karlowicz, "The Architecture of the World's Columbian Exposition," Ph.D. Diss., Northwest-ern University, 1965, pp. 4–5.

5. Burnham and Millet, *World's Columbian Exposition*, p. 12; Daniel H. Burnham, "The Organi-zation of the World's Columbian Exposition," an address delivered before the World's Congress of Architects, Chicago, Aug. 1, 1893, reported in *Inland Architect and News Record*, XXII (Aug. 1893), 5.

6. John Maass, *The Glorious Enterprise: The Centennial Exhibition of 1876 and H. J. Schwarzmann, Architect-in-Chief* (Watkins Glen, N.Y., 1973), pp. 94, 98.

7. Burnham, "The Or-ganization of the World's Columbian Ex-position," 5–6; Freder-ick Law Olmsted, "The Landscape Architecture of the World's Colum-bian Exposition," *Inland Architect and News Rec-ord*, XXII (Sept. 1893), 19; Donald Hoffmann, *The Architecture of John Wellborn Root* (Balti-more, 1973), 223 ff.; Laura Roper, *FLO: A Biography of Frederick Law Olmsted* (Baltimore, 1973), pp. 426–427. The Midway Plaisance, adja-cent to Jackson Park, was the principal entertain-ment area.

8. Monroe, *John Wellborn Root*, pp. 220–221; Charles Moore, *Daniel H. Burnham* (Bos-ton, 1921), I, 34–37; clip-ping from *Chicago Tribune*, Aug. 20, 1890, p. 8, World's Columbian Exposition Scrapbook, HC; quoted from *Chicago Inter-Ocean* in Anon., "The World's Fair Architect," *Architec-ture and Building*, XIII (August 1890), 97; Anon., "Appointment of Consulting World's Fair Architects," *Inland Ar-chitect and News Record*, XVI (Sept. 1890), 14–15; Charles Moore, "Les-sons of the Chicago World's Fair," *Architec-tural Record*, XXXIII (Jan. 1913), 38. There was speculation that others were considered for the position of consulting architect: see Karlowicz, "Architecture of the

World's Columbian Exposition," pp. 32–33. See also Thomas S. Hines, *Burnham of Chicago: Architect and Planner* (New York, 1974), ftn. 8, p. 408.

9. Burnham, "Organization of the World's Columbian Exposition," 6; Moore, *Burnham*, I, 35–37; Monroe, *Root*, pp. 222, 225.

10. Karlowicz, "Architecture of the World's Columbian Exposition," p. 35, with the memorandum, pp. 283–285.

11. Moore, *Burnham*, I, 40–42; quoted in Charles Moore, *The Life and Times of Charles Follen McKim* (Boston, 1929), p. 113; CCHH (HP, p. 231) placed Hunt's resolve not to become involved with the exposition and his change of heart considerably earlier, perhaps at the time when there was speculation that he would be named consulting architect.

12. Moore, *Burnham*, I, 42; quoted in Moore, *McKim*, p. 115; Burnham, "Organization of the World's Columbian Exposition," 6.

13. Monroe, *Root*, pp. 239, 247–248; Dimitri Tselos, "The Chicago Fair and the Myth of the 'Lost Cause,'" *Journal of the Society of Architectural Historians*, XXVI (Dec. 1967), 260; Titus M. Karlowicz, "D. H. Burnham's Role in the Selection of Architects for the World's Columbian Exposition," *Journal of the Society of Architectural Historians*, XXIX (Oct. 1970), 247–254. Robert C. McLean wrote, in 1915, that *even before* Chicago was chosen for the fair, Root had written down a list of those architects who should be asked to contribute designs and that those he then named included all those eventually invited: see "Did John Wellborn Root Design the World's Fair?," 18.

14. Rossiter Johnson, ed., *A History of the World's Columbian Exposition* (New York, 1897), I, 137; Moore, "Lessons of the World's Fair," 38–39; Burnham and Millet, *World's Columbian Exposition*, p. 5.

15. Henry Van Brunt, "Richard Morris Hunt," *Proceedings of the Twenty-Ninth Annual Convention of the American Institute of Architects* (Providence, 1895), p. 77; CCHH, HP, p. 247. Louis Sullivan, *The Autobiography of an Idea* (New York, 1924), p. 320, and Hugh Morrison, *Louis Sullivan:* *Prophet of Modern Architecture* (New York, 1935), p. 182, place the incident described in Sullivan's anecdote quoting RMH at the February meeting of the Board of Architects, though the character of the interchange would indicate that it occurred at the first meeting in January. Hines, *Burnham of Chicago*, pp. 94–95, finds that Burnham was in no way "overly apologetic, deferential, and subservient to the eastern architects."

16. Monroe, *Root*, pp. 248–249; Hoffman, *Architecture of John Wellborn Root*, pp. 234–235.

17. CCHH, HP, pp. 247–248; Monroe, *Root*, pp. 242–243; Johnson, ed., *History of the World's Columbian Exposition*, I, 137–138; Alexander R. Butler, "McKim's Renaissance; A Study in the History of the American Architectural Profession," Ph.D. Diss., Johns Hopkins University, 1953, p. 87. Karlowicz, "Architecture of the World's Columbian Exposition," pp. 56–67, summarizes well the position Root had and the possibility of his influence.

18. Johnson, ed., *History of the World's Co-*

lumbian Exposition, I, 45–46, 138; Moore, Burnham, I, 45–46; Hines, Burnham of Chicago, p. 87; RMH, "Address Delivered at the 25th Annual Convention of the A.I.A. at Boston, Mass.," Inland Architect and News Record, XVIII (Nov. 1891), 40.

19. CCHH, HP, p. 247.

20. Frederick Law Olmsted to Clarence Pullen, Jan. 7, 1891, World's Fair, Box 47, and Frederick Law Olmsted to W. A. Stiles, Mar. 10, 1895, Gen. Corres., Box 25, Olmsted Papers, Library of Congress.

21. Moore, Burnham, I, 46–47; interview with S. S. Beman, quoted in Chicago Journal, Aug. 1, 1895, clipping, World's Columbian Exposition Scrapbook, HC; quoted in CCHH, HP, pp. 224A, 277. Frank Wallis of Hunt's staff recalled that Hunt made his first sketch for the Administration Building on the back of an old envelope and at once laid out the whole scheme. Wallis marveled at Hunt's "complete control of mass and of a problem as a whole": see Frank E. Wallis, "Richard M. Hunt, Master Architect and Man," Architectural Review, n.s. V (Nov. 1917), 240.

22. RMH, "Presentation of the R.I.B.A. Medal and Reply," American Architect and Building News, XLI (July 15, 1893), 41; Burnham and Millet, World's Columbian Exposition, p. 27.

23. Ibid., 29.

24. Moore, Burnham, I, 47; quoted in Burnham and Millet, World's Columbian Exposition, p. 29; Johnson, ed., History of the World's Columbian Exposition, I, 143; Moore, McKim, pp. 118–119; Moore, "Lessons of the World's Fair," 42. The following day, the National Commission approved the designs.

25. D. H. Burnham to RMH, Mar. 28 and June 24, 1891, Burnham Letter Books, Vol. II, Nos. 43 and 331, Burnham Library, The Art Institute of Chicago; CCHH, HP, p. 253.

26. CCHH, HP, pp. 253, 256, 260; Chicago Tribune, Dec. 1, 1891, p. 2, quoted in Karlowicz, "Architecture of the World's Columbian Exposition," p. 113; New-York Daily Tribune, Dec. 6, 1891, p. 28; F. D. Millet to C. F. McKim, June 6, 1892, C. F. McKim Papers (Box 33), Manuscripts and Archives Division, New York Public Library. Hunt's designs were advertised for es-

timates on July 2, 1891: see Karlowicz, supra, p. 311.

27. CCHH, HP, pp. 260–261; C. F. McKim to RMH, Oct. 3, 1892; C. F. McKim to CCHH, Sept. 3 and Oct. 27, 1892; C. F. McKim to Thomas Newbold, Sept. 1, 1892; and C. F. McKim to C. D. Flagg, Sept. 1, 1892, all in McKim Papers (Box 1, Bk. 1), Library of Congress.

28. CCHH, HP, pp. 261–262; New York Times, Oct. 22, 1892, p. 9.

29. Quoted in CCHH, HP, pp. 262–263.

30. C. F. McKim to RMH, Feb. 9, and Mar. 6, 1893, and C. F. McKim to E. H. Kendall, Feb. 13, 1893, McKim Papers (Box 1, Bk. 1), Library of Congress; CCHH, HP, pp. 265–267; Moore, McKim, pp. 122–123; Moore, Burnham, I, 69–70.

31. Quoted in New York Times, Mar. 26, 1893, p. 2; C. F. McKim to RMH, Mar. 7, 1893, C. F. McKim Papers (Box 1, Bk. 1), Library of Congress; Moore, Burnham, I, 72–79.

32. F. L. Olmsted to John Olmsted, Apr. 13 and May 3, 1893, Gen. Corres., Box 24, Olmsted Papers, Library of Con-

gress; *New York Times,* May 2, 1893, pp. 1–3; Roper, *FLO,* p. 448.

33. CCHH, HP, pp. 275–276; Form No. 126, "Information for the Committee of Retrospective Arts," Charles Henry Hart Papers, Manuscripts and Archives Division, New York Public Library; Frank R. Stockton to Esther Hunt, Nov. 8, 1897, Manuscript Collection, Redwood Library, Newport; Theodore Sizer, ed., *The Recollections of John F. Weir* (New York and New Haven, 1957), p. 62.

34. Royal Cortissoz, "Richard Morris Hunt," *New-York Daily Tribune,* Aug. 4, 1895, p. 23, reprinted in *Art and Common Sense* (New York, 1913), p. 398.

35. Charles E. Banks, *The Artistic Guide to Chicago and the World's Columbian Exposition* (Chicago, 1893), p. 242; Henry Van Brunt, "Architecture at the World's Columbian Exposition," *Century,* n.s. XXII (May 1892), 90–94.

36. Banks, *Artistic Guide,* pp. 241–243; Johnson, ed., *History of the World's Columbian Exposition,* I, 163–165; Van Brunt, "Architecture at the World's Columbian Exposition,"

91–92. The central section and the dome of the Administration Building were framed with iron, while the corner pavilions were built entirely of wood.

37. Anon., "Architectural Sculpture: Decorations of the Administration Building of the Columbian Exhibition," *Harper's Weekly,* XXXVI (Jan. 30, 1892), 114; Van Brunt, "Architecture at the World's Columbian Exposition," 92–93; Wayne Craven, *Sculpture in America* (New York, 1968), p. 468; James M. Dennis, *Karl Bitter, Architectural Sculptor, 1867–1915* (Madison, Wis., 1967), pp. 41–42, 45–46.

38. Montgomery Schuyler, "The Works of the Late Richard M. Hunt," *Architectural Record,* V (Oct.–Dec. 1895), 118; C. Howard Walker, "Notes on the Sculpture and Architecture at the Columbian Exposition," *Architectural Review,* I (May 2, 1892), 41; Dudley Arnold Lewis, "Evaluations of American Architecture by European Critics, 1875–1900," Ph.D. Diss., University of Wisconsin, 1962, p. 177; Jacques Hermant, "The World's Fair Buildings Through French Spectacles," *Engineering Magazine,* VI

(Mar. 1894), 768–769; editorial from the *Chicago Inter-Ocean* quoted in "Richard Morris Hunt Memorial Edition," *Inland Architect and News Record,* XXVI (Aug. 1895), 4.

39. For artistic reactions, see, for example, Edwin H. Blashfield, "A Painter's Reminiscences of a World's Fair," *New York Times Magazine,* Mar. 18, 1923, reprinted in William A. Coles and Henry Hope Reed, Jr., *Architecture in America: A Battle of Styles* (New York, 1961), pp. 149–151; Homer Saint-Gaudens, ed., *The Reminiscences of Augustus Saint-Gaudens* (New York, 1913), II, 74; and Moore, *Burnham,* I, 90; see also Hines, *Burnham of Chicago,* pp. 74, 123–124; Montgomery Schuyler, "Last Words About the World's Fair," *Architectural Record,* III (Jan.–Mar. 1894), 291–301; Sullivan, *Autobiography of an Idea,* p. 325.

40. Henry Adams, *The Education of Henry Adams* (Boston, 1918; New York, Mod. Lib. ed., 1931), pp. 340–341, 343, 315.

CHAPTER 23

1. Gifford Pinchot, *Biltmore Forest* (Chicago, 1893), p. 8.

2. Wayne Andrews, *The Vanderbilt Legend* (New York, 1941), p. 333; CCHH, HP, p. 248; ABD, No. 1296 of 1886; NBD, No. 1536 of 1887.

3. Consuelo Vanderbilt Balsan, *The Glitter and the Gold* (New York, 1952), p. 4; Gifford Pinchot, *Breaking New Ground* (New York, 1947), p. 48; Carl Alwin Schenck, *The Biltmore Story: Recollections of the Beginning of Forestry in the United States,* ed. by Ovid Butler (St. Paul, 1955), p. 32; Gifford Pinchot, Diary, Oct. 18, 1891, Pinchot Papers, Manuscript Division, Library of Congress; CCHH, HP, pp. 233, 296; Frederick Law Olmsted to Frederick Kingsbury, Jan. 20, 1891, Gen. Corres., Box 23, Olmsted Papers, Manuscript Division, Library of Congress.

4. Frederick Law Olmsted to Frederick Kingsbury, Jan. 20, 1891, Gen. Corres., Box 23, Olmsted Papers; Pinchot, *Biltmore Forest,* pp. 7–8; quoted in Fannie C. W. Barbour, "A Palace in 'The Land of the Sky,'" *Chautauquan,* XXI (June 1895), 324.

5. Frederick Law Olmsted to Frederick Kingsbury, Jan. 20, 1891, Gen. Corres., Box 23, Frederick Law Olmsted to J. G.

Aster, Oct. 29, 1888, Gen. Corres., Box 22, Frederick Law Olmsted to James Gall, Oct. 30, 1888, Gen. Corres., Box 22, and Frederick Law Olmsted to George W. Vanderbilt, Nov. 6, 1889, Private Estates, Box 43, all in Olmsted Papers.

6. Quoted in CCHH, HP, p. 289; Frederick Law Olmsted to George W. Vanderbilt, Mar. 2, 1889, Private Estates, Box 43, Olmsted Papers; William A. V. Cecil, "Biltmore," pamphlet (Asheville, 1972), pp. 12–27; Edward F. Turberg, "Frederick Law Olmsted at Biltmore," M.A. thesis, University of Virginia, 1973, passim.

7. Frederick Law Olmsted to RMH, Mar. 2, 1889, copy in Private Estates, Box 43, Olmsted Papers; Laura Wood Roper, *FLO: A Biography of Frederick Law Olmsted* (Baltimore, 1973), p. 416.

8. Frederick Law Olmsted to George W. Vanderbilt, Mar. 26, 1889, and Henry S. Codman to RMH, Feb. 7, 1890, Private Estates, Box 43, copies in Olmsted Papers; Roper, *FLO,* p. 416; Turberg, "Frederick Law Olmsted at Biltmore," pp. 30–31.

9. Quoted in CCHH, HP, p. 244; Anon.,

"George Vanderbilt's Southern Home," *Architecture and Building,* XII (May 31, 1890), 258; Anon., "Mr. George Vanderbilt's House at Asheville, N.C.," *American Architect and Building News,* XXIX (July 12, 1890), 18; Roper, *FLO* p. 416.

10. Frederick Law Olmsted to W. A. Thompson, Nov. 6, 1889, Private Estates, Box 43, Frederick Law Olmsted to his partners, Oct. 28, 1893, Gen. Corres., Box 24, Frederick Law Olmsted to his partners, May 3, 1894, Private Estates, Box 43, Olmsted Papers; Frederick Law Olmsted to his partners, Nov. 1, 1893, quoted in Roper, *FLO,* p. 453.

11. Frederick Law Olmsted to John Olmsted, Oct. 24, Oct. 25, Oct. 27, 1890, and Oct. 11, 1891, Private Estates, Box 43, and Oct. 29, 1890, Gen. Corres., Box 23, Olmsted Papers; Gifford Pinchot to his mother, Feb. 28, March 13, 1892, and n.d. [1892], Family Correspondence files, and Gifford Pinchot, Diary, Oct. 14, Dec. 30, and Dec. 31, 1891, and Jan. 1, and Jan. 3, 1892, Pinchot Papers; Roper, *FLO,* p. 419; CCHH, HP, p. 244.

12. CCHH, HP, p. 254; Harold T. Pinkett, "Gif-

ford Pinchot at Biltmore," *North Carolina Historical Review*, XXXIV (July 1957), 346–357; Roper, *FLO*, p. 433; Gifford Pinchot, Diary, Oct. 14, Oct. 15, Nov. 12, Dec. 30, Dec. 31, 1891, and Jan. 1, Jan. 3, Jan. 6, Jan. 9, and Feb. 2, 1892, Pinchot Papers; Gifford Pinchot to his father, Jan. 5, 1892, Family Correspondence files, Pinchot Papers.

13. Pinchot, *Breaking New Ground*, pp. 48–54, 57; E. H. Frothingham, "Forestry on the Biltmore Estate," U.S. Dept. of Agriculture, Appalachia Forest Experiment Station, Technical Note No. 93 (Asheville, Jan. 27, 1941); Anon., "Biltmore House & Gardens," pamphlet (Asheville, 1973), p. 2.

14. M. Nelson McGreary, *Gifford Pinchot: Forester, Politician* (Princeton, 1960), pp. 26–30; Schenck, *Biltmore Story*, passim; Gifford Pinchot, Diary, Jan. 2, 1895, Pinchot Papers; Anon., "The Vanderbilt Arboretum," *Architecture and Building*, XX (Apr. 14, 1894), 181; quoted in Anon., "Biltmore House & Gardens," p. 26.

15. Turberg, "Frederick Law Olmsted at Biltmore," pp. 33–34;

Richard Howland Hunt to Henry G. Marquand, Nov. 13, 1895, Archives (B868), Metropolitan Museum of Art.

16. Turberg, "Frederick Law Olmsted at Biltmore," pp. 38–40; Frederick Law Olmsted to John Olmsted, Feb. 25, 1894, Private Estates, Box 43, and Frederick Law Olmsted to W. A. Stiles, Mar. 10, 1895, Gen. Corres., Box 25, Olmsted Papers. Albert Fein, *Frederick Law Olmsted and the American Environmental Tradition* (New York, 1972), p. 56, concludes that Hunt opposed Olmsted "on almost every aspect of the [Biltmore] project," but the evidence supports exactly the opposite conclusion.

17. Frederick Law Olmsted, "Letter to the Editor," *Lyceum Magazine*, II (Dec. 1891), 6; Norman T. Newton, *Design on the Land: The Development of Landscape Architecture* (Cambridge, Mass., 1971), p. 348. The gardens and nursery and the arboretum at Biltmore were developed under the direction of Chauncey D. Beadle, a graduate of Cornell University, and became the most complete in the southeastern United States.

18. Turberg, "Frederick Law Olmsted at Biltmore," pp. 15, 27–28; CCHH, HP, pp. 255–256; Newton, *Design on the Land*, pp. 346–347. In his work at Biltmore as elsewhere, Olmsted attempted to subordinate the landscaping details to a coherent, overall effect, which would have an unconscious impact on the viewer: see Charles E. Beveridge, "Frederick Law Olmsted's Theory on Landscape Design," *Nineteenth Century*, III (Summer 1977), 42 and passim.

19. Harry W. Desmond and Herbert Croly, *Stately Homes in America* (New York, 1903), p. 431; Montgomery Schuyler, "The Works of the Late Richard M. Hunt," *Architectural Record*, V (Oct.–Dec. 1895), 168.

20. Schuyler, "The Works of the Late Richard M. Hunt," 170; Anon., "The Builders of Biltmore," *Architectural Record*, V (Oct.–Dec. 1895), 200–201.

21. James M. Dennis, *Karl Bitter, Architectural Sculptor, 1867–1915* (Madison, Wis., 1967), pp. 24, 29, 30–33; Anon., "Life Visits the Vanderbilt Mansions," *Life*, XXVIII (Jan. 2, 1950), 90;

Stapleton Dabney Gooch IV, "The Art and Architectural Library at Biltmore," *American Association of Architectural Bibliographers Papers*, IV (1967), 17–46. See Anon., "Biltmore House & Gardens," for a detailed description of the decorations and furnishings of the rooms of Biltmore open to the public.

22. George W. Vanderbilt to Frederick Law Olmsted, May 2, 1895, Gen. Corres., Box 25, Olmsted Papers; Roper, *FLO*, p. 467; William H. Downes, *John S. Sargent: His Life and Work* (Boston, 1925), p. 175; Edward B. Martin, *The Life of Joseph H. Choate* (New York, 1920), II, 206; CCHH, HP, pp. 297–298.

23. Barbour, "A Palace in 'The Land of the Sky,'" 325; Martin, *Life of Joseph H. Choate*, II, 206; quoted in CCHH, HP, p. 290.

24. Quoted in Leon Edel, *Henry James: The Master, 1901–1916* (Philadelphia, 1972), pp. 270–271.

25. Anon., "Biltmore House & Gardens," pp. 2, 26–27; Frothingham, "Forestry on the Biltmore Estate," passim.

CHAPTER 24

1. CCHH, HP, pp. 257–258; *Harvard Graduates' Magazine*, I (Oct. 1892), 93–94.

2. CCHH, HP, pp. 268–269; *New York Times*, Mar. 7, 1893, p. 10 and June 20, 1893, p. 2. In 1903, when Charles F. McKim received the Royal Gold Medal of the R.I.B.A., as the second American recipient, Hunt's old friend Joseph H. Choate was United States ambassador to Great Britain and at the awards ceremony spoke of Hunt's pioneering work improving American building practices: see Charles Moore, *The Life and Times of Charles Follen McKim* (Boston, 1929), p. 240.

3. CCHH, HP, pp. 269–271; Anon., "Royal Institute of British Architects; Presentation of the Royal Gold Medal," *American Architect and Building News*, XLI (July 15, 1893), 39–40; *New York Times*, Aug. 1, 1895, p. 5; Dudley Arnold Lewis, "Evaluations of American Architecture by European Critics, 1875–1900," Ph.D. Diss., Univ. of Wisconsin, 1962, pp. 206, 212, 216.

4. Anon., "Royal Institute of British Architects," 41–42; CCHH, HP, pp. 271–273.

5. CCHH, HP, pp. 273–274.

6. Amable Charles Franquet, comte de Franqueville, *Le Premier Siècle de L'Institut de France* (Paris, 1895–1896), II, 112 and passim; New York *Sun*, Jan. 19, 1894, p. 6; Benjamin Franklin was elected a foreign associate of the old Académie Royale des Sciences in 1772.

7. RMH to J. F. Weir, Apr. 18, 1893, J. F. Weir Papers, Manuscript Division, Yale University; RMH to Alfred Stone, May 20, 1893, Gen. Corres., HC; RMH to Charles W. Eliot, Aug. 6, 1893, Archives, Harvard University; clippings from *Worcester* (Mass.) *Spy*, Aug. 1, 1895, and *Buffalo Courier*, Aug. 3, 1895, Obituaries Scrapbook, HC; CCHH, HP, pp. 247, 256, 299; William A. Stiles to Frederick Law Olmsted, Feb. 28, 1895, and Mar. 5, 1895, and Frederick Law Olmsted to W. A. Stiles, Mar. 10, 1895, Gen. Corres., Box 25, Olmsted Papers, Library of Congress; Laura Roper, *FLO: A Biography of Frederick Law Olmsted* (Baltimore, 1973), p. 464.

8. CCHH, HP, pp 280–281; Nathalie Dana, "The Municipal Art So-

ciety: Seventy-Five Years of Service to New York," *New-York Historical Society Quarterly*, LI (Apr. 1967), 161–183; Charles De Kay, "A Turning Point in the Arts," *Cosmopolitan*, XV (July 1893), 275; Wayne Craven, *Sculpture in America* (New York, 1968), p. 478; Charles De Kay to J. Q. A. Ward, Apr. 26, 1893, and miscellany, June 1, 1894, Ward Papers, New-York Historical Society; Henry Hope Reed, Jr., "Classical New York," *Art in America*, XLV (Summer 1957), 15.

9. Anon., "The Supervising Architect's Office Reorganized," *Inland Architect and News Record*, XXX (August 1897), 3; CCHH, HP, pp. 206–207, 256; RMH to Dankmar Adler, Feb. 8, and May 10, 1892, and RMH to Alfred Stone, Feb. 14, 1893, Gen. Corres., HC.

10. Anon., "The Supervising Architect's Office Reorganized," 3; Glenn Brown, "Government Buildings Compared with Private Buildings," *American Architect and Building News*, XLIV (Apr. 7, 1894), 2–12; CCHH, HP, pp. 287, 298; Jeremiah O'Rourke to RMH, Jan. 17, 1894, Gen. Corres., HC; C. F. McKim to RMH, Mar.

29, Mar. 31, Apr. 4, and June 12, 1894, and C. F. McKim to Richard Olney, Mar. 29, 1894, Box 1, Bk. 3, McKim Papers, Library of Congress; Charles Moore, *Daniel H. Burnham: Architect Planner of Cities* (Boston, 1921), I, 96, 103–105. See also Thomas S. Hines, *Burnham of Chicago* (New York, 1974), 126–133. The Tarsney Act was repealed in 1912 on the grounds of economy.

11. Alexander R. Butler, "McKim's Renaissance: A Study in the History of the American Architectural Profession," Ph.D. Diss., The Johns Hopkins University, 1953, p. 2. For a study of McKim's early designs and architectural ideas, see Richard Guy Wilson, "Charles F. McKim and the Development of the American Renaissance: A Study in Architecture and Culture," Ph.D. Diss., University of Michigan, 1972, 4 vols.

12. Quoted from a working paper by Charles F. McKim, ca. 1895, Archives, American Academy in Rome, New York; see also Moore, *McKim*, p. 129.

13. CCHH, HP, pp. 284–285; C. F. McKim to RMH, May 19, 1894, Box 1, Bk. 3, McKim Papers; C. F. McKim to D. H.

Burnham, May 29, 1894, and McKim to RMH, June 5, 1894, reprinted in Moore, *McKim*, p. 137 (see also p. 140); Butler, "McKim's Renaissance," 104 ff.; "Minutes of the Meetings of the American School of Architecture in Rome," June 6, June 15, Sept. 8, and Nov. 12, 1894, and Feb. 7, Feb. 27, Mar. 9, Apr. 23, May 11, and May 14, 1895, Archives, The American Academy in Rome, New York.

14. John M. Carrère to C. F. McKim, July 18, 1894, and Catharine Hunt to C. F. McKim, Mar. 14, 1895, Old Corres., Archives, American Academy in Rome; C. F. McKim to RMH, Mar. 8, 1895, quoted in Moore, *McKim*, p. 144; Butler, "McKim's Renaissance," chapter 8. See also William Francklyn Paris, "Richard Morris Hunt: First Secretary and Third President of the Institute," *Journal of the American Institute of Architects*, XXV (Jan. 1956), 17.

15. "Minutes," Mar. 9, 1895, Archives, American Academy in Rome; Moore, *McKim*, pp. 144–146.

16. "Minutes," Apr. 23 and May 14, 1895, Archives, American Academy in Rome; RMH

to C. F. McKim, June 24, 1895, and William R. Ware to RMH, July 26, 1895, Old Corres., Archives, American Academy in Rome; Moore, *McKim*, pp. 145–146.

17. "Minutes," May 11, 1895, Archives, American Academy in Rome; "Corporation Book," Apr. 6, Apr. 20, May 17, and May 18, 1895, Archives, American Academy in Rome; Charles F. Boring to C. F. McKim, Aug. 1, 1895, RMH to C. F. McKim, Apr. 2, May 4, and May 26, 1895, R. J. Nevin to RMH, May 8, 1895, Old Corres., Archives, American Academy in Rome; Cablegrams, R. J. Nevin to C. F. McKim, Apr. 9, 1895, and Austin W. Lord to C. F. McKim, July 1, 1895, Archives, American Academy in Rome; C. F. McKim to Thomas Newbold, Aug. 1, 1895, Box 1, Bk. 3, McKim Papers; Moore, *McKim*, pp. 146–148.

18. Butler, "McKim's Renaissance," chapter 7; "Corporation Book," passim., Archives, American Academy in Rome.

19. *New York Times*, Oct. 24, 1899, p. 7; Alan Burnham, ed., *New York Landmarks: A Study and Index of Architecturally Notable Structures in Greater New York* (Middletown, Conn., 1963), p. 194.

20. Winifred E. Howe, *A History of the Metropolitan Museum of Art* (New York, 1913), I, pp. 176, 231–232, 265–266; CCHH, HP, pp. 118–119; Executive Committee Minutes, Dec. 20, 1881 (E3:13) and Trustees Minutes, Feb. 18, 1890 (T3:44), Archives, Metropolitan Museum of Art (hereafter AMMA).

21. RMH to H. G. Marquand, Feb. 18, 1890, and Feb. 15, 1891 (H913), J. Q. A. Ward to H. G. Marquand, Apr. 2, 1890 (H9135), and L. di Cesnola to H. G. Marquand, Aug. 2, 1895 (B868), AMMA; CCHH, HP, p. 119.

22. Joseph Wolf to L. di Cesnola, Jan. 15, 1895; RMH to L. di Cesnola, Feb. 1 and Mar. 27, 1895; L. di Cesnola to RMH, Mar. 27, 1895; RMH to H. G. Marquand, Apr. 3 and Apr. 20, 1895 (B868), AMMA; Building Committee Minutes, Apr. 5, 1895 (B1:65–67), AMMA; CCHH, HP, p. 295.

23. CCHH, HP, pp. 295–296; Metropolitan Museum of Art, *Twenty-Sixth Annual Report of the Trustees of the Association for the Year Ending December 31, 1895* (New York, 1896), p. 645; Executive Committee Minutes, Apr. 27 and Oct. 28, 1895 (E4:259, 272); Building Committee Minutes, Oct. 24 and Oct. 30, 1895 (B868); RMH to L. di Cesnola, May 7, May 13, and May 15, 1895; L. di Cesnola to RMH, Apr. 20, May 10, and May 17, 1895; L. di Cesnola to H. G. Marquand, Aug. 2 and Nov. 5, 1895; H. G. Marquand to L. di Cesnola, Aug. 7 (including quote) and Aug. 24, 1895; Richard Howland Hunt to H. G. Marquand, Aug. 19 and Nov. 14, 1895 (all B868), all AMMA.

24. *New York Times*, Oct. 24, 1899, p. 7; Albert Ten Eyck Gardner, "Those Blocks: Story of the Fifth Avenue Façade of the Museum," *Metroploitan Museum Bulletin*, n.s. XI (May 1953), 252.

25. John Maass, *The Glorious Enterprise: The Centennial Exhibition of 1876 and H. J. Schwarzmann, Architect-in-Chief* (Watkins Glen, N.Y., 1973), pp. 52–53; Henry-Russell Hitchcock, *Architecture: Nineteenth and Twentieth Centuries* (Harmondsworth and Baltimore, 1958; 3d ed., 1968), p. 23; see J. N. L. Durand, *Précis des Leçons d'architec-*

ture données à l'Ecole Polytechnique, 2 vols. (1802–1805).

26. For discussions of the design of the Metropolitan Museum of Art, see, for example, A. D. F. Hamlin and F. S. Lamb, "The New York Architectural League Exhibition," *Architectural Review,* VI (Mar. 1899), 42; Anon., "The New Metropolitan Museum of Art," *Architectural Record,* XII (Aug. 1902), 304–310; Gardner, "Those Blocks," 252–258; Henry Hope Reed, *The Golden City* (New York, 1971), p. 14; Wayne Craven, *Sculpture in America* (New York, 1968), p. 468; James M. Dennis, *Karl Bitter Architectural Sculptor, 1867–1915* (Madison, Wis., 1967), p. 78; Walter C. Kidney, "R. M. Hunt at the Metropolitan Museum," *Progressive Architecture,* XLVII (Oct. 1966), 12.

27. Quoted in CCHH, HP, p. 278.

CHAPTER 25

1. CCHH, HP, p. 296, including quote.

2. CCHH, HP, pp. 246, 248, 252, 264.

3. CCHH, HP, pp. 223, 258, 264, 287, 295; Catharine Howland Hunt to Gifford Pinchot,

Mar. 3, Apr. 29, and May 20, 1892, Gen. Corres., Pinchot Papers, Library of Congress. Esther Hunt was a close friend of Gertrude Vanderbilt, the daughter of Mr. and Mrs. Cornelius Vanderbilt II and later the wife of Harry Payne Whitney, and apparently she had a tremendous "crush" on her wealthy friend: see B. H. Friedman, *Gertrude Vanderbilt Whitney* (Garden City, N.Y., 1978), pp. 46–47 and passim.

4. CCHH, HP, pp. 295–299; C. F. McKim to CCHH, Mar. 14, 1895, McKim Papers (Box 1, Bk. 1), Library of Congress.

5. CCHH, HP, pp. 299–300; *Newport Daily News,* Aug. 1, 1895, p. 1; *Newport Mercury,* Aug. 3, 1895, p. 1; C. F. McKim to E. D. Morgan, Aug. 1, 1895, McKim Papers (Box 1, Bk.1). Hunt's death was reported to have been "the result of a complication of diseases."

6. *New York Times,* Aug. 4, 1895, p. 13.

7. *New York Times,* Aug. 9, 1895, p. 11; *New-York Daily Tribune,* Aug. 9, 1895, p. 7; clippings from *Philadelphia Inquirer,* Aug. 1, 1895, and *Boston Herald,* Aug. 10, 1895, in Obituaries

Scrapbook, HC. The appointment of a third executor, Edward Mitchell, named in the original document, was revoked by a codicil drawn up on June 2, 1893, just before the Hunts started for Europe for the R.I.B.A. award. A copy of the will is in the HP.

8. Two scrapbooks in the HC contain mostly obituaries; see *Newport Daily News,* Aug. 5, 1895, p. 6; quoted in E. H. Kendall, "Richard Morris Hunt," *Proceedings of the Twenty-Ninth Annual Convention of the American Institute of Architects* (Providence, 1895), p. 86; Henry Van Brunt, "Richard Morris Hunt," ibid., 77.

9. Trustees' Resolution (T3:203) and "Annual Report of Trustees for Year 1895" (648), Archives, Metropolitan Museum of Art; Century Association, *Reports, Constitution, By-Laws and List of Members of the Century Association for the Year 1895* (New York, 1896), p. 16.

10. Quoted in Van Brunt, "Richard Morris Hunt," p. 83. The original resolutions are in the HC.

11. Dudley Arnold Lewis, "Evaluations of

American Architecture by European Critics, 1875–1900," Ph.D. Diss., University of Wisconsin, pp. 207, 210, 213–218.

12. Clippings from *Philadelphia Bulletin*, Dec. 31, 1895, in Obituaries Scrapbook, HC; Pennsylvania Academy of Fine Arts, *A Memorial Exhibition of Drawings and Photographs Illustrating the Life and Works of the Late Richard Morris Hunt, Architect, 1827–1895* (Philadelphia, 1896).

13. *New-York Daily Tribune*, Dec. 18, 1898, Illus. Suppl., p. 4.

14. *New-York Daily Tribune*, Feb. 15, 1896, p. 12; Mar. 4, 1896, p. 7; Apr. 4, 1896, p. 4; May 27, 1896, p. 2; Feb. 17, 1897, p. 6; Sept. 26, 1897, Sec. 3, p. 1; and Feb. 12, 1898, p. 3; CCHH, HP, p. 281; Executive Committee Minutes (E4:282, 296–297, 314), Archives, Metropolitan Museum of Art.

15. Catharine Howland Hunt, 1898 Diary, HP; CCHH, HP, pp. 281–283; *New York Times*, Nov. 1, 1898, p. 12.

16. "'Ars Longa, Vita Brevis Est': Richard Morris Hunt. 'Laborare Est Orare,' 1895," newspaper clippings and public statements about RMH, compiled by his widow and presented to her children on the fifth anniversary of their father's death. Privately owned. Deposited 1978 in the Avery Library, Columbia University. Many notes in the HP refer to the gathering of biographical materials.

17. Clippings from the Charles H. Russell Scrapbook, Newport Historical Society; miscellaneous clippings, HP.

18. *New York Times*, Oct. 12, 1924, Sec. X, p. 7, and July 13, 1931, p. 17; William Rhinelander Stewart, *Grace Church and Old New York* (New York, 1924), p. 328; miscellaneous clippings, HP.

19. Clipping from *Boston Transcript*, n.d., n.p., Memoria Cuttings Scrapbook, HC.

20. Montgomery Schuyler, "The Works of the Late Richard M. Hunt," *Architectural Record*, V (Oct.–Dec. 1895), 99, 109, 170.

21. William Francklyn Paris, "Richard Morris Hunt: First Secretary and Third President of the Institute," *Journal of the American Institute of Architects*, XXIV (Dec. 1955), 243–244, 246; Barr Ferree, "Richard Morris Hunt: His Art and Work," *Architecture and Building*, XXIII (Dec. 7, 1895), 271; quoted in Frank E. Wallis, "Richard M. Hunt, Master Architect and Man," *Architectural Review*, n.s. V (Nov. 1917), 240; Peter B. Wight, "Richard Morris Hunt," *Inland Architect and News Record*, XXVI (Aug. 1895), 2.

22. Quoted in CCHH, HP, p. 232.

23. See John Tomsich, *A Genteel Endeavor: American Culture and Politics in the Gilded Age* (Stanford, 1971), pp. 186–194. See also the discussion of Frederick Law Olmsted as a conservative reformer in Geoffrey Blodgett, "Frederick Law Olmsted: Landscape Architecture as Conservative Reform," *Journal of American History*, LXII (Mar. 1976), 869–889.

24. Paul Bourget, *Outre-Mer: Impressions of America* (New York, 1895), p. 53.

APPENDIX

A CHRONOLOGICAL
LIST OF
ARCHITECTURAL
WORK BY RICHARD
MORRIS HUNT

This list of the architectural work of Richard Morris Hunt, including both buildings erected and designs not executed, is probably incomplete. In the absence of office records, the list has been compiled from information left by Hunt's widow and from a variety of other contemporary sources, including materials in the Hunt Collection at the American Institute of Architects Foundation in Washington, D.C., and the privately held Hunt Papers. Wherever possible, the inclusion of a project has been verified from more than one contemporary source. Hunt's student designs have not been included. In the list, the first date given is for the earliest work that Hunt did on the project; this sometimes occurred well before actual construction of a building commenced. Occasionally Hunt also worked on a project after it was "officially" completed. For most commissions executed in New York City from 1866 onward, the building docket numbers are given from the records of the New York City Buildings Department located in the New York City Municipal Building. New buildings are recorded in the New Buildings Dockets file (NBD), while alterations to already existing structures are recorded in the Alterations Buildings Dockets file (ABD). These files serve as an index to the actual building plans and include information as to the location of the building, the architect, the builder, and the owner, along with a brief description of the system of construction and the dates that work was begun and completed. A small number of buildings attributed to Hunt either by contemporaries or by others subsequently have been excluded from this list, since positive evidence for Hunt's authorship was lacking or since the building has been convincingly attributed to another architect.

The author would appreciate hearing from any reader who might have information regarding additions to or corrections for this list.

Pavillon de la Bibliothèque, Palais du Louvre, Paris, France (inspector of works under Hector Martin Lefuel, 1854–1855)

Thomas P. Rossiter house (Dr. Eleazer Parmly house), 11 West Thirty-Eighth Street, New York, N.Y. (1855–1857; demolished)

United States Capitol extension, Washington, D.C. (assistant to Thomas U. Walter, 1856)

Studio Building, 15 (later 51) West Tenth Street, New York, N.Y. (1857–1858; demolished)

Dr. H. H. Williams (with Dr. Morland) houses, 13, 14, and 15 Arlington Street, Boston, Mass. (1859–1860; demolished)

William Beech Lawrence house, stables, and coach house, Ochre Point Avenue, Newport, R.I. (1860; alterations; demolished)

Alexander Duncan house, Providence, R.I. (1860; alterations; probably demolished)

W. P. Wright picture gallery, Hoboken, N.J. (1860–1861; demolished). Also Wright log cabin, sketch at A.I.A. (probably not executed)

Edward Willing house, Bellevue Avenue, Newport, R.I. (1860–1861; alterations; demolished)

Arthur Bronson house, Ocean Drive at Castle Hill, Newport, R.I. (1860–1861; demolished)

Frederic E. Church, "Cosy Cottage," near Hudson, N.Y. (ca. 1860–1861) and house (ca. 1867; not constructed)

Arsenal, Central Park, New York, N.Y. (1860+; alterations)

George Chandler Hall house, Brattleboro, Vt. (1860–1868; demolished)

National Academy of Design, Fourth Avenue at Twenty-Third Street, New York, N.Y. (1861; unsuccessful competition; not constructed)

Gateways for the southern entrances, Central Park, New York, N.Y. (1861+; not constructed)

John N. A. Griswold house, coach house, stables, and barn, 76 Bellevue Avenue, Newport, R.I. (1861–1863; presently The Art Association of Newport)

William Shepard monument, Island Cemetery (?), Newport, R.I. (ca. 1863)

Metropolitan Fair annex building, Union Square, New York, N.Y. (1864; temp. building; interior design; demolished)

Lincoln funeral monument, Union Square, New York, N.Y. (1865; temporary monument; demolished)

Brooklyn Mercantile Library Association building, Brooklyn, N.Y. (1865; unsuccessful competition; not constructed)

New-York Historical Society Museum, New York, N.Y. (1865–1866; not constructed)

Captain Percival Drayton Monument, Trinity Church, Broadway opposite Wall Street, New York, N.Y. (with L. Larmande, 1865–1867)

William Conant Church house, location unknown (1866; probably not constructed)

American Institute, New York, N.Y. (with R. G. Hatfield, 1866; not constructed)

Russell family monument (erected for Caroline Howland Russell), Island Cemetery, Newport, R.I. (1866)

Academy of Music, Fourteenth Street and Irving Place, New York, N.Y. (1866; unsuccessful competition; not constructed)

Mrs. Colford Jones Swiss chalet, barn, and coach house, Halidon Avenue, Newport, R.I. (1866–1867; 1870 [?])

Union League Clubhouse, Fourth Avenue and Twenty-Third

Street, New York, N.Y. (1867; not constructed; also 1879, unsuccessful competition for Fifth Avenue and Thirty-Ninth Street, N.Y.C. location)

Equitable Life Assurance Society building, southeast corner of Broadway and Cedar Street, New York, N.Y. (1867; unsuccessful competition; not constructed)

John W. Bigelow house, Washington Street, Newport, R.I. (1867–1868; alterations; demolished)

Alexander Van Rensselaer house, Miantonomi Avenue, Middletown, R.I. (1867–1868; alterations)

Sara Gibbs tomb, Brattleboro, Vt. (1867–1868)

Seventh Regiment Monument pedestal, Central Park, New York, N.Y. (with J. Q. A. Ward, designed 1867–1868; erected 1873)

Scroll and Key Society clubhouse, Yale University, College and Wall streets, New Haven, Conn. (1867–1869)

Union Theological Seminary, New York, N.Y. (1868; unsuccessful competition; not constructed)

Nielley cottage and barn, Newport, R.I. (1868; probably demolished)

J. C. Bancroft Davis house and barn, Cedarcliff, N.Y. (1868; demolished)

Samuel Tweedy tomb, location unknown (1868)

Anthon Memorial Church rectory, location unknown (1868).

Matthew Calbraith Perry Monument pedestal, Touro Park, Newport, R.I. (with J. Q. A. Ward; erected 1868)

John Quincy Adams Ward, two houses and a studio, 7 and 9 West Forty-Ninth Street, New York, N.Y. (1868–1869; NBD No. 579 of 1868; demolished)

William Shakespeare Monument pedestal, Central Park, New York, N.Y. (with J. Q. A. Ward; 1868–1870; not constructed)

Presbyterian Hospital, Administration Building, North Pavilion, and boiler house, Madison Avenue to Fourth (later Park) Avenue between East Seventieth and Seventy-First streets, New York, N.Y. (1868–1872; NBD No. 128 of 1870; North Pavilion de-

stroyed by fire and replaced; all demolished)

United States Post Office, Broadway and Park Row, New York, N.Y. (with Renwick & Sands, Le Brun, Correja, and Schulze & Schoen; modified and supervised by A. B. Mullett; 1868–1875; demolished)

Levi P. Morton house (Fairlawn) ballroom, Bellevue and Ruggles avenues, Newport, R.I. (1869; alterations)

Lewis M. Rutherfurd house and stables, Harrison Avenue, Newport, R.I. (1869; demolished)

Liberty Bank building (Chambers, Calder & Co.), 9–10 Exchange Place, Providence, R.I. (ca. 1869; demolished)

New York Institute for the Blind, Thirty-Third to Thirty-Fourth streets off Ninth Avenue, New York, N.Y. (1869; unsuccessful competition for an addition; not constructed)

Academic Hall, Hampton Institute, Hampton, Va. (1869–1870; destroyed by fire, 1879, and replaced by Hunt's Second Academic Hall)

East Divinity Hall, Yale Divinity School, northwest corner of College and Elm streets, New

Haven, Conn. (1869–1870; demolished)

Mrs. William F. Coles house, Bellevue Avenue and Dixon Street, Newport, R.I. (1869–1870; alterations; demolished)

Stuyvesant Apartments, 142 East Eighteenth Street, New York, N.Y. (1869–1870; NBD No. 562 of 1869; demolished)

William H. Osborn house and studio, 32 Park Avenue, New York, N.Y. (1869–1870; NBD No. 858 of 1869; demolished)

Jonathan Sturges house, 34 Park Avenue, New York, N.Y. (1869–1870; NBD No. 858 of 1869; demolished)

Richard Morris Hunt house (Hill Top Cottage), Bellevue Avenue at Touro and Church streets, Newport, R.I. (1869–1870; 1877–1878; alterations; demolished)

Rathbone houses, Providence, R.I. (1869–1871; probably demolished)

William R. Travers house (formerly Thomas H. Hitchcock house) and ballroom, Narragansett and Ochre Point avenues, Newport, R.I. (1869–1872; alterations; demolished)

Union Car Spring Company warehouses, location unknown (1869–1872; status unknown)

Eighth Avenue Grand Opera House, northwest corner of Eighth Avenue and Twenty-Third Street, New York, N.Y. (ca. 1869–1872; alterations; demolished)

New York Hospital Asylum for the Insane, White Plains, N.Y. (1869, 1874; not constructed)

Martin Brimmer, two houses, 47 and 48 Beacon Street, Boston, Mass. (1869–1870, 1876; demolished)

George Peabody Wetmore mansion and entrance gates (Château-sur-Mer), Bellevue Avenue, Newport, R.I. (1869–1873; principal work, 1872; 1879+; alterations; presently owned by the Preservation Society of Newport County and open to the public)

Abattoir Company slaughterhouses, Jersey City, N.J. (1870; probably demolished)

Charlotte Cushman house (The Corners), coach house, and stables, 49 Catherine Street, Newport, R.I. (1870; destroyed by fire)

William T. Blodgett house, Newport, R.I.

(ca. 1870; not constructed)

Richard Baker house, Ledge Road, Newport, R.I. (ca. 1870; alterations; demolished)

Travers Block stores and apartments, Bellevue Avenue and (presently) Memorial Boulevard, Newport, R.I. (1870–1871)

Colonel George Waring house (The Hypothenuse), 33 Greenough Place at Catherine Street, Newport, R.I. (1870–1871; older house moved to this site and altered)

Marquand Chapel, Yale Divinity School, Elm Street, New Haven, Conn. (1870–1871; demolished)

Thomas G. Appleton house, Catherine Street, Newport, R.I. (1870–1871; destroyed by fire)

George C. Richardson house, Catherine Street, Newport, R.I. (1870–1871; demolished)

Paran Stevens house, north side of Thirty-Sixth Street between Fifth and Madison avenues, New York, N.Y. (1870–1871; NBD No. 769 of 1870; demolished)

Stevens House (later Victoria Hotel), Fifth Avenue to Broadway on the

south side of Twenty-Seventh Street, New York, N.Y. (1870–1872; NBD No. 811 of 1870; demolished)

Rutherfurd Stuyvesant apartment houses, 236–246 East Thirteenth Street, New York, N.Y. (1870–1871, 1873; alterations; ABD No. 496 of 1870 and ABD No. 775 of 1873)

Lenox Library, east side of Fifth Avenue between Seventieth and Seventy-First streets, New York, N.Y. (1870–1877; NBD No. 415 of 1871; demolished)

Frederick Bronson house, gardener's house, and stables, Greenfield, Conn. (1870, 1881, 1889, 1890; alterations)

Fisk house, Fifth Avenue near Seventieth Street, New York, N.Y. (1871; not constructed)

Major General John F. Reynolds Monument, Gettysburg, Pa. (with J. Q. A. Ward; 1871)

Dr. C. F. Heywood house, coach house, and stables, Middletown, R.I. (1871–1872; demolished)

Church project, Broadway, Tarrytown, N.Y. (1871; not constructed)

Rev. S. W. Bacon tomb, Baltimore, Md. (1871; probably not constructed)

Paran Stevens stable, 3 East Twenty-Eighth Street, New York, N.Y. (1871; alterations; ABD No. 573 of 1871; demolished)

Levi P. Morton stable, north side of East Forty-Second Street between Fifth and Madison avenues, New York, N.Y. (1871; NBD No. 994 of 1871; demolished)

T. W. Phinney house (Hilltop) and stables, Ruggles Avenue, Newport, R.I. (1871–1872; later known as the Grosvenor house)

Paran Stevens store and loft, 1160 Broadway, New York, N.Y. (1871–1872; NBD No. 902 of 1871; demolished)

Alexander Van Rensselaer (iron front) store (Rice, Goodwin, Walker & Co.; also known as Lee, Tweedy & Co. Building), 474–476 Broadway, New York, N.Y. (1871–1872; NBD No. 898 of 1871; demolished)

Presbyterian Church, Amity and Leonard streets, Matteawan (now Beacon), N. Y. (1871–1872; dedicated July 17, 1872; destroyed by fire)

Howland Circulating Library, 477 Main Street, Matteawan (now Beacon), N.Y. (1871–1872; dedicated August 5, 1872)

James Lenox store, 634 Broadway, New York, N.Y. (1871–1873; NBD No. 286 of 1873; demolished)

Marshall Field mansion, 1905 Prairie Avenue, Chicago, Ill. (1871–1873; demolished)

Mrs. J. T. Gibert house and barn, off Bellevue Avenue, Newport, R.I. (1872; alterations and additions)

Allen Library, Pittsfield, Mass. (1872; not constructed)

Royal Phelps store and warehouse, north side of East Fifteenth Street between Fifth Avenue and Union Square, New York, N.Y. (1872; alterations; ABD No. 526 of 1872; demolished)

Trinity Church, Copley Square, Boston, Mass. (1872; unsuccessful competition; not constructed)

Colonel Jerome Bonaparte stables, Harrison Avenue, Newport, R.I. (1872; alterations; probably demolished)

R. V. McKim house, Yznaga Avenue, Newport, R.I. (ca. 1872; altera-

tions; probably not executed)

Schultz and Warker store, northeast corner of Broadway and Seventeenth Street, New York, N.Y. (1872; alterations; ABD No. 581 of 1872; demolished)

Western Union Telegraph Company building, Broadway at Dey Street, New York, N.Y. (1872; unsuccessful competition; not constructed)

Drexel Bank, Broad at Wall Street, New York, N.Y. (1872; not constructed)

Royal Phelps office building and store, No. 25 Union Square West, south of Sixteenth Street, New York, N.Y. (1872; NBD No. 449 of 1872; demolished)

Thomas and John D. Crimmins, five houses, 1031–1039 Third Avenue, east side of Third Avenue, north of Sixty-First Street, New York, N.Y. (1872–1873; NBD No. 878 of 1872; demolished, except for the corner building at 201 East Sixty-First Street)

Henry G. Marquand house (Linden Gate), 140 Rhode Island Avenue, Newport, R.I. (1872–1873; with alterations, 1883, 1891; destroyed by fire)

Virginia Hall, Hampton Institute, Hampton, Va. (1872–1874; dedicated June 11, 1874; interior completed 1879)

Fifth Avenue Presbyterian Church, Fifth Avenue at Fifty-Fifth Street, New York, N.Y. (ca. 1873; not constructed)

George Peabody Wetmore monument, Island Cemetery, Newport, R.I. (1873)

Royal Phelps tomb, location unknown (1873)

Roosevelt Hospital store and warehouses, 21 and 23 Peck Slip at Water Street, New York, N.Y. (1873; NBD No. 261 of 1873)

Joseph Howland mansion (Tioranda) music room addition, Fishkill (now Beacon), N.Y. (1873; presently a part of Craig House)

Sun Association factory and workshop, southeast corner of Nassau and Frankfort streets, New York, N.Y. (1873; alterations; ABD No. 884 of 1873; demolished)

Mrs. William Gammell house, Narragansett Avenue, Newport, R.I. (1873, 1881; not constructed)

Roosevelt Building (iron front) store and

warehouse (also known as Hammerslough Brothers Building and part as the Dolly Varden Store), 478–482 Broadway, New York, N.Y. (1873–1874; NBD No. 285 of 1873; rear façade at 40 Crosby Street)

Thomas and John D. Crimmins house, 203 East Sixty-First Street, New York, N.Y. (1873–1874; NBD No. 12 of 1873; demolished)

Thomas and John D. Crimmins, two houses, 1041–1043 Third Avenue, east side of Third Avenue south of Sixty-Second Street, New York, N.Y. (1873–1874; NBD No. 11 of 1873; demolished)

Thomas and John D. Crimmins, four houses, 219, 221, 223, and 225 East Sixty-Second Street, New York, N.Y. (1873–1874; NBD No. 648 of 1873)

Delaware and Hudson Canal Company Building (Coal and Iron Exchange building), 17–21 Cortlandt Street, New York, N.Y. (1873–1876; NBD No. 287 of 1873; demolished)

Tribune Building, northeast corner of Nassau and Spruce streets, New York, N.Y. (1873–1876; NBD No. 465 of 1873; annex addition,

1881–1883 by Edward Raht of Hunt's office; ABD No. 729 of 1881; nine additional stories added to the main building in 1905; demolished)

Lewis M. Rutherfurd house, 175 Second Avenue, New York, N.Y. (1874; alterations; ABD No. 58 of 1874; demolished)

Henry Ward Beecher house, Peekskill, N.Y. (designed 1874; built 1878; presently St. Peter's School)

John Henry Towne tomb, location unknown (1875; probably not constructed)

Lenox Library, Princeton Theological Seminary, Princeton, N.J. (1876–1879; demolished)

Princeton Theological Seminary, two professors' houses, Library Place, Princeton, N.J. (1876–1879; one house demolished and one presently standing at 31 Library Place)

St. Luke's Church, Saranac Lake, N.Y. (1878; not constructed)

Egerton L. Winthrop house, 23 East Thirty-Third Street at the northwest corner of Madison Avenue, New York, N.Y. (1878–1879; NBD No. 483 of 1878; demolished)

Frederic Bronson house, 174 Madison Avenue, New York, N.Y. (1878–1879; NBD No. 484 of 1878; demolished)

William K. Vanderbilt mansion and service buildings (Idlehour), Oakdale, Long Island, N.Y. (1878–1880, 1883, 1887–1889; destroyed by fire except for the gatehouses)

William K. Vanderbilt mansion, 660 Fifth Avenue, New York, N.Y. (1878–1882; house opened 1883; NBD No. 898 of 1879; alterations, 1887; ABD No. 26 of 1887; demolished)

Union League Clubhouse, northeast corner of Fifth Avenue and Thirty-Ninth Street, New York, N.Y. (1879; unsuccessful competition; not constructed)

St. Mark's Church and rectory, Main Street, Islip, Long Island, N.Y. (1879–1880)

New York Stock Exchange, Broad to New Street, New York, N.Y. (1880; unsuccessful competition; not constructed)

First Presbyterian Church, South Second Street, Palatka, Fla. (1880; destroyed by fire, 1882, and rebuilt with modifications from Hunt's designs)

Second Academic Hall, Hampton Institute, Hampton, Va. (1880–1881)

Marquand Chapel, Princeton University, Princeton, N.J. (1880–1882; destroyed by fire)

Yorktown Monument, Yorktown, Va. (with J. Q. A. Ward and Henry Van Brunt; 1880–1884; dedicated October 19, 1884)

J. Q. A. Ward studio and stables, Urbana, Ohio (1881; probably demolished)

J. Q. A. Ward house and studio, 119 West Fifty-Second Street, New York, N.Y. (1881–1882; NBD No. 442 of 1882; demolished)

Ledyard family tomb, Island Cemetery, Newport, R.I. (1881–1882, 1893)

Guernsey Building, 160–164 Broadway, New York, N.Y. (1881–1882; NBD No. 415 of 1881; alterations, 1894; ABD No. 142 of 1894; demolished)

Charles W. Shields house (Nethercliff Hall), Lawrence and Ruggles avenues, Newport, R.I. (1881–1883)

Association Residence for Respectable Aged Indigent Females, and

two adjoining houses, southeast corner of Amsterdam Avenue and One Hundred Fourth Street, New York, N.Y. (early studies, 1868 and 1873; 1881–1883; NBD No. 934 of 1881; building extended in 1903 to One Hundred Third Street; remodeled in 1965)

Henry G. Marquand house, 8 East Sixty-Eighth Street, and two adjoining houses, northwest corner of Madison Avenue and Sixty-Eighth Street, New York, N.Y. (1881–1884; NBD No. 811 and No. 935 of 1881; demolished)

Statue of Liberty pedestal and base, Bedloes (now Liberty) Island, New York, N.Y. (with Frédéric Auguste Bartholdi; 1881–1885; dedicated October 28, 1886; now a national monument, National Park Service, U.S. Department of the Interior, and open to the public)

Horace Greeley Statue pedestal, northeast corner of Nassau and Spruce streets, New York, N.Y. (with J. Q. A. Ward; 1881–1890; dedicated September 20, 1890; presently in City Hall Park, New York, N.Y.)

William Morris Hunt gravestone, Prospect Hill Cemetery, Brattleboro, Vt. (1882)

Lafayette Statue pedestal, University of Vermont, Burlington, Vt., (with J. Q. A. Ward; 1882; dedicated June 27, 1883)

Church project, location unknown (1883; not constructed)

Washington Statue pedestal, Subtreasury Building steps, northeast corner of Nassau and Wall streets, New York, N.Y. (with J. Q. A. Ward; NBD No. 1089 of 1883; dedicated November 26, 1883)

Paxton house [?] and studio, 12 Library Place, Princeton, N.J. (1883–1884)

Henry G. Marquand stable, 166 East Seventy-Third Street, New York, N.Y. (1883–1884; NBD No. 702 of 1883; presently Central Gospel Chapel)

Sidney Webster house, 245 East Seventeenth Street, New York, N.Y. (1883–1885; NBD No. 890 of 1883; presently offices of Beth Israel Hospital)

Simon Kenton Monument base, Oakdale Cemetery, Urbana, Ohio (1884; statue planned by J. Q. A. Ward but not executed)

William E. Dodge Statue pedestal, Herald Square,

New York, N.Y. (with J. Q. A. Ward; 1884–1885; statue but not Hunt's pedestal moved to Bryant Park, New York, N.Y.)

Pilgrim Statue pedestal, Central Park, New York, N.Y. (with J. Q. A. Ward; 1884–1885; dedicated June 6, 1885)

Robert Hoe Mortuary Chapel, Sleepy Hollow Cemetery, Tarrytown, N.Y. (1884–1885; demolished)

James Pinchot mansion (Grey Towers), Milford, Pa. (1884–1886; presently owned by the Forest Service, U.S. Dept. of Agriculture, and open to the public)

James Garfield Monument pedestal, Maryland Avenue and First Street, S.W., Washington, D.C. (with J. Q. A. Ward; 1884–1887; dedicated May 12, 1887)

Vanderbilt mausoleum, Moravian Cemetery, New Dorp, Staten Island, N.Y. (1884–1889)

William Borden mansion, 1020 Lake Shore Drive at Bellevue Place, Chicago, Ill. (1884–1889; demolished)

Marquand family tomb, Island Cemetery, Newport, R.I. (1885)

Columbus O. D. Iselin house, 11 West Fifty-

Second Street, New York, N.Y. (1885–1886; NBD No. 368 of 1885; demolished)

Ogden Mills mansion, southeast corner of Fifth Avenue and Sixty-Ninth Street, New York, N.Y. (1885–1887; NBD No. 1144 of 1885; demolished)

Chemical Laboratory (Old Chemistry Building), southeast corner of Nassau Street and Washington Road, Princeton University, Princeton, N.J. (1885–1891; now called Green Annex)

Darius O. Mills tomb, Sleepy Hollow Cemetery, Tarrytown, N.Y. (1886)

Soldiers' and Sailors' Monument base, Brooklyn, N.Y. (with J. Q. A. Ward; 1886–1887; not constructed)

George W. Vanderbilt house, 9 West Fifty-Third Street, New York, N.Y. (1886–1887; alterations; ABD No. 1296 of 1886; demolished)

Frederic Bronson tenements, 140–142 Tenth Avenue, New York, N.Y. (1886–1887; NBD No. 1301 and No. 1386 of 1886; demolished)

Levi P. Morton mansion, entrance lodge, and service buildings (Ellerslie),

Rhinecliff-on-Hudson, N.Y. (1886–1887; destroyed by fire)

Archibald Rogers mansion and service buildings (Crumwold Hall), Hyde Park, N.Y. (1886–1889; later Eymard Preparatory Seminary)

Peter T. O'Brien tenements, 226–228 East Thirty-Sixth Street, New York, N.Y. (1887; NBD No. 458 of 1887)

Mrs. Elizabeth Coles house and stables, Glen Cove, Long Island, N.Y. (1887; status unknown)

Henry G. Marquand picture gallery, adjoining 8 East Sixty-Eighth Street, New York, N.Y. (1887; not constructed)

Roosevelt Hospital operating theater, New York, N.Y. (ca. 1887; not constructed)

Soldiers' and Sailors' Monument base, Indianapolis, Ind. (with J. Q. A. Ward; 1887–1888; unsuccessful competition; not constructed)

William K. Vanderbilt stable, 49–51 East Fifty-Second Street, New York, N.Y. (1887–1888; alterations; ABD No. 1250 and No. 2064 of 1887; demolished)

Dr. Lincoln Goodale Monument pedestal, Goodale Park, Colum-

bus, Ohio (with J. Q. A. Ward; 1887–1888)

New York Free Circulating Library, Jackson Square Branch, 251 West Thirteenth Street, New York, N.Y. (1887–1888; NBD No. 1536 of 1887; opened July 6, 1888; remodeled 1971; now occupied by The Great Building Crack-Up/International Headquarters of the First National Church of the Exquisite Panic, Inc.)

Maturin Livingston house, 6 East Sixty-Ninth Street, New York, N.Y. (1887–1888; NBD No. 578 of 1887; demolished)

Wadsworth Memorial Fountain, Main Street, Geneseo, N.Y. (with Antoine Louis Barye [?]; 1887–1888)

George W. Vanderbilt gardener's cottage, dairy, water tower, stables, and barn, New Dorp, Staten Island, N.Y. (1887–1889; demolished)

United States Naval Observatory buildings, Georgetown Heights, Washington, D.C. (1887–1893)

Saint Agnes Church and School, Ninety-First Street, New York, N.Y. (1888; unsuccessful competition; not constructed)

Soldiers' and Sailors' Monument base, Portland, Me. (with Franklin Simmons; 1888–1889; dedicated May 30, 1889)

Thomas Riley tenements, north side of East Seventy-Eighth Street west of York Avenue; New York, N.Y. (1888–1889; NBD No. 301 of 1888; demolished)

William Astor mansion (Beechwood), Bellevue Avenue, Newport, R.I. (1888–1890; alterations; presently Beechwood Museum, open to the public)

Henry Ward Beecher Statue pedestal, Cadman Plaza Park, Brooklyn, N.Y. (with J. Q. A. Ward; 1888–1891; dedicated June 24, 1891; moved from Borough Hall Park, Brooklyn, N.Y.)

William K. and Alva Smith Vanderbilt mansion (Marble House), Bellevue Avenue, Newport, R.I. (1888–1892; presently owned by the Preservation Society of Newport County and open to the public)

Ogden Goelet mansion (Ochre Court), Ochre Point Avenue, Newport, R.I. (1888–1892; stables, 1889; presently part of Salve Regina College)

George W. Vanderbilt mansion and service buildings (Biltmore),

Asheville, N.C. (with Richard Howland Hunt; 1888–1895; presently owned by the Cecil family and open to the public)

Cathedral of St. John the Divine, New York, N.Y. (1889; unsuccessful competition; not constructed)

Theodore A. Havemeyer mansion ballroom, main hall, staircase, and gates, 244 Madison Avenue, New York, N.Y. (1889–1891; alterations; ABD No. 1217 of 1889; demolished)

Joseph R. Busk mansion (also known as the Wrentham house and as Indian Spring; begun for William E. Dorsheimer), gatehouse, stables, and service buildings, Ocean Avenue, Newport, R.I. (1889–1891)

George W. Vanderbilt mansion alterations, picture gallery, and conservatory (formerly the William H. Vanderbilt mansion), 640 Fifth Avenue, New York, N.Y. (1889, 1891; alterations; demolished)

Clark Hall, Adelbert College, Cleveland, Ohio (1889–1892; now Case Western Reserve University)

Gymnasium, United States Military

Academy, West Point, N.Y. (1889–1893; demolished)

Academic Building, United States Military Academy, West Point, N.Y. (1889–1895; now Pershing Barracks)

Mrs. Josephine Schmid mansion, southeast corner of Fifth Avenue and Sixty-Second Street, New York, N.Y. (with Richard Howland Hunt; 1889, 1893–1895; NBD No. 163 of 1894; demolished)

Inman house, location unknown (1890; not constructed)

William V. Lawrence mansion, 969 Fifth Avenue at the southeast corner of Fifth Avenue and Seventy-Eighth Street (with Richard Howland Hunt; 1890–1891; NBD No. 1485 of 1890; demolished)

W. W. Sherman house, Fifth Avenue, New York, N.Y. (1890–1891; not constructed)

August Belmont tomb, Island Cemetery, Newport, R.I. (with Karl Bitter; 1890–1891)

Trinity Church doors, Broadway opposite Wall Street, New York, N.Y. (with Karl Bitter, J. Massey Rhind, and Charles M. Niehaus; 1890–1894;

all installed by 1896; ABD No. 2172 of 1890)

Belmont Chapel, Island Cemetery, Newport, R.I. (1891; alterations)

Elliott F. Shepard house, 37 West Fifty-Seventh Street, New York, N.Y. (1891; alterations; ABD No. 955 of 1891; demolished)

Martin Brimmer family tomb, Mount Auburn Cemetery, Cambridge, Mass. (1891)

Charles H. Russell house, 129 East Thirty-Fourth Street, New York, N.Y. (with Richard Howland Hunt; 1891; alterations; ABD No. 1120 of 1891; demolished)

President's house, Adelbert College, Bellflower Road, Cleveland, Ohio (1891–1892; now Case Western Reserve University)

Ordnance Building, Sandy Hook, N.J. (1891–1892; status unknown)

Worcester R. Warner house, 7780 Euclid Avenue, Cleveland, Ohio (1891–1892; demolished)

Ambrose Swasey house, 7808 Euclid Avenue, Cleveland, Ohio (1891–1892; demolished)

J. J. Townsend tomb, location unknown (1891–1892)

Administration Building, World's Columbian Exposition, Chicago, Ill. (1891–1893; temporary structure; destroyed by fire, 1894)

Oliver H. P. Belmont mansion (Belcourt), Bellevue Avenue, Newport, R.I. (1891–1894; presently owned by the Tinney family and open to the public)

Elbridge T. Gerry mansion, 2 East Sixty-First Street at the southeast corner of Fifth Avenue and Sixty-First Street, New York, N.Y. (1891–1894; NBD No. 537 of 1892; demolished)

Mrs. William Astor and John Jacob Astor IV mansion, a double residence, 840 Fifth Avenue, New York, N.Y. (1891–1895; house opened 1896; NBD No. 36 of 1893; demolished)

Adrian Iselin, Jr., house, 9 East Twenty-Sixth Street, and stables, facing Twenty-Seventh Street, New York, N.Y. (1892; alterations; not constructed)

Cornelius Vanderbilt II mansion tower, west side of Fifth Avenue between Fifty-Seventh and Fifty-Eighth streets, New York, N.Y. (with George B. Post; 1892; demolished)

Thomas Hitchcock house, Westbury, Long Island, N.Y. (with Richard Howland Hunt; 1892–1893; alterations)

H. R. Bishop mansion ballroom, 881 Fifth Avenue, New York, N.Y. (1892–1894; alterations; ABD No. 1007 of 1893; demolished)

General John A. Logan Monument pedestal, Vermont Avenue at Thirteenth and P streets, Washington D.C. (with Franklin Simmons; 1892; dedicated April 9, 1901)

Cornelius Vanderbilt II mansion (The Breakers) and lodge, Ochre Point Avenue, and stables, Coggeshall and Bateman avenues, Newport, R.I. (1892–1895; presently owned by the Preservation Society of Newport County and open to the public)

Warren Delano tomb, New Bedford, Mass. (ca. 1893)

Ambrose Thomas tomb, location unknown (ca. 1893)

Columbia University campus plan, Morningside Heights, New York, N.Y. (1892–1893; unsuccessful competition; not constructed)

Richard Mortimer house, Tuxedo, N. Y. (with Richard Howland Hunt; 1893, 1900+)

Plaza Bank, 2–4 East Fifty-Eighth Street, New York, N.Y. (1893; alterations; ABD No. 742 of 1893; demolished)

Elliott F. Shepard tomb, location unknown (1893)

John Bigelow house, Highland-Falls-on-the-Hudson, N.Y. (ca. 1893–1894; not constructed)

William Rice house, Albany, N.Y. (with Richard Howland Hunt; 1893–1894)

Henry R. Hoyt house, south side of Seventy-Fifth Street, east of Fifth Avenue, New York, N.Y. (1893–1895; NBD No. 1272 of 1893; demolished)

Fogg Museum (later Hunt Hall), Harvard University, Cambridge, Mass. (1893–1895; demolished)

Biltmore Village buildings, including estate office building, railroad station, passenger station, village stores, All Souls' Church, Sunday school, and parsonage, Asheville, N.C. (with Richard Howland Hunt, 1893–1897; later Biltmore Village buildings designed solely by Richard Howland Hunt, 1897, and by Richard Sharp Smith, 1897–1902)

Munson-Williams Memorial Building, Utica, N.Y. (with Richard Howland Hunt; 1894–1895; dedicated 1896; demolished)

Guardhouse, United States Military Academy, West Point, N.Y. (1894; constructed 1897; demolished)

Metropolitan Museum of Art Wing "D" and plan for expansion, Fifth Avenue at Eighty-Second Street, New York, N.Y. (1894–1895; completed by Richard Howland Hunt, 1902)

Library renovations, United States Military Academy, West Point, N.Y. (with Richard Howland Hunt; 1895)

Undated

W. W. Billings house, New London, Conn. (status unknown)

Chauncey house, Dobb's Ferry, N.Y. (status unknown)

David Duncan stables and gatehouse, Staten Island, N.Y. (status unknown)

Mrs. C. J. Everett house, Tenafly, N.J. (probably not constructed)

Robert Fulton Monument (with H. K. Brown; not constructed)

Haskell house, location unknown (status unknown)

United States Trust Company of New York, New York, N.Y. (probably not constructed)

George C. Ward House, location unknown (probably not constructed)

Addenda

Redwood Library, Newport, R.I. (1868; not constructed)

Museum of Natural History, New York, N.Y. (1872; not constructed)

Carnegie Music Hall, W. 57th Street at Seventh Avenue, New York, N.Y. (1889; drawings prepared in collaboration with William B. Tuthill and Adler & Sullivan)

N. P. Bailey tomb, location unknown (probably not constructed)

J. Hobard Warren cottage, location unknown (probably not constructed)

SELECTED SOURCES

A complete bibliography of materials used in this study would involve the listing of several hundred books and articles along with a large number of unpublished items. Rather than naming all the works consulted—the more relevant of which are included in the endnotes—this note on the sources includes descriptions of the principal archival and manuscript collections in which significant Richard Morris Hunt (RMH) materials were located; a list of relevant unpublished theses and dissertations; an enumeration of RMH's published writings; and a list of the most important secondary literature on him. A paragraph on the journals most useful for this study concludes the note. For works relating to general themes and special topics in this book, the reader is referred to the endnotes, which also should be consulted for descriptions and evaluations of specific RMH buildings. Readers are urged, as well, themselves to visit RMH's still remaining buildings, several of which are open to the public.

I. Manuscript Collections

The two principal collections of primary source materials relating to the life and works of RMH are the Hunt Collection in the library at the national headquarters of the American Institute of Architects, The Octagon, Washington, D.C., and the privately held Hunt Papers, dealing with several generations of the Hunt family but largely focusing on RMH.

The Hunt Collection (HC) was formed when Richard Howland Hunt in 1925 donated to the American Institute of Architects, in accord with the terms of his mother's will, the collection of books, photographs, and drawings assembled by RMH and added to by him and Joseph Howland Hunt. Approximately one thousand volumes and probably nearly twenty thousand architectural drawings are included in this repository, along with hundreds of photographs. The work of RMH, Richard Howland Hunt, and Hunt and Hunt (Richard Howland and Joseph Howland Hunt) is represented in the architectural drawings and photographs of the collection, although most of the materials relate to RMH. Some of the HC drawings have not been available for study. Many of the large drawings, however, have been catalogued and placed in boxes and folders; a great many smaller architectural drawings have been placed in large drawings scrapbooks, but the contents of these scrapbooks have not presently been catalogued. The list of HC drawings in George S. Koyle, *American Architectural Drawings* (Philadelphia, 1969) includes only a small proportion of the HC holdings. The HC also contains hundreds of photographs of buildings in Western Europe; stereopticon photographs of buildings and natural scenes and of family members; large framed pictures from the Hunt and Hunt offices; bronze and marble plaques of RMH by Karl Bitter; some watercolors and sketches by William Morris Hunt; some Jane Hunt drawings; and a miscellany of other items from the Hunt offices.

Particularly useful in the HC for this study have been the forty-six RMH sketchbooks, almost all of which were compiled while RMH was in Europe at different times. The sketchbooks are filled with pencil and pen and ink sketches and occasional ink and wash drawings and watercolors. Most of the sketchbooks also include journals of European travels, financial accounts, and notes of names and addresses. Although the sketchbooks are mostly dated, it is evident from the contents that many of them were used at various times; the date for a particular sketchbook does not necessarily coincide with all of the entries. Two of the sketchbooks are primarily account books for the years 1861–1862 and 1867. Also useful for this study have been eleven HC scrapbooks, mostly containing newspaper clippings, but in many cases including letters, programs, and other materials as well. In several of the scrapbooks the contents were loosely inserted and they were never organized. The HC includes as well considerable general correspondence to and from RMH. The Archives of the A.I.A. include the presidential and secretarial files, 1867–1895, with many RMH letters. Ecole des Beaux-Arts materials, including the "Memoirs," design books, and miscellaneous drawings, were helpful in studying RMH's work as a student in Paris. The several hundred photographs of RMH's executed commissions were essential for this study.

Supplementing the Hunt Collection is the very rich body of Hunt Papers (HP), privately held. Some years ago a member of the Hunt family organized many of the HP into loose-leaf notebooks, eleven volumes of which were examined for this study. These large notebooks contain letters, legal documents, journals and diaries, memoirs, notes, some photographs, and occasional historical commentary. Some of the notebooks and contents have been paginated, but in many cases there is no pagination. A miscellany of other HP were also used for this study. The following HP were consulted:

Hunt Family

Vol. I, Jonathan Hunt I–V, 1610–1823

Vol. II, Jonathan Hunt VI, 1787–1820

Vol. III, Jonathan Hunt VI, 1821–1828, Miscellaneous

Vol. IV, Jonathan Hunt VI, 1810–1828, Legal Papers

Vol. V, Jonathan Hunt VI, 1828–1832, including Account Books

Vol. VI, Jane Hunt, 1832–1874

Vol. VII, Pt. I, Jane Hunt, 1822–1903, including six volumes of Diaries, 1844–1848

Vol. VII, Pt. II, Jane Hunt , 1822–1903, including Journals and Memoirs

Vol. VIII, Hunt-Howland, 1620 on

Vol. IX, Leavitt-Hunt, 1609 on

Vol. XVI, Hunt-Hone, 1731 on

Miscellaneous Hunt family materials, including estate inventories, financial statements, letters, and newspaper clippings

Richard Morris Hunt

Journal, 1844–1848

1861 Daybook

Miscellaneous letters

Bills of sale for RMH purchases

Autograph file (letters to RMH and Catharine Clinton Howland Hunt)

"Last Will and Testament of Richard M. Hunt"

Jane Hunt

Journal, 1843–1844 (other journals and diaries in Jane Hunt, HP, Vols. VI and VII)

Holy Bible, including inscriptions

Catharine Clinton Howland Hunt

Passport

Typescript biography of Richard Morris Hunt (1907), similar to the American Architectural Archive holding listed below, transcribed and edited by Alan Burnham, but with minor insertions by family members and slight variations in pagination. (This is referred to in the endnotes as "CCHH, HP")

"Ars Longa, Vita Brevis Est" (1900), newspaper

clippings and public statements about RMH, compiled by CCHH (deposited 1978 in the Avery Library, Columbia University)

Catharine Howland Hunt

European Journal, 1885–1886

Daybook, 1892

Diary, 1898

Esther Morris Hunt

Passport

Other manuscript collections consulted:

American Academy in Rome, Archives, N.Y.C.

Minutes of the meetings of the American School of Architecture in Rome, 1895

Old Correspondence, 1894, 1895

Corporation Book, 1895

Cablegrams, 1895

Miscellaneous Papers, including "Documents and Confidential Letters re. Founding of the American Academy in Rome"

American Institute of Architects, N.Y.C. Chapter

Dues Book

Hobart Upjohn, "The American Institute of Architects: The Early Years, 1860–1900" (1941), MS

American Architectural Archive, Greenwich, Conn.

Catharine Clinton Howland Hunt, typescript biography of RMH and RMH "Nile Diary," transcribed and edited

by Alan Burnham and called "The Richard Morris Hunt Papers"

Miscellaneous clippings, letters, and other materials relating to RMH

Archives de France, Paris

Ecole des Beaux-Arts student dossier of RMH, AJ52 369 (courtesy of Richard Chafee)

Archives of American Art, N.Y.C.

William Morris Hunt, 103–257–316

Martin Brimmer letters, D–32, 137–454

Avery Library, Columbia University, N.Y.C.

Records of Properties owned by Rutherfurd Stuyvesant, 2 vols.

Burnham Architectural Library, Art Institute of Chicago

Daniel H. Burnham Papers

Case Western Reserve University, Archives, Cleveland, Ohio

Clark Hall accounts, miscellaneous memoranda, and application for the National Register of Historic Places

Congress, Library of, Manuscript Division, Washington, D.C.

Charles Follen McKim Papers

Frederick Law Olmsted Papers, including General Correspondence, Central Park, Private Estates, George W. Vanderbilt, and World's Fair files

Gifford Pinchot Papers, including Diaries, General Correspondence, and Family Correspondence

Federal Archives and Records Center, Bayonne, N.J.

U.S. Manuscript Census of 1830 for Brattleboro, Vt. (microfilm)

Harvard University, Archives, Cambridge, Mass.

Newspaper clippings relating to the Fogg Museum

Ewart Wetherall and Robert Newman, "Hunt Hall—An Historical Review" (typescript)

RMH letter

Houghton Library, Harvard University, Cambridge, Mass.

Miscellaneous RMH letters

Massachusetts Historical Society, Manuscript Division, Boston, Mass.

Miscellaneous RMH and Jane Hunt letters

Metropolitan Museum of Art, Archives, N.Y.C.

Collection of Architectural Casts file

Sunday Opening Controversy, 1887–1892

Building, Wing D, 1895

Richard Morris Hunt file

Building AB, 1880–1885

Minutes of Trustees

Minutes of Executive Committee

Minutes of the Corporation

Minutes of the Building Committee

Reports

Annual Reports, 1871–1902

Morgan Library, N.Y.C.

Miscellaneous RMH letters

Museum of the City of New York, Library and Archives

Miscellaneous clippings

Folders on various sections of N.Y.C.

National Archives, Washington, D.C.

Office, Chief of Engineers, Land Papers

Naval Observatory, General Correspondence, 1888–1892

General Records Division Correspondence

Office of the Quartermaster General Consolidated Correspondence File, 1794–1915

File on the Garfield Monument

Cash Book for Army Medical Museum and Library

Files on Architect of the Capitol

Yorktown Monument Correspondence

New York City, Buildings Department

New Buildings Dockets, 1866–1895

Alterations Buildings Dockets, 1866–1895

New-York Historical Society, Manuscript Division, N.Y.C.

Karl Bitter Papers

John Quincy Adams Ward Papers and Scrapbooks

Stanford White Papers

George B. Post Papers

A. J. Bloor Diary, 5 vols.

Miscellaneous RMH letters

New York Public Library, Astor, Lenox and Tilden Foundations

Miscellaneous clippings related to the Statue of Liberty, Local History Division

Karl Bitter Scrapbook, Art Division

William Morris Hunt Scrapbook, Art Division

John Quincy Adams Ward Scrapbook, Art Division

Miscellaneous RMH letters, Manuscripts and Archives Division

A.I.A. Meetings Reports, Manuscripts and Archives Division

Charles F. McKim Papers, Manuscripts and Archives Division

Alexander Jackson Davis Papers, Manuscripts and Archives Division

Charles Henry Hart Papers, Manuscripts and Archives Division

World's Columbian Exposition Papers, 1893, Manuscripts and Archives Division

American Committee of the Statue of Liberty Correspondence, Manuscripts and Archives Division

New York University, Archives, N.Y.C.

Rent Rolls, 1856–1860

Miscellaneous documents

Newport Historical Society, Library and Archives, Newport, R.I.

Newspaper files

Clarence Stanhope Scrapbook

George H. Richardson Scrapbooks

Margery Dean Scrapbook

Scrapbook WW

Specifications for The Breakers, including RMH letters

Jane Hunt drawing

Charles H. Russell Scrapbook

Account book of Oliver Belmont

Files of *Newport History*

Pennsylvania, Historical Society of, Philadelphia, Pa.

RMH letters

Princeton University, Archives, Princeton, N.J.

Trustees Minutes, 1874–1894

Marquand Chapel files

Photographs

RMH letter

Princeton Theological Seminary, Library, Princeton, N.J.

Minutes of the Trustees, 1878–1879

Redwood Library, Newport, R.I.

Letters to RMH and CCHH

Trinity Church Archives, N.Y.C.

Vestry minutes

M. Fornachon letter

Daniel Webster Papers, Dartmouth College, Hanover, N.H.

Jonathan Hunt–Daniel Webster Correspondence

United States Capitol, Office of the Architect of the Capitol, Washington, D.C.

Miscellaneous records

United States Military Academy, Archives, West Point, N.Y.

Superintendent's Letter Books, Nos. 7–10

Adjutant's Letter Book, No. 8

Letters Received, 1889–1893

David Gray, "The Architectural Development of West Point" (1951) (typescript)

Yale University, Archives, New Haven, Conn.

Annual Statements

Carroll Meeks Papers

J. F. Weir Papers

Pictures Collection

II. Unpublished Theses and Dissertations

Brendel, Susanne, "Documentation of the Construction of Biltmore House Through Draw-

ings, Correspondence and Photographs." M.A. Thesis, Graduate School of Architecture and

Planning, Columbia University, 1978.

Brenner, Mildred Frances, "Richard Mor-

ris Hunt: Architect."
M.A. Thesis, Institute of
Fine Arts, New York
University, 1944.

Brown, Thelma Robins,
"Memorial Chapel, The
Culmination of the De-
velopment of the Cam-
pus of Hampton Insti-
tute, Hampton, Vir-
ginia, 1867–1887." M.A.
Thesis, School of Ar-
chitecture, University of
Virginia, 1971.

Butler, Alexander R.,
"McKim's Renaissance:
A Study in the History of
the American Architec-
tural Profession." Ph.D.
Dissertation, The Johns
Hopkins University,
1953.

Danes, Gibson A., "A
Biographical and Critical
Study of William Morris
Hunt, 1824–1879."
Ph.D. Dissertation, Yale
University, 1949.

Farrar, Lloyd J.,
"Richard Morris Hunt:
A Sketch of His Life and
Architecture." M.A.
Thesis, Faculty of Politi-
cal Science, Columbia
University, 1954.

Gooch, Stapleton Dab-
ney, IV, "Richard Morris
Hunt and the Vander-

bilts." M.A. Thesis,
School of Architecture,
University of Virginia,
1966.

Hoppin, Martha Jay,
"William Morris Hunt:
Aspects of His Work."
Ph.D. Dissertation, De-
partment of Fine Arts,
Harvard University,
1974.

Hurst, Harold, "The
Elite Class of Newport,
Rhode Island: 1830–
1860." Ph.D. Disserta-
tion, Department of
History, New York Uni-
versity, 1975.

Karlowicz, Titus M.,
"The Architecture of the
World's Columbian Ex-
position." Ph.D. Disser-
tation, Northwestern
University, 1965.

Kramer, Ellen W., "The
Domestic Architecture of
Detlef Lienau, A Con-
servative Victorian."
Ph.D. Dissertation, In-
stitute of Fine Arts, New
York University, 1957. 3
vols.

Levine, Neil A., "The
Idea of Frank Furness'
Buildings." M.A.
Thesis, Department of
the History of Art, Yale
University, 1967.

Lewis, Dudley Arnold,
"Evaluations of Ameri-
can Architecture by
European Critics, 1875–
1900." Ph.D. Disserta-
tion, University of Wis-
consin, 1962.

Silvergold, Barbara
Kornfeld, "Richard Mor-
ris Hunt and the Impor-
tation of Beaux-Arts Ar-
chitecture to the United
States." Ph.D. Disserta-
tion, University of
California, Berkeley,
1974.

Turberg, Edward F.,
"Frederick Law Olmsted
at Biltmore: A Discus-
sion of the Designs Car-
ried Out at Biltmore,
North Carolina, from the
Correspondence of
Frederick Law Olm-
sted." M.A. Thesis,
School of Architecture,
University of Virginia,
1973.

Wilson, Richard Guy,
"Charles F. McKim and
the Development of the
American Renaissance:
A Study in Architecture
and Culture." Ph.D.
Dissertation, University
of Michigan, 1972. 4
vols.

III. Published Writings of Richard Morris Hunt

Hunt's published writings are very limited. Paraphrases and sometimes direct
quotations of his statements at A.I.A. meetings can be found in various of the
Proceedings of the Annual Conventions of the American Institute of Architects and in
The Crayon, 1857–1860. His only book was *Designs for the Gateways of the Southern
Entrances to the Central Park* (New York, 1866). See, regarding the Philadelphia

Centennial, "The Architectural Exhibits of the International Exhibition," in U.S. Centennial Commission, International Exhibition, 1876, *Reports and Awards*, VII (Washington, D.C., 1880), pp. 530–539 [Group 26, pp. 2–11]; "Building Materials," ibid., pp. 539–546 [Group 26, pp. 11–18]; and Miscellaneous "Reports," ibid., indexed, p. 600. See also his "Paper on the Architectural Exhibit of the Centennial Exhibition," *Proceedings of the Tenth Annual Convention of the American Institute of Architects* (Boston, 1876), 34–38, a distillation of his official report; "The Church Architecture That We Need," *American Architect and Building News*, II (Nov. 24, 1877), 374–376, and ibid., (Dec. 1, 1877), 384–385, a paper read at the Fourth Church Congress held at New York from October 30 to November 2, 1877, and summarized in *The Church Journal and Gospel Messenger*, XXV (Nov. 8, 1877), 708; and RMH with George B. Post, N. Le Brun, Henry Dudley, and Detlef Lienau, "The Experts and the New York Capitol," *American Architect and Building News*, II (March 17, 1877), 85. See further his "Address Given to the Third Annual Convention of the A.I.A.," *Proceedings of the Third Annual Convention of the American Institute of Architects* (New York, 1870), 25–26; "President's Address," *Proceedings of the Twenty-Second Annual Convention of the A.I.A.*, Buffalo, 1888 (New York, 1888), pp. 3–8; "President Hunt's Address," *Convention Proceedings of the American Institute of Architects, the Western Association of Architects, and Consolidation of the American Institute and the Western Association*, Cincinnati, 1889 (Chicago, 1890), pp. 21–22; "President's Address," *Proceedings of the Twenty-Fourth Annual Convention of the A.I.A.*, Chicago, 1890 (Chicago, 1891), pp. 9–14; "President's Address," *Proceedings of the Twenty-Fifth Annual Convention of the American Institute of Architects*, Boston, 1891 (Chicago, 1892), pp. 9–16. See also Anon., "Royal Institute of British Architects; Presentation of the Royal Gold Medal," *American Architect and Building News*, XLI (July 15, 23, 1893), 39–42, 55.

IV. Principal Secondary Accounts

The literature focusing directly on RMH and his work is remarkably sparse. This book constitutes the first extended study. Among earlier writings, Montgomery Schuyler's "The Works of the Late Richard M. Hunt," *Architectural Record*, V (October–December 1895), 97–180, is the only critique of any depth. This essay was reprinted, slightly excerpted, in William H. Jordy and Ralph Coe, eds., *American Architecture and Other Writings by Montgomery Schuyler* (Cambridge, Mass., 1961), II, 502–555, with notes and illustrations. Several other articles by Schuyler touch on aspects of RMH's work.

Other secondary works directly concerned with RMH include the following: Anon., "Influence de l'art français à l'étranger: M. Richard Morris Hunt," *La Construction Moderne*, X (1894–1895), 577–580; Alfred Branam, Jr., "Classical America Presents Newport's Favorite Architects . . . August 18–September 5, 1976" (pamphlet published under the auspices of The Preservation Society of Newport County); Alan Burnham, "The New York Architecture of Richard Morris Hunt," *Journal of the Society of Architectural Historians*, XI (May 1952), 9–14; Mary Cable, "The Marble Cottages," *Horizon*, VII (Autumn 1965), 18–27; William A. Coles, "Richard Morris Hunt and His Library as Revealed in the Studio Sketchbooks of Henry Van Brunt," *Art Quarterly*, XXX (Fall–Winter 1967), 224–238; Royal Cortissoz, "Richard Morris Hunt: The Life and Work of a Distinguished Architect," *New York Tribune*, Aug. 1, 1895, p. 1, and Aug. 4, 1895, p. 23, part of which was reprinted in *American Architect and Building News*, XLIX (Aug. 17, 1895), 70; Herbert Croly, "The Work of Richard Morris Hunt," *Architectural Record*, LIX (January 1926), 88–89; John Walter Cross, "Richard Morris Hunt: A Great of the Profession," *Journal of the American Institute of Architects*, VIII (November 1949), 232–233; Barr Ferree, "Richard Morris Hunt: His Art and Work," *Architecture and Building*, XXIII (Dec. 7, 1895), 271–275; Susan Stein Ganelin, "The Drawings of Richard Morris Hunt," *American Preservation* (April-May 1979), 18–25; Russell Lynes, "Château Builder to Fifth Avenue," *American Heritage*, VI (February 1955), 20–25, 110–111; William Francklyn Paris, "Richard Morris Hunt: First Secretary and Third President of the Institute," *Journal of the American Institute of Architects*, XXIV (December 1955), 243–249, XXV (January 1956), 14–19, and XXVI (February 1956), 74–80, which was reprinted from *American Society Legion of Honor Magazine*, XXIII (Summer 1952), 117–38, and also appeared in *The Hall of American Artists*, IX (New York, 1952), pp. 27–48; Robert S. Peabody, "The Founders of the Institute Who Became Its Presidents," *Proceedings of the Fortieth Annual Convention of the American Institute of Architects* (Washington, D.C., 1907), pp. 168–170; Pennsylvania Academy of Fine Arts, *A Memorial Exhibition of Drawings and Photographs Illustrating the Life and Works of the late Richard Morris Hunt, Architect, 1827–1895* (Philadelphia 1896); George B. Post, "Richard Morris Hunt," *Proceedings of the Twenty-Ninth Annual Convention of the American Institute of Architects* (Providence, 1895), pp. 84–89; J. A. S., "Richard Morris Hunt, A Reminiscence and an Appreciation," *Architectural Record*, XXXIX (March 1916), 295–297; Montgomery Schuyler, "Richard Morris Hunt," *Harper's Weekly*, XXXIX (Aug. 10, 1895), 749; Henry Van Brunt, "Richard Morris Hunt: A Memorial Address," *Proceedings of the Twenty-Ninth Annual Convention of the American Institute of Architects* (Providence, 1895), 71–84, reprinted in *American Architect and Building News*, L (November 2, 1895), 53–56, and in William A. Coles, ed., *Architecture and Society: Selected Essays of Henry Van Brunt* (Cambridge, Mass., 1969), pp. 328–341, and excerpted in *Journal of the American Institute of Architects*, VIII (October 1947), 180–187, and in the *Architect and Contract Reporter*, LIV (November 22, 1895), 339–341; Frank E. Wallis, "Richard M. Hunt, Master Architect and Man," *Architectural Review*, V (1917), 239–240; Frank E. Wallis, "A Tribute to Hunt," *American Architect and Building News*, XLIX (August 17, 1895), 72; P. B. Wight, "Richard Morris Hunt," *Inland Architect and News Record*, XXVI (August 1895), 2–4, followed by other "Press and Personal Tributes" in a special "Richard Morris Hunt Memorial Edition."

Among the more perceptive anonymously written obituary notices are the following: *American Architect and Building News*, XLIX (August 3, 1895), 45; *Architect and Contract Reporter*, LIV (August 16, 1895), 97; *Builder*, LXIX (August 17, 1895), 111–112; *Critic*, XXVII (August 10, 1895), 89–90; *New York Times*, August 1, 1895, p. 5, and August 4, 1895, p. 13; and *Scientific American*, LXXIII (August 10, 1895), 83.

Special mention should be made of the discussion of RMH and his works in Wayne Andrews, *Architecture, Ambition and Americans: A Social History of American Architecture* (Glencoe, Ill., 1964), pp. 176–184; Winslow Ames, "The Transformation of Château-sur-Mer," *Journal of the Society of Architectural Historians*, XXIX (December 1970), 290–306; and John Vredenburgh Van Pelt, *A Monograph of the William K. Vanderbilt House, Richard Morris Hunt, Architect* (New York, 1925).

Van Pelt wrote the short biographical sketch of RMH in the *Dictionary of American Biography* (New York, 1927–1936), IX, 389–391.

See also Ormonde De Kay, Jr., "Richard Morris Hunt," in *Three Centuries of Notable American Architects*, ed. by Joseph J. Thorndike, Jr. (New York, 1981), pp. 88–109; William H. Jordy and Christopher J. Monkhouse, *Buildings on Paper: Rhode Island Architectural Drawings, 1825–1945* (Providence, R.I., 1982); Sarah Bradford Landau, "Richard Morris Hunt, the Continental Picturesque, and the 'Stick Style'," *Journal of the Society of Architectural Historians*, 42 (1983), 272–289; and Susan Stein, ed., *The Architecture of Richard Morris Hunt* (Chicago, 1986).

V. Journals

The files of over one hundred periodicals have been consulted for this study. Among the most useful of the journals for information about RMH and his works were the following: *American Architect and Building News*, later titled *American Architect* and *American Architect and Architectural Review*, *American Builder*, *Architects' and Mechanics' Journal*, *Architectural Record*, *American Architectural Review and American Builders' Journal*, *Architectural Review* (Boston), *Architectural Review* (London), *Art Journal*, *Crayon*, *Harper's New Monthly Magazine*, *Inland Architect and News Record*, *Journal of the American Institute of Architects*, *Journal of the Society of Architectural Historians*, *Nation*, *Real Estate Record and Builders' Guide*, and *Scribners Monthly Magazine*. The files of the *New York Times*, *New York Herald*, [New York] *Evening Post*, and *New-York Daily Tribune* were especially useful for this study.

Over several years my researches into the life and works of Richard Morris Hunt have taken me to many libraries and archives and to many buildings. Almost everywhere in these investigations I have encountered others who not only willingly but also enthusiastically helped me ferret out relevant source materials. In these travels I have discovered considerable general interest in nineteenth-century American architecture and in the makers of American architectural traditions and a particular interest in Richard Morris Hunt, about whom so little has been known. My gratitude and indebtedness are immense for the assistance given me by those whose names follow, as well as by many others who cannot be named. Without the cooperation and support of a great many persons this book could never have been written.

I am most grateful, first of all, to descendants of Richard Morris Hunt for giving me full access to Hunt family papers, including the rich body of materials described in the Selected Sources as the Hunt Papers. Before her death, the late Catharine Hunt Paxton expressed her willingness for me to see the Hunt Papers and other materials in her possession. Subsequently, her daughter, Carley P. Angell, graciously gave me access to the family documents in her possession and arranged for me to see other Hunt Papers and materials that had come to her brother, Michael W. Paxton, and to her sister, Susan Battley. I am particularly indebted to Carley Angell for her frequent gracious hospitality and for her kindness in allowing me to transcribe materials at my own pace in my own home. I thank Joseph H. Hunt for sending R. M. Hunt memorabilia to me for my use and for clarifying some family relationships. Richard Barron Hunt has been supportive of my work from the beginning and has given permission for my use of materials created by his great-grandfather.

I wish to acknowledge next the help and support given me by the library staff of the American Institute of Architects in Washington, D.C. George E. Pettengill, librarian emeritus of the A.I.A. and formerly in charge of the Hunt Collection, first opened up the rich body of materials to me, providing me with many letters, sketchbooks, and journals that are so important for this study, as well as giving me access to the photographs and the drawings of the collection. Susan Holton, the librarian, and her assistants Stephanie Byrnes and Deepa Madhavan have been unfailingly helpful to me and willing to let me investigate the resources of the collection at my own pace. To Jeanne Butler Hodges of the American Institute of Architects Foundation, Inc., and to Susan Stein Ganelin, architectural historian, I am indebted for permission to use the materials of the Hunt Collection.

My entry into the study of the life and work of Richard Morris Hunt was aided considerably by the assistance that Alan Burnham provided me. Not only did Mr. Burnham allow me to read and to quote from Catharine Clinton Howland Hunt's manuscript biography of her husband, but he also gave me access to the miscellaneous Hunt materials in his American Architectural Archive. Alan Burnham's knowledge of Hunt and his works has been a great help to many scholars.

I share with almost all American scholars working in the field of architectural history an immense gratitude for the splendid collection of architectural books and journals gathered in the Avery Library of Columbia University. Adolf K. Placzek, the librarian, has been consistently helpful in providing me access to the resources of the library. In addition to many others on the Avery staff, I wish to thank in particular Herbert Mitchell, Charling Fagan, Neville Thompson, and Carol Falcione for their courteous and knowledgeable assistance in locating hard-to-find books and articles.

The Newport Historical Society, with its rich manuscript and local newspaper collection, has been an important source of materials for this study. Gladys E. Bolhouse provided substantial information on some of Hunt's lesser commissions in Newport. Mrs. Edmund M. Wordell, Mrs. Edward G. Crosby, and Stanley A. Ward helped me in my work there.

Others who have aided me include the following: Dr. David Grayson Allen, The Papers of Daniel Webster; Albert K. Baragwanath, Museum of the City of New York; William Edmund Barrett, architectural photographer; Rev. Robert S. Beaman, Princeton Theological Seminary; Sherry Birk, A.I.A. Foundation; Emily Boland, American Academy in Rome offices, New York; Alfred Branam, Jr.; Frederick Branch, Bloomfield (New Jersey) Public Library; Maynett Breithaupt, preservationist; Susanne Brendel, Biltmore House & Gardens; June Bryant, Brooks Memorial Library, Brattleboro, Vermont; Rev. Arthur M. Byers, Jr., Princeton Theological Seminary; Bainbridge Bunting, University of New Mexico; William A. V. Cecil, Biltmore House & Gardens; Richard Chafee, Courtauld Institute, London University; Richard L. Champlin, Redwood Library and Athenaeum, Newport; David A. Clary, History Section, Forest Service, U.S. Department of Agriculture; Earle E. Coleman, Archives, Princeton University; Elaine Crane, Fordham University; Rev. James H. Edgar, First Presbyterian Church, Beacon, New York; William R. Emerson, Franklin D. Roosevelt Library; Edward Foote, cultural historian; Dennis Steadman Francis, architectural historian; Leon A. Froats, National Park Service, Hyde Park, New York; Commander T. A. W. Frye, USN, U.S. Naval Observatory; Mary Ellen Gadski, architectural historian; Deborah S. Gardner, Department of Records and Information Services, New York City; James Garrison, architectural photographer; Margaret E. Gilmore, historian, Geneseo, New York; Nancy Goeschel, architectural historian; Constance M. Grieff, architectural historian; Patricia B. Hanna, Howland Circulating Library, Beacon, New York; Ruth W. Helmuth, Archives, Case Western Reserve University; William J. Hennessey, Helen Foresman Spencer Museum of Art, University of Kansas; Henry-Russell Hitchcock, New York University; Martha Jay Hoppin, University of Massachusetts, Amherst; Bruce Howe, Art Association of Newport; Father Hunsicker, Trinity Church, New York; James S. Irvine, Speer Library, Princeton Theological Seminary; Charles A. Isetts, The Ohio Historical Society; Jack Jackson, The Boston Athenaeum; Corrine R. Jones, Prospect Hill Association, Brattleboro, Vermont; Gina Kellerman, architectural historian; Sue LaDue, First Presbyterian Church, Beacon, New York; Dennis McFadden, Department of Records and Information Services, New York City; Evelyn McGrath, New York City Chapter, A.I.A.; Fritz J. Malval, Archives, Hampton Institute; William Matheson, Rare Book and Special Collections Division, Library of Congress; Robert Murphy, Department of Records and Information Services, New York City; Thomas Murray; Oliver Orr, Manuscript Division, Library of Congress; Monique Panaggio, Preservation Society of Newport County; Leonard J. Panaggio, Rhode Island Development Council; Margaret Partridge, Hyde Park Historical Association; Phoebe Peebles, Archives, Fogg Art Museum, Harvard University; Patricia Pellegrini, Archives, Metropolitan Museum of Art; Barbara Peters, Mount Gulian Society, Beacon, New York; Wilhelmina B. Powers, Adriance Memorial Library, Poughkeepsie, New York; John Rae, Jr.; Rev. Arthur Wilson Rideout, First Presbyterian Church, Palatka, Florida; Ilonka Rogers, Art Association of Newport; Bonnie B. Salt, Archives, Harvard University; Scott Schaefer, Museum of Fine Arts, Boston; Judith A. Schiff, Archives, Yale University; Lewis I. Sharp, Department of American Paintings and Sculpture, Metropolitan Museum of Art; Nancy Singleton, Madison (New Jersey) Public Library; Dr. Jonathan Slocum, Craig House, Beacon, New York; Capt. Joseph C. Smith, USN, U.S. Naval Observatory; Virginia R. Sperl, Dowling College, Oakdale, Long Island; Janet K. Staats; Ilana Stern, Archives, New York University; Henry L. Swint, Archives, Vanderbilt University; Stanley P. Tozeski, Archives, U.S. Military Academy, West Point, New York; Edward F. Turberg, Division of Archives and History, State of North Carolina; Rev. William H. Wagner, Jr., St. Mark's Episcopal Church, Islip, Long Island; Ewart A. Wetherill, consultant in acoustics; Charles Willard, Speer Library, Princeton Theological Seminary.

To Dean Robert R. Raymo and the Arts and Science Research Fund Committee of New York University, I am grateful for summer research grants which helped defray some of the expenses for travel and for the collection of manuscript materials for this study.

For permission to quote from manuscript materials, I wish to thank the following: Carley P. Angell; Alan Burnham; Michael and Lone Paxton; The American Academy in Rome; The American Institute of Architects Foundation; Burnham Library, Chicago Art Institute; Metropolitan Museum of Art; The New-York Historical Society; Manuscripts and Archives Division, The New York Public Library, Astor, Lenox and Tilden Foundations; and The United States Military Academy Archives.

Finally, I am immensely indebted to the scholars who have read and criticized this work, including Bayrd Still of the History Department, New York University; Marvin Trachtenberg of the Institute of Fine Arts, New York University; James T. Maher, cultural historian; the MIT Press's reader-consultants and editorial staff; and my wife, Elizabeth Kemp Baker, to whom this book is dedicated.

INDEX

PAGE REFERENCES
IN ITALICS REFER TO
ILLUSTRATIONS.